Pennington's Corporate Insolvency Law

Pennington's Corporate Insolvency Law

by Robert Pennington, LLD

Solicitor, Emeritus Professor of Commercial Law at the
University of Birmingham, formerly Adviser on
Company Law to the Commission of the
European Communities

Butterworths
London, Edinburgh, Dublin
1997

United Kingdom	Butterworths a Division of Reed Elsevier (UK) Ltd, Halsbury House, 35 Chancery Lane, LONDON WC2A 1EL and 4 Hill Street, EDINBURGH EH2 3JZ
Australia	Butterworths, SYDNEY, MELBOURNE, BRISBANE, ADELAIDE, PERTH, CANBERRA and HOBART
Canada	Butterworths Canada Ltd, TORONTO and VANCOUVER
Ireland	Butterworth (Ireland) Ltd, DUBLIN
Malaysia	Malayan Law Journal Sdn Bhd, KUALA LUMPUR
New Zealand	Butterworths of New Zealand Ltd, WELLINGTON and AUCKLAND
Singapore	Reed Elsevier (Singapore) Pte Ltd, SINGAPORE
South Africa	Butterworths Publishers (Pty) Ltd, DURBAN
USA	Michie, Charlottesville, VIRGINIA

A CIP Catalogue record for this book is available from the British Library.

ISBN 0 406 08177 8

Printed and bound in Great Britain by Clays Ltd, St Ives plc

Preface to the second edition

The purpose and coverage of the second edition of this book are the same as the first edition, namely to present systematically and in a practical manner the law and practice relating to corporate insolvency under the Insolvency Acts 1986 to 1994. The original legislation of 1986 has been amended little since then; nevertheless, the changes introduced by the two Insolvency Acts of 1994 are of substantial importance, even though they affect only two aspects of insolvency law. More extensive changes have been made since 1986 by a succession of amendments to the Insolvency Rules 1986; these rules are primarily a procedural supplement to the Insolvency Act 1986, but they do also contain important substantive provisions which have undergone several changes over the years.

The primary legislation governing corporate insolvency has undergone no radical revision since the first edition of this book was published in 1991, but the practical effect of the legislation has been extensively affected by judicial decisions and by the adoption or rejection by practitioners and companies of the alternative courses of action available under the legislation when a company becomes insolvent. Judicial interpretation of the provisions of the Insolvency Act 1986 has been of particular importance in respect of the insolvency procedures which were newly introduced by that Act and which had no equivalent beforehand, namely the corporate voluntary arrangement, the administration order procedure and the administrative receivership. Many of the doubts and uncertainties which have arisen in respect of these new procedures have now been set at rest by judicial decision, at least when the matters have been ruled on by the House of Lords (which has rarely happened) or by the Court of Appeal or by a consistent line of decisions at first instance; nevertheless, there still remain many important but unresolved questions of interpretation on which professional opinions differ considerably, and on which this book attempts to throw some light by suggesting likely future judicial rulings.

Corporate insolvency procedures other than those introduced by the 1986 legislation have been governed by statute and by an extensive body of case law for more than 150 years; they comprise winding up of companies by the court, voluntary winding up, and receiverships in general. These traditional procedures were continued by the Insolvency Act 1986 in much their previous form, but subject to modifications and additions to make them fairer and more effective.

The existing body of judicial decisions in respect of these traditional forms of corporate insolvency proceedings has provided valuable assistance in the interpretation of the provisions of the Insolvency Act 1986 relating to them, because the provisions of the Act are extensively expressed in identical or closely similar language and the substantive effect of those provisions is much the same as in the earlier legislation with modifications and extensions. Nevertheless, there has been a substantial volume of new case law in respect of the traditional forms of insolvency, and this will no doubt continue to grow.

Since the Insolvency Act 1986 came into force at the end of 1986, certain trends and commercial preferences have manifested themselves in the use of the various corporate insolvency procedures. Creditors, as they always have done, prefer to resort to winding-up petitions if the indebted company does not respond satisfactorily to pressure to pay up and the company lacks assets on which execution can be levied expeditiously, or details of the company's assets on which execution can be levied are unknown. Nevertheless, creditors have often shown themselves more ready than previously to accede to reasonable corporate voluntary arrangements proposed by the company and to proposals made by the company's administrator under an administration order obtained by the company. When the Insolvency Act 1986 came into force, companies at first showed a strong preference for administration orders as a protection against winding up proceedings or receiverships, but the court has made it clear (by ordering directors of insolvent companies to pay costs thrown away on abortive petitions for administration orders) that the administration order procedure is not available as a long-term alternative to liquidation when a company is hopelessly insolvent. Because of this, insolvent companies which do not passively wait for their creditors to present winding-up petitions have increasingly shown an inclination towards proposing corporate voluntary arrangements, which are procedurally simpler, quicker, and in most cases less expensive than winding-up proceedings, and if reasonable may attract the necessary support of the company's creditors.

Corporate insolvency, however fairly and efficiently regulated by law, can never be entirely satisfactory to the parties concerned. The creditors of the insolvent company are not paid in full; the extent of their loss is outside their control and depends on the success or otherwise of the liquidator, administrator, or receiver (as the case may be) realising as much as possible from the shipwreck of the company's fortunes and keeping the attendant expenses to a minimum. The insolvent company (except in administration order proceedings designed to ensure its survival and in corporate voluntary arrangement proceedings) ceases to have any control, or even influence, over the disposal or application of its assets and the continuation or cessation of its business, and merely has the satisfaction (if that is the correct expression) of knowing that when a final dividend has been paid to the company's creditors, its debts are discharged, and its directors and shareholders are freed from liability, unless they have been guilty of misconduct. These consequences are of course the inevitable result of insolvency; the law can merely attempt to deal as fairly as possible with the company's creditors, shareholders and directors, but it cannot summon up assets to ensure that creditors are paid. Broadly speaking, the Insolvency Acts 1986 to 1994 balance the interests and obligations of these persons in a fair manner, and the areas of dissatisfaction are small in number but nevertheless important, particularly the discontent of unsecured trade creditors with the frequent appropriation of substantially all of the company's assets to pay debts, usually loans, which are secured by fixed or floating charges on the company's whole assets and undertaking, and to satisfy preferential debts and claims.

It is unfortunate that the administrative order procedure introduced by the Insolvency Act 1986 has not been used more successfully than it has. The courts' attitude is salutary when it has held that this new procedure should not be allowed to result in the long-term prolonging of the company's business in the hope of its eventual recovery and the consequential indefinite postponement of payment of the company's debts. The court quite properly intends to avoid the situation which often occurs in the United States where insolvent business corporations are permitted to carry on business almost indefinitely without paying their debts and with the protection of the Federal Bankruptcy Act, Chapter 11 against personal liability on the part of their directors and shareholders. On the other hand, too many companies in the United Kingdom which could be saved still go into liquidation, often on professional advice, in order to protect their directors against personal liability for fraudulent or wrongful trading and against disqualification from being directors or being concerned in the management of any company whatever. A steady disposal of the viable parts of such a company's business undertaking over a period of time under an administration order would often ensure that the company's creditors were paid a larger percentage of their debts than is possible in winding up, and employment for more of the company's workforce than in a winding up would be secured.

The law in this edition is set out as it stood on 1 January 1997.

ROBERT R PENNINGTON

University of Birmingham
June 1997

Preface to the first edition

A sound knowledge of insolvency law has become increasingly important for both legal practitioners and accountants in recent years with the growing number of business failures which have resulted in record annual numbers of liquidations of companies, receiverships and bankruptcies. Because of this, it has become more important than ever before that students for the professional legal and accountancy examinations and undergraduate and postgraduate students of law and commerce (the majority of whom go on to qualify professionally or to take up appointments in business management) should be provided with a range of literature on insolvency law and practice to meet their needs. In recognition of the importance of the subject, many university law faculties have over the last ten years added insolvency law to the options available to their second and third year undergraduates; a knowledge of insolvency law has always been a necessary component in the equipment of students preparing for the professional examinations.

This book has been written with a view to meeting the needs of such students for a logically ordered presentation of the substantive law governing the insolvency of companies, together with a reasonably detailed account of the procedure for initiating and conducting the various kinds of insolvency proceedings. The legislation which predominates here is, of course, the Insolvency Act 1986, and the Insolvency Rules 1986 (as amended) made under the 1986 Act. There is additionally a growing body of case law under the Act and Rules (particularly in respect of the newly introduced administration order proceedings for companies as an alternative to liquidation or receivership). Moreover, the existing body of case law on company liquidations and receiverships is still significant where the new legislation adopts the legislative provisions enacted over the last 150 years since the earliest winding-up legislation of 1848, with greater or less modifications and extensions. An appropriate balance has been sought in this book to presenting the contents of the Insolvency Act 1986 and the Insolvency Rules 1986 (without necessarily including all the details which these contain), and to covering the relevant case law which often adds to or modifies the effect of the legislation, as well as interprets it.

Each of the different insolvency proceedngs which may be initiated in respect of a company (namely, winding up by the court, voluntary winding up, administration order proceedings, compromises and arrangements approved by the court, voluntary arrangements and receiverships) is distinct in character and purpose, and is governed by its own rules and procedure. This does not prevent certain insolvency proceedings being pursued concurrently, however (eg winding up and receivership), but other insolvency proceedings are incompatible with each other and so cannot be pursued concurrently (eg administration order proceedings and winding up or receivership; arrangements approved by the court and voluntary arrangements) although they may occur in succession (eg a winding up following on the termination of an administration order). The reason for this disparity is that certain insolvency proceedings are intended to be terminal and to conclude with the dissolution of the insolvent company or its continuance in a restructured form, whereas other such proceedings are designed to solve the current financial problems of the insolvent company and so enable it to re-establish its business, or at least to dispose of some of its assets and to continue to carry on business with the remainder. In fact, the emphasis given by the 1986 legislation to preserving companies which are in temporary financial difficulties, or which can survive if restructured, is the distinguishing feature of that legislation as compared with the earlier legislation governing company winding up and receivership.

The various corporate insolvency proceedings are different in form and character because of their different purposes, and are necessarily treated separately in this book. Nevertheless, many of the incidental rules governing the different corporate insolvency proceedings are the same or substantially the same. Where this is so, the common features of the proceedings are emphasised in this book and, conversely, where important features of different insolvency proceedings are widely different or contrast markedly, this too is indicated. The differences between the various corporate insolvency proceedings are mostly differences resulting from the purpose of the proceedings; the similarities are mostly procedural, but not exclusively so. The rules relating to the retrospective invalidation of certain transactions entered into by a company which later goes into liquidation or is the subject of an administration order, for example, are substantially the same.

It is too early yet to judge how successful the insolvency legislation of 1986 has proved. In an economic recession such as that of the last two years, the number of liquidations and receiverships of companies whose businesses fail inevitably rises. An interesting question, however, is how many other companies in financial difficulties would have gone into liquidation or receivership if the alternative insolvency proceedings introduced by the Insolvency

Act 1986, had not been available. A further interesting question is to what extent the new legislation and procedures have improved the effectiveness of liquidations in making available more assets to pay creditors' claims and in making the persons responsible for insolvencies accountable both pecuniarily and otherwise. Time and further experience will be necessary to answer these questions.

The law is stated in this book as it stands on 1 May 1991.

ROBERT R PENNINGTON

University of Birmingham
May 1991

Contents

Table of statutes

References in this Table to *Statutes* are to Halsbury's Statutes of England (Fourth Edition) showing the volume and page at which the annotated text of the Act will be found.

Table of statutory instruments

List of cases

CHAPTER 1

Insolvency legislation and insolvency practitioners

INTRODUCTION

The Insolvency Act 1986, which came into force on 29 December 1986,[1] consolidated most of the legislation currently effective in England and Wales governing insolvency proceedings in respect of companies and individuals. The 1986 Act embodied the extensive changes in the provisions of the Companies Act 1985, in respect of the winding up of companies which were made by the Insolvency Act 1985, together with the entirely new system of legislation governing individual insolvencies which was introduced by the Insolvency Act 1985, in place of the now repealed Bankruptcy Acts 1914 and 1926. There came into force at the same time the Company Directors' Disqualification Act 1986[2] consolidating the provisions of the Companies Acts 1985 and the Insolvency Act 1985 in respect of the disqualification of persons by court order from being or acting as directors or acting in various other capacities in relation to a company without leave of the court.[3] The Company Directors' Disqualification Act 1986 also re-enacted the prohibition in the Companies Act 1985, prohibiting undischarged bankrupts from being or acting as directors of any company or taking part in the promotion, formation or management of any company without leave of the court. The Insolvency Act 1986 has been amended in certain respects by subsequent legislation, in particular by the Insolvency Act 1994 and the Insolvency (No 2) Act 1994.

The changes in insolvency law made by the Insolvency Act 1985 (which were incorporated in the consolidating Insolvency Act 1986) originated in two reports of a committee commissioned by the Government in January 1977, to report on and make

---

1 The Act came into force when the provisions of Part III of the Insolvency Act 1985, dealing with individual insolvency, were brought into force by the Insolvency Act 1985 (Commencement No 5) Order 1986 (SI 1986/1924) (Insolvency Act 1986, s 443).

2 Company Directors' Disqualification Act 1986, s 25.

3 For the provisions of the Company Directors' Disqualification Act 1986, see *Pennington's Company Law* (7th) p 717 et seq.

recommendations for changes in insolvency law; this was the Review Committee on Insolvency Law and Practice, whose chairman was Mr (later Sir) Kenneth Cork CBE. The first report of the Review Committee was an interim report presented to Parliament in July 1980;[4] its second report was presented to Parliament in June 1982,[5] and was intended to be the first part of a final report, which was to have been followed by a second part proposing the establishment of an Insolvency Court and dealing with certain matters of substantive law not covered by the first part. In fact, the second part of the Review Committee's final report was never produced; work on it was superseded by a Government White Paper on *A Revised Framework for Insolvency Law*[6] which was published in February 1984, as the basis for legislation. The White Paper adopted many of the proposals in the two reports of the Review Committee, subject to various important modifications, but the White Paper also rejected a number of the Committee's other proposals. It was the White Paper which formed the basis of the bill which became the Insolvency Act 1985.

The work of the Review Committee on Insolvency Law and Practice extended over a period of five years, and its reports contained the most thorough and wide-ranging examination of insolvency law and practice which has ever been undertaken in England. Some of the recommendations of the Review Committee were controversial, and did not receive universal acclaim. Nevertheless, the Committee's core recommendations were accepted by the Government and by the bodies which were representative of trade and industry and practitioners in the insolvency field as marking a greatly needed modernisation of the relevant law, and as providing a sound basis for new legislation.

INSOLVENCY PROCEEDINGS

The varieties of insolvency proceedings governed by the Insolvency Act 1986 fall under two heads, namely, insolvency proceedings in respect of companies registered under the Companies Act 1985 or earlier Companies Acts and unregistered and overseas companies, and insolvency proceedings in respect of individuals. Accordingly, the insolvency proceedings available in respect of companies and in respect of individuals are governed by separate Groups of Parts of the Insolvency Act 1986; the First Group of Parts (ss 1 to 251) relate

4 Bankruptcy – Interim Report of the Insolvency Law Review Committee (Cmnd 7968).

to company and corporate insolvencies and the Second Group of Parts (ss 252 to 385) relate to individual insolvencies; the Third Group of Parts (ss 386 to 444) contains miscellaneous provisions affecting both corporate and individual insolvencies.

The various insolvency proceedings which may be taken in respect of companies are winding up (or liquidation), whether effected under an order of the court, or voluntarily in pursuance of a resolution passed by a general meeting of the company; voluntary arrangements made by a company with its creditors and assented to by a majority of them, with or without the approval of the court; administration order proceedings in respect of companies whose undertakings may be rescued and enabled to survive as going concerns, or companies which have entered into, or propose to enter into, arrangements with their creditors, or companies whose assets may be more beneficially realised in administration proceedings than by winding them up; and receiverships, by which secured creditors of a company may realise their security or recover the amount secured without the company's affairs necessarily being wound up.

The insolvency proceedings which may be taken in respect of insolvent individuals initiated by creditors or by the individual debtor himself are bankruptcy proceedings initiated by a creditor or creditors or by the debtor himself; voluntary arrangements made with the creditors of an individual debtor and assented to by a majority of them; and proceedings for the administration of the insolvent estate of a deceased individual by an administrator appointed under an insolvency administration order made by the court. Partnership insolvencies are dealt with separately by delegated legislation made under the Insolvency Act 1986;[7] by this delegated legislation partnerships may be wound up under orders of the court in the same way as companies, and separate, procedurally connected bankruptcy proceedings may be taken concurrently in respect of the individual partners, or separate winding-up proceedings may be taken in respect of corporate partners.

Despite the structural division of the Insolvency Act 1986, many of its substantive provisions relating to corporate and to individual insolvencies are expressed in similar language and have similar effect; in this book occasional reference will therefore be made to provisions of the Act which relate to insolvent individuals and to the decisions of the court which interpret them, although the subject matter of the book is, of course, confined to corporate insolvency.

5 Insolvency Law and Practice – Report of the Review Committee (Cmnd 8558).
6 Cmnd 9175.
7 Insolvency Act 1986, s 420(1); Insolvent Partnerships Order 1994 (SI 1994/ 2421).

The Insolvency Act 1986, does not contain the whole of the legislation currently in force in respect of insolvency proceedings. Some of the legislation relating to the enforcement and validity of securities over the assets of companies, whether enforcement is by means of receiverships or otherwise, is contained in the Companies Acts 1985 and 1989; arrangements made by companies with classes of their creditors or shareholders subject to the approval of the court are governed by the relevant provisions of the Companies Act 1985, as amended by the Insolvency Act 1985, and this is so whether the arrangement is made in connection with administration order proceedings or not; individual debtors may still enter into deeds of arrangement for the benefit of their creditors under the Deeds of Arrangement Act 1914, as amended. Furthermore, many of the substantive rules relating to insolvency proceedings are not contained in legislation, but are either rules of equity superimposed on the relevant legislation (eg the rule against dual or multiple proofs being lodged in respect of a single obligation in the insolvent winding up of a company or in the bankruptcy of an individual),[8] or are independent equitable rules which preceded the enactment of the present legislation and co-exist with it (eg the rules governing the enforcement of securities for indebtedness and the liabilities of secured creditors and receivers for enforcing them improperly). As in many other branches of English law, the relevant legislation, the Insolvency Act 1986, even though a codifying and consolidating measure, does not contain the whole of the relevant law.

INSOLVENCY PRACTITIONERS

The authorisation requirement

The greatest innovation made by the Insolvency Act 1985, and now contained in the Insolvency Act 1986, is the requirement that the persons who fulfil the principal functions in the administration of debtors' assets in insolvency proceedings should be professionally qualified and authorised insolvency practitioners. Before the Insolvency Act 1986 came into force there were no statutory requirements as to the qualification which persons needed to have in order to act as liquidators or receivers of a company or trustees in bankruptcy of individual debtors. The only safeguards for the protection of creditors and debtors against dishonesty or

8 See p 293.

incompetence in the conduct of insolvency proceedings were the need for liquidators appointed in the winding-up of companies by the court and trustees in bankruptcy appointed by the creditors of individual debtors to give security to the Secretary of State for the proper performance of their duties,[9] the practice of the court to require such security when appointing a receiver,[10] and the fact that the court would not appoint persons to be liquidators of companies unless they were solicitors or members of certain accountancy bodies who had been qualified for a substantial period.[11] The new statutory requirements are far more precise and more exacting.

By the Insolvency Act 1986, it is a criminal offence for a person (other than the official receiver)[12] to act as an insolvency practitioner in relation to a company (including an unregistered or an overseas company or an insolvent partnership), or in relation to an individual if he is not authorised to do so, and if he is not authorised his appointment to act in that capacity is void.[13] A person acts as an insolvency practitioner in relation to a company if he acts as its provisional liquidator or as its liquidator (even in a members' voluntary winding-up, where the company is, or should be, solvent),[14] or as an administrator of a company in respect of which an administration order has been made, or as an administrative receiver appointed to enforce a charge created as a floating charge over the whole, or substantially the whole, of the property of a company,[15] or as a supervisor under a voluntary arrangement with the company's creditors which has been approved by meetings of its creditors and members.[16] A person does not act as an insolvency practitioner in relation to a company, however, if he acts as a special manager appointed by the court in a winding up of the company by the court,[17] nor if he acts as a receiver of any property of the company

---

9 Companies Act 1985, s 534(*a*) (re-enacting Companies Act 1948, s 240(*a*) and Companies Act 1929, s 186(1)); Bankruptcy Act 1914, s 19(2).
10 RSC Ord 30, r 2(2) and (3).
11 *Re Icknield Development Ltd* [1973] 2 All ER 168, [1973] 1 WLR 537.
12 The official receiver is an official of the Department of Trade and Industry appointed by the Secretary of State to carry out functions under the insolvency legislation (Insolvency Act 1986, s 399(1)). There are at present four official receivers attached to the High Court and 34 official receivers attached to county courts throughout the country.
13 Insolvency Act 1986, s 220(1), s 221(1), s 230(1) to (4), s 292(2), s 389(1) and (2), s 420(1); Insolvent Partnerships Order 1994 (SI 1994/2421), art 6(1) to (3), art 7(1), art 8(1) and art 153; Administration of Insolvent Estates of Deceased Persons Order 1986 (SI 1986/1999), Sch 1, para 3(1) and para 36.
14 See p 88, post.
15 Insolvency Act 1986, s 29(2).
16 Ibid, s 388(1).
17 See post, p 160.

otherwise than under an appointment as an administrative receiver.[18] A person acts as an insolvency practitioner in relation to an individual if he acts as the individual's trustee in bankruptcy or as an interim receiver pending the court's decision whether to make a bankruptcy order in respect of him,[19] or if he acts as trustee of a deed of arrangement made for the benefit of an individual's creditors, or as a supervisor under a voluntary arrangement made by an individual with his creditors which has been approved by them, or as an administrator appointed under the Insolvency Act 1986 in respect of the insolvent estate of a deceased individual.[20]

A person is disqualified from acting as an insolvency practitioner in relation to any company or individual if the person so acting is an undischarged bankrupt, or if he is a person against whom there is in force an order made by the court disqualifying him from being or acting as a director of a company or in certain other capacities in relation to it, or he is a mental patient within Part VII of the Mental Health Act 1983.[1] Furthermore, only individuals, and not companies, corporations or partnerships, may be or act as insolvency practitioners.[2]

Qualifications and the grant and withdrawal of authorisation

The positive qualification which an individual must have to be authorised to act as an insolvency practitioner may be either of two alternatives. The first of these is that he is a member of one or more professional bodies recognised by the Secretary of State for Trade and Industry[3] which has issued a current professional practising certificate to him certifying that he has been authorised individually by such a body to act as an insolvency practitioner after satisfying it that he is a fit and proper person to do so and has had adequate practice, training in and experience of insolvency work.[4] The alternative qualification is that he has been authorised to act as an

---

18 For the distinction between an administrative receiver and any other class of receiver, see p 488 post.
19 Insolvency Act 1986, s 286(2).
20 Ibid, s 388(2).
1 Ibid, s 390(4); Company Directors' Disqualification Act 1986, s 1(1).
2 Insolvency Act 1986, s 390(1).
3 Ibid, s 390(2). The bodies currently recognised for this purpose are the Law Society, the Law Society of Scotland, the Institute of Chartered Accountants in England and Wales, the Institute of Chartered Accountants in Scotland, the Institute of Chartered Accountants in Ireland, the Chartered Association of Certified Accountants and the Insolvency Practitioners' Association (Insolvency Practitioners (Recognised Professional Bodies) Order 1986 (SI 1986/1764), art 2 and Sch).
4 Insolvency Act 1986, s 390(2)(*a*).

insolvency practitioner by the Secretary of State after having satisfied himself that he is a fit and proper person to do so, that he has certain minimum educational attainments, and that he has had adequate training in, and experience of, insolvency work.[5] The Insolvency Act 1986 provides for the grant and withdrawal of authorisations to act as an insolvency practitioner by the Secretary of State, for the duration and renewal of authorisations granted by him,[6] and for appeals by applicants whose applications are refused by the Secretary of State, and by practitioners who have been authorised by him but whose authorisations are withdrawn or not renewed.[7] Appeals are heard by the Insolvency Practitioners Tribunal, whose members are appointed from a panel of English and Scottish lawyers who have been qualified professionally for at least seven years and are nominated by the Lord Chancellor and the Lord President of the Court of Session, and from a panel of persons with experience of insolvency matters who are nominated by the Secretary of State.[8] The procedure for the grant, withdrawal and renewal of authorisations to act as insolvency practitioners by the recognised professional bodies, and for appeals against their refusals to grant or renew such authorisations, and against the withdrawal of authorisations by them, are contained in the rules of those recognised bodies. They act as bodies administering public law in exercising such powers, however, and their decisions are therefore subject to judicial review by the High Court.

Guidance notes have been issued by the Secretary of State for Trade and Industry and by the recognised accountancy bodies in respect of applications for authorisation to act as an insolvency practitioner, and in respect of the conduct of authorised practitioners. These guidance notes have no immediate legal effect, but failure to comply with them may result in the refusal of an application for

---

5 Ibid, s 390(2)(*b*) and s 393(1). The Secretary of State may direct that any body or person approved by him shall be a competent authority to grant authorisation to act as an insolvency practitioner in cases of any description directed by the Secretary of State (s 293(2)). The intention is that such directions may be made constituting specialised bodies to authorise persons to act as insolvency practitioners even though they are not members of a recognised professional body, and also to authorise suitable persons to engage in work which calls for skills or experience different from that normally possessed by insolvency practitioners authorised by the recognised professional bodies. As yet, the Secretary of State has given no directions under this provision.

6 All authorisations, including those issued by recognised professional bodies, are granted for a period of not more than three years and are renewable (Insolvency Practitioners' Regulations 1990 (SI 1990/439), reg 10).

7 Insolvency Act 1986, s 393(1) to (5) and s 396(2) and (3) and s 397.

8 Insolvency Act 1985, s 8(6); Insolvency Act 1986, s 396(1) and Sch 7, para 1.

authorisation or the withdrawal or non-renewal of an authorisation.[9] One matter which is specifically dealt with by the guidance notes, but not by the Insolvency Act 1986 or the regulations made under it, is the requirement that an insolvency practitioner should be independent of the company or individual in relation to whom he is acting in insolvency proceedings. In the case of members of the recognised accountancy bodies, this is taken as meaning that they should not act as insolvency practitioners in relation to companies of which they or any of their partners have been auditors, directors or other officers within three years before the onset of the company's insolvency, or in relation to companies with which they or any of their partners have had a continuing professional relationship (eg as an accountant or financial or management adviser) within that time; in the case of individuals, members of the accountancy bodies should not act as insolvency practitioners if the individual is a person with whom they or any of their partners have had a continuing professional relationship within three years before the onset of the individual's insolvency, nor if they or any of their partners are trustees of a trust set up by the individual. These requirements do not, however, inhibit an insolvency practitioner from acting as the liquidator of a company in a member's voluntary liquidation where the company is clearly solvent.

Bonding

Every insolvency practitioner must, before acting in the insolvency of a company or individual, obtain and deposit with the recognised professional body which authorised him or with the Secretary of State if he granted the authorisation, a bond issued by an insurance company by which it makes itself jointly and severally liable with the practitioner for the proper performance of his duties under the Insolvency Act 1986 and the rules and regulations made under it.[10] Where two or more insolvency practitioners are appointed in relation to the same company or individual (eg as joint liquidators or administrators) each of them must have in force and deposit a bond covering his acts and defaults as though he were the sole appointee.[10]

---

9 The statutory grounds for the withdrawal of an authorisation granted by the Secretary of State are that the person concerned is no longer a fit and proper person to act as an insolvency practitioner, or that he has failed to comply with the Insolvency Act 1986 or with rules or regulations made under it, or that he has furnished the Secretary of State with false, inaccurate or misleading information (Insolvency Act 1986, s 393(4)).

10 Insolvency Act 1986, s 390(3); Insolvency Practitioners' Regulations 1990, reg 11 and reg 12(1) and Sch 2, Part II (as amended by the Insolvency Practitioners' (Amendment) Regulations 1993 (SI 1993/221), reg 10).

The bond must be entered into by the insurance company for a general penalty sum of £250,000, and under the terms of the bond, as soon as possible after the insolvency practitioner's appointment to any of the offices for which he requires authorisation to act, a certificate must be issued by the insurance company for the addition to the amount of the bond of a specific penalty in respect of the fraud or dishonesty of the practitioner in relation to that appointment, whether acting alone or in collusion with other persons, and for the fraud or dishonesty of other persons connived at by the practitioner.[10] The amount of the specific penalty addition to the bond must be not less than the estimated value of the assets of the company or individual in relation to whom the insolvency practitioner is appointed, except that if he is appointed to be an administrative receiver of the property of a company, the specific penalty addition must be not less than the estimated value of that part of the assets of the company comprised in the receivership which would appear to be available to the unsecured creditors of the company (ie the amount of the company's debts and liabilities (including preferential debts and liabilities) or, of if it is less, the excess of the company's assets over its specifically secured debts and over its debts secured by a floating charge less the amount by which its preferential debts exceed the value of the company's assets comprised in floating charges). The maximum amount for which a special penalty addition must be made to the bond in respect of each company or individual in relation to whom the insolvency practitioner is appointed is £5m, even if the value of the company's or individual's assets exceeds that amount, and the minimum amount of the special penalty addition is £5,000.[11] If, while acting in any of the capacities for which the appointment of a qualified insolvency practitioner is required, the practitioner forms the opinion that the assets of the company or individual are greater than the amount of the specific penalty currently covered by his insurance bond, he must procure a corresponding increase in the amount of the bond, but not so that the special penalty exceeds £5m.[12]

Insolvency practitioners' records

Insolvency practitioners are required to keep a record of certain prescribed information in respect of each company and individual in relation to whom they act in insolvency proceedings, of the nature

---

11 Ibid, Sch 2, Part II, paras 3 and 4.
12 Insolvency Practitioners' Regulations 1990, reg 12(1) and Sch 2, Part II, para 1 (as amended by the Insolvency Practitioners' (Amendment) Regulations 1993, reg 5).

of the proceedings in each case (liquidation, administration under an order of the court, administrative receivership, bankruptcy, etc) and of the progressive stages reached in each of the proceedings.[13] The record must be kept at a place notified by the insolvency practitioner to the recognised professional body which authorised him to act, or to the Secretary of State if he granted the practitioner's authorisation, and the record must be produced to that body or to the Secretary of State (as the case may be) on request.[14] These obligations are additional to the duties of insolvency practitioners to keep accounts and other records in connection with insolvency proceedings of different kinds which are specifically required by the Insolvency Act 1986, and the rules made under it.

ARRANGEMENT OF MATERIAL

In this book insolvency proceedings in respect of companies will be considered in the following order, namely, the winding up or liquidation of companies (Chapters 2 to 6), administration orders (Chapter 7), arrangements by companies with their creditors (Chapter 8) and the enforcement of securities over companies' assets (including receiverships) (Chapter 9). The interrelationship of the different insolvency proceedings will be dealt with as part of the law relating to them respectively, as will the possibility of them being pursued concurrently or consecutively in respect of a company.

---

13 Ibid, reg 16 and reg 17(1) and Sch 3.
14 Ibid, reg 18(1) and (2) and reg 19.

CHAPTER 2

Winding up of companies by the court

Winding up or liquidation is the process by which the management of a company's affairs is taken out of its directors' hands, its assets are realised by a liquidator, and its debts and liabilities are discharged out of the proceeds of realisation (so far as they are sufficient for the purpose) and any surplus of the company's assets which remain is returned to its members or shareholders. At the end of the winding up the company will have no assets or liabilities, and it will therefore be simply a formal step for it to be dissolved, that is, for its legal personality as a corporation to be brought to an end.

A company may be wound up in either of two ways, namely, by the court making a winding up order,[1] or by the company passing an appropriate resolution for its voluntary winding up at a general meeting of its members.[2] This chapter is concerned solely with liquidations brought about by the court making a winding up order.

JURISDICTION

The High Court has jurisdiction to wind up any company registered in England or Wales under the Companies Act 1985 or any of the earlier Companies Acts enacted between 1862 and 1948[3] and its jurisdiction is exercised by certain judges of the Chancery Division who are nominated by the Lord Chancellor, and are known collectively as the Companies Court.[4]

1 The winding up is then usually known as a compulsory winding up; that expression does not appear in the Insolvency Act 1986, but it contrasts appropriately with the expression 'voluntary winding up' which is used in the Act.
2 Insolvency Act 1986, s 73(1).
3 Ibid, s 117(1). All judges of the High Court have jurisdiction in the winding up of companies, and so any judge may exercise jurisdiction over matters which are incidental to a liquidation (eg giving leave under the Insolvency Act 1986, s 130(2) for an action to be brought against a company in compulsory liquidation) (*Fabric Sales Ltd v Eratex Ltd* [1984] 1 WLR 863n).
4 Jurisdiction in winding up is assigned to the Chancery Division by the Supreme Court Act 1981, s 61(1) and Sch 1, para 1 (11 *Halsbury's Statutes* (4th edn) 819 and 866, (re-enacting the Supreme Court of Judicature (Consolidation) Act 1925, s 56(1)(*a*) (18 *Halsbury's Statutes* (3rd edn) 490), which itself re-enacted the Judicature Act 1873, s 34(2))). The winding up of companies was part of the exclusive jurisdiction of the Court of Chancery under the Companies Act 1862, s 81.

A county court may wind up a company whose registered office
is situate within its district[5] if the company's paid up share capital does
not exceed £120,000,[6] but if any party to the proceedings on the
winding up petition or to proceedings subsequent to the winding up
order wishes to have any question of law or fact or the exercise of any
discretion determined in the first instance by the Companies Court,
he may require the county court judge to state a case for the purpose.[7]
In exercising its concurrent jurisdiction to wind up a company, a
county court has all the powers of the High Court,[8] and it may decide
any question in the course of the winding up, even though the value
of the subject matter in dispute would ordinarily take the matter
outside its jurisdiction.[9] But if an action is brought by or against the
company in liquidation which could have been brought by or against
it if it were not being wound up, the county court which tries the action
does so under its ordinary and not its winding up jurisdiction, and its
jurisdiction is then subject to the normal monetary limits.[10] This may
result in the county court being competent to entertain a claim if
presented in one way, but not if presented in another. For example,
the liquidator may sue in the county court to set aside a floating charge
for any amount on the ground that the charge was created by the
company within a year (or in some cases two years) before the
commencement of the winding up to secure an existing debt,[11] but not
on the ground that it was procured by fraud or misrepresentation, or
that the person entitled to the charge has agreed for consideration to
release it, because the floating charge could be impeached on either
of these latter grounds if the company were not being wound up, and
the county court would then have jurisdiction only if the secured debts
were not more than £30,000.[12] Again, a person who has contracted

---

5 For this purpose, a company's registered office is deemed to be situate at the
  place which has longest been its registered office during the six months preceding
  the presentation of the winding up petition (Insolvency Act 1986, s 117(6)).
6 Insolvency Act 1986, s 117(2). The Lord Chancellor may by order exclude
  the jurisdiction of any county court, or transfer it to any other county court
  (s 117(4)). The county courts which do not have jurisdiction in any bankruptcy
  and winding up and the courts which instead have such jurisdiction in their areas
  are specified in the Civil Courts Order 1983 (SI 1983/713), para 10 and Sch 3
  (as subsequently frequently amended by further statutory instruments). In
  practice, most winding up petitions are presented to the High Court, even
  though the county court has jurisdiction over the company concerned.
7 Insolvency Act 1986, s 119(1).
8 Ibid, s 117(5).
9 *Re F and E Stanton Ltd* [1928] 1 KB 464.
10 *Re Ilkley Hotel Co* [1893] 1 QB 248.
11 Insolvency Act 1986, s 245.
12 County Courts Act 1984, s 23(*d*) and (*g*) and s 147(1) (11 *Halsbury's Statutes*
   (4th edn) 623 and 707) (substituted by the Courts and Legal Services Act 1990
   s 2(1)) (*Halsbury's Statutes* (4th edn) (1991 Reissue) 723).

to purchase property from the company may appeal to the county court against the liquidator's rejection of his proof for damages for non-delivery or failure to transfer, whatever the amount of the damages, but he may seek an order of specific performance only if the property is worth no more than £30,000.[13]

A winding up petition presented to the Companies Court and the proceedings in a winding up following a winding up order made by that court may be transferred by the Companies Court to any county court,[14] and conversely any such petition or proceedings in a county court may be transferred to the Companies Court by order of that court or the county court in question.[15] Furthermore, if such a petition is presented or such proceedings are pending in a county court, it may transfer the proceedings to another county court.[16] This power to transfer proceedings is exercisable whether or not the winding up proceedings were originally brought in the wrong court. Moreover, winding up proceedings are not invalid because they are taken in the wrong county court,[17] and when the court in which winding up proceedings are pending discovers the error, it may nevertheless retain the proceedings instead of transferring them.[18]

If two winding up petitions are presented by different petitioners, the first in the Companies Court and the second in a county court, the Companies Court will, if it makes a winding up order on the first petition, transfer the county court proceedings to the High Court and stay them, for no benefit can accrue to anyone from their continuing.[19] But if the petition in the Companies Court is presented after the presentation of an earlier petition to the county court, the Companies Court will transfer the county court proceedings to itself and make an order on both petitions; if it orders a winding up, the commencement of the liquidation will then relate back to the date of the earlier county court petition.[20]

---

13 County Courts Act 1984, s 23(*d*).
14 Ibid, s 40(1).
15 Ibid, s 41(1) and s 42 (substituted by the Courts and Legal Services Act 1990, s 2(1)).
16 Ibid, s 75(3)(*b*) (as amended by the Courts and Legal Services Act 1990, s 16(2) and s 49(3)) and County Court Rules 1981, Ord 16, r 1.
17 Insolvency Act 1986, s 118(1).
18 Ibid, s 118(2).
19 *Re Audio Systems Ltd* [1965] 2 All ER 919, [1965] 1 WLR 1096.
20 *Re Filby Bros (Provender) Ltd* [1958] 2 All ER 458, [1958] 1 WLR 683. For the retrospective operation of a winding up order, see p 98, post.

PETITIONERS

A petition for a winding up order may be presented:– (*a*) by the company itself; or (*b*) by any of its creditors or contributories, (ie members or past members of the company);[1] or (*c*) by the Secretary of State for Trade and Industry after exercising his powers of investigation or inspection in respect of the company;[2] or (*d*) by the directors of the company acting together (and not merely pursuant to a board resolution passed by a majority of their number);[3] or (*e*) by the administrator of the company appointed under an administration order;[4] or (*f*) by an administrative receiver of the whole or substantially the whole of the company's assets appointed under a floating charge. A joint petition may be presented by two or more creditors or contributories, with or without the company or its directors joining as co-petitioners.

Additionally, the Secretary of State for Trade and Industry may present a petition to wind up a company which carries on insurance business in Great Britain.[5] The Bank of England may present a petition to wind up a company which is an institution which is or has been authorised by the Bank to accept deposits in the course of carrying on a deposit taking business,[6] whether it is authorised to represent itself to be a bank or to carry on a banking business or not.[7] The Securities and Investments Board established under the Financial Services Act 1986 to authorise and regulate companies and other persons who carry on investment business, may petition the court to order the winding up of any company which is, or has been, authorised to carry on investment business under the Act, or of any company which is or has been an authorised representative of such a company or other person so authorised to carry on investment business.[8] Finally, the Attorney-General may present a petition to wind up a company formed for charitable purposes.[9]

1 Insolvency Act 1986, s 124(1).
2 Ibid, s 124(4) and s 124A(1) (substituted by Companies Act 1989, s 60(2) and (3)).
3 Ibid, s 124(1); *Re Instrumentation Electrical Services Ltd* [1988] BCLC 550, 4 BCC 301.
4 Ibid, s 14(1) and s 42(1) and Sch 1, para 21.
5 Insurance Companies Act 1982, s 54(1) (22 *Halsbury's Statutes* (4th edn) 205).
6 Banking Act 1987, s 92(1) (4 *Halsbury's Statutes* (4th edn) 621).
7 An authorised institution is entitled to do this only if it satisfies certain additional conditions (Banking Act 1987, ss 67 and 68).
8 Financial Services Act 1986, s 72(1) and (2); Financial Services Act 1986 (Delegation) Order 1987 (SI 1987/942): art 4 and Sch 2, para 4.
9 Charities Act 1993, s 63 (1)(5 *Halsbury's Statutes* (4th edn)(1993 Reissue) 947.

A petition may not be presented for the winding up of more than one company, unless, possibly, the respondent companies are all members of the same group, whether the parent or holding company of the group is included as a respondent or not.[10] The fact that companies have the same shareholders if they are not part of the same group does not justify the presentation of a single petition against them all.[10]

Company's petition

Petitions by the company itself are rare, because the decision to petition must be taken by its members in the general meeting in all but exceptional cases, and if a majority of the members wish the company to be wound up, it will usually be possible for them to pass a resolution for the company to be wound up voluntarily, which will be far speedier and cheaper than a winding up by the court. There is, of course, the possibility that only a bare majority of the members may want the company to be wound up, in which case they may have sufficient votes to pass an ordinary resolution for the presentation of a winding up petition, but will not be able to pass the special or extraordinary resolution required for a voluntary winding up. This does not give rise to any difficulty, however, because the court cannot make a winding up order merely because an ordinary resolution has been passed expressing a wish that the company should be wound up;[11] if there is some other ground for the company's petition, it will also form the basis for a petition by an individual creditor or by a member petitioning as a contributory, and it is obviously more expedient for the petition to be presented by such a person than by the company itself.

It appears that the power to present a winding up petition in the company's name either cannot be delegated to its directors at all by the company's articles of association,[12] or will only be treated as delegated to the directors if the articles expressly so provide, it being insufficient for the articles merely to delegate to them power to manage the company's business and to exercise the company's powers generally.[13] Consequently, in all but exceptional cases, it will

---

10 *Re a Company* [1984] BCLC 307.
11 *Re Anglo-Continental Produce Co Ltd* [1939] 1 All ER 99.
12 *Smith v Duke of Manchester* (1883) 24 Ch D 611; *Re Galway and Salthill Tramways Co* [1918] 1 IR 62.
13 *Re Emmadart Ltd* [1979] Ch 540, [1979] 1 All ER 599. The Companies (Tables A to F) Regulations 1985 (SI 1985/805), Schedule, Table A, art 70 does not contain an express power for the board to present a winding up petition.

be essential for an ordinary resolution for the presentation of a winding up petition in the company's name to be passed by a general meeting of the members. If the directors present a petition in the company's name without the approval of a general meeting, such a meeting may ratify their action subsequently, however, and if it has not been ratified before the petition is heard, the court will adjourn the hearing so that a general meeting may be held to decide whether the proceedings shall be continued.[14] The presentation of a winding up petition by the directors of a company now presents no difficulty, however, because they may petition in their own names provided that they all concur in doing so.[15]

If a receiver is appointed by or on behalf of secured creditors or by debenture holders or debenture stockholders under the provisions of a debt security agreement, debentures or a trust deed covering an issue of debentures or debenture stock and the receiver's powers extend to taking possession of and preserving and protecting the company's assets, the receiver may, if he is expressed in the debt security agreement or the debentures or covering trust deed to be an agent of the company, present a winding up petition in the company's name, provided that a winding up order will enable the company's assets to be protected from depletion,[16] or possibly, if the company's assets will be augmented for the benefit of the secured creditors or debenture holders or debenture stockholders under the statutory provisions empowering the liquidator to recover assets which the company has disposed of or given as security.[17] An administrative receiver (who is defined as a receiver appointed by or on behalf of the holders of debentures secured by a floating charge or such a charge and any other securities where the appointment extends to the whole or substantially the whole of the company's assets)[18] is deemed to be the agent of the company until it resolves to be wound up voluntarily or has a winding up order made against it, and it would therefore appear that an administrative receiver may petition in the company's name for it to be wound up, unless such a power is impliedly excluded by the administrative receiver's statutory power to petition in his own name.[20] Since a receiver who is appointed by the court is not an agent for the secured creditors or debenture holders for whose benefit he was

14 *Re Galway and Salthill Tramways Co*, supra.
15 Insolvency Act 1986, s 124(1); *Re Instrumentation Electrical Services Ltd*, supra.
16 *Re Emmadart Ltd*, supra.
17 See p 221 et seq, post.
18 Insolvency Act 1986, s 29(2).
19 Ibid, s 44(1) and s 247(2).
20 Ibid, s 42(1) and Sch 1, para 21.

appointed,[1] such a receiver can, of course, in no circumstances present a winding up petition in the company's name.

Creditor's petition

Definition of a creditor

A creditor of a company may petition for a winding up order whatever the amount of his debt, whether it is immediately payable or is payable only at a future time or on the fulfilment of a contingency,[2] and whether it is secured or unsecured.[3] A guarantor of a debt of the company is a contingent creditor for his right to an indemnity by the company, but it has been held that he cannot petition for the company to be wound up unless he has discharged the debt which he has guaranteed in full, because until then the right to petition in respect of the debt is vested exclusively in the creditor to whom it is owed;[4] however, there is authority that a guarantor of a company's obligation can petition for it to be wound up, even though he has not fulfilled the obligation and it remains unfulfilled.[5] An equitable assignee of a debt owed by a company may petition for it to be wound up, and the assignor need not be a party to the petition, even though he would have to be joined in an action brought by the assignee against the company.[6] Conversely, the court will not make a winding up order on the petition of a creditor who has made an equitable assignment of the whole beneficial interest in his debt, unless the assignee joins in the petition.[7] Although an equitable assignee of a debt may petition for a winding up order, a person for whom a debt is held on trust by the company's creditor may not do so, and the petition must be presented by the creditor himself.[8]

A creditor is a person who could enforce his claim against the company by an action of debt, and a person cannot petition for a

1 *Moss SS Co Ltd v Whinney* [1912] AC 254; *Parsons v Sovereign Bank of Canada* [1913] AC 160 (see p 484, post).
2 Insolvency Act 1986, s 124(1).
3 *Moor v Anglo-Italian Bank* (1879) 10 Ch D 681. The creditor need not value his security in his petition, and will be entitled to a winding up order although his debt is adequately covered by the value of his security.
4 *Re Fitness Centre (South East) Ltd* [1986] BCLC 518, 2 BCC 99, 535.
5 *Re Dollar Land Holdings plc* [1994] 1 BCLC 404, [1993] BCC 823.
6 *Re Steel Wing Co* [1921] 1 Ch 349.
7 *Re Pentalta Exploration Co* [1898] WN 55.
8 *Re Uruguay Central and Hygueritas Rly Co of Monte Video* (1879) 11 Ch D 372; *Re Dunderland Iron Ore Co Ltd* [1909] 1 Ch 446.

winding up order as a creditor when he has merely a right of action against the company for unliquidated damaged for breach of contract[9] or tort,[10] or for the restitution of money or property to him in equity.[11] But if such a person obtains judgment against the company for an ascertained sum of money, the judgment itself creates a debt, and he is then able to petition for the company to be wound up. However, a person who has obtained judgment against a third party to whom the company is indebted, does not become a creditor of the company by obtaining a garnishee order against it requiring it to pay the debt which it owes to the third party to his judgment creditor, and this is so even if the garnishee order is made absolute, so that it will be contempt of court for the company not to comply with it.[12] If the judgment creditor cannot or does not wish to enforce the garnishee order by the normal processes of execution, he may sue the company for the amount owed by it to the judgment debtor, relying on the garnishee order absolute as creating a debt owed to him by the company, and when he has obtained judgment against the company for the amount payable under the garnishee order, he may present a winding up petition against it as a judgment creditor of the company itself.[11]

The petitioning creditor's claim against the company must exist at the date he presents his petition. Consequently, if he is a judgment creditor who has levied execution against the company, and unknown to him, the sheriff or other officer of the court has recovered the amount of the judgment debt and the incidental costs before the petition is filed, he is no longer a creditor, and his petition must be dismissed with costs.[13] This is so, even though in the event of the company subsequently being wound up on the petition of another creditor presented before the execution was completed, the original petitioner may have to return to the liquidator any amount which the sheriff or officer of the court recovered for his benefit and prove as a creditor in the winding up of the company for the amount of his judgment debt.[14] Similarly, it has been held that if the Secretary of State for Trade and Industry brings an action in the company's name purporting to act under the powers conferred on him by the Companies Act 1985 (as amended) but in fact without authorisation under those powers, the fact that a liquidator in a winding up of the

9 *Re Milford Docks Co* (1883) 23 Ch D 292.
10 *Re Pen-y-Van Colliery Co* (1877) 6 Ch D 477; doubted by Megarry J in *Re a Company* [1974] 1 All ER 256 at 260, [1973] 1 WLR 1566 at 1572.
11 *Pritchett v English and Colonial Syndicate Ltd* [1899] 2 QB 428.
12 *Re Combined Weighing and Advertising Machine Co* (1889) 43 Ch D 99.
13 *Re William Hockley Ltd* [1962] 2 All ER 111, [1962] 1 WLR 555; contra *Re a Debtor (No 2 of 1977), Debtor v Goacher* [1979] 1 All ER 870, [1979] 1 WLR 956.
14 See p 249 et seq, post.

company may ratify the bringing of the action, and that if the action then fails on the merits, the company may become liable to the defendant in costs, does not make the defendant a contingent creditor for the purpose of presenting a winding up petition.[15] On the other hand, the fact that the petitioning creditor's claim is for a debt incurred on the company's behalf by its liquidator in a voluntary winding up does not prevent the petition from succeeding, even though the company will be treated as having been in liquidation from the commencement of the voluntary winding up if a winding up order is made.[16] Nor is it necessary that the petitioning creditor's claim should be immediately enforceable by an action of debt at the date when his petition is presented. If the claim will be enforceable by an action of debt when a future date arrives (ie if it is for a future debt), or will become so enforceable if a specified contingency is fulfilled (ie if it is a contingent debt), the fact that the creditor will or may be able to bring an action of debt entitles him to present a winding up petition immediately.[17] Consequently, a judgment creditor of the company may petition for it to be wound up in reliance on a court order for payment by it of costs awarded to the creditor in proceedings to which the company was a party, even though the costs have not yet been taxed.[18]

Amount of the debt owed to the creditor

The court will not make a winding up order if the petitioning creditor is owed less than £750,[19] unless the petition is supported by other creditors, and the total of the debts owed to the petitioner and the supporting creditors amounts to at least £750.[20] But if the company has no assets which can be reached by the ordinary processes of execution, and it refuses to call up any capital remaining unpaid on its shares in order to pay the petitioner's debt, the court will make a winding up order even though the debt is less than £750, for this is the only way to ensure that the petitioner's debt is paid.[1]

---

15 *Re SBA Properties Ltd* [1967] 2 All ER 615, [1967] 1 WLR 799.
16 *Re Bank of South Australia (No 2)* [1895] 1 Ch 578.
17 *Re British Equitable Bond and Mortgage Corpn Ltd* [1991] 1 Ch 574; *Re a Company (No 003028 of 1987)* [1988] BCLC 282, 3 BCC 575.
18 *Tottenham Hotspur plc v Edennote plc* [1995] 1 BCLC 65, [1994] BCC 681.
19 *Re Milford Docks Co*, supra. The amount of £750 is adopted judicially from the amount specified in the Insolvency Act 1986, s 123(1) as the minimum amount for which a notice demanding payment may be served by a creditor in order to establish the company's insolvency (see p 42, post).
20 *Re Leyton and Walthamstow Cycle Co* [1901] WN 225.
 1 *Re World Industrial Bank Ltd* [1909] WN 148.

Defences to the creditor's claim

On the hearing of a creditor's petition the court is reluctant to go into the merits of any defence which the company has to the creditor's claim, and if the defence is a substantial one and is put forward in good faith, the court will dismiss the petition, and entertain a fresh petition only when the creditor has successfully sued the company by action and entered judgment against it. The court is unwilling to adjourn the hearing of a creditor's petition so that the validity of his claim that the company is indebted to him may be litigated, because this will prevent other creditors presenting petitions until the first petition has been disposed of, and also because the conduct of the company's business and the disposal of its assets for quite proper purposes may be inhibited meanwhile.[2] Consequently, the court dismissed a petition in which the creditor claimed a sum for goods sold to the company when no price had been agreed upon and the company contended that the sum demanded by the creditor was unreasonable.[3] The court also dismissed a petition by a creditor who claimed payment of an agreed sum for work done for the company when the company contended that the work had not been done properly,[4] or that the terms for payment had been varied by agreement and the amount claimed by the petitioner was not yet due,[5] or that the company was not incorporated when the contract under which the debt to the petitioner arose was entered into, and the contract was therefore made by the petitioner with the company's promoters.[6] Similarly, the court dismissed a petition based on an alleged loan which the company contended was a payment made to it by the petitioner so that it might purchase an investment on his behalf as his agent.[7]

But the court will not dismiss a petition merely because the company alleges that it had a defence to the creditor's claim, unless it also shows that the defence is likely to succeed in point of law, and adduces at least prima facie proof of the facts on which the defence depends. Consequently, the court refused to dismiss a petition by a creditor who had done work for the company, merely because the company alleged that it had a private arrangement with its secretary that he should pay the creditor's claim out of funds in his hands, and that this arrangement was known to the creditor; this allegation would not constitute a defence if the creditor sued the company by

2 *Re Boston Timber Fabrications Ltd* [1984] BCLC 328.
3 *Re London and Paris Banking Corpn* (1874) LR 19 Eq 444.
4 *Re Brighton Club and Norfolk Hotel Co Ltd* (1865) 35 Beav 204.
5 *Re a Company (No 0012209 of 1991)* [1992] 2 All ER 797, [1992] 1 WLR 351.
6 *Re a Company (No 003079 of 1990)* [1991] BCLC 235, [1991] BCC 683.
7 *Re Lympne Investments Ltd* [1972] 2 All ER 385, [1972] 1 WLR 523.

action, and so was no impediment to the petition being heard.[8] For the same reason the court refused to dismiss a petition grounded on the admitted dishonour of a cheque issued by a company when the company contended that its bank had invited the petitioner to re-present the cheque, which the petitioner declined to do, and the cheque would have been paid on re-presentation.[9] Similarly, the court made a winding up order on the petition of a supplier of goods to the company in response to its order, when the company alleged that it ordered the goods as agent for an overseas purchaser, who alone was liable for the price, but the evidence showed that the company had agreed to supply the goods to that purchaser at a higher price than the original supplier had agreed to accept, so that the company could not possibly have ordered the goods as agent for that purchaser.[10] Again, the court refused to dismiss the petition of the holder of a policy issued by an insurance company merely on the strength of an allegation that the petitioner had failed to disclose material facts to it when the policy was taken out, for the company did not support the allegation with any vestige of proof.[11] On the other hand, if the company disputes its indebtedness to the petitioner, but the facts of the case are relatively straightforward and need to be investigated only to determine whether the company's defence is tenable and put forward in good faith, the court may in its discretion decide whether the petitioner's claim is well founded on the hearing of the petition.[12] If a creditor has reason to expect that the company will raise a plausible defence to his claim, his best course is to sue the company by action and to present a winding up petition when he has obtained judgment against it. The company will then be estopped by the judgment from disputing the petitioner's claim on its merits, and the only possible defences which it will be able to plead to the winding up petition, apart from release or satisfaction of the judgment debt, will be that the judgment was obtained fraudulently or by collusion with the company's directors,[13] or that the transaction on which the judgment was based was void because it was ultra vires the company.[14]

8 *Re King's Cross Industrial Dwellings Co* (1870) LR 11 Eq 149.

9 *Re a Company (No 001259 of 1991), ex p Medialite* [1991] BCLC 594.

10 *Re Janeash Ltd* [1990] BCC 250.

11 *Re Great Britain Mutual Life Assurance Society* (1880) 16 Ch D 246.

12 *Brinds Ltd v Offshore Oil NL* (1985) 2 BCC 98, 916; *Re a Company (No 001946 of 1991), ex p Fin Soft Holdings SA* [1991] BCLC 737.

13 *Bowes v Directors of Hope Life Insurance and Guarantee Co* (1865) 11 HL Cas 389.

14 *Re Jon Beauforte (London) Ltd* [1953] Ch 131, [1953] 1 All ER 634. But the defence cannot be relied on if the transaction is validated by the Companies Act 1985, s 35A(1) (inserted by Companies Act 1989, s 108(1)), or if the company pleaded the defence of ultra vires unsuccessfully in the action.

The fact that the company disputes the amount of the debt claimed by the petitioning creditor will not induce the court to dismiss the petition if the company admits that it is indebted to him for an amount which, taken by itself, would be sufficient for the court to make a winding up order.[15] On the other hand, if the company admits and pays part of the amount claimed by the petitioner, but disputes the remainder, the court will not make a winding up order unless the petitioner first obtains judgment for the remainder.[16] If the petitioner has obtained judgment against the company for the claim on which his petition is based, the fact that the company has an appeal pending against the judgment,[17] or has a cross-claim against the petitioner which it is asserting in pending litigation,[18] is no reason for the refusal of a winding up order, but if the cross-claim equals or exceeds the debt claimed by the petitioning creditor, even if it is disputed by him,[19] or if the cross-claim arises under the same transaction as the debt on which the petition is based,[20] the court may in its discretion stay the proceedings on the petition until litigation on the cross-claim has been concluded. On the other hand, if the company's sole asset is a claim for damages against the petitioner and the claim can be more effectively prosecuted by the directors than by a liquidator, the court will not wind the company up at the petitioner's request, unless there are other factors which would make it harmful to the company's creditors generally not to wind it up.[1]

Wishes of other creditors and shareholders

A creditor whose debt is immediately payable and who has not been paid is entitled to a winding up order as of right as between himself and the company.[2] But if there is opposition to the making of a winding up order from other creditors or from shareholders (contributories), the court will consider their wishes, and may in its

---

15 *Re Tweeds Garages Ltd* [1962] Ch 406, [1962] 1 All ER 121; *Re Camburn Petroleum Products Ltd* [1979] 3 All ER 297, [1980] 1 WLR 86; *Re Trinity Insurance Co Ltd* [1990] BCC 235.

16 *Re a Company* [1984] 3 All ER 78, [1984] 1 WLR 1090.

17 *Re Amalgamated Properties of Rhodesia (1913) Ltd* [1917] 2 Ch 115.

18 *Re Douglas (Griggs) Engineering Ltd* [1963] Ch 19, [1962] 1 All ER 498; *Re R A Foulds Ltd* (1986) 2 BCC 99, 269; *Re FSA Business Software Ltd* [1990] BCLC 825, [1990] BCC 465; *Re Leasing and Finance Services Ltd* [1991] BCC 29.

19 *Re LHF Wools Ltd* [1970] Ch 27, [1969] 3 All ER 882; *Re Euro-Hotel (Belgravia) Ltd* [1975] 3 All ER 1075.

20 *McDonald's Restaurants Ltd v Urbandivide Co Ltd* [1994] 1 BCLC 306.

1 *Re LHF Wools Ltd*, supra.

2 *Bowes v Hope Life Insurance and Guarantee Co*, supra: *Re Chapel House Colliery Co* (1883) 24 Ch D 259.

discretion decline to make the order.[3] This is particularly so if the opposing creditors belong to the same class as the petitioning creditor, for example, if they hold debentures of the same series,[4] but the wishes of creditors who rank for payment after the petitioner,[5] and the wishes of shareholders,[6] also merit consideration, although obviously less weight will be attached to them. In taking account of the wishes of opposing creditors and shareholders, the court does not simply compare the total of the debts owing to them or the value of their shares with the total of the debts owing to the petitioner and his supporters.[7] The court also has regard to the reasonableness of the opponents' case,[8] to whether the opponents would gain an unjust advantage over the petitioner by the refusal of a winding up order,[9] to whether the purpose of the opposition is to prevent the company enforcing a claim which it has against the opposing creditors,[10] to whether the petitioner is seeking to gain a priority for payment of his claim over those of other creditors by obtaining a winding up order,[11] to whether greater harm or injustice would be done to the petitioner by refusing a winding up order than to the opponents by making it,[12] to whether there are matters which should be inquired into and which can only be investigated properly if a winding up order is made,[13] and to whether, when a voluntary winding up is proposed as a cheaper and quicker alternative to a winding up by the court, there is any certainty that a winding up resolution would be passed by the controlling shareholders of the company who were also creditors of it and who opposed the making

---

3 The court may have regard to the wishes of the creditors or shareholders generally in exercising any of its powers in connection with a winding up (Insolvency Act 1986, s 195(1)).

4 *Re Western of Canada, Oil Lands and Works Co* (1873) LR 17 Eq 1; *Re St Thomas' Dock Co* (1876) 2 Ch D 116; *Re Chapel House Colliery Co*, supra.

5 *Re St Thomas' Dock Co*, supra; *Re Great Western (Forest of Dean) Coal Consumers' Co* (1882) 21 Ch D 769.

6 *Re Brighton Hotel Co* (1868) LR 6 Eq 339.

7 *Re Vuma Ltd* [1960] 3 All ER 629, [1969] 1 WLR 1283; *Re P and J Macrae Ltd* [1961] 1 All ER 302, [1961] 1 WLR 229.

8 *Re Great Western (Forest of Dean) Coal Consumers' Co* (1882) 21 Ch D 769.

9 *Re Crigglestone Coal Co Ltd* [1906] 2 Ch 327; *Re Alfred Melson & Co* [1906] 1 Ch 841; *Re Clandown Colliery Co* [1915] 1 Ch 369 (winding-up order made on the petition of a trade creditor despite the opposition of debenture holders who had appointed a receiver to carry on the company's business for their own benefit as secured creditors).

10 *Re Allobrogia SS Corpn* [1978] 3 All ER 423.

11 *Re Leigh Estates (UK) Ltd* [1994] BCC 292. The petitioner was a local authority whose claim for unpaid rates in respect of premises occupied by the company would rank as an expense of the liquidation if a winding up order were made.

12 *Re Camburn Petroleum Products Ltd* [1979] 3 All ER 297, [1980] 1 WLR 86.

13 *Re Krasnapolsky Restaurant and Winter Garden Co* [1892] 3 Ch 174; *Re Crigglestone Coal Co Ltd*, supra.

of a winding up order;[14] if the opponents' case appears unmeritorious in the light of any of these considerations, a winding up order will be made. On the other hand, the court cannot exercise a discretion to refuse a winding up order because the closure of the company's business will put its employees out of work, or because the public generally has some interest in the continuation of the company's business.[15]

Winding up order must benefit creditors

It has often been held that a winding up order will not be made on a creditor's petition if it will not benefit him[16] or the company's creditors generally.[17] But the court will not normally refuse to wind a company up merely because the petitioning creditor alone will benefit by a winding up order being made, for example, because the company's only asset is a claim against its insurers which the petitioner will be able to enforce for his own exclusive benefit if the company goes into liquidation.[18] Nevertheless, the court has refused a winding up order when the petitioner was the company's landlord, who would be able to forfeit the company's lease if a winding up order were made; this would benefit the petitioner alone, and would be to the detriment of the other creditors of the company by diminishing its saleable assets available to satisfy the company's debts.[19]

One reason why the court formerly refused to make a winding up order was that the company had no assets, or had only assets which would be consumed in paying secured creditors who ranked before the petitioner. By statute a winding up order cannot now be refused for this reason alone,[20] but there can be little doubt that the general rule that a winding up order will be made only if it will benefit the petitioning creditor or the company's creditors as a whole nevertheless remains intact. Even before the statutory provision was first enacted,[1] it was held that a winding up order would be made against a company which had no assets if, as a result, assets might be recovered from persons who were liable or accountable to the

---

14 *Re Television Parlour plc* (1988) 4 BCC 95.

15 *Re Craven Insurance Co Ltd* [1968] 1 All ER 1140, [1968] 1 WLR 675.

16 *Re St Thomas' Dock Co* (1876) 2 Ch D 116; *Re Great Western (Forest of Dean) Coal Consumers' Co,* supra; *Re Chapel House Colliery Co* (1883) 24 Ch D 259.

17 *Re Greenwood & Co* [1900] 2 QB 306; *Re Rhine Film Corpn (UK) Ltd* (1985) 2 BCC 98, 949.

18 *Re Compania Merabello San Nicholas SA* [1973] Ch 75, [1972] 3 All ER 448.

19 *Re Rhine Film Corpn (UK) Ltd,* supra.

20 Insolvency Act 1986, s 125(1).

 1 Companies Act 1907, s 29.

company, or if mortgages or charges on its property which ranked before the petitioner's claim might be set aside,[2] for then the petitioner would benefit from the order. This has been confirmed in a recent case.[3] If there is no possibility of obtaining such benefits for the petitioner, however, it is submitted that, notwithstanding the statutory provision, a winding up order should not be made even today, and this is particularly so where the company has no realisable assets at present, but does have a good prospect of being able to pay its debts if it is allowed to carry on its business as a going concern for a brief period.[4]

Contributory's petition

Definition of contributory

The statutory term 'contributory' is misleading, because it conveys the impression that contributories are restricted to members of a company who can be called on to contribute a sum of money to its assets to enable it to meet its liabilities when it is wound up, in other words, that they must be either holders of partly paid shares, or members of a company limited by guarantee, or members of an unlimited company. The definition of a contributory in the Insolvency Act 1986, is very much wider than this, however. It is true that the definition section[5] provides that the term 'contributory means every person who is liable to contribute to the assets of the company in the event of it being wound up', but this merely refers back to an earlier section,[6] which provides that 'every present and past member shall be liable to contribute to the assets of the company to an amount sufficient for payment of its debts and liabilities ... and for the adjustment of the rights of the contributories among themselves', subject to certain restrictions on the liability of members of limited companies, and to the complete exemption of persons who ceased to be members of a company a year or more before the commencement of its winding up.[7] This section therefore makes all past and present

---

2 *Re Krasnapolsky Restaurant and Winter Garden Co*, supra; *Re Crigglestone Coal Co Ltd*, supra.
3 *Bell Group Finance (Pty) Ltd v Bell Group (UK) Holdings Ltd* [1996] 1 BCLC 304, [1996] BCC 505.
4 *Re St Thomas' Dock Co*, supra; *Re Great Western (Forest of Dean) Coal Consumers' Co*, supra.
5 Insolvency Act 1986, s 79(1).
6 Ibid, s 74(1).
7 Ibid, s 74(2) and (3).

members contributories, and then goes on to limit the amount which some of them have to contribute and to exempt others of them from contributing at all, but these latter provisions do not take away the status of contributories from the members to whom they apply. Consequently, it has been held that the holders of fully paid shares in a limited company are contributories,[8] as also are persons who ceased to be members more than a year before the commencement of the winding up,[9] and so any such person may petition for a winding up order as a contributory, subject to the statutory and other restrictions dealt with below.

The definition of a contributory does not confine the category to present or past members (ie registered shareholders)[10] of a company, and so other persons who are liable to contribute to its assets in its winding up, such as allottees of shares holding partly paid letters of allotment[11] and allottees of shares whose title rests merely on a resolution of the board of directors for the allotment of shares to them,[12] are included. Although allottees of shares are contributories, transferees by delivery of scrip to bearer and renouncees of letters of allotment are not in any contractual relationship with the company, and so are not contributories, unless they declare that they are willing to be registered as members,[13] nor are persons who have merely agreed to take a transfer of shares from the present registered holders.[14]

The fact that a petitioner's right to be registered as a member is challenged by the opponents of the petition, or that he is alleged by them to hold the shares registered in his name as their nominee, will not induce the court to dismiss the petition or to adjourn the hearing until the petitioner's title to membership has been established in separate proceedings.[15] If the status of a petitioner who claims to be an allottee of shares is challenged by the company, however, his winding up petition will not be heard until he has established his status as a contributory in separate proceedings but the court may in its discretion try the petitioner's claim to be an allottee as a preliminary question on the hearing of the winding-up petition.[12]

---

8 *Re Anglesea Colliery Co* (1866) 1 Ch App 555; *Re National Savings Bank Association* (1866) 1 Ch App 547.

9 *Re Consolidated Gold Fields of New Zealand Ltd* [1953] Ch 689, [1953] 1 All ER 791.

10 Companies Act 1985, s 22(2).

11 *Re Littlehampton, Havre and Honfleur SS Co, Ormerod's Case* (1867) LR 5 Eq 110; *Re Patent Steam Engine Co* (1878) 8 Ch D 464.

12 *Re JN2 Ltd* [1977] 3 All ER 1104, [1978] 1 WLR 183; *Re UOC Corpn, Alipour v Ary* [1997] BCC 377.

13 *Ormerod's Case*, supra. Scrip to bearer is now obsolete in practice.

14 *Re a Company (No 003160 of 1986)* [1986] BCLC 391, 2 BCC 99 276.

15 *Re Garage Door Associates Ltd* [1984] 1 All ER 434, [1984] 1 WLR 35.

Statutory restrictions on contributory's right to petition

A contributory may not present a winding up petition unless[16] (a) the company is a public or unlimited company and its membership has fallen below two; or (b) the shares in respect of which he is a contributory were originally allotted to him, or have been held by him and registered in his name for at least 6 out of 18 months before the commencement of the winding up (ie the date when the contributory's petition is presented), or those shares have devolved on him on the death of a former holder.[17]

If shares were originally allotted to the petitioner, or have devolved on him as the personal representative of a deceased member,[18] or, possibly, as a beneficiary of a deceased member's estate,[19] it is not necessary that the petitioner should be registered as a member himself, but in any other case it seems that he must have been registered as a member for at least six months,[20] although it is not necessary that he should have been the beneficial owner of the shares during any part of that time.[1] A person to whom the allottee of shares has renounced them, or who has otherwise succeeded to the rights of the allottee, but has not been registered as holder of the shares therefore cannot present a winding up petition.[2] If a transferee of shares has presented his transfer to the company for registration and the company has improperly refused or failed to register it, there is authority for treating the qualifying period of six months as running in the transferee's favour from the time when the company was first in default, and not from the date of actual registration.[3] Nevertheless, there are obiter dicta to the contrary,[4] and the

16 Insolvency Act 1986, s 124(2), as amended by the Companies (Single Member Private Companies) Regulations 1992 (SI 1992/1699), reg 2(1)(*b*) and Sch, para 8.
17 This second alternative is clearly inapplicable in the case of a company which has no share capital, and it is submitted that a member of such a company may present a winding up petition however short a time he has been a member.
18 *Re Norwich Yarn Co* (1850) 12 Beav 366; *Re Bayswater Trading Co Ltd* [1970] 1 All ER 608, [1970] 1 WLR 343.
19 The Insolvency Act 1986, s 81(1) provides that the personal representatives of a deceased member shall be contributories in his place, but this does not appear to prevent a beneficiary of his estate in whom the personal representatives have vested the deceased member's shares being also treated as a person on whom they have devolved on the death of a member.
20 The purpose of this requirement is to prevent a person from seeking to wreck a company by purchasing shares in it solely with a view to presenting a winding up petition immediately.
1 *Re Wala Wynaad Indian Gold Mining Co* (1882) 21 Ch D 849.
2 *Re Quickdome Ltd* [1988] BCLC 370.
3 *Re Patent Steam Engine Co* (1878) 8 Ch D 464.
4 *Re a Company* [1894] 2 Ch 349 at 351, per Vaughan Williams J; *Re Gattopardo Ltd* [1969] 2 All ER 344 at 347, [1969] 1 WLR 619 at 623, per Russell LJ.

concession certainly does not apply unless the company is proved to have been in default.[5]

The trustee in bankruptcy of a member or contributory cannot present a winding up petition unless he has been registered as holder of the bankrupt's shares for the requisite six months.[6] This is so, even though by statute the trustee in bankruptcy for all other purposes represents the bankrupt in winding up proceedings and is a contributory in his place.[7] One consequence of this provision is that a bankrupt member or contributory himself cannot present a winding up petition, nor can he make any application to the court in connection with winding up proceedings, and this disability continues even after the termination of his bankruptcy, unless the bankruptcy order made against him is annulled.[8]

The bearer of a share warrant or share certificate in favour of the bearer of the document cannot present a winding up petition unless he was the original allottee of the shares comprised in it.[9] Under the Companies Act 1862, it was held that a transferee of scrip[10] entitling the bearer to call on the company to allot him shares could present a winding up petition on undertaking to submit to being registered as a member of the company.[11] However, it would appear that the renouncee of a letter of allotment who is willing to give the same undertaking may petition only if the company is a public or unlimited company whose membership has fallen below two, because, unlike a transferee of scrip, he is not the person to whom the shares are originally allotted, and ex hypothesi he has not been registered by the company as holder of the shares.

If the membership of a public or unlimited company has fallen below two, a contributory may petition, however short a time he has held his shares,[12] but it is submitted that a transferee of shares can qualify as a petitioner under this provision only if he is registered as

---

5 *Re Gattopardo Ltd*, supra.

6 *Re H L Bolton Engineering Co* [1956] Ch 577, [1956] 1 All ER 799.

7 Insolvency Act 1986, s 82(2).

8 *Re Wolverhampton Steel and Iron Co Ltd* [1977] 3 All ER 467, [1977] 1 WLR 860.

9 *Re Wala Wynaad Indian Gold Mining Co* (1882) 21 Ch D 849.

10 Scrip used to be issued by companies during the last century to applicants for shares. It gave the scripholder, whether the original holder or his transferee, the right to have a specified number of shares allotted to him and to become a member of the company when he had paid the issue price of the shares in full. The difference between scrip and a letter of allotment is that the original allottee under a letter of allotment is contractually bound to the company to take and pay for the shares comprised in it, whereas a scripholder had an option to take them and to be registered as a member when their issue price had been paid.

11 *Re Littlehampton, Havre and Honfleur SS Co, ex p Ellis* (1865) 2 De GJ & Sm 521.

12 Insolvency Act 1986, s 124(2) (as amended by the Companies (Single Member Private Companies) Regulations 1992, reg 2(1) and Sch, para 8).

a member of the company or undertakes to be registered; the provision is obviously intended to protect a member from the personal liability for the company's debts which he will incur if its membership remains below the statutory minimum for six months, and that liability is imposed only on a person who is a member of the company.[13]

Contributory must have an interest in the winding up

The court will make a winding up order on the petition of a contributory only if he has an interest in obtaining it. If he is the holder of partly paid shares, or a member of a company limited by guarantee or of an unlimited company, he will have such an interest, because a winding up order will prevent the directors and other agents of the company from incurring further debts on its behalf, and so will limit the amount of the company's indebtedness towards which he must contribute.[14] If the company is unlimited and is insolvent, the contributory is entitled to a winding up order as of right because of his unlimited liability to contribute to payment of its debts,[15] but in any other case the court has a discretion to refuse a winding up order, and will refuse it unless the petitioner may be called on to contribute a substantial sum.[16]

A petitioner who holds fully paid shares in a company limited by shares has nothing to contribute toward payment of the company's debts, and so will normally have an interest in obtaining a winding up order only if there is a reasonable prospect of the company paying its debts in full and having a surplus of assets to distribute among its members.[17] This is so despite the statutory provision,[18] that a winding up order may not be refused merely because the company has no assets, or because its assets are mortgaged for more than they are worth.[19] But in deciding whether there is a reasonable prospect of the liquidation resulting in there being surplus assets to distribute to the members, money or property which the company may recover from third persons in a

---

13 Companies Act 1985, s 24.

14 *Re Chesterfield Catering Co Ltd* [1977] Ch 373 at 380, [1976] 3 All ER 294 at 297.

15 *Re Norwich Yarn Co* (1850) 12 Beav 366; *Re Electric Telegraph Co of Ireland* (1856) 22 Beav 471.

16 *Re London Suburban Bank* (1871) 6 Ch App 641.

17 *Re Rica Gold Washing Co* (1879) 11 Ch D 36 at 43, per Jessel MR; *Re Instrumentation Electrical Services Ltd* [1988] BCLC 550, 4 BCC 301.

18 Insolvency Act 1986, s 125(1).

19 *Re Kaslo-Slocan Mining and Financial Corpn* [1910] WN 13; *Re Othery Construction Ltd* [1966] 1 All ER 145, [1966] 1 WLR 69; *Re Expanded Plugs Ltd* [1966] 1 All ER 877, [1966] 1 WLR 514.

winding up[20] must be taken into account,[1] and the probability of the company recovering such money or property may give the petitioner an interest in obtaining a winding up order which he would otherwise lack. It has been held, moreover, that a holder of fully paid shares need not prove that there is a prospect of a distributable surplus of assets if his petition is founded upon the company's failure to circulate proper annual accounts to its members, for in that case the petitioner has no means of determining whether there will be a surplus or not.[2] This is also the case if the petition alleges, and the petitioner proves, that there has been misconduct by the persons in control of the company which should be investigated by the court or the official receiver, or that dissension between the members and directors of the company has made it impossible for the company's affairs to be properly managed.[3] If the company opposes a fully paid shareholder's petition on the ground that there will be no surplus of assets to be distributed to shareholders, it should do so by defending the petition on the hearing, and not by applying to the court to strike out the petition and to restrain its advertisement by the petitioner, unless it is obvious or admitted by the petitioner that there will be no surplus.[4]

A fully paid shareholder of a public or unlimited company has an interest in obtaining a winding up order despite the company's insolvency, if its membership has fallen below two; his interest here is in escaping the personal liability for the company's debts which he will incur if the membership continues below the statutory minimum for six months.[5] It would seem, moreover, that other interests of a contributory may qualify him to present a winding up petition, and that the categories of such interests are not closed.[6] The qualifying interest must be one held by the contributory as a member or shareholder, or former member or shareholder, of the company, however, and an interest held by him in some other capacity (eg as a contingent creditor of the company or as the company's landlord) will not suffice.[6]

---

20 Eg, compensation recoverable from directors by misfeasance proceedings, or property subject to a floating charge which will be invalidated by the company being wound up, (see post, pp 237 and 263).
1 *Re Diamond Fuel Co* (1879) 13 Ch D 400.
2 *Re Newman and Howard Ltd* [1962] Ch 257, [1961] 2 All ER 495.
3 *Re Wessex Computer Stationers Ltd* [1992] BCLC 366.
4 *Re Martin Coulter Enterprises Ltd* [1988] BCLC 12, 4 BCC 210.
5 Companies Act 1985, s 24; *Re Chesterfield Catering Co Ltd* [1977] Ch 373 at 380, [1976] 3 All ER 294, at 297.
6 *Re Chesterfield Catering Co Ltd* [1977] Ch 373 at 386, [1976] 3 All ER 294 at 301.

Wishes of other members

Except in the case of a petition by a contributory of an unlimited company which is insolvent, the court has a discretion whether to make or refuse a winding up order on a contributory's petition. In exercising its discretion the court has regard to the wishes of the other members or shareholders of the company, and the court will usually refuse to make a winding up order if a majority in value of the other members or shareholders oppose it for legitimate reasons.[7] But if there is reason to suspect that the holders of a majority of the company's issued shares have been guilty of fraud toward the minority,[8] or that the majority shareholders have not paid for their shares in cash or by an agreed consideration other than cash although the company treats them as fully paid shareholders,[9] or that there are any other matters which ought to be investigated by a liquidator,[9] the wishes of the majority shareholders will be disregarded, and a winding up order will be made. Similarly, if a minority shareholder and director of a private company petitions for it to be wound up because the majority shareholders (who are its other directors) refuse to participate in the management of the company, and confidence between the directors and shareholders has been lost, the court will make a winding up order despite the opposition of the majority shareholders.[10]

Alternative remedies

In some early cases[11] a winding up order was refused because the number of members of the company was small, and it would have been easier and cheaper for the company to be wound up voluntarily.[12] In other cases there were obiter dicta that a contributory should not

---

7 *Re Metropolitan Saloon Omnibus Co Ltd, ex p Hawkins* (1859) 28 LJ Ch 830; *Re London and Suburban Bank*; supra; *Re Professional Commercial and Industrial Benefit Building Society* (1871) 6 Ch App 856.

8 *Re West Surrey Tanning Co* (1866) LR 2 Eq 737.

9 *Re Varieties Ltd* [1893] 2 Ch 235.

10 *Vujnovich v Vujnovich* [1990] BCLC 227.

11 *Re Natal Co Ltd* (1863) 1 Hem & M 639; *Re Sea and River Marine Insurance Co* (1866) LR 2 Eq 545.

12 An additional reason given for the refusal of winding up orders in these cases was that the court was empowered to make such orders by statute principally in order to deal with companies which had numerous members, because such a company could not be wound up under the equity rules in force before the earliest winding up legislation by a representative action being brought by any of the company's members suing on behalf of himself and the other members for the purpose of having its affairs administered in equity like a trust fund (*Long v Yonge* (1830) 2 Sim 369; *Evans v Stokes* (1836) 1 Keen 24). Such reasoning is unlikely to carry conviction today.

petition for a winding up order if there was some other remedy for his grievance.[13] These cases and dicta are now of little importance in view of the statutory provision, that where a contributory petitions for a winding up order on the ground that it is just and equitable that the company should be wound up, the existence of an alternative remedy shall be no bar to the contributory's petition, and that the court may not refuse a winding up order because the contributory has an alternative remedy, unless he is acting unreasonably in not pursuing it.[14]

It is not often that a contributory does have an adequate alternative remedy for his grievance,[15] unless it be by presenting a petition under Companies Act 1985, for relief from the unfairly prejudicial conduct of the company's affairs by its management or controlling shareholders.[16] Consequently, a winding up petition is unlikely to be rejected because the petitioner has an alternative remedy. The possibility of the court giving relief from the alleged unfairly prejudicial treatment of the petitioner will not by itself induce the court to dismiss a winding up petition,[17] and if a petition for relief from unfair treatment is a more appropriate remedy in the circumstances, the court has power to make an order giving such relief on the hearing of the winding up petition instead of dismissing it.[18] It has been held that the alternative remedies open to the petitioner which the court may take into account are not confined to the enforcement of rights which he has by law or under the company's memorandum or articles, and that they include any course of action which is in fact available to him to remedy his grievance.[19] Consequently, a winding up petition by a minority shareholder of a private company on the ground of his effective exclusion from his directorship was dismissed when it was shown that the petitioner had expressed willingness to sell his shares to the majority shareholders, and they were willing to pay a price equal to the fair value of the shares assessed by an impartial and competent valuer.[19] The petitioner's unreasonableness lay in his rejection of this manner of arriving at the price for his shares, and it is clear that

---

13 But in *Loch v John Blackwood Ltd* [1924] AC 783, it was held that the existence of other remedies did not preclude a winding up order.

14 Insolvency Act 1986, s 125(2).

15 A winding up petition will always be the last resort of an aggrieved shareholder of a company which is making profits, because if it is successful it will preclude any possibility of him obtaining a return on his investment in the future.

16 Companies Act 1985, s 459(1); *Virdi v Abbey Leisure Ltd* [1990] BCLC 342, [1990] BCC 60. See *Pennington's Company Law* (7th edn) 885 et seq.

17 *Re a Company (No 001363 of 1988)* [1989] BCLC 579, 5 BCC 18.

18 Insolvency Act 1986, s 125(1).

19 *Re a Company* [1983] 2 All ER 854 [1983] 1 WLR 927.

had he rejected the offer to buy his shares at the outset and no price was specified in the offer, or if the offered price was obviously inadequate, it would not have been unreasonable for him to petition for a winding up order, even though the majority shareholders eventually offered to buy his shares at a fair price.

Provisions of memorandum and articles

A contributory has a statutory right to petition for a winding up order, and any provision in the company's memorandum or articles which attempts to take away his right, or subject it to conditions, is void.[20]

Petitioner in arrears with calls

A contributory may petition for a winding up order even though he has failed to pay calls made on his shares, but his petition will be heard only if he pays the calls to the company or into court, or undertakes to submit to such order as the court may make for their payment.[1] The same rule appears to apply to a contributory who is in arrears with payment of instalments of the issue price of his shares.

Petition by Secretary of State for Trade and Industry

The Secretary of State for Trade and Industry may petition for the winding up of a company on the ground that it is just and equitable that the company should be wound up, but such a petition may be presented only if the company's affairs have been investigated by an inspector appointed by the Secretary of State, or if its books and papers have been inspected by the Secretary of State's officers or persons authorised by him under his statutory powers, and as a result of the investigation or inspection it appears to the Secretary of State expedient in the public interest that the company should be wound up.[2] It is for the Secretary of State to decide whether the presentation of a petition is in the public interest, but it is for the court, after taking account of the interests of members and creditors of the company and of sections of the public who are affected by the company's activities, to decide whether it is in the public interest for

---

20 *Re Peveril Gold Mines Ltd* [1898] 1 Ch 122.
 1 *Re Crystal Reef Gold Mining Co* [1892] 1 Ch 408.
 2 Insolvency Act 1986, s 124(4) and s 124A(1) (substituted by Companies Act 1989, s 60(2) and (3)).

it to order that the company shall be wound up.[3] Nevertheless, the court will attach considerable weight to the Secretary of State's opinion on the question, and will therefore be reluctant to dismiss the petition merely because a majority of the company's creditors or contributories are opposed to a winding up order being made; this is especially so if there are matters to be enquired into or remedies to be pursued which can best be dealt with in a winding up by the court.[4] The Secretary of State must, of course, prove that in all the circumstances it would be just and equitable to wind the company up,[5] and the fact that the investigation or inspection initiated by him has resulted in findings adverse to the company is not conclusive on this question. In proving his case the Secretary of State may rely on information about the company and its management which he has obtained as a result of the investigation or inspection, but he is not confined, as he formerly was,[6] to relying on that information, and so he may now support his petition with allegations and evidence not contained in an inspector's report or brought to light by an inspection of the company's records.

The Secretary of State may also petition for the winding up of a company which was incorporated as a public company on or after 22 December 1980[7] on the ground that it has not obtained from the Registrar of Companies a certificate that it is entitled to do business and to borrow and more than a year has expired since its incorporation.[8] The Secretary of State may likewise petition for the winding up of a company which was a public company immediately before 22 December 1980 and which has not since been re-registered as a public or private company.[9]

The Secretary of State may petition for the winding up of an insurance company on the ground that it is unable to pay its debts, or that it has failed to fulfil any of its obligations under the Insurance Companies Act 1982, or that it has not kept proper accounting records.[10] Creditors and contributories of insurance companies may also present winding up petitions on any of the grounds on which

---

3 *Re a Company (No 007923 of 1994) (No 2)* [1995] 1 BCLC 594, [1995] BCC 641; *Re a Company (No 7816 of 1994)* [1995] 2 BCLC 539; *Re Senator Hanseatische Verwaltungsgesellschaft mbH* [1996] 2 BCLC 562, [1997] BCC 112.
4 *Re Lubin Rosen and Associates Ltd* [1975] 1 All ER 577, [1975] 1 WLR 122.
5 For the discharge of the burden of proof, see p 70, post.
6 Companies Act 1948, s 169(3).
7 This is the date on which the relevant provisions of the Companies Act 1980 came into operation (Companies Act 1980 (Commencement No 2) Order 1980 (SI 1980/1785), para 2).
8 Insolvency Act 1986, s 122(1)(*b*) and s 124(4) (see p 39, post).
9 Ibid, s 122(a)(*c*) and s 124(4) (see p 39, post).
10 Insurance Companies Act 1982, s 54(1) (as amended by Insolvency Act 1986, s 439(2) and Sch 14), (22 *Halsbury's Statutes* (4th edn) 291).

petitions may be presented for the winding up of any kind of company, and with leave of the court at least ten policy holders of an insurance company whose policies are together worth £10,000 or more may petition for the company to be wound up by the court on any of those grounds.[11]

Although a winding up petition is presented by the Secretary of State for Trade and Industry as petitioner, the decision to present the petition need not be taken by him personally, but may be taken by a sufficiently senior official of his department.[12] Furthermore, the affidavit supporting the petition[13] may be made by such an official, and should be made in his own name, and not in that of the Secretary of State.

Bank of England's petition

The Bank of England may petition for the winding up of a company which has been authorised by it under the Banking Act 1987, to take deposits in connection with a deposit taking business.[14] The grounds on which the Bank of England may petition are either that the authorised institution is unable to pay its debts or an amount due and payable in respect of a deposit made with it; or that it is just and equitable that the institution should be wound up.[14] The first of these grounds is established by showing that the authorised institution is insolvent or, although it is solvent, that it has defaulted for any reason in repaying one or more deposits which have become due for repayment, or has defaulted in payment of interest which has accrued on such a deposit; the second ground, that it is just and equitable to wind up the company, has the same wide meaning as in the case of a petition presented against a company which does not take deposits.[15] The power of the Bank of England to petition on these grounds does not exclude or affect the right of a contributory or creditor (including a depositor) or the authorised institution to do so.

Securities and Investments Board's petition

The Securities and Investments Board may petition the court to order the winding up of a company which is or has been authorised

11 Ibid, s 53(1).
12 *Re Golden Chemical Products Ltd* [1976] Ch 300, [1976] 2 All ER 543.
13 See p 57, post.
14 Banking Act 1987, s 92(1), (4 *Halsbury's Statutes* (4th edn) 621).
15 See p 47, post.

to carry on investment business under the Financial Services Act 1986, or which is or has been the authorised representative of a person or company so authorised, and the petition may be presented either on the ground that the company is unable to pay its debts in the sense described below,[16] or on the ground that it is just and equitable that the company shall be wound up.[17]

Attorney General's petition

If a company was formed for a charitable purpose, the Attorney General may petition for it to be wound up on any of the grounds on which the court may make a winding up order.[18]

Improper motive; petition for administration order

The court will make a winding up order only if the petitioner genuinely seeks it in order to recover the debt which the company owes him, or in the case of a contributory's petition, in order to remedy the legitimate grievance of which he complains. Consequently, even if the petitioner makes out his case, the court will refuse to make a winding up order if the petition is presented in order to coerce the company into satisfying some groundless claim made against it by the petitioner,[19] or a claim to which the company has a substantial defence to pleas, as the petitioner is aware;[20] or in order to coerce the directors into buying the petitioner's shares;[1] or with the object of wrecking the company in the interests of a rival concern;[2] or in order to enforce a judgment obtained against the company in collusion with it for the purpose of defrauding its creditors;[3] or to procure the company's dissolution so as to prevent it from enforcing continuing obligations (such as restrictive covenants) against the petitioner or a third party;[4] or in order to

16 See p 42, post.
17 Financial Services Act 1986, s 72(1) and (2).
18 Charities Act 1993, s 63(1), (5 Halsbury's Statutes (4th edn)(1993 Reissue) 947.
19 Re Professional, Commercial and Industrial Benefit Building Society (1871) 6 Ch App 856; Re Planet Benefit Building and Investment Society (1872) LR 14 Eq 441; Charles Forte Investments Ltd v Amanda [1964] Ch 240, [1963] 2 All ER 940; Coulon Sanderson and Ward Ltd v Ward (1985) 2 BCC 99, 207.
20 Mann v Goldstein [1968] 2 All ER 769, [1968] 1 WLR 1091; Re a Company (No 0012209 of 1991) [1992] 2 All ER 797, [1992] 1 WLR 351.
1 Quartz Hill Consolidated Gold Mining Co v Eyre (1883) 11 QBD 674.
2 Re Metropolitan Saloon Omnibus Co Ltd, ex p Hawkins, supra.
3 Re United Stock Exchange Co [1884] WN 251.
4 Re Surrey Garden Village Trust Ltd [1964] 3 All ER 962, [1965] 1 WLR 974.

cause the forfeiture of the company's interest in certain property and to obtain that property for the petitioner himself.[5] A petition will also be dismissed if, although it is probable that the petitioner is entitled to a winding up order on the evidence, the petition deliberately misstates material facts or omits to disclose relevant matters, and no application is made on the hearing to amend it.[6] On the other hand, a creditor's petition for the winding up of a substantial public company will not be stayed or dismissed merely because the company clearly has sufficient resources to pay the petitioner's debt if the company has failed to pay it within a reasonable time after it fell due without giving its reason for not doing so.[7]

When the company contends that a petition for it to be wound up has been presented for an improper purpose, it may apply by motion to the Companies Court to have the petition struck out before the date on which it is due to be heard, and the company may ask the court to restrain the petitioner from advertising the petition pending the hearing of the motion for it to be struck out.[9] If the defendant has merely threatened to present a winding up petition in such circumstances,[10] or has served a written demand for payment of a debt which he alleges the company owes him with the intention of presenting a winding up petition as a creditor,[11] or if the company has obtained an order of the court conditionally setting aside a money judgment in favour of the defendant upon which he threatens to present a winding up petition, the condition in the order setting aside the judgment being the company paying the amount of it into court within a period which has not yet elapsed,[12] the company may apply for an injunction to prevent the defendant from proceeding, and such an application may also be made after a petition has been presented as an alternative to apply to the court by motion for it to be struck out.[13] If the question whether the petitioner is improperly motivated can be more conveniently tried by allowing the petition to be heard in the normal way, however, the court will not issue an injunction, and this is particularly so if the petitioner could properly present a petition in an amended form and leave to amend it is likely

5 *Re a Company (No 001573 of 1983)* [1983] BCLC 492, 1 BCC 937.
6 *Re a Company* [1974] 1 All ER 256, [1974] 1 WLR 1566.
7 *Cornhill Insurance plc v Improvement Services Ltd* [1986] 1 WLR 114, [1986] BCLC 26.
8 *Re Gold Hill Mines* (1882) 23 Ch D 210.
9 *Re a Company* [1894] 2 Ch 349.
10 *Charles Forte Investments Ltd v Amanda* [1964] Ch 240, [1963] 2 All ER 940.
11 *Holt Southey Ltd v Catnic Components Ltd* [1978] 2 All ER 276, [1978] 1 WLR 630.
12 *Re Druce & Co* [1993] BCLC 964.
13 *Mann v Goldstein*, supra.

to be given.[14] On the other hand, if the petitioner's improper motive is clear from acts done by him, or if he admits his motive and the question is whether the petitioner has the capacity to present a petition at all, or whether he has presented it in the correct capacity, the court will decide the matter in issue on hearing the application for an injunction.[15]

If the company takes no steps to prevent the petition being presented or proceeding to a hearing, but defends the petition successfully, it may recover damages from the petitioner if it can show that he had no reasonable or probable cause for presenting the petition, and that he was actuated by an improper motive.[16] On the other hand, the company cannot sue the petitioner for damages after the dismissal of his petition if the petitioner was merely negligent in not realising that the petition was groundless or unsupported by evidence, or if the petitioner merely failed to conform to the procedural requirements for presenting and serving the petition.[17]

It has been held that if a winding up petition is presented by a creditor of the company and is not opposed by it, but its directors present a petition for an administration order to be made in respect of the company, the court will hear the petition for an administration order, and will not hear the winding-up petiton until the petition for an administration order has been disposed of.[18] Furthermore, the court has ordered that a creditor's winding up petition should not be advertised when the company undertook to present a petition for an administration order forthwith, but the court gave permission for the creditor to advertise his petition if the petition for an administration order and a supporting affidavit were not both filed within 14 days.[19]

GROUNDS FOR WINDING UP

The court may make a winding up order on the petition of the company, its directors, a creditor or a contributory on any one or

14 *Holt Southey Ltd v Catnic Components Ltd*, supra; Practice Direction (Chancery 4/88).
15 *Stonegate Securities Ltd v Gregory* [1980] Ch 576, [1980] 1 All ER 241. In that case the question was whether the defendant could proceed with a petition presented by him as a creditor who has served a statutory demand for payment of a debt immediately due (see p 42, post), or whether he should be permitted to petition only as a prospective or contingent creditor.
16 *Quartz Hill Consolidated Gold Mining Co v Eyre* (1883) 11 QBD 674.
17 *Business Computers International Ltd v Registrar of Companies* [1988] Ch 229, [1887] 3 All ER 465.
18 *Re a Company (No 001992 of 1988)* [1989] BCLC 9, 4 BCC 451; secus *Re Manlon Trading Ltd* (1988) 4 BCC 455.
19 *Re a Company (No 001448 of 1989)* [1989] BCLC 715, 5 BCC 706.

more of seven grounds, and such persons may present a petition on any of those grounds.[20] The grounds on which the Secretary of State for Trade and Industry, the Bank of England or the Securities and Investments Board may petition are limited by the statutory provisions which have been mentioned above,[1] but where the grounds on which they may petition are within any of the seven grounds dealt with below, the ground or grounds are interpreted in the same way as if a creditor or contributory were the petitioner.

1. That the company has resolved by a special resolution to be wound up by the court

This is an extremely rare ground for a winding up petition, because if members or shareholders holding sufficient voting rights to pass a special resolution (namely three-quarters of the voting rights exercisable at a general meeting)[2] want the company to be wound up, they can pass a special resolution to wind it up voluntarily,[3] and a voluntary winding up is far cheaper and speedier than a winding up by the court.

2. That the company was registered as a public company on its incorporation on or after 22 December 1980,[4] and that it has not been issued by the Registrar of Companies with a certificate that it is entitled to do business and to borrow within one year after its incorporation[5]

3. That the company was a public company immediately before 22 December 1980,[4] and it has not since been re-registered as a public or private company

A company which was a public company under the Companies Act 1948 (ie a company whose articles did not contain the three

20 Insolvency Act 1986, s 122(1); *Re a Company (No 003028 of 1987)* [1988] BCLC 282, 3 BCC 575.
 1 See p 33 et seq, ante.
 2 Companies Act 1985, s 378(2).
 3 See p 86, post.
 4 This is the date on which the relevant provisions of the Companies Act 1980 came into operation (Companies Act 1980 (Commencement No 2) Order 1980 (SI 1980/1785), para 2).
 5 A public company must obtain such a certificate before it may engage in business transactions or borrow (Companies Act 1985, s 117(1)).

restrictions required to make it a private company[6]) was required by the Companies Act 1980 to re-register as either a public or a private company not later than 22 March 1982.[7] Such a company was, and still is, classed as an 'old public company'[8] and in addition to it and its officers incurring criminal penalties if it is not re-registered, and the company being unable to invite the public to subscribe for its shares and debentures,[9] the court may wind the company up on the ground that it has not been re-registered by the date when the petition is presented.

4. That the company has not commenced its business within a year from its incorporation or has suspended its business for a whole year

A company will not be so moribund as to warrant the court winding it up under this paragraph unless it has ceased to pursue all of its main objects, or has never pursued any of them. Thus, where a company was formed to carry on business in Great Britain and abroad, but in fact only carried on business abroad, it was held that it had in fact commenced business, and a winding up order was refused.[10] To ascertain what is the company's business, regard must be had to its memorandum of association alone, and if its memorandum contains several main objects, although a prospectus issued by the company to raise share capital mentions only one of them, the company will not be wound up because it abandons that one object but continues to pursue the others.[11] On the other hand, a company does not carry on business unless it genuinely attempts to achieve the objects or some of the objects for which it was formed, and so it does not carry on business merely by its directors holding board meetings[10] or exercising ancillary powers set out in the objects clause of its memorandum of association,[12] or by the directors litigating a claim by the company against a third person which arose while the company was carrying on a business which has now ceased.[13] Even if the company's memorandum of association provides

6 Companies Act 1948, s 28(1).
7 Companies Act 1980, s 8(3), (8) and (9).
8 Ibid, s 8(1); Companies Consolidation (Consequential Provisions) Act 1985, s 1(1).
9 Companies Consolidation (Consequential Provisions) Act 1985, s 5(1) and s 7.
10 *Re Capital Fire Insurance Association* (1882) 21 Ch D 209.
11 *Re Langham Skating Rink Co* (1877) 5 Ch D 669.
12 *Re Metropolitan Rly Warehousing Co Ltd* (1867) 36 LJ Ch 827; *Re German Date Coffee Co* (1882) 20 Ch D 169; *Re Kitson & Co Ltd* [1946] 1 All ER 435.
13 *Re Perfectair Holdings Ltd* [1990] BCLC 423, 5 BCC 837.

that each of the powers in the objects clause shall be deemed a main object of the company, the court will discover what objects the company was really formed to pursue, and will wind it up if they have been abandoned and only ancillary powers have been exercised.[14]

The court is reluctant to wind up a company before a year has elapsed from its incorporation, because even though it has not yet commenced business, it may do so within that time.[15] But if it is obvious that the company will never have sufficient resources to commence business, the court will wind it up within the year.[16] On the other hand, even if the company has not begun to carry on business within the year, the court will not wind it up if there are reasonable prospects of it doing so at not too remote a date and there are good reasons for the delay, for example, that the company is waiting for a trade depression to pass,[17] or is awaiting the commencement of the undertaking of another concern on which it is dependent.[18]

5. That the number of members of a public or unlimited company has been reduced below two

This ground is provided to enable a member of a public or an unlimited company to escape the personal liability for the company's debts which he will incur if the membership of the company remains below the statutory minimum of two members for more than six months.[19] In practice petitions are rarely presented on this ground, because a sole member of a public or unlimited company may avoid personal liability for the company's debts by transferring some of his shares to one or more nominees for himself so as to raise the number of members to or above the statutory minimum. The right to petition for a winding up order is useful, however, where the directors have declined to register a transfer of some or a sole member's shares to a nominee under a power conferred on them by the articles, or where there are no directors holding office, so that a transfer cannot be registered at all. The right to petition may also be useful in the case of unlimited companies which have no share

14 *Cotman v Brougham* [1918] AC 514 at 520, per Lord Parker.
15 *Re Langham Skating Rink Co*, supra.
16 *Re London and County Coal Co* (1866) LR 3 Eq 355.
17 *Re Middlesborough Assembly Rooms Co* (1880) 14 Ch D 104.
18 *Re Metropolitan Rly Warehousing Co Ltd*, supra.
19 Companies Act 1985, s 24 (as amended by the Companies (Single Member Private Limited Companies) Regulations 1992 (SI 1922/1699), reg 2(1) and Sch, para 2).

capital; the admission of additional members to such companies is usually a function of the board of directors or a general meeting, and an individual member has no power to raise the number of members to the statutory minimum by his own act.

6. That the company is unable to pay its debts

A company is deemed to be unable to pay its debts in the following circumstances:[20]

(a) If a creditor to whom the company owes more than £750 immediately payable has delivered to it at its registered office a notice in the prescribed form requiring payment,[1] and the company has for three weeks thereafter neglected to pay the debt or to compound for it or to secure it to the reasonable satisfaction of the creditor. The notice must be dated and signed by the creditor or by a person who states in the notice that he is authorised by the creditor to sign it; it must also state the nature and amount of the debt and the consideration for it, and if the debt includes interest not previously notified to the company or any other periodic charge (eg rent), the notice must state the rate of interest or periodic charge, and only interest or a periodic charge accrued due at the date of the notice may be included; finally, the notice must explain to the company the purpose of delivering it, the consequences of the company not complying with it, the period within which the notice must be complied with and the methods by which that may be done.[2]

An assignee of a debt may serve a notice requiring payment of the debt to himself, but not if he is merely an equitable assignee;[3] in that case the notice must be delivered by the assignor in whom the legal title to the debt is still vested; when the assignor has done this the assignee may present a winding up petition based on the company's failure to comply with the notice.[4] Similarly, a person for whom a debt of the company is held in trust (such as a debenture stockholder) cannot serve a notice demanding payment of the debt; the notice must be signed and delivered by or on

---

20 Insolvency Act 1986, s 123(1).
 1 The prescribed form is that of Form 4.1 in Sch 4 of the Insolvency Rules 1986 (SI 1986/1925).
 2 Insolvency Rules 1986, rr 4.5 and 4.6.
 3 *Re Steel Wing Co* [1921] 1 Ch 349.
 4 *Re a Company (No 008790 of 1990)* [1991] BCLC 561.

behalf of the person in whom the legal title to the debt is vested, and a winding up petition based on the company's non-compliance with the notice may be presented only by that person.[5] It appears that a notice is not invalid because the creditor demands payment of a greater sum than the company owes him, if it in fact owes him more than £750,[6] but the creditor's claim must be for a liquidated sum, and so he cannot deliver a notice for payment of the price of goods or any other fixed sum less the amount of any unliquidated damages which the company may claim for breaches by the creditor of the contract under which the price or fixed sum is due.[7]

The notice delivered by the creditor to the company must be proved to have been delivered at the company's registered office, and this is so even if the notice is sent by post, there being no presumption of delivery in the ordinary course of the post;[8] a telex message sent to and received at the company's registered office does not suffice, and is not an effective notice.[9] After delivering the notice the creditor must wait for 21 clear days before presenting his petition; if he presents it before the expiration of that time, he will not be able to rely on the company's failure to comply with his demand for payment in the notice as proof of its inability to pay its debts, even though more than three weeks have elapsed since the delivery of the notice when the petition is heard.[10]

A company does not neglect to satisfy the creditor's claim if it refuses to pay it because it contends that it is not owing, or if the company pays part of the creditor's claim and refuses to pay the balance contending that it is not owing or recoverable by the creditor under the transaction or transactions between the parties, or if the company claims to set off a debt which it alleges is owed to it by the creditor and pays or tenders any balance of the amount claimed by him.[11] If the company contends that it is not liable to the creditor for the whole or the unpaid part of his claim, and can satisfy the court that it

---

5 *Re Dunderland Iron Ore Co* [1909] 1 Ch 446.
6 *Cardiff Preserved Coal and Coke Co v Norton* (1867) 2 Ch App 405.
7 *Re Humberstone Jersey Ltd* [1977] LS Gaz R 31.
8 *Re a Company (No 008790 of 1990)* [1991] BCLC 561.
9 *Re a Company* [1985] BCLC 37.
10 *Re Catholic Publishing and Bookselling Co Ltd* (1864) 2 De GJ & Sm 116; *Re Lympne Investments Ltd* [1972] 2 All ER 385, [1972] 1 WLR 523.
11 *Re a Company* [1984] 3 All ER 78, [1984] 1 WLR 1090.

has a substantial and reasonable defence to plead, the court will hold that it is not in default, and will refuse to make a winding up order.[12] The court will not usually decide on the validity of the company's defence on the hearing of the winding up petition, unless the defence relies upon propositions of law which are incorrect and do not constitute a defence to the petitioner's claim;[12] where the defence depends on questions of fact and the company alleges facts which the petitioning creditor disputes, the court will usually refuse to determine the relevant facts (although it may in its discretion do so where the disputed questions of fact are simple),[13] and the court will therefore normally dismiss the petition. This is so even if the company has not notified the petitioner during the three weeks following the delivery of the statutory notice that it intends to defend any petition which he may present based on the notice.[14] Consequently, as has already been pointed out,[15] a petitioning creditor who anticipates a defence being pleaded to his claim will be wise to sue the company to judgment by action first, and then serve a demand on it for payment of the judgment debt; when the creditor later presents his winding up petition, the company will then be estopped by the judgment from disputing his claim on the merits.

(b) If a judgment creditor of the company has issued a writ or other process of execution which has been returned unsatisfied in whole or part; the sheriff or other relevant officer's return to the process of execution must show that execution was levied and not merely that it was attempted, and so if the return to an execution on the company's goods shows merely that the sheriff's officer could not gain access to them at the premises where they were stored, the return is inadequate and will not provide proof of the company's inability to pay its debts for the purpose of obtaining a winding up order.[16]

12 *Re Brighton Club and Norfolk Hotel Co Ltd* (1865) 35 Beav 204; *Re London and Paris Banking Corpn* (1874) LR 19 Eq 444; *Re Lympne Investments Ltd*, supra; *Re Humberstone Jersey Ltd*, supra; *Re a Company*, supra; *Re a Company (No 0012209 of 1991)* [1992] 2 All ER 797, [1992] 1 WLR 351 (see also p 20, ante).

13 *Brinds Ltd v Offshore Oil NL* (1985) 2 BCC 98, 916; *Re R A Foulds Ltd* (1986) 2 BCC 99, 269.

14 *Re Cannon Screen Entertainments Ltd* [1989] BCLC 660, 5 BCC 207.

15 See p 21, ante.

16 *Re Flagstaff Silver Mining Co of Utah* (1875) LR 20 Eq 268; *Re Yate Collieries and Limeworks Co* [1883] WN 171; *Re a Debtor (No 340 of 1992), The Debtor v First National Commercial Bank plc* [1994] 3 All ER 269, [1994] 2 BCLC 171; affd [1996] 2 All ER 211.

(c) If the court is otherwise satisfied that the company is unable
to pay its debts, in other words, that the company is insolvent.
Two alternative tests of insolvency apply under this head,
and the court may make a winding up order if either test is
satisfied.

Under the first alternative test, a company is unable to pay its debts
if it cannot pay them as they fall due for payment out of cash or
readily realisable assets in its hands, and it is immaterial in applying
this test that the company could pay all its debts over a lengthy
period by a steady realisation of all its assets.[17] On the other hand,
in applying this test, no account is taken of debts and other liabilities
of the company which have not yet accrued due, or are contingent,
or are liabilities for unliquidated damages. A company is unable to
pay its debts under the alternative test if the value of its assets is less
than the total amount of its liabilities, taking its contingent and
prospective liabilities into account as well as its debts which are
immediately due and payable.[18]Under this test a company is unable
to pay its debts and other liabilities if it has no reasonable prospect
of paying all of them, both accrued and prospective, by a steady
realisation of all its assets over the period until they will accrue due
and become payable or, in the case of contingent and unliquidated
liabilities over the period until they are likely to become accrued
liabilities of a fixed amount;[19] in applying this test it will be
immaterial that the company can pay its already accrued debts out
of its immediately available liquid resources. In order to determine
whether the company is insolvent under this alternative test, it must
be supposed that the company will cease carrying on its business
immediately, except for fulfilling contracts which it has already
entered into, and it must then be asked whether the company would
be able to satisfy its accrued liabilities and its liabilities which will or
may accrue in the future under transactions which it has already
entered into if the company were to realise all its assets over a
reasonably long period, so that it does not have to accept reduced
prices because of forced sales.[20] No regard must be paid to the profits
which the company might earn or to any further liabilities which it
might incur under fresh contracts if it continued to carry on its
business during the period of realisation, nor to any assets which the
company may acquire in the future, unless it has already contracted

---

17 Insolvency Act 1986, s 123(1)(*e*); *Re European Life Assurance Society* (1869) LR
9 Eq 122.
18 Insolvency Act 1986, s 123(2).
19 *Re a Company (No 003038 of 1987)* [1988] BCLC 282.
20 *Re European Life Assurance Society* (1869) LR 9 Eq 122; *Byblos Bank SAL v Al-
Khudhairy* [1987] BCLC 232, 2 BCC 549.

to acquire them, nor to any funds which it may obtain by issuing share capital or raising loans in the future, unless reliable persons have already contracted to provide them.[20]

Proof by a creditor that his debt was not paid when it became immediately due and payable and has not been paid since that time is prima facie evidence that the company is insolvent if the company gives no reason for not paying the debt, and this is particularly so if the company has given no reason for failing to comply with a statutory notice demanding payment.[1] An admission by its directors that the company has no assets on which the creditor may levy execution is also prima facie evidence of the company's insolvency.[2] The company may, nevertheless, rebut the presumption of insolvency which thereby arises by proving that it can in fact pay its debts which have accrued due out of money which it has or will have in the immediate future; but even if the company proves that this is so, the court will make a winding up order if the company has admitted that it is indebted to the petitioning creditor, but has failed to pay his debt despite repeated requests for payment.[3] Similarly, if a company has repeatedly failed to pay debts owed to its creditors or to the petitioning creditor when the debts fell due, or has been coerced into doing so only by the threat or the commencement of actions for recovery by its creditors, the court may conclude that the company is insolvent under the first test mentioned above.[4] In deciding whether a company is insolvent under the second test mentioned above, the amount of its unpaid share capital must be taken into account as an asset of the company, but regard must also be had to the possibility that some of its members may not pay the capital unpaid on their shares in full.[5]

A petitioning creditor may prove that the company is insolvent in any of the ways mentioned above without serving a statutory notice on it demanding payment of his debt, even though he is entitled to serve such a notice, and the court will not dismiss his petition or restrain the petitioner from advertising it because he has not done so.[6] Conversely, it has been held that a creditor who has obtained judgment against a company for damages which have not

1 *Re Globe New Patent Iron and Steel Co* (1875) LR 20 Eq 337; *Re Camburn Petroleum Products Ltd* [1979] 3 All ER 297, [1980] 1 WLR 86; *Taylor's Industrial Flooring Ltd v M & H Plant Hire (Manchester) Ltd* [1990] BCLC 216, [1990] BCC 44.
2 *Re Flagstaff Silver Mining Co of Utah* (1875) LR 20 Eq 268.
3 *Re Bradford Tramways Co* (1876) 4 Ch D 18 at 22, per Bramwell JA; *Cornhill Insurance plc v Improvement Services Ltd* [1986] 1 WLR 114, 129 Sol Jo 828.
4 *Re a Company* [1986] BCLC 261.
5 *Re European Life Assurance Society*, supra.
6 *Taylor's Industrial Flooring Ltd v M & H Plant Hire (Manchester) Ltd* [1990] BCLC 216, [1990] BCC 44.

yet been assessed or quantified cannot rely on the company's inability to pay its debts as they fall due as proving its insolvency, but must show that the totality of its assets will not suffice on realisation to satisfy all its liabilities.[7] On the other hand, it has also been held that a creditor for costs awarded to him as the successful defendant in an action brought by the company can prove its insolvency by showing that it is unable to pay its debts as they fall due, even though the costs awarded to the creditor have not been taxed or otherwise quantified.[8]

7. That it is just and equitable that the company should be wound up

This is a separate and independent ground for a winding up order, and for a case to be made out under it, it is not necessary that the circumstances should be analogous to those which justify an order on one of the six more specific grounds already dealt with.[9] Consequently, new kinds of cases may be brought under this seventh head by judicial interpretation. The cases which have so far been decided have fallen into five broad categories, but these categories may be extended by the courts in the future.

Disappearance of company's substratum

A company's substratum is the purpose or group of purposes which it was formed to achieve, in other words, its main objects. If the company has abandoned all of these main objects and not merely some of them,[10] or if it cannot achieve any of its main objects, its substratum has gone, and it will be wound up. The fact that the company is exercising some of the ancillary powers conferred by its

---

7 *Securum Finance Ltd v Camswell Ltd* [1994] BCC 434.
8 *Tottenham Hotspur plc v Edennote plc* [1995] 1 BCLC 65, [1994] BCC 681.
9 *Ebrahimi v Westbourne Galleries Ltd* [1973] AC 360, [1972] 2 All ER 492. In *Re Agriculturist Cattle Insurance Co, ex p Spackman* (1849) 1 Mac & G 170, Lord Cottenham said that this final paragraph of what is now the Insolvency Act 1986, s 123(1) must be construed ejusdem generis with the preceding paragraphs, but the court has never restricted itself in this way, and in *Loch v John Blackwood Ltd* [1924] AC 783 at 788–790, Lord Cottenham's dictum was explained away and shown as not imposing any limitation on the meaning of the final paragraph.
10 *Re Kitson & Co Ltd* [1946] 1 All ER 435. Vaughan Williams J's dictum in *Re Thomas Edward Brinsmead & Sons Ltd* [1897] 1 Ch 45, that the court will wind a company up if a material part of its substratum has gone, appears to be meaningless, because each of its main objects is of equal importance, and it is achieving the purpose for which it was formed even though it is pursuing only one of them.

memorandum of association will not save it, because these powers are intended merely to aid it in achieving its main objects, and not to enable it to carry on a different kind of business or to preserve some appearance of activity.[11] If the company's memorandum of association provides that each of the powers conferred by the objects clause shall be a main object, the court will nevertheless determine the purposes for which the company was really formed, and will wind it up if it has abandoned them; the court will do this despite the fact that the company is still pursuing some of its expressed objects if they are merely ancillary or incidental to its main purpose.[12]

A company may lose the ability to achieve its main objects in a variety of ways. It will do so if it fails to obtain a patent for an invention which it was formed to exploit on the assumption that the patent would be granted,[13] or if it fails to acquire the business which it was formed to purchase,[14] or if it fails to obtain the necessary approval of a local authority for the erection of the building which it was formed to erect.[15] It will also be unable to achieve its main objects if it has insufficient capital,[16] but in deciding whether its capital is insufficient, regard must be had to the unpaid capital which it may call up from its shareholders.[17] However, the mere fact that a company has suffered trading losses will not destroy its substratum, unless there is no reasonable prospect of it ever making a profit in the future, and the court is most reluctant to hold that it has no such prospect.[18] Still less, of course, is a company's substratum destroyed by a bare majority of the members wishing to discontinue its business and wind it up.[19]

Illegality of objects and fraud

If any of a company's objects are illegal, or apparently, if they become illegal by a change in the law, the court will order the company to be wound up on the ground that it is just and equitable to do so.[20]

---

11 *Re German Date Coffee Co* (1882) 20 Ch D 169; *Re Kitson & Co Ltd* [1946] 1 All ER 435; *Re Perfectair Holdings Ltd* [1990] BCLC 423, 5 BCC 837.
12 *Cotman v Brougham* [1918] AC 514 at 520, per Lord Parker.
13 *Re German Date Coffee Co*, supra.
14 *Re Blériot Manufacturing Aircraft Co* (1916) 32 TLR 253.
15 *Re Varieties Ltd* [1893] 2 Ch 235.
16 *Re Diamond Fuel Co* (1879) 13 Ch D 400.
17 *Re National Livestock Insurance Co* (1858) 26 Beav 153.
18 *Re Suburban Hotel Co* (1867) 2 Ch App 737; *Davis & Co v Brunswick (Australia) Ltd* [1936] 1 All ER 299.
19 *Re Anglo-Continental Produce Co Ltd* [1939] 1 All ER 99.
20 *Princess Reuss v Bos* (1871) LR 5 HL 176; *Re International Securities Corpn* (1908) 25 TLR 31.

Similarly, if a company is promoted in order to perpetrate a serious fraud or deception on the persons who are invited to subscribe for its shares, the court will wind it up. Thus, a winding up order was made when the company's prospectus stated that it had agreed to purchase the business of an existing firm, together with the right to use the firm's name, for a very substantial sum, and subscribers for the company's shares were intentionally misled by the name and the amount of the purchase price into thinking that the firm was a different and reputable concern, whose business name the vendor firm had, in fact, successfully but illegally imitated for a number of years.[1] Again, a winding up order was made against a company whose promoters sold a business to it at a gross overvalue, and when the deception was discovered, bought up at a very low price most of the shares subscribed for by the public, so as to prevent the company from suing them for their wrongdoing, and so as to wind the company up voluntarily and distribute its assets among themselves.[2]

Deadlock

If it becomes impossible to manage a company's affairs because the voting power at board and general meetings is divided between two or more dissenting groups, the court will resolve the deadlock by making a winding up order. The most obvious kind of deadlock is where the company has two directors who are its only shareholders and who hold an equal number of voting shares; if they disagree on major questions in respect of the management of the company, their disagreement cannot be resolved at a board meeting or by a general meeting, and management decisions will cease to be made. In this situation the court will make a winding up order, even though there is a provision in the company's articles that one director shall have a casting vote at board meetings,[3] or that disputes shall be settled by arbitration.[4] Nevertheless, the petitioner must show that there is no likelihood of the deadlock being resolved in fact, and for this purpose he should set out in his petition or in his supporting affidavit the relevant provisions of the company's articles (if any) and details of the attempts which he has made to resolve the deadlock.[5] There may also be a deadlock even though the voting power is not equally divided between the dissenting groups. Thus, where there were

---

1 *Re Thomas Edward Brinsmead & Sons Ltd* [1897] 1 Ch 45.
2 *Re West Surrey Tanning Co* (1866) LR 2 Eq 737.
3 *Re Davis and Collett Ltd* [1935] Ch 693, [1935] All ER Rep 315.
4 *Re Yenidje Tobacco Co Ltd* [1916] 2 Ch 426.
5 *Re Davis Investments (East Ham) Ltd* [1961] 3 All ER 926, [1961] 1 WLR 1396; *Re W R Willcocks & Co Ltd* [1974] Ch 163, [1973] 2 All ER 93.

three shareholders with equal shareholdings, and two of them were the company's directors, one of the director/shareholders was held entitled to a winding up order when the other persistently refused to attend board meetings so as to make a quorum competent to transact business; the reason for the other director's absence was his fear that the petitioner would insist on a general meeting being called at which, by the terms of the articles, the petitioner could require the other shareholders to purchase his shares, or if they were unwilling to purchase them, to join with the petitioner in passing a resolution to wind up the company voluntarily; the result of the other director's absence from board meetings, however, was that the company's business could not be carried on at all, and for this reason the court made a winding up order.[6]

Grounds analogous to dissolution of partnerships

If a company is a private one whose share capital is held wholly or mainly by its directors, and they or most of them manage the company's business personally and are remunerated as such by a share of the company's profits or a salary which is dependent on the level of profits, the company is in substance a partnership in corporate form (a quasi-partnership), and the court will order its winding up in the same situations as it would order the dissolution of a partnership on the ground that it is just and equitable to do so.[7] Thus, if one of the directors has been excluded from taking part in the management of the company by the use of the others' majority voting power, or if the directors have lost confidence in each other or disagree so seriously that they cannot carry on business together, or if the directors have ceased to manage the company's business and are not likely to resume doing so, the company will be wound up,[8] and it is not necessary for the petitioner to prove that the controlling shareholder or any of the other directors has been guilty of underhand or improper conduct.[9] But a winding up order will not be made because a controlling director, who has by tacit consent always managed the company's business alone, refuses to allow a fellow director to participate in day-to-day management as distinct from attending and taking part in board meetings.[10] However, the exclusion of a fellow director who has taken a part in managing the company's business from doing so any longer will be cause for

6 *Re American Pioneer Leather Co* [1918] 1 Ch 556.
7 *Re Yenidje Tobacco Co Ltd*, supra.
8 *Re Davis and Collett Ltd*, supra; *Re A and BC Chewing Gum Ltd* [1975] 1 All ER 1017, [1975] 1 WLR 579; *Vujnovich v Vujnovich* [1990] BCLC 227.
9 *Re R A Noble & Sons (Clothing) Ltd* [1983] BCLC 273.
10 *Re Fildes Bros Ltd* [1970] 1 All ER 923, [1970] 1 WLR 592.

winding the company up if the company was formed on the understanding that he should participate in managing its business,[11] or if the director was appointed after the company's formation and on his appointment he subscribed for or purchased shares in the company, and incurred personal liability as a guarantor of the company's debts and made loans to the other directors so that they might increase their shareholdings on the understanding that he would be entitled to participate in managing the company's business.[12] Likewise, the failure of the majority shareholders to appoint the petitioner to be a director when he subscribed for shares in the company on the understanding that he would be made a director, will justify a winding up order.[13] Furthermore, the failure of a director of a private company who is its majority shareholder to take an active part in the management of the company, which was intended when it was formed, will induce the court to wind up the company on the petition of a minority shareholder who is a fellow director.[14]

In contrast to these decisions, a winding up order will not be made because a director has been excluded from management of the company's affairs, if the director has expressed willingness to sell his shares to the remaining directors and shareholders and they have offered to buy them at their fair market value as assessed by an independent expert.[15] A winding up order will also not be made merely because a director or shareholder has become bankrupt, at least if the company's articles of association provide for the transmission of his shares to his trustee in bankruptcy,[16] but in this situation a winding up order may be made if the directors or controlling shareholders of the company impede the proper realisation of the bankrupt's shares for the benefit of his creditors.[17] Also a winding up order will not be made to enable a director who has resigned to realise the amount he invested in the company if the other shareholders wish to continue carrying on its business; this is because the resignation of a director, unlike the termination of a partnership by notice given by one of the partners, does not affect the director's position as a shareholder in the company.[16]

If the understanding between the shareholders when the company was incorporated was that it should be used to carry out a single venture which has in fact been completed (eg the development and

11 *Ebrahimi v Westbourne Galleries Ltd* [1973] AC 360, [1972] 2 All ER 492.
12 *Tay Bok Choon v Tahansan Sdn Bhd* [1987] 1 WLR 413, [1987] BCLC 472.
13 *Re Zinotty Properties Ltd* [1984] 3 All ER 754, [1984] 1 WLR 1249.
14 *Vujnovich v Vujnovich* [1990] BCLC 227.
15 *Re a Company* [1983] 2 All ER 854, [1983] 1 WLR 927.
16 *Re K/9 Meat Supplies (Guildford) Ltd* [1966] 3 All ER 320, [1966] 1 WLR 1112.

disposal of one piece of land), a winding up order will be made if the majority shareholders and the directors other than the petitioner decide to invest the proceeds of the venture in another similar venture, or to use the proceeds of the first to make interest free loans to other companies in which they, but not the petitioner, are interested.[18] A winding up order will likewise be made if the understanding between the shareholders when the company was incorporated was that it should carry on a certain kind of business at certain premises and not elsewhere, and the majority shareholders now intend, against the petitioner's wishes, to dispose of those premises and to carry on a similar business together with other business activities of a different kind on a larger scale at other premises to be acquired by the company.[19]

It would seem that wilful or persistent breaches of the company's articles of association by the other directors will be a ground on which a director or former director who is also a shareholder may seek a winding up order, and because the company is a quasi-partnership; it would not seem necessary for the petitioner to show that the breaches amounted to an oppressive course of conduct directed against him.[18] Cases of oppression are now recognised as a separate category from situations analogous to those where the court would dissolve a partnership, even though originally oppression was adopted as a ground for making a winding up order by analogy with partnership law.

The special circumstances indicated above in which the court will order the winding up of a company which is a quasi-partnership will not induce the court to wind up a company which is not a quasi-partnership although it has the same persons as its directors and shareholders and has issued shares which are not freely transferable; but of course, a winding up order may be sought by the contributories of such a company if they can prove that any of the other situations exist which would justify the court ordering the winding up of the company because it would be just and equitable to do so (eg deadlock, oppression).[20]

Oppression

A winding up order will be made if the persons who control a company have been guilty of oppression toward its minority shareholders, whether in the latters' capacity as shareholders or in

17 *Ebrahimi v Westbourne Galleries Ltd* [1973] AC 360 at 387, [1972] 2 All ER 492 at 506, per Lord Cross of Chelsea.
18 *Re Zinotty Properties Ltd*, supra.
19 *Virdi v Abbey Leisure Ltd* [1990] BCLC 342, [1990] BCC 60.
20 *Re a Company (No 007936 of 1994)* [1995] BCC 705.

some other capacity (eg as directors).[1] Thus, a company was wound up on the petition of minority shareholders when the directors, who held a majority of the issued shares, had persistently refused to call annual general meetings, or to submit accounts to the petitioners, or to have auditors appointed, or to give the petitioners any information about the company's affairs, all this being part of a scheme to coerce the petitioners into selling their shares to the directors at a price which was less than a quarter of their worth.[2] Similarly, in Scotland a winding up order was made at the instance of a minority shareholder who was a director, when the majority shareholder, who was the other director, excluded the petitioner from taking any part in the management of the company, refused to allow him to inspect the company's books and records, denied him any information relating to its affairs, and generally managed the company's undertaking as though it were the majority shareholder's own property.[3] In these two cases, the persons responsible for the oppression obviously knew that their conduct was improper, but malevolence or a desire on their part for an improper gain at the expense of the petitioner is not an essential part of his case. Thus, a winding up order was made when the petitioner merely showed that for several years no annual general meeting of the company had been held, and no annual audits of the company's accounts had taken place, and that assets which the company had agreed to purchase from its majority shareholders had not been transferred to it although the price for them had been paid.[4] The court reasoned that every shareholder is entitled to have the company's business managed properly according to law, and if the persons who control the company show a persistent unwillingness to do this, any minority shareholder is entitled to have the company wound up.[5] Oppression in the conduct of the company's affairs may now often be remedied more effectively by the court exercising the powers given to it to relieve minority shareholders from the unfairly prejudicial conduct of the company's affairs,[6] but this alternative remedy does not

---

1 *Ebrahimi v Westbourne Galleries Ltd,* supra. Contrast the position in the case of petitions under the Companies Act 1985, s 459(1) for relief from the conduct of the company's affairs in a manner which is unfairly prejudicial to the interests of some of its members (see *Pennington's Company Law* (7th edn) 885).
2 *Loch v John Blackwood Ltd* [1924] AC 783.
3 *Thomson v Drysdale* 1925 SC 311.
4 *Baird v Lees* 1924 SC 83.
5 *Baird v Lees,* supra, at 92, per Lord Clyde. Compare *Re H R Harmer Ltd* [1958] 3 All ER 689, [1959] 1 WLR 62.
6 Companies Act 1985, s 459(1) and s 461(2). The remedy is more effective because it does not involve bringing the company's business to an end, as winding up does.

preclude the petitioner from seeking a winding up order, and the court must make such an order unless the petitioner is acting unreasonably in not seeking the alternative remedy instead.[7]

Acts of oppression by the persons who promote or control a company must be of a serious character for the court to wind the company up. Isolated acts of misconduct by the directors will not suffice,[8] nor will the application of the company's funds by them for an ultra vires purpose on isolated occasions,[9] and the court will not make a winding up order merely because the promoters of the company have issued a false prospectus or have made a profit out of the promotion without the shareholders' consent.[10] A winding up order was also refused to the executors of a deceased shareholder whom the directors, in reliance on a power in the articles, declined to register as members of the company in his place, even though the directors were the only other members and the result of their refusal was that they alone could vote at general meetings.[11] Although the directors had clearly exercised their power to refuse registration in a way which benefited themselves by keeping the control of the company in their hands, and although they had shown their desire to perpetuate their control by offering to purchase the deceased's shares, the court would not infer that they had been guilty of oppression.[11] This decision has, however, been disapproved of by the House of Lords, although not expressly overruled,[12] and it would seem unlikely that it will be followed in the future. Again, a winding up order was refused when the directors had issued bonus shares although the company had earned no profits which could be capitalised to pay for them, with the consequence that the value of all the company's shares was diminished, and the petitioner had suffered a loss by buying shares from an existing shareholder at par.[13] In this latter case it was held that the directors had at most been guilty of a breach of duty owed to the petitioner personally, but it could not be inferred from that breach of duty that they were managing the company's affairs oppressively so as to justify winding the company up. If the directors have been guilty of a breach of duty to the petitioner, such as improperly refusing to register a transfer of shares to him, the court will also refuse to make a winding up order

---

7 Insolvency Act 1986, s 125(2); *Virdi v Abbey Leisure Ltd* [1990] BCLC 342, [1990] BCC 60.
8 *Re Diamond Fuel Co* (1879) 13 Ch D 400.
9 *Re Irrigation Co of France, ex p Fox* (1871) 6 Ch App 176; *Re Professional Commercial and Industrial Benefit Building Society* (1871) 6 Ch App 856.
10 *Re Haven Gold Mining Co* (1882) 20 Ch D 151 at 164, per Jessel MR.
11 *Re Cuthbert Cooper & Sons Ltd* [1937] Ch 392, [1937] 2 All ER 466.
12 *Ebrahimi v Westbourne Galleries Ltd* [1973] AC 360, [1972] 2 All ER 491.
13 *Re Gold Co* (1879) 11 Ch D 701.

if some other more appropriate remedy is provided for such a breach of duty, even though it may not be available in the case before the court because of its peculiar circumstances.[14]

PROCEDURE

The procedure for obtaining a winding up order and for winding up the company's affairs after the order has been made is governed by the Insolvency Rules 1986 (as amended).[15] These rules govern the procedure in all the courts which have jurisdiction to wind up companies, but it will be assumed in this and the four following chapters, unless otherwise stated, that the company against which a petition for winding up order is presented is the Companies Court.

The petition for a winding up order

Presentation of the petition

A petition for a winding up order to be made against a company which is presented by any person other than a contributory must be in the standard form set out in the Insolvency Rules 1986.[16] The petition must be headed with the full designation of the court to which the petition is addressed; if this is the High Court, the heading will be 'In the High Court of Justice/Chancery Division/Companies Court'. The petition formally commences with its title, namely 'In the Matter of [name of company] And in the matter of the Insolvency Act 1986'.[17] There then follows the address of the petition to the court to which it is presented; in the Companies Court this will be 'To Her Majesty's High Court of Justice'. The address to the court is followed by a description of the petition as presented by the petitioner, giving his or its full name and address or their full names and addresses.

The substantive contents of the petition, setting out the grounds on which it is presented and the relevant facts, are presented in

14 *Charles Forte Investments Ltd v Amanda* [1964] Ch 240, [1963] 2 All ER 940.
15 SI 1986/1986. The Insolvency Rules 1986, have been amended by the Insolvency (Amendment) Rules 1987 (SI 1987/1919), the Insolvency (Amendment) Rules 1989 (SI 1989/397), the Insolvency (Amendment) Rules 1991 (SI 1991/495), the Insolvency (Amendment) Rules 1993 (SI 1993/602) and the Insolvency (Amendment) Rules 1995 (SI 1995/586).
16 Insolvency Rules 1986, r 12.7(1) and Sch 4, Form 4.2.
17 Ibid, r 7.26(1).

numbered paragraphs, the first four of which state the name of the company, the date of its incorporation and the Companies Act in force at that time, the present registered office of the company, the nominal and paid-up capital of the company, the nominal value of the shares into which its capital is divided and the principal objects of the company. The fifth and following paragraphs of the petition set out the relevant facts and the statutory grounds on which a winding up order is sought; the relevant facts are elaborated in a number of paragraphs presenting them comprehensively, but nevertheless concisely. For example, a creditor's petition will recite the company's indebtedness to him and the transaction or transactions which gave rise to it (eg it will state that the company owes the creditor a specified amount as the price of goods sold and delivered, or that the company owes him the specified amount of a loan made by the petitioner to the company together with interest at a specified rate or rates calculated to a specified date or dates and also costs properly incurred by the petitioner of a specified amount). Additionally, the creditor's petition will state, where applicable, that on a certain date the petitioner served on the company a statutory notice requiring payment of the debt owed to him, specifying the date when the debt fell due for payment, that the creditor has demanded payment but without satisfaction, and that the company has neglected to comply with the statutory notice; or, alternatively, that the petitioner obtained judgment for a specified sum against the company in a named court and the petitioner has issued execution thereon which has been returned unsatisfied; or that the company has ceased to pay its debts as they fall due because of its inability to do so; or that the company's liabilities (giving an estimate of their total amount) exceed the value of its assets (briefly describing them and giving their approximate realisable value), and that consequently the company is unable to pay its debts. This part of the creditor's petition concludes with a separate formal paragraph stating that the company is insolvent and unable to pay its debts, unless this has already been included in the narrative. The prescribed form of petition also requires the inclusion of a formal statement in a separate ensuing paragraph that 'in the circumstances it is just and equitable that the company should be wound up': this is inserted whether the petitioner intends to rely on the statutory ground that the winding up of the company is justified by the circumstances making it just and equitable, or whether he intends to rely exclusively on the more specific statutory ground previously specified in the petition. The reference to the justice and equity of a winding up order in the latter circumstances can be interpreted as referring to matters which the court takes into account in exercising its discretion to make or refuse a winding-up order, such as support or absence of support for a creditor's petition by a majority in value of the company's creditors.

The petition concludes with a formal prayer by the petitioner that the company may be wound up by the court under the provisions of the Insolvency Act 1986, or that such other order may be made as the court thinks fit. This is followed by a note of the persons, in addition to the company, on whom it is intended to serve the petition. It is not necessary for the petition to be dated, signed or witnessed.

Affidavit in support of the petition

Unless the petition for a winding-up order is presented by a contributory, it must be accompanied, when filed in the court to which it is presented, by an affidavit verifying the statements contained in it.[18] The supporting affidavit must be made by the petitioner or one of the petitioners, if there are more than one of them, or by a person who has been concerned in the matters giving rise to the petition (such as a director, secretary or other officer of a petitioning company, or a solicitor engaged to recover the debt owed to the petitioning creditor), or by a responsible person who has been authorised by the petitioner or petitioners to make the affidavit and who has the requisite knowledge of the matters on which the petition is based.[19] The deponent of the supporting affidavit must state in it that the statements in the petition are true, or that they are true to the best of his knowledge, information and belief (as the case may be); and if the deponent is not the petitioner or one of the petitioners, he must state the capacity in which, or the authority from the petitioner by which, he makes the affidavit and his means of knowing that the statements made in it are true.[20] The petition must be exhibited to the affidavit verifying it.[1]

If the petition is presented in respect of debts owed to different creditors of the company, the debts owed to each petitioning creditor must be separately verified; and if this necessitates affidavits being made by more than one deponent, several affidavits must be filed.[2] On the other hand, when several petitions are presented concurrently against two or more companies based upon the same grounds and supporting facts, a single affidavit by one deponent may be filed if he can verify the statements contained in all the

18 Ibid, r 4.7(1) and r 4.12(1) and Sch 4, Form 4.3.
19 Ibid, r 4.12(4).
20 Ibid, r 4.12(1) and (5).
 1 Ibid, r 4.12(3).
 2 Ibid, r 4.12(2).

petitions; but a photocopy of the affidavit must then be filed with each of the petitions.[3] This may occur when the concurrent petitions are based on a single debt for which the respondent companies are jointly liable, or on a debt of one of the companies which has been guaranteed by all the others. If a single winding-up petition is presented against two or more companies, as it may be when the debt on which the petition is based is one for which all the respondent companies are liable,[4] only one affidavit is required in support of the petition, provided that the deponent is able to verify all the statements contained in the petition.

Filing of the petition

When a petition for a winding-up order is presented by any person other than a contributory, the petition and the supporting affidavit must be filed in the court to which the petition is presented, accompanied by a receipt issued by the court office for payment of the deposit of £500 which must be made as security for the Official Receiver's fee of £640;[5] this fee is payable to the official receiver for the performance of his general duties after the winding up order is made; but if the winding-up petition is withdrawn or dismissed, the deposit of £500 as security for the fee is repaid.[6]

Unless the company itself is the petitioner, there must be delivered to the court with the petition an additional copy of it for service on the company and a further additional copy which will be exhibited to the affidavit of service on the company; also, whether the company is the petitioner or not, further copies of the petition must be delivered to the court so that a copy of the petition may be sent to the liquidator of the company if it is already in voluntary liquidation, or to the administrator of the company if an administration order has been made in respect of it, or to the administrative receiver if one has been appointed to realise the company's assets comprised in a floating charge over the generality of its assets, or to the supervisor of any voluntary arrangement between the company and its creditors which is effective under the Insolvency Act 1986.[7]

The original petition is retained by the court, and the other copies are sealed by it and delivered to the petitioner, with an

3 Ibid, r 4.12(7).
4 *Re Chancery Lane Registrars Ltd* [1984] BCLC 307 referred to in *Re a Company* [1984] BCLC 307.
5 Insolvency Rules 1986, r 4.7(1) and (2).
6 Ibid, r 4.14(1) and (4); Insolvency Fees Order 1986 (SI 1986/2030), arts 3, 8, 9 and 11(1) and (2) and Sch 1, (as amended by Insolvency Fees (Amendment) Order 1994 (SI 1994/2541)).
7 Insolvency Rules 1986, r 4.7(3) and (4).

endorsement on each of them showing the date on which the petition was filed and the time, date and place when and where it will be heard, together with the names and addresses of the petitioner's solicitors and their London agents.[8]

Contributory's petition

If the winding-up petition is presented by a contributory, it is in almost the same form as a creditor's petition. However, its third paragraph, in addition to setting out the company's nominal and paid-up capital and the nominal value of its shares, must state the number of shares held by the petitioner, and show that he is qualified to present the petition by being the allottee of those shares, or by them having been registered in his name for at least six out of the preceding 18 months, or by the shares having devolved on him on the death of a former holder of the shares.[9] The fifth and following paragraphs of the petition must set out the facts on which the petitioner relies for a winding-up order to be made, and they conclude with a paragraph which states that 'in the circumstances it is just and equitable that the company should be wound up'.[9] There then follows a prayer by the petitioner, in the same form as in a creditor's petition, that the company shall be wound up by the court under the provisions of the Insolvency Act 1986.

A contributory's petition is filed in the court to which it is presented without a supporting affidavit, but a copy of the petition for service must be delivered to the court for sealing together with the original petition and a receipt issued by the court office for payment of the same deposit toward the Official Receiver fee as on the presentation of a creditor's petition.[10] On receiving the petition, the court fixes a day and time when the petitioner and the company by its representative must appear before the registrar in chambers (in the Companies Court, before the Chief Clerk of the court in chambers)[11] for directions to be given as to the proceedings to be taken on the petitioner, endorsed with the date and time of the hearing in chambers, so that the petitioner may serve that copy on the company at least 14 days before the return date.[12]

On or after the return day for the hearing in chambers, the court may give such directions as it thinks appropriate as to: (a) service of the petition on persons other than the company (which will already have been served); (b) whether particulars of claim and defence shall

8 Ibid, r 4.12(5) and (6) and Sch 4, Form 4.2.
9 Ibid, r 4.22(1) and Sch 4, Form 4.14.
10 Ibid, 4.4.22(1) and (1A).
11 Ibid, r 13.2(2) and Practice Direction dated 10 December 1986, para 4.
12 Insolvency Rules 1986, r 4.22(2) to (4).

be delivered by the petitioner and the company to each other; (c) whether and how the petition is to be advertised; (d) the manner in which evidence in support of and against the petition shall be adduced on the hearing of the petition, and in particular, whether evidence shall be given wholly or partly by affidavit or orally, whether deponents of affidavits may be cross-examined, and finally, what questions of fact are to be covered by the evidence; and (e) any other matter affecting the procedure on the petition and the hearing and disposal of it.[13] Because the court has jurisdiction to decide whether and how a contributory's petition shall be advertised, it is an abuse of process for a contributory to inform creditors or customers of the company or persons having dealings with it of the presentation of the petition otherwise than on the court's direction, and if the contributory does this, the court may order that the petition shall be struck out.[14]

Service and advertisement of the petition

The rules governing the service of a winding-up petition apply whenever the petitioner is a person other than the company itself or a contributory, and the rules as to the advertisement of the petition apply if the petition is presented by a person other than a contributory.[15] On the return day endorsed on a contributory's petition the registrar of the court (or the Chief Clerk of the Companies Court) will give directions as to the service and advertisement of the petition; such directions correspond to the rules that apply automatically when the petition is presented by a creditor or any other petitioner, and those rules may be embodied in the court's directions (expressly or by reference with suitable modifications according to the circumstances).[13] A sealed copy of a contributory's petition must, in any case, be served on the company before the return day for directions, and presumably service on the company is effected in the same way as when the petition is presented by a creditor.

Service on the company of a petition presented by a creditor must be effected at the company's registered office most recently notified to the Registrar of Companies.[15] Service may be effected by delivering a sealed copy of the petition (endorsed with the date and place where it will be heard) to a person at the appropriate address

---

13 Ibid, r 4.23(1) and (2).
14 *Re Doreen Boards Ltd* [1996] 1 BCLC 501.
15 Insolvency Rules 1986, r 4.8(2).

who acknowledges himself to be a director, officer or employee of the company, or who is such a director, officer or employee to the best of the server's knowledge, information and belief; alternatively, service may be effected by delivering the copy petition to a person at the appropriate address who acknowledges himself to be authorised to accept service of documents on behalf of the company; if no such director, officer or employee or person authorised to accept service is present at the appropriate address, the petition may be served by leaving it at the company's registered office or if that is not practicable, at the company's last known principal place of business, and in either case the petition must be left in a manner which makes it likely that it will come to the notice of a person attending there (eg by being left in a mail collecting box), or by delivering it to the secretary or a director, manager or principal officer of the company, wherever such a person may be found.[16] If it is impracticable to serve the petition on the company in any of the foregoing ways, it may be served on it in such other manner as the court may direct on an ex parte application made by the petitioner;[17] consequently, the court may direct substituted service on the company in any of the ways in which it may direct substituted service of a writ. It appears that the company may agree to accept service of a petition in a manner other than those prescribed by the Insolvency Rules 1986 (eg by service on the company's solicitor).[18] If a winding up order is made by the court on a petition which was not properly served on the company, the order is effective, but the court will on the application of a creditor or contributory of the company order the winding up to be stayed.[19]

In addition to serving the petition on the company, the petitioner must send a copy of the petition to the company's liquidator, if the petitioner knows that the company is in voluntary liquidation; or to an administrative receiver whom the petitioner knows has been appointed by or on behalf of a creditor or creditors secured by a floating charge over the generality of the company's assets; or to an administrator appointed under an administration order which the petitioner knows has been made in respect of the company; or to the supervisor under a voluntary arrangement which the petitioner knows has been made by the company with its creditors under the Insolvency Act 1986.[20] Strictly speaking, a petition is not served on a liquidator, administrative receiver, administrator or supervisor

16 Ibid, r 4.8(3) and (4).
17 Ibid, r 4.8(6) and (7).
18 *Re Regent United Service Stores Ltd* (1878) 8 Ch D 75.
19 *Re Intermain Properties Ltd* [1986] BCLC 265, 1 BCC 99, 555.
20 Insolvency Rules 1986, r 4.10(1) to (3).

under this provision, and so the rules dealt with above governing service on the company do not apply. The rules merely provide that a copy of the petition must be sent to such a person by prepaid post or delivered to him personally; and if a copy petition is sent by post, it must be despatched on the next business day after the petition is served on the company.[1]

Service of the petition on the company is proved by filing in court immediately after service an affidavit in the prescribed form by the person who effected service, stating how it was effected; the affidavit must have exhibited to it a sealed copy of the petition and, if the court has ordered substituted service of the petition, a sealed copy of the court order.[2] No affidavit need be filed in respect of the despatch or delivery of a copy petition to a liquidator, administrative receiver, administrator or supervisor.

Unless the court otherwise directs, a winding-up petition must be advertised once in the London Gazette not less than seven business days after the service of the petition on the company (except where the company is itself the petitioner), and not less than seven business days before the date appointed for the hearing of the petition.[3]

The obligatory postponement of the advertisement to seven days after the petition is served on the company provides the company with an opportunity to apply to the court to strike out the petition or to stay the proceedings on the ground that the company has a defence to the petitioning creditor's claim which it intends to plead.[4] The court may in its discretion permit the petition to proceed to hearing even though it has been advertised before seven days have elapsed after it was served on the company, but the court will do this only if the company will suffer no harm from the premature publicity.[5] It has been held in one case that notification of the petition to the company's bank within seven days after it was served on the company was a breach of the postponement rule,[6] but in another case it was held that this is not so, because advertisement of the petition for the purpose of the rules means advertisement in the London Gazette or a newspaper directed by the court, and not any other form of publicity.[7] The advertisement of the winding up petition in the London Gazette must state the name of the company and the address of its registered office, the name and address of the

1 Ibid, r 4.10(5), r 12.10(1) and r 13.3(1) and (3).
2 Ibid, r 4.9(1) and (2).
3 Insolvency Rules 1986, r 4.11(1) and (2).
4 See p 20, ante.
5 *Re Roselmar Properties Ltd* (1986) 2 BCC 157.
6 *Re a Company (No 001127 of 1992)* [1992] BCC 477.
7 *SN Group plc v Barclays Bank plc* [1993] BCC 506.

petitioner, the date when the petition was presented, the time, date and place fixed for the hearing of the petition, and the name and address of the petitioner's solicitors; and it must also state that any person intending to appear on the hearing of the petition, whether to support or oppose it, must notify the petitioner or his solicitor of his intention to do so not later than 4 pm on the business day immediately before the day fixed for the hearing.[8] The court may permit the petition to be advertised in a specified newspaper, instead of the London Gazette, if it is not reasonably practicable to advertise it there within the time limits prescribed; and the court then fixes the time limits between which the advertisement must appear in the alternative newspaper.[9]

The publicity given to the presentation of a winding up petition by its advertisement may obviously result in damage to the company's interests, for example, by its bank refusing to allow its directors to continue operating its bank account, or calling for immediate repayment of money advanced by the bank on overdraft, or by the company's suppliers refusing further credit and calling for immediate payment of the debts which it already owes them, or by persons who are indebted to the company deferring payment until the outcome of the winding up petition is known. The court will consequently order that the petition shall not be advertised if its presentation is an abuse of the process of the court (eg if the petitioner is aware that the company has a defence which it intends in good faith to plead to the petitioner's claim),[10] but the court will not intervene unless the company tenders prima facie evidence of the abuse of process.[11] The court may also restrain the advertisement of a winding up petition on the ground that the company would suffer serious prejudice if the petition were advertised, and that prejudice outweighs the interest of creditors or members of the company or of the public in being informed that the petition has been presented.[12]

The petitioner or his solicitor must file in court at least five days before the date fixed for the hearing of the petition a certificate that

8 Insolvency Rules 1986, r 4.11(4) and Sch 4, Form 4.6.
9 Ibid, r 4.11(3).
10 *Re a Company (No 003079 of 1990)* [1991] BCLC 235, [1991] BCC 683; *Re a Company (No 0012209 of 1991)* [1992] 2 All ER 797, [1992] 1 WLR 351; *Re a Company (No 004502 of 1988), ex p Johnson* [1992] BCLC 701.
11 *Coulon Sanderson and Ward Ltd v Ward* (1985) 2 BCC 207. The fact that the petitioning creditor has not delivered a statutory notice requiring the company to pay or compound for the debt he claims before presenting his petition is not an abuse of process, because he may prove the company's inability to pay its debts by other means (*Taylor's Industrial Flooring Ltd v M & H Plant Hire (Manchester) Ltd* [1990] BCLC 216.
12 *Re a Company (No 007923 of 1994)* [1995] 1 WLR 953, [1995] 1 BCLC 440.

the rules relating to service and advertisement of the petition have been complied with; the certificate must state the date of presentation of the petition, the date fixed for the hearing and the dates on which the petition was served on the company and advertised in the London Gazette or any other newspaper directed by the court;[13] and the certificate of compliance must be accompanied by a copy of the published advertisement of the petition.[14]

If the petitioner does not wish to proceed with the petition, he may apply to the court ex parte, not later than five days before the date fixed for the hearing, for leave to withdraw the petition; and if the petitioner satisfies the registrar (the Chief Clerk in the Companies Court) that the petition has not been advertised, that no notices of an intention to appear on the hearing of the petition have been received by him (whether supporting or opposing it), and the company consents to the withdrawal of the petition, the court may give leave for the petition to be withdrawn on such terms as to costs as the petitioner and the company agree.[15] If the petition is not withdrawn in this way, it may be withdrawn only with leave of the court on the hearing.

If the petitioner fails to advertise his petition or consents to the withdrawal of his petition or to it being dismissed, the registrar of the court to which the petition was presented (the Chief Clerk of the Companies Court) may order that any creditor or contributory who is qualified to present a winding-up petition against the company shall be substituted for the original petitioner. The registrar of the court may make a similar order if the petitioner does not appear on the date fixed for the hearing of the petition, or does appear but does not apply for an order that the company shall be wound up.[16] This may be done even though the substituted petitioner relies on different grounds for seeking a winding up order than the original petitioner, and even though he could not have presented a petition himself when the original petition was presented (eg because he is the assignee of the debt to which the original petitioner was entitled at the date of the original petition).[17] However, the court will not permit the substitution of a creditor or contributory of the company as the petitioner where the petition was presented by the Secretary of State for Trade and Industry on the ground that it is expedient in

---

13 *Re Signland Ltd* [1982] 2 All ER 609n.
14 Insolvency Rules 1986, r 4.14(1) and (2) and Sch 4, Form 4.7.
15 Insolvency Rules 1986, r 4.15 and Practice Direction dated 10 December 1986, para 4.
16 Insolvency Rules 1986, r 4.19(1) to (3) and Practice Direction dated 10 December 1986, para 4.
17 *Perak Pioneer Ltd v Petroliam Nasional Bhd* [1986] AC 849, 2 BCC 128.

the public interest that the company should be wound up, and the Secretary of State proposes not to proceed with the petition.[18]

Notification of intention to appear on the hearing

Any person who intends to appear on the hearing of the petition, whether in support of it or in opposition to a winding up order being made, must notify his intention to do so to the petitioner or his solicitor not later than 4 pm on the business day immediately preceding the day fixed for the hearing of the petition.[19] The notification must be in writing, must state whether the person giving it intends to support or oppose the petition, must specify the amount and nature of the company's indebtedness to him if he is a creditor, and must give his name, address and telephone number and any reference required for communicating with him or any other person named in the notice who is authorised to speak or act on his behalf.[20] If no such notification is given, a person who wishes to appear on the hearing of the petition may do so only with leave of the court.[1] The petitioner must hand to the court on the date fixed for the hearing of the petition a list of the persons who have notified their intention to appear at the hearing, showing whether they intend to support or to oppose the petition.[2] To enable interested persons to decide whether to appear on the hearing to support or oppose the petition, every director, contributory or creditor of the company is entitled to be furnished by the petitioner or his solicitor with a copy of the petition within two days after requesting it on payment of 15 pence for each A4- or A5-sized page supplied or 30 pence per A3-sized page supplied.[3]

The rules set out above as to the notification to the petitioner of an intention to appear on the hearing of the petition and the handing to the court by the petitioner of a list of persons who have given such a notification, apply also when the petition has been presented by a contributory;[4] but the obligation of the petitioner to supply a copy of the petition to a director, contributory or creditor who requests it applies in that case only if the court so orders when giving directions as to the conduct of the proceedings.[5]

18 *Re Xyllyx plc* [1992] BCLC 376.
19 Insolvency Rules 1986, r 4.16(1).
20 Ibid, r 4.16(2).
 1 Ibid, r 4.16(5).
 2 Ibid, r 4.17(1) to (3) and Sch 4, Form 4.10.
 3 Ibid, r 4.13 and r 13.11(*b*).
 4 Ibid, r 4.24.
 5 Ibid, r 4.23(2).

The company against which a winding-up order is sought need not notify its intention to appear on the hearing in order to oppose the making of an order, but it will be heard in opposition only if its board of directors so resolve, and if the petitioner is a director, he is deemed to consent to the company opposing his petition by issuing and serving it on the company.[6]

Filing of further affidavits

If the company intends to oppose the petition, it must file in court an affidavit in opposition made by a director or other person who can depose to the facts, and the affidavit must set out the facts on which the company relies for the dismissal of the petition; the affidavit must be filed not less than seven days before the date fixed for the hearing, and the company must send a copy of it to the petitioner immediately after filing.[7] If the petition is presented by a contributory, the company will file an affidavit in opposition only if the court so orders on giving directions for the conduct of the proceedings.[8]

There is no provision in the rules for the filing of an affidavit by the petitioner in reply to the company's affidavit, but such an affidavit or affidavits by other persons supporting or opposing the petitioner's case may under the general rules governing procedure in the High Court[9] be submitted on the hearing only if they have been filed in court and the other party to the proceedings (ie the company) has been notified of that fact.[9] If the petitioner is a contributory, however, the filing of affidavits made by the parties or by other persons in support of their respective cases will be dealt with by the directions given by the court on the return day for such directions.[8]

Provisional liquidator

At any time after the presentation of a winding-up petition and before the making of a winding-up order, the court on the application of the petitioner, or of any creditor or contributory, or of the company itself, or of the Secretary of State for Trade and Industry,

---

6 *Re Fletcher Hunt (Bristol) Ltd* [1989] BCLC 108, 4 BCC 703.
7 Insolvency Rules 1986, r 4.18(1) and (2).
8 Ibid, r 4.23(1)(*d*).
9 Rules of the Supreme Court, Ord 32, r 17, Ord 38, r 2(3) and Ord 41, r 9(3) and (4).

may appoint the official receiver or a qualified insolvency practitioner to be the provisional liquidator of the company, and the court may confer such functions on him and limit the powers normally exercisable by him as a liquidator as it thinks fit.[10]

An application for the appointment of a provisional liquidator must be made in the prescribed form, and must be supported by an affidavit by the applicant stating the grounds on which the application is made (eg a risk that the company's assets may be disposed of or dissipated by its directors or other persons before the winding up petition is heard).[11] The affidavit must also depose that the person proposed for appointment has consented to act as provisional liquidator, and, unless the application is for the appointment of the official receiver, that to the best of the applicant's belief the person proposed is qualified to act as an insolvency practitioner in relation to the company; whether the official receiver has been informed of the application and furnished with a copy of it; whether to the applicant's knowledge there has been proposed or is in force a voluntary arrangement with the company's creditors; whether an administrator or an administrative receiver has been appointed in respect of the company; whether a liquidator has been appointed if the company has resolved to go into voluntary liquidation; and, finally, the applicant's estimate of the value of the assets of the company of which the proposed provisional liquidator would take possession.[12] A copy of the application for the appointment of a provisional liquidator and the supporting affidavit must be sent to the official receiver, who may appear on the hearing and make representations to the court.[13]

The application for the appointment of a provisional liquidator is heard in chambers by the judge of the court to which the winding up petition was presented;[14] he may appoint a provisional liquidator on such terms as he thinks fit, and in his order making the appointment there must be specified the functions which the provisional liquidator shall fulfil.[15] If the official receiver is appointed to be the provisional liquidator, the applicant for the appointment must deposit with him or secure to his satisfaction such sum as the

---

10 Insolvency Act 1986, s 135(1), (2), (4) and (5), s 388(1) and s 389(1); Insolvency Rules 1986, r 4.25(1) and (4). The official receiver is an official of the Department of Trade and Industry attached to the courts with insolvency jurisdiction. (Insolvency Act 1986, s 399(1) and (2)).
11 Insolvency Rules 1986, r 4.25(2), r 7.2(2) and r 7.3(1) and Sch 4, Form 7.2.
12 This estimate is omitted if the person proposed for appointment is the official receiver.
13 Insolvency Rules 1986, r 4.25(3).
14 Ibid, r 7.6(1); Practice Direction dated 17 November 1996, para 4.
15 Ibid, r 4.25(4) and r 4.26(1).

court orders to cover the official receiver's remuneration and expenses, and the court may later increase the amount ordered to be deposited or secured if the original amount proves insufficient; if a winding up order is made, the amount deposited is returned to the applicant, unless it is required to satisfy a deficiency of the company's assets to meet the official receiver's remuneration and his expenses incurred as provisional liquidator.[16] If a qualified insolvency practitioner is appointed to be the provisional liquidator, he must give such security for the proper fulfilment of his duties as the court orders, and he is entitled to be reimbursed out of the company's assets for the cost of providing that security.[17] The provisional liquidator is entitled to such remuneration out of the company's assets as the court orders.[18]

The purpose of appointing a provisional liquidator is to conserve the assets of the company if there is a risk of their being dissipated or diminished in value by the directors or other persons, and the court will normally exercise its discretion to appoint a provisional liquidator only if the company is, or is likely to become, insolvent or if it is obvious that a winding up order will be made.[19] However, the court may also appoint a provisional liquidator if there is an interest of the public to be protected, such as that of the policyholders of an insurance company which may become insolvent if it is allowed to continue to issue policies and carry on business,[20] or if there is substantial evidence that the company has throughout its existence misled investors so as to induce them to make hazardous speculations on vague terms which have enabled the company to impose excessive charges on them for its services.[1]

In practice the powers of a provisional liquidator are confined by the court to taking possession of the company's assets and preserving and protecting them,[2] but it has been held that a provisional liquidator who has been given power to preserve the company's assets may close down a branch of its business which is making losses, and may dismiss employees working in that branch, because by avoiding further losses which would be made if the

16 Ibid, r 4.27(1) to (3).
17 Ibid, r 4.28(1) and (2).
18 Ibid, r 4.30(1).
19 *Re Railway Finance Co Ltd* (1866) 35 Beav 473; *Re Hammersmith Town Hall Co* (1877) 6 Ch D 112.
20 *Re Union Accident Insurance Co Ltd* [1972] 1 All ER 1105, [1972] 1 WLR 640. It is doubtful whether a provisional liquidator may close down the whole of the company's business without the authorisation of the court.
1 *Re Highfield Commodities Ltd* [1984] 3 All ER 884, [1984] 1 WLR 149; *Re Pinstripe Farming Co Ltd* [1996] 2 BCLC 295.
2 *Re Bound & Co Ltd* [1893] WN 21.

branch were to continue carrying on business, the provisional liquidator preserves the company's assets generally.[20] The appointment of the provisional liquidator is superseded by that of the official receiver as liquidator if the court makes a winding up order,[3] but it is necessary for the court to make a formal order removing the provisional liquidator,[4] and this is done as a matter of course when a winding up order is made or the winding up petition is dismissed.[5]

The hearing and consequential proceedings

The hearing of a winding up petition takes place in open court, whether it is opposed or unopposed.[6] The hearing is before a judge of the court to which the petition was presented; but in the Companies Court unopposed petitions are heard by the registrar of the court, who may make or refuse to make a winding up order or adjourn the petition for hearing by a judge.[7] If the petitioner does not appear and is not represented on the hearing, the petition is normally dismissed. If the petitioner does appear or is represented, after hearing him and, if the petition is opposed, after hearing the company and any creditors and contributories who appear in support of or against the petition after notifying their intention to do so to the petitioner or his solicitor, and also after hearing any other persons to whom the court gives leave to appear, the court may make a winding up order, or may dismiss the petition, or make an interim order (eg appointing a provisional liquidator) or adjourn the hearing conditionally or unconditionally.[8]

If the court adjourns the hearing, it is not necessary for the petitioner to advertise the time and place of the adjourned hearing, unless the court so orders. Any person who could have appeared at the original hearing, but who did not give proper notice of his intention to do so to the petitioner or his solicitor before the hearing, may give a similar notice in writing of his intention to appear at the adjourned hearing in support of or against the petition; but such a notice must be given not later than 4 pm on the business day immediately preceding the day of the adjourned hearing.[9] The court

3 Insolvency Act 1986, s 136(1) and (2).
4 Ibid, s 172(1) and (2).
5 *Re Dry Docks Corpn of London* (1888) 39 Ch D 306.
6 Practice Direction dated 10 December 1986, para 3.
7 Practice Direction dated 22 October 1986.
8 Insolvency Act 1986, s 125(1).
9 Insolvency Rules 1986, r 4.16(5).

is reluctant to adjourn the hearing of a petition repeatedly, particularly when it is opposed by the company or by a substantial number of its creditors, because until the petition is disposed of the company cannot make dispositions of any of its assets or incur further obligations with the certainty that they will not be upset if a winding up order is eventually made, and other creditors who have stronger cases for obtaining a winding-up order are prejudiced because no other winding up petition may be presented until the first petition has been disposed of.

If on the hearing or adjourned hearing of a petition the court finds that the petitioner is not entitled to present a petition, or the petitioner consents to withdraw his petition or to allow it to be dismissed, or fails to appear in support of his petition, or appears but does not apply for a winding up order, the court may, instead of dismissing the petition, order that some other person who would be entitled to petition for a winding up order as a creditor or contributory shall be substituted as the petitioner, and that the original proceedings shall be continued by the substituted petitioner on such terms as the court thinks just.[10]

Evidence on the hearing of a winding up petition

The evidence tendered to the court on the hearing of a winding up petition is confined to the affidavits filed in support of and in opposition to the petition, unless the court permits testimony to be given orally (eg to facilitate the cross-examination of the deponent of an affidavit). The affidavit verifying the petition is prima facie proof of the facts alleged by it and suffices to prove the petitioner's case unless there are affidavits filed in opposition.[11] However, it has been held that if the petition alleges fraud on the part of the company or its promoters, directors or controlling shareholders, or if a winding up order is sought so that irregularities in the company's management may be investigated, the petitioner's affidavit should be supplemented by a statement of the facts and evidence on which he relies, even though there are no affidavits filed in opposition.[11]

There is a conflict of judicial opinion as to whether the court may accept the adverse findings in the report of inspectors appointed by the Secretary of State for Trade and Industry in exercise of his

---

10 Ibid, r 4.19(1) and (2). Such an order will be made in favour of a person to whom the petitioning creditor assigns the debt on which the petition is based (*Perak Pioneer Ltd v Petroliam Nasional Bhd* [1986] AC 849, 2 BCC 128).

11 *Re S A Hawken Ltd* [1950] 2 All ER 408.

powers of investigation under the Companies Act 1985 (as amended) as sufficient evidence of those facts; and whether the court may make a winding up order on a petition presented by the Secretary of State in consequence of the report without him adducing direct evidence to support those findings.[12] In two cases decided by Pennycuick J[13] it was held that this may be done, but in an earlier case[14] Buckley J held that the inspectors' report may be admitted, although it is only hearsay evidence, but a winding up order should not be made unless the report is corroborated by direct testimony. In a fourth case decided after Pennycuick J's two judgments, however,[15] Buckley J held that the report may be accepted as the basis for making a winding up order if no evidence is tendered in opposition to the petition. Despite this conflict of opinion, both judges were agreed that it is not necessary for an affidavit by the inspectors verifying their report to be filed in the winding up proceedings, and that the company cannot cross-examine them. Pennycuick J further held that if the company adduces evidence rebutting the inspectors' findings, a winding up order may not be made unless the Secretary of State presents direct evidence supporting the findings, but he did not express an opinion as to the weight to be attached to the inspectors' findings in the event of the company tendering conflicting direct evidence.[15] Megarry and Templeman JJ have affirmed the view taken by Buckley J, and have also ruled that the inspectors' report can be considered by the court only if the company does not challenge it by presenting evidence rebutting the inspectors' findings; if the company does contest the inspectors' findings in this way, Megarry and Templeman JJ concurred with Buckley J in holding that the inspectors' conclusions must be proved by direct evidence alone.[16] This view has been followed in a later case where it was held that the inspectors' report may be relied on by a petitioner other than the Secretary of State, and has the same evidentiary value as it does in proceedings initiated by the Secretary of State.[17] On the other hand, the Court of Appeal has held that the

---

12 In litigation other than winding up proceedings and applications for disqualification orders against directors consequential on an adverse report by inspectors, the inspectors' report is merely evidence of their opinion, and not of the facts found by them (Companies Act 1985, s 441(1), as amended by Insolvency Act 1986, s 109 and Sch 6, para 3).

13 *Re Travel and Holiday Clubs Ltd* [1967] 2 All ER 606, [1967] 1 WLR 711; *Re SBA Properties Ltd* [1967] 2 All ER 615, [1967] 1 WLR 799.

14 *Re ABC Coupler and Engineering Co Ltd (No 2)* [1962] 3 All ER 68, [1962] 1 WLR 1236.

15 *Re Allied Produce Co Ltd* [1967] 3 All ER 399n, [1967] 1 WLR 1469.

16 *Re Koscot Interplantary (UK) Ltd* [1972] 3 All ER 829; *Re Armvent Ltd* [1975] 3 All ER 441, [1975] 1 WLR 1679.

17 *Re St Piran Ltd* [1981] 3 All ER 270, [1981] 1 WLR 1300.

burden of proof is on the Secretary of State to satisfy the court that the findings of the inspectors' report are justified and that the winding up of the company is expedient in the public interest, in the same way as in other civil proceedings, and that the inspectors' findings are not sufficient proof by themselves if they are unsupported by affidavit evidence of the underlying facts.[18]

Service of the winding up order

When a winding up order has been made, the court must immediately notify the official receiver.[19] The order is formally drawn up by the court without an appointment being made for the parties to attend in order to settle its contents, unless the court considers this necessary.[20] The order formally recites the presentation of the petition, and that the court has heard the parties and supporting and opposing creditors and contributories (if that is so) and has read the affidavits which had been filed before or submitted at the hearing, and goes on to order that the company (naming it) shall be wound up by the court under the provisions of the Insolvency Act 1986, and that the costs of the petitioner and of persons appearing on the hearing who were awarded costs shall be paid out of the assets of the company.[20] Three sealed copies of the winding up order are sent by the court to the official receiver, and he must serve one copy on the company by post addressed to its registered office, and must send another copy to the Registrar of Companies for inclusion in the company's file at the Companies Registration Office; the official receiver must also advertise the winding-up order in the London Gazette and may advertise it in such other newspaper as he thinks fit.[1]

Costs

If the court makes a winding up order, the successful petitioner will, in all but exceptional circumstances, be awarded his costs against the company to be paid out of its assets in the liquidation; if the petition is dismissed, the company will usually be awarded its costs against the petitioner. An unsuccessful petitioner will in practice only be awarded his costs against the company if it has misled him

18 *Re Walter L Jacob & Co Ltd* [1989] BCLC 345, 5 BCC 244.
19 Insolvency Rules 1986, r 4.20(1).
20 Ibid, r 4.20(3) and Sch 4, Form 4.11.
 1 Ibid, r 4.21(1) and (4).

in some way into presenting his petition (eg if the company was incorporated with exactly the same name as a dissolved company which was indebted to the petitioner and carried on the business which the respondent company acquired),[2] or if the company has allowed judgment for the petitioning creditor's debt to be entered against it in default of appearance or defence, and has since the issue of the petition obtained leave to defend the action on the merits and to set aside the judgment in default.[3] The court has a discretion to order that the costs of a petitioning creditor shall be paid out of the company's assets when the only reason for the dismissal of his petition is the opposition of the majority in value of the company's creditors to a winding up order being made.[4]

However, the court will not order the costs of an unsuccessful petitioning creditor to be paid out of the company's assets, if he has served a statutory notice demanding payment of his debt on the company, which did not respond to it within the three-week period, and the creditor then presented his petition without first obtaining judgment against the company, and on the hearing of the petition the company, has satisfied the court that it had a good defence to the creditor's claims.[5] Furthermore, the court will not award the costs of a first winding up petition to a creditor when the petition is dismissed because the company relies on an alleged defence to the creditor's claim, and he then obtains judgment against the company in an action on his claim and presents a second successful winding up petition based on the judgment.[6]

If the company appears on the hearing of a winding up petition to consent to a winding up order, its costs will always be ordered to be paid out of its assets, but if it unsuccessfully opposes the petition on the hearing without good reason for doing so, the court will either not make any order for the payment of its costs out of its assets, or will order payment of its costs only after all its creditors have been paid in full.[7] In such a case the successful petitioner's increased costs of the contested hearing will be allowed in full out of the company's assets, but it has been held that the court has no power to order the company's directors to pay those costs personally.[8] This latter ruling is now questionable in view of the courts' present statutory power to

2 *Re M McCarthy & Co (Builders) Ltd (No 2)* [1976] 2 All ER 339.
3 *Re Lanaghan Bros Ltd* [1977] 1 All ER 265.
4 *Re Arrow Leeds Ltd* [1986] BCLC 538, 2 BCC 991.
5 *Re Cannon Screen Entertainment Ltd* [1989] BCLC 660, 5 BCC 207.
6 *Re Fernforest Ltd* [1990] BCLC 693, [1991] BCC 680.
7 *Re Bathampton Properties Ltd* [1976] 3 All ER 200, [1976] 1 WLR 158; *Re Esal (Commodities) Ltd* [1985] BCLC 450.
8 *Re Reprographic Exports (Euromat) Ltd* (1978) 122 Sol Jo 400.

order persons other than the parties to litigation to pay the costs of the proceedings.[9] However, the court will not order the costs of a winding up petition to be paid by the respondent company's directors personally unless they have acted improperly, for example, by defending the petition in order to avoid enquiries into their conduct of the company's affairs in their own interests, and not the shareholders'.[10]

The court usually orders the losing party, whether the company or the petitioner, to pay one set of costs to contributories who appeared against him or it on the hearing, and also one set of costs to creditors who so appeared.[11] If a petitioner consents to the withdrawal of his petition at the hearing, he will usually be ordered to pay the company's costs,[12] and four separate sets of costs to the contributories and creditors who respectively supported and opposed the petition and appeared on the hearing for that purpose.[13] But if the petition is withdrawn or dismissed, not on its merits, but simply because the majority of the creditors or contributories do not want the company to be wound up, no costs will be awarded against the petitioner,[14] unless he was aware when he presented his petition that the majority of the creditors or contributories had reasonable grounds for opposing a winding up order,[15] or unless the petition was founded on a claim against the company the validity of which had not been established by agreement or litigation before the petition was presented, for in such a case it is impossible to be sure that the petition would have been successful even if it had not been opposed by the majority of the creditors or contributories.[16] Also a petitioner will not be ordered to pay any costs if the presentation of his petition was justified, and another creditor of the company is substituted for him by order of the court; this is so whether a winding up order is made or not.[17]

A petitioning creditor should withdraw his petition if the company offers to pay his debt and costs and is in a position to do

---

9 Supreme Court Act 1981, s 51(1), as substituted by Courts and Legal Services Act 1990, s 4(1); (11 *Halsbury's Statutes* (4th edn) (1991 Reissue) 1217).

10 *Re Tajik Air Ltd* [1996] 1 BCLC 317, [1996] BCC 368.

11 *Re Anglo-Egyptian Navigation Co* (1869) LR 8 Eq 660; *Re New Gas Co* (1877) 5 Ch D 703.

12 If the petitioner has good cause for withdrawing his petition (eg because the company has paid his debt) the court will not order him to pay the company's costs (*Re Tyneside Permanent Benefit Building Society* [1885] WN 148).

13 *Re Home Assurance Association* (1871) LR 12 Eq 59; *Re Hereford and South Wales Waggon and Engineering Co* (1874) LR 17 Eq 423.

14 *Re R W Sharman Ltd* [1957] 1 All ER 737, [1957] 1 WLR 774. But in that case the petitioner bears his own costs.

15 *Re A E Hayter & Sons (Portchester) Ltd* [1961] 2 All ER 676, [1961] 1 WLR 1008.

16 *Re Sklan Ltd* [1961] 2 All ER 680, [1961] 1 WLR 1013.

17 *Re Esal (Commodities) Ltd,* supra.

so before the hearing; the creditor will then not be allowed his costs of the hearing if he continues with his petition.[18] However, if the petitioning creditor's debt remained unpaid when his petition was presented to the court, but is paid immediately before the date fixed for hearing the petition without any prior offer to pay the debt in full, the court will dismiss the petition on the hearing date and order that the petitioner's costs up to and including the hearing shall be paid by the company.[19] A creditor or contributory should not present a winding up petition once a petition has been presented by someone else and has been advertised,[20] but he should instead appear in support of that other petition when it is heard. If he presents a second petition of his own, he will not be allowed any costs, unless he had good reason to believe that the first petition was groundless and bound to fail, or that it was presented in collusion with the company in order to deter the presentation of genuine petitions.[1]

If interlocutory or incidental proceedings take place in connection with a winding up petition, the court usually directs that the costs of such proceedings shall be treated as part of the costs of the petition (ie that the costs shall follow the event). But if the interlocutory or incidental proceedings are taken or defended without justification, the court may order the person who initiates or defends them, knowing that this is so, to pay the costs of those proceedings, irrespective of the courts' award of the general costs of the winding up petition.[2] Also, in one case the court ordered the costs of an application by the company to restrain further steps on a winding up petition to be paid by the solicitors acting for the petitioner, who were aware that the company intended to defend the winding up petition on a legitimate ground, but nevertheless on behalf of the petitioner opposed an application for an injunction to restrain proceedings.[3]

Appeals

If a winding up order is made against a company by a judge of the Companies Court or a county court, the company may appeal

18 *Re Times Life Assurance and Guarantee Co* (1869) LR 9 Eq 382.
19 *Re Nowmost Co Ltd* [1996] 2 BCLC 492.
20 If the first petition was presented to the Companies Court, the registrar of the court will refuse to accept a second petition until the first one has been disposed of, unless the court otherwise directs. Nevertheless, it is possible to have two or more pending petitions if one, both or all of them are presented in different county courts.
1 *Re Building Societies' Trust Ltd* (1890) 44 Ch D 140.
2 *Re Brackland Magazines Ltd* [1994] 1 BCLC 190, sub nom *Gamlestaden plc v Brackland Magazines Ltd* [1993] BCC 194.
3 *Re a Company (No 0022 of 1993)* [1993] BCC 726.

against it to the Court of Appeal, which may quash the order or make any order which the judge could have made.[4] If a company appeals against a winding up order made on a contributory's petition, the court may order that security for the petitioner's costs of the appeal shall be given by the company, or shall be given personally by its directors or shareholders who initiate the appeal. In this situation, if the appeal is dismissed the petitioner's costs of the appeal will not be met out of the company's assets, which would mean that a proportion of them would in effect be met at the expense of the petitioner himself.[5]

An appeal against the refusal of a winding up order by a judge of the Companies Court or a county court, lies to the Court of Appeal.[4]

An appeal against the making or refusal of a winding up order by the registrar of the Companies Court or by a county court lies to a single judge of the Companies Court, and not to the Court of Appeal.[6] On an appeal from the registrar, the judge does not rehear the petition de novo (although in his discretion he may do so), but merely decides the questions raised by the grounds for the appeal.[7] A further appeal lies to the Court of Appeal, but only with the leave of the judge who heard the initial appeal or of the Court of Appeal.[8]

Stay of winding up

On the application of a creditor or contributory or the official receiver or the liquidator, the court may stay proceedings on an order it has made for the winding up of a company.[9] In exercise of this power the court may discharge the liquidator and allow the directors to resume the management and administration of the company as though it had not been ordered to be wound up. A winding up may be stayed in this way at the request of the contributories if all the creditors of the company have been paid in full,[10] or if adequate provision has been made for the few creditors who have not been paid and whose claims are not admitted by the company,[11] or if all the creditors have agreed to an arrangement with the company for the satisfaction of their claims,[12] or if it is found that

---

4 Supreme Court Act 1981, s 16(1) (11 *Halsbury's Statutes* (4th edn)(1991 Reissue) 982).
5 *Re E K Wilson & Sons Ltd* [1972] 2 All ER 160, [1972] 1 WLR 791.
6 Insolvency Rules 1986, r 7.47(2); *Re Calahurst Ltd* [1989] BCLC 140, 5 BCC 318; *Midrome Ltd v Shaw* [1994] 1 BCLC 180.
7 *Re Industrial and Commercial Securities plc* (1988) 5 BCC 320.
8 *Midrome Ltd v Shaw*, supra.
9 Insolvency Act 1986, s 147(1).
10 *Re South Barrule Slate Quarry Co* (1869) LR 8 Eq 688.
11 *Re Baxters Ltd* [1898] WN 60.

the winding up order was procured by a person who purported to act on behalf of the named petitioner but who had in fact no authority to present a petition in his name or on his behalf,[13] or if the petition on which the winding up order was made was not served on the company[14] or if the judgment upon which the winding up order was based is set aside by the court and the company's assets will suffice to satisfy its debts and liabilities in full.[15] But a stay of the winding up proceedings will not be ordered unless the liquidator's remuneration and expenses have been paid or provided for, nor unless the application for a stay is either supported by an overwhelming majority of the contributories, or is reinforced by a scheme of arrangement which has been approved by the court and is consequently binding on all the contributories.[16]

As an alternative to staying a winding up by order of the court, the winding up order may be rescinded by the court,[17] and it is not necessary that the company should be solvent for this to be done, as it is for a stay.[18] So far, however, a winding up order has been rescinded only when the company intended to propose a voluntary arrangement with its creditors under the Insolvency Act 1986, on which an insolvency practitioner had reported favourably and which was likely to be accepted by the statutory majority of creditors[19] so as to become binding on them all.[18]

Actions and proceedings against the company

The fact that a petition has been presented to the court for a winding up order against a company does not automatically prevent creditors or claimants against the company from commencing or continuing litigation or other proceedings against it. However, if a winding up petition has been presented, the court may in its discretion stay any action or proceeding which is pending against the company, whether commenced before or after the presentation of the petition; if the action or proceeding is in the High Court or the Court of Appeal, the

---

12 *Re Stephen Walters & Sons Ltd* [1926] WN 236.
13 *R v Robinson* [1990] BCC 656. The winding up order cannot be treated as a nullity, however.
14 *Re Intermain Properties Ltd* [1986] BCLC 265, 1 BCC 555. If the winding up order has not been drawn up, the court may rescind it in exercise of its inherent jurisdiction.
15 *Re Lowston Ltd* [1991] BCLC 570.
16 *Re Calgary and Edmonton Land Co Ltd* [1975] 1 All ER 1046, [1975] 1 WLR 355.
17 Insolvency Rules 1986, r 7.47(1).
18 *Re Dollar Land (Feltham) Ltd* [1995] 2 BCLC 370, [1995] BCC 740.
19 See p 411, post.

application for a stay must be made to it, and if the action or proceeding is any other court, the application must be made to the court to which the winding up petition has been presented.[20] The court may stay any pending litigation against the company under this provision, whatever its form, and may also restrain the initiation or continuance of any proceedings for the enforcement of a claim otherwise than by litigation, for example by process of execution to recover a judgment debt[1] or by the levying of distress.[2]

The court will exercise its discretion to stay an action or other proceeding only where there are special circumstances making it equitable to do so, for example some unfair dealing by the claimant.[3] The fact that the claimant, if allowed to proceed, may gain an advantage over other creditors of the company is not, of itself, sufficient to justify the imposition of a stay of proceedings. The reason for this is that at the time the application for a stay is made the court has not yet heard the winding up petition, and consequently it would be unjust to prevent a creditor or other claimant from pursuing his normal legal remedies against a company which is not yet in liquidation when it is uncertain whether a winding up order will be made.

If the court makes a winding up order, or appoints a provisional liquidator after a winding up petition has been presented but before a winding up order is made, no action or proceeding against the company or its property may be commenced or continued without leave of the court, and leave may be given on such terms as the court thinks fit.[4] The court to which an application must be made for leave to initiate or continue an action or proceeding is the court which made the winding up order, or which appointed the provisional liquidator. It has been held at first instance by Rattee J that an action initiated without the necessary leave of the court is a nullity, and cannot be validated by the court subsequently giving the plaintiff leave to sue the company; this was held to be so, whether or not the plaintiff was aware that winding up proceedings had been brought against the company, and he must therefore bring a new action against the company after obtaining leave of the court, which he may

20 Insolvency Act 1986, s 126(1).
 1 *Thomas v Patent Lionite Co* (1881) 17 Ch D 250; *Westbury v Twigg & Co* [1892] 1 QB 77; *Gerard v Worth of Paris Ltd* [1936] 2 All ER 905.
 2 *Re Roundwood Colliery Co* [1897] 1 Ch 373; *Re Bellaglade Ltd* [1977] 1 All ER 319; *Re Memco Engineering Ltd* [1986] Ch 86, [1985] 3 All ER 267.
 3 *Venner's Electrical Cooking and Heating Appliances Ltd v Thorpe* [1915] 2 Ch 404; *Re Bellaglade Ltd*, supra.
 4 Insolvency Act 1986, s 130(2).

do only if the limitation period for suing the company has not expired by then.[5] On the other hand, it has been held by Lindsay J in another case[6] that an action brought against a company after a winding up petition has been presented against it on which a winding up order is subsequently made is not a nullity, and if the plaintiff obtains leave of the court to continue the action either before or after the winding up order is made, the action is retrospectively treated as though leave to bring it had been given by the court before it was commenced. The statutory provision for the automatic stay of proceedings supersedes the power of the court to order the stay of proceedings brought against a company against which a winding up petition is pending, and so when a provisional liquidator is appointed it is necessary for the claimant against the company to apply for leave to proceed if the action or other proceeding which he has commenced is to be continued pending the hearing of the winding up petition.

The expressions 'action' and 'proceeding' in the present context have the same meaning as in the provision which empowers the court to stay actions and proceedings against a company before the hearing of a winding up petition. Consequently, a prosecution for a criminal offence cannot be brought against a company ordered to be wound up by the court unless leave of the court is first obtained.[7] Likewise, a distress cannot be levied on a company without leave of the court when a winding up order has been made against it or a provisional liquidator has been appointed,[8] and an execution against the company's assets cannot be initiated or continued without leave of the court in those circumstances. A separate provision retrospectively invalidates executions and distraints levied on the assets of a company which is wound up under an order of the court if the execution or distress is initiated after the successful winding up petition is presented,[9] but the provision currently under consideration also applies to executions and distraints which are commenced before the presentation of a winding up petition.[8]

The purpose of the automatic stay on actions and proceedings against a company when a winding up order has been made or a provisional liquidator has been appointed is to ensure that all claims which can be proved in the liquidation and qualify for payment of a dividend out of the company's assets, are enforced by the cheap

5 *Re National Employers' Mutual General Insurance Association Ltd* [1995] 1 BCLC 232.
6 *Bristol and West Building Society v Saunders* [1997] BCC 83.
7 *R v Dickson* [1991] BCC 719. In this case the Court of Appeal held that the requirement of the court's leave was directory only, and so the initiation of the prosecution was not invalid and the court could give leave for it to be continued.
8 *Re Memco Engineering Ltd*, supra.

and expeditious process of submitting proofs to the liquidator, and not by bringing actions or levying executions or distraints. Because of this, the court does not readily give leave for an action to be brought or an execution to be levied when a winding up order has been made or a provisional liquidator has been appointed. It will nevertheless do so if the claimant seeks to enforce a mortgage or other security for his debt or claim by bringing an action for foreclosure, or for an order that the security shall be sold or that a receiver shall be appointed;[10] leave will also be given if the claimant seeks specific relief, such as an order for specific performance or rescission of a contract entered into with the company,[11] or for an injunction against it,[12] or for an order that specific property shall be returned or delivered,[13] but leave will be given only if the claimant shows a prima facie case for the relief he seeks.

There was formerly a conflict of authority as to whether the court should permit the initiation or continuance of an action for damages for a tort to be brought against a company in liquidation under a winding up order. In two cases it was held that leave should be given, because as the law then stood, claims for damages for tort could not be proved in the liquidation of an insolvent company, and were therefore excluded from the liquidation,[14] but in a third case it was held that leave should not be given because the legislative intention was that tort claims for damages should not be enforceable in any way, apart from enforcing any security, if the company were insolvent.[15] Now that claims against a company for damages in tort are no longer excluded from the claims which may be proved in the company's liquidation,[16] there appears to be no good reason why the court should permit the claimant to enforce his claim by action against such a company, unless the question of liability or the quantification of damages cannot be conveniently dealt with by an appeal to the court from the liquidator's rejection of the claimant's proof.

9 Insolvency Act 1986, s 128(1).
10 *Re David Lloyd & Co* (1877) 6 Ch D 339; *Re Joshua Stubbs Ltd* [1891] 1 Ch 187, on appeal [1891] 1 Ch 475; *The Zafiro* [1960] P 1, [1959] 2 All ER 537; *Re Lineas Navieras Boliviarnas SAM* [1995] BCC 666.
11 *Thomas Plate Glass Co v Land and Sea Telegraph Construction Co* (1871) 6 Ch App 643; *Re Pacaya Rubber and Produce Co* [1913] 1 Ch 218.
12 *Wyley v Exhall Coal Mining Co* (1864) 33 Beav 538.
13 *Re Strand Hotel Co* [1868] WN 2.
14 *Post Office v Norwich Union Fire Insurance Society Ltd* [1967] 2 QB 363, [1967] 1 All ER 577; *Re Berkeley Securities (Property) Ltd* [1980] 3 All ER 513, [1980] 1 WLR 1589.
15 *Re Islington Metal and Plating Works Ltd* [1983] 3 All ER 218, [1984] 1 WLR 14.
16 Insolvency Act 1986, s 143(1); Insolvency Rules 1986, r 13.12(1), (2) and (4).

THE WINDING UP OF
UNREGISTERED COMPANIES

Unregistered companies generally

The court has jurisdiction to make a winding up order against a company or association which is not registered under the Companies Act 1985, or any of the earlier Companies Acts and which carries on a trade or business[17] unless it is a railway company incorporated by Act of Parliament.[18] Unregistered companies include trustee savings banks and companies incorporated or formed under the law of a country outside Great Britain.[18] The grounds for making a winding up order in respect of such an unregistered company or association are:[19]

(a) that it has been dissolved, or has ceased to carry on its business, or is carrying on its business only for the purpose of winding up its affairs; or

(b) that it is unable to pay its debts;[20]

(c) that it is just and equitable that the company or association should be wound up.

The winding up proceedings, both before and after the making of a winding up order, are subject to the same rules and are conducted in the same way as in the case of a company registered under the Companies Act 1985, except so far as the Insolvency Act 1986 otherwise provides.[1]

In the winding up of an unregistered company the definition of contributories is different from that in the corresponding rules governing registered companies. A contributory of an unregistered company is anyone who is liable under the company's constitution (Act of Parliament, charter, letters patent, statutes, articles of incorporation, deed of settlement, etc) to contribute toward the

---

17 The Insolvency Act 1986, s 220(1) and s 221(1) refers simply to 'an association', but it was held in *Re St James' Club* (1852) 2 De GM & G 383, *Re Bristol Athenaeum* (1889) 43 Ch D 236 and *Re Witney Town Football and Social Club* [1994] 2 BCLC 487, [1993] BCC 874 that an association not formed for profit or gain cannot be wound up as an unregistered company.

18 Insolvency Act 1986, s 220(1).

19 Ibid, s 221(5).

20 The company is deemed unable to pay its debts in circumstances similar to those set out in the Insolvency Act 1986, s 123(1) and (2), in respect of a company formed under the Companies Act 1985 (Insolvency Act 1986, ss 222 to 224).

1 Insolvency Act 1986, s 221(1).

payment of its debts and liabilities, or toward the adjustment of the rights of its members among themselves, and a contributory includes anyone who is personally liable to any creditor of, or claimant against, the company or association under the terms of any contract or rule of law.[2] Under the first of these heads, a person is a contributory only if his fellow members can compel him to contribute, and so a contractual arrangement between members and the company that past members shall not be liable to contribute may exonerate them in a winding up.[3] Under the second head, however, a person may be caught as a contributory although he escapes under the first head; for example, a member of an unincorporated company may be personally liable to creditors whose debts are incurred while he is or was a member, and so be jointly liable with all the other members; he will then be a contributory for the total of such debts which remain unpaid.[4]

No distinction is made in the winding up of an unregistered company between the liabilities of present and past members to contribute to the company's assets. Consequently, it would seem that calls should be made on them in proportion to the total amounts of the company's indebtedness for which they are respectively responsible, and if there is any difference between the amount which their fellow members can require them to contribute and the total amount for which creditors of the company can sue them individually, the higher figure should be taken as the measure of their liability to contribute in a winding up. As in the winding up of a company registered under the Companies Act 1985, creditors of an unregistered company rank equally for payment of their claims out of amounts collected by the liquidator from contributories, irrespective of the dates when the claims respectively accrued,[5] but this is subject to the provisions of the Insolvency Act 1986, as to preferential and deferred payments.[6]

Unregistered companies and associations cannot be wound up voluntarily under the Companies Act 1985.[7]

Insolvent partnerships could not formerly be wound up by the court, but the court now has jurisdiction to make winding up orders in respect of them under the Insolvent Partnerships Order 1994,[8]

2 Ibid, s 226(1).
3 *Re Pennant and Craigwen Consolidated Lead Mining Co, Fenn's Case* (1854) 4 De GM & G 285; ibid, *Mayhew's Case* (1854) 5 De GM & G 837.
4 *Re Wheal Emily Mining Co, Cox's Case* (1863) 4 De GJ & Sm 53; *Re Hoylake Rly Co, ex p Littledale* (1874) 9 Ch App 257.
5 *Webb v Whiffin* (1872) LR 5 HL 711 (see p 271, post).
6 Insolvency Act 1986, s 175(1) and (2) and s 386(1) and Sch 6 (see p 303, post).
7 Ibid, s 221(4).
8 SI 1994/2421.

which incorporates many of the provisions of the Insolvency Act 1986 with appropriate modifications. The winding up of partnerships is not dealt with in this book.

Overseas companies

Jurisdiction of the court

Under its jurisdiction to wind up unregistered companies, the court may wind up companies which are formed or incorporated outside Great Britain, whether or not they have been wound up or dissolved in their own countries. The Insolvency Act 1986 expressly provides that the court may wind up a company incorporated outside Great Britain which has carried on business in Great Britain but has ceased to do so, notwithstanding the dissolution of the company in its own country.[9] This does not limit the jurisdiction of the court, however, and so a winding up order may be made in respect of an overseas company, even though it has never carried on business in Great Britain, if the company has assets in England which the court can administer,[10] and the realisation of those assets will benefit the petitioner or other persons who are or were interested in the company.[11] The character of the assets is immaterial; they need not be connected with the company's business, and they may consist of claims against third persons, such as claims under insurance policies which will benefit the petitioner alone if they are enforced by the liquidator.[11] Even if a company has assets in England, however, the court may decline to make an order if the company's affairs can be more satisfactorily wound up in its own country.[12]

It has also been held that the court may order the winding up of an overseas company if its affairs have been managed from England and the debt on which the winding-up petition is based was incurred there, even though the company has no assets in England.[13] Furthermore, a winding up order may be made against an overseas company which has ceased to carry on business in Great Britain but has incurred debts there, if there is a likelihood that proceedings

9 Insolvency Act 1986, s 225.
10 *Banque des Marchands de Moscou v Kindersley* [1951] Ch 112, [1950] 2 All ER 549; *Re Azoff-Don Commercial Bank* [1954] Ch 315, [1954] 1 All ER 947; *Re Real Estate Development Co* [1991] BCLC 210.
11 *Re Compania Merabello San Nicholas SA* [1973] Ch 75, [1972] 3 All ER 448; *Re Allobrogia SS Corpn* [1978] 3 All ER 423.
12 *Re Hibernian Merchants Ltd* [1958] Ch 76, [1957] 3 All ER 97.
13 *Re a Company (No 003102 of 1991), ex p Nyckeln Finance Co Ltd* [1991] BCLC 539.

brought against directors or shadow directors of the company in its winding up in England[14] may result in the recovery of amounts which would be available to meet its creditors' claims.[15]

A winding up order may, moreover, be made against an overseas company which has no assets in England if the order would benefit the petitioner by making the assets of a third person available to him, or by imposing a liability on a third person to make a payment to him, and it is immaterial that the assets or payment would not be receivable by the liquidator or applied for the benefit of all creditors or members of the company.[16]

Rules governing the liquidation

The winding up of an overseas company is governed by the same rules as the winding up of an unregistered English company, whether the company is also being wound up in the country in which it was incorporated or not, and whether the law of that country has different rules for the application of the company's assets or not.[17] Although the winding up is conducted in the same way as the winding up of a company incorporated under the Companies Act 1985. The court may by the terms of the winding-up order require the liquidator to seek its directions before taking certain steps. The assets which the liquidator may collect apply and distribute are those owned by the company at the commencement of the winding up, or if it had previously been dissolved under the system of law which governed it, the assets owned by the company at the date of its dissolution.[17] If the company has been dissolved, its assets in the United Kingdom will have vested in the Crown as bona vacantia,[18] but on the making of a winding up order the liquidator has power to take possession of all such assets and to sell or otherwise realise them,[17] and the court can vest the legal title to them in him.[19]

---

14   *Re Eloc Electro-Optieck and Communicatie BV* [1982] Ch 43, [1981] 2 All ER 1111. A winding up order was made in this case to enable the petitioners, as former employees of the company, to recover compensation for unfair dismissal from the Department of Employment under the Employment Protection (Consolidation) Act 1978, ss 121 and 127 (16 *Halsbury's Statutes* (4th edn) 347 and 354).

15   For example, under the Insolvency Act 1986, s 213 or s 214 (see pp 253 and 259, post).

16   *Re a Company (No 00359 of 1987)* [1988] Ch 210, sub nom *International Westminster Bank plc v Okeanos Maritime Corpn* [1987] 3 All ER 137.

17   *Re English, Scottish and Australian Chartered Bank* [1893] 3 Ch 385; *Re Suidair International Airways Ltd* [1951] Ch 165; *Re Bank of Credit and Commerce International SA (No 10)* [1996] 4 All ER 796, [1997] 1 BCLC 80.

18   In the case of freehold land, it will have escheated to the Crown (*Re Wells* [1933] Ch 29).

19   Insolvency Act 1986, s 145(1).

The company is treated for the purpose of the winding up as though it still existed, notwithstanding its dissolution under the law of the country in which it was formed or incorporated. Consequently, the liquidator may bring actions in the company's name to enforce causes of action which accrued to it before or since its dissolution.[20] With leave of the court, actions may be brought against the company after a winding up order has been made in respect of it,[1] but actions may not be brought by its creditors against contributories personally unless the court permits.[2] Contracts which are terminated or broken by or in consequence of the company being wound up are treated as terminated or broken only when the winding up order is made, and not when the company was earlier dissolved in its own country.[3]

Winding up orders against overseas companies have invariably been sought by creditors, and after their debts have been paid the Crown has claimed the residue of the companies' assets as bona vacantia, even though the companies had already been dissolved under the law of the country where they were incorporated. In one case[4] this claim was upheld, but in another case it was held that the Crown's claim to the assets is completely extinguished by the winding up order, and the residual assets of the company are distributable among its members in accordance with the system of law which governed the company before its dissolution.[5] If such members or persons claiming under them cannot be traced, however, it would seem that the Crown would still be entitled to claim the residual assets of the company in the United Kingdom in right of its members, on the assumption that they have died without heirs and their assets in the United Kingdom are therefore bona vacantia.[6] If any person can prove his right to a share of the company's residual assets, either as a member or in succession to a member, however, the Crown must concede his claim to that share.

---

20 *Russian and English Bank v Baring Bros & Co* [1936] AC 405 at 426–7, [1936] 1 All ER 505 at 518, per Lord Atkin; *Re Azoff-Don Commercial Bank*, supra.
1 Insolvency Act 1986, s 130(2).
2 Ibid, s 228.
3 *Re Russian Commercial and Industrial Bank* [1955] Ch 148, [1955] 1 All ER 75.
4 *Re Banque Industrielle de Moscou* [1952] Ch 919, [1952] 2 All ER 532.
5 *Re Banque des Marchands de Moscou* [1958] Ch 182, [1957] 3 All ER 182.
6 The Crown's right excludes any similar claim by the government of the country where the company was formed or where its shareholders were domiciled (*Re Barnett's Trusts* [1902] 1 Ch 847; *Re Musurus* [1936] 2 All ER 1666).

CHAPTER 3

Voluntary winding up

WINDING UP RESOLUTIONS

A company may be put into voluntary liquidation by its members in general meeting passing one of the three statutory resolutions for a voluntary winding up. These resolutions are:[1]

(a) An ordinary resolution passed by a simple majority vote that the company shall be wound up voluntarily because the period fixed for the duration of the company by its articles of association has expired, or because an event has occurred on the occurrence of which the articles provide that the company shall be dissolved. It is rare nowadays to find a company whose articles prescribe a period for its duration or make express provision for its dissolution, and so an ordinary resolution for a voluntary winding up is unlikely to be encountered in practice. It should be noted, however, that a company is not automatically wound up or dissolved on the expiration of any period for its duration or on the occurrence of the event specified in its articles for the company's dissolution.[2] Moreover, the court is not bound to make a winding up order in those circumstances, although it may take the provisions of the articles into account in deciding whether it is just and equitable to make a winding up order.[3]

(b) A special resolution that the company shall be wound up voluntarily.[4] No particular reason need be assigned for the passing of the resolution, nor need any particular circumstances exist for it to be passed. Consequently, the

---

1 Insolvency Act 1986, s 84(1).
2 Contrast the Partnership Act 1890, s 32(a) (32 *Halsbury's Statutes* (4th edn) (1996 Reissue) 801) in the case of partnerships.
3 *Re American Pioneer Leather Co* [1918] 1 Ch 556.
4 A special resolution is defined by the Companies Act 1955, s 378(2) as one which is passed by a three-quarters' majority vote of members of a company who vote in person or by proxy at a general meeting of which at least 21 days' notice of an intention to propose it as a special resolution has been given to the members. On a poll the requisite majority is the holders of three-quarters of the votes attached to the shares of the company which carry voting rights and which are cast in favour of the resolution; unless the company's articles otherwise provide, each share of the company carries one vote (s 370(6)).

persons who control at least three-quarters of the voting
power at a general meeting of the company may wind it up at
any time for any reason they think fit, and in practice it is
unusual for the resolution to express the reason which
motivated it. The only grounds on which the special resolution
can be set aside by the court, apart from any defects in the
proceedings which led to it being passed, are that it was part
of a scheme to defraud or oppress minority shareholders[5] or,
possibly, that it was not passed in the interests of the
members of the company as a whole.

(c) An extraordinary resolution[6] that the company shall be
wound up voluntarily because it cannot continue its business
by reason of its liabilities. When an extraordinary resolution
is passed the company is usually insolvent, but this need not
always be so, for a company may find it impossible to
continue its business because the payment of its debts would
leave it with insufficient working capital. In practice, however,
in that situation the company would pay its debts, and its
members would then pass a special resolution to wind it up.

When a company has passed a resolution for voluntary winding up
it must advertise the resolution in the London Gazette within 14
days after it is passed,[7] and must deliver a copy of the resolution to
the Registrar of Companies within 15 days after it is passed.[8]

Once a resolution for voluntary winding up has been passed, the
members of the company cannot rescind it and restore the directors'
powers to them so as to enable the company to carry on its business
as before.[9] But an application may be made to the court to stay the
winding up in the same way, and with the same consequences, as if
the company were being wound up under an order of the court.[10]

---

5 *Menier v Hooper's Telegraph Works Ltd* (1874) 9 Ch App 350; *Re Langham
  Skating Rink Co* (1877) 5 Ch D 669 at 685–6, per James LJ; *British Water Gas
  Syndicate Ltd v Notts and Derby Water Gas Co Ltd* [1889] WN 204.

6 An extraordinary resolution is defined by the Companies Act 1985, s 378(1) as
  one which is passed by a three-quarters majority vote calculated in the same way
  as for a special resolution, but only 14 days' notice need be given to the members
  of the company of the intention to propose it at a general meeting as an
  extraordinary resolution (s 369(1)).

7 Insolvency Act 1986, s 85(1).

8 Companies Act 1985, s 380(1) and (4), as amended by Insolvency Act 1986, s
  439(1) and Sch 13, Part I.

9 The directors may continue to exercise their powers in certain events despite the
  winding up, but only for the purpose of winding up the company's affairs (see
  p 103, post).

10 Insolvency Act 1986, s 112(1) and s 147(1). An example of such a stay is found
   in *Re Stephen Walters & Sons Ltd* [1926] WN 236 (see p 76, ante).

MEMBERS' AND CREDITORS' VOLUNTARY WINDING UP

Although a voluntary winding up is initiated by the members of the company, the Insolvency Act 1986 gives exclusive control of the liquidation to them only if the company is solvent. If it is not, the creditors have an interest in the liquidation being properly conducted, and so control over it is shared between them and the members, with the creditors' wishes predominating.

Members' voluntary winding up

Although a members' voluntary winding up presupposes that the company is solvent, the distinction between a members' and a creditors' voluntary winding up is determined by a procedural and not by a substantive factor. A members' voluntary winding up is defined as one where the directors or a majority of them (if more than two in number) have within five weeks before the winding up resolution is passed made a statutory declaration as to the company's solvency at a board meeting, and have in that declaration stated that, after making a full examination of the company's affairs, they have formed the opinion that the company will be able to pay its debts in full (together with the recoverable interest thereon) within a period specified in the declaration, not exceeding twelve months from the date on which the winding up resolution is passed.[11] If no such declaration of solvency is made before the winding up resolution is passed, the winding up is a creditors' voluntary winding up.[12] The declaration of solvency (if there is one) must be delivered to the Registrar of Companies within 15 days after the winding up resolution is passed together with a copy of the resolution,[13] but failure to file the declaration or a copy of the resolution merely involves the company and its directors in liability to a fine,[14] and does not impair the validity of the resolution or the nature of the liquidation as a members' voluntary winding up.

If directors make a declaration of solvency without having reasonable grounds for the opinion they express in it that the company will be able to pay its debts in full (with the recoverable

---

11 Insolvency Act 1986, s 89(1) and (2). Recoverable interest means the amount of interest which may be claimed under the Insolvency Act 1986, s 189 (see p 289, post).
12 Insolvency Act 1986, s 90.
13 Ibid, s 89(3).
14 Ibid, s 89(6).

interest thereon) within the period stated in the declaration, they are
guilty of a criminal offence.[15] For this purpose. if the company's
debts are not in fact paid or provided for in full within that period,
it is presumed, unless the directors prove otherwise, that they did
not have reasonable grounds for their expressed opinion.[13] However,
neither the fact that the company's debts are not paid or provided
for within the period stated in the declaration, nor the fact that the
directors made the declaration without reasonable cause for their
expressed belief that the company would be able to pay its debts
within that period, or their conviction for doing so, converts the
members' voluntary winding up into a creditors' voluntary winding
up.[16] The solvency or insolvency of the company either at the
commencement of the voluntary winding up or during its continuance
does not determine whether the liquidation is or becomes a creditors'
voluntary winding up. This is determined exclusively by whether a
statutory declaration of solvency has or has not been made by the
directors before the winding up resolution is passed. However, if it
appears to the liquidator during a members' voluntary winding up
that the company's debts will not be paid or provided for in full
(together with the recoverable interest thereon) within the period
stated in the declaration of solvency, the liquidator is bound to take
steps to convert the liquidation into a creditors' voluntary winding
up.[17]

Creditors' voluntary winding up

If no statutory declaration of solvency is made within five weeks
before a voluntary winding up resolution is passed, and the liquidation
is therefore a creditors' voluntary winding up, the company must
call a meeting of its creditors to be held not later than 14 days after
the day on which the general meeting which passes the winding up
resolution will be held; the company must send notices of the
creditors' meeting by post to each creditor of the company not less
than seven days before it is to be held, and the company must also
advertise the creditors' meeting in the London Gazette and in at
least two newspapers circulating in the locality or localities of the
company's principal place or places of business in Great Britain at
the date when the notices of the meeting are sent to creditors and
during the preceding six months.[18] The notices and advertisements

15 Ibid, s 89(4) and (5).
16 *De Courcy v Clement* [1971] Ch 693, [1971] 1 All ER 681.
17 Insolvency Act 1986, p 91, post.
18 Ibid, s 98(1), (4) and (5).

of the creditors' meeting must contain the name and address of a qualified insolvency practitioner[19] who will provide creditors free of charge with such information about the company's affairs as they reasonably require, and the notices and advertisements must also indicate a place within the locality or each of the localities in which the newspaper or newspapers containing the advertisement of the creditors' meeting circulate where a list of the names and addresses of all the company's creditors will be available for inspection by creditors, and apparently, by anyone else.[20]

The directors must also prepare a statement of the company's affairs in the prescribed form, showing details of the company's assets, debts and liabilities, the names and addresses of its creditors and the securities (if any) held by them respectively and the dates of such securities, and the statement of affairs must be verified by the affidavits of one or more of the directors.[1] The statement of affairs must be laid before the creditors' meeting, which is presided over by one of the directors appointed by the board of the company.[2] If the director appointed by the board fails to attend the creditors' meeting, the creditors who attend may appoint a person to preside over it by a resolution passed by a simple majority, and the person so appointed need not himself be a creditor.[3]

Non-compliance with the rules governing the creditors' meeting result in the company and its directors being guilty of criminal offences punishable by fine,[4] but the status of the liquidation as a creditors' voluntary winding up is not affected. However, until the creditors' meeting is held, any liquidator appointed by a general meeting of the company,[5] whether the general meeting which passes the winding up resolution or a subsequent general meeting, cannot without leave of the court exercise any of the powers of a liquidator, other than his powers to take the company's assets into his custody or under his control, to dispose of goods of the company which are perishable or likely to diminish in value if they are not immediately disposed of, and to do all acts necessary for the protection of the company's assets,[6] such as notifying the company's agents and trustees and persons in possession of the company's assets of his

---

19 The insolvency practitioner must be qualified to act as such in relation to the company, and he therefore may not be a director or an officer of it.
20 Insolvency Act 1986, s 98(2), (3) and (5).
1 Ibid, s 99(1) and (2); Insolvency Rules, r 4.34 and Sch 4. Form 4.19.
2 Insolvency Act 1986, s 99(1).
3 *Re Salcombe Hotel Development Co Ltd* [1991] BCLC 44, 5 BCC 807.
4 Ibid, s 98(6) and s 99(3).
5 For the appointment of a liquidator in a creditors' voluntary winding up, see p 136, post.
6 Insolvency Act 1986, s 166(1) to (3).

appointment. The purpose of this provision is to prevent a liquidator appointed by the general meeting which passes a winding up resolution from exercising the substantive powers of a liquidator before the creditors' meeting has had an opportunity to appoint its own nominee as liquidator in his place. This was possible under the law before the Insolvency Act 1985 came into operation,[7] but is no longer so.

Conversion of a members' into a creditors' voluntary winding up

If during a members' voluntary winding up the liquidator forms the opinion that the company will be unable to pay its debts in full (together with recoverable interest thereon) within the period specified in the statutory declaration of solvency made before the winding up resolution was passed, the liquidator must call a meeting of creditors of the company to be held not later than 28 days after he forms that opinion; the liquidator must send a notice of the meeting to each creditor and advertise it in the London Gazette and in at least two local newspapers circulating in the localities of the company's principal place or places of business, in the same way as the directors must do if a winding up resolution has been passed, or is to be passed, without a declaration of solvency being made at all.[8] The liquidator must also prepare and verify by affidavit a statement of the company's affairs in the same form and containing the same information as a statement of affairs prepared by directors at the commencement of a creditors' voluntary winding up, and he must lay the statement of affairs before the creditors' meeting which he calls.[9] During the period before the creditors' meeting is held, the liquidator must provide creditors free of charge with all the information about the company's affairs which they reasonably require.[10] The liquidator must attend and preside at the creditors' meeting.[11] As from the date when the creditors' meeting is held, the voluntary liquidation becomes a creditors' voluntary winding up,[12] with the consequence that the creditors may appoint their own

---

7 *Re Centrebind Ltd* [1966] 3 All ER 889, [1967] 1 WLR 377; *E V Saxton & Sons Ltd v R Miles (Confectioners) Ltd* [1983] 2 All ER 1025, [1983] 1 WLR 952.
8 Insolvency Act 1986, s 95(1), (2) and (5).
9 Ibid, s 95(3) and (4); Insolvency Rules 1986, r 4.34 and Form 4.18.
10 Insolvency Act 1986, s 95(2).
11 Ibid, s 95(3).
12 Ibid, s 96.

nominee as liquidator, and may exercise the powers of control over the liquidation which creditors may exercise in a voluntary liquidation which begins as a creditors' voluntary winding up.[13]

Comparison with winding up by the court

The procedure to initiate a voluntary winding up is obviously far simpler than the procedure for obtaining a winding up order. No provisional liquidator may be appointed in a voluntary winding up; the official receiver has no part to play; and although applications to the court in voluntary liquidations are possible,[14] a voluntary winding up may be carried out without the intervention of the court at any point.

There is a useful provision in the Insolvency Act 1986, however, by which the aid of the court may be invoked in a voluntary winding up. The liquidator or any contributory or creditor may apply to the court to determine any question arising in the winding up, or to exercise any of the powers which the court could exercise if the company were being wound up by the court, and the court may make such order as it thinks just.[14] Under its jurisdiction to determine questions, the court may, for example, compel the liquidator to pay regard to the wishes of the liquidation committee, representing creditors and contributories, or to the wishes of the creditors and contributories themselves in exercising his powers.[15] Under its jurisdiction to exercise the powers which it has in a winding up by the court, the court may stay the voluntary winding up,[16] or may stay actions or proceedings which were pending against the company when the winding up resolution was passed, or which are brought against it thereafter.[17]

In a voluntary winding up actions and proceedings against the company are not automatically stayed, as they are on the making of a winding up order, and so it is always necessary for the liquidator in a voluntary winding up to apply to the court for an order imposing a stay. The liquidator must show good cause for the proceedings to be stayed, and the court will not impose a stay if the liquidator repudiates all liability of the company to the plaintiff, for in that

---

13 See p 136, post.
14 Insolvency Act 1986, s 112(1) and (2).
15 The liquidator is under no statutory obligation to have regard to their wishes, but the court may do so, and may direct the liquidator accordingly (Insolvency Act 1986, s 195(1)).
16 *Re Calgary and Edmonton Land Co Ltd* [1975] 1 All ER 1046, [1975] 1 WLR 355.
17 Insolvency Act 1986, s 126(1).

event if the plaintiff were remitted to proving in the winding up, the liquidator would certainly reject his proof, and the court would have to try the issue on an appeal from the liquidator's decision.[18] Furthermore, in no circumstances will the court stay an action by a creditor if the company is solvent, because it will not prejudice the company's other creditors to allow him to proceed, and the members have no justification for depriving him of his right to exact payment by obtaining judgment and levying execution in the normal way.[19] Finally, the court may make an order on an application by the liquidator or by a creditor or contributory in a voluntary winding up only if it would be just and beneficial to do so: this means just and beneficial to the creditors or contributories generally or, at least, to certain of them, and the court will therefore not make an order if its only effect will be to protect directors of the company from a personal liability to a creditor by statute or otherwise.[20]

WINDING UP BY THE COURT OF A COMPANY IN VOLUNTARY LIQUIDATION

The fact that a company is in voluntary liquidation does not prevent the court from making a winding up order against it on the petition of a creditor or contributory or any other person who could present a winding up petition if the company were not in voluntary liquidation. A creditor may petition even though the debt on which he relies was incurred by the liquidator in the voluntary winding up which he seeks to terminate.[1] However, a contributory who petitions for a winding up order must satisfy the court that the rights of contributories will be prejudiced if the voluntary winding up continues.[2] The official receiver may petition for a winding up order against a company which is being wound up voluntarily, but the court may not make a winding up order on the petition of the official receiver or (it would seem) any other person unless it is satisfied that the existing liquidation cannot be continued with due regard to the interests of the creditors or contributories.[3] This may be because of the liquidator's manifest incompetence and his failure to fulfil his statutory duties, coupled with the unwillingness of the majority of

---

18 *Currie v Consolidated Kent Collieries Corpn* [1906] 1 KB 134; *Cook v X Chair Patents Co Ltd* [1959] 3 All ER 906, [1960] 1 WLR 60.
19 *Gerard v Worth of Paris Ltd* [1936] 2 All ER 905.
20 *Re J Burrows (Leeds) Ltd* [1982] 2 All ER 882, [1982] 1 WLR 1177.
 1 *Re Bank of South Australia (No 2)* [1895] 1 Ch 578.
 2 Insolvency Act 1986, s 116.
 3 Ibid, s 124(5).

the contributories or creditors to procure his replacement.[4] But the court will not make an order on the official receiver's petition if the voluntary winding up has been all but formally completed, and the liquidator is willing to make good any losses of assets found by the court to have been caused by his failure to exercise proper care.[5] The liquidator appointed in the voluntary winding up may appear and be heard on the hearing of the winding up petition, but he should confine his submissions to pointing out relevant facts, and should not adopt a partisan stance for or against the petition; if he does so, the court will not award him his costs out of the company's assets.[6]

The petitioner for a winding up order against a company in voluntary liquidation must prove that one of the statutory grounds for making such an order exists,[7] and additionally, whether he is a contributory, a creditor or the official receiver, he must show that the continuation of the voluntary liquidation will be in some way harmful. This additional burden of proof rests on a contributory or creditor even though his petition was presented before the winding up resolution was passed.[8] In certain early cases the court held that a contributory petitioner showed that the contributories would be prejudiced by the continuation of the voluntary liquidation when the liquidator refused to investigate a prima facie case of wrongdoing by the directors or promoters;[9] when there appeared to be serious irregularities in the management of the company which ought to be investigated;[10] when there was a likelihood of some of the contributories not being compelled to pay the capital unpaid on their shares and of some of the company's assets not being collected so that the company's debts might be paid;[11] and when the liquidator in the voluntary winding up had been guilty of inexcusable delay in winding up the company's affairs.[12] But it is doubtful whether the

---

4 *Re Ryder Installations Ltd* [1966] 1 All ER 453n, [1966] 1 WLR 524; *Re Hewitt Brannan (Tools) Co Ltd* [1991] BCLC 80.

5 *Re J Russell Electronics Ltd* [1968] 2 All ER 559, [1968] 1 WLR 1252.

6 *Re Medisco Equipment Ltd* [1983] BCLC 305; *Re Roselmar Properties Ltd (No 2)* (1986) 2 BCC 99, 157; *Re Pinstripe Farming Co Ltd* [1996] 2 BCLC 295.

7 See p 39 et seq, ante.

8 *Re New York Exchange Ltd* (1888) 39 Ch D 415.

9 *Re United Service Co* (1868) LR 7 Eq 76; *Re Gold Co* (1879) 11 Ch D 701; *Re National Distribution of Electricity Co Ltd* [1902] 2 Ch 34.

10 *Re Gutta Percha Corpn* [1900] 2 Ch 665 (the company had disposed of practically all its stock in trade for which it had paid £30,000 two years previously, and its total receipts during that time amounted to only £14).

11 *Re Northumberland and Durham District Banking Co* (1858) 2 De G & J 357 at 378, per Turner LJ.

12 *Re Fire Annihilator Co* (1863) 32 Beav 561. Possibly the appropriate remedy nowadays would be to seek the appointment of another liquidator by the court or by a specially converted meeting of creditors.

court would make a winding up order in such circumstances under the present legislation in view of the far more extensive powers which the court and the creditors now possess to remove a liquidator who is unsatisfactory and to recover compensation from him or from the company's directors for breaches of their duties by taking misfeasance proceedings in the voluntary liquidation.[13] Moreover, even when it is shown that there are matters concerning the management of the company or the conduct of the voluntary liquidation which require investigation, a winding up order will not be made unless the investigation is likely to result in the company recovering money or assets for the benefit of its creditors or contributories.[14] On the other hand, if the conduct of the company or the liquidator in the voluntary liquidation casts doubts on the liquidator's impartiality, even though not on his competence, or if reasonable suspicions have been aroused that the liquidator may not fully investigate and seek redress for possible misapplications of the company's assets despite the lack of a reasonable explanation for its insolvency,[15] or if the liquidator has admitted inflated or groundless claims against the company in the voluntary winding up,[16] the court will make a winding up order, particularly when the petition for it is supported by a majority of the company's creditors who are not connected with its management.

The one petitioner who need not prove any additional factor in order to obtain a winding up order against a company which is already in voluntary liquidation, is the Secretary of State for Trade and Industry, if he presents a winding up petition on the ground that it appears to him to be expedient in the public interest that the company shall be wound up in the light of a report on the company's affairs made by inspectors appointed by the Secretary of State, or in the light of information or documents obtained as a result of the Secretary of State requiring the production of books and papers relating to the company.[17] The matters which the Secretary of State must prove in order to obtain a winding up order are exactly the same as if the company were not already in liquidation, and the court will not dismiss his petition because it is opposed by a majority of the company's creditors, unless they can prove that the conclusions

13 *Re Hadleigh Castle Gold Mines Ltd* [1900] 2 Ch 419, at 423, per Cozens Hardy J.
14 *Re National Distribution of Electricity Co* [1902] 2 Ch 34.
15 *Re Lowestoft Traffic Services Ltd* [1986] BCLC 81, 2 BCC 99, 945; *Re Palmer Marine Surveys Ltd* [1986] 1 WLR 573, [1986] BCLC 106; *Re Falcon RJ Development Ltd* [1987] BCLC 437, 3 BCC 146.
16 *Re Gordon & Breach Science Publishers Ltd* [1995] 2 BCLC 189, [1995] BCC 261; *Re Magnus Consultants Ltd* [1995] 1 BCLC 203.
17 Insolvency Act 1986, s 124(4) and (4A) (substituted by Companies Act 1989, s 60(1)).

reached by the inspectors or the Secretary of State are totally unfounded.[18]

On hearing a creditor's petition for a winding up order against a company in voluntary liquidation (except on a petition by the Secretary of State for Trade and Industry), the court takes into consideration the wishes of the company's other creditors, and if the majority in value of all its creditors wish the voluntary winding up to continue, and there is no advantage to be obtained or detriment to be avoided by making a winding up order, the court will normally refuse it.[19] Where a winding up petition is opposed by a majority in value of the creditors and the company is not already in voluntary liquidation, the burden of showing that there is good reason for the court to refuse a winding up order rests on the opposing creditors;[20] but where the company is already in voluntary liquidation, the burden of proof is shifted, and the petitioning creditor must then show that there is a good reason for disregarding the opposition of the majority of the creditors,[21] for example, that the majority creditors are directors of the company or persons closely connected with them,[1] or that the majority creditors are also shareholders of the company and are suspected of having disposed of the company's assets to an associated company at an undervalue or of having been guilty of fraudulent trading.[2] It is rare for the court to dismiss a creditor's petition against a company which is already in voluntary liquidation if it is supported by a majority in value of the creditors or if the petitioner is himself the majority creditor, but the court may nevertheless do so in special circumstances, for example, if the supporting creditors are companies in the same group as the petitioning company and the transaction with the respondent company on which the petition is based may be voidable;[3] or if the petitioner is the majority creditor and the only advantage which will result from the court making a winding up order is that he will be able to replace the liquidator in the voluntary liquidation by his own nominee.[4]

The costs of proceedings on a petition for a winding up order in respect of a company in voluntary liquidation are awarded by the

18 *Re Lubin Rosen and Associates Ltd* [1975] 1 All ER 577, [1977] 1 WLR 122.

19 *Re Home Remedies Ltd* [1943] Ch 1, [1942] 2 All ER 552; *Re J D Swain Ltd* [1965] 2 All ER 761, [1965] 1 WLR 909.

20 *Re P and J Macrae Ltd* [1961] 1 All ER 302, [1961] 1 WLR 229.

21 *Re J D Swain Ltd*, supra.

 1 *Re Lowestoft Traffic Services Co Ltd* [1986] BCLC 81, 2 BCC 98, 945; *Re MCH Services Ltd* [1987] BCLC 535, 3 BCC 179.

 2 *Re Palmer Marine Surveys Ltd*, supra; *Re Lowestoft Traffic Services Co Ltd*, supra.

 3 *Re Southard & Co Ltd* [1979] 3 All ER 556, [1979] 1 WLR 1198.

 4 *Re Medisco Equipment Ltd* [1983] BCLC 305.

court in the same way as if the company were not already in liquidation.[5] But if majority creditors who oppose the making of a winding up order do not voice their opposition until the hearing of the petition has been adjourned, and the petition is dismissed because of that opposition, the court may in its discretion award the petitioner his costs out of the company's assets up to and including the adjourned hearing.[6]

5 See p 72, ante.
6 *Re Arrow Leeds Ltd* [1986] BCLC 538, 2 BCC 99, 991.

CHAPTER 4
The conduct of a liquidation

The rules governing the conduct of liquidations are similar, whether
the winding up is by order of the court or voluntary, and although
in some respects, particularly as regards procedural matters, there
are differences between the two kinds of liquidation, the substantive
rules governing them are largely the same, and in many respects are
identical. In this chapter, therefore, the two kinds of liquidation will
be treated together so as to avoid repetition where the law is the same
for both of them, and so as to bring out clearly the matters in respect
of which they differ.

EFFECT OF A WINDING UP ORDER
OR RESOLUTION

Commencement of winding up

When a company is wound up by order of the court, the winding up
is deemed to have commenced when the winding up petition was
presented on which the winding up order was made.[1] This does not
mean that a company is in liquidation as soon as a winding up
petition is presented in respect of it; it means instead that if the
petition is successful and a winding up order is made, the
commencement of the winding up is ante-dated to the date of the
petition, and the company is treated retrospectively as having been
in liquidation on and from that date.

A voluntary winding up is deemed to commence when the
resolution for winding the company up voluntarily is passed.[2]
However, if a winding up order is subsequently made against the
company, the winding up is still deemed to have commenced on the
passing of the winding up resolution, unless the successful winding
up petition was presented before the resolution was passed, in which
case the winding up will be deemed to have commenced on the
presentation of the petition.[3] All dispositions of the company's

1 Insolvency Act 1986, s 129(2).
2 Ibid, s 86.
3 Ibid, s 129(1).

assets by the liquidator in the voluntary winding up in exercise of his statutory powers will be effective, and the liquidator will be entitled to be paid his costs and expenses in connection with the voluntary liquidation as the first item of expenditure to be met out of the company's assets.[4]

Notification that company is in liquidation

When a company is being wound up, every invoice, order for goods, or business letter issued by or on behalf of the company or its liquidator or by any receiver or manager of its property must, in addition to stating the company's name,[5] also state that the company is being wound up.[6]

Transfers of shares

Any transfer of shares in a company and any alteration in the status of its members[7] made after the commencement of its winding up is void unless sanctioned by the court in the case of a winding up by the court,[8] or in the case of a voluntary winding up, by the liquidator[9] or by the court on his refusal to consent.[10]

The effect of this provision is merely to invalidate a transfer of shares as between the company and the transferor, and the provision is obviously designed to prevent the transferor from evading his liability to pay the capital unpaid on his shares by transferring them at the last moment to a person without sufficient means to pay that unpaid capital. Indeed, the court has gone further than the statutory provision in this respect, and has held that it will not compel the company to register a transfer of partly paid shares made after the company had stopped payment of its debts, even though no winding up petition had yet been presented against it and no meeting to pass

---

4 *Re AV Sorge & Co Ltd* [1986] BCLC 490.

5 Companies Act 1985, s 349(1).

6 Insolvency Act 1986, s 188(1). If a receiver or manager has been appointed, a statement to that effect must also appear (ibid, s 39(1)).

7 For example, a member of a company which has no share capital ceasing to be a member under the provisions of the company's articles of association, or the holders of partly paid shares ceasing to hold them by their being forfeited or surrendered for failure to pay the unpaid part of the issue price.

8 Insolvency Act 1986, s 127.

9 Ibid, s 88.

10 Ibid, s 112(1).

a winding up resolution had been called.[11] As between the transferor and transferee, however, a transfer of shares executed after the commencement of the winding up is effective, whether it is executed in performance of a contract made before[12] or after[13] that time. Furthermore, if a person who has contracted to purchase shares refuses to carry out his contract after the commencement of the winding up, the court will, on the application of the seller, compel him to take a transfer of them, to take all steps within his power to procure his registration by the company and to indemnify the transferor against calls.[14] However, in conflict with this ruling, it has also been held that, unless an order has been made compelling the liquidator to register a transfer of the shares to the purchaser, the seller cannot obtain an order for specific performance of the contract of sale by the purchaser, but can only sue him for damages.[15] If the contract for the sale of the shares is entered into after the winding up began and the purchaser is ignorant of that fact when he agrees to buy, he may rescind the contract in equity because of his mistaken belief that the company was a going concern, and the court will not compel him to submit to registration as a member of the company.[16] The purchaser has no right to rescind the contract if he knows of the winding up, of course,[17] but the constructive notice of a winding up petition which is given by its advertisement in the London Gazette and the press is not sufficient for this purpose,[18] nor is the notification of a winding up order or resolution to the Registrar of Companies,[19] and only actual knowledge by the purchaser of the presentation of the petition will prevent him from rescinding.

The court has a discretion in deciding whether to compel the liquidator to register a transfer of shares which was not registered before the winding up commenced, and an application for the court's directions may be made by the liquidator himself.[20] If an

---

11 *Re Overend, Gurney and Co, Walker's Case* (1866) LR 2 Eq 554; *Re City of Glasgow Bank, Mitchell's Case* (1879) 4 App Cas 548 at 578, per Lord Selborne.
12 *Chapman v Shepherd* (1867) LR 2 CP 228.
13 *Rudge v Bowman* (1868) LR 3 QB 689.
14 *Evans v Wood* (1867) LR 5 Eq 9; *Paine v Hutchinson* (1868) 3 Ch App 388.
15 *Sullivan v Henderson* [1973] 1 All ER 48, [1973] 1 WLR 333.
16 *Re London, Hamburg and Continental Exchange Bank, Emmerson's Case* (1866) 1 Ch App 433.
17 *Re London, Hamburg and Continental Exchange Bank, Emmerson's Case* (1866) LR 2 Eq 231.
18 It would seem that the advertisement of a winding up order or resolution by the Registrar of Companies in the London Gazette under the Companies Act 1985, s 711(1) no longer gives even constructive notice of it to third persons (*Official Custodian for Charities v Parway Estates Developments Ltd* [1985] Ch 151, [1984] 3 All ER 679).
19 Companies Act 1985, s 711A(1) (inserted by Companies Act 1989, s 142(1)).
20 Insolvency Act 1986, s 112(1) and s 127.

instrument of transfer of the shares was presented to the company before the winding up commenced, and the reason for the transfer not being registered was the directors' default, the court will order the liquidator to register the transfer, and the application for the court's directions may be made either under the provisions of the Insolvency Act 1986, now being discussed[1] or under the general provision of the Companies Act 1985, relating to proceedings for the rectification of the register of members.[2] Furthermore, if the instrument of transfer was executed but not presented to the company for registration before the commencement of the winding up, but the transferee had sufficient time to present it, the court will usually order the liquidator to register the transfer.[3] But if an instrument of transfer of shares is executed after the commencement of the winding up, the court will order the liquidator to register the transfer only if the transferee's membership of the company would benefit it or the persons entitled to share in its assets,[4] and registration will not be ordered simply because the transferor and transferee are willing that it should take place.[5] Moreover, whether the instrument of transfer is executed before or after the commencement of the winding up, the court will not compel the company to register it if, by the company's articles, the directors have a power by the company's articles of association to refuse to register transfers, either for specified reasons or for any reason they think fit, because to do so would deprive the directors or the liquidator, as successor to the directors, of their discretion to refuse registration.[6]

If the court will not compel the liquidator to register a transfer of shares, the purchaser is not entitled to repudiate the contract to purchase them, unless the seller has expressly undertaken that the transfer would be registered; this is because a seller only impliedly undertakes to do everything in his power to enable the purchaser to be registered, and does not undertake that the company will in fact register the transfer to him.[7] On the other hand, if the company's articles of association require the seller to obtain the directors' approval of the purchaser before transferring shares to him, the seller does impliedly undertake that he will obtain that approval,[8] and if it cannot be obtained because the company is in liquidation,

---

1 *Re Joint Stock Discount Co, Fyfe's Case* (1869) 4 Ch App 768.
2 Companies Act 1985, s 359(1); *Re Sussex Brick Co* [1904] 1 Ch 598.
3 *Re Overend, Gurney and Co, Ward and Garfit's Case* (1867) LR 4 Eq 189.
4 For example, because the transferee is more likely to pay the capital unpaid on the shares than the transferor.
5 *Re Onward Building Society* [1891] 2 QB 463.
6 *Re Overend, Gurney and Co, Walker's Case* (1866) LR 2 Eq 554.
7 *London Founders Association and Palmer v Clarke* (1888) 20 QBD 576.
8 *Wilkinson v Lloyd* (1845) 7 QB 27.

the purchaser may repudiate the contract to purchase the shares, and is not bound to take a transfer of them.[9]

Directors and agents

If the court makes a winding up order or appoints a provisional liquidator, the appointments of all directors,[10] employees[11] and agents[12] of the company automatically cease, and their service contracts or contracts of employment are terminated. Whether a resolution for voluntary winding up has the same effect is unsettled,[13] but it is submitted that it does not,[14] although events subsequent to the winding up resolution, such as the sale of the company's business by the liquidator, may operate as a dismissal. This view is strengthened by the fact that the Insolvency Act 1986 enables directors to continue to exercise their powers conferred by the company's articles of association in certain circumstances, notwithstanding the voluntary winding up of their company, thus clearly contemplating that they, at least, do not automatically cease to hold office on the passing of the winding up resolution.[15]

In a winding up by the court the dismissal of directors as the result of a winding up order or the appointment of a provisional liquidator means that they cease to have any power to act on the company's behalf after the order or appointment is made.[16] Nevertheless, acts done by them thereafter may be ratified by the liquidator and thereby made binding on the company, and ratification may be implied from the liquidator carrying out part of the transaction

9 *Bermingham v Sheridan Co (No 4)* (1864) 33 Beav 660.
10 *Measures Bros Ltd v Measures* [1910] 2 Ch 248.
11 *Re General Rolling Stock Co, Chapman's Case* (1866) LR 1 Eq 346.
12 *Re Oriental Bank Corpn, ex p Guillemin* (1884) 28 Ch D 634; *Re Mawcon Ltd* [1969] 1 All ER 188, [1969] 1 WLR 78. A power of attorney given by a company to secure a proprietary interest of the attorney or an obligation owed to him is not terminated by the winding up of the company if the power is expressed to be irrevocable (Powers of Attorney Act 1971, s 4(1) (1 *Halsbury's Statutes* (4th edn) 57).
13 In *Midland Counties District Bank Ltd v Attwood* [1905] 1 Ch 357, it was held that directors of a solvent company were not dismissed by it going into voluntary liquidation for the purpose of amalgamating with another company.
14 In *Deaway Trading Ltd v Calverley* [1973] 3 All ER 776, it was held that employees were not dismissed by the company going into voluntary liquidation, but in that case a receiver for a debenture holder had already taken possession of the company's assets and was running its business as a going concern with a view to selling it.
15 Insolvency Act 1986, s 91(2) and s 103.
16 *Fowler v Broad's Patent Night Light Co* [1893] 1 Ch 724; *Gosling v Gaskell* [1897] AC 575 at 587, per Lord Watson.

which the directors initiated, or from the liquidator accepting benefits under the transaction on the company's behalf.[17] Subject to what is said in the next section of this chapter, however, directors' powers do not cease merely because a winding up petition is presented in respect of the company, even if a winding up order is subsequently made,[18] and so between the date of the petition and the winding up order or the appointment of a provisional liquidator, the directors are still competent to exercise their powers, and may accept transfers and delivery of property to the company,[19] and may receive payment on its behalf of debts owed to the company, so discharging the debtors from liability.[20] The authority of agents of the company, other than directors, ceases only when they are notified of the winding up order, and so they may bind the company by contracts negotiated by them in the meantime.[17]

In a voluntary winding up the directors' powers cease on the passing of the winding up resolution, but they may continue to exercise any of their powers in a members' voluntary winding up with the consent of the liquidator,[1] and in a creditors' voluntary winding up with the consent of the liquidation committee, or if there is no such committee, with the consent of a meeting of the company's creditors.[2]

Dispositions of the company's property

In a winding up by the court, the Insolvency Act 1986 provides that any disposition of the company's property after the commencement of the winding up is void, unless the court otherwise orders.[3] Consequently, a disposal of any property of the company by its directors or any person purporting to act on its behalf is invalid if it is made after the presentation of the petition on which the court makes a winding up order, but the disposition is validated if it is approved by the court beforehand or is confirmed by it afterwards. An application for the court's approval or confirmation of a disposition may be made by the company itself, by a contributory or by any other person who has a particular interest in the matter.[4] The purpose of

---

17 *Re Mawcon Ltd* [1969] 1 All ER 188, [1969] 1 WLR 78.
18 *Re Oriental Bank Corpn, ex p Guillemin* (1884) 28 Ch D 634.
19 *Re Barned's Banking Co, ex p Contract Corpn* (1867) 3 Ch App 105.
20 *Mersey Steel and Iron Co v Naylor Benzon & Co* (1882) 9 QBD 648; affd (1884) 9 App Cas 434.
1 Insolvency Act 1986, s 91(2).
2 Ibid, s 103.
3 Ibid, s 127.
4 *Re Argentum Reductions (UK) Ltd* [1975] 1 All ER 608, [1975] 1 WLR 186.

this provision and the occasions on which the court should give its approval to dispositions of the company's property were explained by Cairns LJ in the following passage:[5]

> 'This is a wholesome necessary provision, to prevent, during the period which must elapse before a petition can be heard, the improper alienation and dissipation of the property of a company in extremis. But where a company actually trading, which it is in the interests of everyone to preserve, and ultimately to sell, as a going concern, is made the object of a winding up petition which may fail or may succeed, if it were to be supposed that transactions in the ordinary course of its current trade, bona fide entered into and completed, would be avoided, and would not in the discretion given to the court, be maintained, the result would be that the presentation of a petition, groundless or well-founded, would, ipso facto, paralyze the trade of the company, and great injury, without any counter-balance of advantage, would be done to those interested in the assets of the company.'

Dispositions and payments in the ordinary course of business

In the light of this interpretation, the court will sanction dispositions of the company's property by its directors during the interval between the presentation of a petition and the making of a winding up order only if they are made in good faith for the purpose of carrying on the company's business and if the disponee acted reasonably.[6] If the winding up petition is presented by a creditor, the burden of proving that this is so rests on the company, but if the petitioner is a contributory and the company is not clearly insolvent, a disposition will be presumed to have been made or proposed in good faith and for the company's benefit, unless the contrary is alleged and proved.[7] Good faith on the part of the disponee, whether a purchaser, mortgagee or payee, is essential, but is not of itself sufficient to save the disposition from avoidance if the disponee did not act reasonably in the circumstances, or if the company did not benefit from the disposition. Thus, where a receiver appointed by the debenture holders of a parent or holding company made advances to its subsidiary after the presentation of a winding up petition against it, but failed to enquire whether the advances would in fact enable the subsidiary to continue carrying on its business or

---

5 *Re Wiltshire Iron Co* (1868) 3 Ch App 443 at 446–447.
6 A Practice Direction dated 22 February 1990 prescribes a standard form of order which the court will make in respect of a company which is or has been carrying on business as a going concern. The order permits the payment of money into or out of its bank accounts and the disposition of any property of the company for value in the ordinary course of its business between the date on which the winding up petition was presented and the date when a winding up order is made.
7 *Re Burton and Deakin Ltd* [1977] 1 All ER 631, [1977] 1 WLR 390.

to check the subsidiary's records of receipts and payments in order
to confirm that it continued to be solvent, it was held that the
receiver could not retain a subsequent repayment of the advances
made by the subsidiary's directors, despite the receiver's own good
faith and the legitimacy of the purpose he intended to achieve.[8]
Again, where a director of a company paid out of his own resources
part of the debt which was the subject of the winding up petition in
order to procure its adjournment, and then drew on the company's
bank account to reimburse himself, it was held that he should not be
absolved from restoring the amount which he had drawn out,
because a winding up order was eventually made on the petition,
and so the company did not in fact benefit by the director's part
payment of the debt.[9] On the other hand when the court is asked to
confirm a disposition of the company's property, it is immaterial
that the person who takes the disposition was aware at the time that
a winding up petition had been presented if he otherwise acted in
good faith. Consequently, the court has upheld the issue of debentures
by the directors of a company despite the debenture holder's
knowledge of a pending winding up petition, when the debentures
were issued to secure loans made to enable the company to pay its
workmen's wages,[10] or to purchase goods so that it might continue
trading.[11]

The payment of a debt owed by the company after the
presentation of a winding up petition will be upheld if it is made in
good faith for the purpose of carrying on the company's business,
and not simply in order to prefer the creditor or to discharge the
company's indebtedness, when it obtains no benefit other than the
termination of its liability to that creditor.[12] Consequently, where
the company had obtained a temporary overdraft facility from its
bank to finance its current trading, and had undertaken to reduce
the overdraft by paying into its account the proceeds of sale of
certain goods which it bought and paid for by means of the overdraft,
it was held that the bank might retain the amount so paid in to the
company's bank account, even though the payment was made after
a winding-up petition was presented.[13] Likewise, the Court of
Appeal held that the payment of a debt owed by the company to a
supplier of goods essential for the continued carrying on of the
company's business (fuel oil supplied to a transport company)

8 *Re Clifton Place Garage Ltd* [1970] Ch 477, [1969] 3 All ER 892.
9 *Re Webb Electrical Ltd* [1988] BCLC 382, 4 BCC 230.
10 *Re Park Ward & Co Ltd* [1926] Ch 828.
11 *Re Steane's (Bournemouth) Ltd* [1950] 1 All ER 21.
12 *Re J Leslie Engineers Co Ltd* [1976] 2 All ER 85, [1976] 1 WLR 292.
13 *Re TW Construction Ltd* [1954] 1 All ER 744, [1954] 1 WLR 540.

should be validated when the supplier was unaware that a winding up petition had been presented against the company and insisted that the payment must be made if further supplies to the company on credit were to be made.[14] In another case,[15] however, the court refused to allow a creditor of the company to retain payment of a trade debt made after presentation of a winding-up petition, even though the creditor promised to supply further goods to the company if the debt were paid. It is true in the first two of these three cases, the bank and the supplier were unaware of the winding-up petition when the payment was made, whereas in the third case the creditor was aware of it, but the creditor's right to retain the payment in the first two cases did not depend solely on that. The ignorance of the petition by the bank or supplier in those cases merely helped to show that it did not seek to be preferred over other creditors, whereas in the third case the creditor's knowledge of the petition persuaded the court that the real purpose of the payment was to prefer him. It does not follow, therefore, that a creditor who is paid his debt in the ordinary course of business will never be allowed to retain it, merely because he knows of a pending winding up petition.

Completion of the disposition before winding up order

The court cannot approve a disposition of property which is made after the presentation of a winding up petition unless the title to the property has passed to the purchaser, mortgagee or other disponee before a winding up order is made. Consequently, if a contract by the company to sell goods[16] or to pay money[17] is still executory when the winding up order is made, the other party must prove in the winding up for his debt or for damages for breach of contract, unless the liquidator voluntarily chooses to carry out the contract, or the court makes an order of specific performance in an appropriate case.[18] However, if before a winding up order is made the legal or equitable title to the property has been unconditionally transferred by the company to the purchaser or other disponee and the company has received the agreed consideration, the court will not invalidate the disposition if it was made in good faith and for adequate consideration.[19]

---

14 *Denney v John Hudson & Co Ltd* [1992] BCLC 901, [1992] BCC 503.
15 *Re Civil Service and General Store Ltd* (1887) 57 LJ Ch 119.
16 *Re Wiltshire Iron Co* (1968) 3 Ch App 443.
17 *Re Oriental Bank Corpn, ex p Guillemin* (1884) 28 Ch D 634.
18 After a winding up order has been made the other party can seek such an order
    only if the court gives him leave to do so (Insolvency Act 1986, s 130(2) (see p
    80, ante)).
19 *Re French's (Wine Bar) Ltd* [1987] BCLC 499, 3 BCC 173.

When application for the court's approval must be made

It was held in one case that the court's approval of a disposition of the company's property made after the presentation of a winding up petition cannot be sought until after the winding up order is made, because until then it is impossible to predict whether the disposition will be invalidated by the statutory provision, and whether the approval of it by the court will be necessary to make it effective.[20] This reasoning was not followed in another case,[1] where the court permitted the company to dispose of a lease pending the hearing of the winding up petition in order that the provision contained in the lease for its forfeiture if the company were wound up should not take effect. This latter decision is undoubtedly preferable, for the protection of persons dealing with the directors or other agents of the company in good faith and the ordinary course of the company's business should be the paramount consideration. The second decision was followed in a third case,[2] and the court in that case exercised its powers there even more extensively by permitting the directors to carry on the company's business in the ordinary way pending the hearing of a creditors' winding up petition, and by authorising them in doing so to dispose of the company's assets and to pay its debts without it being necessary for the court's approval to be sought for each transaction. The Court of Appeal has more recently held, however, that an order permitting the continued carrying on of the company's business should only be made if there is a real probability that the business will be saleable as a going concern if a winding up order is made,[3] and it would appear that proof that the company will be able to discharge all its liabilities in full out of the proceeds would suffice to satisfy this condition, unless the sale of its business will be impossible or impracticable for other reasons (eg the termination of the lease of the premises where the business is carried on). Leave to dispose of the company's property in the course of carrying on its business will not be given, however, if the company has suffered recent trading losses and is likely to continue to do so.[4] On the other hand the court will permit any disposal of a company's assets if it is shown that it will be able to pay all its creditors in full after the disposal has been completed, or if the disposal will be made in the ordinary course of the company's

20 *Re Miles Aircraft Ltd, Barclays Bank Ltd's Application* [1948] Ch 188, [1948] 1 All ER 225.
1 *Re AI Levy (Holdings) Ltd* [1964] Ch 19, [1963] 2 All ER 556.
2 *Re Operator Control Cabs Ltd* [1970] 3 All ER 657n.
3 *Re Gray's Inn Construction Co Ltd* [1980] 1 All ER 814, [1980] 1 WLR 711.
4 *Re a Company (No 007523 of 1986)* [1987] BCLC 200, 3 BCC 57; *Re McGuinness Bros (UK) Ltd* (1987) 3 BCC 571.

business and will be beneficial for all the company's unsecured creditors, and not merely some of them.[5]

If a winding up petition is presented by a creditor who discontinues the proceedings on being paid his debt and costs by the company, but the court substitutes another creditor as petitioner[6] and makes a winding up order, the first creditor must repay the amount paid to him by the company, because the payment was made after the commencement of the winding up proceedings in which the order was made, and the court will allow him to retain only such part of the amount paid as represents his costs incurred in taking steps toward obtaining the winding up order which the substituted petitioner eventually obtained.[7]

Consequences of refusal of court's approval

If the court refuses to approve or confirm a disposition of the company's property made after the presentation of a winding up petition, the liquidator may not only recover the property itself from the disponee, or the proceeds of the resale of the property in the hands of the disponee or a third person,[8] but may also recover the value of the property from the directors or the other persons who disposed of it in the company's name or on its behalf.[9] It is uncertain, however, which of these remedies should be sought first, and if either may be pursued at the liquidator's choice, whether the disponee or a third person who is compelled to return the property or the proceeds of its resale may seek an indemnity from the directors or the other person who effected the disposition. If property of the company is disposed of a second time by the disponee, or if money belonging to the company is paid out after the presentation of a winding up petition, and the proceeds of resale of the property or the amount or amounts paid out come into the hands of a third person in circumstances where it is not possible to trace the proceeds or the company's money directly (for example, because the proceeds or the amounts or amounts paid out have been mixed with other funds in a bank account), the liquidator may recover the amount of the proceeds or the amount or amounts paid out from the third person by a personal claim in equity.[8] The liquidator's claim is based on the rule that the assets of the company in liquidation are

---

5 *Re Fairway Graphics Ltd* [1991] BCLC 468.
6 Insolvency Rules 1986, r 4.19(1) and (2).
7 *Re Bostels Ltd* [1968] Ch 346, [1967] 3 All ER 425; *Re Western Welsh International System Buildings Ltd* (1985) 1 BCC 296.
8 *Re J Leslie Engineers Co Ltd* [1976] 2 All ER 85, [1976] 1 WLR 292.
9 *Re Neath Harbour Smelting and Rolling Works* [1887] WN 87.

treated as a fund held in trust for its creditors and members according to their respective claims.[10] However, the liquidator cannot recover the proceeds of the second disposal or the amount or amounts paid out if the third person has given value or has cancelled an obligation owed to him in consideration of the disposal or the payment and has otherwise acted in good faith, nor if the liquidator has not exhausted available claims against other persons who can be made personally liable for the disposal of the company's property or the payment out of its funds (such as the directors who made it, the immediate disponee of the property in question, or the company's bank which honoured a cheque drawn on its account by means of which the payment was made).[8]

If a disposition of a company's property after the presentation of a winding up petition is not approved and validated by the court, a person who is compelled to return the property to the liquidator, or whose interest in it becomes void, may be able to pursue secondary remedies in relation to the property in certain situations. For example, if the directors sell property of the company to a purchaser, and use the proceeds of sale to discharge a mortgage or charge created by the company over the property so as to transfer an unincumbered title to the purchaser, on the invalidation of the transfer the purchaser can claim to be subrogated to the rights and remedies conferred by the mortgage or charge, which is treated as though it had been transferred to him by the person who held it.[11] Similarly, if such a purchase of the company's property after the presentation of a winding up petition is financed by the purchaser himself mortgaging or charging the property to a lender whose advance is used to discharge an existing mortgage or charge created by the company over the property, that mortgage or charge is treated as having been transferred to the lender whose advance is made to the purchaser, if the mortgage or charge created by him in favour of the lender is itself invalidated by the court refusing to approve the transfer of the property from the company.[11] Such secondary remedies would seem to be confined to situations where the equitable remedy of subrogation is available, however, and if there are no third party rights to which the purchaser or lender can be subrogated, it would not seem possible for him to trace the purchase money or the mortgage advance which the lender has made into the company's assets generally, so as to make them recoverable in the company's liquidation by means of a tracing order.[11]

10 *Ayerst v C & K (Construction) Ltd* [1976] AC 167, [1975] 2 All ER 537.
11 *Re Tramway Building and Construction Ltd* [1988] Ch 293, [1987] BCLC 632.

Operation of the company's bank account

The invalidation of dispositions of a company's assets between the presentation of a winding up petition and the making of a winding up order raises particular problems for a bank at which the company has a current account. If when the petition is presented the account is overdrawn, the payment of amounts into the account thereafter, whether in cash or by cheques payable to the company, will be dispositions of the company's property, since the overdraft will thereby be reduced.[12] Furthermore, whether the account is in credit or is overdrawn when the petition is presented, all subsequent payments out of the account by the bank will be dispositions of the company's property, since the credit balance which the company may claim from the bank is thereby reduced or the debit balance which it owes the bank is thereby increased.[12] However, the court will not order the bank to pay to the liquidator the sum of the amounts paid into and out of the account after the presentation of the petition, but will limit the recoverable amount to the loss suffered by the company as a result of the continued operation of the account after the presentation of the petition, including the amount of the company's debts owing at that date which have been paid out of the account after the bank became aware of the petition, but only to the extent that those payments exceed the amount which the creditors would have received in respect of their debts if they had not been paid but had proved in the liquidation.[12] Furthermore, amounts paid to third persons after the bank became aware of the petition will only be repayable by the bank if they prove irrecoverable from those third persons.[12] On the other hand, if a debit balance on the company's bank account when the petition is presented is subsequently discharged or reduced by the payment of amounts into the account,[13] the amounts so paid in will be recoverable in full by the liquidator, so preventing the bank paying itself the whole or part of the company's indebtedness to it to the prejudice of the company's other creditors.[12] Additionally, the bank will not be entitled to charge interest or bank charges in respect of any increase in the debit balance of the account after presentation of the winding up petition,[12]

---

12 *Re Gray's Inn Construction Co Ltd* [1980] 1 All ER 814, [1980] 1 WLR 711; *Re Barn Crown Ltd* [1994] 2 BCLC 186, [1994] BCC 381.

13 Payments into the account will under the general rules governing current bank accounts be credited against debit items in the account in the chronological order in which they were incurred (*Devaynes v Noble, Clayton's Case* (1816) 1 Mer 529).

except possibly where such increases result from the company's existing debts owing to third parties being paid by the bank and the bank, acting in ignorance of the winding up petition, is entitled to be subrogated to the rights of those third persons. Although the court can in special circumstances relieve the bank from liability to account to the liquidator in full for payments made out of the company's account or items debited to it, the court will not do so merely because the bank has acted carefully in satisfying itself that the continued operation of the company's account was exclusively for the purpose of carrying on its business in the usual way.[12] A bank should therefore protect itself in all cases by obtaining, or requiring the company's directors to obtain, the court's authorisation in advance for the continued operation of the company's account when the bank becomes aware of the presentation of a winding up petition against the company.

Voluntary liquidations

In a voluntary winding up there are no problems in connection with dispositions of the company's property by the directors or other persons acting on the company's behalf before a winding up resolution is passed, because the commencement of the winding up is not ante-dated to a time before the passing of the winding up resolution, and there is therefore no hiatus period during which dispositions of the company's property may be made which will subsequently be invalidated.[14] On the other hand, no disposition made by the directors after the date of the winding up resolution is binding on the company, unless they are authorised to continue exercising their powers by the liquidator, the committee of inspection, or the creditors, as the case may be.[15] If dispositions are made by persons other than directors without the approval of the liquidator after the date of the winding up or resolution, the court may invalidate the, or may restrain the persons concerned from carrying them out if they have not been completed.[16]

14 Nevertheless, the provisions of the Insolvency Act 1986, ss 239 and 245, enable the court to set aside payments and dispositions to creditors as voidable preferences and provide for the invalidation of certain floating charges (see post, pp 225 and 237).
15 See p 103, ante.
16 Insolvency Act 1986, s 112(1) and s 127; *Re Roundwood Colliery Co, Lee v Roundwood Colliery Co* [1897] 1 Ch 373.

PROCEEDINGS CONSEQUENT ON A WINDING UP ORDER OR RESOLUTION

The official receiver as liquidator in a winding up by the court

When a winding up order is made against a company, the official receiver becomes its liquidator, and continues to be the liquidator until another person is appointed in his place.[17] Any provisional liquidator appointed by the court before the winding up order is made is removed by order of the court at the same time as the winding up order is made.[18] The functions of the official receiver at this stage of the winding up of the company are, first to decide whether to call first meetings of the company's creditors and contributories so that they may resolve whether one or more persons shall be appointed to be the liquidator or liquidators in place of the official receiver, and whether to constitute a liquidation committee to supervise the liquidator's conduct of the winding up;[19] and secondly, to investigate the causes of the company's insolvency or its failure to pay its debts if that has happened, and also to investigate generally the promotion, formation, business, dealings and affairs of the company and to make such report or reports to the court as the official receiver thinks fit.[20]

If the official receiver considers that any director or shadow director of a company which has been ordered to be wound up by the court when it was insolvent, has been guilty of conduct which makes him unfit to be concerned in the management of a company, he must report the matter to the Secretary of State for Trade and Industry with a view to proceedings being taken by the Secretary of State or the official receiver for obtaining an order of the court disqualifying the director or shadow director from being or acting as a director of any company or in various other capacities in relation to any company, unless the court gives him leave to do so.[1]

Statement of affairs

When the court has made a winding up order or appointed a provisional liquidator, the official receiver may require certain

---

17 Insolvency Act 1986, s 136(1) and (2).
18 Ibid, s 72(1) and (2); *Re Dry Docks Corpn of London* (1888) 39 Ch D 306.
19 See below, pp 115 and 127.
20 Insolvency Act 1986, s 132(1).
 1 Company Directors' Disqualification Act 1986, s 1(1), s 6 and s 7(3). See *Pennington's Company Law* (7th edn), p 717 et seq.

persons who are or have been connected with the company to make or concur in making a statement of the company's affairs verified by affidavit.[2]

The statement of affairs must be in the prescribed form, and must contain particulars of the company's assets, debts and liabilities; the names and addresses of the company's creditors, the nature and dates of creation of any securities held by them for the debts or liabilities of the company to them, and the individual and total amounts of preferential debts of the company, which are payable in priority to its other debts and liabilities;[3] the estimated surplus of the company's assets over its preferential debts and over its other debts and liabilities, or (as the case may be) the deficiency of the company's assets to satisfy its preferential debts and, separately, to satisfy the company's other debts and liabilities; and the names and addresses of the company's shareholders, the number, nominal values and classes of shares held by them respectively, and the amounts (if any) remaining to be called up in respect of those shares (including unpaid instalments of the issue price).[4]

The persons whom the official receiver can require to make or concur in making the statement of affairs are: (a) present and former directors and officers of the company; (b) persons who took part in the company's formation within one year before the date of the winding up order; (c) persons who are, or who within one year before the date of the winding up order or the earlier appointment of a provisional liquidator have been, employees of the company and whom the official receiver considers to be capable of giving the information required; and (d) persons who are, or who within one year before that date have been, officers or employees of a company which is, or has within that year been, an officer of the company in liquidation.[5] If the official receiver requires any such person to make or concur in making the statement of affairs, he must send a notice to him to that effect, setting out the names and addresses of all other persons to whom he has sent similar notices, the time within which the statement of affairs must be delivered to the liquidator (being not less than 21 clear days from the day when the notice is given), the penalty for failing to make or concur in making the statement of affairs (ie a fine and daily default fine after first conviction), and the statutory obligation of all persons to whom the notice is given to provide the official receiver with such information about the company

2 Insolvency Act 1986, s 131(1) and (2).
3 See p 303, post.
4 Insolvency Act 1986, s 131(2); Insolvency Rules 1986, r 4.33(1) and Sch 4, Form 4.17.
5 Insolvency Act 1986, s 131(3) and (6).

and its affairs which he is able, and to attend on the official receiver when so required.[6] The official receiver, or the court on appeal from him, may absolve any person whom he has required to join in making the statement of affairs from doing so, or may extend the time for delivering the statement of affairs.[7] Although the obligations of any person who is required to concur in making the statement of affairs is prima facie to verify the whole of its contents by his affidavit, he may qualify his verification in respect of statements in it with which he does not agree, or which he considers to be wrong or misleading, or about which he lacks the direct knowledge necessary for concurring.[8]

When he has received the completed statement of affairs and the affidavits verifying it, the official receiver must file the documents at the court which made the winding up order, and circulate to creditors and contributories a report summarising the statement of affairs with the official receiver's comments on it and on the company's affairs in general.[9] The filed statement of affairs, like all other records of the court in respect of the winding up of the company, is open to inspection by any person;[10] but should the official receiver consider that it would prejudice the conduct of the liquidation if the whole or part of the filed statement of affairs were disclosed, he may apply to the court for an order either that the statement of affairs or a part of it shall not be filed, or that the statement or part of it shall be separately filed and not made available for public inspection.[11]

The official receiver may authorise the reimbursement out of the company's assets of expenses incurred by any person who concurs in making the statement of affairs if he necessarily incurs those expenses; and if such a person is unable to prepare a statement of affairs at all (eg because of disability), the official receiver may employ some other person to assist him to make it, and the cost may be met out of the company's assets.[12]

Information and accounts

The persons whom the official receiver could require to make or concur in making a statement of affairs are additionally under an

6 Ibid, s 131(4) and (7) and s 235(1) to (4); Insolvency Rules 1986, r 4.32(1) to (4).
7 Insolvency Act 1986, s 131(5); Insolvency Rules 1986, r 4.46(1) and (2).
8 Insolvency Rules 1986, r 4.33(2) and (3).
9 Ibid, r 4.33(6) and r 4.45(1).
10 Ibid, r 7.28(1).
11 Ibid, r 4.35(1) and (2).
12 Ibid, r 4.37(1) and (2).

obligation at the request of the official receiver, of a provisional liquidator or of the liquidator for the time being of a company in liquidation, to give him such information about the company and its promotion, formation, business, dealings, affairs and assets as he reasonably requires, and to attend on him so as to assist him in carrying out his functions at such times and places as he reasonably calls on them to do, and they are punishable by fine if they fail to comply with such requirements.[13] The same persons may be required by the official receiver to provide him with accounts of the company for any period he specifies; but if the period begins more than three years before the date when the petition for the winding up of the company was presented, the obligation is imposed only if the court so orders.[14]

The accounts called for by the official receiver must be verified by affidavit if he so requires, and the accounts must be submitted to him in duplicate within 21 days after he calls for them or within such extended period as he, or the court on appeal from him, allows.[15] One copy of the accounts and the verifying affidavit must be filed in court by the official receiver after they have been submitted to him.[14] Furthermore, the official receiver can require any person who has concurred in making the statement of affairs in respect of the company to submit to him further information in writing, amplifying, modifying or explaining any matter contained in the statement of affairs, or in any accounts submitted to the official receiver or the liquidator by any person under the Insolvency Act 1986 or the Insolvency Rules 1986, and he may require the information to be verified by affidavit.[16]

THE LIQUIDATOR AND THE LIQUIDATION COMMITTEE IN A WINDING UP BY THE COURT

Procedure for the appointment of the liquidator

First meetings of creditors and contributories

Within twelve weeks after an order for the winding up of a company is made, the official receiver must decide whether to call separate first meetings of the company's creditors and contributories to

13 Insolvency Act 1986, s 235(1) to (3) and (5).
14 Insolvency Rules, 1986, r 4.39(1) to (3).
15 Ibid, r 4.39(3) and (6).
16 Ibid, r 4.42(1) to (3).

nominate an individual or individuals qualified to act as an insolvency practitioner to be the liquidator or liquidators of the company, and to decide whether to establish a liquidation committee representative of both creditors and contributories.[17] The functions of the liquidation committee are to receive periodic and other reports from the liquidator, to give or withhold its consent to the exercise of certain of the liquidator's powers and to convene and consult meetings of creditors and contributories when it considers it desirable to do so.[18]

If the official receiver decides to call first meetings of creditors and contributories, he must fix the date or dates on which they will respectively be held, which must not be later than four months after the date of the winding up order; he must then give notice of the time and place of the meetings to the court, and send by post or deliver a notice of the creditors' meeting to every creditor of the company who is identified in the company's statement of affairs, or who is otherwise known to the official receiver; and the official receiver must also deliver or send by post a notice of the contributories' meeting to every person who appears from the company's register of members or other records to be a contributory.[19] The notices sent or delivered to creditors and contributories must be despatched by post or delivered to them at least 21 days before the date fixed for the meeting, and must be accompanied by proxy appointment forms for use by those of them who wish to appoint representatives to attend the meetings in their place.[20] The official receiver must furthermore give notice of the first meetings of creditors and contributories by public advertisement; on the official receiver's application the court may order that this shall be the only form of notice of the meetings which need be given, and that it shall not be necessary to send individual notices to creditors and contributories.[1] Any creditor who wishes to vote at the first meeting of creditors must lodge a proof of his claim against the company not later than the time specified in the notice of the meeting (which cannot be earlier than four days before the date fixed for the meeting); and if the creditor is to be entitled to vote, his claim must be admitted for the purpose of voting by the chairman of the meeting.[2] Contributories have the same voting rights at meetings of contributories as they have in their capacity as members of the company at general meetings of the

17 Insolvency Act 1986, s 136(4) and (5) and s 141(1); Insolvency Rules 1986, r 4.52(1) and (2).
18 Insolvency Act 1986 s 167(1) and Insolvency Rules 1986, r 4.155.
19 Insolvency Rules 1986, r 4.50(1) and (2) and r 13.3(1) to (3).
20 Ibid, r 4.50(3) and r 4.60(3).
 1 Ibid, r 4.50(5) and r 4.59(1).
 2 Ibid, r 4.54(4), r 4.67(1) and r 4.70(1).

company.[3] Creditors and contributories who wish to vote by proxy at their respective meetings must lodge their proxy appointments at the place and by the time and date specified in the notice of the meeting (not being earlier than four days before the date fixed for the meeting).[4]

The chairman at the first meetings of creditors and contributories is the official receiver or some other person nominated by him.[5] The quorum for the first or any other meeting of creditors is one creditor present in person or by proxy, and the quorum for the first or any other meeting of contributories is two contributories or (if there is only one contributory) the sole contributory present in person or by proxy; the representative of a corporate creditor or contributory appointed to represent it by its board of directors or governing body is counted as one person present at any meeting of creditors or contributories for each of the companies or corporations which he represents.[5]

Resolutions are passed at the first meetings in the same ways as at all other meetings of creditors or contributories, namely, by the vote of a majority in value of those persons who are present in person or by proxy and who vote on the resolution. Resolutions for the appointment of the liquidator are, however, subject to special rules. If two persons are nominated for appointment as liquidator, the one of them who obtains the greater number of votes is the choice of the meeting; and if there are three or more persons nominated, the successful nominee must obtain more than one half of the total number of votes which are cast for all the nominees.[6] If no nominee obtains such a majority, the nominee who obtains the least number of votes is eliminated, and the chairman must take a further vote for the appointment of one of the remaining nominees; this process is repeated as necessary if there were four or more nominees originally, the nominee who obtained the least number of votes on a resolution, being eliminated on a subsequent vote.[6] In addition to this complex procedure for the appointment of a liquidator, the appointment of the successful nominee on a first or subsequent vote is valid only if the resolution for his appointment is supported by the votes of creditors or contributories (as the case may be) who between them may cast more than one half of the total votes which can be all the creditors or contributories (as the case may be) who are present or represented at the meeting.[6]

3 Ibid, r 4.69.
4 Ibid, r 4.50(4).
5 Ibid, r 12.4A (1) to (3).
6 Ibid, r 4.63(1), and (2A).

Resolutions to appoint a liquidator

If at their meeting the creditors resolve that a person nominated at the meeting shall be the liquidator, he becomes the liquidator, whether the appointment is agreed to by the meeting of contributories or not; but if no person is nominated or supported by the necessary majority vote at the creditors' meeting, the person chosen by the meeting of contributories becomes the liquidator.[7] If different persons are chosen to be liquidator by the two meetings, any creditor or contributory may, within seven days after the meeting of creditors makes its nomination, apply to the court which made the winding up order for an order that the contributories' chosen nominee shall be the liquidator in place of, or jointly with, the creditors' chosen nominee, or that some person other than the creditors' chosen nominee shall be the liquidator.[8]

Where the official receiver calls no first meetings

The procedure for the appointment of the liquidator or liquidators set out above is the one which is normally followed, and in practice it is rare for more than two persons to be nominated for appointment at each of the meetings of creditors and of contributories. Whether this procedure is in fact followed, however, depends on the official receiver deciding to call first meetings of creditors and contributories; if he decides not to call such meetings, he must give notice of his decision to the court which made the winding up order and to each of the company's creditors and contributories before the expiration of twelve weeks from the date of the winding up order.[9] In that situation, creditors of the company who represent at least one-quarter of the company's total indebtedness may require the official receiver to call meetings of creditors and contributories, and the official receiver must then call such meetings to be held not later than three months after he receives the creditors' request; the meetings have the same functions and are governed by the same rules as if they were first meetings of creditors and contributories called by the official receiver of his own volition.[10] The notice which the official receiver gives to creditors, notifying them of his decision not to call first meetings of creditors and contributories, must inform them of their right to require such meetings to be called if

---

7 Insolvency Act 1986, s 139(2) and (3).
8 Ibid, s 139(4). The application is heard by the registrar in chambers, but in the Companies Court it may be heard by the Chief Clerk (Insolvency Rules 1986, r 7.6 (1) and (2); Practice Direction dated 10 December 1986, paras 2 and 4).
9 Insolvency Act 1986, s 136(5).
10 Ibid, s 136(5); Insolvency Rules 1986, r 4.50(6) and (7).

their requisition is supported by one quarter in value of all the creditors.[11]

If the official receiver decides not to call first meetings of creditors and contributories, and he receives no requisition to do so from the appropriate fraction of creditors, or if at any time the official receiver is liquidator of the company (eg because the liquidator has resigned or has ceased to be qualified professionally or has become disqualified),[12] the official receiver may apply to the Secretary of State for Trade and Industry to appoint another person to be the liquidator in his place; and if first meetings of creditors and contributories are held but they fail to choose a liquidator, the official receiver must decide whether to refer the need to appoint a liquidator to the Secretary of State.[13] The Secretary of State may on such an application or reference by the official receiver appoint another person to be the liquidator of the company in place of the official receiver; or he may decline to do so, in which case the official receiver remains the liquidator.[14] A liquidator so appointed by the Secretary of State must send a notice of his appointment to each creditor and contributory, or if the court so directs on his application, he must instead advertise his appointment in some other manner.[15]

Co-liquidators

Although the Insolvency Act 1986 generally speaks of the liquidator of the company in the singular, it is possible for the meeting of creditors or contributories which is entitled to choose a liquidator, or for the court or the Secretary of State when exercising their powers to make the appointment, to appoint two or more persons to be co-liquidators, and they are then properly described as 'the liquidators' of the company in question.[16] If such an appointment is made, all the co-liquidators must be individuals qualified as insolvency practitioners and must hold current authorisations to act as such,[17] and the appointment must state whether any act required or authorised by any enactment to be done by a liquidator shall be done by all the co-liquidators, or by any one or more of the co-liquidators for the time being holding office.[18] The appointment may therefore

11 Insolvency Act 1986, s 136(2).
12 Ibid, s 136(6).
13 Ibid, s 137(1) and (2).
14 Ibid, s 136(2) and s 137(3).
15 Ibid, s 137(4).
16 Interpretation Act 1978, s 6; Insolvency Act 1986, s 163.
17 Insolvency Act 1986, s 388(1), s 390(1) and (2) and s 393(1) and (3).
18 Ibid, s 231(1) and (2).

provide that the co-liquidators shall act jointly, or that they may act separately, or that any act or certain specified acts to be done by them may be done by a certain minimum number of them, and it would also seem possible to make certain of the co-liquidators' powers exercisable jointly, and other of their powers exercisable separately or by a certain minimum of their number.

Vacation of office by a liquidator

A liquidator in a winding up by the court may cease to hold office by resigning, by being removed from office, or by ceasing to be qualified professionally to act as a liquidator or by being disqualified from acting as a liquidator, and, of course, a vacancy in the office of liquidator occurs if he dies.

Resignation

A liquidator may resign only because of ill health, or because he intends to cease practising as an insolvency practitioner, or because there is a conflict of interest or change of personal circumstances which prevents him continuing to fulfil his duties as liquidator or makes it impracticable for him to do so; his resignation must be accepted by a meeting of creditors, or if the meeting refuses to accept it, he must obtain leave of the court to resign.[19] Additionally, where there are two or more co-liquidators in office, any of the liquidators may resign in the same circumstances as a sole liquidator, and also any co-liquidator may resign because all the liquidators are of the opinion that it is no longer expedient that there should continue to be the present number of liquidators; in both of these situations, it is necessary that the resignation of any one or more of the liquidators should be accepted by a meeting of creditors or by the court.[20]

If a liquidator wishes to resign, he must call a meeting of creditors by a notice which indicates to them that if the meeting accepts his resignation, it may grant or refuse his release from liability for any breaches of duty committed by him as a liquidator; a copy of the notice must be sent by the liquidator to the official receiver.[1] The notice of the meeting sent to creditors must be accompanied by an account of the liquidator's administration of the winding up, including a summary of his receipts and payments and

---

19 Ibid, s 172(6); Insolvency Rules 1986, r 4.108(1) and (4), r 4.109(1) and (6), r 4.111(1).
20 Insolvency Rules 1986, r 4.108(5), r 4.109(1) and (2) and r 4.111(1).
 1 Ibid, r 4.108(1) and (2).

a statement by the liquidator that he has reconciled his account with the account or accounts which he has delivered to the Secretary of State for Trade and Industry.[2] The meeting of creditors may be called both to accept the liquidator's resignation, and to appoint a new liquidator in place of the resigning liquidator, and to give the latter his release.[3] Whether these further matters are included in the notice of the meeting or not, the meeting may resolve to accept the resignation of the liquidator, and if the further matters are included, the meeting may also resolve that a new liquidator shall be appointed and that the resigning liquidator shall, or shall not, be given his release.[3] The resigning liquidator may then give notice of his resignation to the court, accompanied by a copy of the account which he presented to the meeting of creditors; and a copy of the notice of resignation must also be sent to the official receiver, which he, too, must file in court if it is in order; the liquidator's resignation then takes effect as from the date when the official receiver files the copy notice of resignation in court, and the date of filing must be endorsed on it.[4]

If the creditors' meeting refuses to accept the liquidator's resignation, he may apply to the court for leave to resign.[5] If the court gives the liquidator leave to resign, it may determine the date from which his release shall be effective.[6] The liquidator is provided with two copies of the court's order giving him leave to resign, one of which he must send to the official receiver; the liquidator may then file his resignation in court, whereupon it takes effect, and the liquidator must at the same time send a copy of his notice of resignation to the official receiver.[7]

The resignation of a liquidator need not be separately advertised in a newspaper, but if a new liquidator is appointed by the meeting of creditors, he must state in the newspaper advertisement relating to his own appointment that his predecessor has resigned and (if it is the case) has been given his release.[8]

Removal of a liquidator

A liquidator may be removed from office by an order of the court or by a meeting of creditors called for the purpose; however, a provisional

2 Ibid, r 4.108(3).
3 Ibid, r 4.108(1). For the release of a liquidator, see p 174, post.
4 Ibid, r 4.109(1) and (4) to (6).
5 The application is heard by the registrar of the court in chambers, but in the Companies Court it may be heard by the Chief Clerk (Insolvency Rules 1986, r 7.6(1) and (2); Practice Direction dated 10 December 1986, paras 2 and 4).
6 Insolvency Rules 1986, r 4.111(1), (2) and (5).
7 Ibid, r 4.111(1), (3) and (5).
8 Ibid, r 4.106(1) and r 4.112.

liquidator may be removed only by order of the court.[9] If the liquidator was appointed by the court otherwise than on an application made to it when the first meeting of creditors and contributories chose different persons for appointment, a meeting of creditors will be called for the purpose of removing and replacing the liquidator only if the liquidator thinks fit, or if the court so orders, or if the meeting is requested by at least one quarter in value of the creditors.[10] If the liquidator was appointed in any other way (ie by a meeting of creditors or contributories in the case of the first liquidator, or by a meeting of creditors in the case of a second or subsequent liquidator), the liquidator must call a meeting of creditors to consider a proposal for his removal if such a meeting is requisitioned by at least one-tenth in value of the company's creditors.[11] A meeting of creditors called to remove a liquidator may pass other resolutions specified in the notice calling it which are related to the removal, such as the appointment of a new liquidator and the release from liability of the liquidator who is to be removed, and the notice calling the meeting must then state that the meeting is able to grant or refuse his release.[12] A copy of the notice calling the meeting must be sent to the official receiver.[13] The liquidator whose removal is sought, or someone nominated by him, may preside at the meeting of creditors; but the meeting may resolve to elect as chairman instead someone other than the liquidator or his nominee, because the liquidator has an obvious conflict of interest.[14] If the liquidator or his nominee does act as chairman and the resolution for the liquidator's removal is proposed, he may not adjourn the meeting without the consent of at least one half in value of the creditors present at the meeting in person or by proxy and entitled to vote.[14]

An application to the court for an order removing a liquidator, or directing the liquidator to call a meeting of creditors to consider a proposal for the liquidator's removal, must be made ex parte in the first instance if the court so directs; on the hearing of the ex parte application, the court may dismiss it if the applicant does not make out a prima facie case.[15] In the case of any such application, the court may require the applicant to give security for the costs which the liquidator may incur in connection with it,[16] and whether there has

---

9 Insolvency Act 1986, s 172(1) and (2).
10 Insolvency Act 1986, s 172(3).
11 Ibid, s 168(2).
12 Insolvency Rules 1986, r 4.113(1). For the release of the liquidator, see p 174, post.
13 Insolvency Rules 1986, r 4.113(2).
14 Ibid, r 4.114(3).
15 Ibid, r 4.119(1) and (2).
16 Ibid, r 4.119(3).

been an ex parte hearing or not, the applicant must, at least 14 days before the date fixed for the hearing of the application send to the liquidator and the official receiver a notice of the time and place of the hearing and a copy of the evidence which the applicant intends to adduce.[17] The application is heard by the registrar of the court in chambers, but he may refer it to a judge for decision.[18] The court will remove a liquidator not only if he has been guilty of misconduct,[19] but also where it is in the interests of the persons between whom the company's assets are divisible (ie its creditors if the company is insolvent) that another person should be appointed as liquidator,[20] for example, where the liquidator has a conflict of interests or duties.[1] It has been held that if an insolvency practitioner who is a member of a partnership resigns from it and becomes a partner in another firm, the court will not order his removal as liquidator of companies which he was winding up while a partner in the first firm, or order that he shall replace a concurrently retiring partner in the second firm as liquidator of companies which he was winding up unless meetings of the creditors of those respective companies resolve to approve these changes being made, and the court orders will be made conditional on this being done.[2] However, in another case[3] the court made a removal and replacement order in similar circumstances without requiring the approval of the creditors of the companies concerned; it therefore appears that it is a matter for the court's discretion whether to require the creditors' approval.

If the court makes an order removing the liquidator it sends copies of the order to the liquidator and the official receiver, and if the court appoints a new liquidator in place of the one it removes, the court also sends the official receiver and the liquidator a copy of its order making the appointment.[4] If on hearing the application the court directs that the liquidator shall call a meeting of creditors to consider a proposal for the liquidator's removal, it may give directions as to the time and place at which the meeting shall be held; but, subject to those directions, the meeting is called and held and consequential steps are taken as though the liquidator had called the meeting without a court order.[5] A liquidator appointed by such a

---

17 Ibid, r 4.119(4).
18 Ibid, r 7.6(1) to (3).
19 *Re Charterland Goldfields Ltd* (1909) 26 TLR 132; *Re Keypak Homecare Ltd* [1987] BCLC 409, 3 BCC 558.
20 *Re Adam Eyton Ltd* (1887) 36 Ch D 299.
 1 *Re Corbenstoke Ltd (No 2)* [1990] BCLC 60, 5 BCC 767.
 2 *Re Sankey Furniture Ltd, ex p Harding* [1995] 2 BCLC 594.
 3 *Re Bullard and Taplin Ltd* [1996] BCC 973.
 4 Insolvency Rules 1986, r 4.119(6).
 5 Ibid, rr 4.113 and 4.115.

meeting of creditors must advertise his appointment in such newspaper as he thinks most appropriate to ensure that it comes to the attention of the company's creditors and contributories, and he must notify his appointment to the Registrar of Companies.[6]

A liquidator appointed by the Secretary of State for Trade and Industry on the application of the official receiver while he is acting as liquidator may be removed in the same way as a liquidator appointed in any other way, and may additionally be removed from office by direction of the Secretary of State.[7] The Secretary of State must notify the liquidator and the official receiver of his provisional decision to remove a liquidator appointed by him and of the grounds for doing so; the notice must specify a period within which the liquidator may make representations against the provisional decision, and the Secretary of State must consider any representations which the liquidator makes before reaching his final decision.[8] If the Secretary of State decides to remove the liquidator, he must file the document containing his decision in the court which made the winding up order, and send a notice of it to the liquidator and the official receiver.[9]

Other causes for a liquidator ceasing to hold office

Apart from resigning or being removed from office, a liquidator ceases to hold office if he is no longer qualified to act as the liquidator of the company (ie if he ceases to be a qualified insolvency practitioner, or there ceases to be in force the appropriate security for the liquidator's proper performance of his duties in respect of the liquidation); or if he becomes disqualified from acting as an insolvency practitioner by becoming bankrupt; or if a disqualification order is made against him by the court under the Company Directors' Disqualification Act 1986; or if an order is made by the court for the administration of his property under the Mental Health Act 1983.[10] When a liquidator ceases to hold office by ceasing to be qualified to act, or by becoming disqualified from acting, he must give notice of that fact to the official receiver, who must notify the Secretary of State for Trade and Industry and must also file a copy of the liquidator's notice in court.[11]

---

6 Ibid, r 4.106(1) and (4).
7 Insolvency Act 1986, s 172(1) and (4).
8 Insolvency Rules 1986, r 4.123(1).
9 Ibid, r 4.123(2).
10 Insolvency Act 1986, s 172(5) and s 390(2) to (4). For disqualification orders, see *Pennington's Company Law* (7th edn) p 717.
11 Insolvency Rules 1986, r 4.134(1) and (2).

On the death of a liquidator, his personal representatives or, if he was a partner in a firm, another partner who is a qualified insolvency practitioner must notify the official receiver of the fact and date of the liquidator's death, and the official receiver must then give notice of the liquidator's death to the court.[12]

Consequences of a vacancy in the office of liquidator

Whenever a vacancy occurs in the office of liquidator, and no new liquidator is appointed during the proceedings resulting in the vacancy (as may happen when a liquidator resigns or is removed), the official receiver again becomes the liquidator of the company, and he may either call meetings of creditors and contributories to make an appointment of a new liquidator or liquidators, or may apply to the Secretary of State for Trade and Industry to make such an appointment.[13] If the calling of a meeting of creditors and contributories for the purpose of appointing a new liquidator is requisitioned by one quarter in value of the company's creditors, the official receiver must call meetings of creditors and contributories for a date not later than three months after receiving the requisition.[14]

Whether meetings of creditors and contributories are the result of the official receiver's own initiative or of a requisition, the meetings are called by him giving at least 21 days' notice to the creditors and contributories respectively, and the notice calling the meeting must inform them of their right to appoint proxies to represent them at the meetings by lodging proxy appointments at a specified address by a certain time and date not more than four days before the date of the respective meetings.[15] The remaining rules governing the meetings and voting at them are the same as for the first meeting of creditors and contributories.[16] If the meetings of creditors and contributories choose different persons for appointment as liquidator, the appointee will be the person chosen by the creditors' meeting, unless the court otherwise orders on an application made by a creditor or contributory within seven days after the date of the creditors' meeting.[17] If the creditors' meeting does not choose a person to be appointed as liquidator, the person chosen by the contributories' meeting will be the liquidator; and if neither meeting makes a choice the official receiver continues to be the liquidator.[18]

12 Ibid, r 4.132(1), (2) and (4).
13 Insolvency Act 1986, s 136(3) and (4) and s 137(1).
14 Ibid, s 136(5).
15 Insolvency Rules 1986, r 4.54(3) and (4).
16 Ibid, r 4.55(2), r 4.60(1) to (4).
17 Insolvency Act 1986, s 139(1) to (4).
18 Ibid, s 136(3) and s 139(3).

The liquidator's remuneration

The liquidator in a winding up by the court is entitled to remuneration for his services consisting of either a percentage of the company's assets which he realises, or a percentage of its assets which he distributes, or a combination of both. On the other hand, the liquidator's remuneration may take the form of a fee calculated by reference to the time devoted by him and his staff (if any) to the winding up of the company's affairs.[19] The form and rate of the liquidator's remuneration is decided upon by the liquidation committee, or if there is no such committee, by a meeting of creditors.[20] In deciding on the form and rate of the liquidator's remuneration, the liquidation committee must take into account the complexity of the liquidation, whether it involves responsibility on the part of the liquidator of an exceptional kind or degree, the effectiveness with which the liquidator is carrying out his duties and the value and nature of the company's assets with which he has to deal.[1] The official receiver, as a salaried government official, is not personally entitled to remuneration for acting as liquidator of a company, but is entitled to charge remuneration on the government's behalf, the principal item of which is payable for the performance of his general duties as liquidator at diminishing percentage rates on successive bands of the total amount realised and distributed in the liquidation.[2] If the remuneration of a liquidator other than the official receiver is not fixed by the liquidation committee or a meeting of creditors, it is calculated in the same way as the official receiver's remuneration.[3]

The liquidator's remuneration can be altered on his initiative if he considers it too low, or on the initiative of a group of creditors if they consider it too high. The liquidator can require the liquidation committee to reconsider the rate of his remuneration already fixed by it; and whatever the method by which his remuneration was calculated, the liquidator can apply to the court to order an increase in his remuneration.[4] The liquidator must give the liquidation committee at least 14 days' notice of his application to the court, and the liquidation committee may nominate one or more of its members to appear or be represented on the hearing of the application.[5] If

19 Insolvency Rules 1986, r 4.127(1) and (2).
20 Ibid, r 4.127(3) and 95).
 1 Ibid, r 127(4).
 2 Insolvency Regulations 1994 (SI 1994/2507), reg 33 and Sch 2, Table 9.
 3 Insolvency Rules 1986, r 4.127(6).
 4 Ibid, rr 4.129 and 4.130(1).
 5 Ibid, r 4.130(3).

there is no liquidation committee, the liquidator must send notice of his application to such of the company's creditors as the court directs, and they may nominate one or more of their number to appear or be represented on the hearing of the application.[6] Conversely, any creditor may, with the support of other creditors who together with himself account for at least one-quarter of the company's total indebtedness apply to the court for an order that the liquidator's remuneration shall be reduced because it is excessive.[7] The court may require the applicant for a reduction in the liquidator's remuneration to make out a prima facie case on an initial ex parte application before the court directs that the application shall be heard on a specified date; and in any case the applicant must serve a copy of this application on the liquidator, accompanied by a copy of the evidence he intends to use, at least 14 days before the hearing.[8] Applications to increase or reduce the liquidator's remuneration are heard in chambers by the registrar, but he may refer such an application for decision to a judge of the court which made the winding up order.[9] The remuneration of the official receiver cannot be altered from the scale fixed by regulations.

The liquidation committee in a winding up by the court

Constitution of the liquidation committee

A liquidation committee may be constituted to supervise the conduct of the liquidator in the winding up of a company by the court to receive certain periodic and other reports from him and to give or withhold its consent to the exercise of certain of his powers. If no such committee is constituted, its powers and functions are exercised by the Secretary of State for Trade and Industry, who acts through the official receiver.[10] If the official receiver is himself the liquidator, the powers and functions of the liquidation committee are exercised by the Secretary of State.[11]

The decision whether to constitute a liquidation committee is taken by the first meetings of creditors and contributories called to appoint a liquidator.[12] If the meeting of contributories resolves to establish a liquidation committee but the creditors' meeting does

6 Ibid, r 4.130(4).
7 Ibid, r 4.131(1).
8 Ibid, r 4.131(2) and (3).
9 Ibid, r 7.6(1) to (3).
10 Insolvency Act 1986, s 141(5); Insolvency Rules 1986, r 4.172(2).
11 Insolvency Act 1986, s 141(4).
12 Ibid, s 141(1).

not resolve to do so, or resolves that there shall be no liquidation committee, the meeting of contributories may appoint one of their number to apply to the court for an order directing that a further creditors' meeting shall be held to resolve that a liquidation committee shall be established and to appoint the creditors' representatives to it; the court may make such an order if it considers that there are special circumstances justifying it; if the creditors' meeting ordered by the court does not resolve to constitute a liquidation committee, the contributories' meeting may do so, and they may appoint between three and five contributories to be its members.[13]

If the first meeting of creditors resolves to establish a liquidation committee, the meeting may appoint as members of the committee representing the creditors between three and five creditors who have lodged proofs of their claims against the company for voting or dividend purposes, provided their proofs have not been rejected; and if the company is solvent (ie the winding up order was not made on the ground that the company is unable to pay its debts), the first meeting of contributories may add not more than three of their own members to be their representatives on the liquidation committee.[14] If a liquidation committee is not constituted by the first meetings of creditors and contributories, and the liquidator for the time being is not the official receiver, the liquidator may at any time call meetings of creditors and contributories for the purpose of establishing a liquidation committee and appointing its members, and he must do this if the court directs, or if he is requested to do so by creditors who are entitled to at least one-tenth of the company's total indebtedness.[15]

No person becomes a member of the liquidation committee unless he agrees to do so, and the liquidator cannot issue a certificate that the committee has been duly constituted (so as to bring it into being) until at least three creditors' representatives have been appointed to it, and if the company is solvent and the first meeting of contributories resolves to appoint members of the committee to represent contributories, until that meeting has appointed not more than three contributories to be such representatives.[16] The liquidator's certificate that the liquidation committee has been duly constituted must be filed in court.[17]

Any member of a liquidation committee may resign by giving written notice to the liquidator, and membership is automatically terminated by a member becoming bankrupt or making a composition

13 Ibid, s 141(3); Insolvency Rules 1986, r 4.154(1) to (4).
14 Insolvency Rules 1986, rr 4.151 and 4.152(1) and (3).
15 Insolvency Act 1986, s 168(2) and s 195(2).
16 Insolvency Rules 1986, r 4.154(1) to (4).
17 Ibid, r 4.153(5).

or arrangement with his creditors, or failing to attend three consecutive meetings of the committee either personally or by representative, unless the committee resolves that the absence of the member shall not terminate his membership.[18] If a member becomes bankrupt, his place on the committee is taken by his trustee in bankruptcy.[19] A representative of creditors on the liquidation committee additionally ceases to be a member if a meeting of creditors so resolves, and a representative of the contributories on the committee similarly ceases to be a member if a meeting of contributories so resolves.[20] A vacancy among the creditors' or contributories' representatives on the liquidation committee may be filled by resolution of a meeting of creditors or contributories (as the case may be), or by the liquidator with the consent of a majority of the members of the committee representing creditors or contributories (as the case may be). Nevertheless, the liquidator and a majority of the members of the committee representing creditors or contributories (as the case may be), may decide not to fill the vacancy, provided that the committee still comprises at least three creditors, or if the creditors have not appointed members of the committee at all, at least three contributories.[1]

Meetings of the liquidation committee

The liquidator must call the first meeting of the liquidation committee within three months after the committee is constituted, and must thereafter call meetings on the dates or at the intervals resolved on by the committee, and additionally whenever he is requested to do so by a creditors' representative on the committee, in which case the meeting must be held within 21 days after the liquidator receives the request.[2] The liquidator may also call a meeting of the liquidation committee at any time he thinks fit (eg to consent to the exercise by him of powers of which he requires the approval of the committee or the court).[2] Meetings of the committee are called by the liquidator giving at least seven days' written notice of the time and place of the meeting to each member of the committee, but members may individually waive notice or accept shorter notice.[3]

Members of the liquidation committee may attend committee meetings in person or by representatives appointed in writing by

18 Ibid, rr 4.160 and 4.161(1).
19 Ibid, r 4.161(2).
20 Ibid, r 4.162(1).
 1 Ibid, r 4.163(1) to (4) and r 4.164(1) to (4).
 2 Ibid, r 4.156(1) and (2).
 3 Ibid, r 4.156(3).

them individually, and for this purpose a proxy appointment to vote at meetings of creditors or contributories given by a member of the liquidation committee is deemed also to be an appointment of the proxy to be the representative of that member at meetings of the liquidation committee, unless the contrary is stated; representatives of members of the liquidation committee must be individuals, but need not be other members of the committee; any one individual (whether a committee member or not) may not represent more than one committee member, and a representative of a member of the committee may not attend committee meetings if he is an undischarged bankrupt or if he has made a composition or arrangement with his creditors.[4] Companies and other corporations may be members of a liquidation committee, but they can only attend at meetings of the committee by individuals appointed to represent them; the appointment by a corporate creditor or contributory of an individual to be its representative at meetings of creditors or contributories is deemed also to be the appointment of that individual to be the representative of the corporate creditor or contributory at meetings of the liquidation committee of which it is a member, unless the contrary is stated.[5]

The quorum at meetings of a liquidation committee is two creditors' representative members attending in person or by their representatives, but it would seem that if the creditors have declined to constitute a liquidation committee, there is a quorum if two members representing contributories, or the individual representatives of such members, attend the meeting.[6] The chairman at meetings of the committee is the liquidator or a person nominated by him who is a qualified insolvency practitioner in relation to the company, or an employee of the liquidator or his firm who is experienced in insolvency matters.[7]

At meetings of the liquidation committee, each member of it present in person or by representative has one vote, and resolutions are passed by a majority of the votes cast by the members of the committee who are or represent creditors, regardless of the respective amounts owing to them.[8] Members of the committee who are or represent contributories may vote and their votes must be recorded, but their votes do not count in determining whether a resolution has been passed, unless the creditors have not appointed any members of the committee to represent them, or unless the liquidator of the

4 Ibid, r 4.159(1), (2), (4) and (5).
5 Ibid, r 4.152(5) and r 4.189(2).
6 Ibid, r 4.158(1); *Sharp v Dawes* (1876) 2 QBD 26.
7 Insolvency Rules 1986, r 4.157(1) and (2).
8 Ibid, r 4.165(1) and (2).

company has filed in court a certificate by him that the company has paid all of its debts and liabilities in full (including interest from the commencement of the liquidation), whereupon the creditors' representatives cease to be members of the committee.[9] In these situations a resolution is passed if it is supported by a majority in number of the members of the liquidation committee representing contributories.[10]

The liquidator may obtain the consent of the liquidation committee to a proposed resolution by sending a copy of it by post to each member of the committee or his designated representative, and the resolution is deemed to be passed without a meeting being held when the liquidator has received written notifications from a majority in number of the members of the committee representing creditors or their respective representatives that they consent to it.[11] However, a resolution may not be passed by a postal vote if, within seven business days after the liquidator sends copies of the proposed resolution to members of the committee or their representatives, any member of the committee representing creditors requires the liquidator to call a meeting of the committee to consider the proposal.[12]

Information for the liquidation committee

The liquidator is under a duty to communicate to the liquidation committee all matters which appear to him to be of concern to the committee, or which the committee indicates to him it considers to be of concern to it.[13] However, the liquidator need not comply with a request for information made by the committee, if he considers that the request is frivolous or unreasonable, or that the cost of complying with the request would be excessive or that the company's resources are insufficient to cover the costs of complying with the request;[14] nor can the liquidation committee require the liquidator to disclose to it the statutory reports which he is required to make to the Secretary of State for Trade and Industry of conduct by directors of the company which may justify proceedings for their disqualification from being directors of any company.[15] The liquidator must report to the liquidation committee on the progress of the liquidation at intervals fixed by it, or on its calling for a report; but

9 Ibid, r 4.165(3) and r 4.171(1), (2) and (4).
10 Ibid, r 4.165(3).
11 Ibid, r 4.167(1), (2) and (5).
12 Ibid, r 4.167(3).
13 Ibid, r 4.155(1).
14 Ibid, r 4.155(2).
15 *Re W and A Glaser Ltd* [1994] BCC 199. The reports are made by the liquidator under the Company Directors' Disqualification Act 1986, s 7(3) and (4).

the liquidator cannot be required to report more frequently than once every two months, and if the committee does not give the liquidator directions as to his reports, he must report to it at least once every six months.[16]

Interests of members of the liquidation committee

Because members of the liquidation committee are appointed to protect the interests of the creditors and contributories of the company in liquidation, members of the committee, the persons they appoint as their representatives to attend committee meetings, the associates of members of the committee and of their representatives,[17] and persons who have been members of the committee within the preceding twelve months are prohibited from receiving any remuneration or consideration for their services out of the company's assets, and they are also prohibited from obtaining any profit out of the liquidation and from acquiring any of the company's assets.[18] These prohibitions do not apply if the court gives prior leave for the remuneration to be paid or for the transaction to be entered into, or if the transaction originated in a contract entered into before the winding up order was made and the committee member concerned obtains the court's leave to carry it out without undue delay, or if the liquidation committee gives its prior approval to the payment of the remuneration or the conclusion of the transaction by a resolution on which interested members of the committee and their representatives do not vote, or if the remuneration or transaction is justified by urgency.[18]

THE LIQUIDATOR AND LIQUIDATION COMMITTEE IN A VOLUNTARY WINDING UP

Appointment and vacation of office by the liquidator in a members' voluntary winding up

Appointment

The appointment of the liquidator or liquidators in a members' voluntary winding up is made by an ordinary resolution passed by

16 Insolvency Rules 1986, r 4.168(1) and (2).
17 Associates are defined by the Insolvency Act 1986, s 435, and include relatives by blood or marriage, partners, employers and employees, beneficiaries of a trust of which the person concerned is a trustee, and companies controlled by the person and his associates.
18 Insolvency Rules 1986, r 4.170(1) to (4).

a general meeting of the company, which may be either the general meeting which resolves to wind up the company or a later general meeting.[19] The Insolvency Rules 1986 do not apply to a members' voluntary winding up, except in certain limited respects;[20] and consequently, the resolution appointing the liquidator or liquidators is passed by a simple majority vote of the company's members voting in person or by proxy in accordance with the voting rights conferred on them by the company's articles of association or the Companies Act 1985.[1] Two or more individuals may be appointed to be co-liquidators in a members' voluntary winding up, and the same rules then apply as if the appointment were in a winding up by the court.[2]

If a vacancy occurs in the office of liquidator in a members' voluntary winding up, a general meeting of members or contributories of the company (which in a members' voluntary winding up means the members of the company at the date of the winding-up resolution, or the persons to whom they later transfer their shares with the consent of the liquidator)[3] may, subject to any arrangement made by them with the company's creditors, appoint a new liquidator or liquidators by ordinary resolution; a general meeting may be called for this purpose by any contributory, or if there is a liquidator or liquidators still holding office, by the liquidator or any of the liquidators.[4]

When a liquidator is appointed by a general meeting of contributories, the chairman of the meeting must certify the appointment in writing upon the liquidator providing him with a written statement that he is an insolvency practitioner holding a current authorisation to act as such, that he is qualified to act as the liquidator of the company, and that he consents to being appointed.[5] The qualifications for acting as a liquidator of a company in a members' voluntary liquidation are the same as for acting as a liquidator in a winding up by the court.[6] The liquidator must publish his appointment in the London Gazette and deliver a notice of it to the Registrar of Companies within 14 days after the date when his appointment is made, and must give notice of it to all creditors of the company of whom he is aware within 28 days after that date.[7]

19 Insolvency Act 1986, s 91(1).
20 Insolvency Rules 1986, r 4.1(1).
 1 Companies Act 1985, s 370(6).
 2 Interpretation Act 1978, s 6; Insolvency Act 1986, s 163, s 231(1) and (2), s 390(1) and (2) and s 393(1) and (3) (see p 119, ante).
 3 Insolvency Act 1986, s 88.
 4 Ibid, s 92(1) and (2).
 5 Insolvency Rules 1986, r 4.139(1) and (2).
 6 Insolvency Act 1986, s 388(1) and s 390(1) to (4) (see p 5, ante).
 7 Ibid, s 109(1); Insolvency Rules 1986, r 4.139(4).

If for any reason there is no liquidator of the company for the time being, the court may appoint a liquidator or liquidators on the application of a contributory, creditor or any other interested person (eg a liquidator who has ceased to be qualified as an insolvency practitioner);[8] and on the person appointed filing in court a statement that he is an insolvency practitioner qualified to act as the liquidator of the company and that he consents to act, the court issues a sealed copy of the order making the appointment to the liquidator, who must publish it in the London Gazette and give notice of it to the Registrar of Companies and to the creditors of the company in the same way as if he had been appointed by a general meeting of contributories.[9]

Resignation

A liquidator in a members' voluntary winding up may resign his office by giving notice to that effect to the Registrar of Companies, but before doing so, the liquidator must call a general meeting of contributories to accept his resignation.[10] The meeting is called in the same way as an extraordinary general meeting of the company while it was a going concern;[11] and the notice of the meeting sent to the contributories must be accompanied by an account of the liquidator's administration of the winding up, including a summary of his receipts and payments and a statement by him that he has reconciled his account with that held by the Secretary of State for Trade and Industry.[12]

The liquidator may resign only because of ill health, or because he intends to cease practising as an insolvency practitioner, or because of a conflict of interest or a change in personal circumstances which makes it impossible or impracticable for him to continue to discharge the functions of liquidator; if there are two or more liquidators acting jointly, a liquidator may also resign because, in the opinion of the resigning liquidator or the other liquidators, it is no longer expedient for all the liquidators to remain in office.[13]

If the general meeting does not accept the liquidator's resignation, it would appear that he may resign only if the court so decides on his satisfying it that one or more of the grounds set out above are applicable.[14] If the meeting called to accept the liquidator's resignation

---

8 *Re A J Adams (Builders) Ltd* [1991] BCLC 359, [1991] BCC 62.
9 Insolvency Act 1986, s 108(1) and s 109(1); Insolvency Rules 1986, r 4.140(1) to (4).
10 Insolvency Act 1986, s 171(5); Insolvency Rules 1986, r 4.142(1).
11 Companies Act 1985, s 369, s 370(2) and s 372(3).
12 Insolvency Rules 1986, r 4.142(2).
13 Ibid, r 4.142(3) and (4).
14 Insolvency Act 1986, s 112(1).

appoints a new liquidator in his place, the newly appointed liquidator must, when giving notice of his appointment to the creditors of the company, also give them notice of the resignation of his predecessor.[15]

Removal

The liquidator in a members' voluntary winding up may be removed from office by order of the court, or by an ordinary resolution passed by a general meeting of contributories; but if the liquidator was appointed by the court, a general meeting to remove the liquidator may be called only if the liquidator thinks fit, or if the court so directs, or if the meeting is requested by contributories who can exercise at least one half of the voting rights of all the contributories entitled to vote at a general meeting.[16] The court may require that when an application made to it to order the removal of the liquidator, or to direct that a meeting of contributories shall be held to resolve on his removal, the application shall be made ex parte in the first instance; and the court will then permit the applicant to serve a copy of the application on the liquidator only if a prima facie case is made for his removal on the hearing of the ex parte application.[17] The court may also order that the applicant for the removal of the liquidator, or the applicant for a meeting to be called to remove him, shall give security for the liquidator's costs incurred in connection with the application.[18] The applicant must send to the liquidator a notice of the time and place of the hearing directed by the court at least 14 days before the date of the hearing, and the notice must be accompanied by a copy of the evidence which the applicant intends to submit to the court.[19]

An application for an order removing the liquidator, or an order directing the calling of a general meeting to consider a proposal for his removal, is heard by the registrar of the court which would have jurisdiction to order the winding up of the company, but he may refer the application to a judge for decision.[20] If the court removes the liquidator from office, it sends two copies of the order of removal to him, one of which he must send to the Registrar of Companies together with a notice that he has ceased to act as liquidator.[1] The court may appoint a new liquidator in place of the liquidator whom it removes, and the new liquidator must then give the creditors of the

15 Insolvency Rules 1986, r 4.142(6).
16 Insolvency Act 1986, s 171(2) and (3).
17 Insolvency Rules 1986, r 4.143(1) and (2).
18 Ibid, r 4.143(3).
19 Ibid, r 4.143(4).
20 Ibid r 7.6(1) to (3).
 1 Ibid, r 4.143(5).

company notice of the removal of his predecessor when he gives them notice of his own appointment.[2]

Other causes for vacation of office

A liquidator in a members' voluntary winding up also ceases to hold office if he ceases to be qualified to act as an insolvency practitioner in relation to the company, or if he becomes disqualified from so acting.[3] On that happening, he must forthwith give notice of the fact to the Secretary of State for Trade and Industry and the Registrar of Companies.[4] If the liquidator dies, his personal representatives, or a partner in the firm of which the liquidator was a member and who is a qualified insolvency practitioner, must give notice of the liquidator's death to the Secretary of State for Trade and Industry and the Registrar of Companies.[5]

Appointment and vacation of office by the liquidator in a creditors' voluntary winding up

Appointment

If a company calls a general meeting of its members to pass a winding up resolution when a statutory declaration of solvency has not been made by its directors, it must, as explained above, also call a meeting of its creditors to be held not later than 14 days after the general meeting at which the winding up resolution is passed or proposed.[6] The members of the company and its creditors at their respective meetings may nominate one or more qualified insolvency practitioners to be the liquidator or liquidators of the company; the liquidator or liquidators will then be the person or persons resolved upon by the creditors' meeting, or if no such person is chosen, the liquidator or liquidators will be the person or persons resolved upon by the general meeting which passes the winding up resolution.[7] However, if different persons are chosen for appointment as liquidator by the two meetings, or if two or more persons are nominated by each of the meetings and they are not identical, any director, creditor or member of the company may, within seven days after the resolution

2 Ibid, r 4.140(4) and r 4.143(5).
3 Insolvency Act 1986, s 171(4).
4 Insolvency Rules 1986, r 4.146(2).
5 Ibid, r 4.145(1) and (2).
6 Insolvency Act 1986, s 98(1) (see p 89, ante).
7 Insolvency Act 1986, s 100(1) and (2).

of the creditors' meeting is passed, apply to the court having jurisdiction to wind up the company for an order either that the person or persons chosen for appointment as liquidator by the general meeting of members shall be the liquidator or liquidators of the company instead of, or jointly with, the person or persons chosen by the creditors' meeting, or that some other person or persons shall be appointed to be the liquidator or liquidators.[8] The application is heard by the registrar of the court, who may refer it to a judge for decision.[9]

The same rules apply, and the same application can be made to the court to appoint as liquidator the person chosen to be the liquidator by the contributories, or to appoint a person other than the liquidator appointed by the creditors' meeting, when the liquidator in a members' voluntary liquidation calls a meeting of creditors because he forms the opinion that the company will be unable to discharge its debts and liabilities in full within the period specified in the directors' declaration of solvency made before the winding up resolution was passed initiating the liquidation.[10]

Two or more individuals may be appointed to be co-liquidators in a creditors' voluntary winding up and the same rules then apply as in a winding up by the court.[11] When a person is chosen to be the liquidator by a meeting of creditors or contributories, the chairman of the meeting must certify the resolution of appointment on the person chosen providing a statement that he is an insolvency practitioner who is qualified to act as the liquidator of the company, and that he consents to act; if the meetings of creditors and contributories are held on the same day, however, the chairman of the meeting of contributories need not certify the appointment of the person chosen by them to be the liquidator if the creditors' meeting appoints a different person on the same day.[12] If the court appoints someone other than the person chosen by the creditors of the company, the court's order is issued only when the person appointed by it has filed in court a statement that he is an insolvency practitioner who is qualified to act as the liquidator of the company, and that he consents to act.[13]

If for any reason there is no liquidator acting in a creditors' voluntary winding up, the court may on the application of a contributory, creditor or other interested person (eg a liquidator

8 Ibid, s 100(3).
9 Insolvency Rules 1986, r 7.6(1) to (3).
10 Insolvency Act 1986, s 95(1) to (3) and s 96 (see p 91, ante).
11 Interpretation Act 1978, s 6; Insolvency Act 1986, s 163, s 231(1) and (2), s 388(1), s 390(1) and (2) and s 393(1) and (3) (see p 119, ante).
12 Insolvency Rules 1986, r 4.101(1), (2) and (4).
13 Ibid, r 4.103(1) and (2).

who has ceased to be qualified as an insolvency practitioner) appoint a qualified person to be the liquidator.[14]

A liquidator appointed by the court in a creditors' voluntary winding up must notify his appointment to all creditors of the company of whom he is aware within 28 days of his appointment, or if the court permits, he may instead advertise his appointment in the manner directed by the court.[15] If the liquidator is appointed by a meeting of creditors or contributories, he must advertise his appointment in such newspaper as he thinks most appropriate to bring it to the notice of the company's creditors and contributories.[16] In whatever manner the liquidator is appointed, he must publish his appointment in the London Gazette and notify it to the Registrar of Companies.[17]

Resignation

The liquidator in a creditors' voluntary winding up may resign by giving notice of his resignation to the Registrar of Companies in the same circumstances and with the same approval of a meeting of creditors or, alternatively, with the leave of the court, as is required in a winding up by the court.[18] When the liquidator resigns after a meeting of creditors has approved his proposal to do so, he must give notice of his resignation to the Registrar of Companies immediately following that meeting; and if the meeting appoints a new liquidator in place of the resigning liquidator, the chairman of the meeting must deliver a certificate of his appointment to the new liquidator.[19] If the court gives leave for the liquidator to resign, the court sends two sealed copies of its order to the liquidator, who must send one of them to the Registrar of Companies with his notice of resignation.[20] If a new liquidator is appointed in place of a liquidator who has resigned with leave of the court, he must give creditors of the company of whom he is aware notice of his predecessor's resignation when he gives them notice of his own appointment.[1]

Removal

A liquidator in a creditors' voluntary winding up may be removed from office by order of the court or by resolution of a meeting of

---

14 Insolvency Act 1986, s 108(1); *Re A J Adams (Builders) Ltd* [1991] BCLC 359, [1991] BCC 62.
15 Insolvency Rules 1986, r 4.103(3) and (4).
16 Ibid, r 4.106(1).
17 Insolvency Act 1986, s 109(1).
18 Ibid, s 171(1) and (5); Insolvency Rules 1986, r 4.108(1) and (3) to (5).
19 Insolvency Rules 1986, r 4.110(1) to (3).
20 Ibid, r 4.111(4).
 1 Ibid, r 4.103(4) and r 4.112.

creditors; such a meeting of creditors to resolve on the removal of the liquidator must be called if it is requested by one quarter in value of the company's creditors other than those who are connected with it (ie creditors who are directors or shadow directors of the company, or associates of such persons, or creditors which are companies controlled by the same persons as control the company in liquidation).[2] However, if the liquidator was appointed by the court because there was no liquidator acting at the time, a meeting of creditors must be called to remove him only if the liquidator thinks fit, or if the court so directs, or if the meeting is requested by not less than one half in value of the creditors.[3]

The liquidator or a person nominated by him may preside at a meeting of creditors which is called to resolve on his removal, but he may not adjourn the meeting without the consent of creditors entitled to at least one half of the company's total indebtedness to all the creditors present in person or by proxy and entitled to vote at the meeting.[4] Moreover, in that situation the creditors may elect a chairman other than the liquidator or a person nominated by him.[4] If the creditors' meeting resolves that the liquidator shall be removed, the chairman of the meeting must send a certificate of the liquidator's removal to the Registrar of Companies; but if a new liquidator is appointed by the meeting in place of the liquidator who is removed, the chairman must deliver the certificate of removal to the new liquidator, so that he may advertise the removal of his predecessor at the same time as the advertisement of his own appointment.[5]

The grounds and procedure for the removal of a liquidator by the court in a creditors' voluntary winding up are the same as on a removal by the court of a liquidator in a winding up by the court, as is the procedure on an application to the court for an order directing the liquidator to call a meeting of creditors to consider a proposal for his removal.[6] In particular, the court may remove the liquidator if he has been guilty of misconduct, or if he has lost the confidence of most of the company's creditors by acting in accordance with the wishes of the company's principal creditor without exploring the possibility of conducting the liquidation in a way more beneficial to the generality of its creditors.[7] If the court orders the removal of the liquidator, it sends him two sealed copies of the order, one of which

---

2 Insolvency Act 1986, s 171(1) and (2), s 249 and s 435(6); Insolvency Rules 1986, r 4.114(1).
3 Insolvency Act 1986, s 171(3).
4 Insolvency Rules 1986, r 4.114(3).
5 Ibid, r 4.106(1), r 4.117 and r 4.118.
6 Ibid, r 4.120(1) to (4) (see p 122, ante).
7 *Re Edennote Ltd, Tottenham Hotspur plc v Ryman* [1995] BCC 389; revsd [1996] BCC 718.

he must send to the Registrar of Companies; if the court appoints a
new liquidator in place of the one it removes, the new liquidator
must provide a statement that he is an insolvency practitioner
qualified to act as the liquidator of the company, and that he
consents to act, and he must give notice to all the creditors of the
company of whom he is aware that he has been appointed in place
of the former liquidator.[8]

Other causes for vacation of office

A liquidator in a creditors' voluntary winding up vacates office if
he ceases to be qualified to act as an insolvency practitioner in
relation to the company; upon this occurring, he must forthwith
give notice of the fact to the Registrar of Companies and the
Secretary of State for Trade and Industry.[9] On the death of a
liquidator in a creditors' voluntary winding up, his personal
representatives or, alternatively, a partner in the firm of which the
deceased liquidator was a member and who is himself a qualified
insolvency practitioner, must give notice of the liquidator's death
to the Registrar of Companies and to the liquidation committee (if
any) or to a member of it.[10]

The liquidator's remuneration in a voluntary winding up

In a members' voluntary winding up, it would appear that the form,
rate or amount of the liquidator's remuneration will be fixed by a
meeting of contributories, or if the liquidator is appointed by the
court because there is no liquidator acting, it will be fixed either by
the court or by such a meeting.[11] A power to fix the liquidator's
remuneration would appear to be incidental to the power to appoint
him. In a creditors' voluntary liquidation, the liquidator's
remuneration is fixed in the same way as in a winding up by the
court; and the same rules apply as to the form and rate of his
remuneration, the fixing and variation of his remuneration by the
liquidation committee (if any) and the increase or reduction of the
remuneration by the court.[12]

8 Insolvency Rules 1986, r 4.120(6).
9 Insolvency Act 1986, s 171(4); Insolvency Rules 1986, r 4.135(1) and (2).
10 Ibid, r 4.133(1) and (2).
11 Insolvency Act 1986, s 91(1) and s 108(1).
12 Insolvency Rules 1986, rr 4.127 to 4.131 (see above p 126, ante).

The liquidation committee

A liquidation committee may be established in a creditors' voluntary winding up on the initiative of the creditors, but not in a members' voluntary winding up.[13] The functions of the liquidation committee in a creditors' voluntary winding up are the same as in a winding up by the court, namely to supervise the liquidator's conduct of the winding up, to receive periodic and other reports from him, and to give or withhold its consent to the exercise of certain of his powers, although the number of powers in respect of which the committee's consent is required is smaller than in a winding up by the court.[14]

At the meeting of creditors that must be called within 14 days after the date of the general meeting which resolves that the company shall go into a creditors' voluntary liquidation, or at the meeting of creditors called by the liquidator in a members' voluntary liquidation when he forms the opinion that the company's debts and liabilities will not be fully discharged within the period specified in the directors' statutory declaration of solvency,[15] or at any subsequent meeting of creditors, the creditors may resolve to constitute a liquidation committee and to appoint as the creditors' representatives on the committee not more than five creditors who have lodged proofs for their claims which the liquidator has not rejected.[16] If the creditors constitute a liquidation committee, a meeting of contributories may, either at the meeting which passes the winding up resolution or at a subsequent general meeting, resolve to appoint up to five persons to represent contributories on the committee; however, a meeting of creditors may resolve that all or any of the persons nominated by the contributories shall not be members of the liquidation committee; they do not then become members of it unless the court so orders on an application made by any contributory, and on such an application the court may order that any person rejected by the creditors' meeting, or some other person or persons in his place, shall be members of the liquidation committee.[17] The application is heard by the registrar of the court in chambers, but he may refer it to a judge for decision.[18] In practice, the members or contributories usually resolve to appoint their representatives on the

13 Insolvency Act 1986, s 101(1) and (2).
14 See p 148, post.
15 Insolvency Act 1986, s 95(1) and (2) and s 98(1) (see pp 89 and 91, ante).
16 Ibid, s 101(1) and s 102; Insolvency Rules 1986, r 4.152(3).
17 Insolvency Act 1986, s 101(2) and (3).
18 Insolvency Rules 1986, r 7.6(1) to (3).

liquidation committee at the general meeting which passes the winding up resolution, in anticipation that the creditors at their first meeting will resolve to constitute a liquidation committee.

The rules governing meetings of the liquidation committee in a creditors' voluntary winding up are the same, or substantially the same, as the rules applicable to a liquidation committee in a winding up by the court.[19] This includes the rules governing the person who acts as chairman, the quorum for the holding of a meeting, the appointment of representatives by members of the committee, the representatives of corporate creditors and contributories who are members of the committee, vacancies on the committee and the filling of them, postal resolutions, reports by the liquidator to the committee and his obligation to provide it with information about the liquidation, the prohibition on dealings connected with the liquidation by members of the committee and their associates, and the reconstruction of the committee when the debts and liabilities of the company have been fully discharged. The only material differences are, first, that if a meeting of contributories in a creditors' voluntary winding up appoints a person to fill a vacancy among the contributories' representatives on the committee, the members of the committee representing creditors may resolve that the appointee shall not be a member of it; he does not then become a member unless the court so directs, and the court may appoint another person or persons to fill the vacancy instead.[20] Secondly, each member of the committee or his representative has one vote on a resolution proposed at a committee meeting; a resolution is passed by a meeting of the committee if a majority of the members of it (and not only those members who represent creditors) who are present in person or by representative vote in favour of it.[1] Additionally if it is proposed to pass a resolution of the committee by the affirmative postal vote of a majority of its members, any member of the committee (and not only one representing creditors) may require a meeting of the committee to be held instead; in the absence of such a request, the resolution is deemed to have been passed if a majority in number of all the members of the committee (and not only those members who represent creditors) assent to it in writing.[2]

---

19 Ibid, r 152(4) and (5), r 153, r 4.155 to 4.164 and rr 4.166 to 4.171 (see pp 128 to 132, ante).
20 Ibid, r 4.164(5).
 1 Ibid, r 4.166(1).
 2 Ibid, r 4.167(4) and (6).

THE STATUS AND POWERS OF THE LIQUIDATOR

The status of the liquidator

The liquidator in the winding up of the company under an order of the court or in a voluntary winding up is the person who is responsible for carrying out the winding up process. In fulfilling his functions he acts as an agent of the company, and is therefore not personally liable for the breach of contracts which he enters into in carrying out his functions,[3] provided he does not enter into personal commitments and makes it clear that he enters into the contracts in a representative and not in a personal capacity.[4] To enable a liquidator to manifest the representative capacity in which he acts and so avoid personal contractual liability, the Insolvency Act 1986 directs that in all transactions which he concludes or carries out he shall be described as 'the liquidator', and that he shall not be described by his individual name.[5] This provision is merely directory, however, and if a liquidator is a party to a deed or document in which he is described by his own name, he is not taken to be a party in his personal capacity if the document makes it clear that he is acting as liquidator, or if the document will be effective only if he is treated as acting in that capacity (eg a conveyance of land belonging to the company).

A liquidator (other than the official receiver in a winding up by the court) may be appointed by a meeting of creditors, by a meeting of contributories or members of the company, or by the Secretary of State or the court in accordance with the rules already dealt with. The manner of his appointment in no way affects the status of the liquidator, however. He acts as an agent of the company, but he is also an officer of the company for the purposes of the Companies Act 1985.[6] The company's assets do not vest in him, in the way that the assets of a person against whom a bankruptcy order has been made vest in his trustee in bankruptcy on his appointment.[7] Consequently, the liquidator disposes of and deals with the company's assets in exercise of the statutory powers conferred on him, and not

---

3 *Re Anglo-Moravian Hungarian Junction Rly Co, ex p Watkin* (1875) 1 Ch D 130, 133 per James LJ; *Re Silver Valley Mines Ltd* (1882) 21 Ch D 381, 386 per Jessel MR; *Stead, Hazel & Co v Cooper* [1933] 1 KB 840.
4 *Plant Engineers (Sales) Ltd v Davis* (1969) 113 Sol Jo 484.
5 Insolvency Act 1986, s 163.
6 *Re X Co Ltd* [1907] 2 Ch 92; *Re Windsor Steam Coal Co (1901) Ltd* [1929] 1 Ch 151, 167 per Lawrence LJ.
7 Insolvency Act 1986, s 306(1).

as the owner of those assets, or as a trustee of those assets for the company or its creditors' contributories or members.

Nevertheless, it has been held that when a company goes into liquidation, its assets are impressed with a trust for the benefit of its creditors, and if it is solvent, also for the benefit of its members or contributories.[8] This does not make the liquidator a trustee, however, despite the fact that in carrying out his functions he is subject to fiduciary duties similar to those of trustees.[9] The trust is imposed on the company, which remains the legal owner of its assets, and not on the liquidator personally.

Despite the rule that the assets of the company in liquidation do not vest in its liquidator by operation of law, it is possible for the court to order that any assets owned or held in trust for the company shall vest in the liquidator by his official name, and he may then bring or defend legal proceedings relating to those assets, or for the purpose of recovering or dealing with them in the liquidation, by suing, defending or acting in his official name.[10] In practice, it is rarely necessary for the court to make an order vesting any of the company's assets in the liquidator, and no advantage is obtained by such an order being made.

The functions and powers of the liquidator

The functions of a liquidator are stated by the Insolvency Act 1986 to be to recover and realise the company's assets and to distribute the assets or the proceeds of realisation between the company's creditors, and if there is a surplus after discharging the company's debts and liabilities in full, among the company's shareholders or the other persons entitled.[11] The statutory functions define the scope of the liquidator's task in the same way as the objects set out in a company's memorandum of association define the purposes for which the powers conferred on its directors by statute and the company's articles of association may be used. It follows, therefore, that since a liquidator's powers are wholly statutory, being defined exhaustively by the Insolvency Act 1986, he can do an act or enter

---

8 *IRC v Olive Mill Spinners Ltd* [1963] 2 All ER 130, [1963] 1 WLR 712; *Pritchard v MH Builders (Wilmslow) Ltd* [1969] 1 WLR 409; *Ayerst v C & K (Construction) Ltd* [1976] AC 167, [1975] 2 All ER 537.
9 See p 172, post.
10 Insolvency Act 1986, s 145(1) and (2).
11 Ibid, s 143(1). This relates to a winding up by the court. The liquidator's functions in a voluntary liquidation are similarly described by the Insolvency Act 1986, s 91(1) and s 100(1).

into a transaction only if it is both expressly authorised by the Act and if the purpose to be achieved in the particular instance is the fulfilment of one or more of the liquidator's functions. It is for this reason that the liquidator can exercise his statutory power to carry on the company's business so far as may be necessary for the beneficial winding up of the company only if his purpose is to discover whether such a sale may eventually be a practical possibility, but not for the purpose of making the company's business viable as a going concern so that a new company with the same shareholders as the company in liquidation may take it over.[12]

General powers

The liquidator in every winding up, whether by order of the court or voluntary, is given a wide range of powers which he may exercise on his own initiative and at his own discretion without the need for any preliminary authorisation by any other person.[13] These powers enable the liquidator in most liquidations to carry out all the operations required for a complete winding up of the company's affairs without the need to seek the approval or concurrence of the court, the liquidation committee or a meeting of creditors or contributories. These general powers, which the liquidator can exercise without prior authorisation, comprise the following:[13]

(1) to sell any of the company's property and assets by auction or private contract, and either piecemeal or in parcels or as a whole, and to transfer the company's assets in the same way; this power enables the liquidator to sell the company's business undertaking, or any of its separate business undertakings, or parts of them as going concerns, or to sell individual assets or packages of assets (such as stock in trade), and also to give effect to contracts of sale by transferring the company's title to the purchasers;

(2) to do all acts and to execute in the name and on behalf of the company all deeds and other documents, and for that purpose to use the company's seal; this power enables the liquidator to give legal effect to all transactions into which he enters in order to carry out the winding up of the company's affairs, for example, to transfer title to the company's goods by delivery to the transferee, to give consents on the company's behalf to

---

12 *Re Wreck Recovery and Salvage Co* (1880) 15 Ch D 353; *Re Great Eastern Electric Co Ltd* [1941] Ch 241, [1941] 1 All ER 409.
13 Insolvency Act 1986, s 165(1) and (3), s 167(1) and Sch 4, Part III, paras 6 to 13.

acts by other persons, to convey the company's land or to assign intangible personal property, such as patents, trade marks, copyright and know-how;

(3) to prove, rank and claim in the insolvency of any person, firm or company against whom or which the company in liquidation has a claim, and to receive dividends in the insolvency;

(4) to draw, accept, make and indorse bills of exchange, cheques or promissory notes in the name and on behalf of the company, with the same effect as regards the company's liability as though the instrument had been drawn, accepted, made or indorsed by the company itself in the course of its business; the liquidator of a bank may, for example, accept a bill of exchange in its name under a letter of credit issued by it before the winding up began, or a liquidator may draw a cheque on the bank account of a company in liquidation in order to fulfil a contract which it entered into before it went into liquidation, or in order to fulfil a contract which the liquidator has entered into for the purpose of the winding up; the liquidator's signature should be accompanied by words which not only describe him as liquidator of the company, but also state that he signs for or on behalf of the company so as to avoid him incurring personal liability on the instrument;[14]

(5) to raise any money required for the purpose of the liquidation on the security of any of the assets of the company; the form of security is left to the discretion of the liquidator, and so if the borrowing is for a proper purpose, the security is valid whether it is a pledge of goods or documents relating to them (eg bills of lading, warehouse warrants), a legal or equitable mortgage or charge over land, a mortgage by assignment (whether legal or equitable) of things in action or intangible personal property or an equitable charge over such property, or even, it would seem, a floating charge over a class of the company's assets, such as a floating charge over present and future book debts of the company's business which the liquidator is carrying on with a view to selling it as a going concern;

(6) to extract in his official name as liquidator, letters of administration to the estate of a deceased contributory, and to do in his official name as liquidator any other act which is necessary to obtain payment of any money due from a contributory or his estate, if the act cannot be done conveniently in the name of the company; the liquidator

---

14 *Dutton v Marsh* (1871) LR 6 QB 361; *Landes v Marcus and Davids* (1909) 25 TLR 478; *Rolfe Lubell & Co v Keith* [1979] 1 All ER 860.

would in such a situation extract letters of administration in his own name, but expressly as the representative of the company to which the deceased contributory owed the unpaid part of the issue price of his shares; the liquidator could similarly extract letters of administration to the estate of a deceased debtor of the company in exercise of his powers under (8) below;

(7) to appoint an agent to do any business which the liquidator is unable to do personally; this power appears to be wide enough to enable the liquidator to employ any professional or other agent whose services are requisite for carrying out the winding up of the company's affairs, and in appropriate situations this would include accountants, banks, auctioneers, surveyors, brokers, shipping and forwarding agents and debt collection agencies; coupled with his power to execute deeds in the company's name and on its behalf, this power would appear to enable the liquidator to execute a power of attorney conferring powers on an agent, including the power to execute deeds in the company's name; and

(8) to do all such other things as may be necessary for winding up the company's affairs and distributing its assets; this appears to be an independent power, and should not be construed as restricted to matters which are ejusdem generis with the preceding specific powers; on the other hand, if specific powers are conferred on a liquidator by the Insolvency Act 1986, subject to the fulfilment of certain conditions, the conditions cannot be disregarded by the liquidator purporting to act in exercise of the present power.[15]

Qualified powers in a winding up by the court

There are two powers which a liquidator in a winding up by the court can exercise only with the approval of the court or of the liquidation committee,[16] or if there is no such committee or if the official receiver is the liquidator, with the approval of the court or the Secretary of State for Trade and Industry.[17] In a voluntary winding up the liquidator can exercise the powers on his own initiative and without any approval.[18] The powers are:[19]

15 *Re Phoenix Oil and Transport Co Ltd (No 2)* [1958] Ch 565, [1958] 1 All ER 158.
16 Insolvency Act 1986, s 167(1).
17 Ibid, s 141(4) and (5) and s 167(1).
18 Ibid, s 165(3).
19 Ibid, Sch 4, paras 4 and 5.

(1) to bring or defend any action or other legal proceedings in the name and on behalf of the company; in exercise of this power the liquidator can sue in the company's name to enforce all rights of action vested in it at the date of the winding up order or subsequently accruing to the company; on the other hand, applications to the court in the liquidation proceedings are brought under the provisions of the Insolvency Act 1986 and the Insolvency Rules 1986, and are made by or against the liquidator in his official name, and not by or against the company, despite the fact that its name appears in the title for the application, and so the liquidator requires no consent to bringing or defending such applications;[20] and

(2) to carry on the business of the company so far as may be necessary for its beneficial winding up; as has already been observed, this power cannot be used by the liquidator to carry on the company's business indefinitely or with the object of rendering an insolvent company solvent, and the court will give approval for the continuance of the company's business, but only for a limited period, if the liquidator shows that there is a prospect of selling the business as a going concern or of selling the assets comprised in it piecemeal, and in either case it is likely that a higher price will be realised than if the company's assets were sold piecemeal immediately.[1]

Qualified powers in all liquidations

Whether the liquidation is by order of the court or voluntary, there are three powers which a liquidator can exercise only with approval. In a winding up by the court, the approval must be given by the court or by the liquidation committee,[2] or if there is no liquidation committee or the official receiver is the liquidator, by the court or the Secretary of State for Trade and Industry.[3] In a members' voluntary winding up the approval must be given by the members in general meeting passing an extraordinary resolution, and in a creditors' voluntary winding up, approval must be given by the court or the liquidation committee, but if there is no such committee, approval may be given in its place by a meeting of the company's creditors.[4] The powers which the liquidator may exercise only with such approval are:[5]

---

20 *Re Silver Valley Mines Ltd* (1882) 21 Ch D 381.
 1 See p 145, ante.
 2 Insolvency Act 1986, s 167(1).
 3 Ibid, s 141(4) and (5) and s 167(1).
 4 Ibid, s 165(2).
 5 Ibid, s 165(1) and s 167(1) and Sch 4, paras 1 to 3.

(1) to pay any class of creditors in full; the liquidator must ensure that the remaining assets of the company are sufficient to enable him also to pay all debts and liabilities of the company which rank for payment in priority to, or equally with, the debts and liabilities of the company which the liquidator pays in full, and so the liquidator's power to pay a class of debts in full extends only to determining the chronological order in which different classes of liabilities are discharged, and he cannot make payments so as to give a class of creditors priority for payment over other classes when it is not given to them by law;

(2) to make compromises or arrangements with any creditors or claimants against the company, whether their debts or claims are liquidated or unliquidated, and whether they are accrued due or payable only in the future or subject to fulfilment of a contingency; it has been held that this power does not enable the liquidator to compel creditors or claimants to accept a compromise or arrangement, even if it is accepted by a majority of all the creditors or claimants, but merely enables the liquidator to make compromises or arrangements with creditors or claimants to which they individually agree;[6] on the other hand the Court of Appeal has held that the court may approve a compromise or arrangement binding on the companys creditors despite the dissent of a majority or minority in value of their number if the liquidator's proposals are the best which can be devised without protracting the liquidation excessively and incurring disproportionate costs;[7]

(3) to agree to compromises with any contributories in respect of their liability for the amount unpaid on their shares, or otherwise in respect of their liabilities as contributories (eg as shareholders in an unlimited company), or in respect of the company's liabilities to them (eg for declared but unpaid dividends, and for accrued amounts payable by the company on the purchase or redemption of its shares), and to agree to compromises with contributories in respect of questions relating to, or affecting, the assets or the winding up of the company (eg questions as to the ownership or entitlement to the use of assets); again under this power the liquidator cannot compel contributories or other persons to submit to compromises which they do not accept individually.[6]

---

6 *Re Trix Ltd* [1970] 3 All ER 397, [1970] 1 WLR 1421. For compromises and arrangements which may be made binding by a majority accepting them, see chapter 8.

7 *Re Bank of Credit and Commerce International SA (No 3)* [1993] BCLC 1490, [1992] BCC 715.

Notification of the exercise of powers

In a winding up by the court, if the liquidator (other than the official receiver) appoints a solicitor to assist him in carrying out his functions, or if the liquidator disposes of any assets of the company in liquidation to a person who is connected with it (ie a director or shadow director[8] of the company, or an associate of such a director or shadow director, or an associate of the company itself),[9] the liquidator must notify the liquidation committee that he has exercised his power to do either of these things and give it particulars of the action he has taken.[10]

A person is an associate of another person who is a director or a shadow director of the company in liquidation if the first mentioned person is his spouse, or a relative of him or his spouse, or is his partner or the spouse of his partner, or is his employer or employee, or is the trustee of a trust in which he is beneficially interested (other than a trust in respect of a pension scheme or an employees' share scheme); a company is an associate of another company if the person who, or the group of persons which, controls one of them also controls the other, either alone or with his or its associates; and a company is an associate of another individual or company if that person either alone or with his or its associates controls the first company.[11]

The obligation of the liquidator under the present provision is merely to notify the liquidation committee when he appoints a solicitor or makes a disposition of the company's assets to a person connected with it; the provision does not require the liquidator to consult the liquidation committee or to obtain its approval. If there is no liquidation committee, the liquidator need not inform the Secretary of State for Trade and Industry as the repository of the powers of a liquidation committee if none has been appointed. The notification requirement does not apply to a creditors' voluntary winding up.

8 A shadow director is a person in accordance with whose directions or instructions the directors of a company are accustomed to act (Companies Act 1985, s 741(2); Insolvency Act 1986, s 251).

9 Insolvency Act 1986, s 167(2) and ss 249 and 435. For the court's power to set aside transactions of a liquidator with his associate and the accountability of such persons for profits made from such transactions, see p 172, post.

10 Insolvency Act 1986, s 167(2).

11 Ibid, s 435(1) to (7).

The power of disclaimer

Scope of the power

In any liquidation, whether under an order of the court or voluntary, the liquidator may by giving the prescribed notice[12] to the persons interested in any onerous property of the company exercise a statutory power to disclaim it, and he may exercise the power of disclaimer even though he has taken possession of the property, attempted to sell it, or otherwise exercised rights of ownership over it.[13] Onerous property which may be disclaimed comprises unprofitable contracts entered into by the company, and any other property of the company which is not saleable or not readily saleable, or which may give rise to a liability to pay money or to perform any other onerous act.[14]

A contract is unprofitable if the cost of performing the company's obligations under it is likely to exceed the amount of any payment or the value of any benefit which the company is entitled to receive in return. A contract is not unprofitable, however, if the profit likely to be obtained from it is small, or if the liquidator could obtain a greater profit by entering into an identical contract proposed by a third person who is willing to pay a higher price or give a more valuable consideration to the company than it would obtain under the original contract.[15] In judging whether a contract is unprofitable, it would seem that the amount or value of the consideration which the company is entitled to receive under the contract is the only relevant factor to be compared with the cost of the liquidator of carrying out the contract. The fact that the other party to the contract is unable or unwilling to provide that consideration, so that the company will be left with a claim for damages if it performs its part of the contract, would not seem to justify the liquidator in disclaiming the contract. The proper course in that situation would appear to be for the liquidator to call for an assurance from the other party that he will perform his obligations notwithstanding that the company has gone into liquidation, and on this assurance being refused or the other party failing to fulfil his obligations under the contract, the liquidator should terminate the contract under the

12 For the form of the prescribed notice see Insolvency Rules 1986, r 4.187(1) and Sch 4, Form 4.53.
13 Insolvency Act 1986, s 178(1) and (2).
14 Ibid, s 178(3).
15 *Re Bastable* [1901] 2 KB 518.

general rules of contract law and, if appropriate, claim damages from the other party.

Under the former legislation, the liquidator's power of disclaimer extended to land of any tenure burdened with onerous covenants, to shares or stock in companies and to any other property which was unsaleable or not readily saleable by reason of its binding its possessor to the performance of any onerous act or to the payment of money.[16] The present power of disclaimer is wider in that it extends to property of any kind which is not saleable or not readily saleable for any reason (eg the collapse or disappearance of a market for it), and it is no longer necessary that the property should be burdened by continuing obligations, or that its possession or ownership should expose the company or the liquidator to a substantial risk of liability to third persons in contract or tort.[17] Conversely, if the property is burdened by continuing obligations, which include restrictive covenants imposed on land,[18] it is possible for the liquidator to disclaim the property even though it is not unsaleable, although in that situation he would be best advised to sell the property for whatever price he can get without giving an indemnity undertaking to the purchaser. Shares held by the company in liquidation in other companies may be disclaimed on the ground that they are unsaleable, even though they are fully paid and were issued by limited companies so that there is no outstanding liability for any part of the issue price, and probably this was so under the previous legislation. On the other hand, there is nothing to be gained by disclaiming such shares, unless the company may incur a collateral liability in respect of them, for example because the company in liquidation has become the sole remaining member of a public company in which the shares are held, and so may become statutorily liable for its future debts.[19]

There is now no limit on the time within which a liquidator may disclaim onerous property after the commencement of the liquidation or the date of his appointment, as there was under the former legislation,[20] but the liquidator cannot disclaim any contract or property more than 28 days (or such longer period as the court directs) after any person interested in the contract or property has applied in writing to him or any previous liquidator of the company

---

16 Companies Act 1985, s 618(1).
17 See *Re Potter's Oils Ltd* [1985] BCLC 203; *Re Potter's Oil Ltd (No 2)* (1985) 1 BCC 593.
18 *Re Mercer and Moore* (1880) 14 Ch D 287.
19 Under the Companies Act 1985, s 24, as amended by Companies (Single Member Private Limited Companies) Regulations 1992 (SI 1992/1699), reg 2(1) and Schedule, para 4.
20 Companies Act 1985, s 618(3).

to decide whether he will disclaim it or not, and so unless a notice
of disclaimer has been given within that period to one or more of the
persons who are interested in the contract or property, it cannot be
disclaimed.[1]

There are additional special provisions governing the disclaimer
of leases and underleases of land by a liquidator. A disclaimer of a
lease or underlease vested in the company does not take effect,
unless the liquidator serves a copy of the prescribed notice of
disclaimer on every person claiming under the company as an
underlessee or mortgagee whose address is known to the liquidator,
and either no application to the court for a vesting order is made by
any person who is interested in the lease or underlease or under a
liability in respect of it within 14 days after the last copy of the notice
of disclaimer is served, or if such an application is made, the court
nevertheless directs that the disclaimer shall take effect.[2] The only
power which the court has if such an application is made within the
period of 14 days is to make an order vesting the lease or underlease
in the applicant or in one of the applicants if there are more than
one,[3] and so the disclaimer will take effect if no successful application
for a vesting order is made.

The court may set aside any exercise of the liquidator's power
of disclaimer if it considers that the liquidator has acted in bad faith,
or has misused the power of disclaimer, or has exercised the power
wholly unreasonably (eg where the disclaimed contract or property
has a substantial and realisable value).[4] The effect of the court's
order setting aside the disclaimer will be to restore the position of the
company and other interested parties to that which existed before
the liquidator disclaimed.

The effect of a disclaimer

The effect of a disclaimer of an unprofitable contract or any onerous
property by the liquidator is to terminate as from the date of the
disclaimer the rights, interests and liabilities of the company in, or
in respect of, the contract or property, but the disclaimer does not
affect the rights or liabilities of any other person, except so far as
necessary for the purpose of releasing the company from liability.[5]

The result of the termination of the company's interest in
disclaimed property is that its interest becomes ownerless, and

1 Insolvency Act 1986, s 178(5).
2 Ibid, s 179(1).
3 Ibid, s 181(3).
4 *Re Hans Place Ltd* [1993] BCLC 768, [1992] BCC 737.
5 Insolvency Act 1986, s 178(4).

consequently vests in the Crown under the general law,[6] or in the case of freehold land, escheats the Crown.[7] It was formerly held that this applied also to a lease or underlease granted to the company,[8] but it has more recently been held that if the company is the original lessee or underlessee and the lease or underlease has not been assigned, the lease or underlease simply terminates.[9] It has also been held that where the company has granted an underlease out of the lease granted to it and its liquidator disclaims the lease, the lease is simply terminated, as are the company's and the underlessee's covenants in the underlease; the underlessee then has merely a status of irremovability by the company's lessor until the expiration of the term granted by the underlease, but the lessor may nevertheless forfeit the underlease and re-enter the property comprised in it under a proviso for forfeiture contained in the lease, and the underlessee's status or irremovability will terminate if he does not apply to the court for an order vesting the lease in himself.[10]

Whether personal rights of the company, such as rights under a disclaimed contract, vest in the Crown is uncertain, but it would appear that such rights simply terminate, and it is certain that contractual rights do so.[9] This question is of little importance in practice, however, because the Crown would have no reason to adopt these rights or the contract under which they arise in view of the unprofitability of the contract, and it is clear that the Crown incurs no liability in connection with disclaimed property or a disclaimed contract until it does exercise or claim rights in respect of it.[11]

Of more importance is the question whether and to what extent third persons are released by a disclaimer from obligations collateral to those of the company, such as those of a guarantor of the company's obligations under a disclaimed contract, the liability of the original lessee of property to the lessor under a lease which has been assigned to the company and disclaimed by its liquidator, and the liability of a intermediate assignee of a lease which has subsequently been assigned to the company and disclaimed by its liquidator when the intermediate assignee has given a general indemnity undertaking to his assignor in respect of the future

6 *Re Mercer and Moore* (1880) 14 Ch D 287; *Re Levy* (1881) 17 Ch D 746.
7 *Scmlla Properties Ltd v Gesso Properties (BVI) Ltd* [1995] BCC 793.
8 *Re Wells, Swinburne-Hanham v Howard* [1933] Ch 29.
9 *Warnford Investments Ltd v Duckworth* [1979] Ch 127, [1978] 2 All ER 517; *Hindcastle Ltd v Barbara Attenborough Associates Ltd* [1997] AC 70, [1996] 1 All ER 737.
10 *Re Thompson and Cottrell's Contract* [1943] Ch 97, [1943] 1 All ER 169; *Re AE Realisations (1985) Ltd* [1987] 3 All ER 83, [1988] 1 WLR 200. See also *Hindcastle Ltd v Barbara Attenborough Associates Ltd*, supra.
11 See Insolvency Act 1986, s 180(2), exonerating the Crown from liability for a rentcharge on disclaimed land, unless it takes possession or control of the land.

payment of rent and the future fulfilment of the lessee's other obligations under the lease.

It was held that under the former bankruptcy legislation (which was identical in this respect to the former winding up legislation) and under the former winding up legislation itself, that a guarantor of the company's obligations under a contract (including a lease or underlease or an assignment of it) was released from his obligations as a surety by the disclaimer of the contract or lease by the company's liquidator, because if he were not released and were compelled to fulfil those obligations, he would have a claim to an indemnity from the company, and so the company would not be effectively released, as the legislation intended.[12] Consequently, the court would not give leave under the former legislation for a liquidator to disclaim a lease where a surety had guaranteed the payment of rent and the fulfilment of the company's obligations as lessee, because if the disclaimer were permitted, the lessor would lose his rights against the surety as well as against the company. Consistently with this, it was held in another case that if the reversion on the lease to the company had been conveyed by the original lessor to a purchaser who did not take an express assignment of the guarantee given by the surety to the original lessor, and so was not entitled to the benefit of the guarantee, the court would permit the liquidator to disclaim the lease because the purchaser of the reversion would not thereby be deprived of the guarantee.[13] It has now been held by the House of Lords, however, that a guarantee of a company's obligations is not terminated by the disclaimer of the contract, lease or other transaction to which the guarantee relates; the surety remains liable under the guarantee as though the contract etc were still effective, but the company's obligations are terminated.[14] The present legislation does not require leave of the court to be obtained for any disclaimer by the liquidator, and there is consequently no impediment to a liquidator disclaiming, even though a consequence of him doing so would be the termination of the company's obligations under the lease and the continuance of any guarantee of those obligations without any right for the surety to claim an indemnity out of the company's assets.[15]

It was held by the House of Lords under the former bankruptcy legislation,[16] and has been confirmed by the House of Lords[14] and

12 *Stacey v Hill* [1901] 1 KB 660; *Re Katherine et Cie Ltd* [1932] 1 Ch 70; *Warnford Investments Ltd v Duckworth*, supra.
13 *Re Distributors and Warehousing Ltd* [1986] BCLC 129, 1 BCC 570.
14 *Hindcastle Ltd v Barbara Attenborough Associates Ltd* [1997] AC 70, [1996] 1 All ER 737.
15 *Re Yarmarine (IW) Ltd* [1992] BCLC 276 [1992] BCC 28; *Re Hans Place Ltd* [1993] BCLC 768, [1992] BCC 737.
16 *Hill v East and West India Dock Co* (1884) 9 App Cas 448.

courts of first instance under the present legislation governing both bankruptcy and company liquidations,[17] that the obligations of the original grantee of a lease or underlease which has been assigned (whether immediately or by a succession of assignments) to an individual whose trustee in bankruptcy, or to a company whose liquidator, disclaims the lease or underlease are not discharged, and that the lease or underlease continues in existence so as to preserve the original lessee's or underlessee's obligations to the lessor or underlessor by privity of contract. It would appear that the same reasoning would apply to preserve the obligation of an intermediate assignee of a lease or underlease which is subsequently assigned to a company whose liquidator disclaims it where the intermediate assignee has given a general indemnity undertaking to his assignor in respect of the future payment of rent and the future performance of the lessee's or underlessee's covenants in the lease or underlease. Because the obligations of an original lessor or underlessor under a lease or underlease which has been assigned to a company and then disclaimed by its liquidator are based upon the continuance of the disclaimed lease or underlease, it follows that the lease or underlease must on the disclaimer vest in the Crown as ownerless property, subject to the power of the court (dealt with below) to make vesting orders in respect of it.

The problem of the liability of an original lessee or underlessee who has assigned the lease or underlease to an assignee whose trustee in bankruptcy or in the case of a corporate assignee, whose liquidator, disclaims the lease or underlease, will be less taxing in future because if the lease or underlease is granted on or after 1 January 1996, the original lessee or underlessee will be automatically discharged from liability for future rent and the future fulfilment of the lessee's or underlessee's covenants upon the lease or underlease being assigned.[18]

Vesting orders and damage claims

When a liquidator has disclaimed a contract or property, any person who claims an interest in it, or who is under a liability in respect of it which is not released by the disclaimer, may apply to the court to make an order vesting the disclaimed contract or property in him or

---

17 *Warnford Investments Ltd v Duckworth*, supra; *W H Smith Ltd v Wyndham Investments Ltd* [1994] 2 BCLC 571, [1994] BCC 699; *Hindcastle v Barbara Attenborough Associates Ltd* [1997] AC 70, [1996] 1 All ER 737.
18 Landlord and Tenant (Covenants) Act 1995, s 1(1) and (3), s 5(1) and (2), and s 31(1).

in a trustee for him, and the court may make such a vesting order on such terms as it thinks fit.[19] For this purpose an interest in a disclaimed lease includes that of an underlessee or subtenant whose own tenancy has terminated but who remains in possession of property comprised in the lease as a statutory tenant protected by the Rent Acts.[20] Where the applicant claims no interest in the disclaimed contract or property but remains under a liability in respect of it, the court may make a vesting order only for the purpose of compensating him for the liability,[1] and so if the liability is a purely nominal one and is unlikely to be enforced, or has ceased to exist,[2] the court will refuse to make a vesting order.

If the liquidator disclaims a lease or underlease vested in the company, the court may make an order vesting it in an underlessee or mortgagee only on terms that he shall take the lease or underlease subject to the same liabilities and obligations as the company was under in respect of it at the commencement of the liquidation, or, alternatively, that he shall take the lease or underlease subject to the same liabilities and obligations as if the company had assigned it to him at the commencement of the liquidation.[3] The difference between these alternative orders is that under the first the person in whose favour a vesting order is made is liable to the lessor or underlessor for rent accrued due and breaches of lessee's obligations under the lease or underlease occurring before the commencement of the company's liquidation but after it acquired the lease or underlease by grant or assignment, and also for all rent accruing due and breaches of the lessee's or underlessee's obligations occurring at any subsequent time, including a period after the liquidator disclaims the lease or underlease, unless the lease was granted on or after 1 January 1996,[18] or the company is an assignee of the lease or underlease;[18] under the second alternative, however, the person in whose favour the vesting order is made is liable to the lessor or underlessor only for rent accruing due and breaches of the lessee's or underlessee's obligations occurring between the commencement of the company's liquidation and the time when that person assigns the lease or underlease to someone else.

If no underlessee or mortgagee is willing to accept a vesting order on the terms which the court is prepared to order, his own interest in the property ceases to exist without the need for a court

19 Insolvency Act 1986, s 181(1) to (3).
20 *Re Vedmay Ltd* [1994] 1 BCLC 676.
1 Insolvency Act 1986, s 181(4).
2 *Re No 1 London Ltd* [1991] BCC 118.
3 Insolvency Act 1986, s 182(1).

order to that effect (so that declining to apply for a vesting order is an effective way to terminate an underlease which the underlessee finds burdensome); the court may then vest the company's lease or underlease in any person who is liable to perform the lessee's or underlessee's obligations under it.[4] The exclusion of the underlessee or mortgagee who is unwilling to take a vesting order therefore opens the way to the court making such an order in favour of an original lessee when the company was an assignee of the lease or underlease, or it would seem, an intermediate assignee who has given an indemnity undertaking to his assignor in respect of the future payment of rent and the future fulfilment of the lessee's obligations and has then later assigned the lease or underlease to the company.

Any person who suffers loss or damage in consequence of the disclaimer of any contract or onerous property by the liquidator may prove as a creditor in the liquidation of the company, and is entitled to receive the same dividend in respect of that loss or damage as an ordinary unsecured creditor.[5] If a vesting order is made in favour of the claimant, the value of the property or rights conferred by it must be taken into account when assessing the loss or damages which he may prove for in the liquidation.[6] If the liquidator disclaims a lease or underlease, the lessor's or underlessor's claim for damages in the liquidation if no vesting order is made is calculated by taking the total amount payable by the company for rent, cost of repairs, insurance etc, during the unexpired period of the lease or underlease (if it had not been disclaimed) discounted by the market risk rate (ie the anticipated market interest rate until those amounts would have become payable) and deducting the total amount of similar items in consideration of which the lessor or underlessor could grant a lease or underlease on the same terms immediately after the disclaimer (ie the market rental).[7] If the market rental value of the property at the date of the disclaimer is less than the rent payable under the lease or underlease, the lessor's or underlessor's claim will in effect be for the capitalised value of the difference. If repairs to the property are needed to enable it to be re-let, and the rent for the re-letting is calculated on the assumption that the lessor or underlessor will carry out those repairs, he may additionally claim the cost of doing so.[7]

4 Ibid, s 182(3) and (4).
5 Ibid, s 178(6).
6 Ibid, s 181(5).
7 *Re Park Air Services plc* [1996] 1 BCLC 547, [1996] BCC 556.

THE ANCILLARY POWERS OF THE LIQUIDATOR

Summary enforcement of liabilities to the company

The liquidator is given power by several provisions of the Insolvency Act 1986, to enforce the liabilities of various persons to the company by taking summary proceedings in the winding up, thus saving the additional expense of suing them by action. In addition to compelling contributories to pay the capital unpaid on their shares in this way,[8] the liquidator may recover compensation for breaches of duty from promoters, directors and other officers of the company by taking summary proceedings against them.[9]

By another provision of the Act[10] the liquidator in a winding up of a company by the court and, if the court so directs, in a voluntary winding up may obtain a summary order against a contributory to pay to the liquidator any money due from him to the company otherwise than in respect of a call made by the liquidator in the winding up for the payment of unpaid capital. This power was originally given to enable the liquidator to collect calls made or instalments of unpaid share capital which became due for payment before the commencement of the winding up,[11] but it has also been used to enable a liquidator to recover dividends wrongfully paid to members out of the company's capital,[12] and to recover amounts paid to a contributory in the winding up in repayment of the capital of his shares when liabilities of the company were subsequently discovered and the amounts paid to the contributory were required to discharge them.[13] But the court will not allow the liquidator to use his powers of summary recovery as a means of collecting debts other than unpaid calls or instalments of the issue price of shares, or as a means of obtaining the restitution of amounts other than improper distributions made by the company; the liquidator must sue for such other debts or amounts in the normal way by action.[14] This is important, because a contributory who is sued summarily for

---

8 See p 272, post.
9 Insolvency Act 1986, s 212(1) to (3), s 213(1) and (2) and s 214(1) to (7) (see p 254 et seq, post.
10 Insolvency Act 1986, s 112(1) and (2) and s 149(1).
11 It is immaterial that the calls or instalments are owing from persons who ceased to be members of the company more than a year before the commencement of the winding up, so that the liquidator could not himself make a call on them (see p 269, post) (*Re Bangor and North Wales Mutual Protection Association, Baird's Case* [1899] 2 Ch 593).
12 *Re Mercantile Trading Co, Stringer's Case* (1869) 4 Ch App 475.
13 *Re Aidall Ltd* [1933] Ch 323.
14 *Re Marlborough Club Co* (1868) LR 5 Eq 365.

unpaid share capital or for restitution of distributions has no right
to set off any debt or other amount which the company owes him,[15]
unless the company is an unlimited one,[16] whereas he has such a
right of set-off if he is sued by action. It is only just that there should
be no set-off when the liquidator is suing for unpaid calls or the
return of assets improperly distributed to a contributory, but it
would be grossly unjust to deprive the contributory of the right of
set-off which a defendant normally has when his liability to the
company is simply a trading or other debt.

Special manager

In a winding up by the court or in a voluntary winding up, the court
may on the application of the liquidator appoint any person (not
necessarily a qualified insolvency practitioner) to be the special
manager of the business or any of the property of the company in
liquidation.[17] An application for such an appointment may also be
made by a provisional liquidator appointed by the court at any time
after the presentation of a winding up petition and before a winding
up order is made.[17] The application may be made if the liquidator
or provisional liquidator considers that the nature of the company's
business or property, or the interests of its creditors or contributories,
require the appointment of someone other than the liquidator or
provisional liquidator to manage it; the application must be supported
by a report to that effect by the applicant, which must also include
an estimate by him of the value of the assets for which the appointment
of a special manager is sought.[18] The application is made to the
registrar of the court which made the winding up order or, in a
voluntary liquidation, the registrar of the court which would have
jurisdiction to wind up the company; the application is heard in
chambers, but the registrar may refer the application for decision by
a judge.[19]

If the court appoints a special manager, it may confer on him
such powers as it thinks fit, and may direct that any provision of the
Insolvency Act 1986, which relates to a liquidator or to a provisional
liquidator (including the powers conferred on him by law) shall

---

15 *Re Overend, Gurney & Co, Grissell's Case* (1866) 1 Ch App 528; *Re Whitehouse
& Co* (1878) 9 Ch D 595; *Re Hiram Maxim Lamp Co* [1903] 1 Ch 70.
16 Insolvency Act 1986, s 149(2).
17 Ibid, s 177(1) and (2).
18 Ibid, s 177(2); Insolvency Rules 1986, r 4.206(1) and (2).
19 Insolvency Rules 1986, r 7.6(1) to (3).

apply to the special manager so as to enable him to carry out any of the functions which the liquidator or provisional liquidator would otherwise carry out.[20] The order appointing a special manager must specify the duration of the appointment, which may be until the occurrence of a specified event (eg the sale of the company's business, if the special manager is appointed to manage it), or until further order of the court; and the appointment can in any case be extended one or more times by a later order of the court.[1] The remuneration of a special manager is fixed by the court,[2] and may be calculated on any basis which the court thinks fit (eg a salary, a percentage or commission calculated on turnover or on the profits realised from carrying on the company's business, or a combination of those elements).

A special manager must give security for the proper performance of his functions in an amount not less than the value of the assets which he is appointed to manage, as estimated by the liquidator or provisional liquidator in the report filed in support of the application for the appointment.[3] A special manager may not act as such until he has given security, or if the court permits, until he has undertaken to do so; and if he fails to give the required security within the time limited by the court, or if he fails to maintain his security, the liquidator must report the failure to the court, which may terminate the order for the special manager's appointment.[4]

A special manager must keep accounts of his receipts and payments, and during his appointment must submit accounts for successive periods of three months for the liquidator's approval; after his approval has been given, the liquidator must incorporate the special manager's accounts in his own accounts.[5]

A special manager's appointment procured by a provisional liquidator terminates if the pending winding up petition is dismissed or withdrawn, or if the provisional liquidator's own appointment is terminated by the court; if a liquidator considers that a special manager's appointment is no longer necessary or advantageous, or if a meeting of the company's creditors resolves that the appointment should be terminated, the liquidator must apply to the court for directions, and it may then terminate the special manager's appointment.[6]

20 Insolvency Act 1986, s 177(3) and (4).
 1 Insolvency Rules 1986, r 4.206(3) and (4).
 2 Ibid, r 4.206(5).
 3 Insolvency Act 1986, s 177(5); Insolvency Rules 1986, r 4.207(3).
 4 Insolvency Rules 1986, r 4.207(1) and r 4.208(1) and (4).
 5 Ibid, r 4.209(1) to (3) (see p 191, post).
 6 Ibid, r 4.210(1) to (3).

Meetings of creditors and contributories

Liquidator's power and obligations to call meetings

The liquidator in a winding up by the court or in a creditors' voluntary winding up may call meetings of creditors or contributories in order to ascertain their wishes with regard to any matter arising in the liquidation. The court is directed to have regard to the wishes of creditors and contributories in all liquidations (although in the liquidation of an insolvent company, the creditors' wishes will obviously predominate); and in order to ascertain their wishes, the court may in any liquidation direct a meeting or meetings of creditors or of contributories to be held, and may appoint a chairman to preside at a meeting or meetings so directed and to report the result of the meeting or meetings to the court.[7]

A liquidator in a winding up by the court must call a meeting of creditors or contributories if a meeting of creditors or contributories (as the case may be) so resolves, or if the holders of one-tenth in value of the interests of the creditors or contributories (as the case may be) so require in writing.[8]

In a members' voluntary winding up, the liquidator must call a general meeting of the company (ie its contributories) within three months after each anniversary of the resolution to wind up the company, and in a creditors' voluntary winding up, the liquidator must at the same intervals call separate meetings of creditors and contributories.[9] However, if the liquidator in a members' voluntary winding up calls a meeting of creditors to be held within three months before the first anniversary of the winding up resolution because he forms the opinion that the company's debts and liabilities will not be discharged in full within the period stated in the directors' statutory declaration of solvency, the liquidator need not call an additional creditors' meeting within three months after that first anniversary, but he must call both creditors' and contributories' meetings within three months after each succeeding anniversary of the winding up resolution.[10] The Secretary of State for Trade and Industry may, at the liquidator's request, extend the period of three months from any or each of the anniversaries of the winding up resolution within which annual meetings of contributories or of contributories and creditors must be held.[11]

---

7 Insolvency Act 1986, s 195(1).
8 Ibid, s 168(1) and (2).
9 Ibid, s 93(1) and s 105(1).
10 Ibid, s 105(4).
11 Ibid, s 93(1) and s 105(1).

The annual meetings in a voluntary liquidation are held so that the liquidator may fulfil his obligation to lay before the contributories, or before the contributories and creditors (as the case may be), an account of his acts and dealings and of the conduct of the winding up during the previous year.[12] If a voluntary liquidation is completed within a year after the winding up resolution is passed, there is no need to hold an annual meeting of contributories or creditors at the end of the year; instead, the liquidator will call a final meeting of contributories or, in a creditors' voluntary winding up, final meetings of contributories and creditors on the conclusion of the winding up.[13]

Rules governing meetings; requisition of meetings

Some of the rules relating to meetings in a liquidation were dealt with above, in connection with the first meetings of creditors and contributories which are held at the beginning of a winding up by the court.[14] It is now necessary to deal in some detail with the general rules that apply to all kinds of meetings of creditors and contributories which may be held during a winding up by the court or in a creditors' voluntary winding up.[15]

Meetings are called by the liquidator, but as indicated above, he may be compelled to call a meeting because the court so directs, or because the meeting is in a winding up by the court and has been requisitioned by the appropriate fraction of creditors or contributories.[16] If the meeting is requisitioned by creditors, the written requisition must be accompanied by a list of the creditors who concur in it and the amount of their respective claims, written confirmation by each of the requisitioning creditors of his concurrence and a statement of the purpose of the proposed meeting.[17] Upon receiving a requisition which is properly made, the liquidator must call the meeting to be held not more than 35 days after receiving the requisition.[17] Similar rules apply when a meeting of contributories is requisitioned by the appropriate fraction of contributories.[18]

Notices of meetings

All meetings, whether requisitioned or not, are called by the liquidator, giving at least 21 clear days' notice of them in writing; in

12 Ibid, s 93(2) and s 105(2).
13 See pp 198 and 199 post.
14 See p 116, ante.
15 Insolvency Rules 1986, r 4.1(1).
16 Insolvency Act 1986, s 168(2) and s 195(1).
17 Insolvency Rules 1986, r 4.57(1) and (2) and Sch 4, Form 4.21.
18 Ibid, r 4.57(4).

the case of a creditors' meeting, notice must be given to each creditor who is known to the liquidator or who is identified in the company's statement of affairs; in the case of a contributories' meeting, notice must be given to every person who appears by the company's books (ie register of members) or otherwise to be a contributory of the company.[19] The notice must specify the time and place of the meeting and the purpose of holding it, and also the place where and the time within which proofs must be lodged by creditors and proxy appointments must be lodged by creditors or contributories (as the case may be), but in a winding up by the court, and as regards proxy appointments by creditors in a creditors' voluntary winding up, that time must not be earlier than four days before the date on which the meeting is held.[20]

Notice of a meeting of creditors or contributories may be given to the persons entitled to receive it by delivery to them personally, or by sending it by prepaid post addressed to the person concerned at his last known address; if notice is given by post, unless the contrary is shown, it is deemed to be given on the second business day after posting, or if sent by second class post, on the fourth business day after posting.[1] If notice of the meeting is not received by all the persons to whom notice of it should have been given, the meeting is nevertheless presumed to have been validly called and held.[2] In addition to the notices of a meeting sent to creditors or contributories individually, the liquidator may advertise a meeting publicly by newspaper advertisement or otherwise, and he must do so if the court so directs.[3] On the other hand, the court may direct that notice of a meeting shall be given only by public advertisement, and that no individual notices need be given to creditors or contributories.[4]

Chairman

The chairman of a meeting of creditors or contributories will be the liquidator, or the official receiver if the meeting is one called by him in a winding up by the court; the liquidator or official receiver may nominate another person to be the chairman, however, provided that he is qualified to act as an insolvency practitioner in relation to the company, or is an employee of the liquidator or his firm and is

19 Ibid, r 4.54(2) and (3), r 4.57(3) and Sch 4, Forms 4.22 and 4.23.
20 Ibid, r 4.54(3) to (5).
 1 Ibid, r 12.10(1) to (3) and r 13.3(1) to (3).
 2 Ibid, r 12.16.
 3 Ibid, r 4.54(6).
 4 Ibid, r 4.59(1).

experienced in insolvency matters.[5] If the meeting is ordered by the court, the chairman will be the person directed by the court.[6]

Creditors' and contributories' voting rights

A creditor is entitled to vote at a meeting of creditors only if he has lodged a proof of his claim, together with any proxy appointment made by him, by the time indicated in the notice of the meeting; but in a creditors' voluntary winding up, the chairman may allow a creditor to vote even though he has not lodged a proof of his claim, or has lodged it late, if this was due to circumstances beyond the creditor's control.[7] Moreover, the court may in exceptional circumstances permit all the creditors or the creditors of a certain class (eg employees of the company as creditors for wages or salaries) to vote without proving their debts.[8]

The chairman of a meeting of creditors has power to admit or reject creditors' proofs for the purpose of voting, subject to an appeal to the court, and a proof may be admitted for part of a creditor's claim and rejected for the remainder; if the chairman is in doubt as to whether to admit or reject a proof by a creditor, he must allow the creditor to vote, but mark his vote as objected to, so as to enable the court to declare it invalid in subsequent proceedings if that is appropriate.[9] If, on appeal against a rejection of a proof, the court holds that the rejection was unfounded, or if the court declares a creditor's vote invalid when the chairman has allowed it but marked it as objected to, the court may order another meeting to be called or make such other order as it thinks just.[10] Appeals against rejections of proofs and challenges to votes which the chairman has admitted but marked as objected to are heard in chambers by the registrar of the court which made the winding up order or, in a creditors' voluntary winding up, by the registrar of the court which could have ordered the company to be wound up.[11]

A creditor can prove his claim for the purpose of voting only if it is for a liquidated amount, but if it is unliquidated or its value is unascertained, the chairman may agree to admit the claim for an estimated minimum amount.[12] There has been a conflict of authority as to whether this provision means that the chairman may admit the

5 Ibid, r 4.55(1) to (3) and r 4.56(1) and (2).
6 Insolvency Act 1986, s 195(1).
7 Insolvency Rules 1986, r 4.67(1) and r 4.68.
8 Ibid, r 4.67(2).
9 Ibid, r 4.70(1) to (3).
10 Ibid, r 4.70(4).
11 Ibid, r 7.6(1) to (3).
12 Ibid, r 4.67(3).

creditor's claim for an estimated amount only if the chairman and the creditor agree on that amount (as was held in one case),[13] or whether the only agreement required is the unilateral assent of the chairman to admit the claim for voting purposes at his estimate of its value and the acceptance of that estimate by the creditor is not required (as was held in another case);[14] the latter view, which now has the support of the Court of Appeal would appear to be the correct one.[15] A secured creditor may vote only in respect of the excess of his claim over his estimate of the value of his security; and a creditor who proves in respect of a bill of exchange or a promissory note to which the company is a party (other than as the acceptor of the bill or the maker of the note) can prove only for the excess of the amount of the bill or note over the creditor's estimate of the value of his claim against every solvent party to the bill or note prior to the company.[16]

The value of the rights of contributories for the purpose of voting at their meetings is ascertained by reference to the number of votes they are respectively entitled to cast at general meetings of the company in accordance with its articles of association.[17]

Resolutions

Resolutions within the scope of the business stated in the notice calling a meeting of creditors or contributories may be moved by any person properly present (including a proxy).[18] If the chairman holds a proxy appointment requiring him to vote for a particular resolution and no other person present at the meeting moves it, the chairman must move the resolution himself, unless he considers that there is good reason for not doing so; if he does not move the resolution, he must immediately after the meeting inform the creditor or contributory who gave him the proxy appointment of his reasons for not doing so.[19]

Resolutions are passed at a meeting of creditors or contributories by the votes of a majority in value of the persons present at the meeting who vote in person or by proxy or, if they are corporations, by their duly appointed representatives.[20] The requisite majority need not comprise a majority in number of those attending and

---

13 *Re Cranley Mansions Ltd, Saigol v Goldstein* [1995] 1 BCLC 290, [1994] BCC 576.
14 *Doorbar v Alltime Securities Ltd* [1995] 1 BCLC 316, [1994] BCC 994 and *Re a Debtor, Doorbar v Alltime Securities Ltd (No 2)* [1995] 2 BCLC 513, [1995] BCC 728.
15 [1996] 1 BCLC 487, [1995] BCC 1149.
16 Insolvency Rules 1986, r 4.67(4) and (5).
17 Ibid, r 4.63(1).
18 Ibid, r 8.1(1) and (6).
19 Ibid, r 4.64.
20 Ibid, r 4.63(1); Companies Act 1985, s 375(1) and (2).

voting at the meeting, as it did under the former law,[1] and so the vote on a resolution is necessarily taken by a poll, and not by a show of hands. On the poll, each creditor has the right to cast a number of votes proportionate to the amount of his claim admitted by the chairman for voting purposes, and each contributory is entitled to cast the number of votes attributed to his shares by the company's articles of association.[20]

Adjournment

If a meeting of creditors or contributories does not complete the business for which it was called, it may resolve to adjourn for a period not exceeding 21 days; the chairman may in his discretion adjourn the meeting for not longer than that period, and must do so if the meeting so resolves.[2] Proxies given for use at a meeting may also be used at adjournments of it.[3]

Minutes

The chairman at a meeting of creditors or contributories must cause minutes of the proceedings to be kept, and he must sign them at the conclusion of the meeting; the minutes must include, or be accompanied by, a list of the creditors or contributories present at the meeting in person or by proxy or by corporate representatives.[4] The signed minutes, the list of creditors or contributories attending the meeting and the proxy appointments used at the meeting must be delivered to and retained by the liquidator.[5] In a winding up by the court, the chairman of the meeting must file in court particulars of all resolutions passed by the meeting within 21 days after its conclusion.[6]

In both a winding up by the court and a voluntary winding up the liquidator must keep administrative records in respect of the company, containing the minutes of all meetings of creditors and contributories (including a record of every resolution passed at such meetings), the minutes of all meetings of the liquidation committee, a record of every resolution passed at such meetings (including resolutions of the committee passed by postal voting) and a record of all other matters necessary to provide an accurate record of the liquidation.[7]

1 Companies (Winding Up) Rules 1949, r 134.
2 Insolvency Rules 1986, r 4.65(1), (3) and (5).
3 Ibid, r 8.3(1).
4 Ibid, r 4.71(1) to (3).
5 Ibid, r 4.71(1) and r 8.4(1) and (2).
6 Ibid, r 4.71(4).
7 Insolvency Regulations 1986 (SI 1986/1994), regs 8 and 26.

CONTROL OVER THE LIQUIDATOR

The liquidator's autonomy

The liquidator is in general in sole control of the conduct of the winding up of a company's affairs, and except in those situations where he requires the consent of the liquidation committee, a meeting of creditors, the Secretary of State for Trade and Industry or the court to exercise certain powers,[8] he acts on his own initiative and uses his own discretion in the management and disposal of the company's assets and the distribution of the proceeds of realisation among the creditors.[9] Nevertheless, as has been shown above, the liquidator may call meetings of creditors or contributories in a winding up by the court or in a voluntary winding up in order to ascertain their wishes, and he may then act in accordance with their expressed wishes if he thinks fit, and he is in any case bound to take them into account.

In a winding up by the court the liquidator is obliged to call meetings at such times as the creditors or contributories direct by passing a resolution at a meeting of their number,[10] for example, periodical meetings of creditors at which the liquidator will report on the progress of the liquidation. As indicated above, a liquidator in a winding up by the court is also obliged to call a meeting of creditors of contributories when required to do so by the holders of one tenth in value of the total of their interests.[10] At any meeting called by the liquidator in a winding up by the court or in a creditors' voluntary winding up he may require any present or former directors or officers of the company to attend, and also he may require the attendance of any persons who are or who have within one year preceding the date of the winding up order been promoters or employees of the company, or officers or employees of companies which are or have been directors or officers of the company within that time, so that questions may be put to them.[11]

Despite the liquidator's duty to call meetings of creditors or contributories in certain circumstances, in general, meetings called in a liquidation are merely consultative, and except in those situations where the Insolvency Act 1986 requires the consent of creditors or contributories to action proposed by the liquidator, he is not bound to give effect to their expressed wishes, or even to consult them before acting.

8 See pp 147 and 148, ante.
9 Insolvency Act 1986, s 165(3) and s 168(4).
10 Ibid, s 168(1) and (2).
11 Insolvency Rules 1986, r 4.58(1) and (2).

Directions by the court

On an application by the liquidator in a winding up by the court the court may give him directions in relation to any particular matter arising in the winding up,[12] and may also give directions to the liquidator on his application in a voluntary liquidation in exercise of the court's powers to make any order which it could make in a winding up by the court.[13] The court exercises its power to give directions sparingly, and will do so only when a doubtful question of law is involved, or when the liquidator could be involved in personal liability for loss resulting from an alleged breach of his duties if he carried out a proposed act or transaction, or if the liquidator's action or proposed action is clearly not in the interests of the company's creditors (if it is solvent) or its contributories taken as a whole.[14] The court will not substitute its own discretion for the liquidator's when the proposed act or transaction is one which the Insolvency Act 1986 clearly empowers the liquidator to carry out and is relevant to the winding up of the company and is not wholly unreasonable. The court will not intervene when the only question is whether the act or transaction is desirable or will be beneficial.

Again, both in a winding up by the court and in a voluntary liquidation any person who is aggrieved by an act or decision of the liquidator may apply to the court, which may confirm, reverse or modify the act or decision, and make such order as it thinks just.[15] This would appear to give the court a wider discretion than it has on hearing an application by the liquidator for directions, but the court will in fact intervene only if the liquidator proposes to act illegally or in breach of his duties or wholly unreasonably, or has already done so, and the court will not interfere with the fair and reasonable exercise by the liquidator of his discretionary powers.[16]

The Insolvency Act 1986 additionally provides that in a winding up by the court the liquidator exercises his powers subject to the control of the court, and any creditor or contributory may apply to the court with respect to the exercise or proposed exercise of those powers.[17] However, it has been held that this in no way enlarges the court's power to interfere with the exercise of the liquidator's

---

12 Insolvency Act 1986, s 168(3).
13 Ibid, s 112(1).
14 *Re Edennote Ltd, Tottenham Hotspur plc v Ryman* [1995] 2 BCLC 248, [1995] BCC 389; revsd [1996] BCC 718.
15 Insolvency Act 1986, s 112(1) and s 168(5).
16 *Stead, Hazel & Co v Cooper* [1933] 1 KB 840; *Harold M Pitman & Co v Top Business Systems (Nottingham) Ltd* [1984] BCLC 593, 1 BCC 345; *Re Hans Place Ltd* [1993] BCLC 768, [1992] BCC 737; *Re Edennote Ltd*, supra.
17 Insolvency Act 1986, s 167(3).

discretion.[16] It is true that the court is authorised by the Insolvency Act 1986, in any liquidation, whether under an order of the court or voluntary, to have regard to the wishes of the creditors or contributories of the company as shown by resolutions passed by meetings of their number or otherwise,[18] but it has been held that this applies only when the court exercises discretionary powers vested in it by the Act, and does not mean that it will overrule the exercise of a discretion by the liquidator merely because it does not conform to the creditors' wishes.[16]

THE DUTIES AND LIABILITIES OF THE LIQUIDATOR

Statutory provisions

The statutory description of the functions of the liquidator in a compulsory or a voluntary liquidation[19] does not of itself impose a statutory duty on him to carry out the liquidation, nor does the enumeration of the powers which he may exercise in carrying out his functions.[20] If the liquidator fails to carry out those functions, the proper remedy is for him to be removed by the court or otherwise and for a new liquidator to be appointed.[1] Specific statutory duties are nevertheless imposed on the liquidator in connection with a winding up (eg the duty in a winding up by the court to call meetings of creditors or contributories when requisitioned by a certain fraction of their number)[2] or by rules made under the Insolvency Act 1986 (eg the duty in a winding up by the court or in a creditors' voluntary winding up to declare and distribute dividends to the company's creditors when the liquidator has funds available).[3] The court in a winding up by the court is under a statutory duty to settle a list of contributories and to cause the company's assets to be collected and applied in discharge of its liabilities,[4] and by rules made under the Insolvency Act 1986, the liquidator is to fulfil the court's duties in this respect as its delegate subject to its control.[5] In a voluntary winding up the liquidator is under a duty to pay the

18 Ibid, s 195(1).
19 Ibid, s 91(1), s 100(1) and s 143(1), (see p 144, ante).
20 Insolvency Act 1986, ss 165 and 167.
1 See pp 121, 135 and 138, ante.
2 Insolvency Act 1986, s 168(2).
3 Insolvency Rules 1986, r 4.180(1).
4 Insolvency Act 1986, s 148(1).
5 Ibid, s 160(1); Insolvency Rules 1986, r 4.179(1), r 4.195 and r 4.196(1).

company's debts out of its assets and to adjust the rights of contributories among themselves,[6] and he must do so in conformity with the statutory provision that, subject to the priority claims of preferential creditors, the company's debts and liabilities must be paid pari passu out of its assets and any surplus assets must be distributed among the contributories in accordance with their rights.[7]

Liquidator's common law and equitable duties

Despite the absence of any general statutory duty imposed on a liquidator to carry out the liquidation properly, the liquidator in any kind of winding up is under a common law or equitable duty to apply the company's assets in the proper manner and to discharge its liabilities in the proper order out of those assets.

If the liquidator makes an error in administering the company's assets (eg pays a claim for which the company is not legally liable, or declines to enforce a claim which the company has against a third person), any creditor or contributory who disputes the propriety of the liquidator's act or decision may apply to the court to give directions to the liquidator in order to correct the error by taking whatever remedial action is appropriate in the further administration of the company's assets.[7] This is the proper course of action for a creditor or contributory if the liquidator's erroneous action can be corrected by applying the company's assets in the future, and so if the liquidator admits a claim against the company for too large an amount, but has so far paid only a small dividend on all admitted claims, the court will order him to withhold future dividends in respect of that over-large claim and so ensure that all the company's creditors receive a rateable distribution in respect of the proper amounts of their claims.[8]

On the other hand, if the liquidator's error cannot be corrected by an application of the company's as yet undistributed assets, and the liquidator does not take any action open to him to rectify the error (eg by suing for the repayment of an amount paid to a claimant who has no valid claim against the company as money paid to him by the liquidator under a mistake of fact), the court will order the liquidator to make good himself the loss which the company has suffered. This may be ordered by the court only if the liquidator is

6 Insolvency Act 1986, s 165(5).
7 Ibid, s 107.
8 *Re Armstrong Whitworth Securities Co Ltd* [1947] Ch 673, [1947] 2 All ER 479.

shown to have acted wilfully, or at least negligently, and his liability is not an absolute one. Consequently, liquidators have been held personally liable to pay compensation for losses caused by paying claims out of the company's assets for which it was not legally liable and which the liquidator should have known were invalid,[9] for compromising claims against the company which were clearly doubtful without seeking the directions of the court,[10] for transferring the company's assets to its sole shareholder in return for an undertaking by him to indemnify the liquidator in respect of the company's outstanding debts, which the shareholder did not honour,[11] and for distributing the balance of the company's assets without ascertaining from its accounting records whether there were any outstanding debts which had not been proved in the liquidation, and failing to notify the creditors for such debts so that they might claim.[8]

Fiduciary duty to the company

A liquidator, as an agent of the company, occupies a fiduciary position, and must therefore use his powers in the interests of the company and its creditors and contributories generally, and not in the interests of himself or third persons. He must therefore account for any profit or gain which he obtains personally from the carrying out of his functions in excess of the remuneration properly allowed to him. The rules made under the Insolvency Act 1986 expressly make the liquidator liable to compensate the company for any loss which it suffers as a result of the liquidator entering into a transaction in the course of the liquidation with an associate of his, and the court may set aside any such transaction and require the liquidator or his associate to restore any money or assets of the company which they have obtained under it; these rules do not apply if the court gives the liquidator leave to enter into the transaction or if the transaction was for value and the liquidator was unaware that it was entered into with a person who was an associate of his.[12] Furthermore, the Insolvency Rules 1986 enable the court to enforce the liquidator's obligations at common law and equity against him in respect of a transaction with his associate which is not within either of the

9 *Re Home and Colonial Insurance Co Ltd* [1930] 1 Ch 102.
10 *Re Windsor Steam Coal Co (1901) Ltd* [1929] 1 Ch 151.
11 *Re AMF International Ltd (No 2)* [1996] 2 BCLC 9, [1996] BCC 335.
12 Insolvency Rules 1986, r 4.149(1) and (2). For the meaning of associate, see p 150, ante.

exceptions mentioned above.[13] On the other hand, a liquidator owes no fiduciary duties to individual creditors and contributories of the company,[14] and so can be made personally liable to them only in the manner stated in the next paragraph.

Remedies for liquidator's breach of duties

Where a liquidator has misapplied, retained or become accountable for any money or property of the company of which he is liquidator, or has caused a loss to the company's assets by a breach of his duties, the court may on an application by a creditor or contributory, or by the official receiver or any liquidator subsequently appointed, order the liquidator in default to repay, restore or account for any property which he has misapplied or retained or for which he has become accountable, or to contribute such sum to the company's assets by way of compensation for his wrongdoing or misfeasance or breach of his duties as the court think just.[15] This provides a speedy, informal remedy to compel liquidators to account for any personal gains obtained in breach of their duties, or to pay compensation for losses caused to the company's assets by their wilful or negligent acts or omissions.

Summary proceedings cannot be brought against a liquidator for breaches of his duties during the winding up after the company has been dissolved, because the winding up terminates upon the company's dissolution, and misfeasance proceedings can only be brought summarily in the course of a liquidation.[16] Nevertheless, after the company's dissolution an action for damages for negligence may be brought by a creditor or contributory against the liquidator for any loss caused to the creditor or contributory personally by the liquidator's misapplication of the company's assets in the liquidation, for example, by his failure to pay a claim by a creditor of which he was or should have been aware.[17] Such an action by a creditor or contributory must be brought by writ, and if the plaintiff is successful, judgment is given in his favour against the liquidator personally. An action of this kind cannot be brought against the liquidator before

13 Insolvency Rules 1986, r 4.149(3).
14 *Knowles v Scott* [1891] 1 Ch 717; *Re Hill's Waterfall Estate and Gold Mining Co* [1896] 1 Ch 947.
15 Insolvency Act 1986, s 212(1) to (3). A contributory may make an application only with leave of the court (s 212(5)).
16 Insolvency Act 1986, s 212(1).
17 *Pulsford v Devenish* [1903] 2 Ch 625; *Argylls Ltd v Coxeter* (1913) 29 TLR 355; *James Smith & Sons (Norwood) Ltd v Goodman* [1936] Ch 216; *Lamey v Winram* 1987 SLT 635, 3 BCC 156.

the company has been dissolved however;[18] the creditor or contributory in that situation must either initiate summary proceedings against the liquidator in the liquidation or apply to the court to give directions to the liquidator as to the future application of the company's assets.[19]

Release of the liquidator from liability

Release in a winding up by the court

The liquidator in a winding up by the court which is concluded in the normal way by the liquidator calling and holding the final meeting of the company's creditors,[20] obtains his release when he vacates office, that is, when he notifies the court and the Registrar of Companies that the final meeting has been held.[1] If the final meeting resolves that the liquidator shall not be released, however, he obtains his release only if the Secretary of State for Trade and Industry so orders on the liquidator's application.[1]

If the liquidator in a winding up by the court is removed by a meeting of creditors of the company, he obtains his release when the official receiver delivers to the court a certificate given by the chairman of the meeting that the liquidator has been so removed.[2] But if the meeting of creditors which resolves to remove the liquidator also resolves that he shall not be given his release, or if the liquidator is removed by the court or the Secretary of State, he obtains his release only if the Secretary of State so orders on an application made to him by the liquidator, which he must notify to the court and the official receiver.[3]

A liquidator in a winding up by the court may resign only after calling and holding a meeting of creditors to receive his resignation, and if the meeting accepts it, the resignation takes effect when the official receiver delivers to the court a certificate by the chairman of the meeting to that effect.[4] If the meeting resolves that the liquidator shall not be released, however, he obtains his release only if the Secretary of State so orders.[5]

---

18 *Pulsford v Devenish*, supra.
19 Insolvency Act 1986, s 112(1), s 168(5) and s 212(1) to (3).
20 Ibid, s 146(1).
1 Ibid, s 172(8) and s 174(4); Insolvency Rules 1986, r 4.125(6), (see p 197, post).
2 Insolvency Act 1986, s 174(4); Insolvency Rules 1986 r 4.121(2).
3 Insolvency Act 1986, s 174(4); Insolvency Rules 1986, r 4.121(3) to (5) and r 4.123(2) and (3).
4 Insolvency Act 1986, s 172(6); Insolvency Rules 1986, rr 4.109(6) and 4.121(1).
5 Insolvency Rules, r 4.121(3) to (5).

Release in a voluntary winding up

If a liquidator in a members' voluntary liquidation completes the winding up of the company's affairs and holds the final meeting of members, or in a creditors' voluntary winding up, completes the winding up of the company's affairs and holds the final meetings of creditors and contributories, the liquidator vacates office when he notifies the Registrar of Companies that the final meeting or meetings have been held, informs the Registrar of the resolutions passed at them, and delivers to the Registrar a copy of the account of the liquidation which he presented to the meeting or meetings.[6] Upon vacating office the liquidator obtains his release, but if in a creditors' winding up the final meeting of creditors resolves that he shall not be given his release, he obtains it only if the Secretary of State for Trade and Industry so directs.[7]

Similarly, a liquidator in a voluntary winding up who is removed by a resolution passed by a general meeting of members or by a meeting of creditors, obtains his release when he notifies the Registrar of Companies of his removal, but if he is removed by a meeting of creditors which resolves against giving him his release, he obtains it only if the Secretary of State so directs and the release then takes effect from the date of the Secretary of State's certificate of release.[8]

A liquidator in a voluntary winding up who resigns obtains his release in the same way and at the same time as though he had been removed.[9]

Effect of release

As from the time when a liquidator's release takes effect, he is discharged from all liability in respect of his acts and omissions in the winding up and in relation to his conduct as liquidator, but this does not prevent the court from exercising its power to order the restitution of any of the company's property or the payment of compensation by the liquidator in proceedings taken summarily against him in the liquidation.[10] The immediate consequence of the liquidator's release, therefore, is that no proceedings commenced by writ may be brought against him, and it would seem that no

6 Insolvency Act 1986, s 94(3), s 106(3) and s 171(6); (see pp 198, and 199, post).
7 Ibid, s 173(2); Insolvency Rules 1986, r 122(4) and (5), and r 126(3).
8 Insolvency Act 1986, s 171(1) and (2) and s 173(2); Insolvency Rules 1986, r 4.122(3) or (5).
9 Insolvency Act 1986, s 171(5) and s 173(2); Insolvency Rules 1986, r 4.122(1) to (5).
10 Insolvency Act 1986, s 173(4) and s 174(6).

directions can be given to him by the court to rectify errors or misapplications of the company's assets which he has made in the course of the liquidation and for which he would be liable if the release had not been given. When the company is dissolved[11] it becomes impossible even for summary proceedings in the liquidation to be brought against the released liquidator and the liquidator's discharge is then complete. Moreover, the release of the liquidator discharges him from liability to creditors and contributories of the company after its dissolution for loss suffered by them as a result of his failure to wind up the company's affairs properly.[12]

The liquidator's release will normally take effect before the company is dissolved,[13] and since his personal liability to creditors or contributories can be enforced only after the dissolution of the company, the release of the liquidator prevents the creditors' or contributories' personal rights of action arising at all. The only occasion when they can sue the liquidator after the dissolution of the company, therefore, is where the liquidator can obtain his release only if the Secretary of State for Trade and Industry so orders, and either the liquidator fails to apply for his release or the Secretary of State refuses to grant it.

Under the former legislation the release of a liquidator in a winding up by the court had to be obtained by express grant from the Secretary of State when the liquidation was completed or the liquidator ceased to hold office, but the Secretary of State could revoke the release if it was obtained by fraud or the suppression or concealment of material facts.[14] There is no provision in the present legislation for the revocation of a release, but it would appear that the court could rescind or annul it in exercise of its equitable jurisdiction if the release were obtained by fraudulent misrepresentation or concealment, or if full disclosure of material facts has not been made by the liquidator on applying for his release. Because the grant of a release does not prevent summary proceedings for restitution of assets to the company or for compensation being taken against the liquidator while the company continues to exist,[15] the effect of a judicial rescission of a release would be confined to enabling creditors or contributories of the company to pursue individual claims against the liquidator after its dissolution.

11 See pp 194, 196, 198 and 200, post.
12 See p 174, ante.
13 For the date of dissolution, see pp 177, 181, 183 and 184, post.
14 Companies Act 1948, s 251(1) and (3); Companies Act 1985, s 545(1) to (3) and (5).
15 Insolvency Act 1986, s 173(4) and s 174(6).

INSPECTIONS, INVESTIGATIONS AND EXAMINATIONS

The Insolvency Act 1985 makes a number of provisions to enable the court, the official receiver (in a winding up by the court), the liquidator and other persons interested in the winding up of a company to discover the real state of the company's affairs and the events leading up to its liquidation so that the winding up may be more effectively carried out, and so that any legal remedies available to the company or to its creditors or members may be effectively pursued.

Inspection of company's books

When a company is ordered to be wound up by the court, the liquidator is entitled to take possession of all its books, records and papers, except documents of title to mortgaged property which are in the hands of mortgagees,[16] and the liquidator may recover such books, records and papers from any officer or agent of the company or any other person who has possession or control of them by obtaining an order for the purpose on making a summary application to the court.[17] If a person who possesses any books, papers or other records of the company has a lien or other right to retain the possession of them, that lien or other right is ineffective against the liquidator, except where it is a lien on documents which give a title to property and are held as such.[18] The exception enables a person who has a lien over documents relating to proprietary interests of the company (such as documents of title to land vested in the company or to shares or investments held by the company) to retain them as security for undebtedness of the company to him.[19]

Whether the liquidator in a winding up by the court has recovered books and other documents belonging to the company or not, the court may allow any creditor or contributory to inspect them if they are in the possession of the company,[20] but creditors and

---

16 *Engel v South Metropolitan Brewing and Bottling Co* [1892] 1 Ch 442.
17 Insolvency Act 1986, s 144(1) and 234(1) and (2); Insolvency Rules 1986, r 7.2(1).
18 Insolvency Act 1986, s 246(1) to (3).
19 *Re SEIL Trade Finance Ltd* [1992] BCC 538; *Brereton v Nicholls* [1993] BCLC 593.
20 Insolvency Act 1986, s 155(1). Documents in the possession of the company's present officers, employees or agents would appear to be in its possession for this purpose.

contributories have no absolute right of inspection. The power of
the court to order inspection is undoubtedly wider than when the
company was a going concern, but inspection will be ordered in a
winding up only when it is required for the purpose of the liquidation,[1]
and not when the applicant merely wishes to enforce a personal
claim for damages against the directors for misrepresentations in a
prospectus issued by the company.[2] Furthermore, the rights of
members or creditors or the public to inspect the various registers
and documents which the Companies Act 1985 requires companies
to keep open for inspection, cease when the company is wound up,[3]
as also does any right of inspection conferred on members by the
company's articles of association,[4] and so the information desired
can be obtained only by inspecting returns and documents filed by
the company at the Companies Registry, or by obtaining an order
of the court for inspection.

The powers of the Secretary of State for Trade and Industry or
inspectors appointed by him to call for books, records and information
in connection with the investigation of a company's affairs, or to
require the production of its books and papers to his officers or
persons authorised by him,[5] are unaffected by the company being in
liquidation, and are exercisable in the same way and for the same
purposes as though it were still a going concern.

Private examinations

The power of the official receiver or liquidator in a winding up by the
court to call for information and accounts which has already been
referred to,[6] is reinforced by a more general power of the court which
made a winding up order or a court which could order the winding
up of a company which is in voluntary liquidation to make an order
on the application of the liquidator, or alternatively, if the company
is being wound up by the court, on the application of the official
receiver or a provisional liquidator or of the liquidator for the time

1 *Re DPR Futures Ltd* [1989] 1 WLR 778. For example, inspection will be ordered
   to assist the discovery of assets, to defeat groundless claims made against the
   company, and to obtain evidence in support of misfeasance proceedings against
   the company's officers.
2 *Re North Brazilian Sugar Factories Ltd* (1887) 37 Ch D 83.
3 *Re Kent Coalfields Syndicate Ltd* [1898] 1 QB 754.
4 *Re Yorkshire Fibre Co* (1870) LR 9 Eq 650.
5 Companies Act 1985, s 434(1) and (2) and s 447(2) to (4) (as amended by
   Companies Act 1989, s 56(1) and s 63(1)).
6 See p 114, ante.

being of the company, requiring any officer of the company, or any person known or suspected to be in possession of assets of the company or to be indebted to it, or any person whom the court thinks capable of giving information about the promotion, formation, business, dealings or assets of the company, to appear before the court and to answer such questions as it puts to him orally or by interrogatories, or to make a statement about matters within his knowledge on affidavit.[7] Under this provision the court may order the examination of solicitors or other agents who act for a person who could himself be ordered to undergo an examination if it appears that they have or have access to information which he possesses and act entirely on his instructions; solicitors in this position may not rely on the solicitor/client relationship between themselves and the person for whom they act in order to decline to answer the questions put to them.[8] If the person sought to be examined offers to supply written answers to the questions intended to be put to him, the court may order an oral examination if it considers that such an examination would be more likely to elicit the information sought by the liquidator.[9] The court may direct that a person ordered to appear before it who fails to do so shall be arrested, and that any books, papers, records, money or goods in his possession shall be seized and brought before the court to be disposed of as it orders.[10] The court may also order that the person ordered to be examined shall deliver any property of the company in his possession to the liquidator or that he shall pay to the liquidator any debt owed by him to the company.[11]

An application by the official receiver or the liquidator for the examination of an officer of the company or other person concerned may be made ex parte in the first instance; it must state whether the applicant seeks an order that the respondent shall be examined orally by the court, or by answering interrogatories, or by filing an affidavit, and whether he should be required to produce books, papers or records to the court.[12] The applicant may obtain an order for a private examination without proving even a prima facie case against the person whom it is proposed to have examined by the court.[13] Moreover, if disclosure of the matters on which it is proposed that the respondent should be examined might enable him

7 Insolvency Act 1986, s 236(1) to (3) and s 237(4).
8 *Re Murjani* [1996] 1 BCLC 272, [1996] BCC 278.
9 *Re Bishopsgate Investment Management Ltd (No 2)* [1994] BCC 732.
10 Insolvency Act 1986, s 236(4) to (6).
11 Ibid, s 237(1) and (2).
12 Insolvency Rules 1986, r 9.2(3) and (4).
13 *Re Gold Co* (1879) 12 Ch D 77.

to take evasive action to prevent the official receiver or liquidator from recovering reparation for wrongs to the company which are alleged to have been committed, an order for an examination may be made on the strength of written allegation by the applicant without revealing their contents to the respondent.[14] In general the court will not order that the statement of the reasons for an application for a private examination which the applicant files with his application shall be disclosed to the person sought to be examined, but the court may do this if such disclosure is needed to enable that person to identify the documents which he is required to produce or to answer the questions which are to be put to him.[15]

If the registrar of the court orders the respondent to appear before it, the order must fix a date for the examination, being not less than 14 days from the date of the order; if the registrar orders that the respondent shall answer questions by interrogatories or shall submit an affidavit, or shall produce books, papers or other records, the order must specify the questions to be answered by the respondent, or the matters with which the respondent's affidavit must deal, or the time and manner in which the respondent shall produce the relevant books, papers or records.[16] Because failure to comply with the court's order is a contempt of court, the order must be served personally on the respondent.[17]

An oral examination of the respondent by the court takes place before the registrar, but he may adjourn it to be held before a judge.[18] If an oral examination before the court is ordered, the respondent may be represented at his own expense by a solicitor or counsel, who may put such questions to the respondent as the court allows so that he may explain or qualify his answers to the questions put to him by the official receiver or the liquidator.[19] The record of the respondent's examination, his answers to any interrogatories administered to him and the statements in any affidavit made by him are not filed in court unless the court so orders; they are therefore not open to inspection by anyone other than the official receiver and the liquidator of the company for the time being, unless the court gives leave.[20]

A private examination will be ordered only if it will assist the official receiver or the liquidator to fulfil his functions under the

14 *Re Rolls Razor (No 2)* [1970] Ch 576, [1969] 3 All ER 1386.
15 *Re British and Commonwealth Holdings plc (No 2)* [1992] BCLC 641, [1992] BCC 172.
16 Insolvency Rules 1986, r 9.3(2) to (4).
17 Ibid, r 9.3(5).
18 Ibid, r 7.6(1) to (3).
19 Ibid, r 9.4(5).
20 Ibid, r 9.5(1) and (2).

Insolvency Act 1986,[1] including inquiring into the causes of the company's insolvency, but not if the purpose of the examination is to elicit evidence to support a personal claim by a creditor of the company against the person whose examination is sought.[2] A private examination will, in particular, be ordered to enable the liquidator to discover facts or evidence which will enable him to decide whether to bring proceedings on the company's behalf for damages or reparation or restitution of assets against the person examined or other persons,[3] or to decide whether to proceed with an action which he has already resolved to bring,[4] but not if the examination is intended merely to obtain evidence in support of an action by the company which is already pending, since the normal processes of discovery should be employed for that purpose.[5] The fact that the company has previously litigated against the person proposed to be examined about the matters which are to be the subject of the private examination or related matters, however, will not prevent the court from ordering such an examination if the liquidator needs to decide whether to bring further proceedings for the recovery of assets or damages which, if the proceedings are successful, will become available to satisfy the company's debts and liabilities.[6]

A private examination will not be ordered, if after giving due weight to the liquidator's need to obtain the information sought, the court considers that to order an examination would be unfair or oppressive for the person proposed to be examined,[7] particularly when the liquidator already has sufficient information to enable him to judge whether he should institute proceedings for the recovery of damages by the company from that person.[8] However, the fact that the person to be examined will need to undertake a heavy burden of work in order to answer the questions to be put to him, or to identify the documents, which he is required to produce, will not, of itself,

---

1 *British and Commonwealth Holdings plc v Spicer and Oppenheim* [1993] BCLC 168, [1992] BCC 977.
2 *Re Movitex Ltd* [1990] BCLC 785, [1990] BCC 491.
3 *Re Spiraflite Ltd* [1979] 2 All ER 766, [1979] 1 WLR 1096n; *Re Castle New Homes Ltd* [1979] 2 All ER 775, [1979] 1 WLR 1075.
4 *Re Cloverbay Ltd (No 3)* [1990] BCC 414; affd [1991] BCLC 135; *British and Commonwealth Holdings plc v Spicer and Oppenheim*, supra.
5 *Re Bletchley Boat Co Ltd* [1974] 1 All ER 1225, [1974] 1 WLR 630; *Re John T Rhodes Ltd (No 2)* (1987) 3 BCC 588.
6 *Re J T Rhodes Ltd* [1987] BCLC 77; *Re John T Rhodes Ltd (No 2)* (1987) 3 BCC 588.
7 *Re Embassy Art Products Ltd* [1988] BCLC 1, 3 BCC 292; *Re Adlards Motor Group Holdings Ltd* [1990] BCLC 68; *Re Cloverbay Ltd (No 3)* supra; *British and Commonwealth Holdings plc v Spicer and Oppenheim*, supra.
8 *Re Cloverbay Ltd (No 3)* [1990] BCLC 471, [1990] BCC 414.

induce the court to dispense with the oral examination or the production of documents, or to restrict the extent of the examination or the required disclosure.[9]

A person who is ordered to be privately examined is not absolved from answering questions put to him because his answers are likely to incriminate him,[10] and the transcript of his answers may be used as evidence against him in criminal proceedings.[11]

Public examination

The public examination of persons connected with a company is designed to elicit information about the company's promotion and management which may be used for the purpose of recovering assets of the company, or of enforcing claims by it against the persons examined or against third persons, or of initiating criminal proceedings. The official receiver may at any time before the dissolution of a company apply to the court which made a winding up order against the company to order the public examination of any person who is or has been a director or officer of the company, or who has acted as a liquidator of the company in a voluntary winding up or as a receiver or manager of its property, or who has been concerned or taken part in the promotion, formation or management of the company.[12] Although the initiative rests with the official receiver, he must apply to the court to order the public examination of any such person if he is requested to do so by one half in value of the company's creditors or three-quarters in value of the company's contributories, but the court may absolve him from his duty to apply in these circumstances.[13]

Unless the court permits him to make an ex parte application, the official receiver must serve a copy of his application on the person whom he seeks to have publicly examined, and if he is a person who is alleged to have been concerned or to have taken part in the promotion, formation or management of the company, the application must be accompanied by a report by the official receiver setting out the grounds for that allegation and stating whether in his opinion service of an order for the public examination of that person

9 *British and Commonwealth Holdings plc v Spicer and Oppenheim*, supra.
10 *Re Jeffrey S Levitt Ltd* [1992] BCLC 250, [1992] BCC 137; *Re AE Farr Ltd* [1992] BCLC 333, [1992] BCC 150; *Re Bishopsgate Investment Management Ltd* [1993] Ch 1, [1992] BCLC 475.
11 *R v Kansal* [1992] BCLC 1009, [1992] BCC 615.
12 Insolvency Act 1986, s 133(1).
13 Ibid, s 133(2); Insolvency Rules 1986, r 4.213(5).

can be effected by post at a known address.[14] If the report states that it is unlikely that service by post at that address can be effected, the court may direct that its order for a public examination shall be served by some means other than, or in addition to, service by post.[15] In all other cases where the court orders the public examination of any person, he must be served with the order personally, or if the court directs, by post or other form of substituted service.[16]

The official receiver must also give at least 14 days' notice of the time and place of the public examination by post to the liquidator of the company if one has been appointed, to any special manager of the company's business who has been appointed,[17] and to every creditor and contributory who is known to the official receiver or named in the statement of affairs.[18] The official receiver may also advertise the order in one or more newspapers at least 14 days before the date of the public examination; the advertisement must be published not earlier than seven days after the order for the public examination is served, so as to give the person who is ordered to be publicly examined an opportunity to appeal against it.[19]

A public examination ordered by the court must be held in open court before the registrar of the Companies' Court or the court which made the winding up order, or if the registrar so directs, before a judge.[20] At the examination, questions concerning the promotion, formation or management of the company which the court allows may be put to the person examined by the official receiver, or by the liquidator or special manager of the company (if any), or by any creditor who has tendered proof of his claim, or by any contributory, and any such person may with the court's approval be represented by a solicitor or counsel.[1] If the person to be examined fails to attend for his public examination without having a reasonable excuse for his failure, he is guilty of a contempt of court,[2] and he is also guilty of contempt if he refuses to answer any question which the court allows to be put to him, it being no excuse that his answer would or might incriminate him.[3] The person examined may at his own expense employ a solicitor or counsel to

14 Insolvency Rules 1986, r 4.211(2) and r 7.3(3) and (4).
15 Ibid, r 4.211(3).
16 Ibid, r 4.211(1).
17 See p 160, ante.
18 Insolvency Rules 1986, r 4.212(2).
19 Ibid, r 4.212(3).
20 Ibid, r 7.6(1) to (3); Practice Direction dated 10 December 1986, paras 2 and 3.
 1 Insolvency Act 1986, s 133(3) and (4); Insolvency Rules 1986, r 4.215(1) and (2).
 2 Insolvency Act 1986, s 134(1).
 3 *Re Bishopgate Investment Management Ltd* [1993] Ch 1, [1992] BCLC 375.

put to him such questions as the court allows, to enable him to explain or qualify any answers given by him.[4] A written record of the questions put to the person examined and of his answers to them must be made and read over to him, and he must sign the record as correct and verify his answers by affidavit.[5] The written record of the examination may then be used as evidence against the person examined in any civil or criminal proceedings, whether under the Insolvency Act 1986 or not.[6] If criminal proceedings are initiated against a person whom the court has ordered to undergo a public examination, the court may adjourn the examination if it considers that its continuance would be calculated to prejudice a fair trial.[7]

The expenses incurred in holding a public examination are normally payable out of the assets of the company as part of the official receiver's general expenses; but if an application for a public examination is made by the official receiver at the request of one half in value of the company's creditors or three-quarters in value of its contributories, the court may order that the expenses of the examination shall be met wholly or partially out of the deposit which the requisitionists are required to make with the official receiver as security for expenses when they lodge the requisition with him.[8]

Investigations and examinations in a voluntary liquidation; liquidator's reports on directors' conduct

The official receiver has no functions to fulfil in the early stages of a voluntary winding up comparable to his functions of inquiry and investigation at the commencement of a winding up by the court. If the voluntary winding up begins as a creditors' voluntary winding up because the directors of the company do not make a statutory declaration of solvency before the winding up resolution is passed, the directors are required to prepare and lay before the meeting of creditors which they must call at the time of, or shortly after, the passing of the winding up resolution a statement of the company's affairs verified by affidavit in a similar form to, and containing the same detailed information as, the statement of its affairs which directors in a winding up by the court are called on to prepare by the official receiver.[9] This information provides a basis on which the

4 Insolvency Rules 1986, r 4.215(3).
5 Ibid, r 4.215(4).
6 Ibid, r 4.215(5).
7 Ibid, r 4.215(6).
8 Insolvency Rules 1986, r 4.213(3), r 4.217(1) and r 4.218(1)(*b*).
9 Insolvency Act 1986, s 98(1) and s 99(1) and (2); Insolvency Rules 1986, r 4.34(1) and Sch 4, Form 4.19 (see p 112, ante).

liquidator appointed by the meeting of creditors or by the general meeting which passes the winding up resolution can make his own inquiries to ascertain whether the directors or other persons concerned with managing the company have committed criminal offences or breaches of duty for which they can be compelled to compensate the company in the winding up proceedings.

If the voluntary winding up commences as a members' voluntary liquidation, but the liquidator forms the opinion that the company will be unable to discharge its debts and liabilities in full in the period specified in the directors' statutory declaration of solvency which was made before the winding up resolution was passed, the liquidator is required to call a meeting of creditors and to prepare and lay before it a verified statement of the company's affairs, containing the same items of information as a statement of affairs laid by directors before the meeting of creditors which is held when a company resolves to go into a creditors' voluntary liquidation.[10]

The liquidator in a liquidation which commences as a creditors' voluntary winding up, or which is converted into one, should therefore have a considerable quantity of basic information enabling him to plan the conduct of the liquidation and to initiate proceedings against persons who are liable to the company to pay debts and satisfy obligations which they owe it, or in order to compensate the company for breaches of duty which they have committed and to restore assets of the company in their possession or control. The liquidator is able to augment this basic information by exercising the same powers as the official receiver or a liquidator in a winding up by the court to compel persons who are or have been directors, officers or employees of the company in liquidation or of another company which is or has been an officer of the company, and persons who have taken part in the promotion or formation of the company in liquidation, to provide the liquidator with such information about the company's promotion, formation, business, dealings, affairs or property as he reasonably requires.[11] As indicated above,[12] the liquidator may also apply to the court to order the private examination by the court of any officer of the company, or of any person known or suspected of being in possession of any of its assets or of being indebted to it, or of any person whom the court thinks capable of giving information about the company's promotion, formation, business, dealings or assets.[13] Finally, the liquidator may

---

10 Insolvency Act 1986, s 95(1) to (4); Insolvency Rules 1986, r 4.34(1) and Sch 4, Form 4.18, (see p 91, ante).
11 Insolvency Act 1986, s 235(1) to (3) (see p 114, ante).
12 See p 178, ante.
13 Insolvency Act 1986, s 236(1) and (2).

apply to the court for an order that any present or former director or officer of the company, or any person who has been concerned or taken part in the promotion, formation or management of the company, shall undergo a public examination by the court, but this is rare when the company is in voluntary liquidation and the court has not already made a winding up order in respect of it.[14] The powers of the court and the rules of procedure governing an application for a private or public examination and the holding of such an examination are the same as when such an examination is applied for or held in connection with a winding up by the court.

There is a further function of a liquidator in a voluntary winding up, which has no exact counterpart in a winding up by the court,[15] but may result in information being obtained to assist the liquidator in enforcing liabilities against directors and shadow directors of the company, and also to support criminal proceedings against them or proceedings to disqualify them from being or acting as directors of any company. A liquidator in a members' or creditors' voluntary winding up is under an obligation to send a report in the prescribed form to the Secretary of State for Trade and Industry if it appears to him in the course of the liquidation that the company is or has at any time been insolvent, and that any person to whom the report relates is, or was at the time of the company's insolvency or within three years beforehand, a director or shadow director of the company and that he has been guilty of conduct which makes him unfit to be a director of any company.[16] The report which the liquidator is required to make must list all the directors and shadow directors of the company during the period to which the report relates, must summarise the financial condition of the company during that period and give detailed information about the individual directors or shadow directors to whom the report relates, indicating the remuneration, expense allowances and other benefits received by them during the three years preceding the commencement of the liquidation, all other companies of which they were directors or shadow directors during those three years, and the conduct of any of the directors or shadow directors which in the liquidator's opinion shows him to be unfit to be a director of any company.[17]

14 Ibid, s 133(1); *Re Campbell Coverings Ltd (No 2)* [1954] Ch 225, [1954] 1 All ER 222; (see p 182, ante).
15 The nearest equivalent is the report which the official receiver (not the liquidator) is required to make in respect of the conduct of directors and shadow directors of a company which is being wound up by the court; (see p 112, ante).
16 Company Directors' Disqualification Act 1986, s 6(1), s 7(3) and s 22(4) and (5).
17 Insolvent Companies (Reports on Conduct of Directors) Rules 1996 (SI 1996/1909), r 3(1) and (2) and Schedule, Form D1.

To ensure that liquidators in a voluntary liquidation fulfil their obligation to report on conduct by directors which shows them to be unfit to be directors of any company, a liquidator in a creditors' voluntary winding up must, within six months after the resolution to wind up the company is passed, and the liquidator in a members' voluntary winding up who forms the opinion that the assets of the company at the date of the resolution to wind it up were not sufficient to discharge its debts and liabilities in full within the period specified in the directors' statutory declaration of solvency, must within six months after forming that opinion, send a report in the prescribed form to the Secretary of State.[18] The report must state why the liquidator has not yet made a report about all the persons who are at the commencement of the six month period, or who have been within the preceding three years, directors or shadow directors of the company; and the reasons given for the absence of a report must fall under one of the three alternative heads, namely, that the company has in fact sufficient assets to pay its debts and the expenses of the winding up in full, or that the liquidator is unaware of any matters concerning the directors which call for a report, or that the liquidator does not yet have sufficient information to make a report.[19]

The principal use which is made of the liquidator's reports under these provisions is to seek disqualification orders or orders imposing personal liability on directors and shadow directors to contribute towards payment of the debts and liabilities of the company under the provisions of the Insolvency Act 1986, dealt with in Chapter 5,[20] but the information obtained by the liquidator for the purpose of making the reports may, of course, be used by him for other purposes of the liquidation.

Director of Public Prosecutions and Department of Trade and Industry

If in a winding up by the court it appears that any past or present officer or member of the company has committed a criminal offence in relation to the company, the court may of its own motion, or on the application of a creditor or contributory, direct the liquidator to refer the matter to the Director of Public Prosecutions.[1] The

---

18 Ibid, r 4(1) to (5) and Schedule, Form D2.
19 Ibid, Sch, Form D3.
20 See pp 254 and 259 and *Pennington's Company Law* (7th edn), p 717.
 1 Insolvency Act 1986, s 218(1) and (2).

liquidator in a winding up by the court must report to the official receiver any such criminal offence which appears to him to have been committed by any past or present officer of the company[2] so that the official receiver may take appropriate action to initiate a prosecution or proceedings for the disqualification of the officer concerned from acting as a director of any company.[3]

If in a voluntary winding up it appears to the liquidator that any such criminal offence has been committed, he must refer the matter to the Director of Public Prosecutions, and give him access to all relevant information and documents in the liquidator's possession or under his control.[4] If a report is made to the Director of Public Prosecutions by the liquidator in a voluntary winding up, the Director may refer the matter to the Secretary of State for Trade and Industry for further inquiry, and the Secretary of State may for the purpose of investigating the allegations in the report exercise any of the powers conferred on an inspector appointed by the Secretary of State under the Companies Act 1985,[5] to investigate the affairs of a company,[6] or alternatively he may appoint an inspector to carry out the investigation.[7] Any answers given by a person in response to questions put to him by the Secretary of State may be used in evidence against him.[8]

PAYMENTS AND ACCOUNTS

Payments by and to the liquidator

Winding up by the court

The liquidator in a winding up by the court must pay all money received by him in the course of the liquidation into the Insolvency Services Account kept by the Secretary of State for Trade and Industry at the Bank of England, except in so far as he is authorised by the Secretary of State to pay money received in connection with carrying on the company's business into an account with the local branch of a recognised bank.[9] The liquidator must remit money

2 Ibid, s 218(3).
3 For disqualification proceedings, see *Pennington's Company Law* (7th edn) p 717.
4 Insolvency Act 1986, s 218(4).
5 See *Pennington's Company Law* (7th edn) p 912.
6 Insolvency Act 1986, s 218(5).
7 Companies Act 1985, s 432(1).
8 Insolvency Act 1986, s 219(2).
9 Insolvency Act 1986, s 411(1) and (2) and Sch 8, para 16; Insolvency Regulations 1994 (SI 1994/2507), reg 5(1) and reg 6(1) to (4).

received by him to the Insolvency Services Account once every 14 days, but if he receives an amount of £5,000 or more on any one occasion, he must remit it immediately.[10] A remittance by the liquidator must be made through the Bank Giro system (ie by credit transfer or through the Bankers' Automated Clearing Service), or by being sent directly to the Bank of England, Threadneedle Street, London EC2R 9AH by a cheque drawn in favour of 'Insolvency Services Account' and crossed 'A/c payee only'.[11] Presumably, it is also permissible for the liquidator to indorse any cheque he receives which is payable to the company or to himself as its liquidator, and to send it to the Bank of England for collection, but the indorsement should be a special one to 'Insolvency Services Account'; the liquidator need not make his indorsement 'without recourse', provided that he indorses his cheque expressly as liquidator of the company. A receipt is issued by the Bank of England for each remittance made by the liquidator to the Insolvency Services Account if the liquidator requests.[11]

The liquidator makes payments out of moneys standing to the company's credit in the Insolvency Services Account by applying to the Department of Trade and Industry for the issue of cheques, money orders or warrants in favour of the respective payees, and by forwarding the cheques etc to the persons to whom they are made payable when he has received them from the Department.[12] If a liquidator meets necessary disbursements or expenses out of his own pocket, or out of funds other than the company's, he may obtain reimbursement out of the amount standing to the company's credit in the Insolvency Services Account by applying to the Department of Trade and Industry and submitting a requisition for payment, detailing the expenses; if the liquidator vacates office before receiving reimbursement, he may claim payment from the official receiver or his successor as liquidator out of the same credit balance.[13] If any person claims to be entitled to any money paid into the Insolvency Services Account (eg as a creditor of the company in liquidation), he may, on the liquidator's failure to procure its payment to him, apply to the Secretary of State for Trade and Industry for payment on submitting such evidence of his claim as the Secretary of State requires; and if the Secretary of State declines to make the payment, the claimant may appeal to the court which made the winding up order.[14]

10 Insolvency Regulations 1986, reg 5(1).
11 Ibid, reg 5(3).
12 Ibid, reg 7(2).
13 Ibid, reg 7(1) and (5).
14 Ibid, reg 32(1) and (2).

If a liquidator in a winding up by the court exercises his power to carry on the company's business with a view to its realisation as a going concern after having obtained the consent of the liquidation committee or the court to do so,[15] he may apply to the Secretary of State for Trade and Industry for an authorisation to open and operate a specified account with a local branch of a recognised bank for the purpose of carrying on the company's business; the Secretary of State may authorise the liquidator to make payments into and out of such a specified account, instead of the Insolvency Services Account, for the purposes of carrying on the company's business, subject to a limit fixed by the Secretary of State on the balance which may be maintained in the account from time to time.[16] An insolvency practitioner who is authorised as the liquidator of two or more insolvent companies to maintain local bank accounts while carrying on their respective businesses must maintain separate bank accounts for each such company, and must pay into and out of the bank account for each of the companies only money belonging to it or payable by it in respect of the carrying on of its business.[16] If the liquidator of a company ceases to carry on the company's business, or ceases to carry on practice as an insolvency practitioner, or vacates office as liquidator, or if the Secretary of State revokes his authorisation to maintain a local bank account for carrying on the company's business, he must immediately close the bank account and remit any balance standing to its credit to the Insolvency Services Account.[18] The insolvency practitioner must keep proper records of amounts paid into and out of each local bank account which he is authorised to maintain.[19]

Voluntary winding up

The rules governing the holding and disposal of moneys received by the liquidator of a company which is in voluntary liquidation are less stringent than those applicable in a winding up by the court. The liquidator must, within 14 days after the expiration of each succeeding period of six months from the date of his appointment and on vacating office, pay into the Insolvency Services Account to the credit of the company in liquidation the balance of money belonging to it which is in his hands or under his control, but he may retain any part of that balance which he considers necessary for the immediate

15 Insolvency Act 1986, s 167(1).
16 Insolvency Regulations 1994, reg 6(1) and (2).
17 Ibid, reg 7(3) and (4).
18 Ibid, reg 7(8).
19 Ibid, reg 7(6).

purposes of the liquidation.[20] If the liquidator requires a payment to be made out of the Insolvency Services Account in connection with the liquidation, he must apply in writing to the Secretary of State for Trade and Industry, who may authorise the payment of a sufficient sum to the liquidator, or may direct that payment instruments in favour of the intended payees shall be delivered to the liquidator for transmission to them.[1]

Liquidator's financial records and audit

The liquidator in a winding up by the court or in a creditors' voluntary winding up must keep separate financial records in respect of each company of which he is the liquidator, and must enter receipts and payments daily in those records.[2] If the liquidator carries on the company's business with a view to its ultimate sale, he must keep separate trading accounts in respect of the business, including particulars of payments made into and out of any local bank account which he maintains; and he must enter in the main financial record which he keeps for the liquidation the total weekly amounts of his receipts and payments in respect of the business, in addition to the daily entries which he is required to make in the record in respect of other payments and receipts.[3] The liquidator must submit his main financial record for the liquidation to the liquidation committee whenever it requires,[4] and if the committee is not satisfied with the record, it may inform the Secretary of State for Trade and Industry and request him to have it audited when it is submitted to him by the liquidator at the end of the current period for which he is required to submit an account.[4]

The liquidator in a winding up by the court or in a creditors' voluntary winding up must send to the Secretary of State an account of his receipts and payments in connection with the liquidation for such a period or successive periods of the liquidation as the Secretary of State directs and must certify the accounts as correct if the Secretary of State requires.[5] In a winding up by the court the account must be accompanied by a summary of the statement of affairs made at the commencement of the winding up, or if no statement of affairs was prepared, it must be accompanied by a summary of the known

20 Ibid, reg 5(2).
 1 Ibid, reg 7(3).
 2 Ibid, reg 10(1).
 3 Ibid, reg 12(2).
 4 Ibid, reg 10(4).
 5 Ibid, reg 14(1).

assets of the company and a statement of the amount so far realised
from those assets; in either case, the liquidator must explain why the
remaining assets of the company have not yet been realised.[6] In a
winding up by the court, within 14 days after vacating office or
holding the final meeting of creditors at the conclusion of the
winding up, the liquidator must send to the Secretary of State his
final account in the same form as a periodic account, but covering
the period from the date to which the preceding periodic account
was made up to the date when the liquidator vacates office or the
date when the final meeting of creditors is held (as the case may be);
if the liquidator vacates office or the final meeting of creditors is held
before the liquidator has delivered his first periodic account to the
Secretary of State, his final account must cover the whole period of
the liquidation.[7]

The Secretary of State may have the liquidator's periodic or
final account audited;[8] but whether he does so or not, he may require
the liquidator to produce vouchers and give information in relation
to the account, and also to produce for inspection any accounts,
books or records which he or any of his predecessors in office has
kept in connection with the liquidation.[9] Any creditor, contributory
or director of the company in liquidation may require the liquidator
to supply him with a copy of the liquidator's periodic accounts sent
to the Secretary of State covering the one year period ending on the
most recent anniversary of him becoming a liquidator of the
company.[10]

THE CONCLUSION OF A LIQUIDATION

Introductory

A liquidation is technically concluded when the company is dissolved,
and so ceases to be a legal person, or when the assets of the company
are completely disposed of (eg by the remaining proceeds of the
realisation of its assets being paid into the Insolvency Services
Accounts at the Bank of England), whichever is the later.[11] The final

6 Ibid, reg 14(4) and (5).
7 Ibid, reg 14(2) and (3).
8 Ibid, reg 14(6).
9 Ibid, reg 15(1).
10 Ibid, reg 11(1) and (2).
11 Insolvency Rules 1986, r 4.223(2). This rule applies only in the creditors'
   voluntary liquidation, but a winding up by the court is concluded at the same
   time.

steps to be taken by the liquidator to complete the winding up may be considered for practical purposes as dating from the time when he declares and pays the final dividend to the creditors of the company out of the company's remaining assets or, if the company is solvent, when he distributes its remaining assets among its contributories after discharging the company's debts and liabilities in full (including the statutory interest calculated up to the date of payment).[12] In a winding up by the court, there is provision for the summary conclusion of the liquidation if the official receiver is satisfied that the company's assets are insufficient to meet the cost of winding it up,[13] but there is nothing equivalent to this in a voluntary liquidation. For this and other reasons, the procedure to conclude a liquidation differs in a winding up by the court from the procedure in a voluntary winding up, and in this chapter the two procedures will be dealt with separately.

Winding up by the court

Summary dissolution

If in a winding up of a company by the court the official receiver is the liquidator (whether because no liquidator has ever been appointed or because the liquidator previously holding office has ceased to do so and no other qualified insolvency practitioner has been appointed in his place), the official receiver may apply to the Registrar of Companies for the early dissolution of the company, if it appears to him that the company's realisable assets are insufficient to discharge the expenses of the liquidation, and that the affairs of the company do not require any further investigation (eg because of the likelihood that directors or officers of the company have been guilty of conduct for which they could be prosecuted in criminal proceedings, or for which they could be disqualified by the court from being directors of any company, or because further investigation might reveal assets which could be recovered or payments which could be exacted to supplement the assets of the company).[14]

Before making an application to the Registrar of Companies, the official receiver must give to the company's creditors and contributories at least 28 days' notice of his intention to do so, by sending them individual notices by post or by delivering such

12 Insolvency Act 1986, s 189(1) to (4).
13 Ibid, s 202.
14 Ibid, s 202(1) and (2).

notices to them.[15] When he has given notice of his intention to apply for the early dissolution of the company, the official receiver ceases to be required to perform any further duties in the winding up of the company, apart from making the application to the Registrar of Companies.[16] The Registrar must register the official receiver's application on receiving it, and at the expiration of three months from the date of registration, the company is automatically dissolved.[17]

When notice of the official receiver's intention to apply for the early dissolution of the company has been given to its creditors and contributories, either the official receiver or any creditor or contributory may apply to the Secretary of State for Trade and Industry to give directions that the winding up shall proceed as though no application for an early dissolution of the company had been made, or to direct that the date of the dissolution shall be deferred for such time as the Secretary of State decides.[18] The grounds on which such an application may be made are that the realisable assets of the company are sufficient to cover the costs of the liquidation, or that the affairs of the company do in fact require further investigation, or that for any other reason the early dissolution of the company is inappropriate.[19] The Secretary of State must send to the applicant two copies of the direction which he gives, and the applicant must deliver one of these copies to the Registrar of Companies for registration.[20] No time limit is set by the Insolvency Act 1986, on the making of an application to the Secretary of State to give directions, but it would appear not to be possible for the Secretary of State to give a direction that the winding up shall proceed, or that the date of the dissolution shall be deferred, later than three months after the official receiver made his application for early dissolution to the Registrar of Companies. If the company has already been dissolved at the expiration of that time, it would seem that the only way in which it can be revived is by an order of the court.[1]

Whether the Secretary of State, on a application to defer the dissolution of the company, gives directions that the winding up shall proceed, or that the dissolution of the company shall be deferred, or that the official receiver's application to the Registrar shall have its normal effect, an appeal lies to the court against the Secretary of State's directions, apparently at the instance of any

15 Ibid, s 202(3); Insolvency Rules 1986, rr 12.10 and 13.3(1) to (3).
16 Insolvency Act 1986, s 202(4).
17 Ibid, s 202(5).
18 Ibid, s 202(5) and s 203(1) and (3).
19 Ibid, s 203(2).
20 Ibid, s 203(5); Insolvency Rules 1986, r 4.224(1) and (2).
 1 Companies Act 1985, s 651(1); (see p 204, post).

interested person.[2] The appeal is heard by the registrar of the court in chambers, but he may refer it to a judge for decision.[3] The court may dispose of the appeal by substituting its directions for those of the Secretary of State, or by confirming his directions. The court sends two sealed copies of the order which it makes to the person in whose favour the appeal is decided, and he must deliver one of them to the Registrar of Companies for registration.[4]

Normal conclusion of a winding up by the court

Where the winding up of a company by the court is carried out in the normal way and no application is made by the official receiver to the Registrar of Companies for the early dissolution of the company, the liquidator (if not the official receiver) must, when the winding up of the company's affairs is complete for practical purposes, call a final meeting of the company's creditors to receive the liquidator's report of his conduct of the winding up and to decide whether the liquidator shall have his release.[5] The liquidator may call the meeting at the same time as he gives notice to the creditors of the final dividend to be paid to them or, if the company is solvent, at the same time as he gives notice to the contributories of his intention to distribute the company's remaining assets to them; but if the creditors' meeting is called for an earlier date than that on which the notice of a final distribution is sent out, the meeting must be adjourned until the liquidator is able to report to the meeting that the winding up of the company is for practical purposes complete.[6]

The liquidator calls the final meeting of creditors by giving at least 28 clear days' notice of it to each creditor who has lodged a proof of his debt or claim against the company; the notice is given in the same way as notices of other meetings of creditors, and it must be advertised in the London Gazette.[7] The report laid by the liquidator before the meeting must contain a summary of the liquidator's receipts and payments and a statement by him that he has reconciled his account with the account of the liquidation which he has delivered to the Secretary of State for Trade and Industry.[8]

---

2 Insolvency Act 1986, s 203(4).
3 Insolvency Rules 1986, r 7.6(1) to (3).
4 Ibid, r 4.225.
5 Insolvency Act 1986, s 146(1).
6 Ibid, s 146(2).
7 Insolvency Rules 1986, r 4.125(1), r 12.4(1), r 12.10(1) to (3) and r 13.3(1) to (3).
8 Ibid, r 4.125(2).

At the final meeting of creditors, the liquidator may be questioned in respect of any matters contained in his report, and the meeting may resolve that he shall or shall not have his release.[9]

After the final meeting of creditors has been held, the liquidator must give notice of the fact to the court and to the Registrar of Companies, stating whether the meeting gave him his release or not, and the liquidator must also deliver copies of the report which he laid before the meeting to the Registrar of Companies and to the official receiver.[10] The liquidator vacates office when he has given notice of the final meeting of creditors to the court and the Registrar; the company is then dissolved at the expiration of three months from the registration of the notice by the Registrar.[11] However, on the application of the official receiver or any other interested person, the Secretary of State for Trade and Industry may direct that the dissolution of the company shall be deferred for such time as the Secretary of State thinks fit.[12] The Secretary of State must send two copies of the direction which he gives to the liquidator, who must send one of them to the Registrar of Companies for registration.[13] An appeal lies to the court against the direction given by the Secretary of State, whether he has directed that the date of the company's dissolution shall be deferred or not, and it would seem that any interested person may bring such an appeal.[14] The appeal is heard by the registrar of the court in chambers, but he may refer it to a judge for decision.[15] The court sends two sealed copies of its decision on the appeal to the person in whose favour it was decided, and he must send one of the copies to the Registrar of Companies for registration.[16]

If at the time when a winding up of a company by the court is completed the official receiver is the liquidator, he does not call a final meeting of creditors, but merely gives notice to the Secretary of State for Trade and Industry and to the Registrar of Companies that the winding up is for practical purposes complete so as to obtain his release.[17] Before applying for his release, however, the official receiver must give notice of his intention to do so to each creditor of the company who has lodged a proof of his debt or claim, and the notice must be accompanied by a summary of the official receiver's

---

9 Ibid, r 4.125(3). For the release of the liquidator, see p 197, ante.
10 Insolvency Act 1986, s 182(8); Insolvency Rules 1986, r 4.125(4).
11 Insolvency Act 1986, s 172(8) and s 205(1) and (2).
12 Ibid, s 205(3).
13 Insolvency Rules 1986, r 4.224(2).
14 Insolvency Act 1986, s 205(4).
15 Insolvency Rules 1986, r 7.6(1) to (3).
16 Insolvency Act 1986, s 205(6); Insolvency Rules 1986, r 4.225.
17 Insolvency Act 1986, s 146(1), s 174(3) and s 205(1).

receipts and payments.[18] The release of the official receiver takes effect from a date determined by the Secretary of State; the Secretary of State must notify the court when he has given the release, and must file in court a copy of the summary of the official receiver's receipts and payments which has been circulated to creditors.[19]

The company is dissolved three months after the Registrar of Companies registers the notice which he has received from the official receiver that the winding up of the company is completed for practical purposes, but the Secretary of State may on the application of the official receiver or any interested party defer the date of dissolution for such time as he thinks fit.[20] An appeal lies to the court against the Secretary of State's decision on an application to defer the dissolution of the company.[1] The procedure on such an application and on an appeal against the Secretary of State's decision is the same as in a winding up by the court when the liquidator has given notice to the Registrar of Companies that a final meeting of creditors has been held.[2]

Release of a liquidator in a winding up by the court

At the conclusion of a winding up by the court, the liquidator obtains his release from liability to the company and its creditors and contributories in connection with the liquidation at the time when he vacates office, that is, when he gives notice to the court and the Registrar of Companies of the holding of the final meeting of creditors.[3] However, if the final meeting of creditors resolves that the liquidator shall not be given his release, he is released from liability only if the Secretary of State for Trade and Industry so determines, and the release is then effective as from the date specified in the certificate of release which the Secretary of State issues to the liquidator.[4] The certificate must be sent by the Secretary of State to the official receiver so that he may file it in court, and he must send a copy of the certificate to the liquidator.[4]

The manner in which the official receiver obtains his release on the completion of the winding up was indicated in the preceding

18 Insolvency Rules 1986, r 4.124(1) and (2).
19 Insolvency Act 1986, s 174(3); Insolvency Rules 1986, r 4.124(3).
20 Insolvency Act 1986, s 205(2) and (3).
 1 Ibid, s 205(4).
 2 Insolvency Rules 1986, rr 4.224 and 4.225.
 3 Insolvency Act 1986, s 172(8) and s 174(4); Insolvency Rules 1986, r 4.125(6). For the effect of the release of a liquidator in a winding up by the court, see p 175, ante.
 4 Insolvency Act 1986, s 174(4); Insolvency Rules 1986, r 4.121(4) and (5).

paragraph, where it was shown that the release is given by the Secretary of State as part of the procedure for the dissolution of the company. There is no provision for the release of the official receiver if the company is summarily dissolved by the official receiver applying to the Registrar of Companies for early dissolution because of an insufficiency of the company's assets to cover the expenses of the liquidation.

Voluntary winding up

Members' voluntary winding up

When a members' voluntary winding up the company's affairs are fully wound up, the liquidator must prepare an account of the winding up, showing how it has been conducted and how the company's assets have been disposed of; he must then call a general meeting of the members of the company in order to lay the account before them and to explain the account to them.[5] The general meeting of members must be called in the same way as a general meeting of the company before it went into liquidation; additionally, it must be advertised in the London Gazette at least 28 days before it is held; notices and advertisements of the meeting must specify the time and place of the meeting and state that it will be the final general meeting of the company in the liquidation.[6]

Within one week after the meeting is held, the liquidator must send to the Registrar of Companies a copy of the account he laid before the meeting, and must make a return to the Registrar of the holding of the meeting and of its date, or if a quorum of members was not present or represented at the meeting, the liquidator must make a return to that effect.[7] The return incorporates a form of account of the proceeds of realisation of the various classes of the company's assets, and of the various expenses which the liquidator has incurred during the liquidation; the form of account, although not mandatory, can usefully be employed in preparing the account which the liquidator lays before the final meeting.[8] On receiving a copy of the account of the liquidation laid before the final meeting and the return relating to the holding of the meeting, the Registrar of Companies must register them; at the expiration of three months

5 Insolvency Act 1986, s 94(1).
6 Ibid, s 94(2).
7 Ibid, s 94(3) and (5); Insolvency Rules 1986, Sch 4, Form 4.71.
8 Insolvency Act 1986, s 94(1).

from the date of registration, the company is automatically dissolved.[9] However, the court may, on the application of the liquidator or any other interested person, order that the date of the company's dissolution shall be deferred until such time as the court thinks fit; the successful applicant for an order deferring the company's dissolution must deliver an office copy of the order to the Registrar of Companies for registration.[10]

When the company has been dissolved and any remaining assets of the company have been distributed or paid into the Insolvency Services Account, the liquidator must send a final statement in the prescribed form to the Registrar of Companies.[11] The statement must cover the whole of the liquidation, showing the amounts realised from all the company's assets, the nature and amounts of the expenses incurred in the liquidation, any cash remaining in the liquidator's hands and the balance of the company's money in the Insolvency Services Account.[12] A final statement need not be sent by the liquidator to the Registrar of Companies if the liquidator has made a return of the holding of the final meeting of the members of the company to the Registrar, and that return shows that no assets or funds of the company remain unclaimed or undistributed in the hands or under the control of the liquidator or any former liquidator of the company, but the liquidator must then deliver a copy of the return to the Secretary of State for Trade and Industry.[13]

Creditor's voluntary winding up

A creditors' voluntary liquidation is concluded in the same way as a members' voluntary winding up, but the liquidator must call final meetings of both creditors and of members or contributories and lay before both meetings an account of the liquidation which he must prepare, and the liquidator must answer questions relating to the account which are put to him in the meeting of creditors.[14] Both meetings are governed by the relevant provisions of the Insolvency Rules 1986 relating to creditors' and contributories' meetings, but at least 28 days' notice of the final meeting of creditors must be given to each creditor who has lodged a proof for a debt or claim against the company.[15] Furthermore, both meetings must be advertised in the London Gazette at least one month before they are held,

9 Ibid, s 201(1) and (2).
10 Ibid, s 201(3) and (4).
11 Ibid, s 192(1).
12 Insolvency Rules 1986, r 4.1(1) and r 4.223(1) to (3) and Sch 4, Form 4.68.
13 Ibid, r 4.223(3A).
14 Insolvency Act 1986, s 106(1); Insolvency Rules 1986, r 4.126(2).
15 Insolvency Rules 1986, r 4.126(1).

specifying the times, dates and places at which they will be held and stating that they will be the final meetings of creditors and contributories respectively.[16]

Within one week after holding the meetings of creditors and of members or contributories (or the later of the two meetings if they are held on different dates) the liquidator must send to the Registrar of Companies a copy of the account which he laid before both meetings, and he must make a return to the Registrar of the holding of the meetings, or if a quorum was not present at either meeting, a return to that effect.[17] The return incorporates a form of account of the proceeds of realisation of the company's assets, and of the various expenses incurred by the liquidator in the liquidation; this form of account can usefully be employed in preparing the account of the liquidation to be laid before the meetings of creditors and contributories.[18] The Registrar of Companies must register the copy of the account and the notice of the final meetings of creditors and of members or contributories when he receives them; on the expiration of three months from the date of registration the company is automatically dissolved.[18] The court has the same power to defer the date of dissolution as it has in a members' voluntary winding up, and the successful applicant for a deferment must deliver an office copy of the court's order to the Registrar of Companies.[19]

When the company has been dissolved and its remaining assets (if any) have either been distributed or paid into the Insolvency Services Account, the liquidator must send a final statement to the Registrar of Companies in the same prescribed form and containing the same information as in a members' voluntary winding up.[20] However, the liquidator need not send such a final statement to the Registrar of Companies if the liquidator has made a return of the holding of the final meetings of creditors and of members or contributories to the Registrar, and that return shows that no assets or funds of the company remain unclaimed or undistributed in the hands or under the control of the liquidator or any former liquidator of the company, but the liquidator must then deliver a copy of the return to the Secretary of State for Trade and Industry.[1]

16 Insolvency Act 1986, s 106(2).
17 Insolvency Act 1986, s 106(3) and (5); Insolvency Rules 1986, Sch 4, Form 4.72.
18 Insolvency Act 1986, s 106(1).
19 Ibid, s 201(3) and (4).
20 Ibid, s 192(1); Insolvency Rules 1986, r 4.223(1) to (3) and Sch 4, Form 4.68.
 1 Insolvency Rules 1986, r 4.223(3A).

Release of the liquidator in a voluntary winding up

A liquidator in a members' voluntary winding up obtains his release from further liability to the company and its creditors and members or contributories when he vacates office on making a return to the Registrar of Companies of the holding of the final meeting of members or contributories in the liquidation.[2] A liquidator in a creditors' voluntary winding up similarly obtains his release when he makes a return to the Registrar of Companies of the holding of the final meetings of creditors and contributories; but if the final meeting of creditors resolves that the liquidator shall not be given his release, he must apply to the Secretary of State for Trade and Industry to grant it to him.[3] If the Secretary of State gives the liquidator his release, he must certify it accordingly, and send the certificate to the Registrar of Companies and a copy of the certificate to the liquidator; the release is effective from the date of the certificate.[4]

Dissolution and revival of a company

Effect of dissolution

On the dissolution of a company in liquidation in any of the ways mentioned above, the company's legal personality terminates. After its dissolution, the company no longer exists, and can no longer have or acquire rights or property, or incur or be subject to obligations or liabilities. Consequently, a person who has had a claim for damages against a company before its dissolution cannot enforce the company's rights under an insurance policy taken out by it to cover such a liability, because the statutory vesting of the company's rights under the policy in the claimant[5] cannot take effect after its dissolution, and those rights are thereby terminated if they have not been established against the company by judgment or compromise before the dissolution.[6] Likewise, an insurance company which settles a claim by a company cannot after its dissolution bring an action against a third person who was liable to the company for the loss

---

2 Insolvency Act 1986, s 171(6) and s 173(2). For the effect of the release of a liquidator in a voluntary liquidation, see p 175, ante.
3 Ibid, s 171(6) and s 173(2); Insolvency Rules 1986, r 4.126(3).
4 Insolvency Rules 1986, r 4.122(4) and (5) and r 4.126(3).
5 Third Parties (Rights Against Insurers) Act 1930, s 1(1) (4 *Halsbury's Statutes* (4th edn) 688).
6 *Bradley v Eagle Star Insurance Co Ltd* [1989] AC 957, [1989] 1 All ER 961.

insured against, by relying on the insurer's right to be subrogated to the company's right of action against the third person, because that right of action ceased to exist on the company's dissolution.[7]

In order to give public notice of the incipient dissolution of a company, the Registrar of Companies must advertise in the London Gazette the filing of the return made by the liquidator of the final meetings of creditors and of members or contributories at the end of a liquidation;[8] but no notice is published of the actual dissolution of the company when it occurs three months afterwards, or on any later date which is ordered by the Secretary of State for Trade and Industry or by the court.

When a company is dissolved, all items of property and rights vested in it or held in trust for it immediately beforehand (including leasehold property, but not property held by the company in trust for any other person) are deemed to be bona vacantia or ownerless property, and accordingly vest in the Crown or, if locally situate in the Duchies of Lancaster or Cornwall, vest in the Crown in right of the Duke of Lancaster or in the Duke of Cornwall.[9]

The Crown may disclaim any property which has vested in it on the dissolution of a company by a notice of disclaimer signed by the Treasury Solicitor within one year after the property comes to his notice, or within three months or such longer period as the court permits after any interested person calls on the Treasury Solicitor to elect whether to disclaim or not; the Crown may waive its right of disclaimer expressly, or by taking possession of, or asserting a right to, the property in question.[10] A notice of disclaimer by the Treasury Solicitor must be delivered to the Registrar of Companies, who must advertise it in the London Gazette and send copies of it to persons who have given notice that they claim to be interested in the property disclaimed.[11]

When property has been disclaimed by the Crown, it is deemed not to have vested in it, and the court may then make a vesting order in respect of the property on the application of any person who claims to have an interest in it or to be under a liability in respect of it; the court makes the order on the same conditions, and the order has the same effect, as if the liquidator had disclaimed the property in the course of the winding up.[12] Whether the Crown comes under

7 *M H Smith (Plant Hire) Ltd v Mainwaring* (1986) 2 BCC 262.
8 Companies Act 1985, s 711(1)(r); Insolvency Act 1986, s 94(3), s 106(3) and s 172(8); (see pp 195 and 198, ante).
9 Companies Act 1985, s 654(1).
10 Ibid, s 656(1) to (3).
11 Ibid, s 656(5).
12 Ibid, s 657(1) and (2) (as amended by Insolvency Act 1986, s 109(1) and Sch 6, para 46).

any liability in respect of the property if it has neither taken possession of it nor disclaimed it, is uncertain, but it is expressly provided that the Crown is not liable to pay a rentcharge in respect of land which vests in it unless it takes possession of the land.[13] Property held by the company on trust for other persons vests in the Crown, subject to the trust by the general law.[14] Whatever the nature of the trust property, however, the court may appoint a new trustee and vest the property in him, and if the trust property is land, the court may vest it in him for such estate as it thinks fit.[15]

Alternative method of dissolution

If a company is being wound up by the court or voluntarily and the Registrar of Companies has reasonable cause to believe that no liquidator is acting, or that the affairs of the company have been fully wound up, and no return has been made to the Registrar by the liquidator in respect of the liquidation for more than six months, the Registrar must publish in the London Gazette and send to the company or its liquidator (if any) a notice that, after the expiration of three months from the date of the notice, the company will be struck off the register of companies unless cause to the contrary is shown, and that the company will then be dissolved.[16] At the end of three months from the publication and despatch of the notice, the Registrar of Companies will strike the company's name off the register, unless cause has been shown to him why he should not do so or that he should defer the striking off; if cause is not shown, the Registrar must, on the expiration of the three months, publish a notice of the striking off of the company in the London Gazette.[17] On the publication of that notice, the company is dissolved, but this does not affect the power of the court to wind it up, nor does it relieve any director, managing officer or member of the company from any liability, and any such liability may be enforced as though the company had not been dissolved.[18]

If a company is dissolved by being struck off the register, a resolution subsequently passed by a meeting of its members to wind up the company voluntarily is, of course, ineffective because the company

---

13 Insolvency Act 1986, s 180.
14 *Re Strathblaine Estates Ltd* [1948] Ch 228, [1948] 1 All ER 162.
15 Trustee Act 1925, s 41(1) and (3) (48 *Halsbury's Statutes* (4th edn) (1995 Reissue) 311).
16 Companies Act 1985, s 652(4).
17 Ibid, s 652(5).
18 Ibid, s 652(5) and (6).

is no longer in existence;[19] but if the company is later restored to the register by order of the court under the provisions dealt with below, it appears that the winding-up resolution and acts done in the winding up of the company's affairs are thereby retrospectively validated.

Revocation of a dissolution

If a company has been dissolved in the normal way at the conclusion of its winding up, or if it has been dissolved by the Registrar of Companies striking its name off the register, the court may, on the application of the liquidator or any interested person within two years after the dissolution, make an order on such terms as it thinks fit declaring the dissolution void, and thereupon such proceedings may be taken as might have been taken if the company had not been dissolved.[20] The commonest ground for applications to the court to declare the company's dissolution void is that the liquidator was unaware at the date of the dissolution of assets of the company which will re-vest in it and be realisable for the benefit of its creditors or contributories on the dissolution of the company being avoided.[1] If an application for an order declaring the dissolution void is made in order that an action for damages in respect of personal injuries may be brought against the company, the application may be made at any time, but the court will refuse to accede to it if the limitation period allowed for bringing the action has already expired.[2]

A person is interested for the purpose of making an application for the revival of a company which has been dissolved only if he would have some claim against its assets if they were re-vested in it.[3] An application cannot be made therfore by the solicitor or agent of such a claimant, or by a person who has no interest capable of quantification in money terms.[4] However, it has been held that the Secretary of State for Trade and Industry has a sufficient interest to apply for the revocation of the dissolution of a company so that he may take proceedings for the disqualification of its former directors from being directors of, or taking part in the management of any company without leave of the court under the Company Directors'

---

19 *Re Wood and Martin (Bricklaying Contractors) Ltd* [1971] 1 All ER 732, [1971] 1 WLR 293.
20 Companies Act 1985, s 651(1), (2) and (4), as amended by Companies Act 1989, s 141(1) to (3). The application for the declaration by the court is made by originating summons (RSC Ord 102, r 3(1)).
1 *Re Oakleague Ltd* [1995] 2 BCLC 624, [1995] BCC 921.
2 Companies Act 1985, s 651(5) (added by Companies Act 1989, s 141(3)); *Re Workvale Ltd* [1991] 1 WLR 294, [1991] BCC 109.
3 *Re Belmont and Co Ltd* [1952] Ch 10, [1951] 2 All ER 898; *Re Test Holdings (Clifton) Ltd* [1970] Ch 285, [1969] 3 All ER 517.
4 *Re Roehampton Swimming Pool Ltd* [1968] 3 All ER 661, [1968] 1 WLR 1693.

Disqualification Act 1986.[5] If after a company's name has been struck off the register by the Registrar of Companies, its shareholders pass an ineffective winding up resolution and appoint a liquidator, the liquidator cannot apply in that capacity to have the dissolution revoked, for his appointment as liquidator is as ineffective as the winding up resolution; but if he has done work or incurred expense or liabilities in winding up the company's affairs, and so could claim an indemnity out of its assets if they were re-vested in it, he may apply for the revocation of its dissolution as an interested person.[6] An application to the court for the revocation of the dissolution of a company has also succeeded where the company was the grantee of a lease by the applicant, and the purpose of the application was to enable the applicant to enforce the company's liability for unpaid rent and breaches of the lessee's covenants occurring after the company had assigned the lease.[7] On the other hand, the court cannot on revoking the dissolution of a company order that an action brought against it while it was dissolved shall be retrospectively validated so that the action may be continued after the revocation of the dissolution.[8]

If a company is dissolved by the Registrar of Companies striking its name off the register, the company or any member or creditor of the company may apply to the court within 20 years after the publication of the notice of the striking off in the London Gazette for an order that the company shall be restored to the Register, and the court may in its discretion order the restoration.[9] Upon an office copy of the order being delivered to the Registrar, the company is deemed to have continued in existence as though its name had not been struck off the register; the court may give such directions as seem just for placing the company and all other persons so far as possible in the same position as if the company had not been dissolved.[10] In exercise of this power the court has directed that leases or sub-leases granted by the company which terminated on the disclaimer of the dissolved company's freehold or leasehold interest by the Treasury Solicitor shall be restored on the company itself being restored to the register.[11]

5 *Re Townreach Ltd* [1995] Ch 28, [1994] BCC 933.
6 *Re Wood and Martin (Building Contractors) Ltd*, supra; *Re Portrafram Ltd* [1986] BCLC 533, 2 BCC 160.
7 *Stanhope Pension Trust Ltd v Registrar of Companies* [1994] 1 BCLC 628, [1994] BCC 84.
8 *Re Mixhurst Ltd* [1994] 2 BCLC 19, [1993] BCC 757.
9 Companies Act 1985, s 653(1) and (2).
10 Ibid, s 653(3).
11 *Shire Court Residents Ltd v Registrar of Companies* [1995] BCC 821.

An application for the restoration of a company to the register may be made only by a person who was a member or creditor of the company at the date when it was struck off; consequently, an application may not be made by a person who has paid money to the company or for its benefit since it was struck off,[12] or who has since then acquired the shares or other interests in the company of a member or creditor.[13] However, the personal representatives or the trustee in bankruptcy of a member who dies or becomes bankrupt before or after the dissolution of the company may make an application by virtue of the statutory provision which places them in the same position as the deceased or the bankrupt in a winding up,[14] and it is immaterial whether they have themselves been registered as members.[15]

If an action is brought against a company after it has been struck off the register, the action is a nullity and will be dismissed by the court, but if an application has been made to the court to restore the company to the register, the court will stay the action until the application for restoration to the register is heard, and if the court orders its restoration the action may then proceed.[16]

For the purpose of both the statutory provisions empowering the court to revoke the dissolution of a company and to order its restoration to the register, the expression 'creditor' includes all claimants for sums of money, whether liquidated or unliquidated, whether the claim arises under a contract, in tort or under any other head, and whether the claim is certain or contingent.[17] Furthermore, if an application is made to the court under either of the statutory provisions, the Registrar of Companies must be made the sole respondent to the application and, apart from the applicant, is the only person entitled to be heard when the court considers the application.[18] The Registrar is empowered to appear so that he may draw the court's attention to any matters affecting the public interest, and may suggest conditions which should be imposed in the order granting the application. The applicant will be ordered to pay the Registrar's costs, unless the court thinks fit to impose this burden on any other person who appears on the hearing; but the

---

12 *Re AGA Estate Agencies Ltd* [1986] BCLC 346, 2 BCC 257.
13 *Re New Timbiqui Gold Mines Ltd* [1961] Ch 319, [1961] 1 All ER 865.
14 Insolvency Act 1986, s 81(1) and s 82(1) and (2).
15 *Re Bayswater Trading Co Ltd* [1970] 1 All ER 608, [1970] 1 WLR 343.
16 *Steans Fashions Ltd v Legal and General Assurance Society Ltd* [1995] 1 BCLC 332, [1995] BCC 510.
17 *Re Harvest Lane Motor Bodies Ltd* [1969] 1 Ch 457, [1968] 2 All ER 1012.
18 *Re Wood and Martin (Bricklaying Contractors) Ltd* [1971] 1 All ER 732, [1971] 1 WLR 293; *Re H Clarkson (Overseas) Ltd* (1987) 3 BCC 606.

costs may not be imposed on the company,[19] unless the company is itself the applicant and it has been dissolved by its name being struck off the register.[20]

Effect of revocation of dissolution

Whether the court declares a dissolution void or orders a company's name to be restored to the register, the effect of its order is to re-vest in the company all its property which vested in the Crown as ownerless property on its dissolution. But if the court merely makes a winding up order against a company whose name has been struck off the register, its former property will not re-vest in it, and so the proper course is for an application to be made to revoke its dissolution or to restore the company's name to the register before the winding up petition is presented.[1] Nevertheless, the court may in its discretion revoke the dissolution or order the restoration of the company's name to the register when a winding-up order has already been made against the company since its dissolution, but the court will do this only if an application is made with reasonable promptness after the making of the winding-up order.[2]

Although property vested in the Crown as ownerless property automatically re-vests in the company on the court declaring its dissolution void or ordering its restoration to the register, this is not so if the Crown has disposed of the property since it vested in the Crown on the company's dissolution. In that case the disposition by the Crown remains effective, and the only claim which the revived company may make against the Crown is for a sum equal to the consideration which the Crown received for the disposition or, if it received no consideration, a sum equal to the value of the property at the time of the disposition.[3]

The court will declare a dissolution void only so as to enable a company to regain assets or enforce claims which belonged to it at the date of its dissolution, or so that a person who had a claim against the company at the time of its dissolution, or possibly a person to whom he has since transferred the claim, may enforce the claim against the company's assets.[4] If the company had at the date of its

---

19 *Re Test Holdings (Clifton) Ltd* [1970] Ch 285, [1969] 3 All ER 517.
20 *Re Court Lodge Development Co Ltd* [1973] 3 All ER 425, [1973] 1 WLR 1097.
 1 *Re C W Dixon Ltd* [1947] Ch 251, [1947] 1 All ER 279; *Re Cambridge Coffee Room Association Ltd* [1952] 1 All ER 112n.
 2 *Re Thompson and Riches Ltd* [1981] 2 All ER 477, [1981] 1 WLR 682.
 3 Companies Act 1985, s 655(1) and (2).
 4 *Re Roehampton Swimming Pool Ltd* [1968] 3 All ER 661, [1968] 1 WLR 1693; *Re Oakleague Ltd* [1995] 2 BCLC 624, [1995] BCC 921.

dissolution a mere spes successionis or expectation not amounting even to a contingent or conditional interest in property, such as a bequest under the will of a testator who was then alive, the court will not revive the company when the testator later dies so that it may take the bequest and prevent it from passing to the persons entitled to the testator's residuary estate.[5] It would seem that the court would also not order the restoration of the company's name to the register in such a situation if it has been struck off by the Registrar of Companies.

If the court declares the dissolution of a company void, no act done or litigation conducted in the company's name and no litigation initiated or continued against the company after its dissolution is thereby validated and made binding on it or effective against it,[6] but such an act is validated and made binding if the company was dissolved by its name being struck off the register and the court subsequently orders its restoration to the register.[7] Similarly, a contract made on behalf of a company during the period between the date when it was struck off the register and the date of its restoration will become binding on the company as though it had originally been valid, provided, of course, that the contract was negotiated by the board of directors or the liquidator of the company in office at the date of striking off, or by some other agent who had the authority to bind the company on that date.[8] When the contract was made, the company had no real legal existence and the contract was then void, with the consequence that the person or persons who negotiated it became liable to the other contracting party in damages for breach of warranty of authority. This liability is destroyed by the restoration of the company to the register, however, and the court will not preserve it for the benefit of the other contracting party by inserting a condition to that effect in the order for restoration.[8]

If a dissolved company whose name has been struck off the register is restored to the register, the court may order that rights of action existing against it at the date of its dissolution shall not be barred under the Limitation Act 1980 by the passage of time meanwhile.[9] However, the court will do this only if the application for restoration is made by a member or by a creditor whose claim would otherwise have become statute-barred between the date of

5 *Re Servers of Blind League* [1960] 2 All ER 298, [1960] 1 WLR 564.
6 *Morris v Harris* [1927] AC 252; *Re Lewis and Smart Ltd* [1954] 2 All ER 19, [1954] 1 WLR 755; *Re Mixhurst Ltd* [1994] 2 BCLC 19, [1993] BCC 757.
7 *Morris v Harris*, supra, per Lord Blanesburgh at 268–269; *Tyman's Ltd v Craven* [1952] 2 QB 100, [1952] 1 All ER 613.
8 *Re Lindsay Bowman Ltd* [1969] 3 All ER 601, [1969] 1 WLR 1443.
9 *Re Donald Kenyon Ltd* [1956] 3 All ER 596, [1956] 1 WLR 1397.

the dissolution and the restoration of the company to the register; the court will not make such an order if the applicant's right of action would not have become statute-barred before the date of the court's order restoring the company to the register, because on the restoration the applicant will still have part of the limitation period unexpired within which he may commence proceedings.[10] The court may make an order extending the limitation period where it would have expired before the order for the company's restoration to the register in exercise of the court's jurisdiction to put the company and other persons so far as possible in the same position as if the company's name had not been struck off the register,[11] but where the court's intervention is unnecessary for that purpose, no order will be made.[10] Consequently, the court will not order the suspension of the limitation period if the company was already in liquidation when the Registrar struck its name off the register, for in such a situation the limitation period had already ceased to run by reason of the company going into liquidation.[12] It would also seem possible for the court to make an order suspending the running of limitation periods after the dissolution of a company when the court declares the dissolution void, in exercise of its power to impose such terms as it thinks fit when it makes the declaration.[13]

10 *Re Huntingdon Poultry Ltd* [1969] 1 All ER 328, [1969] 1 WLR 204.
11 Companies Act 1985, s 653(3).
12 *Re Vickers and Bott Ltd* [1968] 2 All ER 264n.
13 Companies Act 1985, s 651(1) and (3) (as amended by Companies Act 1989, s 141(1) and (3)).

CHAPTER 5

Assets of a company in liquidation

THE BASIC ASSETS

General

The assets of a company in liquidation out of which, or the proceeds of which, the liquidator may satisfy the company's debts and liabilities and repay share capital to its members (so far as those assets permit) are the assets which the company owns or to which it is entitled at the commencement of the winding up and the assets which the company acquires or becomes entitled to during the winding up. From this are excluded assets which the directors have disposed of with the court's sanction before the date of the winding up order in a winding up by the court.[1] If the liquidator disposes of assets of the company in exercise of his powers, or if secured creditors sell such assets in order to realise their securities, or if assets are sold by order of the court, such assets cease to be available for the benefit of members and creditors because they thereupon cease to be assets of the company, but are replaced by the proceeds of sale or realisation except so far as appropriated to discharge securities held by secured creditors. The liquidator may recover any assets in the liquidation by applying summarily to the court for an order that they shall be paid, delivered or transferred to him by the person in possession of them.[2]

The assets of a company in liquidation must be applied first in meeting the costs and expenses of the liquidation, including the costs of the petitioner for the winding up order by means of which the company is put into liquidation and the costs of supporting or opposing creditors which are directed by the court to be paid out of the company's assets. The company's assets after satisfying the expenses of the liquidation are applied in paying the company's debts and other liabilities so far as they suffice to do so, and if and when those debts and liabilities have been fully discharged, any remaining assets are distributed among the members or shareholders of the company in accordance with their rights.[3]

1 Insolvency Act 1986, s 127 (see p 103, ante).
2 Ibid, s 234(1) and (2).
3 Ibid, s 107, s 143(1), s 148(1) and s 154.

Under certain provisions of the Insolvency Act 1986, the liquidator may recover certain assets of the company which have been disposed of before the commencement of its liquidation, or may have certain securities or charges over its assets created before that time set aside by the court, or may recover certain amounts which have been paid by the company before that time, or may enforce certain claims which the company has for wrongful acts which diminish its assets. The assets or amounts recovered in this way augment the basic assets of the company in the liquidator's hands, and are applied by him for the same purposes. These special provisions enabling the liquidator to recover assets and amounts which the company could not have recovered itself are dealt with later in this chapter.

The assets of a company in liquidation do not vest in its liquidator in the way that the assets of a bankrupt vest in his trustee in bankruptcy, but the court may by order vest any of the company's assets in the liquidator by his official name, including assets held by trustees for the company, and the liquidator can then bring or defend actions in respect of those assets in his own name.[4] In practice it is rarely necessary for the court to make such vesting orders, because the liquidator can dispose of the company's assets and enforce rights of action vested in it under his statutory power to act in the company's name. The only occasions when the court's power is useful are when the company is an unincorporated one wound up under the provisions of the Act relating to unregistered companies, or when the company is a foreign one which has been dissolved in its own country before its affairs are wound up in Great Britain.[5]

Although a company in liquidation remains the legal owner of its assets unless the court vests them in the liquidator, it ceases to be their beneficial owner as from the commencement of the winding up. This is because the Insolvency Act 1986 directs that the company's assets (after meeting the expenses of the liquidation) shall be applied in satisfying its liabilities, and that any assets remaining after doing so shall be distributed among its members or contributories.[6] Consequently, the company holds the legal title to its assets on behalf of its creditors and contributories or shareholders collectively according to their respective entitlements under the Insolvency Act 1986 and the Insolvency Rules 1986 and, in the case of its members or contributories, according to their entitlements under the company's memorandum and articles of association.[7]

---

4 Insolvency Act 1986, s 112(1) and s 145(1) and (2).
5 Ibid, ss 220 to 229.
6 Insolvency Act 1986, s 107, s 143(1) s 148(1) and s 154.
7 *IRC v Olive Mill Spinners Ltd* [1963] 2 All ER 130, [1963] 1 WLR 712; *Pritchard v MH Builders (Wilmslow) Ltd* [1969] 2 All ER 670, [1969] 1 WLR 409; *Ayerst v C & K (Construction) Ltd* [1976] AC 167, [1975] 2 All ER 537.

These statutory provisions do not impose a trust in the normal sense, however, and creditors and contributories have no specific equitable interests in the company's assets until their claims have been quantified and the appropriate authorisation for payment has been given; but the fact that the creditors and contributories are the only persons who can henceforth be beneficially entitled to the company's global assets (subject to the rights of its secured creditors) and that the company has ceased to be the beneficial owner of those assets, can have important consequences in connection with taxation.[7]

Contracts by the company to acquire or dispose of assets

The title of the company to assets already acquired by it before the commencement of the liquidation and its rights in respect of assets which it has contracted to acquire or dispose of remain valid and effective despite the company going into liquidation and are not altered by it doing so. Consequently, if the company is entitled to acquire a title to assets but has not yet done so (eg under a contract to purchase goods by which the ownership is to be retained by the seller until the price of the goods or the current indebtedness of the company to the seller is discharged in full), the title to the assets does not vest in the company merely because it goes into liquidation, but the liquidator can obtain a title to the goods for the company by fulfilling the contractual conditions on which the company is entitled to acquire it.[8]

Where a company has contracted to purchase goods the title to which will pass to it only on payment of the price or on the discharge of the company's total indebtedness to the seller, the liquidator must pay the price or the amount which the company owes in full if the company is to acquire a title to the goods, and it is not sufficient that he pays the same dividend in respect of that price or amount as he pays the company's unsecured creditors in respect of their respective debts. If the liquidator is not able or willing to pay the price or amount in full, the seller may recover the goods from the liquidator by terminating the contract of sale and with it the company's right to possess them.[8] This is so even if the company has incorporated the goods in question in a larger product or piece of equipment, provided that the goods are still identifiable and can be physically

---

8 *Aluminium Industrie Vaassen BV v Romalpa Aluminium Ltd* [1976] 2 All ER 552, [1976] 1 WLR 676; *Clough Mill Ltd v Martin* [1984] 3 All ER 982, [1985] 1 WLR 111; *Armour v Thyssen Edelstahlwerke AG* [1991] 2 AC 339, [1990] 3 All ER 481.

separated without doing substantial damage,[9] but the seller may not recover the goods if they have been integrated with other goods so as to lose their identity, or if they have been processed so as to result in a distinct product, or if they have lost their original economic identity (ie if the purpose for which they are intended to be used has changed in consequence of the processing to which they have been subjected); in that event the goods will have passed into the ownership of the company.[10] Conversely, where the company in liquidation has supplied goods to a customer subject to the retention of ownership of the goods by the company until the price or other indebtedness of the buyer to the company is paid, and this has not been done, the liquidator can recover the goods or their value as damages for their wrongful detention by terminating the contract of sale because of the buyer's default, unless the goods have already been integrated or processed by the buyer so as to result in a distinct product, or have otherwise lost their original identity.

If a company has entered into any contract to dispose of any of its assets, the contract is not terminated by the company going into liquidation, but if the contract is repudiated by the liquidator, the other party's remedies are normally confined to proving in the liquidation for damages for breach of contract, the measure of such damages being the same as if the company had not gone into liquidation. In the rare cases where a purchaser can seek the remedy of specific performance under the general law, however, the purchaser can seek such an order against the company in liquidation, but in a winding up by the court he must obtain leave of the court to commence litigation for that purpose.[11] It is not possible to evade the need to obtain the leave of the court by applying to the court in the liquidation proceedings for its approval of the disposition of the company's assets after the commencement of its liquidation,[12] because such an application can be made only when directors or other agents of the company purport to transfer title to the purchaser before a winding up order is made, and not where the company has done no more than contract to make the disposition before a winding up order is made against it.[13]

9 *Hendy Lennox (Industrial Engines) Ltd v Grahame Puttick Ltd* [1984] 2 All ER 152, [1984] 1 WLR 485 (diesel engines attached by bolts to generators).
10 *Borden (UK) Ltd v Scottish Timber Products Ltd* [1981] Ch 25, [1979] 3 All ER 961 (resinous adhesive mixed with sawdust to make chipboard); *Re Peachdart Ltd* [1984] Ch 131, [1983] 3 All ER 204 (leather sheets fabricated into ladies' handbags); *Modelboard Ltd v Outer Box Ltd* [1993] BCLC 623, [1992] BCC 945 (cardboard sheets folded by machinery in order to make boxes).
11 Insolvency Act 1986, s 130(2).
12 Ibid, s 127.
13 *Re Wiltshire Iron Co* (1868) 3 Ch App 443; *Re Oriental Bank Corpn, ex p Guillemin* (1884) 28 Ch D 634.

Assets belonging to third persons

Assets which the company holds as an agent, bailee or trustee for another person cannot be applied by the liquidator in paying the company's debts or liabilities, or otherwise for the purpose of its winding up.[14] Such assets do not belong beneficially to the company and therefore cannot be applied for its own purposes, but must be delivered or accounted for to the persons who are their beneficial owners. Consequently, if a company offers shares for subscription and undertakes to pay money received from the subscribers into a separate bank account until a Stock Exchange listing is obtained for the shares and meanwhile to hold the money on the subscribers' behalf, the money remains the property of the subscribers in equity, and cannot be used to pay the company's creditors or for the purposes of its winding up.[15] Likewise, if a company advertises goods for sale to the public by mail order, and undertakes to pay into a separate account all amounts received by it from persons who respond to its advertisement, and to withdraw money from that account only when the goods paid for are available for delivery, the money will be held in trust while in the separate account, and will be returnable to the persons who paid it to the company if it goes into liquidation.[16]

Again, if a loan is made to a company so that it may purchase equipment, and the lender permits the company to make an advance payment to the supplier in anticipation that the equipment will be manufactured and delivered, but this is not done and the supplier returns the advance payment to the company after it has gone into liquidation, the liquidator holds the returned advance payment in trust for the lender because the purpose for which the loan was made has not been fulfilled.[17] Conversely, if a company pays money to a third person to be used for a limited purpose which in the event is not, or cannot be, achieved, the money remains the company's property beneficially, and if the company goes into liquidation the money can be reclaimed in full by its liquidator from the person who received it without him being entitled to deduct from it a debt which the company owes him.[18] On the other hand, if trustees deposit trust

---

14 *Re Marwalt Ltd* [1992] BCC 32; *Re Fleet Disposal Services Ltd* [1995] 1 BCLC 345, [1995] BCC 605.
15 *Re Nanwa Gold Mines Ltd* [1955] 3 All ER 219, [1955] 1 WLR 1080.
16 *Re Kayford Ltd* [1975] 1 All ER 604, [1975] 1 WLR 279; *Re Eastern Capital Futures Ltd* [1989] BCLC 371, 5 BCC 223.
17 *Re EVTR Ltd* [1987] BCLC 646, 3 BCC 389.
18 *Re Mid-Kent Fruit Factory* [1896] 1 Ch 567; *Barclays Bank Ltd v Quistclose Investments Ltd* [1970] AC 567, [1968] 3 All ER 651; *Carreras Rothman Ltd v Freeman Mathews Treasure Ltd* [1985] Ch 207, [1985] 1 All ER 155.

money in a bank account, the relationship between the bank and the trustees is the normal one of debtor and creditor,[19] and the beneficiaries of the trust cannot claim to have part of the bank's assets equal to the credit balance of the account segregated in the liquidation of the bank and treated as trust property held by it in trust for the beneficiaries.[20]

At common law a liquidator who took possession of any goods or land in the name of the company in liquidation, or who disposed or purported to dispose of such property, was personally liable in tort if the property in fact belonged to a third person who did not consent to the disposal, and it was no defence to an action for damages brought by the owner against the liquidator that the liquidator honestly and reasonably believed that the property was owned by the company.[1] On the other hand, if the liquidator innocently purported to dispose of intangible personal property or things in action (such as debts, investments or industrial property rights) to which a person other than the company was entitled, he committed no wrong at common law, and the only consequence was that the person to whom he made the disposition acquired no title. The only occasion when the liquidator could be made liable in damages for such a disposal was when the intangible personal property was represented by a certificate or document, whether negotiable or not, and the liquidator delivered the document to the disponee in connection with the disposition. If the owner of the intangible personal property was also entitled to the certificate or document (as he would be if it were a share certificate in respect of shares registered in his name), the liquidator was liable to him for its conversion if he delivered the certificate or document to the person to whom he purported to dispose of the property, and the value of the certificate or document for the purpose of calculating the damages recoverable by the owner was taken to be the current market value of the rights which it represented.[2]

However, liquidators are now protected by the Insolvency Act 1986, if they make honest but wrongful disposals of property which belongs to persons other than the company in liquidation. If a liquidator takes possession of any property which is not that of the

19 *Foley v Hill* (1848) 2 HL Cas 28.
20 *Space Investments Ltd v Canadian Imperial Bank of Commerce Trust Co (Bahamas) Ltd* [1986] 3 All ER 75, [1986] BCLC 485.
 1 *Hollins v Fowler* (1875) LR 7 HL 757; *Consolidated Co v Curtis & Son* [1892] 1 QB 495.
 2 *Alsager v Close* (1842) 10 M & W 576; *Morison v London County and Westminster Bank Ltd* [1914] 3 KB 356; *Midland Bank Ltd v Eastcheap Dried Fruit Co Ltd* [1962] 1 Lloyd's Rep 359; *BBMB Finance (Hong Kong) Ltd v Eda Holdings Ltd* [1991] 2 All ER 129, [1990] 1 WLR 409.

company, or if he disposes of such property, he is not liable in damages to any person who suffers loss in consequence, if at the time when the liquidator took possession of the property or disposed of it he believed on reasonable grounds that he was entitled to do so.[3] Although the Act absolves the liquidator from personal liability to pay damages in these circumstances, it does not validate the wrongful possession or disposal by the liquidator, and so the owner of the property, whether goods, land or a document of title to intangibles, may recover it in specie. A purchaser of the property from the liquidator obtains no better title to it than the liquidator has to give, unless he is a purchaser for value of a negotiable instrument without notice of any defect in the liquidator's title to it. As an alternative to recovering the property in specie, the person entitled to it may trace the proceeds of the disposal into the liquidator's hands in equity and recover them in whatever form they now take (eg the purchase price of the property which the liquidator has paid into a bank account in his official name, or land, goods or investments purchased by the liquidator with the purchase price).[4]

Executory contracts

The assets of the company which the liquidator may apply or dispose of for the purpose of the liquidation include contracts entered into by the company before the liquidation began which have not been fully carried out by both or all the parties. Executory contracts made by the company are not terminated automatically by the commencement of its liquidation, unless they so provide expressly, or unless they are personal in character (such as contracts of employment) or create rights or obligations the extent of which are determined by the personal characteristics of the original parties.[5] Nevertheless, a person who has entered into a contract with a company which has gone into liquidation may treat the contract as terminated by the company's breach if the liquidation makes the company incapable of performing its obligations under the contract,[6]

---

3 Insolvency Act 1986, s 234(3) and (4).
4 *Banque Belge pour l'Etranger v Hambrouck* [1921] 1 KB 321; *Chase Manhattan Bank NA v Israel-British Bank (London) Ltd* [1981] Ch 105, [1979] 3 All ER 1025.
5 *British Waggon Co v Lea* (1880) 5 QBD 149; *Tolhurst v Associated Portland Cement Manufacturers Ltd* [1903] AC 414; *Nokes v Doncaster Amalgamated Collieries Ltd* [1940] AC 1014, [1940] 3 All ER 549; *Bank of Credit and Commerce International SA v Malik* [1996] BCC 15.
6 *Re Asphaltic Wood Pavement Co, Lee and Chapman's Case* (1885) 30 Ch D 216; *Sale Continuation Ltd v Austin Taylor & Co Ltd* [1968] 2 QB 849, [1967] 2 All ER 1092.

or if the liquidator repudiates the contract, or fails or refuses to perform the company's obligations under it, or does an act which is inconsistent with its continuance.[7]

If a contract is not terminated by the company going into liquidation, the other party is not entitled to an immediate decision from the liquidator on his appointment whether he intends to carry out the company's obligations under the contract or not, and the uncertainty created by the liquidator's failure to make his intentions clear does not justify the other party delaying or refusing performance of his own obligations. The only pressure which the other party can bring to bear on the liquidator is to require him to decide whether to disclaim the contract as unprofitable within 28 days after the other party serves a notice calling on him to make a decision, with the consequence that the liquidator cannot disclaim the contract after the expiration of that time.[8] If the liquidator is precluded from disclaiming the contract by the lapse of the 28 days, however, there is no certainty that he will perform the company's obligations under the contract, even if he has stated that he will not disclaim, and if he does not in fact perform the company's obligations, the other party will then only be able to prove in the winding up for damages for breach of those obligations, having possibly missed participating in distributions which the liquidator has already made to the company's creditors.[9] To give relief to parties to executory contracts in this and other situations, statute provides that any person who is as against the liquidator entitled to the benefit, or subject to the burden, of a contract made with the company before a winding up order was made or a winding up resolution was passed in respect of it, may apply to the court to rescind (ie terminate) the contract on such terms as to payment of damages for non-performance by either party to the other, or as to any other matter, as the court thinks just, and the other party may prove in the winding up for any damages so awarded to him.[10]

The assets of a company in liquidation do not, of course, include the benefit of contracts which it entered into before it went into liquidation, if before that time it had assigned the benefit of such contracts to other persons, and if the company had mortgaged or charged the benefit of such contracts before it went into liquidation, the liquidator can deal with them in the liquidation only subject to

7 *Fowler v Commercial Timber Co Ltd* [1930] 2 KB 1; *Re T N Farrer Ltd* [1937] Ch 352, [1937] 2 All ER 505.
8 Insolvency Act 1986, s 178(5) (see p 151, ante).
9 For the position of the claimant who does not prove in the winding up until after the liquidator declares and pays a dividend, see p 287, post.
10 Insolvency Act 1986, s 186(1) and (2).

the rights of the mortgagee or chargee. Where a contract has not been carried out by either party before the winding up order is made or the winding up resolution is passed, however, or where the contract is wholly or partly executory as regards the company's obligations, the question arises whether the assignee or mortgagee may enforce the company's rights against the other party, and leave the liquidator to bear the expense of fulfilling the company's obligations under the contract out of the company's other assets. In a number of bankruptcy cases it has been held that in order to avoid this result, the assignment or mortgage of the benefit of contracts made by the bankrupt before his bankruptcy will not be treated as extending to contracts under which the bankrupt's obligations remain substantially unperformed, and the trustee in bankruptcy, who must meet the expense of performing the bankrupt's obligations under the contracts, is therefore entitled to enforce the bankrupt's rights under the contracts as part of his assets.[11]

In the one case where the question has arisen in the winding up of a company, however, the court held that the assignee or mortgagee of an executory contract entered into by the company is entitled to the full benefit of the company's contractual rights in this situation, and the expense of fulfilling the company's obligations under the contract must be met out of the company's assets unless the assignment or mortgage otherwise provides.[12] It would seem that the liquidator cannot avoid this result by disclaiming the contract on the ground that it is unprofitable; the contract itself is not unprofitable, even though the company's general assets will not in the circumstances be increased by the liquidator performing its obligations under the contract.

Contracts of employment

If a liquidator sells or disposes of the whole or part of a company's business undertaking as a going concern, the rights, powers, obligations and liabilities of the company as regards its employees (whether employed before the commencement of the liquidation or by the liquidator subsequently, and whether the rights etc arise under a contract of employment, statute or otherwise) are transferred by law to the purchaser or disponee of the business undertaking or part of it concerned.[13] Such sales or dispositions occur most frequently

---

11 *Re Jones, ex p Nichols* (1883) 22 Ch D 782; *Wilmot v Alton* [1897] 1 QB 17; *Re Collins* [1925] Ch 556.

12 *Re Asphaltic Wood Pavement Co, Lee and Chapman's Case* (1885) 30 Ch D 216.

13 Transfer of Undertakings (Protection of Employment) Regulations 1981 (SI 1981/1794), reg 3 (1) and (2) and reg 5(1) and (2) (as amended by Trade Union Reform and Employment Rights Act 1993, s 33).

in connection with receiverships and the effects of the relevant statutory provisions will therefore be dealt with in that connection.[14]

Insurance contracts

When a company which has insured against a certain risk goes into liquidation, the benefit of the insurance contract forms part of its general assets, and if claims arise or have arisen under the insurance, the liquidator must apply the amounts received from the insurers in the same way as the company's other assets. The only exception to this is where the insurance contract covers the liabilities of the company to third parties either in tort (eg liability for damage caused by the company's officers or employees to third parties' property, and liability of the company for injuries to its own employees) or under contracts entered into by the company (other than reinsurance contracts).[15]

In these situations if the company incurs a liability to a third party which is covered by the insurance, whether the liability arises before or after the company goes into liquidation, the company's rights under the insurance contract vest in the third party by operation of law when a winding up order is made or a winding up resolution is passed in respect of the company or when the company's liability arises, whichever is the later.[16] No provision in the insurance contract and no agreement between the company and the insurer made after the company's liability has been incurred to the third party, whether before or after the winding up has commenced, can waive or modify the third party's rights.[16] The result of these statutory provisions is that where they apply, the third party can enforce the company's contractual rights against the insurer for the third party's own benefit, and the liquidator of the company cannot recover any amount under the insurance as part of the company's general assets until the third party's claim has been met in full.

Company's rights of action

Following a number of decisions in bankruptcy law, the court has held in three cases that the liquidator of a company may sell and

---

14 See p 516, post.
15 Third Parties (Rights against Insurers) Act 1930, s 1(1) and (5), (4 *Halsbury's Statutes* (4th edn) 688).
16 Ibid, s 1(3) and s 3.

assign a right of action belonging to the company, and may lawfully agree to divide any amount recovered with the purchaser without infringing the common law prohibitions on maintenance and champerty.[17] The reason for these decisions is that the liquidator is empowered by the Insolvency Act 1986 to sell any of the company's property, which is defined as including 'things in action', which are themselves interpreted as comprising, not only intangible movables, but also bare rights of action for breach of contract, tort or any other cause.[18] A liquidator cannot, however, agree merely to permit another person to initiate or conduct litigation in the company's name in consideration of the liquidator sharing in any amount recovered, but if the company's right of action is sold and assigned in equity to the purchaser, the liquidator may agree to co-operate with him by bringing and conducting proceedings in the company's name as plaintiff.[17] The purchaser of the company's right of action may be met by any defence which could be pleaded against the company itself, including the insolvency rule of set-off applicable in the company's liquidation.[19] The power of a liquidator to sell and assign rights of action belonging to a company facilitates the financing of litigation for which the company's resources are insufficient; the usual arrangement is that the purchaser shall be indemnified for the costs and expenses of the litigation out of any amount recovered, and that any surplus shall be divided between the purchaser and the company in agreed proportions.

Although a liquidator may sell and assign a right of action vested in the company at the commencement of the liquidation or later accruing to it, he cannot assign any of the statutory powers exercisable by the liquidator under the Insolvency Act 1986 (eg the power to apply to the court to set aside voidable preferences or dispositions of assets at a significant undervalue by the company, or to treat charges created by the company over its assets as void against the liquidator because not registered under the Companies Act 1985;[20] or to order that directors guilty of wrongful trading shall pay compensation to the

---

17 *Bang and Olufsen UK Ltd v Ton Système Ltd* (16 July 1993, unreported), CA; *Grovewood Holdings plc v James Capel & Co Ltd* [1994] 2 BCLC 782, [1995] BCC 760; *Re Oakleague Ltd* [1995] 2 BCLC 624, [1995] BCC 921; *Norglen Ltd v Reeds Rains Prudential Ltd* [1996] 1 BCLC 690; *Circuit Systems Ltd v Zuken-Redac (UK) Ltd* [1996] 3 All ER 748 (in the latter two cases the assignee was an individual shareholder who intended to seek legal aid to prosecute the action; this was held not to affect the validity of the assignment).
18 Insolvency Act 1986, s 165(1) and (3) and s 167(1) and Sch 4, para 6; Insolvency Act 1986, s 436.
19 *Farley v Housing and Commercial Developments Ltd* [1984] BCLC 442; 1 BCC 150; *Stein v Blake* [1995] 2 BCLC 94, [1995] BCC 543.
20 *Re Ayala Holdings Ltd (No 2)* [1996] 1 BCLC 467.

company).[1] Consequently the liquidator cannot transfer the prospective title to assets or property which he may recover by the exercise of such powers, but only the title to assets which are so recoverable when the liquidator has himself recovered them.[20]

THE STATUTORY INVALIDATION OF CERTAIN TRANSACTIONS

Introductory

Under a number of provisions of the Insolvency Act 1986, the court is empowered to invalidate or reverse certain transactions which have taken place within a limited time before a company goes into liquidation in an insolvent condition, where the transaction involved a disposal of assets of the company without it receiving a substantially equivalent consideration, or where the transaction would, if allowed to stand, result in an inequality of treatment between the company's creditors. Where transactions come within these provisions the court may order that assets which the company has disposed of shall be revested in it and so added to the company's assets comprised in its liquidation, or the court may alternatively order that property representing assets so disposed of shall be vested in the company with the same effect, or that an amount shall be paid to the company by way of restitution of benefits received from it or payments made by it, the amounts so to be paid being held by the company as part of its general assets in the liquidation.[2] The result of such a restoration or restitution order is that the assets of the company available to meet its debts and other liabilities are augmented, and the liquidator is thereby enabled to make correspondingly larger distributions toward satisfying the company's liabilities to its creditors and persons who have claims against it.

Transactions at an undervalue

The court may on the application of the liquidator in any winding up[3] make such order as it thinks fit to restore the company and the

---

1 *Re Oasis Merchandising Services Ltd* [1995] 2 BCLC 493, [1995] BCC 911; affd [1997] BCLC 282.
2 Insolvency Act 1986, s 241(1), s 244(4) and s 425(1).
3 The application to the court is made by an originating application (Insolvency Rules 1986, r 7.2(1) and r 7.3(2)).

other parties to a transaction to their original position if the company
has within a limited period before the commencement of the
liquidation entered into a transaction at an undervalue, that is, if the
transaction was a gift by the company, or a transaction under which
the company was to receive no consideration (even if another party
was to do so), or if the transaction was one under which the company
received a consideration whose monetary value was significantly less
than the monetary value of the consideration given by the company.[4]
The court cannot make an order, however, if the company entered
into the transaction in good faith for the purpose of carrying on its
business, and at the time of the transaction there were reasonable
grounds for believing that it would benefit the company.[5]

Conditions for setting transactions aside

A transaction may be made the subject of an order restoring the
parties to their original position only if it was entered into within two
years before the commencement of the winding up of the company,
or (if an administration order had been made in respect of the
company before it went into liquidation and that order was terminated
immediately before it did so),[6] within two years before the presentation
of the petition on which the administration order was made.[7]

Furthermore, the court may make an order in respect of a
transaction entered into during the relevant period only if at the time
of the transaction the company was unable to pay its debts as they
fell due out of its liquid assets, or if the value of the whole of its assets
was then less than the total amount of its liabilities (taking into
account its contingent and prospective liabilities), or if, in
consequence of the transaction, the company became unable to pay
its debts as they fell due or its assets became insufficient to satisfy its
total liabilities.[8] To determine whether the company was insolvent
or whether it became insolvent in consequence of the transaction,
the value of any consideration given by the company and of any
consideration received by it must be taken as at the date of the
transaction, and the existence of facts at that time which would
suffice to prove that the company was unable to pay its debts and
liabilities if a petition for a winding up order had then been presented

4 Insolvency Act 1986, s 238(1) to (4).
5 Ibid, s 238(5).
6 The administration order will have been made under the Insolvency Act 1986,
   Part II and will have been discharged under the Insolvency Act 1986, s 18,
   immediately before the making of the winding up order or the passing of the
   winding up resolution.
7 Insolvency Act 1986, s 240(1) and (3).
8 Ibid, s 240(2) and (3), applying s 123(1) and (2).

against it,[9] must be taken as establishing that it was or became insolvent at that time. If the transaction was entered into with a person who was at the time connected with the company (otherwise than by reason only of being its employee), that is, if the company entered into the transaction with a director or shadow director of the company, or with an associate of such a director or shadow director or of the company itself,[10] it must be presumed until the contrary is proved that the company was unable to pay its debts at the time of the transaction, but if the other party or parties were not connected with the company, the burden of proof that the company was then insolvent rests on the liquidator.[11]

Objectivity of the test of a significant undervalue

The test for determining whether the court will invalidate a transaction at an undervalue and make a restoration or restitution order is an objective one, and it is unnecessary for the liquidator to prove that the company intended to defraud or injure its creditors, or that it was aware that it was insolvent at the time of the transaction, or that the transaction would make it insolvent. To show that the transaction was at a significant undervalue as regards the company, however, the liquidator must prove the respective values in money terms of the consideration which it gave and which it received and must show that there was a significant difference between the two.[12] It follows that if the total realisable value of the company's assets was not diminished by the transaction, it cannot be invalidated by the court. Consequently, where a company creates a mortgage or charge over the whole or any of its assets to secure an existing unsecured debt, the mortgage or charge cannot be invalidated as a transaction at an undervalue, because no assets of the company have ceased to be its property, and the total value of its assets has not been reduced because the company may discharge the mortgage or charge by paying the debt secured by it.[12] Whether similar reasoning applies if a company incurs an obligation for a consideration which does not benefit the company financially (eg a guarantee of a third person's indebtedness which a company gives to his creditor for a consideration which benefits the third person but not the company) is uncertain, as also is the immunity from invalidation of a mortgage or charge given by a company over its property to secure such an obligation.

9 See p 42, ante.
10 For the full definition of an associate, see p 150, ante.
11 Insolvency Act 1986, s 240(2), s 249 and s 435.
12 *Re MC Bacon Ltd* [1990] BCLC 324, [1990] BCC 78; *National Bank of Kuwait v Menzies* [1994] 2 BCLC 306, [1994] BCC 119.

The comparison which the court must make between the realisable value of the assets disposed of by the company and the consideration received by it in return is not confined to assessing the cash value of the consideration. Consequently, where a company which had taken leases of aircraft from their owners in order to sub-lease them to users, assigned the leases to an associated company in consideration of an undertaking by the company to pay to the assignor the capitalised value of the rental payable to the owners at a remote future date and meanwhile to maintain the aircraft, it was held that the assignment was made at a significant undervalue.[13] Again, where a company which owned the freehold of agricultural property granted a lease of it at a full market rent payable only in arrear and the tenant was empowered to terminate the lease on giving short notice, it was held that the lease was granted at a significant undervalue.[14] The whole of the terms and circumstances of the transaction must therefore be examined to discover whether the real value of the consideration given to the company was significantly less than the value which it gave. It was therefore held that where a company sold property which was subject to a mortgage for the price of £1 plus an undertaking by the purchaser to keep the company indemnified against its liability for the mortgage debt, the transaction was at a significant undervalue only if the saleable value of the property unincumbered by the mortgage was significantly greater than the mortgage debt, interest and costs.[15]

The court has no discretion to exercise if it finds that a transaction has been entered into by a company at a significant undervalue. If the company entered into the transaction within the relevant period before the commencement of its liquidation or the making of an administration order in respect of it, and the company was already insolvent in the statutory sense or was rendered insolvent by carrying out the transaction, and the transaction was a gift or was entered into for a consideration of significantly less value than that which the company was to receive, the court must make a restoration or restitution order.

Validation of transactions in good faith

Proof by the persons who seek to uphold an impugned transaction that the company entered into it in good faith and for a sound business purpose, and that the company had reasonable grounds for

---

13 *Arbuthnot Leasing International Ltd v Havelet Leasing Ltd* [1990] BCLC 802; *Same (No 2)* [1990] BCC 636.
14 *Barclays Bank plc v Eustice* [1995] 4 All ER 511, [1995] BCC 978.
15 *Pinewood Joinery v Starelm Properties Ltd* [1994] 2 BCLC 412, [1994] BCC 569.

believing that the transaction would as a whole benefit the company, will prevent the court from setting it aside as one entered into at a significant undervalue.[16] This too, involves an objective test, because it must be shown that the company expected to obtain a business advantage from the transaction which was proportionate, if not equal, in value to the consideration it gave. An example of such justifiable business dealing would be the sale of the whole or a large part of the company's stock in trade, manufactured products or investments at a substantially reduced price, but for immediate payment, so that the company might discharge its debts which had fallen due or reduce its bank overdraft in response to pressure by its bank. Another example would be a sale of stock or products at a substantial discount in the expectation of benefits resulting from the sale, such as the introduction of the company's products on an overseas market where they had not previously been sold, or the expectation of repeat orders at normal prices.

The terms of the statutory provision empowering the court to invalidate transactions at a significant undervalue itself shows that the provision is not intended to upset transactions which could, with the benefit of hindsight, have been negotiated on better and more profitable terms for the company, but which were nevertheless entered into in what the directors of the company reasonably believed at the time was in the company's best interests. It is impossible to prescribe in advance how large a discount off normal prices a transaction by the company must concede before it becomes a transaction at a significant undervalue. All the circumstances, including the company's financial condition, its need for immediate cash receipts, the reasonableness of the terms of the transaction and the circumstances in which it was entered into, must be taken into account. The transaction will come within the condemnation of the statutory provision only if in the light of all these circumstances the company agreed to take very much less in value than it could reasonably be expected to have obtained, and it will only then be necessary, in order to save the transaction, for the other party to it to prove that the transaction was entered into by the company for justifiable business reasons.

Voidable preferences

In addition to seeking the invalidation of transactions at a significant undervalue, the liquidator of a company in liquidation may apply to

16 Insolvency Act 1986, s 238(5).

the court[17] to set aside a preference given by the company to any of
its creditors, or to a surety or guarantor for any of its debts or
liabilities, within a limited period before the commencement of the
liquidation, and if the preference is set aside the court will make a
restoration or restitution order so as to return the parties to their
original position before the preference was given.[18] A company gives
a preference if it does anything, or suffers anything to be done, which
has the effect of putting a creditor of the company or a surety for any
of its obligations in a position which, in the event of the company
going into an insolvent liquidation in an insolvent condition, will be
better than the position which he would have occupied if that thing
had not been done; but the court cannot make a restoration or
restitution order, unless in giving the preference the company was
influenced by a desire to put the creditor or surety in such a better
position in the event of the company being wound up.[19]

Examples of preferences

The act which constitutes a voidable preference may be anything
which brings about the result that the creditor or surety is or would
be preferred. Obvious examples of preferences are the company
paying an unsecured debt or giving security for an unsecured debt
when it is insolvent, so that the creditor is paid in full or will be able
to pay himself in full out of the proceeds of his security. If the
company's debt is guaranteed by a surety, it will also be a preference
of the surety if the company pays the debt or gives security for it, so
that the surety is released, or will on the realisation of the security
be released, from liability to the creditor. A partial payment of a debt
by the company, or the giving by it of a security which is worth less
than the amount of the debt, is still a preference if the company's
assets at the time would not suffice to pay an equal proportion of all
its other debts and liabilities.

A preference may also take a more oblique form, as it could
under the previous legislation governing the setting aside of fraudulent
preferences in a liquidation.[20] For example, a creditor is preferred if
the company at a time when it is already insolvent gives him a
security which it contracted to give him when the debt was incurred,
even though the obligation to give the security created an immediate
equitable mortgage or charge over the assets concerned as from the

---

17 The application to the court is made by an originating application (Insolvency
   Rules 1986, r 7.2(1) and r 7.3(2)).
18 Insolvency Act 1986, s 239(1) to (3).
19 Ibid, s 239(4) and (5).
20 Companies Act 1948, s 320(1); Companies Act 1985, s 615(1).

moment the company acquired them.[1] Again, the company giving
its consent or withdrawing its opposition to an application to the
court by a mortgagee or holder of a charge over its property for leave
to register the mortgage or charge at the Companies Registry after
the period allowed for doing so has expired, may be a preference,
because the effect of the late registration of the mortgage or charge
is to make it effective against other creditors of the company when
the company is later wound up, which it would not be if it remained
unregistered.[2] But it is not a preference if a company exercises a
contractual or other right of set-off against one of its creditors who
is indebted to the company even though the set-off in effect results
in the creditor being paid in full to the extent of the company's
indebtedness to him, and reduces correspondingly the amount for
which he will prove in the liquidation and receive the same dividend
in the £ as the other creditors of the company receive in respect of
the whole of the company's indebtedness to them.[3]

The act, forbearance or acquiescence which is alleged to be a
preference must be that of the company, and not that of the creditor
or surety without the concurrence or collaboration of the company.
It is therefore not a preference for a secured creditor of an insolvent
company to realise his security and pay himself out of the proceeds,
even if his security would have been void against the company's
other creditors for want of registration at the Companies Registry
had it not been realised before the company went into liquidation.[4]
Nor is it a preference for a company's bank to require that its
unsecured overdraft shall be secured by a fixed or a floating charge
over its assets if a mortgage which the company proposes to give to
its employees' pension fund trustees is to be created to secure a loan
to the company, and for the bank also to require that the mortgage
to the trustees shall be expressly subordinated to the bank's floating
charge.[5] Likewise, it is not a preference for a company to create a
fixed or floating charge over its assets to secure a loan by a person
who has guaranteed the company's bank overdraft, even though
part of the loan is to be used to discharge the overdraft, if the purpose
of the loan is to enable the company to continue carrying on its
business and the lender is unwilling to make the loan without

1 *Re Eric Holmes (Property) Ltd* [1965] Ch 1052, [1965] 2 All ER 333. If the creditor
  relies on his equitable mortgage or charge and not on the security which the
  company later gives him, however, no question of a voidable preference will arise.
2 *Peat v Gresham Trust Ltd* [1934] AC 252. Registration was required in this case
  by the Companies Act 1948, s 95(1) and (2) (now Companies Act 1985, s 396(1)
  and (2) and s 398(1)).
3 *Re Exchange Travel (Holdings) Ltd (No 3)* [1996] 2 BCLC 524, [1996] BCC 933.
4 *Re Cardiff Workmen's Cottage Co Ltd* [1906] 2 Ch 627.
5 *Re MC Bacon Ltd* [1990] BCLC 324, [1990] BCC 78.

security.[6] If the preference is not the result of a positive act of the company, it must at least be the consequence of the company suffering something being done, which means that the company must have authorised, permitted, or concurred in its being done, or collaborated in doing it. The mere fact that the company knows that an act is being done by its creditor which improves the creditor's or a surety's position will not be a preference if the company is powerless to prevent it.

The company's motives

To be a preference the act, forbearance or acquiescence of the company must have been influenced by a desire to put the creditor or surety in a better position than he would otherwise occupy in the company's liquidation.[7] Under the previous legislation the company's act had to be done 'with a view' to giving a preference, that is, the company's primary motive must have been to prefer the creditor or surety over its other creditors.[8] Such a motive is not required by the present legislation, which merely requires the company to have been influenced by a desire to put the preferred creditor or surety in an improved position.[9] At most this will require proof that one of the company's motives was to produce this result, even though its principal motive may have been something else, such as a wish to obtain further credit or the postponement of the date for payment of a debt, which the creditor would agree to only if he were given security or some other advantage. However, it may be that a company will be held to have been influenced by a desire to improve a creditor's or surety's position if at the time it gives the alleged preference the company realises, or must realise from facts known to it, that one of the consequences of its act, forbearance or acquiescence will be to improve the position of the creditor or surety.[10] If this is the interpretation of the new statutory provision which the court adopts, the motive or purpose of the company will be irrelevant, because the company will be taken to have intended the known or foreseeable consequences of what it did. On the other hand, it will not be a preference for a company to fulfil an obligation which it is already under to appropriate money or assets received by it as an agent or trustee in satisfaction of its fiduciary duty to its principal or the beneficiary of the trust, because the company is then

6 *Re Fairway Magazines Ltd* [1993] BCLC 643, [1992] BCC 924.
7 Insolvency Act 1986, s 239(5).
8 Bankruptcy Act 1914, s 44(1); Companies Act 1985, s 615(1); *Re Inns of Court Hotel Co* (1868) LR 6 Eq 82; *Peat v Gresham Trust Ltd*, supra.
9 Insolvency Act 1986, s 239(5).
10 *Re DKG Contractors Ltd* [1990] BCC 903.

never beneficially entitled to the money or property.[11] Nor will it be a preference for a company to put its directors in funds to pay the rent of premises leased to them but occupied by the company, if the company has loan facilities available which are sufficient to discharge its indebtedness to its creditors and they are not pressing for payment.[12]

If the creditor or surety who is given an alleged preference or whose position is knowingly improved by the company's act or sufferance is a person who is connected with the company (otherwise than by reason only of being the company's employee), that is, if the preferred person is a director or shadow director of the company or an associate of such a person or of the company itself, it is to be presumed until the contrary is shown that the company was influenced by a desire to prefer him.[13]

For a preference of a creditor of the company or of a guarantor or surety of any of its debts or obligations to be set aside it is not necessary that the directors or other agent acting for the company in giving the preference should know or have cause to believe that the company will shortly become insolvent, and if they erroneously believe that the company is solvent the transaction constituting the preference will nevertheless be set aside.[14] Moreover, the fact that the recipient of the preference believes that the asset of the company by which it is made is his property in equity because the company is a trustee or fiduciary for him, will not prevent the invalidation of the preference.[14]

Date of the preference

A preference may be set aside by the court only if it was given to a creditor or surety within six months before the commencement of the winding up of the company, or (if an administration order had been made in respect of the company which was terminated immediately before it went into liquidation) within six months before the presentation of the petition on which the administration order was made.[15] However, if the preference was also a transaction at a significant undervalue, or was a preference given to a person who was at the time connected with the company (otherwise than by reason only of being its employee), that is, a director or shadow director of the company or an associate of such a director or of the

11 *Re Lewis's of Leicester Ltd* [1995] BCC 514.
12 *Re Beacon Leisure Ltd* [1991] BCC 213.
13 Insolvency Act 1986, s 239(6), s 249 and s 435. For the definition of an associate, see p 150, ante.
14 *Re Exchange Travel (Holdings) Ltd (No 3)* [1996] 2 BCLC 524, [1996] BCC 933.
15 Insolvency Act 1986, s 240(1) and (3).

company itself,[12] the court may set aside the preference if it was given within two years before the commencement of the company's liquidation or the prior presentation of a petition on which an administration order was made in respect of the company, which was terminated immediately before it went into liquidation.[15]

The company's insolvency

An act or sufferance by the company cannot be treated as a preference unless at the time the company was unable to pay its debts as they fell due out of its liquid assets, or unless it became unable to pay its debts as they fell due in consequence of the preference, or unless the company's total assets were insufficient to satisfy all its debts and liabilities at the time of the preference or became insufficient to do so in consequence of the preference.[16] The value of the company's assets must be taken as at the date of the alleged preference for the purpose of ascertaining whether it was insolvent or became insolvent in consequence of the preference, and the existence of facts at that time which would suffice to prove that the company was unable to pay its debts if a petition for a winding up order had then been presented against it,[17] and that its assets would additionally suffice to meet the costs and expenses of winding it up,[18] must be taken as establishing its insolvency at that time for the purpose of the present provision.[15] The burden of proving the company's insolvency rests on the person who alleges it; even if the preference was given to a person who was at the time connected with the company, there is no presumption (as there is when a transaction is impugned as one entered into by the company at a significant undervalue) that the company was unable to pay its debts at the time of the preference, or was unable to do so without the aid of the property comprised in the transaction.[19]

Restoration and restitution orders

When the court invalidates a transaction at an undervalue or sets aside a preference under the statutory provisions dealt with above, it may make any one or more of the following orders in order to restore the company and the other persons involved to the position which they originally occupied, namely orders:[20]

16 Ibid, s 240(2), applying s 123(1) and (2).
17 Ibid, s 123(1) and (2) (see p 42, ante).
18 *West Mercia Safetyware Ltd v Dodd* [1988] BCLC 250, 4 BCC 30.
19 Insolvency Act 1986, s 240(2).
20 Ibid, s 241(1).

(1) requiring any property transferred or money paid as part of a transaction at a significant undervalue or in connection with a preference to be vested in the company;

(2) requiring any property to be so vested if it represents the application of the proceeds of sale of property transferred as part of such a transaction at a significant undervalue or in connection with a preference; the proceeds of sale of property transferred by the company itself cannot be caught by such an order, but only property acquired with it, which would presumably include the credit balance of a bank account into which the proceeds of sale have been paid;

(3) releasing or discharging in whole or part any security given by the company (eg a mortgage or charge to secure a sum in excess of an advance actually made to a company and interest thereon and the lender's reasonable expenses, or a mortgage or charge given to prefer an unsecured creditor);

(4) requiring any person to pay to the liquidator of the company such amount as the court thinks fit in respect of benefits received by him from the company; such an order has a purely personal effect on the person against whom it is made, and does not affect any assets acquired by him, but it could usefully be employed when a company has provided services for the person in question gratuitously or at a significant undervalue or as a preference, or where a person still has in his possession the proceeds of disposition of property transferred to him by the company at a significant undervalue or as a preference;

(5) imposing new or revived obligations on a surety or guarantor whose original obligations to a creditor of the company or to a co-surety have been discharged in whole or part under a transaction at an undervalue or by the giving of a preference (eg the imposition of the same obligations under a guarantee or substituted obligations on a surety who has been released from his liability to a creditor to pay a debt which the company has discharged by a transaction at a significant undervalue or by giving a preference);

(6) requiring security to be provided for any obligation imposed by the court's order (eg for a payment ordered under (4) or (5) above), or for such an obligation to be charged on any property, and for any such security or charge to have the same priority as any security or charge which was released or discharged by the transaction at a significant undervalue or by the giving of the preference which is set aside; it is questionable whether under this head the court could order the revival or reconstitution of a mortgage or charge given by

a third person to secure a debt of the company which it has discharged by paying the creditor in circumstances which amount to a preference to the creditor, but the third person has not personally guaranteed the debt;

(7) providing for the extent to which any person whose property is vested in the company under heads (1) or (2), or on whom any obligation is imposed by the court's order, may prove in the winding up of the company for any debt or other liability which arose from, or was released or discharged under, a transaction at a significant undervalue or a preference which the court sets aside (eg the court may permit a creditor who has been paid by the giving of a preference, or a surety who has been discharged from liability by such a preference, to prove in the liquidation for the whole or part of the amount which he is required to repay to the liquidator, or the court may permit a purchaser of a company's property at a significant undervalue to prove in the liquidation for the amount which he paid the company for it).

Orders for the restoration of assets to the company, or for the payment of money to its liquidator by way of restitution, may be made by the court against persons who were not parties to the transaction at a significant undervalue or to the giving of a preference, but such an order may not require any person to make a payment to the liquidator if he has obtained a benefit from the transaction or preference in good faith and for value; nor may such an order prejudice any interest in property acquired by any third person from someone other than the company (eg an interest acquired from the person to whom the company transferred assets at a significant undervalue) if the third person acquired the interest in good faith and for value.[1]

A person who obtains a benefit from a transaction at a significant undervalue or a preference, or a person who has acquired an interest in property from a person other than the company who himself acquired it under a transaction at a substantial undervalue or a preference, is not deemed to have acted in good faith if he had notice of the relevant circumstances (ie the fact that the transaction was at a significant undervalue or that a preference was given by the company) and of the presentation of a petition on which a winding up order was subsequently made against the company or of a winding up resolution subsequently passed by a general meeting of the company; if the company went into liquidation immediately following the discharge of an administration order made against it,

1 Ibid, s 241(2), as amended by the Insolvency (No 2) Act 1994, s 1(1).

the notice of insolvency proceedings which will deprive the person who benefits from the transaction or preference or who acquires an interest in property from a person other than the company, will be notice of the presentation of a petition for an administration order or the making of an administration order or of the company going into liquidation.[2] Notice for the purpose of these provisions presumably means actual knowledge or knowledge of such facts and circumstances as inevitably induce the conclusion that the matter in question exists.

Transactions to avoid payment of debts

In addition to the provisions of the Insolvency Act 1986, which enable the court in the liquidation of an insolvent company to set aside transactions entered into by it at a significant undervalue and preferences which it has given to its creditors or sureties within a limited time before the liquidation of the company began, the Act contains a general provision by which the court may set aside and make restoration and restitution orders in respect of certain transactions entered into by a company at any time whatsoever by which it makes gifts, or under which it receives no consideration or a consideration which is significantly less than the consideration which it gives in return itself.[3] The significant features of this general provision are, first, that the company need not be in liquidation, and if it is not, an application for restitution may be made to the court by any person who is, or is capable of being, prejudiced by the transaction,[4] (including a person who has a claim against the company which it disputes or to which it pleads a counterclaim),[5] and secondly, that if the company is in liquidation, although an application to the court may be made only by its liquidator,[6] it is not necessary that the transaction by way of gift or at a significant undervalue should have been entered into within two years before the commencement of the company's liquidation, or that the company should have been insolvent at the time of the transaction, or that it should have been made insolvent by the transaction.

The burden of proof on the applicant under this general provision is, however, greater than on an application made by a

2 Ibid, s 241(3), (3B) and (3C), inserted by Insolvency (No 2) Act 1994, s 1(2) and (3).
3 Ibid, s 423(1).
4 Ibid, s 423(5) and s 424(1).
5 *Pinewood Joinery v Starelm Properties Ltd* [1994] 2 BCLC 412, [1994] BCC 569.
6 Insolvency Act 1986, s 424(1).

liquidator to set aside a transaction at a significant undervalue under the provision applicable in a liquidation which was dealt with above.[7] The court may make an order setting aside a transaction at an undervalue under the present general provision only if the court is satisfied that the company entered into it either for the purpose of putting its assets beyond the reach of a person or persons who have made, or may make, claims against it (eg present and prospective creditors), or for the purpose of prejudicing the interests of such a person or persons in relation to the claims which they have made, or may make, against it.[8] In other words, the applicant for an order under the general provision must prove that the company intended to prevent its creditors or a particular creditor being paid, or being paid in full, or that the company intended to make it more difficult or expensive for its creditors or a particular creditor to obtain payment.

Acts which may manifest such an intention are transferring assets gratuitously or at a substantial undervalue to nominees, or to other companies with substantially the same shareholders (the phoenix company phenomenon), transferring assets to countries where it will be difficult or impossible for creditors to recover them, and transferring assets under sham transactions where it is not intended that the transferee shall provide the company with the consideration which he promises. The court has under this provision set aside an assignment of leases of aircraft held by a company to an associated company in consideration of a promise by the associated company to pay to the assignor company a sum equal to the future rent payable under the leases at a remote future date, when the assignment was accompanied by an agreement by the associated company to manage the remaining aircraft held on lease by the assigning company for a very substantial fee, the purpose of the arrangement being to protect the assigning company against proceedings for the recovery of rent due under the assigned leases brought by the owners of the aircraft.[9] Likewise, the court has under this provision set aside a lease of agricultural property owned by a debtor where the rent reserved was less than the annual value of the property, which resulted in a substantial reduction in the value of the freehold reversion.[10] The court has also set aside the transfer of a business at a price equal to its current market value, but payable only at a remote future date, and the concurrent grant of a lease of the

---

7 See p 221, ante.
8 Insolvency Act 1986, s 423(3).
9 *Arbuthnot Leasing International Ltd v Havelet Leasing Ltd* [1991] 1 All ER 591, *(No 2)* [1990] BCC 636.
10 *Agricultural Mortgage Corpn plc v Woodward* [1995] 1 BCLC 1, [1994] BCC 688.

premises where the business was carried on at a rent equal to the annual value of the premises but payable substantially in arrear with an option for the lessee to terminate the lease on giving short notice.[11]

Because a liquidator can recover property transferred under the present provision only if he can prove fraud or something akin to it on the part of the persons who control the company or its management, he will resort to the general provision only when the transaction at a significant undervalue was entered into by the company more than two years before the commencement of its liquidation or the presentation of the petition on which an administration order was made against the company before it went into liquidation. If an application is made successfully under the present provision, the court will make such orders as it thinks fit to restore the company to the position which it would have occupied if the transaction at a significant undervalue had not been entered into;[12] and in exercising its jurisdiction the court may make any order which it could make when setting aside a transaction at a significant undervalue under the specific provision applicable only in a liquidation which was dealt with above,[12] but subject to similar safeguards for persons who were not parties to the transaction and who acted in good faith and for value.[13]

Extortionate credit transactions

On an application made by the liquidator of a company which has gone into liquidation in an insolvent condition,[14] the court may make an order setting aside a transaction to which the company was a party and which involved the provision of credit to the company on extortionate terms.[15] The court may invalidate such a transaction which was entered into within three years before a winding up order was made against the company or a winding up resolution was passed by a general meeting of its members, or, if an administration order has been made in respect of the company and was terminated immediately before it went into liquidation, within three years before that order was made.[16]

---

11 *Barclays Bank plc v Eustice* [1995] 2 BCLC 630, [1995] BCC 978.
12 Insolvency Act 1986, s 423(2).
13 Ibid, s 425(1) to (4) (see p 231, ante); *Chohan v Saggar* [1994] 1 BCLC 706, [1994] BCC 134.
14 The application to the court is made by an originating application (Insolvency Rules 1986, r 7.2(1) and r 7.3(2).
15 Insolvency Act 1986, s 244(1).
16 Ibid, s 244(2).

The court may set a credit transaction aside, however, only if it was extortionate, that is, not only unreasonable but also oppressive.[17] A credit transaction is extortionate if, having regard to the risk borne by the person who provided the credit, the terms of the transaction required grossly exorbitant payments to be made in respect of the provision of the credit, whether such payments are payable in any event or only contingently (eg on the company defaulting in making a payment of principal or interest), or if the transaction otherwise grossly contravenes ordinary principles of fair dealing (eg because the company is required by the lender to enter into an onerous collateral transaction as a condition of obtaining the credit).[17]

If the court intervenes on the liquidator's application, it may set aside the whole or part of any obligation created by the transaction, or may vary its terms or the terms of any security created by the transaction, or may order any party to the transaction to repay to the liquidator any amounts paid by the company to him under it, or may order any person to surrender any property held by him as security for the purpose of the transaction, or may direct accounts to be taken between any persons.[18] The powers of the court also extend to releasing or modifying the obligations of sureties for the company's obligations under the transaction, and to discharging or modifying the terms of any security given by a third person for the company's obligations under the transaction.[19]

Although the court can order the repayment of money paid by the company under the transaction, it appears that it cannot order the repayment of an amount paid by a surety for the company, or by a person who has mortgaged or charged his own property as security for the company's obligations, in order to discharge the guarantee or mortgage given by him. Furthermore, there are no provisions for the protection of third persons who acquire interests in or under the extortionate credit transaction, even if they act in good faith (eg an assignee of the benefit of the transaction from the person who provided credit under it), but on the other hand, such third persons, whether acting in good faith or not, cannot be ordered to return payments made to them by the company.

The provision of the Insolvency Act 1986, which empowers the court to set aside extortionate credit transactions operates concurrently with, and not to the exclusion of, the provisions of the Act under which transactions at a significant undervalue and

17 Ibid, s 244(3).
18 Ibid, s 244(4).
19 The court cannot exercise such powers under s 241(1) when setting aside a transaction at a significant undervalue by the company or a preference given by it (see p 231, ante).

preferences may be invalidated,[20] and consequently an extortionate credit transaction may also be attacked under any of those provisions, but on different grounds.

Invalidation of certain floating charges

A transparent device by which a company in financial difficulties may seek to prefer an unsecured creditor, or a creditor whose security is inadequate, is by giving him a floating charge over the whole of its assets and undertaking, or over a class or classes of its assets (eg book debts owing to it at any time, or investments held by it at any time in other companies), as security for the company's indebtedness to him. Under the rules of equity governing floating charges,[1] the existence of the charge will not impede the company in continuing to carry on its business, and will not prevent it from disposing of its assets free from the charge in the course of doing so; but on the company going into liquidation the floating charge will crystallise and attach specifically to the assets then owned by the company, or to the assets then owned by it of the class or classes which are comprised in the floating charge, and the creditor or a receiver appointed by him or the court will be able to take and realise such assets and apply the proceeds of realisation in payment of what the company owes the holder of the floating charge in priority to its unsecured creditors, other than creditors for preferential debts.[2] This device has been combatted since the Companies Act 1929, by statutory provisions which invalidate such floating charges created for no new consideration within a limited period before the commencement of the company's liquidation.[3]

Extent of invalidation

By the Insolvency Act 1986, a charge over a company's undertaking or property (including a class or classes of its assets) which was created as a floating charge within a limited period before the commencement of the company's liquidation in an insolvent condition is invalid as a security, except for an amount equal to the aggregate of:

---

20 Insolvency Act 1986, s 244(5).
1 See *Pennington's Company Law* (7th edn), p 569 et seq.
2 For preferential debts, see Insolvency Act 1986, s 175(1) and (2), s 386(1) and Sch 6; (see p 303, post).
3 Companies Act 1929, s 266; Companies Act 1948, s 322(1); Companies Act 1985, s 617(1).

(1) the value of so much of the consideration for the creation of the charge as consists of money paid, or goods or services supplied, to the company at the same time as, or subsequently to, the creation of the charge;

(2) the value of so much of that consideration as consists of the discharge or reduction of any debt of the company at the time when the charge was created or subsequently (eg a floating charge given to secure the right to an indemnity of a surety for a debt of the company which the surety has wholly or partly discharged, or the similar right to reimbursement of a third person who has paid a debt of the company at its request); and

(3) interest on amounts falling under (1) and (2) at the rate reserved by the agreement under which the money was paid, or the goods or services supplied, or under which the debt was discharged or reduced.[4]

The result of a charge created as a floating charge being preserved as a valid security for the excepted debts and liabilities is that such a charge created within the limited period before the company's liquidation is invalid as a security only in respect of debts and liabilities of the company which existed before the charge was created and which were not discharged or reduced as the consideration for the charge. Such a charge created within the same limited period is also invalid in the company's liquidation as a security for the indebtedness of persons other than the company, whether arising before or after the creation of the charge (eg debts of subsidiaries of a parent or holding company which creates a floating charge over its assets and undertaking. However, as indicated below, a floating charge is invalidated under the present provision as regards a person who is not connected with the company only if the company is insolvent when the charge is created, or if the company becomes insolvent in consequence of the charge being created to secure them.[5]

The wording of the present provision appears to produce two curious consequences. The first is that a floating charge created within the relevant limited period is invalid as a security for existing indebtedness of the company which the charge is expressed to secure, but it is valid as a security for the amount of that indebtedness, or part of it, if the indebtedness is expressed to be discharged or reduced in consideration of the company creating the floating charge as security for an equivalent sum, or more directly, if the

4 Insolvency Act 1986, s 245(1), (2) and (5) and s 251.
5 Ibid, s 245(3).

creditor makes a new advance to the company out of which it is required to discharge or reduce its existing indebtedness to him.[6] Such a new advance made on that condition is not treated as money paid to the company under the present provision, even if the advance is made by a cheque which is matched by a cheque issued by the company to the lender for the same or a smaller amount,[7] but this does not preclude the consideration for the floating charge being created under the present legislation as being the discharge or reduction of an existing debt of the company.

The second curious consequence is that although a floating charge created by the company within the limited period as security for the existing or future indebtedness of a third person is generally invalid under the present provision, it will be saved if the indebtedness which it secures, is also indebtedness of the company which is validly secured by the charge, as it will be if the company is personally liable in respect of it as a surety for the third person at the time when the charge is created or when the indebtedness subsequently arises; but if the indebtedness of the third person for which the company is surety already exists when it creates the charge, for the reason given in the preceding paragraph, to be valid the charge must be expressed to be given in consideration of the discharge or reduction of the company's liability for that indebtedness, and the charge must be expressed to secure an equivalent sum for which the company makes itself a surety, or the creditor must make a fresh advance to the company which it must then re-lend or pass on to the third person so that he may discharge the original indebtedness out of it.

Legislation which confers validity on transactions which achieve acceptable results only if they are carried out only in such a contorted fashion hardly deserves approbation; this is even more so when the purpose of the legislation is to invalidate the same transaction if it is carried out by direct means. The former law was more commendable in this respect, because it invalidated floating charges only if they were given to secure existing indebtedness of the company, whether as a principal or a surety, and whether the transaction was effected directly or by way of a fresh advance which was earmarked to discharge or reduce the company's existing indebtedness.

---

6 Under the earlier legislation mentioned in footnote 3, the new advance made on terms that the company must discharge its existing indebtedness to the creditor out of it, was identified with the company's existing indebtedness to the creditor, and the floating charge was therefore invalid as a security for the new advance (*Re Destone Fabrics Ltd* [1941] Ch 319, [1941] 1 All ER 545).

7 *Re Fairway Magazines Ltd* [1993] BCLC 643, [1993] BCC 924.

The time when the floating charge is created

A charge created as a floating charge is invalid when given to secure existing indebtedness of the company, or existing or subsequent indebtedness of a third person, only if the charge is created within 12 months before the commencement of the company's liquidation, or within 12 months before or after the presentation of a petition for an administration order in respect of the company on which such an order is made; but if the charge is created in favour of a person who is connected with the company, at the time of its creation or who is then an associate of such a person or of the company itself,[8] the period of 12 months is extended to two years.[9]

If the creation of the floating charge was preceded by an unconditional agreement by the company to create it in consideration of money paid to it then or thereafter, it was formerly held that the period of 12 months or two years must be calculated with reference to the date of the agreement,[10] but if the agreement was conditional (eg to secure any amount paid by a surety for a debt of the company, but only when payment to the creditor is made), the period must be calculated with reference to the date when the floating charge was actually created.[11] These decisions have now been overruled, however, by a decision of the Court of Appeal (affirming a judgment of Hoffmann J) under the present legislation, in which it was held that a loan or other consideration for the creation of a floating charge created by a company can be treated as made or given contemporaneously with the creation of the charge only if it is made or given substantially at the same time.[12] If there is first, an agreement to make the loan to the company on the security of a floating charge, and secondly and separately the fulfilment of the agreement by the creation of the charge, the lender is entitled in equity to have the charge granted as soon as the agreement is entered into; the charge is therefore treated in equity as created when the agreement is made, and particulars of it must be presented for registration at the Companies Registration Office within 21 days thereafter to prevent its invalidation in the company's subsequent liquidation or on an administration order being made against it by

8 For the definition of a connected person and an associate, see p 150, ante.
9 Insolvency Act 1986, s 245(3) and (5).
10 *Re Columbian Fireproofing Co Ltd* [1910] 2 Ch 120; *Re F and E Stanton Ltd* [1929] 1 Ch 180.
11 *Re Gregory Love & Co* [1916] 1 Ch 203.
12 *Re Shoe Lace Ltd, Power v Sharp Investments Ltd* [1994] 1 BCLC 111, [1993] BCC 609. The judgment of Hoffmann J is reported at [1992] BCLC 636, [1992] BCC 367.

the court.[13] If there was no such agreement when the loan was made, or if there was such an agreement but the lender's right to call for the creation of a floating charge (which vested an equitable security in him) was not notified for registration at the Companies Registration Office within 21 days of the agreement, the subsequent creation of the floating charge will be treated as effected under a separate agreement entered into at that time, and since the loan will then already have been made, the floating charge given to secure it will be invalidated under the provisions of the Insolvency Act 1986 under consideration if the company goes into liquidation within the following one or two years (as the case may be). The same reasoning applies where the consideration for the creation of the floating charge is an agreement to provide goods or services to the company.

The company's insolvency

A floating charge created within 12 months before the commencement of the company's liquidation in favour of a person who is neither connected with the company nor an associate of such a person or of the company itself, is invalid only if at that time the company is unable to pay its debts as they fall due out of its liquid assets, or if the value of the whole of the company's assets is then less than the total amount of its liabilities (taking its contingent and prospective liabilities into account), or if the company later becomes unable to pay its debts as they fall due or its assets become insufficient to satisfy its total liabilities in consequence of the transaction under which the floating charge is created.[14] This limitation on the scope of the invalidating provision does not apply if the floating charge is created in favour of a person who is at the time connected with the company or who is then an associate of such a person,[14] and so the invalidating provision applies whether the company is then insolvent in this sense or not.

In determining the company's solvency or insolvency, the value of the company's assets must be taken as at the date when the floating charge was created; the existence of facts at that time which would suffice to prove that the company is unable to pay its debts if a petition for a winding up order were then presented against it[15] must be taken as establishing its insolvency at that time for this purpose.[14]

On the other hand, in order to ascertain whether the company becomes unable to pay its debts as they fall due or otherwise

13 Companies Act 1985, s 395(1).
14 Insolvency Act 1986, s 245(4).
15 Ibid, s 123(1) and (2); (see p 42, ante).

becomes insolvent in consequence of the creation of the charge (the alternative insolvency test), it would seem that the ability of the company to pay its debts as they fall due out of its liquid assets other than those comprised in the charge, alternatively, the sufficiency of the company's assets other than those comprised in the charge to satisfy the total of its liabilities, must be judged at the date when the floating charge crystallises, and not when it is created. This is because at the date when the charge is created the company is in no way inhibited by the existence of the charge from applying any of its assets (including those subject to the charge) in satisfying its other debts and liabilities. Consequently, if at the date when the floating charge crystallises by a receiver being appointed under it, or the company going into liquidation, or some other event occurring which by the terms of the charge causes it to crystallise, the company's assets not comprised in the charge, plus any surplus of the realisable value of its assets subject to the charge over the amount secured by it, is insufficient to satisfy the company's other debts and liabilities in full, the company will have become unable to pay its debts in consequence of the creation of the charge, and the statutory invalidating provision will apply. This interpretation of the alternative insolvency test is consistent with the purpose which underlies the statutory provision, namely to protect the unsecured creditors of companies which go into liquidation in an insolvent condition against the claims of creditors who have taken floating charges over the company's assets to secure previously unsecured indebtedness within the relevant period before their liquidation; so far as such unsecured creditors are concerned, the appropriate date to determine whether the company is insolvent is when its liquidation commences.

If the floating charge extends to the company's liquid assets, it is uncertain whether the company would be treated under the first insolvency test as unable to pay its debts as they fall due when the floating charge crystallises merely because the appropriation of those liquid assets to satisfy its secured debts and liabilities which have accrued due would leave insufficient assets to pay its unsecured debts which have also so accrued. It is submitted that this result may be avoided by an application of the equitable principle of marshalling[16] if the liquid assets of the company are at the time of crystallisation sufficient to satisfy the company's unsecured debts which have

---

16 The principle is that, if there are two creditors or classes of creditors, one of which can resort to two funds or properties for payment and the other to only one of those funds or properties, the first creditor or class is compelled in equity to resort primarily to the fund or property to which the other cannot resort, so as to ensure that as much as possible of the fund or the proceeds of the property to which both creditors or classes can resort is left available to satisfy the other's claims.

accrued due, and the discounted[17] realisable value of its non-liquid assets plus any surplus of its liquid assets after satisfying its accrued unsecured debts will suffice to meet the indebtedness secured by the floating charge and the company's other debts and liabilities.

In the light of the foregoing considerations, it would appear that the application of the test of the company's insolvency to a floating charge created within 12 months before the commencement of the company's liquidation in favour of a person who is not connected with the company will result in the charge being invalidated as a security for the company's existing indebtedness at the time when the charge was created, or as security for the existing or subsequent indebtedness of a third person, only if the company is already insolvent at the date when the charge is created, or if it cannot discharge the indebtedness secured by the charge at the date when the floating charge crystallises plus all its other indebtedness and liabilities at that time out of the totality of the assets which the company then owns, or if at the date when the floating charge crystallises the company's liquid assets do not suffice to pay its indebtedness which has already fallen due for payment.

Floating charges to secure bank advances

One of the commonest uses of a floating charge over the whole of the assets and undertaking of a company is as a security for a bank overdraft or for all moneys owing at any time by a company to its bank, and the charge is then given to secure all advances made by the bank to the company before, at the time of, or subsequently to, the creation of the charge. If the charge is given to the bank within 12 months before the commencement of the company's liquidation, and the company is insolvent when the charge is created or subsequently becomes insolvent in consequence of the creation of the charge, the charge will effectively secure advances made by the bank at the time it is created or subsequently, but not advances already made before the charge is created. However, the part of the company's total indebtedness to the bank equal to advances made before the creation of the floating charge will be effectively secured by it if the company has, since the creation of the charge, paid into the credit or its account with the bank an amount equal to or

17 That is, discounted at the current market rate of interest for the period from the commencement of the company's liquidation or the date when a petition on which an administration order is made in respect of the company (whichever is the earlier) until the anticipated date or dates by which the company's assets will be realised and the proceeds of realisation recovered.

exceeding the outstanding bank advances immediately before the charge was created.[18] This is because the payments which the company makes into the account after the creation of the charge, will be treated as discharging its drawings and other items debited to its account in the chronological order in which they were made, earlier drawings or advances being discharged before later ones.[19] Consequently, if payments into the company's account after it creates the floating charge equal or exceed the debit balance on the account at the date when the charge is created, there will be no indebtedness of the company to its bank which existed when the charge was created and remains undischarged.

The debit balance of the company's account when it subsequently goes into liquidation will then represent exclusively advances or overdrawings made at the time of, or subsequently to, the creation of the charge, and those advances or overdrawings will be validly secured by it, despite the company's insolvency at the time when the floating charge was created.[18] If the amounts paid to the credit of the account are less in total than the advances or overdraft outstanding immediately before the creation of the floating charge, the charge will be invalidated as a security only for the amount by which the advances or the amount overdrawn which were outstanding immediately before the creation of the floating charge exceed the total of payments subsequently made to the credit of the company's account.[18]

The foregoing assumes, of course, that the bank was not a person connected with the company, or an associate of such a person or of the company itself, when the floating charge was created.[20] If the bank was such a person, the charge will be invalid as security for advances made before its creation and not since repaid if the charge was created within two years before the commencement of the company's liquidation, and this will be so even if the company was solvent at the time when the charge was created, but becomes insolvent by the time it goes into liquidation.[1] Whether the bank is connected with the company or not, however, it would appear to be possible to make a floating charge an effective security for advances made by the bank to the company before the charge was created, even though the company was then insolvent. This can be done, it seems, by the bank opening a new account with

---

18 *Re Yeovil Glove Co Ltd* [1965] Ch 148, [1964] 2 All ER 849.
19 *Devaynes v Noble, Clayton's Case* (1816) 1 Mer 529.
20 For the definition of a connected person and an associate, see p 132, ante.
 1 Insolvency Act 1986, s 245(3) and (4).

the company when the charge is created and crediting it with a new advance equal to the company's existing indebtedness to the bank, and then, with the company's agreement, discharging that existing indebtedness by setting it off against the credit to which the company is entitled under the new account, so eliminating the debit balance on the company's former account.[2] The floating charge then secures consideration given by the bank in the form of a discharge of the company's existing indebtedness, and so the charge appears to be valid as a security for the new advance on the company subsequently going into liquidation, whether the company was solvent at the time or not.[3]

It has been suggested that a floating charge created in favour of a company's bank to secure advances made to the company at the time when the floating charge is created or subsequently will, if the company is insolvent and goes into liquidation within the relevant period, be invalid as a security for advances made after the creation of the charge, unless the bank contracted at that time to make the advances and the charge was expressed to secure them, a mere statement in the document creating the floating charge that it was intended to secure further advances which the bank chooses to make, without being bound to make them, being insufficient. The conclusion is reached by relying on the provision in the Insolvency Act 1986, that the floating charge is valid in the liquidation only as security for 'the value of so much of the consideration for the charge as consists of money paid ... to the company at the same time as, or after, the creation of the charge';[4] it is contended that advances made by the bank after the charge was created which it had not contracted to make are not made in consideration of the creation of the charge, because the company makes them voluntarily, and not in fulfilment of an obligation entered into by it in consideration of the creation of the charge. It would seem that such an interpretation of the statutory provision is too narrow, and involves reading into it words which it does not contain. The interpretation relies on the difference between the wording of the present provision and its predecessor (now repealed) which preserved the floating charge as a valid security only for 'cash paid to the company at the time of or subsequently to the creation of, and in consideration for, the charge';[5] this was interpreted by the court as preserving the charge as a valid security for advances made at the same time as or

2 *Deeley v Lloyds Bank Ltd* [1912] AC 756.
3 Insolvency Act 1986, s 245(2)(*b*).
4 Ibid, s 245(2)(*a*).
5 Companies Act 1985, s 617(1).

subsequently to, and as a result of, the creation of the charge, because the parties intended that such advances, although not made under a contractual obligation, were to be secured by it.[6] The word 'consideration' in the former statutory provision[5] was read by the court as not having its technical meaning in the law of contract, but as meaning that the creation of the charge provided the cause or reason for the bank making the contemporaneous or subsequent advances. The same interpretation of the word consideration should be given in the present statutory provision.[4]

There is an alternative reason for concluding that the altered wording of the present statutory provision does not result in uncovenanted but contemplated advances made after the creation of the charge being excluded from the security of the charge if the company is insolvent at the time it is created and later goes into an insolvent liquidation. The required consideration for the charge under the present provision is not the obligation of the bank to make advances to the company at the time when the charge is created or subsequently, but the actual making of such advances. In other words, the consideration for the floating charge is an executed, and not an executory, one, and an executed consideration is not necessarily one which is furnished when the contract is made, but it may be provided in the future, the effect of the delay being merely to postpone the time when the contract becomes legally binding or in the present case, where the contract is binding when the initial advance is made to the company, to postpone the floating charge extending to further advances until those advances are respectively made by the bank to and accepted by the company. The result under the statutory provision is, therefore, that the floating charge is initially a security only for the advance made by the bank at the time it is created, but because the charge is expressed to be a security also for advances subsequently made, it becomes a security additionally for those advances when they are made in consideration of them being made. There is only one floating charge, but the consideration for its creation is now, not only the original advance (which was only part of that consideration), but also the subsequent advances, which are further consideration for the creating of the charge, not because they were promised, but because they were made (ie they were 'money paid ... to the company ... after the creation of the charge').[4] The contract for the creation of the floating charge is, therefore, one which becomes effective in stages, and the contract expands when each subsequent advance is made; the single floating charge initially secures only the original advance, but when the subsequent advances

6 Re Yeovil Glove Co Ltd, supra.

which it is also expressed to secure are made, the further consideration for which the charge was created is furnished as executed consideration, and the contract automatically extends the floating charge to secure that further consideration.

This interpretation is consistent with the purpose underlying the statutory provision, namely, to invalidate floating charges given by an insolvent company only where they are given to secure existing unsecured debts. It does not assist the fulfilment of this purpose to invalidate a floating charge which is given to a bank in anticipation of money being advanced to the company, if the money is in fact subsequently advanced by the bank, but only because the floating charge already exists to secure it.

Conversion of floating charges into fixed charges

A charge which is created as a floating charge to secure existing indebtedness is invalid under the provision of the Insolvency Act 1986 which invalidates such floating charges created within a certain time before the commencement of the company's liquidation,[7] whether the charge is still a floating charge when the company goes into liquidation or not, at least, if the amount secured by the charge has not been paid to, or recovered by, the secured creditor before that time.

If the company repays the whole or part of the loan or indebtedness secured by a floating charge before the commencement of its liquidation, the liquidator cannot recover the amount paid to the secured creditor, even though the charge would have been invalid if it had not been discharged before the liquidation commenced.[8] It is possible, however, that the liquidator may be able to recover the amount repaid as a voidable preference if it was paid within six months before the liquidation commenced, or within two years beforehand if the creditor secured by the floating charge was connected with the company.[9] If the creditor who holds a floating charge realises his security and pays himself the amount owing out of the proceeds of realisation before the commencement of the company's liquidation, he cannot be compelled to account to the liquidator,[10] and in this situation there is no risk that the liquidator may recover the proceeds of realisation as a preference if the

7 Insolvency Act 1986, s 245(1) to (3).
8 *Re Parkes Garage (Swadlincote) Ltd* [1929] 1 Ch 139.
9 Insolvency Act 1986, s 239(1) to (4); (see p 225, ante).
10 *Mace Builders (Glasgow) Ltd v Lunn* [1986] Ch 459, [1985] BCLC 154.

company did not concur or acquiesce in the realisation. On the other hand, if the creditor secured by a floating charge has an option to convert his charge into a fixed charge by the terms of the agreement creating the charge, and he exercises that option before the commencement of the company's liquidation,[11] or if the floating charge has crystallised before the commencement of the liquidation (eg by the appointment of a receiver), the now crystallised charge will be invalid as a fixed charge in the liquidation if the other conditions for invalidation are fulfilled, because the statutory provision applies to any charge which 'as created' was a floating charge, even though it has become a fixed charge before the commencement of the liquidation.[12]

Effect of statutory invalidation provisions

Where statute invalidates an act or transaction by a company on it going into liquidation, the assets which the liquidator is thereby enabled to recover are added to the company's general assets for the benefit of all its creditors. If the company has created a floating charge over the whole of its assets and undertakings, the creditor secured by the charge therefore cannot claim the assets recovered as part of his security[13] even though in general it is possible for a floating charge to extend to assets acquired by a company after it goes into liquidation.[14] Assets recovered by the liquidator in connection with transactions at an undervalue, voidable preferences, transactions to avoid payment of a company's debts or extortionate credit transactions therefore augment the general assets of a company available to satisfy all its debts and liabilities.

This is not necessarily so, however, when a floating charge created by a company within a limited period before its liquidation is invalidated by the Insolvency Act 1986; the effect of the charge becoming invalid as a security may be to give priority to another valid charge created by the company over the same assets,[15] and if satisfaction of that other charge will exhaust the assets comprised in

---

11 Insolvency Act 1986, s 245(2) and s 251. This was not so under the Companies Act 1985, s 617(1) (see *Re Woodroffes (Musical Instruments) Ltd* [1986] Ch 366, [1985] BCLC 227; *Re Brightlife Ltd* [1987] Ch 200, [1986] BCLC 418).

12 Insolvency Act 1986, s 251.

13 *Willmott v London Celluloid Co* (1886) 31 Ch D 425; *Re Yagerphone Ltd* [1935] Ch 392; see also *Re Oasis Merchandising Services Ltd* [1995] 2 BCLC 493, [1995] BCC 911.

14 *NW Robbie & Co Ltd v Witney Warehouse Ltd* [1963] 3 All ER 613, [1963] 1 WLR 1324.

15 *Capital Finance Co Ltd v Stokes* [1968] 1 All ER 573, [1968] 1 WLR 1158, 1165.

the invalidated floating charge, no addition will be made to the assets of the company in the hands of the liquidator which are available to satisfy the company's unsecured debts and liabilities.

THE INVALIDATION OF EXECUTIONS

Introductory

The provision of the Insolvency Act 1986 enabling the court to stay or prevent the continuance of an execution or distress levied on a company's assets after the presentation of a winding up petition against it,[16] together with the prohibition on the levying of execution or distress on a company's assets without leave of the court after a winding up order has been made in respect of it, and the retrospective invalidation of executions and distress levied after the presentation of a winding up petition on which a winding up order is made,[17] have already been dealt with,[18] as has the power of the court after the passing of a resolution for the voluntary winding up of a company to order the stay or discontinuance of any execution or distress levied before or after the resolution is passed.[19] Nevertheless, there are two further provisions of the Act relating to executions which remain to be considered. These provisions have the effect of invalidating executions and requiring the assets taken in execution or their proceeds to be delivered to the liquidator so as to be applied by him as part of the company's general assets, and the two provisions apply both in liquidations under an order of the court and in voluntary liquidations.

Uncompleted executions

A judgment creditor of a company is not entitled without leave of the court to retain as against its liquidator the benefit of any execution levied by him on the company's assets if he has not completed the execution before the commencement of the liquidation, or in the case of a voluntary liquidation, before he has notice that a general meeting of the company has been called at which a resolution to

16 Insolvency Act 1986, s 126(1).
17 Ibid, s 128(1).
18 See pp 78 and 79, ante.
19 Insolvency Act 1986, s 112(1) and (2); (see p 92, ante).

wind it up voluntarily is passed.[20] An execution against a company's goods is completed by their seizure and sale, whether the sheriff or, in the case of execution under a county court judgment, the officer charged with the execution has accounted to the judgment creditor for the proceeds of the execution or not.[1] An execution against shares or debentures or other debt securities held in other companies by a company which goes into liquidation is completed by the court making a charging order in respect of them under the Charging Orders Act 1979.[2] Execution against a debt owed to the company is completed by the making of a garnishee order absolute against the debtor and payment of the debt by him to the judgment creditor.[3] Execution against land is completed by seizure under a writ of possession, by the appointment of a receiver by way of equitable execution, or by the court making a charging order under the Charging Orders Act 1979.[4]

The effect of the execution not being completed by the commencement of the company's liquidation or before the judgment creditor has notice of a meeting having been called to pass a voluntary winding up resolution, is that the judgment creditor loses the benefit of the right which he would otherwise have to complete the execution, and any assets in his hands or the hands of the sheriff or the county court officer charged with the execution must be delivered to the liquidator.[5]

Nevertheless, if the judgment creditor has already received payment of the whole or part of the judgment debt and the costs of the execution from the company in order to avoid an execution or a sale by the sheriff or, in the county court, the officer charged with the execution, or if the judgment creditor or the sheriff has received part of the judgment debt as the result of the sheriff or bailiff selling the whole or part of the goods seized, or as the result of a debtor of the company making payment under a garnishee order nisi, the judgment creditor may retain the amount so far recovered.[6] The

---

20 Ibid, s 183(1) and (2). The section refers to executions against the goods or land of the company or the attachment of debts owed to it by way of execution, but goods are defined as including all chattels personal (s 183(4)), and so the section applies to executions against all kinds of assets of a company.

1 Insolvency Act 1986, s 183(3)(a).

2 Ibid, s 183(3)(a). The order need not have been made absolute (Roberts Petroleum Ltd v Bernard Kenny Ltd [1982] 1 All ER 685, [1982] 1 WLR 301, revsd on other grounds [1983] 2 AC 192, [1983] 1 All ER 564).

3 Insolvency Act 1986, s 183(3)(b). Re Walkden Sheet Metal Co Ltd [1960] Ch 170, [1959] 3 All ER 333.

4 Insolvency Act 1986, s 183(3)(c).

5 Re Andrew, ex p Official Receiver [1937] Ch 122, [1936] 3 All ER 450.

6 Ibid, Re Walkden Sheet Metal Co Ltd [1960] Ch 170, [1959] 3 All ER 333; Re Caribbean Products (Yam Importers) Ltd [1966] Ch 331, [1966] 1 All ER 181.

reason for this is that the statutory provision[20] merely deprives the judgment creditor of the right to pursue the execution process further against assets of the company which have been taken in execution;[6] if money has been received by the judgment creditor in whole or partial satisfaction of his judgment debt and costs, no further steps are needed on his part to pursue the execution and the judgment creditor then simply retains what he has received.

The court may in its discretion set aside the liquidator's right to recover assets taken under an uncompleted execution on such terms as it thinks fit,[7] but it will not do so in practice unless the judgment creditor has delayed levying or completing the execution at the company's request,[8] or unless the company has delayed the execution by appealing against the judgment in favour of the execution creditor on grounds which it must have known were baseless.[9] However, the fact that an execution has been completed by the relevant time and so cannot be attacked as an uncompleted execution, will not prevent the court setting it aside as a preference if it was carried out with the concurrence, collaboration or acquiescence of the company within six months (or two years, if the judgment creditor is a person connected with the company) before the commencement of the company's liquidation at a time when the company was insolvent or was thereby made insolvent.[10] On the other hand, the court will not restrain a judgment creditor of the company from levying execution on assets of the company in a foreign country under a process of execution issued by a court of that country in respect of a judgment registered or recorded by it to give effect to the judgment of an English court.[11]

Executions against goods

Where an execution is levied on goods owned by a company and before the sheriff or the county court officer charged with the execution sells them, or before the execution is completed by the sheriff or county court officer receiving the full amount for which execution is levied (eg by the company paying the judgment debt and the costs of the execution to the sheriff or county court officer to avoid a sale), notice is served on the sheriff or the county court officer that a provisional liquidator has been appointed under a

7 Insolvency Act 1986, s 183(2).
8 *Re Grosvenor Metal Co Ltd* [1950] Ch 63, [1949] 2 All ER 948.
9 *Re Suidair International Airways Ltd* [1951] Ch 165, [1950] 2 All ER 920.
10 Insolvency Act 1986, s 239(1), (2) and (4) and s 240 (1) and (2) (see p 225, ante).
11 *Re Buckingham International plc* [1997] BCC 71.

petition to wind up the company, or that a winding up order has been made, or that a winding-up resolution has been passed in respect of the company, the sheriff or county court officer must deliver any goods seized or any money received by him to the liquidator (after deducting or recovering his costs of the execution).[12] Furthermore, if the judgment debt for which the execution is levied exceeds £500 and the sheriff or the county court officer receives the proceeds of the execution or money paid by the company to him to avoid a sale, he must deduct the costs of the execution and retain the balance for 14 days before accounting to the judgment creditor, and if during that time notice is served on him of the presentation of a winding up petition on which a winding up order is subsequently made, or of the calling of a general meeting of the company to pass a winding up resolution and such a resolution is passed by that meeting or an adjournment of it, the sheriff or the county court officer must account to the liquidator for the balance of the money in his hands.[13] For this latter provision to apply, notice must be served on the sheriff or the county court officer within the 14-day period either of a petition for a winding up order on which such an order is eventually made, or of a meeting being called to pass a winding up resolution at which such a resolution is in fact passed; notice of a petition is ineffective if the petition is abandoned and a winding up resolution is passed instead, and notice of a meeting to pass a winding up resolution is ineffective if no such resolution is passed but a winding up order is made instead, either before or after the date of the meeting.[14] Moreover, giving notice to the sheriff or the county court officer of a meeting being called to pass a winding up resolution is ineffective if the meeting has not in fact been called,[15] but it has been held that if such a meeting has been validly called to pass a resolution that the company shall go into a creditors' voluntary liquidation, a notice served on the sheriff is effective if it refers only to the meeting of creditors which the company has called in compliance with the statutory requirement that such a meeting must be held within 14 days after the general meeting which passes the winding up resolution.[16]

For the purpose of the provisions dealt with above a company's goods are defined as its chattels personal,[17] which in this context are

12 Insolvency Act 1986, s 184(1), (2) and (6).
13 Ibid, s 184(3) and (4); Insolvency Proceedings (Monetary Limits) Order 1986 (SI No 1986/1990), art 2(1).
14 *Bluston and Bramley Ltd v Leigh* [1950] 2 KB 548, [1950] 2 All ER 29.
15 *Re T D Walton Ltd* [1966] 2 All ER 157, [1966] 1 WLR 869.
16 *Engineering Industry Training Board v Samuel Talbot (Engineers) Ltd* [1969] 2 QB 270, [1969] 1 All ER 480.
17 Insolvency Act 1986, s 184(6).

treated as meaning its tangible movable property; consequently, the provisions apply to movable property of a company on which execution may be levied under a writ of fieri facias, such as investments in bearer form and negotiable instruments, as well as goods in the strict sense. The effect of the statutory provisions is that the judgment creditor loses the benefit of his execution, and the goods seized by the sheriff or the county court officer, or the proceeds of the execution or the amount paid by the company to avoid a sale, are delivered by the sheriff or county court officer to the liquidator and become part of the company's general assets. This is so, even though no winding up order has been made and no winding up resolution has been passed before the execution is completed, and the judgment creditor has no notice of the presentation of a winding up petition or of a meeting being called to pass a winding up resolution before that time. Nevertheless, the court may in its discretion set aside the rights of the liquidator in favour of the judgment creditor on such terms as it thinks fit,[18] and in deciding whether to exercise its discretion the court will be influenced by the same considerations as when an application is made by a judgment creditor to set aside the rights of the liquidator in connection with an execution which was uncompleted at the commencement of the company's liquidation.[19]

COMPENSATION FOR FRAUDULENT AND WRONGFUL TRADING AND MISFEASANCE

Introductory

The Insolvency Act 1986 contains two provisions which enable the liquidator of a company to recover contributions which will augment its assets available to satisfy its debts and liabilities from persons who have been responsible for the improper management of the company's affairs (fraudulent and wrongful trading), even though the company may have had no statutory or other cause of action against them while it was a going concern. The Act also contains a number of procedural provisions which enable the liquidator to recover damages, compensation or other payments from persons closely associated with the company whom it could have sued while it was a going concern, but the liquidator is empowered to proceed by making

18 Ibid, s 184(5).
19 See p 251, ante.

summary applications to the court[20] instead of bringing actions commenced by writ. The most important of these summary applications is the so-called misfeasance application, which is brought against persons responsible for the management and administration of the company's affairs who have committed breaches of their fiduciary or other obligations toward it in carrying out their functions.

Fraudulent trading

If when a company is wound up it appears that its business has been carried on with intent to defraud its creditors or the creditors of another person, or for any fraudulent purpose, the court may on the application of the liquidator order that any persons who were knowingly parties to carrying on its business in that way shall be liable to make such contributions to the company's assets as the court thinks proper.[1] The amount ordered to be contributed will not normally exceed the amount of the company's indebtedness incurred during the period while the company's business has been carried on fraudulently,[2] but if the respondent's conduct has been particularly reprehensible, the court may include a punitive element in the amount of the contribution which it directs to be paid.[3] The court may charge the amount which it orders a person to contribute to the assets of the company on any debt due from the company to him, or on any mortgage or charge on the company's assets to which he is entitled; the amount ordered to be paid may also be charged on any debt due from the company or on any mortgage or charge on its assets if the debt, mortgage or charge is vested in a trustee for the person against whom the order is made, or in anyone in whose favour it was created on the direction of that person, or if it is vested in or is held in trust for an assignee (other than an assignee for money or money's worth) from the person against whom the order is made or from his trustee or a person so nominated by him.[4] The primary purpose of this complex supplementary provision is to enable the court to charge debentures or other debt securities with payment of

---

20 The application is made by an originating application supported by evidence on affidavit (Insolvency Rules 1986, r 7.2(1) and r 7.3(2)).
1 Insolvency Act 1986, s 213(1) and (2). The application to the court is made by an originating application (Insolvency Rules 1986, r 7.2(1) and r 7.3(2)).
2 In *Re Cyona Distributors Ltd* [1967] Ch 889 at 902, [1967] 1 All ER 281, 284, Denning MR said obiter that under the former legislation the court could order a payment not exceeding the whole of the company's outstanding indebtedness, whenever incurred, but it is doubtful whether the court would do so under the present statutory provision.
3 *Re a Company (No 001418 of 1988)* [1991] BCLC 197, [1990] BCC 526.
4 Insolvency Act 1986, s 215(2) and (3).

the amount of the order if they were issued to the person against whom the order is made, or were issued or transferred at his direction to nominees for himself. The court may also order that the whole or part of any debt owed by the company to a person who is ordered to make a contribution to the assets of the company shall rank for payment in the liquidation of the company after all its other debts and interest on those debts.[5]

The court cannot make an order under the statutory provision simply because the company is insolvent, or because the company was formed to enable the shareholders to avoid incurring personal liability for debts incurred in carrying on a business. It is only where the persons responsible for directing or managing the company's business have been guilty of dishonesty that personal liability may be imposed on them,[6] but a single act of dishonesty which they commit or in which they participate suffices for an order to be made against them.[7] The dishonest intentions of the respondents may be apparent from the circumstances in which the company's business was carried on. Thus, in a case where a company had become insolvent, but its directors continued to carry on its business and purchased further goods on credit, Maugham J, declaring them personally liable for the price of those goods, said:[8]

'... If a company continues to carry on business and to incur debts at a time when there is to the knowledge of the directors no reasonable prospect of the creditors ever receiving payment of those debts, it is, in general, a proper inference that the company is carrying on business with intent to defraud.'

Too much emphasis should not be placed on the word 'ever' in this passage. A person is guilty of fraudulent trading if he has no reason to believe that the company will be able to pay its creditors in full by the dates when their respective debts become payable or within a short time thereafter.[9] On the other hand, the mere fact that directors in the course of disposing of the company's assets with a view to its ultimate winding up have made a payment which would be voidable as a preference of a creditor in the winding up[10] does not

---

5 Ibid, s 215(4).
6 *Re Patrick and Lyon Ltd* [1933] Ch 786, [1933] All ER Rep 590; *R v Cox and Hodges* (1982) 75 Cr App Rep 291, [1983] BCLC 169.
7 *Re Gerald Cooper Chemicals Ltd* [1978] Ch 262, [1978] 2 All ER 49.
8 *Re William C Leitch Bros Ltd* [1932] 2 Ch 71 at 77.
9 *R v Grantham* [1984] QB 675, [1984] 3 All ER 166; *Re a Company (No 001418 of 1988)* [1991] BCLC 197, [1990] BCC 526.
10 That is, a fraudulent preference, voidable in the insolvent winding up of the company under the Companies Act 1985, s 615(1), which is now repealed and replaced by the Insolvency Act 1986, s 239 as to preferences made or given by a company within a limited period before the onset of its insolvency.

necessarily mean that they have carried on its business with intent to defraud its other creditors.[11]

A person is not a party to carrying on a company's business with intent to defraud its creditors unless he actively participates in its management. If he is an officer of the company or its professional adviser who merely fails to warn its directors that it is insolvent and that no further debts should be incurred on its behalf, he cannot be made liable under the statutory provision, even though he is guilty of negligence in failing to give that advice, and could be sued by the company for breach of his duty as an officer of the company or for breach of a contract to advise it properly.[12] Furthermore, a shareholder cannot be made personally liable for a company's debts by an order of the court, however large his holding, merely because he was in a position to influence the conduct of its affairs, or merely because he nominated or procured the appointment of directors who are guilty of fraudulent trading. To impose liability on a shareholder it must be shown that he took part in making management decisions which were intended to defraud creditors or were known to be likely to cause them loss, or that he gave instructions to the directors which he knew would produce such results and he knew that the directors would carry out those instructions.

Moreover, the directors of the company or the persons who manage its affairs must have acted fraudulently themselves, and so no liability can be imposed by the court on directors of a parent or holding company which undertakes informally to give the necessary financial support to enable a loss-making subsidiary company to continue trading, if the directors of the parent company honestly believe that company is able to give that financial support but are prevented from doing so by unforeseen events.[13] But a third person who knowingly participates in an act of fraudulent trading committed by a company's directors (for example, a creditor of the company who accepts payment of his debt out of money which he knows its directors have obtained by fraud), may be compelled personally to repay the amount so applied to the liquidator of the company.[14] For liability to be imposed on a person under the statutory provision it is essential that he personally should have acted fraudulently in the direction or management of its affairs, and so even if the directors of a company have carried on its business with knowledge of its insolvency, the court cannot impose liability for its debts on its parent company, which has given a temporary informal undertaking

11 *Re Sarflax Ltd* [1979] Ch 592, [1979] 1 All ER 529.
12 *Re Maidstone Buildings Provisions Ltd* [1971] 3 All ER 363, [1971] 1 WLR 1085.
13 *Re Augustus Barnett & Son Ltd* [1986] BCLC 170, 2 BCC 904.
14 *Re Gerald Cooper Chemicals Ltd*, supra.

to support its current trading activities at a time when the parent company was financially able to do so, if the parent company declines to extend the undertaking when the subsidiary later becomes insolvent.[13]

Although an order by the court imposing personal liability on an individual who has knowingly participated in the fraudulent carrying on of company's business takes away the protection from personal liability afforded to directors and shareholders by the company's separate legal personality, it does not entirely disregard the company's existence. The effect of the order is not to make the person subject to it personally liable to a creditor of the company who has been defrauded; instead, the person against whom the order is made must pay the sum ordered by the court to the liquidator, who will apply it with the other money of the company and the proceeds of realising its assets in paying all its creditors rateably, and the creditors who have been defrauded have no preferential claim to the sum ordered to be paid.[15] Similarly, if the court charges the sum ordered to be paid on any mortgage of the company's assets held by or on behalf of the person in default, the sole effect is to destroy his priority as a secured creditor to that extent, and no defrauded creditor of the company is thereby subrogated to his rights as a mortgagee.

On the other hand, it has been held under the former provisions of the Companies Act relating to fraudulent trading[16] that if a creditor of the company obtains payment of his debt from directors out of their own resources by threatening to take proceedings against them for an order making them personally liable, the payment is not impressed with a trust in favour of the company's creditors as a whole, and so the liquidator cannot require the recipient to account for it to him.[17] In the same case Denning MR said obiter that in making an order under the statutory provision, the court may direct that payment of the sum ordered to be paid by the directors shall be made to the defrauded creditors individually for their own exclusive benefit, instead of to the liquidator for the benefit of the company's creditors generally.[18] The court later held under the same legislation in a case where a defrauded creditor sought an order imposing liability on a company's directors and others who had participated in their fraud, that the court did indeed have power to make an order for payment by the respondents directly to the defrauded creditor.[19] Such an order in favour of a

15 *Re William C Leitch Bros Ltd (No 2)* [1933] Ch 261.
16 The decision was given under the Companies Act 1948, s 332(1), which was re-enacted by the now repealed Companies Act 1985, s 630(1) and (2).
17 *Re Cyona Distributors Ltd* [1967] Ch 889, [1967] 1 All ER 281.
18 Ibid, [1967] Ch 889 at 902, [1967] 1 All ER 281 at 284.
19 *Re Gerald Cooper Chemicals Ltd*, supra.

particular creditor cannot now be made under the provisions of the present legislation, which confine the court to making orders imposing an obligation on persons responsible for fraudulent trading to make such contributions to the company's assets as the court thinks fit, and an application for such an order can be made only by the company's liquidator.[20]

A liquidator who has applied to the court for an order that a person alleged to have carried on a company's business fraudulently shall make a contribution to the company's assets may agree to a compromise with the respondent under which he undertakes to contribute a particular amount; such a compromise is effective despite the disapproval of creditors of the company, unless the court sets it aside as an abuse of the liquidator's functions or because it is wholly unreasonable.[1] However, the liquidator cannot agree to sell or transfer his right to apply to the court for a contribution order, nor can he sell or dispose of the right to the proceeds of recovering a contribution ordered by the court in return for the disponee making a payment or agreeing to finance the proceedings.[2] The application to the court does not relate to a right of action vested in the company, which the liquidator is exceptionally able to sell,[3] but is made under a statutory provision which takes effect only when the company has gone into liquidation.

If a person against whom the court could make a contribution order dies before the liquidator applies to the court for such an order, the liquidator may apply to the court for an order that his personal representatives shall pay an amount out of his estate equal to the contribution which the court would have ordered him to make to the company's assets.[4]

An application by a liquidator for an order that a person alleged to be guilty of fraudulent trading shall make a contribution to the company's assets is a proceeding for the recovery of a sum of money, and must therefore be made within the appropriate limitation period of six years from the occurrence of the latest event which completes the liquidator's right to make the application, namely, the company being ordered by the court or resolving to be wound up.[5]

A person who is a party to carrying on a company's business with intent to defraud its or another person's creditors, or for any other

---

20 Insolvency Act 1986, s 213(1) and (2).
1 *Re Esal (Commodities) Ltd, London and Overseas (Sugar) Co Ltd v Punjab National Bank* [1993] BCLC 872.
2 *Re Oasis Merchandising Services Ltd* [1995] BCC 911; affd [1997] BCC 282.
3 See p 219, ante.
4 *Re Sherborne Associates Ltd* [1995] BCC 40.
5 *Re Farmizer (Products) Ltd* [1995] BCC 926.

fraudulent purpose is guilty of a criminal offence.[6] A prosecution may be brought for the offence, whether the company is being, or has been, wound up or not.[6] The offence is committed if the accused carries on a company's business with intent to defraud its customers, who are potential creditors of the company for the claims they will have against it for reparation in respect of the fraud.[7]

Wrongful trading

If, in the winding up of a company which has gone into insolvent liquidation,[8] it appears that a person who was a director or shadow director of the company at some time before the commencement of the winding up, knew or ought to have concluded that there was no reasonable prospect that the company would avoid such an insolvent liquidation, the court may on the application of the liquidator order that person to contribute such amount to the assets of the company as the court thinks fit.[9] The court may not make such an order, however, if the director or shadow director satisfies it that after he first realised or should have concluded that the company would inevitably be wound up in an insolvent condition, he took every step to minimise the potential loss to the company's creditors which he ought to have taken.[10]

A shadow director of a company is a person in accordance with whose directions or instructions the directors of the company are accustomed to act, but a person is not a shadow director by reason only that the company's directors act on advice given by him in a professional capacity.[11] A bank may therefore become a shadow director of a company and responsible for wrongful trading if, in order to protect a loan made by it to the company, it induces the directors to conduct the company's business in accordance with the bank's directions during a period of adverse trading conditions which result in the company's insolvency, and the bank should have realised that this would happen.[12] A bank will not become a shadow

6 Companies Act 1985, s 458.
7 *R v Kemp* [1988] QB 645, [1988] BCLC 217.
8 A company goes into an insolvent liquidation if at the time when a winding up order is made, or a winding up resolution is passed in respect of it, its assets are insufficient for the payment of its debts and liabilities and the expenses of the winding up (Insolvency Act 1986, s 214(6)).
9 Insolvency Act 1986, s 214(1), (2) and (7). The application to the court is made by an originating application (Insolvency Rules 1986, r 7.2(1) and r 7.3(2)).
10 Ibid, s 214(3).
11 Ibid, s 251.
12 *Re a Company (No 005009 of 1987)* (1988) 4 BCC 424.

director of a company to which it makes a loan, however, if it confines itself to requiring the company's indebtedness to other creditors to be kept within prescribed limits, prohibits the company giving security to its other creditors and requires the company to pay its cash receipts into an account designated by the bank.[13] A parent company will be a shadow director of its wholly owned subsidiary if the board of the subsidiary habitually conforms to the directions of the board of the parent company in managing the subsidiary's business, but individual directors of the parent company will not be shadow directors of the subsidiary in concurring in giving such directions, because in that respect they act as directors of the parent company which gives the directions, and not as shadow directors of the company.

The court may make an order for a contribution by a director or shadow director in circumstances where it cannot be proved that he knowingly and fraudulently carried on the company's business with intent to defraud the company's creditors, and that he was therefore guilty of fraudulent trading; liability for wrongful trading can be imposed if it is proved that the respondent ought by the exercise of proper skill and care to have concluded that the company's insolvent liquidation could not be avoided. Once that is established, however, the respondent can escape having an order to contribute made against him only by showing that he took every possible step which he reasonably believed to be appropriate, or which he ought to have concluded was appropriate, to minimise the loss suffered by the company's creditors.[10]

To determine whether the respondent director or shadow director ought to have concluded that the company's insolvent liquidation was inevitable and whether he then took every step to minimise loss to creditors, the following will be considered by the court, namely: the facts which the respondent knew or should have known or ascertained, the conclusions which he should have reached, and the steps which he should have taken, as compared with those which would be known, ascertained, reached or taken by a reasonably diligent person who had the general knowledge, skill and experience which may reasonably be expected of a person carrying out the respondent's functions in relation to the company, together with any additional general knowledge and experience which the respondent actually had.[14] The respondent's functions in relation to the company include those which were entrusted to him, even if he

---

13 *Re Hydrodam (Corby) Ltd* [1994] 2 BCLC 180, [1994] BCC 161.
14 Insolvency Act 1986, s 214(4).

did not carry them out personally (eg functions which he delegated) or at all.[15]

The standard of awareness, perspicacity and diligence required of a director or shadow director if he is to resist an application for an order to contribute to the company's assets is therefore that of a person who is competent to fulfil the functions he was appointed to fulfil (eg as a director responsible for a particular sector of the company's operations and activities, as well as a member of the board responsible for directing and supervising the management of the company's affairs generally) and who manifests appropriate skill and care in doing so. It will be no defence to show that the respondent lacked the skills and abilities requisite for fulfilling those functions properly, or that his level of intelligence, knowledge and experience was below that required for comprehending the company's commercial and financial condition adequately, and if the company is or will unavoidably become insolvent, for apprehending the steps which were necessary to prevent it becoming insolvent, or to minimise the loss suffered by its creditors. On the other hand, if the respondent had a higher level of knowledge, intelligence or ability than would normally be expected of a director or shadow director in his position, the standard of performance required of him is correspondingly higher (eg a finance director who is a professionally qualified accountant, or a production director who is a qualified and experienced engineer).

The nature, size and circumstances of the company will be relevant in determining the standard of performance required of its directors. Directors of companies engaged in complex, expensive or risky business activities and directors of companies with high turnover or large scale operations (particularly, if they are correspondingly well remunerated) will be expected to manifest an appropriately enhanced degree of competence, skill and care. On the other hand, the fact that the company is a small one, that it has been carrying on business for only a short time, that its directors are inexperienced or that it has few resources will not diminish the minimum standard of competence and performance expected by the court of its directors.

In one of the small number of cases on liability for wrongful trading which have so far been reported,[16] Knox J held that where directors were aware that their company had made losses in two successive years, that its turnover was contracting and that it was

---

15 Ibid, s 214(5).

16 *Re Produce Marketing Consortium Ltd* [1989] 3 All ER 1, [1989] BCLC 513; see also *Re Purpoint Ltd* [1991] BCC 121. and *Re Sherborne Associates Ltd* [1995] BCC 40.

likely that its liabilities exceeded its assets, an order requiring them to contribute to the company's assets in its subsequent liquidation should be made when they had continued to carry on the company's business and incur further liabilities on the company's behalf, and this was so even though it was not until later that the company's insolvency was revealed by its audited annual accounts. This decision shows that the court will make orders imposing liability for wrongful trading even though there is no suspicion of dishonesty on the part of directors, and that the standard of attentiveness to the company's financial condition required of them is a high one. In the same case, Knox J held that the amount of the contribution ordered to be paid by directors guilty of wrongful trading should be measured by the increase in the indebtedness of the company outstanding during the period of wrongful trading, in the same way as the contribution usually ordered to be paid by directors guilty of fraudulent trading.[17] Knox J also held that the contributions recovered by the liquidator from the directors should be applied as part of the assets of the company in paying equal dividends to its creditors generally, and as in the situation where liability for fraudulent trading is established, the contributions should not be applied primarily in satisfying creditors whose debts were incurred during the period of wrongful trading.[18]

The court which orders the payment of contributions by directors or shadow directors who are liable for wrongful trading may charge the contribution ordered on any debt owed by the company to the respondent or his nominee, trustee or assignee, or on any mortgage or charge on assets of the company held by the respondent or such a person, in the same way as the court may do when it orders the payment of contributions by persons guilty of fraudulent trading.[18] Likewise, the court may order that the whole or any part of a debt owed by the company to a director or shadow director who is ordered to make a contribution to the company's assets shall in its liquidation rank for payment only after all other debts of the company and interest thereon have been discharged in full.[19] Again, the same limitation period of six years from the date of the winding up order or resolution in respect of the company applies to an application by the liquidator for a contribution order against a director or shadow director liable for wrongful trading as applies to an application for such an order against a person guilty of fraudulent trading.[20]

17 See p 254, ante.
18 Insolvency Act 1986, s 215(2) and (3); (see p 254, ante).
19 Ibid, s 215(4).
20 Re Farmizer (Products) Ltd [1995] 2 BCLC 462, [1995] BCC 926.

An application by a liquidator for a contribution order may be made against the personal representatives of a director or shadow director against whom such an order could have been made had he survived, the order against the personal representatives being confined to ordering payment of the amount of the contribution out of his estate.[1]

A liquidator may not sell or transfer his right to apply for a contribution order against a person liable for wrongful trading or may he sell or transfer the right to the proceeds of such an application which succeeds.[2]

Misfeasance proceedings

Grounds for proceedings

In the winding up of a company an application may be made to the court in summary proceedings brought by the official receiver, the liquidator or by any creditor or, with leave of the court, by any contributory, for an order that any present or past officer of the company, or any person who has acted as a liquidator, administrator or administrative receiver of the company, or any other person who has been concerned or taken part in the promotion, formation or management of the company, and who has misapplied or retained or become accountable for any money or property of the company, or has been guilty of any misfeasance or breach of any fiduciary or other duty in relation to the company, shall repay, restore or account for the money or property or any part of it with interest at such rate as the court orders, or shall contribute such sum to the company's assets by way of compensation for the misfeasance or breach of duty as the court thinks just.[3] Such summary proceedings against a liquidator or former liquidator of a company who has obtained his release[4] may be brought only with leave of the court, and must be concluded before the company is dissolved, it being impossible to continue them afterwards.[5] Summary proceedings brought under the statutory provision are, as the result of long usage, known as misfeasance proceedings, although that expression is not used in the Insolvency Act 1986.

---

1 *Re Sherborne Associates Ltd* [1995] BCC 40.
2 *Re Oasis Merchandising Services Ltd* [1995] 2 BCLC 493, [1995] BCC 911.
3 Insolvency Act 1986, s 212(1), (3) and (5). The application to the court is made by an originating application (Insolvency Rules 1986, r 7.2(1) and r 7.3(2)).
4 See p 154, ante.
5 Insolvency Act 1986, s 212(4).

Misfeasance proceedings lie only when the company itself could have sued the respondent in an action commenced by writ,[6] and so a member of a company cannot enforce a right of action vested in himself personally by this means.[7] Moreover, even if an action could be brought by the company itself, it does not always follow that misfeasance proceedings may be restored. Not all rights of action vested in a company may be enforced by misfeasance proceedings,[8] and the claims enforceable in this way are limited to those which satisfy certain conditions in respect of their nature and the persons against whom they are made.

The only orders which the court may make in misfeasance proceedings are for the return of property to the company or for the payment of compensation or damages for losses wrongfully inflicted on it.[9] Consequently, the court cannot rescind a contract,[10] or order the payment of a debt owed to the company[11] in misfeasance proceedings. Nor can it order a director to make a payment to the company, unless he has misappropriated its property or has caused it loss by failing to perform a duty which he owed to it.[12] Thus, misfeasance proceedings cannot be brought against a director who has failed to acquire his share qualification fixed by the articles, because he is under no obligation imposed by law to take them from the company.[12] On the other hand, misfeasance proceedings may be brought to recover a secret profit from a director, even though the company has suffered no loss; this is because the profit belongs to the company in equity, and the director is accountable to the company for it.[13]

Under the former legislation which has been replaced by the Insolvency Act 1986, it was held that misfeasance proceedings will not lie against a director for negligence in managing a company's affairs,[14] although misfeasance proceedings were permitted to be brought against a liquidator who negligently paid an invalid claim

6 *Re Canadian Land Reclaiming and Colonizing Co, Coventry and Dixon's Case* (1880) 14 Ch D 660.
7 *Re Hill's Waterfall Estate and Gold Mining Co* [1896] 1 Ch 947, where a member unsuccessfully claimed compensation from a liquidator who had wrongfully disposed of shares in another company which should have been allotted to the member.
8 *Re Etic Ltd* [1928] Ch 861 at 871, per Maugham J.
9 Insolvency Act 1986, s 212(3).
10 *Re Centrifugal Butter Co Ltd* [1913] 1 Ch 188.
11 *Re Etic Ltd* [1928] Ch 861.
12 *Re Canadian Land Reclaiming and Colonizing Co, Coventry and Dixon's Case,* supra.
13 *Re North Australian Territory Co, Archer's Case* [1892] 1 Ch 322.
14 *Re B Johnson & Co (Builders) Ltd* [1955] Ch 634, [1955] 2 All ER 775.

against the company,[15] and against auditors who were guilty of negligence in certifying the company's accounting records as having been properly kept and its annual accounts as properly prepared.[16] The present legislation authorises the bringing of misfeasance proceedings against present or past officers, liquidators, administrators, administrative receivers and other persons concerned in the promotion, formation or management of a company now in liquidation for breach of 'any fiduciary or other duty in relation to the company',[17] and so misfeasance proceedings may now be brought to recover compensation for any loss suffered by the company, whatever the breach of duty may be (including negligence)[18] and whether the duty which is breached is statutory or arises at common law or in equity, but not if the duty is purely contractual.

Respondents

The only persons who may be made respondents in misfeasance proceedings are those mentioned in the statutory provision.[17] The broadest class of these, 'officers of the company', has given rise to some difficulty of definition. The legislation is unhelpful in this respect, because it merely defines 'officers' as including directors, managers and secretaries, without confining the expression to those persons.[19] It has been held that auditors are officers for the purpose of misfeasance proceedings,[16] and it seems that managers are to be considered as officers if they have authority to carry out or supervise the execution of the company's business policy or the general administration of its business, as distinct from managing a department of that business.[20] However, trustees for debenture or debt security holders[1] and receivers and managers appointed by debenture or debt security holders or by the court[2] (other than administrative receivers) are not officers for the purpose of misfeasance proceedings,

---

15 *Re Windsor Steam Coal Co (1901) Ltd* [1929] 1 Ch 151; *Re Home and Colonial Insurance Co Ltd* [1930] 1 Ch 102; but an unjustifiable payment may also have been a breach of fiduciary duty, because the liquidator had misapplied the company's funds, even though done unintentionally.

16 *Re London and General Bank* [1895] 2 Ch 166.

17 Insolvency Act 1986, s 212(1).

18 *Re Welfab Engineers Ltd* [1990] BCLC 833, [1990] BCC 600; *Re D'Jan of London Ltd* [1994] 1 BCLC 561, [1993] BCC 646.

19 Companies Act 1985, s 744; Insolvency Act 1986, s 251.

20 *Re a Company* [1980] Ch 138, [1980] 1 All ER 284; revsd sub nom *Re Racal Communications Ltd* on other grounds [1981] AC 374, [1980] 2 All ER 634; *Woodhouse v Walsall Metropolitan Borough Council* [1994] 1 BCLC 435.

1 *Astley v New Tivoli Ltd* [1899] 1 Ch 151 at 154.

2 *Re B Johnson & Co (Builders) Ltd* [1955] Ch 634, [1955] 2 All ER 775.

nor are the company's solicitors[3] or its bank,[4] or presumably, any other agent employed by it. On the other hand, a person who acts as a director, even though not properly appointed or qualified to act, is amenable to misfeasance proceedings,[5] and it would appear that the extension of misfeasance proceedings by the present legislation to persons who are or have been concerned in the promotion, formation or management of a company[17] will make all persons who are concerned in the overall direction of a company's affairs, either by participating in it themselves, or by giving instructions to which directors habitually conform (ie shadow directors), amenable to such proceedings.

Because the classes of persons who may be made respondents in misfeasance proceedings are limited, however, a respondent to such proceedings may not have a person added as a third party so as to enforce a claim for contribution or an indemnity in connection with the misfeasance alleged to have been committed by him, and this is so even if that other person could have been made one of the original respondents in the proceedings.[6] But if such a person has been made a respondent by the person who initiated the misfeasance proceedings, the court can order him to pay such contribution or indemnity as it thinks fit to the other respondents, and so avoid the need for them to take separate proceedings against him.[7]

Compensation recoverable

The compensation recoverable in misfeasance proceedings is normally the amount of the loss suffered by the company as a result of the wrongful act or breach of duty complained of, that is, the amount by which the company's assets are less than they would have been if the wrongful act or breach of duty had not been committed, or the neglect or failure to act had not occurred.[8] However, the court has a discretion in fixing the amount of compensation which the respondent is ordered to pay to the company, and it need not require him to make good the whole of the resulting loss to the company. Thus, where a liquidator satisfied a claim against the company on

---

3 *Re Great Western Forest of Dean Coal Consumers Co, Carter's Case* (1886) 31 Ch D 496.
4 *Re Imperial Land Co of Marseilles, Re National Bank* (1870) LR 10 Eq 298.
5 *Re Canadian Land Reclaiming and Colonizing Co, Coventry and Dixon's Case* (1880) 14 Ch D 660.
6 *Re A Singer & Co (Hat Manufacturers) Ltd* [1943] Ch 121, [1943] 1 All ER 225.
7 *Re Morecambe Bowling Ltd* [1969] 1 All ER 753, [1969] 1 WLR 133.
8 *Bishopsgate Investment Management Ltd v Maxwell (No 2)* [1993] BCLC 814, [1993] BCC 120, affd [1994] 1 All ER 261, [1993] BCLC 1282, CA.

an insurance policy issued by it which was technically void, the court merely ordered him to make good so much of the amount so paid as was necessary to pay the company's debts.[9] This was because the company would have honoured the policy voluntarily if it had continued as a going concern, and because the members had resolved that the company should be wound up on the footing that it was insolvent because of its liability on the policy; it would therefore have been inequitable to require the liquidator to repay the whole amount which he had paid out on the policy when the part of that amount not required to meet the company's debts would then be passed on to its members, who had acquiesced in the policy being honoured.[9] In another case[10] a director was allowed to keep a payment made to him under a voidable contract, because the company had benefited from the contract, and almost all the members wished the director to retain the payment.

If a respondent in misfeasance proceedings has a claim against the company, the court cannot allow him to set it off against the amount which the court orders him to pay to the company as compensation for his wrongdoing or breach of duty, even though set-off would have been possible if the company had sued him in an action commenced by writ.[11] The exclusion of set-off does not apply, however, if the proceeds of the misfeasance (eg an improper commission taken by a director) have been applied in discharging a debt of the company to a third person which the respondent had guaranteed; the result in that situation is simply that any right of the respondent to an indemnity by the company is cancelled.[12]

Contributory's application

A contributory will be given leave by the court to bring misfeasance proceedings only if he has an interest in the property or compensation claimed being returned or paid to the company.[13] He will have such an interest only if the company is solvent, so that there will be assets divisible amongst its members after its debts and liabilities have been discharged, or if his shares are partly paid, so that the property or compensation recovered in the misfeasance proceedings will help to reduce the amount of unpaid capital which will have to be called up from him. But a fully paid shareholder of an insolvent limited

9 *Re Home and Colonial Insurance Co Ltd* [1930] 1 Ch 102.
10 *Re Sunlight Incandescent Gas Lamp Co* (1900) 16 TLR 535.
11 *Re Anglo-French Co-operative Society, ex p Pelly* (1882) 21 Ch D 492; *Re Exchange Banking Co, Flitcroft's Case* (1882) 21 Ch D 519.
12 *Re Derek Randall Enterprises Ltd* [1990] BCC 749.
13 *Cavendish-Bentinck v Fenn* (1887) 12 App Cas 652; *Re B Johnson & Co (Builders) Ltd* [1955] Ch 634, [1955] 2 All ER 775.

company will not be permitted to bring misfeasance proceedings, because he has no interest to protect, unless of course, the amount likely to be recovered in the misfeasance proceedings is so substantial that it will not only enable the company to discharge its debts and liabilities in full, but will also result in a surplus being available for distribution between the company's shareholders.

PAYMENTS BY CONTRIBUTORIES

Extent of contributories' liability

If the assets of a company in liquidation are insufficient to meet its debts and liabilities of the company and the expenses of the winding up and to repay the nominal value of the company's shares, the contributories may be called upon to make good the difference.[14] If the company is a company limited by shares, however, the contributories cannot be required to contribute more than the capital unpaid on the shares which they hold or formerly held;[15] if the company is limited by guarantee, the maximum liability of the contributories is the amount which they have undertaken to contribute by the terms of the company's memorandum of association;[16] if the company is limited by guarantee and has a share capital, the contributories' maximum liability is the capital unpaid on their shares plus the amount they have undertaken to contribute by the company's memorandum.[17] But if the company is an unlimited one, the contributories can be called upon not only to pay the capital unpaid on their shares (if any), but also to contribute personally until sufficient money is raised to pay the company's debts and liabilities and the expenses of the liquidation in full.

The contributories who are primarily liable to satisfy the deficiency of the company's assets are those who are members of it at the commencement of the winding up, and they are known as the A List contributories. But if the court, or the liquidator in a voluntary winding up, approves a transfer of shares after the commencement of the winding up, the transferee, or if there are successive transfers, the latest transferee will be the A List contributory

14 Insolvency Act 1986, s 74(1).
15 Ibid, s 74(2)(d).
16 Ibid, s 74(3).
17 It is doubtful whether any such company still exists. No company limited both by shares and by guarantee may be incorporated since 22 December 1980 (Companies Act 1985, s 1(4), re-enacting Companies Act 1980, s 1(2)).

in respect of the shares.[18] In a company limited by shares, the only limit on an A List contributory's liability is the amount unpaid on his shares, and in a company limited by guarantee, the only limit is the maximum amount guaranteed, plus the amount unpaid on his shares if the company has a share capital.

Any person who was a member of the company within a year before the commencement of the winding up may also be called on to contribute,[19] and such contributories are known as B List contributories. A B List contributory's liability is limited by one or more of five further restrictions in addition to those which limit the liability of an A List contributory. These are:

(1) In a company limited by shares, a B List contributory cannot be called upon to contribute more than the amount remaining unpaid on the shares formerly held by him which the A List contributory in respect of those shares has failed to pay.[20] Consequently, if the A List contributory has paid the whole of the unpaid capital in respect of his shares, the B List contributory is under no liability, and if the A List contributory had paid part of the unpaid capital, the B List contributory's liability is limited to the balance. But if the B List contributory held shares which were forfeited or surrendered while the company was a going concern, there will be no A List contributory, unless the shares have been reissued, and the B List contributory's liability, if there has been no re-issue, will therefore be the amount unpaid on the shares at the date of the forfeiture or surrender.[1]

(2) A B List contributory cannot be called upon to contribute unless it appears that the A List contributories are unable to satisfy the contributions required of them.[2] But in a winding up by the court the liquidator will not be required to give a detailed account of the steps which he has taken against the A List contributories before the court approves the making of a call on the B List contributories; it is sufficient that it appears probable that the A List contributories will not satisfy their liabilities in full.[3] On the other hand, if a call is made on B List contributories in the expectation that A List contributories will default, but in fact they satisfy their

---

18 *Re National Bank of Wales, Taylor, Phillips and Rickards' Cases* [1897] 1 Ch 298.
19 Insolvency Act 1986, s 74(1).
20 Ibid, s 74(2)(*d*).
1 *Re North Hallenbeagle Mining Co, Knight's Case* (1867) 2 Ch App 321; *Re Blakely Ordnance Co, Creyke's Case* (1869) 5 Ch App 63.
2 Insolvency Act 1986, s 74(2)(*c*).
3 *Helbert v Banner* (1871) LR 5 HL 28.

liability in full, the money received from the B List contributories must be returned to them, even though the company's debts have not been fully discharged.[4] If there are two or more B List contributories in respect of the same shares, it is uncertain whether they must be called on to contribute the unpaid balance of capital in the reverse of the order in which they ceased to be members,[5] or whether the liquidator may call on them to contribute in any order he thinks fit, leaving each earlier member to seek an indemnity from his immediate transferee.[6] The latter would seem the preferable rule, for the Insolvency Act 1986 draws no distinction between B List contributories according to the order in which they ceased to be members, but treats them as one class equally amenable to a call. Moreover, the relationship between an A List contributory and the corresponding B List contributory is not that of principal debtor and surety, but that of persons who are primarily and secondarily liable in respect of the same obligation. Consequently, if the liquidator compromises with the A List contributory, the B List contributory is not released (as he would be if he were a guarantor), but remains liable for the amount which is still unpaid on the shares.[7]

(3) A B List contributory cannot be called on to contribute in respect of debts and liabilities of the company incurred since he ceased to be a member,[8] and he can only be called upon to contribute in respect of debts and liabilities incurred before he ceased to be a member so far as they have not since been discharged by payment, by a release given by the creditor,[9] or by a dividend in the winding up.[10] If there are several B List contributors in respect of different shares who ceased to be members at different dates, they will contribute rateably[11] in respect of the debts and liabilities for which they are collectively liable to contribute, but if any B List contributory is unable to pay his rateable share, his fellow

---

4 *Re City of London Insurance Co* [1932] 1 Ch 226.
5 *Re Land Credit Co of Ireland, Humby's Case* [1872] WN 126.
6 *Kellock v Enthoven* (1874) LR 9 QB 241 at 248.
7 *Helbert v Banner* (1871) LR 5 HL 28. But the B List contributory may require the A List contributory to indemnify him against the amount he has to pay, notwithstanding the compromise with the liquidator (*Roberts v Crowe* (1872) LR 7 CP 629).
8 Insolvency Act 1986, s 74(2)(b).
9 *Re Apex Film Distributors Ltd* [1960] Ch 378, [1960] 1 All ER 152.
10 *Re Blakely Ordnance Co, Brett's Case* (1873) 8 Ch App 800.
11 Ie in proportion to the respective amounts of capital unpaid on their shares.

contributories must contribute it between them.[12] Although the liability of B List contributories is measured by the company's indebtedness when they respectively ceased to be members, their contributions are paid into one common fund with the payments made by the A List contributories, and are available to pay all the debts of the company irrespective of the chronological order in which they were incurred, earlier creditors being given no priority over later ones.[13]

(4) In a company limited by guarantee without a share capital, the members of the company at the commencement of the winding up are not regarded as the successors in title of former members in the same way as in a company limited by shares, and this is so even if the memorandum or articles of the company permit members to nominate a person to replace them on their own retirement from membership. Consequently, the B List contributories of a company limited by guarantee without a share capital are protected only by rule (3) above, and they can therefore be called on to contribute individually an amount not exceeding the amount required to be contributed by them individually, not exceeding the amount specified the company's memorandum of association, so far as such contributions are needed to satisfy the company's debts and liabilities incurred before they respectively ceased to be members.[14] If a company limited by

---

12 *Re Oriental Commercial Bank, Morris' Case* (1871) 7 Ch App 200. For example, if X, Y and Z are B list contributories, £2,000 capital being unpaid on the shares which X formerly held, £3,000 on Y's former shares, and £7,000 on Z's and when X and Y transferred their shares on the same day the company's indebtedness amounted to £6,000, and when Z transferred his shares later, it had increased by £4,000 to £10,000, the contributions which may be required from X, Y and Z will be calculated as follows:

  (a) Z alone contributes toward the increase in the company's indebtedness of £4,000, reducing the balance which he can be called on to contribute to £3,000 (£7,000–£4,000);

  (b) X, Y and Z contribute toward the original indebtedness of £6,000 in the proportions 2:3:7, making Z's contribution £3,500;

  (c) but Z can only be called on to contribute a further £3,000, and so X and Y contribute the balance of £3,000 in the proportion 2:3, X's contribution being £2,200, and Y's £1,800.

13 *Webb v Whiffin* (1872) LR 5 HL 711.

14 Insolvency Act 1986, s 74(2)(*b*) and (3). It is logical to treat s 74(2)(*c*) (see p 269, ante) as applicable only to companies limited by shares, because if it were applied to companies limited by guarantee, the total amount guaranteed could be reduced during the year preceding the company's liquidation by a reduction in the number of its members, and if it had no members at the commencement of the winding up the amount recoverable from former members would be nil.

guarantee has a share capital, the liability of the B List contributories in respect of the guarantee must be calculated in the same way, and they are additionally liable to make contributions in respect of the shares which they formerly held as though the company were one limited by shares. It would appear, however, that the proper order in which calls should be made in that case is first, on the A List contributories for the amount unpaid on their shares, secondly on the A List contributories for the amounts which the company's memorandum of association requires to contribute, thirdly, on the B List contributories in respect of the capital unpaid on their respective shares which each corresponding A List contributory fails to pay, and finally on the B List contributories in respect of the contribution required by the company's memorandum.

(5) The Insolvency Act 1986 does not state to what extent B List contributories must contribute toward the expenses of the winding up in addition to contributing toward the company's debts. There is a dictum by Lord Chelmsford[15] in the House of Lords that B List contributories are liable to contribute toward all those expenses, but on the other hand it has been held in lower courts that they are liable only for the expense of realising the company's assets and paying its debts and satisfying its liabilities.[16] It is certain, however, that B List contributories cannot be called on to contribute toward the repayment of share capital. Such a contribution would be for the benefit of the A list contributories, who are the present holders of the shares, but they are the persons who are primarily liable to pay the capital unpaid on their shares, and they are therefore unable to require the B List contributories to make good their own default.[17]

Enforcement of contributories' liability

Winding up by the court

In a winding up by the court the liquidator must settle a list of contributories as soon as possible after his appointment, unless the

---

15 *Webb v Whiffin*, supra at 726.
16 *Re Greening & Co, Marsh's Case* (1871) LR 13 Eq 388; *Re Blakely Ordnance Co, Brett's Case* (1873) 8 Ch App 800.
17 *Re Blakely Ordnance Co, Brett's Case* (1873) 8 Ch App 800.

court dispenses with such a list.[18] The list must distinguish between A and B List contributories, and must also distinguish contributories who, as the personal representatives of a deceased member or the trustee in bankruptcy of a bankrupt member,[19] are only liable to a limited extent for unpaid capital.[20]

After settling the list of contributories, the liquidator must give notice to every person whom he includes in it of the number and class of shares for which he has been included, the amount called up and paid up in respect of those shares, and that the contributory may be called on to pay the capital remaining unpaid.[1] Any such person may within 21 days object to his inclusion or to the amount of unpaid capital or other contribution for which the list shows him as liable.[2] The liquidator must within 14 days after receiving an objection either accept or reject it and notify his decision to the objector.[3] The objector may then appeal to the court within the following 21 days,[4] but subject to this right of appeal, the list is conclusive evidence of the liability of the persons appearing in it to contribute the amounts of unpaid capital attributed to them, and those persons cannot dispute their liability when the liquidator later makes calls upon them.[5]

In a winding up by the court the liquidator can make calls on contributories only with the sanction of the liquidation committee (if there is one) or the court.[6] If he seeks the sanction of the liquidation committee, he must call a meeting of the committee by giving at least seven days' notice to each of its members stating the amount of the proposed call and the purpose for which it will be made.[7] If the liquidator seeks the sanction of the court, he must

18 Insolvency Act 1986, s 148(1) and (2); Insolvency Rules 1986, r 4.195. In practice a list of contributories is not prepared if the company's shares are fully paid and the company is a limited one; if the shares are partly paid, the B List of contributories is prepared only when it appears that the A List contributories will not satisfy their obligations. A list of contributories is always necessary in the case of a company limited by guarantee and of an unlimited company if its liabilities exceed its assets.
19 Such persons are liable for unpaid capital on shares held by them but not registered in their names, only to the extent of the deceased's or bankrupt's assets vested in them (*James v Buena Ventura Nitrate Grounds Syndicate Ltd* [1896] 1 Ch 456).
20 Insolvency Act 1986, s 81(1), s 82(3) and s 148(3); Insolvency Rules 1986, r 4.197.
1 Insolvency Rules 1986, r 4.198(1) and (2).
2 Ibid, r 4.198(3).
3 Ibid, r 4.198(4).
4 Ibid, r 419(1) and (2).
5 Insolvency Act 1986, s 152(1).
6 Ibid, s 150(1) and s 160(1); Insolvency Rules 1986, rr 4.202 to 4.204.
7 Insolvency Rules, r 4.203.

apply to it ex parte, and his application must specify the amount of the intended call and the contributories on whom it will be made.[8]

When the appropriate sanction has been given, the liquidator makes the call by notifying each contributory on whom it is made of the amount payable by him and whether the call was made with the sanction of the liquidation committee or the court.[9] The court may direct that its order sanctioning a call shall be advertised.[10] If the call is not paid, the liquidator may obtain an order for payment against the contributory by applying summarily to the court.[11]

Voluntary winding up

In a voluntary winding up, the liquidator may settle a list of contributories, but the list is only prima facie evidence of the liability of the persons included in it,[12] and because those persons can dispute that they are contributories when calls are subsequently made on them, it is not necessary for the liquidator to give notice to them before including their names on the list.[13] After settling the list of contributories, the liquidator may make calls,[12] and may recover them by summary proceedings in the same way as in a winding up by the court.[14]

Rules common to all liquidations

In both compulsory and voluntary liquidations a call cannot be made on B List contributories unless the A List contributories are unable to satisfy a call already made on them.[15] Consequently, the liquidator cannot make a single call on both classes of contributories and seek to recover from the B list contributories if the A List contributories do not pay the call. He must instead defer making a call on the B List contributories until the A List contributories have defaulted.[16] Calls may, nevertheless, be made before an insufficiency of the company's assets to satisfy its liabilities has been ascertained,[17] and an estimate of the company's liabilities may be used as the basis for calculating the amount of the call, without the liabilities having

---

8 Ibid, r 4.204(1) and (2).
9 Ibid, r 4.205(1).
10 Ibid, r 4.204(3).
11 Ibid, r 4.205(2).
12 Insolvency Act 1986, s 165(4).
13 *Brighton Arcade Co v Dowling* (1868) LR 3 CP 175.
14 Insolvency Act 1986, s 112(1).
15 Ibid, s 74(2)(c).
16 *Re Apex Film Distributors Ltd* [1960] Ch 378, [1960] 1 All ER 152.
17 Insolvency Act 1986, s 150(1).

been proved by the creditors or admitted by the liquidator.[18] The contributories will not suffer by too large a call being made, for the excess of the amount contributed by them after payment of the company's liabilities will be returned to them. Furthermore, in deciding on the amount of a call, the liquidator may take into account the probability that some of the contributories may not pay it,[19] and he may increase the amount of the call to counteract the effect of their expected default.

A liquidator cannot require interest to be paid on calls, even though the directors might have charged interest on calls made while the company was a going concern in exercise of a power conferred by the company's articles of association,[20] but the court may order a contributory to pay interest at such rate as it thinks fit from the date when the call became payable,[1] and if the call is made under an order of the court, it bears interest at such rate as is for the time being prescribed by regulations (currently 8 per cent) from the date of the court's order.[2] A liquidator may make successive calls for instalments of unpaid capital payable in accordance with the terms of the issue of shares, and, of course, the contributories become liable to pay such instalments only as and when they are called for.

If a contributory is bankrupt, the liquidator may prove in his bankruptcy for the whole of the amount which he may be called on to contribute, even though no call has been made on the contributories generally,[3] and on the contributory's trustee in bankruptcy discharging his liability for that amount by paying a dividend out of his estate, the contributory and his estate cease to be liable for future calls.[4] However, if there turns out to be a surplus of the company's assets distributable among its shareholders after paying its debts, the bankrupt's shares are not treated as fully paid, but only as paid up to the extent of the amount actually received by the company or the liquidator, and the unpaid balance of capital must be brought into account in calculating the share of the surplus which is distributable to the trustee in bankruptcy.[5] The liquidator's power to prove in a shareholder's bankruptcy for calls is subject to the trustee in

18 *Re Contract Corpn* (1866) 2 Ch App 95.
19 Insolvency Act 1986, s 150(2).
20 *Re Welsh Flannel and Tweed Co* (1875) LR 20 Eq 360.
 1 Insolvency Act 1986. The court's power is now contained in the Supreme Court Act 1981, s 35A(1), inserted by the Administration of Justice Act 1982, s 15(1) and Sch 1 (11 *Halsbury's Statutes* (4th edn) 1088).
 2 Judgments Act 1838, s 17 (22 *Halsbury's Statutes* (4th edn) 263); Judgment Debts (Rate of Interest) Order 1993 (SI 1993/564), para 2.
 3 Insolvency Act 1986, s 82(3) and (4).
 4 Ibid, s 281(1).
 5 *Re West Coast Gold Fields Ltd, Rowe's Trustee's Claim* [1906] 1 Ch 1.

bankruptcy's power to disclaim the shares, thereby terminating the liability of the bankrupt and his estate.[6] After a disclaimer neither the bankrupt nor his trustee may be included in the list of contributories, either as a present or as a former member or shareholder,[7] but the liquidator can still prove in the bankruptcy for the amount of capital unpaid on the shares as damages resulting from the disclaimer.[8]

Set-off against calls and release of debts

If the company is indebted to a contributory, he cannot set off the debt against a call made on him by the liquidator in the winding up,[9] nor against an unpaid call made by the directors or an instalment of the issue price of the shares which fell due before the winding up began,[10] but this is permissible if all the creditors of the company have been paid in full,[11] or if the company is an unlimited one.[12] The reason for this rule is that the call or instalment of the issue price forms part of the fund out of which the liabilities of the company must be paid rateably, and if the contributory were entitled to withhold the whole or part of the call in satisfaction of the debt owed to him by the company, he might recover a larger fraction of his debt than the company's other creditors, which would result in an inequality. If the company is an unlimited one, however, the other creditors do not suffer by the contributory setting off the company's debt to him against the call, because he is liable to the last penny of his fortune to contribute to the payment of the company's debts, and if he is insolvent, the contribution which can be exacted from him will be the same whether he is permitted to set off the company's debt to himself or not.[13]

There is an exception to the general rule prohibiting set-off against calls when the contributory is bankrupt. Whether the call payable by him exceeds the debt owed to him by the company, so that the liquidator is compelled to prove against his estate in the

---

6 Insolvency Act 1986, s 315(1) and (2).
7 *Re Hooley, ex p United Ordnance and Engineering Co Ltd* [1899] 2 QB 579.
8 Insolvency Act 1986, s 315(5).
9 *Re Overend, Gurney & Co, Grissell's Case* (1866) 1 Ch App 528; *Re General Works Co, Gill's Case* (1879) 12 Ch D 755.
10 *Re Whitehouse & Co* (1878) 9 Ch D 595; *Re Hiram Maxim Lamp Co Ltd* [1903] 1 Ch 70.
11 Insolvency Act 1986, s 149(3).
12 Ibid, s 149(2); *Re International Life Assurance Society, Gibbs and West's Case* (1870) LR 10 Eq 312.
13 *Re International Life Assurance Society, Gibbs and West's Case*, supra.

hands of his trustee in bankruptcy,[14] or whether the debt owed to the bankrupt exceeds the call, so that his trustee in bankruptcy proves as a creditor in the winding up of the company,[15] the bankruptcy rule applies which requires debts and other amounts payable by the bankrupt to be set off against debts and other amounts payable to him.[16] The call and the debt must therefore be set off against each other, and the balance only proved for. This is quite logical, because in the administration of the bankrupt's estate the call and the debt are simply two undifferentiated mutual claims; it is the provisions of the Insolvency Act 1986, governing the winding up of the company, which draw a distinction between them, but the distinction is clearly irrelevant in the contributory's bankruptcy.

In theory, the same reasoning should apply where a company in liquidation is indebted to another company which is also in liquidation and holds shares in the first company on which calls made before or during its liquidation are unpaid. If the other company seeks to set off the debt owed to it against the calls owing in respect of the shares held by it and to pay only the excess of the calls over that debt to the liquidator of the first company, it has been held that it may not do so, because the relevant rules are those applicable in the winding up of the first company, and they do not permit the set-off of calls against the first company's indebtedness.[17] If the liquidator of the first company proved in the liquidation of the second company for the unpaid calls, however, it would seem that the second company could set off the debt owed to it by the first company against its liability for the call, which would be discharged by the liquidator of the second company paying the same dividend on any excess of the calls over the debt as he pays to creditors of the second company generally.[18] On the other hand, if the liquidator of the first company does not prove in the second company's liquidation for the unpaid calls, it has been held that he may retain the amount of the calls in full out of any dividend which he pays in respect of the debt owed to the second company.[19]

A situation somewhat different from that where a right of set-off is asserted arises when a contributory releases a debt owed to him by the company. The release reduces the total amount of the indebtedness of the company, and may therefore diminish the amount of the call which has to be made to satisfy its remaining

---

14 *Re Duckworth* (1867) 2 Ch App 578.
15 *Re Universal Banking Corpn, ex p Strang* (1870) 5 Ch App 492.
16 Insolvency Act 1986, s 323(1) and (2).
17 *Re Auriferous Properties Ltd* [1898] 1 Ch 691.
18 See *Re Peruvian Railway Construction Co Ltd* [1915] 2 Ch 442.
19 *Re Auriferous Properties Ltd (No 2)* [1898] 2 Ch 428.

liabilities. Unlike a claim of set-off, such a release benefits not only the contributory who gives it, but also all other contributories by diminishing the amount of the call which has to be made on them to satisfy the company's now reduced total indebtedness. It has been held that the release is effective, even though the contributory who gives it is a B List contributory and the debt released was incurred before he ceased to be a member, so that by the release he diminishes the liability to contribute of himself and his fellow B List contributories, and thus reduces the fund available to pay all creditors of the company, including those whose debts were incurred after he ceased to be a member.[20] But it seems that such a release will not diminish the B List contributories' liability if a call has already been made on them before the release is given, because the obligation created by the call can then only be discharged by paying it.[1]

Floating charges and calls

If a company has created a floating charge over its assets (including uncalled capital), the charge attaches to calls for unpaid capital made by the liquidator in the winding up of the company, and the proceeds of calls must therefore be applied in discharging the debt secured by the floating charge in priority to the company's ordinary unsecured debts.[2] This would appear to apply not only to calls which the company could have made on its shareholders at the date of the call before it went into liquidation, but also to calls on former shareholders who are B List contributories. It does not apply to calls made on members of an unlimited company for amounts in excess of the capital unpaid on their shares, however,[3] and it would appear not to apply to calls made on members of a company limited by guarantee in respect of the liability to contribute which is imposed on them by the company's memorandum of association.

20 *Re Greening & Co, Marsh's Case* (1871) LR 13 Eq 388; *Re Apex Film Distributors Ltd* [1960] Ch 378, [1960] 1 All ER 152.
 1 *Re Apex Film Distributors Ltd* [1960] Ch 378, [1959] 2 All ER 479; revsd on another ground [1960] Ch 378, [1960] 1 All ER 152.
 2 *Re Anglo-Austrian Printing and Publishing Union* [1895] 2 Ch 891.
 3 *Re Mayfair Property Co, Bartlett v Mayfair Property Co* [1898] 2 Ch 28.

CHAPTER 6

The application and distribution of the assets of a company in liquidation

INTRODUCTION

The assets of a company in liquidation, including property and amounts recovered by the liquidator under the provisions of the Insolvency Act 1986 (such as assets disposed of by the company at a significant undervalue or by way of preference of particular creditors) and amounts collected from contributories in respect of unpaid share capital, are applied as a single fund, first in meeting the costs and expenses of the liquidation, secondly in satisfying the debts and liabilities of the company incurred before it went into liquidation, and finally, if there is any surplus remaining, in making distributions to the members of the company at the date when it went into liquidation or to the persons to whom they have since effectively transferred their shares.

The basic principle is that, subject to meeting the expenses of the liquidation, creditors of an insolvent company are paid out of its assets rateably in proportion to the admitted amount of their claims.[1] Nevertheless, certain creditors are statutorily entitled to payment of their claims in full before the company's other debts are paid,[2] and other creditors may be able to claim a more beneficial treatment of their claims than the generality of creditors, either because they have securities on which they can rely,[3] or because they are themselves indebted or liable to the company and can satisfy the whole or part of their own claims by setting off the company's claim against their own.[4]

---

1 Insolvency Act 1986, s 107, s 143(1) and s 148(1); Insolvency Rules 1986, r 4.181.
2 Insolvency Act 1986, s 175(1); (see p 303, post).
3 Insolvency Rules 1986, r 4.88; (see p 326, post).
4 Ibid, r 4.90; (see p 317, post).

COSTS AND EXPENSES OF THE LIQUIDATION

Relevant costs and expenses

The expenses properly incurred by a liquidator in winding up the affairs of a company, whether it is wound up by the court or voluntarily, are payable out of the company's assets in priority to the debts, obligations and liabilities of the company incurred before the liquidation began. The liquidator has the right to be indemnified out of the company's assets for expenses of the liquidation properly incurred by him, and persons who are employed by the liquidator to do work or to supply goods or services in connection with the liquidation are entitled to be subrogated to his claim to be indemnified, and so may recover their claims out of the company's assets if the liquidator does not pay them.[5]

Costs of initiating the winding up

Expenses of the winding up include the taxed costs and expenses of the creditor or contributory who successfully sought the winding up order under which the company is being wound up if the court orders that those costs and expenses shall be paid out of the company's assets, as it invariably does, and the expenses of the winding up also include the costs of supporting or opposing creditors or contributories which the court orders to be paid by the company.[6]

It has never been judicially decided whether the expenses incurred in calling and holding meetings of members and creditors at the commencement of a voluntary winding up should be treated as expenses of the liquidation. The expenses of the meeting of creditors held in consequence of the passing of a winding up resolution at the beginning of a creditors' voluntary liquidation are undoubtedly costs of liquidation, because the company is already in liquidation when the meeting is held and the calling and holding of the meeting is required by law.[7] The expenses of the general meeting which passes the winding up resolution are, of course, incurred by the directors of the company, and not by the liquidator, but the directors can ensure that the company bears the expenses by using its resources to meet them, as they may quite properly do in exercise of their powers as directors up to the time when the winding up

---

5 *Re Anglo-Moravian Hungarian Junction Rly Co, ex p Watkin* (1875) 1 Ch D 130; *Stead, Hazel & Co v Cooper* [1933] 1 KB 840; Insolvency Act 1986, ss 115 and 156.

6 See p 72, ante.

7 Insolvency Act 1986, s 98(1).

resolution is passed. The expenses properly incurred by the liquidator who is appointed by the general meeting which passes the winding up resolution, whether in connection with that meeting or the meeting of creditors which is held because the liquidation is a creditors' voluntary winding up are payable as expenses of the winding up, even though the creditors' meeting appoints another person to be the liquidator.[8] If a voluntary liquidation is superseded by the court making a winding up order against the company, the proper remuneration and expenses of the liquidator in the voluntary liquidation up to the date of the winding up order are payable out of the company's assets in priority to the expenses incurred in obtaining the winding up order and in carrying out the winding up by the court.[9] If a liquidator in a voluntary winding up is aware on his appointment that substantial creditors of the company intend to petition for an order that the company shall be wound up by the court, the liquidator should confine his activities to collecting and preserving the company's assets until the outcome of the petition is known, and the court will not allow his remuneration or expenses in respect of other matters (eg investigating the application of the company's assets by its directors) if a winding up order is made.[10]

General expenses of the liquidation

The expenses incurred by the liquidator in carrying out his functions are, of course, all payable out of the company's assets, provided that the liquidator does not incur them in connection with matters or transactions which involve breaches of duty on his part. Consequently, such expenses include essential and inevitable expenses (such as those of the company's directors in preparing a statement of the company's affairs, the liquidator's expenses in connection with selling and realising the company's assets and in recovering debts and other amounts payable to it, and the expenses of advertising for creditors to submit details of their claims against the company) together with the liquidator's remuneration for the work done by him, and the liquidator's costs of making applications to the court, appearing on the hearing of applications to the court made by creditors or contributories, and calling and holding meetings of creditors to ascertain their wishes.[11] All these expenses are met in priority to satisfying the claims of the company's creditors.

8 *Re Sandwell Copiers Ltd* [1988] BCLC 209, 4 BCC 227.
9 *Re A V Sorge & Co Ltd* [1986] BCLC 490, 2 BCC 306; Insolvency Rules 1986, r 4.219.
10 *Re Tony Rowse NMC Ltd* [1996] 2 BCLC 225, [1996] BCC 196.
11 See Insolvency Rules 1986, r 4.218(1).

On the other hand, the liquidator cannot use the company's assets to meet the cost of employing agents or others to do work which he should do himself and for which he is remunerated. Moreover, if the liquidator makes an application to the court in the liquidation when he has no reasonable cause for doing so, or if he incurs costs in unreasonably opposing such an application properly made to the court by another person, the court may order that he shall bear the costs himself, and he is then not entitled to be indemnified out of the company's assets.[12]

Expenses of carrying out the company's contracts

A liquidator may incur expense in a liquidation in carrying out contracts which the company entered into but had not carried out before it went into liquidation, and unless the liquidator has acted improperly (eg by paying a creditor an amount owed to him for goods or services already supplied to the company before the winding up began, instead of treating the claim as a debt provable in the liquidation), the expense of fulfilling the contract is treated as an expense of the liquidation. Difficulties arise, however, when the other party to the pre-liquidation contract which is still wholly or partly executory applies to the court for an order directing that the payment in question shall be made as an expense of the liquidation in priority to satisfying the company's other debts and liabilities. The other party's claim will then rank as an allowable expense of the liquidation only if the liquidator has voluntarily continued to carry out the contract for the proper purposes of the liquidation, or if the court has ordered him to do so (eg in an action of specific performance), but not merely because the company's obligations under the contract fell due for performance during the liquidation.

Consequently, a liquidator who takes possession of premises held under a lease granted to the company for the purpose of continuing to carry on the company's business, or in order to sell the lease or equipment of the company kept on the premises, will be directed by the court to pay the rent accruing under the lease and to perform the lessee's covenants contained in it while he is in possession of the premises as an expense of the liquidation.[13] But if the liquidator simply takes formal possession of premises held by the

---

12 *Re Silver Valley Mines Ltd* (1882) 21 Ch D 381; *Re R Bolton & Co, Salisbury-Jones and Dale's Case* [1895] 1 Ch 333; *Re Wilson Lovatt & Sons Ltd* [1977] 1 All ER 274.

13 *Re Silkstone and Dodworth Coal and Iron Co* (1881) 17 Ch D 158; *Re Oak Pitts Colliery Co* (1882) 21 Ch D 322; *Re Linda Marie Ltd* [1989] BCLC 46, 4 BCC 463.

company under a lease so as to protect the company's goods or equipment situate there, without any intention of using the premises or the goods or equipment for the purpose of carrying on the company's business, or for the purpose of selling the goods or equipment immediately or as soon as possible, the court will not direct the liquidator to pay accruing rent and to incur the cost of performing the lessee's covenants as an expense of the liquidation.[14] Other persons may also be liable to pay such accruing rent or to see that the lessee's covenants are performed as well as the company (eg guarantors of the company's obligations under the lease, or an original lessee of a lease granted before 1 January 1996 who assigned the lease to the company), and the fact that the company is in liquidation does not relieve them of their liability. Their right to recover an indemnity out of the company's assets for rent paid by them or the cost of fulfilling lessee's covenants depends on whether the liquidator would or would not have been able to treat the expenditure as an expense of the liquidation if he had incurred it himself.[15]

Involuntary expenses

If a liquidator incurs liabilities imposed by law in carrying on the company's business or in occupying premises for the purpose of the liquidation (eg liability for corporation tax on profits earned or capital gains realised by the company during the liquidation, or for value added tax on goods or services supplied to the company's customers by the liquidator), the cost of satisfying those liabilities is an expense of the liquidation, and must be paid accordingly in priority to the debts and liabilities of the company incurred before it went into liquidation.[16]

In this connection the suppliers of certain public utility services (namely, gas, electricity, water and telecommunication services) may, as a condition of continuing to supply the service for which they are responsible, require the liquidator to give a personal guarantee for the payment of charges for services supplied after the date of the winding up order or resolution in respect of the company,[17] and the liquidator is, of course, entitled to an indemnity out of the company's assets against his personal liability if he requires the services for the purpose of the liquidation. However, a

14 *Re ABC Coupler and Engineering Co Ltd (No 3)* [1970] 1 All ER 650, [1970] 1 WLR 702.
15 *Re Downer Enterprises Ltd* [1974] 2 All ER 1074, [1974] 1 WLR 1460.
16 *Re Beni-Felkai Mining Co Ltd* [1934] Ch 406; *Re Mesco Properties Ltd* [1980] 1 All ER 117, [1980] 1 WLR 96.
17 Insolvency Act 1986, s 233(1) to (4).

supplier of such a public utility service may not make it a condition for a continuation of the service that charges for the supply of the service to the company before it went into liquidation shall be paid by the liquidator or anyone else,[17] and so the suppliers of such services must prove as ordinary creditors in the liquidation for their charges in respect of such earlier supplies.

Order of payments of expenses

In a winding up by the court, if the company's assets are insufficient to satisfy all the expenses incurred by the liquidator in carrying out the liquidation, the expenses properly incurred by him are paid in the order of priority directed by the court.[18] There is no similar provision in respect of voluntary liquidations, and the statutory direction that in a voluntary winding up such expenses and the liquidator's remuneration shall be paid in priority to all other claims[19] seems to indicate that the liquidation expenses (including the liquidator's remuneration) must be paid rateably if the company's assets are insufficient to satisfy them in full. It has been held, however, that the expenses of a voluntary winding up should be paid in the same order as the expenses of a winding up by the court so far as possible, but the court may direct a different order of priority.[20] Furthermore, the provision of the Insolvency Rules 1986 (as amended) which sets out the order in which the particular expenses of the winding up are to be met out of the company's assets is not confined to winding up by the court, and apparently therefore applies also to voluntary liquidations.

The expenses of winding up a company by the court are directed to be paid in the following order, unless the court otherwise orders.[1] The same order of priority must apparently be observed in respect of a voluntary winding up, but most of the expenses for which priority is given by the Insolvency Rules 1986 can be incurred only in a winding up by the court. In a winding up by the court, the expenses of the official receiver and the liquidator in preserving and realising the company's assets are paid first, and then the other expenses and disbursements of the official receiver, including those

---

18 Ibid, s 156.
19 Ibid, s 115.
20 *Re Beni-Felkai Mining Co Ltd* [1934] Ch 406; *Re Linda Marie Ltd* [1989] BCLC 46, 4 BCC 463.
 1 Insolvency Rules 1986 r 4.218(1) (as amended by Insolvency (Amendment) Rules 1995 (SI 1995/586), r 3 and Sch, para 1) and r 4.220(1).

incurred in carrying on the business of the company. Then follow the fees paid to the court in connection with the winding up petition and other applications made to the court in respect of the company under the Insolvency Act 1986, and any fees payable to the official receiver (other than the fee for the performance of his general duties in the winding up); this fee is paid next out of the company's assets, and the deposit paid into court when the winding up petition was presented is repaid rateably with the official receiver's fee. There follow next in the following order the remuneration of any provisional liquidator appointed by the court, the taxed costs of the petitioner for the winding up order which the court orders to be paid, and the costs of other persons in connection with the hearing of the winding up petition which the court directs to be paid out of the company's assets. After these items there must be paid successively the remuneration of any special manager appointed by the court, the cost of preparing the statement of the company's affairs, the remaining expenses of the liquidator in winding up the company (including the expenses of the liquidation committee), the remuneration of any person employed by the liquidator to assist him in carrying out his functions, the liquidator's remuneration (not exceeding that which would have been payable to the official receiver if he had been the liquidator), any corporation tax on capital gains payable on the realisation of assets of the company in the course of the liquidation and, finally, any balance of the remuneration to which the liquidator is entitled.

There is now provided a summary method by which the official receiver may apply to the Registrar of Companies for the early dissolution of a company which is wound up by the court if its realisable assets are insufficient to meet the expenses of winding it up.[2] It would seem that before or at the time when the official receiver seeks a summary dissolution, he should apply to the court for an order directing how the assets of the company in his possession shall be applied in meeting the expenses of the liquidation and his remuneration. There is no corresponding provision for the summary dissolution of a company in voluntary liquidation, but if the company's assets will be inadequate to meet the costs of the liquidation, the liquidator may apply to the court for directions as to how the company's assets shall be applied toward meeting the expenses of the liquidation which have so far been incurred (including his remuneration) and for his own removal from office.[3]

2 Insolvency Act 1986, s 202(1), (2) and (5) (see p 193, ante).
3 Ibid, s 108(2) and s 112(1) and (2); Insolvency Rules 1986, r 4.120.

DEBTS AND LIABILITIES OF THE COMPANY

Valuation of debts and liabilities

When the costs and expenses of winding up the affairs of a company in liquidation have been satisfied, the balance of the proceeds of realising its assets and its cash balances must be applied in discharging the company's debts, obligations and liabilities incurred before a winding up order was made or a winding up resolution was passed.[4]

It is essential that an obligation or liability of the company should exist on the date when it goes into liquidation if it is to be proved and its amount paid out of the company's assets in the liquidation, but it is not necessary that the obligation or liability should be for a definite or liquidated amount, or that it should be due for payment immediately, or that it should be unconditional.[4] Consequently, liabilities of the company for unliquidated damages for breaches of contracts by it before or after a winding up order is made, or a winding up resolution is passed, may be proved in the liquidation, and now that the exclusion by the previous legislation of claims for damages for torts for which the company is responsible has disappeared, liabilities of the company for unliquidated damages for torts committed before it went into liquidation may also be proved.[4]

Contingent and conditional liabilities

The fact that a monetary claim against the company is contingent or conditional does not exclude it from participation in the company's liquidation, and the liquidator must admit such a claim at his estimate of its value.[5] Consequently, a proof may be lodged by a person whom the company has agreed to indemnify against loss caused by an event which has not yet happened but which may occur in the future,[6] or by the holder of a fire or accident insurance policy in the liquidation of the insurance company which issued it, even though no claim under the policy has yet arisen.[7] All claims which it is sought to prove against the company in liquidation must be valued by the liquidator as at the date of the winding up order or resolution,[8] but if the value of a

---

4 Insolvency Act 1986, ss 107 and 115, s 143(1) and s 148(1); Insolvency Rules 1986, r 4.1, 3.12(1) to (4).
5 Insolvency Rules 1986, r 4.86(1).
6 *Butler v Broadhead* [1975] Ch 97, [1974] 2 All ER 401.
7 *Re Northern Counties of England Fire Insurance Co, Macfarlane's Claim* (1880) 17 Ch D 337.
8 *Re European Assurance Society's Arbitration, Wallberg's Case* (1872) 17 Sol Jo 69; *Re Law Car and General Insurance Corpn* [1913] 2 Ch 103; *Re Parana Plantations Ltd* [1946] 2 All ER 214.

provable claim is later increased by the occurrence of an event or the fulfilment of a contingency (eg a claim arising under a fire or accident insurance policy), the claimant may with the agreement of the liquidator or on the direction of the court revise his proof so that it is now made for an increased amount.[9] Similarly, if the liquidator rejects a proof for a contingent liability because it is not susceptible to valuation at the date of the winding up order or resolution, and the contingency then occurs during the course of the liquidation, the claimant may prove for the present full amount of his claim. The liquidator may revise his initial valuation of a debt or liability which lacks a definite value because it is subject to a contingency or is otherwise uncertain, and may do this without the consent of the claimant, even though his claim has already been admitted by the liquidator for a greater or smaller amount.[10]

If a claim has been rejected by the liquidator as incapable of valuation, or has been admitted for a reduced amount because it is contingent or conditional, and the claim is later admitted by the liquidator on it becoming capable of valuation or is revised on the contingency or condition occurring, the claim then ranks for future dividends as a debt of a company for its admitted or revised amount. If the liquidator has sufficient assets in hand at any time after he admits or revises the proof, he must first apply those assets in paying dividends to the claimant at the rate he has already paid to the other creditors of the company in respect of their admitted claims, before he pays a further dividend on all the claims now admitted by him (including the new claim).[11] However, the new claimant cannot require other claimants who have already proved and received a dividend in the liquidation to repay any part of the amount which they have received so as to equalise dividends between himself and them.[11]

Amounts involving liability to tax

If a claim is made in a liquidation in respect of an amount payable by the company on which the recipient would have borne income tax if the company had not gone into liquidation and had paid the amount to him in fulfilment of its obligation, an estimate must be made of the tax which the claimant would have borne, and the properly discounted equivalent of that tax must be deducted from

---

9 Insolvency Rules 1986, r 4.84; *Re Northern Counties of England Fire Insurance Co, Macfarlane's Claim*, supra.
10 Insolvency Rules 1986, r 4.86(1) and (2).
11 *Re R-R Realisations Ltd* [1980] 1 All ER 1019, [1980] 1 WLR 805; Insolvency Rules 1986, r 4.182(2).

the nominal or present value of his claim.[12] This applies only for the purpose of quantifying the claim for which the claimant proves in the liquidation, however, and does not affect the amount which he may claim from third persons (eg guarantors of the company's obligation).[12] Moreover, no deduction is made from the amount of a claim in respect of a claimant's potential tax liability if the claimant will be taxable on the dividends which he receives from the liquidator.[12] This rule applies whether the claim which is proved in the liquidation is for damages in tort or for breach of contract, but only if in quantifying the damages the court would under the rules of common law make a deduction for the tax which the claimant would have borne on the amount of his prospective income, profits or capital gains which is taken as the basis for assessing the damages (eg prospective earnings of the claimant under a service contract which the company wrongfully repudiates, or the claimant's prospective income from any employer which the claimant is prevented from earning because of any personal injuries caused by a person for whom the company is responsible in tort).[12]

Recurrent obligations

If the company before its liquidation has contracted to make a series of payments, or to do or abstain from a series of acts (eg covenants by a company in a lease to pay the rent reserved and to fulfil the lessee's obligations throughout the lease), the person with whom the company contracted may prove in its liquidation for the losses which he has suffered in consequence of breaches of contract by the company before it went into liquidation,[13] and also for the loss which he will prospectively suffer by not being able to enforce the company's contractual obligations in the future.[14] If the other contracting party will gain from the contract with the company being terminated, however, the value of the resulting benefit to him must be deducted from the prospective value of the future performance of the company's obligations.[14] Consequently, if the liquidator surrenders, or is willing to surrender, a lease granted to the company, and the lessor can immediately grant a new lease to another lessee at the same or an enhanced rent or on the same or more advantageous terms than the company's lease, the prospective benefits of the surrender to the lessor will equal or exceed the loss which he suffers by the company

---

12 *Houghton v Trafalgar Insurance Co Ltd* [1954] 1 QB 247, [1953] 2 All ER 1409; *Bold v Brough, Nicholson and Hall Ltd* [1963] 3 All ER 849, [1964] 1 WLR 201; *Shove v Downs Surgical plc* [1984] 1 All ER 7.
13 Insolvency Rules 1986, r 4.92(1).
14 *James Smith & Sons (Norwood) Ltd v Goodman* [1936] Ch 216; *Re House Property and Investment Co Ltd* [1954] Ch 576, [1953] 2 All ER 1525.

ceasing to be liable for the future payment of rent and the performance of its covenants under the lease granted to it, and the lessor will then be unable to prove for the value of the prospective fulfilment of the company's obligations.[14]

On the other hand, if the liquidator disclaims a lease held by the company,[15] he presumably does so because the lease is valueless, or because the cost of paying the rent reserved and performing the lessee's other obligations exceeds the value of the lease, and the lessor will then find it impossible to grant a new lease to a third person on the same terms as the disclaimed lease. In that situation the lessor may prove in the liquidation for the difference between the present value of the amounts of rent payable in the future under the disclaimed lease, plus the present value of the future fulfilment of the lessee's obligations (on the assumption that the company would satisfy its obligations in full), and the value of the diminished rent (if any) and the less onerous obligations which the lessor will have to concede to a new lessee if it is possible to find one.[16] If the company is solvent, the court may require the liquidator to set aside a sum which, with interest earned by it in the future, will be sufficient to satisfy the future rent payable under the lease and to provide for the future fulfilment of the lessee's other obligations;[17] but the court will do this only in exceptional circumstances,[18] and certainly not if the company is insolvent, because in that situation the lessor would be put in a preferred position to that of other creditors and claimants if an order for setting up such a fund were made.

Interest

Interest prior to the liquidation

If a debt or other amount payable by a company under a contract carries interest by express agreement, the other party may prove in the winding up of the company for interest at the contractual rate calculated up to the date when the court ordered the company to be wound up or a general meeting of the company resolved to wind it up voluntarily, but if the company is solvent, contractual interest may be claimed up to the later date when the principal of the debt is paid, or up to the date to which interest is payable by the terms of

---

15 Insolvency Act 1986, ss 178, 179 and 182 (see p 151, ante).
16 Ibid, s 178(6); *Re Park Air Services plc* [1996] 1 BCLC 547, [1996] BCC 556.
17 *Oppenheimer v British and Foreign Exchange and Investment Bank* (1877) 6 Ch D 744.
18 *Re House Property and Investment Co Ltd*, supra.

the contract.[19] This applies also to the claim of a creditor of a third person whose indebtedness has been guaranteed by the company where the creditor proves in the company's liquidation for the amount payable under the guarantee.[20]

If the debt is payable by the company by virtue of a written instrument which does not provide for the payment of interest, the creditor may prove in the liquidation of the company for interest calculated from the date on which the debt became due for payment up to the date when a winding up order was made against the company or a resolution to wind it up was passed; interest may be claimed for that period at the rate currently prescribed as the rate of interest payable in respect of judgment debts on the latter date (at present 8 per cent).[1] If a debt is payable by a company under an oral agreement which does not provide expressly for the payment of interest, interest may be claimed if a written demand for payment of the debt was made by the creditor after it became payable stating that interest would be claimed from the date on which the notice was given; under such a notice interest may be claimed from the date when the written demand was made up to the date when a winding up order was made or a winding up resolution was passed; the rate of interest is the same as that payable in respect of judgment debts on the date when the company is ordered to be wound up or resolves to be wound up.[2]

Capitalisation of interest

By capitalisation provisions in a loan agreement, amounts of interest due periodically in respect of the loan are added to the principal of the loan and themselves bear interest at the contractual rate from the due date. Contractual provisions for the capitalisation of interest falling due for payment by a company before the commencement of its liquidation but remaining unpaid after the due date apply in quantifying a creditor's claim, but unless the company is solvent, interest ceases to accrue when a winding up order is made or a winding up resolution is passed, and so capitalisation provisions cannot be applied to interest payments which by the terms of the

---

19 *Re Humber Ironworks and Shipbuilding Co, Warrant Finance Co's Case* (1869) 4 Ch App 643; *Re Amalgamated Investment and Property Co Ltd* [1985] Ch 349, [1984] BCLC 341.

20 *Re Amalgamated Investment and Property Co Ltd, supra.*

1 Insolvency Rules 1986, r 4.93(2), (3) and (6); Judgments Act 1838, s 17; Judgment Debts (Rate of Interest) Order 1993 (SI 1993/564), para 2.

2 Insolvency Rules 1986, r 4.93(4) to (6).

contract would fall due after that time.[3] The same rule would appear to apply when by the terms of a loan to a company provide that it shall have the option to treat amounts of interest which fall due as additions to the principal of the loan instead of paying them, or which provide that interest shall accumulate and be added to the principal in any event.

Interest for period after winding up order or resolution

When all the debts of a company have been paid in full in a solvent liquidation, interest is payable out of the company's remaining assets on all its debts and liabilities which have been proved for the period of the liquidation (ie from the date of the winding up order or resolution to the date of payment).[4] Interest is payable rateably without any priority for interest on preferential debts, and is calculated at the higher of the rate of interest payable on judgment debts on the date when a winding up order was made or a winding up resolution was passed in respect of the company and the contractual rate of interest payable on the debt.[4]

Non-sterling debts

If debts or contractual claims proved against a company are expressed in a currency other than sterling, or if the court has given judgment against a company in such a currency, the amount of the debt or claim must be converted into sterling for the purpose of proof in the liquidation at the official rate of exchange prevailing on the date when the winding up order was made or the winding up resolution was passed,[5] but in the case of a winding up by the court, the court may direct that the rate of exchange to be applied shall instead be that prevailing on the date when the successful winding up petition was presented.[6] The official rate of exchange for this purpose is the middle market rate on the date in question as published by the Bank of England, or if no such rate has been published, the rate of exchange directed by the court.[4] The same rate of exchange is applied when converting interest payments calculated in a foreign currency, and this is so whether the interest payments became due

3 *Re Amalgamated Investment and Property Co Ltd*, supra.
4 Insolvency Act 1986, s 189(1) to (4).
5 Insolvency Rules 1986, r 4.91(1) and (2).
6 *Re Dynamics Corpn of America* [1976] 2 All ER 669, [1976] 1 WLR 757; *Re Lines Bros Ltd* [1983] Ch 1, [1982] 2 All ER 183.

before the company went into liquidation, or, if the company is solvent, afterwards.[7]

Discounts

A creditor of a company must deduct from the amount of his proof all trade and other discounts which would have been available to the company if it had not gone into liquidation, whether the discount was expressly or impliedly agreed upon or was allowed by trade usage, but no deduction need be made of discounts allowed for immediate, early or cash settlement.[8]

For the purpose of calculating a dividend in a liquidation, discount in a more general sense must be deducted from the nominal amount or face value of a debt which was not due for payment at the date when the winding up order was made or the winding up resolution was passed.[9] The proper deduction is interest at an annual rate of five per cent calculated on the nominal or face value of the debt from the date when the dividend is declared until the later date on which the debt would normally have become payable.[9] It is uncertain whether such a discount from the nominal amount of a debt payable at a future date must be deducted when by the express terms of the contract under which it arose interest is payable on the debt calculated up to until the date when it accrues due for payment, because if the company is insolvent, no such interest may be claimed for any period after the commencement of the winding up.[10] However, it is certain that no deduction need be made from the nominal amount of the debt if the contract under which it arose provides for the date on which it becomes payable to be accelerated in the event of the company's liquidation, because the debt then automatically becomes due for payment when a winding up order is made or a winding up resolution is passed.

Guarantees and indemnities

A person who has given a guarantee or an indemnity undertaking to a creditor of the company in respect of any of its obligations cannot prove in the liquidation of the company for the indemnity to which

---

7 *Re Lines Bros Ltd (No 2)* [1984] Ch 438, [1984] BCLC 227.
8 Insolvency Rules 1986, r 4.89.
9 Ibid, r 4.94 and r 11.13(1).
10 Ibid, r 4.93(1).

he is entitled either by the terms of the contract between them or by law, unless he has discharged the company from liability to the creditor by satisfying its obligation to him in full before or after the company goes into liquidation.[11] This is so even if the surety or giver of the indemnity undertaking has agreed to be liable to the creditor only up to a maximum amount (eg a guarantee of the whole of the company's indebtedness to the creditor, but so that the surety shall not be liable to the creditor for more than £100,000), and the surety has paid that maximum amount.[12]

The reason for the inability of the surety or the person to prove in the company's liquidation is that only one proof can be admitted in the liquidation for the same obligation, and if the creditor were able to prove for the whole or part of the debt which neither the company nor the surety or giver of the indemnity undertaking has paid, and the surety or giver of that undertaking were also permitted to prove in the company's liquidation for an indemnity in respect of any amount which he has already paid the creditor and also for any amount which he may have to pay to the creditor in the future in respect of the unpaid part of the company's debt, two proofs would be admissible for the same principal obligation. This would inflate the total amount provable in respect of the same debt to up to possibly twice its amount, and would result in the other creditors of the company receiving an artificially reduced dividend.

If the surety has guaranteed only part of the company's debt, however, (eg the repayment of 25 per cent of a loan made to the company plus interest thereon, or the first £100,000 of the company's indebtedness to the creditor), the surety may prove in the company's liquidation for an indemnity in respect of the part of the company's debt for which he is liable if he has paid that part in full, and the creditor may also prove in the company's liquidation for the remainder of the debt.[12] The splitting of a proof for the whole of the company's obligation is permitted in these circumstances, because there is no possibility of the surety also claiming an indemnity from the company for any prospective liability on his part to pay the balance of the company's debt to the creditor.[12]

Similarly, if a person gives security over his property for a debt owed by the company to a third person who realises the security and discharges part of the company's debt out of the proceeds, the giver

11 *Re Oriental Financial Corpn v Overend, Gurney & Co* (1871) 7 Ch App 142; *Re Fenton, ex p Fenton Textile Association Ltd* [1931] 1 Ch 85; *Re Fenton (No 2), ex p Fenton Textile Association Ltd* [1932] 1 Ch 178; *Barclays Bank Ltd v TOSG Trust Fund Ltd* [1984] AC 626, [1984] 1 All ER 628.
12 *Re Sass, ex p National Provincial Bank of England Ltd* [1896] 2 QB 12; *Barclays Bank Ltd v TOSG Trust Fund Ltd*, supra.

of the security may prove in the company's liquidation for an indemnity in respect of the part of the debt which has been so discharged and the creditor may prove only for the unpaid balance of the debt.[13]

Limitation period

A claim cannot be proved against a company in liquidation if the claimant could not bring an action against the company to enforce it immediately before the commencement of the winding up because the limitation period for suing had already expired and the claim had consequently been extinguished.[14] However, if a claim has not become barred by the expiration of the appropriate limitation period before the commencement of the liquidation, it may be proved at any time during the liquidation, even if the limitation period has by then run out.[15] The reason for this is that the running of the limitation period is suspended when the company goes into liquidation, because the claimant now has no absolute right to sue the company,[16] and the fact that he does not attempt to sue or to prove his claim in the liquidation until a remote date does not prevent him from asserting it.[15] The only risk which a creditor runs by not proving promptly is that he may miss dividends which the liquidator declares before he does prove his claim.[17]

Non-provable claims

A debt or claim can be proved in a winding up only if it could have been recovered or enforced by an action brought against the company before it went into liquidation. Consequently, a debt or claim which is avoided by statute or the general law (eg an illegal debt), or which is made unenforceable by statute (eg an oral guarantee)[18] or by a rule of public policy, cannot be proved in a

13 *Re Butler's Wharf Ltd* [1995] 2 BCLC 43, [1995] BCC 717.
14 *Re Art Reproduction Co Ltd* [1952] Ch 89, [1951] 2 All ER 984.
15 *Re General Rolling Stock Co, Joint Stock Discount Co's Claim* (1872) 7 Ch App 646;
    Re Cases of Taffs Well Ltd [1992] BCLC 11, [1991] BCC 582.
16 The creditor cannot sue after a winding up order has been made without leave
    of the court, and in a voluntary winding up the court may stay an action brought
    by the creditor (Insolvency Act 1986, s 112(1) and (2) and s 130(2); (see pp 77,
    and 92, ante).
17 See p 287, ante.
18 Statute of Frauds (1677), s 4.

liquidation. The one remaining instance of a valid debt or claim being non-actionable by a rule of public policy is that claims for criminal or civil penalties or for taxes or imposts made by or on behalf of the government of an overseas country or of a political subdivision of it (eg local taxes) cannot be enforced by action in an English court or proved in a liquidation, and this applies in respect of both foreign and Commonwealth countries.[19] Fines and penalties imposed by United Kingdom courts in civil or criminal proceedings can be proved in the winding up of the company on which they are imposed.[20] On the other hand, a confiscation order made against a company under the Drug Trafficking Offences Act 1986 or under s 71 of the Criminal Justice Act 1988 cannot be enforced by proof in the winding up of the company for the amount or value of the confiscation.[1]

The former exclusion from proof in the liquidation of an insolvent company of claims for unliquidated damages which arose otherwise than by reason of a contract, promise or breach of trust (ie tort claims) no longer applies, and consequently all claims for unliquidated damages which can be enforced by an action for contract, tort, breach of statutory duty or breach of trust may now be proved in a company's liquidation.[2]

Proof of claim and dividend

A creditor or claimant in a winding up by the court who wishes to have the company's assets applied in payment of his claim must deliver a proof of it in writing to the liquidator, unless the court has, because of exceptional circumstances, ordered that it shall not be necessary to prove the claim or claims of the class to which it belongs.[3] In a members' or a creditors' voluntary winding up, the liquidator may require a person who makes a claim against the company to lodge a written proof of his claim with the liquidator.[4]

A proof in the winding up by the court must be in the prescribed form, or in substantially the same form, and must be signed by the claimant or by a person authorised by him.[5] If the liquidator so

19 *Government of India v Taylor* [1955] AC 491, [1955] 1 All ER 292.
20 *Treasury v Harris* [1957] 2 QB 516, [1957] 2 All ER 455.
 1 Insolvency Rules 1986, r 12.3(2).
 2 Insolvency Act 1986, s 107, s 143(1) and s 148(1); Insolvency Rules 1986, r 13.12(1) and (4).
 3 Insolvency Rules 1986, r 4.67(2) and 4.73(1).
 4 Ibid, r 4.73(2).
 5 Ibid, r 4.73(4) and Sch 4, Form 4.25.

requires, the claimant must verify his proof by an affidavit exhibiting the proof.[6] In a winding up by the court the official receiver or liquidator must send out forms of proof to all creditors and claimants of whom he is aware, or who are identified in the company's statement of affairs; and to ensure that creditors receive them as soon as possible after the company goes into liquidation, they must be sent out with the earliest to be despatched of the official receiver's notice of the first meeting of creditors, the notice by the official receiver that he does not intend to call first meetings of creditors and contributories (if that is the case), or the notice of the liquidator's appointment sent to creditors by a liquidator appointed by the court.[7] If a liquidator is appointed by the court because the first meetings of creditors and contributories nominate different persons to be the liquidator, and the court permits him to advertise his appointment instead of giving individual notices of it to creditors and contributories, the liquidator must ensure that forms of proof are sent to creditors and claimants not later than four months after the date of the winding up order.[8] The court may in an appropriate situation (eg where there are few creditors, or where the company has been dormant for a long time) dispense with the need to send forms of proof to creditors, or the court may alter the time within which forms of proof must be sent out.[9]

In a winding up by the court, a proof lodged by a creditor or claimant must state the creditor's name and address, the total amount of his claim at the date when the company went into liquidation (showing separately any value added tax and any interest which has not been capitalised and added to the principal of the debt), and the proof must also state whether the whole or part of the creditor's claim is a preferential payment ranking in the liquidation before other debts and liabilities of the company; the proof must also contain particulars of how and when the debt or liability was incurred by the company and of any security held by the creditor for the claim, and must state the date of the claim and the name and address and authority of the person who signs the proof (if it is signed by someone other than the claimant).[10] The proof must also specify any documents by which the creditor's claim can be substantiated, but it is not necessary to lodge any such documents with the proof, although the liquidator or the chairman of any meeting of creditors may require documents substantiating or supporting the claim to be

6 Ibid, r 4.77(1) and Sch 4, Form 4.26.
7 Ibid, r 4.74(1) and (2).
8 Ibid, r 4.74(3).
9 Ibid, r 4.74(4).
10 Ibid, r 4.75(1).

produced to him.[11] If the liquidator acknowledges an informal proof in a winding up by the court, the proof must be treated as valid and effective for all purposes, and the creditor or claimant is entitled to participate in all dividend distributions subsequent to the acknowledgment.[12] Moreover, if the liquidator is aware of a claim by a creditor or claimant who has not submitted a formal proof, it is the liquidator's duty to invite him to submit such a proof if the liquidator can communicate with him.[12]

In a voluntary winding up, a creditor or claimant may submit a proof in any form (apparently even orally), but the liquidator may call on him to submit a written proof, or to verify his claim by affidavit; additionally the liquidator or the chairman of a meeting of creditors may call on the creditor or claimant to provide any of the particulars which have to be contained in a proof in a winding up by the court, and also to produce such documentary or other evidence in support of his claim as the liquidator or chairman considers necessary to substantiate it.[13]

Unless the court otherwise orders, the cost of proving and substantiating a debt or claim in a liquidation is borne by the creditor or claimant, but costs incurred by the liquidator in quantifying a claim of uncertain amount are met out of the company's assets.[14] Any creditor or claimant who has lodged a proof and any contributory of the company may inspect any of the proofs lodged with the liquidator.[15]

The liquidator may admit a proof for dividend, or for voting at meetings of creditors, or for both purposes; and if the proof is for a claim ranking wholly or partly as a preferential payment, the liquidator may admit it as a preferential claim.[16] If the liquidator rejects a proof in whole or in part, or rejects a claim for it to rank as a preferential payment, he must send a written statement of his reasons for doing so to the creditor or claimant, who may appeal to the court against the liquidator's decision within 21 days after he receives the statement.[17] A contributory or another creditor or claimant may likewise appeal to the court against the admission or

---

11 Ibid, r 4.75(2) and (3).
12 *Re Compania de Electricidad de la Provincia de Buenos Aires Ltd* [1980] Ch 146, [1978] 3 All ER 668.
13 Insolvency Rules 1986, r 4.73(2) and (6), r 4.76 and r 4.77
14 Ibid, r 4.78(1) and (2).
15 Ibid, r 4.79.
16 Ibid, r 4.70(1) and r 4.82(1). If a creditors' meeting is presided over by a person other than the liquidator, that person may admit proofs of claims for the purpose of voting at that meeting.
17 Insolvency Rules 1986, r 4.82(2) and r 4.83(1).

rejection of a proof in whole or in part; the appeal must be brought within 21 days after the appellant becomes aware of the liquidator's decision.[18]

Appeals in respect of proofs are heard by the registrar of the court in chambers, but he may refer the matter to the judge for decision.[19] The hearing of the appeal involves a consideration de novo of the appellant's claim, and not merely a reconsideration of the reasons why the liquidator rejected the proof or refused to recognise it as a preferential claim: consequently, the proof or the claim in it that it is in respect of a preferential payment may be rejected on the hearing of an appeal for reasons which the liquidator did not take into account, or for reasons other than those which caused him to reject the proof or the contention that it related to a preferential payment.[20]

After a liquidator admits a proof, he may apply to the court to expunge it if he considers that it should not have been admitted, or that the amount for which it was admitted ought to be reduced; and if another creditor or claimant requests the liquidator to make such an application but he declines to do so, the creditor may make the application himself.[1] The court fixes a time for the hearing of the application, which must be notified together with the place of the hearing to the creditor or claimant who lodged the proof; and if the application is made by another creditor or claimant, the time and place of the hearing must also be notified to the liquidator.[2] Applications to expunge proofs are heard by the registrar of the court in chambers, but in the Companies Court applications may be heard by the Chief Clerk of the court.[3]

Distribution of dividends

Declaration of dividends to creditors

Whenever the liquidator has sufficient money in his hands, he must declare and distribute a dividend to the company's creditors, but he may retain out of the money available an amount which he considers necessary to discharge the expenses of the liquidation.[4] In calculating the amount of a dividend which he proposes to declare, the liquidator

18 Ibid, r 4.83(2).
19 Ibid, r 7.6(1) to (3).
20 *Re Kentwood Constructions Ltd* [1960] 2 All ER 655n, [1960] 1 WLR 646.
 1 Insolvency Rules 1986, r 4.85(1).
 2 Ibid, r 4.85(2).
 3 Ibid, r 7.6(1) to (3); Practice Direction dated 10 December 1986, para 4.
 4 Insolvency Rules 1986, r 4.180(1).

may make provision for claims of which he is aware, but for which proofs have not yet been lodged because the claimants may not have had sufficient time to do so by reason of the distance of their residence (at the present day this can relate only to overseas creditors), and the liquidator may also make provision for claims which have not yet been determined and for disputed claims (eg when a claim rejected by the liquidator is subject to an appeal).[5] The result of making provision for such unproved, undetermined and disputed claims is that the liquidator calculates the dividend which he will declare by reference to the total of the claims against the company which have been admitted to proof, plus the liquidator's estimate of the total value of the unproved, undetermined and disputed claims, and the dividend in the pound which he declares is consequently smaller than it would be if he took into account only debts and claims which have been admitted.

When the liquidator has realised all of the company's assets, or so much of them as he considers can be realised without needlessly protracting the liquidation, he must give notice of his intention to declare a final dividend, or if there are no remaining assets available, he must give notice that no dividend, or no further dividend, will be declared.[6] The notice of the liquidator's intention to declare a dividend (whether final or not) must be given to all creditors and claimants who have not proved their claims in the liquidation and of whose identities and addresses the liquidator is aware; the notice must specify a date not less than 21 days from the date of the notice by which such creditors and claimants must lodge proofs of their debts or claims if they are to be included in the declaration of any dividend which the liquidator states that he intends to make within four months after the period for proving expires.[7] If the dividend is the first which the liquidator declares, he must before declaring it invite creditors and claimants to prove their debts and claims by publishing an advertisement (eg in a newspaper or newspapers with an appropriately wide circulation), and specify in the advertisement the last date for proving claims against the company, which must be not earlier than 21 days after the publication of the advertisement.[8] Within seven days of the final date specified by the liquidator in the notices given by him to creditors or claimants who have not already proved, the liquidator must decide whether to admit or reject proofs lodged by that date, or alternatively, if he neither admits nor rejects

5 Ibid, r 4.182(1).
6 Ibid, r 4.186(1).
7 Ibid, r 11.2(1) to (3).
8 Ibid, r 11.2(1A) and (2).

a claim, he may decide to make provision for it.[9] The liquidator is not obliged to deal with proofs lodged after the final date for proving, but he may do so if he thinks fit.[9]

If during the four months after the final date notified for lodging proofs, the liquidator rejects a proof and the creditor or claimant appeals to the court against the rejection, or if during that time an application is made to the court for the liquidator's decision on a proof to be reversed or altered, or for a proof to be expunged, or for the amount of an admitted proof to be reduced, the liquidator may postpone or cancel the declaration of a dividend.[10]

Notification of a dividend

At the end of the four-month period or such longer period during which the liquidator postpones the declaration of a dividend, or after all pending appeals against the liquidator's decisions on proofs and all pending applications to the court to reverse or vary his decisions, or to expunge or reduce proofs, have been disposed of (whichever is the latest), the liquidator must declare the dividend which he proposes to pay, and must give notice of the declaration of the dividend to all creditors and claimants who have proved their debts and claims.[11] If the dividend is payable only to creditors or claimants for preferential payments whose claims have been admitted, the liquidator need notify only them (and not the other creditors) of the declaration of the dividend.[12]

With the leave of the court, the liquidator may declare and notify a dividend, or expunge or reduce the amounts of proofs appeals which are still pending and undecided, or even though an outstanding claim against the company has not been quantified; the court may give leave for this purpose on condition that the liquidator makes provision for those debts and claims, but the court will not give leave for the liquidator to declare a dividend if no provision is made at all, or if the provision proposed will not be adequate to cover the maximum possible amount of any outstanding unquantified claim.[13]

The notice of the declaration of a dividend must state the total amount realised by the sale of the company's assets and, so far as practicable, from the sale of particular assets; the total amount of payments made by the liquidator for the purpose of carrying out the

9 Ibid, r 11.3(1) and (2).
10 Ibid, r 11.4.
11 Ibid, r 11.5(1) and (2) and r 11.6(1).
12 Ibid, r 11.12(1).
13 Insolvency Rules 1986, r 11.5(2); *Re R-R Realisations Ltd (formerly Rolls-Royce Ltd)* [1980] 1 All ER 1019, [1980] 1 WLR 805.

liquidation; the amount of any provision made by him for unsettled claims against the company and the amount of money retained by him for particular purposes; the total amount to be distributed as dividend and the rate in the pound of the dividend; and finally, whether and when any further dividend is expected to be declared.[14]

Payment of a dividend

In a winding up by the court, payment instruments for the payment of a dividend declared by the liquidator out of the Insolvency Services Account are prepared by the Department of Trade and Industry at the request of the liquidator, and he may send them to the creditors and claimants whose claims have been admitted to proof with the notice of the dividend.[15] In a voluntary winding up, the liquidator pays dividends to creditors and claimants by cheques drawn on the bank account which he maintains for the purpose of the liquidation, but if by reason of the six monthly payments of the current balance of that account into the Insolvency Services Account which he is required to make,[16] the liquidator has insufficient money left in the bank account maintained by him to pay the dividend, he requests the Department of Trade and Industry either to remit to him out of the company's credit balance in the Insolvency Services Account sufficient money to pay the dividend which he has declared, or to have payment instruments prepared in favour of the creditors or claimants who are entitled to the dividend so that the liquidator may deliver them to those persons.[17]

If a proof by a creditor or claimant is withdrawn or expunged, or if its amount is reduced after it has been admitted, the creditor or claimant must repay any excess dividend which he has already been paid; and the same applies if a creditor or claimant revalues upwards any security for his debt or claim after a dividend has been declared on the basis of his lower valuation, resulting in the payment of a larger amount in respect of the difference between the original value put by him on the value of his security and the higher amount of his secured debt (the unsecured amount for which he has proved).[18]

If a liquidator gives notice to creditors or claimants who have proved their claims that he is unable to declare a dividend or (as the case may be) a further dividend, the notice must state that no money

14 Insolvency Rules 1986, r 11.6(1) and (2).
15 Ibid, r 11.6(3); Insolvency Regulations 1994, reg 8(1).
16 See p 190, ante.
17 Insolvency Regulations 1994, reg 8(3).
18 Insolvency Rules 1986, r 11.8(3) and r 11.9(1) and (2).

has been realised from the company's assets, or (as the case may be) that the money so realised has already been consumed in discharging the expenses of the liquidation.[19]

When a company is dissolved after the conclusion of its liquidation, the liquidator must, in both a winding up by the court and a voluntary winding up, and whether he has vacated office or not, pay any money of the company remaining in his hands into the Insolvency Services Account.[20] Any person who claims a payment out of such money or any other amount credited to the company in the Insolvency Services Account (eg a creditor who has not yet received payment of a final dividend declared by the liquidator) may apply to the Secretary of State for Trade and Industry for payment of the amount of his claim, and may appeal to the court against a decision of the Secretary of State refusing to make the payment requested.[1]

Distributions to members or shareholders

In a winding up of a company by a court, after its debts and liabilities have been satisfied in full together with interest for the period of the liquidation,[2] the distribution of the company's remaining assets (if any) to its members or shareholders is a function of the court.[3] Consequently, before making a distribution, the liquidator must apply to the court for an order authorising the distribution to the persons specified in a list of members or shareholders prepared by the liquidator which sets out the amounts to be paid to them respectively and is filed with the application.[3] When the court has made an order authorising the distribution, it sends a sealed copy of it to the liquidator,[4] who effects the distribution by requesting the Department of Trade and Industry to issue payment instruments drawn on the Insolvency Services Account for the amounts payable to the members or shareholders included in the list approved by the court, in the same way as the Department issues such instruments for the payment of dividends to creditors in the liquidation.[5]

The distribution in a voluntary winding up of the assets of the company remaining after the costs and expenses of the liquidation and the debts and liabilities of the company have been discharged

---

19 Insolvency Rules 1986, r 11.7.
20 Insolvency Regulations 1994, reg 18.
 1 Ibid, reg 32(1) and (2).
 2 See p 291, ante.
 3 Insolvency Act 1986, s 143(1); Insolvency Rules 1986, r 4.221(1) to (3).
 4 Insolvency Rules 1986, r 4.221(4).
 5 Insolvency Regulations 1994, reg 8(2).

in full is a function of the liquidator;[6] Consequently, in order to effect the distribution, the liquidator must draw cheques on the bank account maintained by him for the purpose of the liquidation, or if he has insufficient funds to do so because he has paid surplus money in his hands into the Insolvency Services Account, he must apply to the Department of Trade and Industry to issue payment instruments for the amounts payable to the members or shareholders so that he may forward the instruments to them.[7]

PREFERENTIAL AND DEFERRED DEBTS AND CLAIMS

Priority of preferential debts

Certain debts and liabilities of a company in liquidation must be satisfied in full before payments may be made in respect of other, non-preferential debts and claims.[8] These preferential debts and claims rank equally between themselves,[9] and are listed exhaustively in the Insolvency Act 1986;[10] no debt or claim which is not included in the statutory list may be treated as preferential in reliance on a privilege otherwise conferred by law.[11] If the company's assets are insufficient to pay all the preferential debts in full, the liquidator must declare and pay a rateable dividend in respect of them out of the balance of the company's assets remaining after meeting the expenses of the liquidation.[12]

In addition to being paid in full in priority to ordinary unsecured debts of the company out of its assets, in a liquidation preferential debts and claims are payable out of assets comprised in a charge created by the company as a floating charge, whether it crystallises or is converted into a fixed charge before or after the company goes into liquidation, if the remaining assets of the company not comprised in the charge are insufficient to satisfy the preferential claims, and the claims of the persons secured by the charge are then postponed to those of the preferential creditors.[13] Creditors secured by a

6 Insolvency Act 1986, s 107.
7 Insolvency Regulations 1994, reg 8(3).
8 Insolvency Act 1986, s 175(1).
9 Ibid, s 175(2).
10 Ibid, s 386(1) and Sch 6.
11 *Food Controller v Cork* [1923] AC 647.
12 Insolvency Act 1986, s 175(2).
13 Ibid, s 175(2) and s 251.

floating charge whose claims have been postponed in this way are then entitled to resort to the general assets of the company by subrogation in order to obtain an indemnity for the amount secured by their charge which has been paid to the preferential creditors out of assets comprised in that charge.[13] The right of such creditors to recover an indemnity is, of course, of no value if the floating charge extends to the whole assets and undertaking of the company and the preferential debts exceed the value of those assets; the rights of the creditors secured by the floating charge are then simply subordinated to the prior payment of the preferential debts, and the holders of the floating charge receive nothing.

The provision for the prior payment of preferential debts and claims in the liquidation of a company out of assets subject to a floating charge created by the company formerly did not apply if the floating charge had crystallised before a winding up order was made or a winding up resolution was passed in respect of the company.[14] Now, however, this priority for preferential creditors applies if the floating charge was created as such, whether or not the charge has crystallised or been converted into a fixed charge by the terms on which the charge was created.[13] Moreover, if the floating charge has crystallised by the holders of the charge or trustees for them or the court appointing a receiver of the assets comprised in the charge, or by the holders of the floating charge or trustees for them taking possession of those assets on the occurrence of an event specified in the instrument creating the charge as one which will cause the charge to crystallise or to be converted into a fixed charge claims which would rank as preferential in a winding up and which exist when a receiver is so appointed or possession of the assets comprised in the charge is so taken have priority for payment out of the assets comprised in the charge, whether at that time or subsequently.[15] If the floating charge has crystallised, a receiver appointed by the holders of the charge or trustees for them or by the court, or the holders secured by the floating charge or trustees for them who take possession of the company's assets, must pay out of the assets coming to his or their hands the debts of the company which would have been preferential claims if the company had gone into liquidation on the date when the receiver was appointed or the holders of the floating charge or their trustees took possession of the company's assets, and the holders of the floating charge or the persons entitled

14 *Re Griffin Hotel Co Ltd* [1941] Ch 129, [1940] 4 All ER 324; *Re Brightlife Ltd* [1987] Ch 200, [1986] 3 All ER 673.
15 Companies Act 1985, s 196(1), (3) and (4) (as substituted by the Insolvency Act 1986, s 439(1) and Sch 13, Part I); Insolvency Act 1986, s 40(1) to (3), s 386(1) to (3) and s 387(4).

to the benefit of it (as the case may be) are entitled to be indemnified against the preferential claims so paid out of any other unencumbered assets of the company.[15]

Under the present law the persons who are entitled to preferential claims have a double priority if a charge created by the company as a floating charge crystallises or is converted into a fixed charge before the company goes into liquidation. Claimants for preferential debts at the date when the receiver is appointed, or when the holders of the charge or their trustees take possession of the assets comprised in it, have priority for payment out of the assets which are comprised in the charge at that date or which subsequently come to their hands.[15] Furthermore, claimants for preferential debts at the date when the company subsequently goes into liquidation have priority for payment of their debts out of the assets which are comprised in the charge at that date or subsequently, whether the floating charge crystallises by the company going into liquidation, or whether it has already crystallised or been converted into a fixed charge for any reason whatsoever (eg by the operation of a provision in the instrument creating the charge for its automatic crystallisation on the occurrence of a specified event, or by the holders of the floating charge exercising an option to convert it into a fixed charge).[13] The two sets of preferential claims will not necessarily be the same, however, because they will be calculated by reference to different periods, namely, the period ending on the date when a receiver was appointed or the holders of the charge or their trustees took possession of the assets comprised in the charge for the first set of claims, and the period ending on the date when the company went into liquidation for the second. It would seem that preferential claims which fall only into the second set will be deferred to the prior satisfaction of the preferential claims which fall into the first set out of the assets comprised in the charge at the date when the receiver was appointed, or the holders of the charge or their trustees took possession of the assets comprised in the charge, together with assets which were subsequently included in the charge (eg by the company acquiring them before it goes into liquidation) and which come to the hands of the receiver or such other persons who take possession of the company's assets, and that the two sets of claims by the different sets of preferential creditors do not rank pari passu. This is because the assets of the company of which a receiver for the holders of the floating charge, or such holders themselves or trustees for them, take possession will be applied by them primarily in paying the first set of preferential debts, and the liquidator in the subsequent liquidation of the company will pay the second set of preferential payments out of the remaining assets of the company after that application.

The problem dealt with in the preceding paragraph does not arise of course, if the floating charge crystallises by a receiver being appointed or in any other way after the company has already gone into liquidation. The preferential creditors at the date when the company went into liquidation are then entitled to payment out of the assets comprised in the floating charge and the company's other assets not subject to specific or fixed mortgages or charges,[16] and there will be only one set of preferential claims to be satisfied by the liquidator.

It has been held by the Court of Appeal that if a charge created as a floating charge crystallises on a company going into liquidation, not only the preferential debts and claims against the company, but also the expenses of the liquidation, are payable out of the assets comprised in the floating charge in priority to the amount secured by the charge, whether those assets are realised by the liquidator or by a receiver appointed under the floating charge after the winding up order is made or the winding up resolution is passed,[17] but the correctness of the decision is questionable. On the other hand, if the floating charge crystallises before the company goes into liquidation, it has been held that only preferential payments calculated up to the date when a receiver is appointed, or when the holders of the floating charge or their trustees take possession of the company's assets, are payable out of the assets comprised in the floating charge at that time or subsequently in priority to the debt secured by the charge,[18] and not also the expenses of the liquidation of the company. This would appear still to be correct. Furthermore, it has been held that if a floating charge crystallises by the company going into liquidation, the costs and expenses of the liquidator in applying unsuccessfully to set the floating charge aside under the provisions of the Insolvency Act 1986, do not rank as an expense of the liquidation, and so are not payable out of the company's assets in priority to the amount secured by the floating charge.[19]

Preferential claims have no priority for payment out of assets of a company which are comprised in a fixed or specific mortgage or charge, and so a secured creditor who has both a fixed and a floating charge over different assets of the company may satisfy the amount owing to him out of the assets subject to the fixed charge (so far as

16 Insolvency Act 1986, s 175(1) and (2) and s 387(3).
17 *Re Barleycorn Enterprises Ltd* [1970] Ch 465, [1970] 2 All ER 155.
18 Companies Act 1985, s 196(1) to (3); Insolvency Act 1986, s 40(1) and (2), s 251 and s 386(1); *Re Christonette International Ltd* [1982] 3 All ER 225, [1982] 1 WLR 1245, not followed in *Re Portbase (Clothing) Ltd* [1993] 3 All ER 829, [1993] BCLC 796.
19 *Re MC Bacon Ltd* [1991] Ch 127 [1990] BCC 430.

they are sufficient for the purpose) without having to account to the company's preferential creditors.[20] Likewise, the holder of a floating charge over assets of a company who is entitled to priority over a later fixed charge on certain of those assets in favour of another person who takes that charge with knowledge of a provision in the instrument creating a fixed charge which prohibits the company from creating later mortgages or charges ranking in priority to the floating charge, can, by relying by way of subrogation on the fixed charge to which he has priority, recover the amount owed by the company to him (not exceeding the amount secured by the fixed charge) free from the claims of the company's preferential creditors.[1] Likewise, if the fixed charge is itself charged by the person entitled to it with payment of the amount secured by the floating charge, the holder of the floating charge can enforce the fixed charge for his own benefit by way of subrogation, and may recover the amount owing to him out of the proceeds of realisation of that charge (so far as they are sufficient) without having to account to the company's preferential creditors.[1] This is not so, however, if the holder of the fixed charge and the floating charge merely agree that the amount secured by the floating charge shall be paid out of the proceeds of realisation of the company's assets on which the fixed charge is secured in priority to the amount secured by the fixed charge; in that situation the preferential claims are payable in priority out of the proceeds of realisation to the extent of the amount secured by the floating charge.[2]

The categories of preferential debts

There are eight categories of debts and liabilities of a company in a liquidation which rank as preferential debts.[3] References in the categories to the 'relevant date' are to the date of the winding up order or resolution under which the company is being wound up; but if a winding up order is made after the company has resolved to be wound up voluntarily, or is made immediately after the court discharges an administration order in respect of the company,

---

20 *Re Lewis Merthyr Consolidated Collieries Ltd* [1929] 1 Ch 498.
 1 *Re Woodroffes (Musical Instruments) Ltd* [1986] Ch 366, [1985] BCLC 227; *Griffiths v Yorkshire Bank plc* [1994] 1 WLR 1427.
 2 *Re Portbase Clothing Ltd* [1993] BCLC 796, [1993] BCC 96.
 3 Insolvency Act 1986, s 386(1) and s 387(3) and Sch 6. If after a petition for a winding up order is presented against a company which is not already in voluntary liquidation, a provisional liquidator is appointed, the 'relevant date' is the date on which the provisional liquidator is appointed.

references to the 'relevant date' are to the date of the voluntary winding up resolution or the date of the administration order (as the case may be).[3]

The eight classes of preferential debts are as follows:

(1) sums due from the company to the Inland Revenue at the relevant date for deductions of income tax which were made, or should have been made, from remuneration or pensions paid by the company during the preceding period of 12 months to persons employed or formerly employed by the company or their dependants, and also similar deductions which the company made, or should have made, from remuneration paid to sub-contractors engaged by it to do building or construction work;[4]

(2) value added tax and insurance premium tax payable by the company which is attributable to the period of six months preceding the relevant date (the amount of tax for an accounting period partly before and partly after the commencement of the six-month period being apportioned on a time basis for this purpose);[5]

(3) car tax, general betting duty, pool betting duty, bingo duty, gaming licence duty and lottery duty becoming due from the company within 12 months before the relevant date and excise duty on beer and air passenger duty becoming due within six months before the relevant date;[6]

(4) contributions under the Social Security Contributions and Benefits Act 1992, in respect of employees of the company, which became due within 12 months before the relevant date;[7]

(5) contributions owing by the company under the Pension Schemes Act 1993, in respect of an occupational pension scheme or as premiums under the state pension scheme which became due within 12 months before the relevant date;[8]

(6) remuneration owing by the company to employees or former employees of the company in respect of the period of four months preceding the relevant date (including remuneration payable to employees during a holiday period or a period of sickness), but not exceeding in total in respect of any one person such amount as is prescribed for the time being by the

---

4 Insolvency Act 1986, s 386(1) and Sch 6, paras 1 and 2.
5 Ibid, Sch 6, paras 3 and 3A (inserted by Finance Act 1994, s 40(2) and Sch 6, para 13(1)).
6 Ibid, Sch 6, paras 4, 5, 5A, 5B and 5C (as amended by Finance Act 1991, Sch 2 and Finance Act 1993, s 36(2)).
7 Ibid, Sch 6, para 6.
8 Ibid, Sch 6, para 8.

Secretary of State (at present £800); accrued holiday remuneration owing by the company to employees whose employment has been terminated before, on or after the relevant date where the holiday remuneration relates to a period of employment before the relevant date, and also holiday remuneration which would have accrued to such employees if their employment had continued until they became entitled to it, and additionally, any amounts owing by the company in respect of money advanced to enable it to pay remuneration or accrued holiday remuneration to employees or former employees which would have been a preferential debt if it had not been paid out of the advance;[9]

(7) any amounts owing by the company to employees or former employees in respect of certain payments claimed by them under the Employment Protection (Consolidation) Act 1978, or the Trade Union and Labour Relations (Consolidation) Act 1992 for the period of four months preceding the relevant date, but not exceeding in respect of any one person the amount for the time being prescribed by the Secretary of State; these payments are guaranteed remuneration for days on which an employee had no work to do, remuneration for days on which an employee was suspended from working on medical grounds, payments for time taken off by an employee in connection with trade union duties, while looking for work or (in the case of a female employee) while undergoing ante-natal care and remuneration payable under a protective award of an industrial tribunal to an employee who has been dismissed as redundant; and additionally, any amounts owing by the company in respect of moneys advanced to enable it to make such payments to an employee or former employee, in so far as the payments would have been preferential debts if they had not been paid;[10] and

(8) any amount which the company has before or after the relevant date been ordered to pay to employees or former employees under the Reserve Forces (Safeguard of Employment) Act 1985, or which it has been so ordered to pay in respect of defaults by the company under that legislation before the relevant date.[11]

In addition to the above claims, the claim to reimbursement of certain payments made by the Secretary of State for Employment to

9 Ibid, Sch 6, paras 9 to 11, para 14(2) and para 15(a).
10 Ibid, Sch 6, paras 9, para 11 and para 13(1) and (2).
11 Ibid, Sch 6, para 12.

employees of the company on its failure to pay them itself ranks equally with those claims as a preferential debt in a company's liquidation.[12] These payments comprise wages or salary for up to eight weeks; remuneration payable during the period after a notice of resignation or dismissal has been given by or to any employee, or the period for which the company should have given such a notice of dismissal; up to six weeks' holiday pay in respect of a holiday period or periods to which any employee was entitled during the 12 months preceding the relevant date; the amount of any basic award of compensation for unfair dismissal made by an industrial tribunal in favour of any employee; and amounts which employees of the company could claim as preferential payments under paragraph (7) above, but which have in fact been paid by the Secretary of State.[13]

The Secretary of State for Employment's indemnity claim is a preferential one only to the extent that the employees who have been paid by him would themselves have had preferential claims under paragraphs (6) and (7) above if the Secretary of State had not paid them.[14] This means that preferential claims by an employee and the Secretary of State under paragraph (6) in respect of unpaid remuneration cannot together exceed the amount for the time being prescribed by the Secretary of State (at present £800). Furthermore, the Secretary of State can claim priority only for payments made by him which would themselves have been preferential claims by the employee if they had not been paid by the Secretary of State.[14] An indemnity claim in respect of remuneration for a period while a notice of dismissal or resignation was running and a payment by the Secretary of State of a basic award for unfair dismissal are therefore not preferential claims at all. When the Secretary of State has a preferential claim, the employee's own preferential claims under paragraphs (6) and (7) above is replaced by the Secretary of State's preferential claim.[15] This means that the dividends payable by the liquidator in respect of the employee's and the Secretary of State's claims must be distributed so that the total amount of the preferential claims by the employee and the Secretary of State together are not increased to more than the employee's original preferential claim.[15]

---

12 Employment Protection (Consolidation) Act 1978, s 125(1) to (2A) (as amended by Employment Act 1989 s 19(1) and (2)) (16 *Halsbury's Statutes* (4th edn) 352.

13 Employment Protection (Consolidation) Act 1978, s 122(3) and (4) (as amended by Employment Act 1989, s 21(2) and Sch 3, Part I, para 4).

14 Employment Protection (Consolidation) Act 1978, s 125(2) and (2A) (substituted by Employment Act 1989, s 19(1)).

15 Employment Protection (Consolidation) Act 1978, s 125(2A) (substituted by Employment Act 1989, s 19(1)).

Application of the preferential debt rules

A surety for a debt of the company which would have been preferential if the surety had not paid it, is entitled to be subrogated to the rights which the creditor would have had, and the surety can claim an indemnity in the liquidation of the company as a preferential creditor for the amount which he has paid.[16] On the other hand, a person who lends money to a company which later goes into liquidation is not generally entitled to treat his loan as a preferential debt merely because it was made to enable the company to pay a debt or debts which would otherwise have been preferential, or merely because the company in fact uses the loan to pay such a debt or debts.

The one exception to this is where the loan is made so that the company may pay employees' or former employees' remuneration or accrued holiday remuneration or any of the other amounts which employees may claim as preferential payments in their capacity of employees.[17] The terms of the preference for the lender in this case have been altered slightly as compared with the former law. Formerly, the lender could claim the amount advanced by him as preferential to the extent that the employees' own preferential claim was diminished by payments made out of the advance,[18] whereas under the Insolvency Act 1986, the loan is now preferential to the extent that the amount owed to the employees which has been paid out of the loan would itself have been preferential.[19] Consequently, under the present law if the company owes an employee an amount for remuneration or accrued holiday remuneration or any of the other amounts which could rank as preferential payments, and any such amount would have been partly preferential and partly an ordinary debt (eg arrears of remuneration greater than the maximum claimable as preferential or for a period longer than four months before the relevant date), payments made by the company to the employee out of the loan are treated as being applied primarily toward satisfying the preferential part of the employee's claim, so as to preserve the preferential status of the part of the loan which is so applied, whereas formerly the lender could claim preference only for the part of his loan which reduced the total amount owed to the employee to below the maximum limit of the preferential claim which he would otherwise have had.

16 *Re Lamplugh Iron Ore Co Ltd* [1927] 1 Ch 308.
17 Insolvency Act 1986, s 386(1) and Sch 6, paras 9 to 11 and para 13(1) and (2).
18 Companies Act 1985, Sch 19, para 13.
19 Insolvency Act 1986, s 386(1) and Sch 6, para 11.

A loan need not be made exclusively for the purpose of paying remuneration or accrued holiday remuneration or other amounts to employees which rank as preferential in order that the loan shall rank as preferential, provided that the lender agrees that the loan may be used for one or more of those purposes. Consequently, where a bank allowed a company to overdraw on its current account for its general business purposes (including the payment of wages and salaries to its employees), it was held that the bank could claim preference in the company's liquidation for drawings on the account which were in fact used by the company to pay remuneration to employees which would have been preferential if it had remained unpaid.[20]

Difficult problems can arise in this connection when a company has had several accounts with the same bank, and the debit balance on one or more of the accounts when the company goes into liquidation could rank as a preferential claim because it comprises advances made to enable the company to pay remuneration or holiday remuneration to its employees, or to make other payments to them which would rank as preferential if they had not been paid. If the company has had a separate account with its bank to which drawings to enable the company to pay wages and salaries or other payments to employees which are potentially preferential in a liquidation are debited, and one or more other accounts some or all of which are in credit when the company goes into liquidation, a balance must be struck on all the accounts taken together, and if the net debit balance is less than the amount overdrawn on the account which is used for making payments to employees which, if not advanced by the bank, would be preferential payments, the bank may claim preference only for that net debit balance.[1] On the other hand, the fact that the company has had a separate account with the bank to which potentially preferential payments to employees are debited, does not limit the advances which the bank can treat as made to enable the company to pay preferential remuneration, and so if the company has drawn on one of its other accounts to pay wages and salaries or other payments to employees which, if not paid, would have been preferential, or if the debit balance on the account designated for the payment of employees' remuneration has been reduced by the bank periodically making transfers from the amounts standing to the credit of the company's other account or accounts, the whole of the net debit balance on all of the company's accounts which represents drawings to pay remuneration or other payments to employees which would have been preferential if they

20 *Re Primrose (Builders) Ltd* [1950] Ch 561, [1950] 2 All ER 334; *Re Rampgill Mill Ltd* [1967] Ch 1138, [1967] 1 All ER 56.
1 *Re E J Morel (1934) Ltd* [1962] Ch 21, [1961] 1 All ER 796.

had remained unpaid may be claimed by the bank as a preferential debt in the company's liquidation.[2]

If a company has two accounts with its bank both of which have debit balances when it goes into liquidation, and it also has a third account which has a credit balance, it has been held that the credit balance must be applied first to reduce or eliminate that part of the debit balance which would rank as a preferential debt for remuneration or other payments to employees in the company's liquidation (ie the preferential part of the debit balance on the account designated for the payment of employees' remuneration), so leaving a net balance owing to the bank which consists primarily of the bank's non-preferential claim.[1] On the other hand, it has more recently been held that the credit balance on the third account must be apportioned between the debit balances which represent advances to the company to enable it to make payments to its employees which would have been preferential debts if they had remained unpaid, and the amount of those debit balances which represent other advances.[3] It would, nevertheless, appear that the company and the bank may effectively agree before the company goes into liquidation that any credit balance on an account of the company with the bank shall be appropriated so as to reduce the debit balances on any other of the company's accounts with the bank in a manner different from the way in which it would be applied under whichever of the two judicial decisions mentioned above is correct.

If a company has two or more bank accounts with debit balances when it goes into liquidation and both or all the debit balances are secured by a mortgage or charge to the bank, it has been held that the bank can apply the proceeds of sale of the property comprised in the security in whatever order it chooses in the absence of an agreement to the contrary.[4] Consequently, the bank may apply the proceeds of sale primarily in discharging the debit balance which does not represent an amount for which the bank could make a preferential claim in the liquidation of the company, so as to preserve as much as possible of the bank's preferential claim which the proceeds of sale are not sufficient to discharge.[4]

Preferential debts and distraints

If a landlord or other person has distrained on goods of a company within three months before a winding up order is made against it,

2 *Re James R Rutherford & Sons Ltd* [1964] 3 All ER 137, [1964] 1 WLR 1211.
3 *Re Unit 2 Windows Ltd* [1985] 3 All ER 647, [1985] 1 WLR 1383.
4 *Re William Hall (Contractors) Ltd* [1967] 2 All ER 1150, [1967] 1 WLR 948.

preferential debts in the company's liquidation are charged on the goods distrained and the proceeds of selling them if the company's other assets are insufficient to satisfy its preferential debts in full.[5] The goods and proceeds of sale are expressed to be charged with these debts 'for the benefit of the company',[5] which appears to mean that the charge is treated as part of the company's assets in the liquidation, and that the charge may be enforced by the liquidator, but not by the preferential creditors individually. The person who has distrained is subrogated to the rights of the company's preferential creditors in the liquidation to the extent that their claims are satisfied out of the distrained goods or the proceeds of selling them,[6] and it has been held (probably incorrectly) that this means that such proceeds must be distributed rateably between the preferential creditors and the person who has distrained in proportion to their respective claims.[7]

The provision creating a charge over distrained goods and the proceeds of selling them does not apply in a voluntary liquidation,[8] and the only power which the court has in such a liquidation is to order that a distress which was levied before the passing of the winding up resolution shall not be completed by a sale of the distrained goods thereafter, or that a distress shall not be levied after that time.[9]

Deferred debts

There are four classes of debts of a company which are deferred for payment in a liquidation until all its other debts and liabilities have been satisfied in full. These classes of debts are as follows, and (apart from classes (1) and (2) which rank equally as between themselves) they rank as between themselves in the order in which they are set out, and not rateably, as do preferential debts:

(1)   the amount of loans made to the company at a rate of interest varying with the profits of the company, or in consideration of a share of the company's profits in lieu of interest, plus any interest or share of profits so accruing; also the amount of any profits of the company to which the seller of the goodwill of

5 Insolvency Act 1986, s 176(1) and (2).
6 Ibid, s 176(3).
7 *Re Memco Engineering Ltd* [1986] Ch 86, [1985] 3 All ER 267.
8 *Herbert Berry Associates Ltd v IRC* [1978] 1 All ER 161, [1977] 1 WLR 1437.
9 *Re Roundwood Colliery Co* [1897] 1 Ch 373.

a business to the company is entitled as consideration for the sale;[10]

(2) amounts payable under an order of the court in respect of profits made from carrying on investment business without proper authorisation under the Financial Services Act 1986, or from carrying on such business in contravention of certain provisions of the Act or of rules or regulations made under it;[11] and amounts payable under an order of the court in respect of profits made from taking deposits in the course of carrying on a deposit-taking business without authorisation from the Bank of England,[12] but claims for damages or compensation in those situations are not deferred;[13]

(3) any amount payable by the company to the holders of its redeemable shares or of shares in itself which it has lawfully purchased where the date agreed for the redemption or payment of the purchase price is not later than the commencement of the company's liquidation, and the company has at some time since that date had profits available for distribution at least equal to the amount payable to the holders of such shares; amounts falling under this head are payable in the company's liquidation only after all its other debts and liabilities (other than those payable to its members as such) have been paid in full;[14]

(4) amounts due to members of the company in their character as members by way of profits, dividends or otherwise;[15] such amounts are payable only after all other debts and liabilities of the company have been paid in full, but before the capital paid up on the company's issued shares is repaid to shareholders; the debts within this category comprise advance payments to the company made by the holders of partly paid shares before the capital unpaid on them is called up or falls due for payment together with interest thereon,[16] and also dividends declared in respect of shares or falling due for

10 Partnership Act 1890, s 2(3)(*d*) and (*e*) and s 3 (32 *Halsbury's Statutes* (4th edn) 638); Insolvency Rules 1986, r 12.3(2A)(*c*).

11 Financial Services Act 1986, s 6(3) and s 61(3) (30 *Halsbury's Statutes* (4th edn) 173 and 234).

12 Banking Act 1987, s 49(1) (4 *Halsbury's Statutes* (4th edn) 582).

13 Insolvency Rules 1986, r 12.3(2A)(*a*) and (*b*).

14 Companies Act 1985, s 178(3) to (6).

15 Insolvency Act 1986, s 74(2)(*f*).

16 *Re Exchange Drapery Co* (1888) 38 Ch D 171. Such payments are in practice never made at present because of the universal practice of making the issue price of shares payable in full on or shortly after allotment.

payment without a declaration before the commencement of the company's liquidation,[17] unless the unpaid dividends have by agreement with the members to whom they are owing been recognised by the company as money retained by it on loan from the members, in which case they rank as ordinary and not deferred debts.[18] Claims against the company for damages or compensation by subscribers for its shares who were induced to subscribe by misrepresentations or non-disclosure of material facts for which the company is responsible are claims by members in their capacity as such, and are therefore deferred in the company's liquidation[19] but not claims for damages for misrepresentation made by the company to the claimant in connection with the acquisition of shares in the company under a takeover offer made by the claimant to the company's existing shareholders.[20]

Wholly apart from statutory provisions for the deferment of certain debts and claims for payment in a company's liquidation, contractual provisions for the postponement of subordination of certain debts to payment of all other claims in the debtor company's liquidation, or subordination to certain categories of such other claims, are effective, whether the contractual arrangements are made by the company with a trustee acting on behalf of the persons who are bound by the subordination arrangements, or directly by the company with those persons themselves,[1] and the liquidator must satisfy the claims of its subordinated and other creditors out of the company's assets in accordance with those arrangements.

Such arrangements do not conflict with the rule invalidating contractual provisions which purport to modify the statutory rule that debts and liabilities of a company in liquidation must be paid rateably out of its assets, except where legislation otherwise provides.[2] This is because the rule applies only where a claimant seeks to rely on such a contractual modification of the rule in his own favour,[2] and contractual postponement or subordination arrangements do not have that effect, but merely subject the contracting party's claim to the prior satisfaction of the claims of other creditors; the fact that

17 *Re Consolidated Goldfields of New Zealand Ltd* [1953] Ch 689, [1953] 1 All ER 791.
18 *Re L B Holliday & Co Ltd* [1986] BCLC 227, 2 BCC 99, 31.
19 *Re Addlestone Linoleum Co* (1887) 37 Ch D 191.
20 *Soden v British and Commonwealth Holdings plc* [1996] 2 BCLC 207, affd [1997] BCC 249.
 1 *Re British and Commonwealth Holdings plc (No 3)* [1992] BCLC 322, [1992] BCC 58; *Re Maxwell Communications plc (No 2)* [1994] 1 BCLC 1, *(No 3)* [1993] BCC 369.
 2 *British Eagle International Airlines Ltd v Compagnie Nationale Air France* [1975] 2 All ER 390, [1975] 1 WLR 758.

the other creditors benefit by the operation of the subordination arrangements does not affect their validity, because the other creditors have no contractual right to be paid first out of the company's assets, but receive prior payment merely in consequence of the restrictions undertaken by the subordinated creditors on the right which they would otherwise have to payment rateably with the company's other creditors.

SET-OFF IN A LIQUIDATION

Nature of set-off

The rule under the general law by which each of two parties who have claims against each other may, subject to certain conditions, set off the amount of his claim against the other one and either claim or tender the difference in full settlement, is extended in the winding up of an insolvent company so that almost all mutual claims between the company and the other party may be set off, and a proof for the net balance may be made by the other party if the balance is in his favour, or the net balance may be recovered by the liquidator from the other party in the converse situation.

The rule under the general law permits parties who have claims against each other to set them off only if both claims are for debts or other liquidated sums which are immediately due and payable, or if both claims are for liquidated or unliquidated amounts arising under the same or related contracts and both claims are immediately recoverable by action.[3] On the other hand, the wider insolvency rule applies in a liquidation when there have been mutual credits, mutual debts or other mutual dealings between an insolvent company and a claimant against it before a winding up order was made or a winding up resolution was passed in respect of the company, and the rule requires an account to be taken of the amount due from each party to the other in respect of such mutual dealings and a set-off effected between them.[4] Only the balance of the mutual claims may be proved in the liquidation or recovered by the liquidator, as the case may be.[5] However, an amount due from the company to the other party may not be included in the set-off if the other party had

3 *British Anzani (Felixstowe) Ltd v International Marine Management (UK) Ltd* [1980] QB 137, [1979] 2 All ER 1063; *McDonald's Restaurants Ltd v Urbandivide Co Ltd* [1994] 1 BCLC 306.
4 Insolvency Rules 1986, r 4.90(1) and (2).
5 Ibid, r 4.90(4).

notice at the time when the amount became due that a petition had been presented for the winding up of the company, or that a meeting had been called to pass a resolution for its voluntary winding up.[6]

The effect of the insolvency set-off rule is normally to benefit the claimant against the company, because to the extent that he sets off the amount which the company is entitled to claim from him against the amount which he is entitled to claim from the company, he recovers the amount which he claims in full, and his loss is limited to the amount by which any surplus of his claim which is not set off exceeds the dividend which the liquidator pays in respect of that surplus. The only situation in which the set-off rule operates to the advantage of the company is where the person who has a claim against it is more insolvent than the company, so that the cost to the company of paying the dividend which its liquidator declares in respect of the whole of the claim against it, less the amount of the dividend which the company would receive in the claimants' insolvency in respect of the whole of its claim against him, would exceed the amount which the company would pay to the claimant by operating the insolvency set-off rule. There is, in fact, no choice about the application of the rule for either the claimant or the company. The insolvency set-off rule, unlike the general set-off rule, is mandatory and cannot be contracted out of by the parties; furthermore, in the liquidation of an insolvent company the insolvency set-off rule supersedes the set-off arrangements which would otherwise apply between the parties under the general law or under a contract between them.[7]

Claims which may be set off

Requirement of mutuality

A claim of a person against a company in liquidation must be set off against a claim which the company has against him if there have been mutual debts between them (ie each owes the other a liquidated sum, whether payable immediately or not), or if they have given credit to each other (ie each has contracted to allow the other to pay a liquidated sum which he owes at a deferred date or by instalments over an agreed period, or to pay the amount or only on the fulfilment of agreed conditions or contingencies), or if they have had mutual

6 Insolvency Rules 1986, r 4.90(3).
7 *National Westminster Bank Ltd v Halesowen Presswork and Assemblies Ltd* [1972] AC 785, [1972] 1 All ER 641; *Coca Cola Financial Corpn v Finsat International Ltd* [1996] 2 BCLC 626.

dealings giving rise to liabilities to each other (ie if there have been transactions in which they were both interested and liabilities between them have been incurred under any one or more of those transactions).

The broadest ground for set-off is, of course, the third one, mutual dealings, which includes the other two grounds and is itself more extensive than both of them. Consequently, it has been held that a set-off in insolvency is possible on this ground when there is no contractual relationship between the parties, but they both have interests in a single transaction, for example, where they are the acceptor and indorsee of a bill of exchange.[8] Set-off is also possible on this ground when there are contractual or non-contractual liabilities of the parties to each other under different transactions, for example, where there are mutual statutory liabilities under different statutory provisions.[9] Furthermore, although it is necessary that the mutual liabilities which it is sought to set off should have arisen before a winding up order is made or a winding up resolution is passed in respect of the insolvent company, it is not necessary that the liabilities should be for liquidated amounts (eg a liability for damages for breach of contract or tort may be set off),[10] nor that they should be immediately due and enforceable (eg a liability for amounts payable in the future may be set off),[11] nor that the liabilities should be unconditional and indefeasible (eg a contractual liability which will accrue only if an agreed contingency occurs, or which will cease to exist if a condition is fulfilled, may be set off.)[12] Where it is sought to set off a claim for a sum payable at a future date, the amount of the claim may be appropriately discounted to ascertain its value at the date when the company goes into liquidation, and that value should be used for the purpose of effecting a set-off.[13] Similarly, an estimate of the value of a contingent or conditional claim at the date when the company goes into liquidation should be taken for the purpose of set-off if the contingency has not occurred or the condition has not yet been fulfilled, but if the claim is against the company (and not against the other party) and the condition or contingency is fulfilled before the set-off is effected, the claim must be valued as at the date when that occurs (ie at the amount to which the claimant is now immediately entitled).[13]

8 *McKinnon v Armstrong Bros & Co* (1877) 2 App Cas 531.
9 *Re D H Curtis (Builders) Ltd* [1978] Ch 162, [1978] 2 All ER 183.
10 *Eberle's Hotels and Restaurant Co v Jonas* (1887) 18 QBD 459; *Re Daintrey, ex p Mant* [1900] 1 QB 546.
11 *Eberle's Hotels and Restaurant Co v Jonas*, supra.
12 *Sovereign Life Assurance Co v Dodd* [1892] 2 QB 573; *Re National Benefit Assurance Co Ltd* [1924] 2 Ch 339; *Re City Life Assurance Co Ltd* [1926] Ch 191.
13 *Stein v Blake* [1995] 2 BCLC 94, [1995] BCC 543.

Because of the wide range of mutual claims which must be set off against each other in the winding up of an insolvent company, the reference in the relevant legislation to an account being taken of what is 'due' from each party to the other, and to the sums 'due' from one party being set off against the sums 'due' to him,[14] cannot be taken in the literal sense of calling for the set-off only of liquidated sums immediately due and payable between the parties; if this were so, the insolvency set-off rule would be narrower even than the set-off rule under the general law. The use of the word 'due' must be construed in the context of the insolvency set-off operation, namely, the set-off of liabilities between the parties arising from 'mutual credits, mutual debts or other mutual dealings';[15] and the reference to sums shown as 'due' from each party to the other by the account which is directed to be taken must mean the amounts which are debited to each party in the account after their mutual liabilities have been properly valued. This conclusion is reinforced by the provision that only the balance shown by the account shall be proved in the liquidation or paid to the liquidator (as the case may be),[16] because it is the present values, and not the nominal amounts of the mutual claims, which are set off in the account.

Cross-claims must exist when the company goes into liquidation

Although the insolvency set-off rule requires liabilities to pay sums in the future and conditional and contingent claims to be brought into account, it is essential that the claims should exist when the company goes into liquidation, and that they should then be vested in the person who seeks to prove in the liquidation and in the company respectively. A surety for a debt owed by the company to a third person does not acquire a right to be paid the amount of the debt by the company, unless and until he has himself paid the debt in full to the creditor. Consequently, whether the debt becomes due to the creditor before or after the company goes into liquidation, the surety cannot by paying it to the creditor after the company has gone into liquidation acquire a right to set off a debt which he owed the company before it was wound up against his claim against the company for an indemnity.[17]

It is true that a surety also has an equitable right to be indemnified by the company immediately the guaranteed debt becomes due to

---

14 Insolvency Rules 1986, r 4.90(1) and (2).
15 Ibid, r 4.90(1).
16 Ibid, r 4.90(4).
17 *Re Fenton, ex p Fenton Textile Association Ltd* [1931] 1 Ch 85; *Re Cushla Ltd* [1979] 3 All ER 415.

the creditor, but this is merely a right for the surety to have the company pay the amount of the debt to the creditor or to have the company make that amount available in order to pay the creditor, and not a right of the surety to have the company pay that amount to himself; moreover, the surety's equitable right arises only when he calls on the company for an indemnity.[18] A surety who has not paid the debt to the creditor before the liquidation, therefore, cannot improve his position by relying on his right to an indemnity from the company, and he cannot set off against the amount of the indemnity a liability of his own to the company which existed before it went into liquidation.[19]

If liabilities are to be set off in the liquidation of a company, the liabilities must not only exist when the company goes into liquidation, but the corresponding rights to enforce them must be vested in the company and the other party at that time. Consequently, a person who is indebted to a company before it goes into liquidation cannot set off against his indebtedness a debt then owed by the company to a third person which the debtor later acquires by assignment from that third person, because the company's debtor has no right to recover that acquired debt from the company when it goes into liquidation.[20] For the same reason, a creditor of the company before it goes into liquidation cannot set off a debt which he incurs to it under a contract made with its liquidator (eg a contract to purchase assets of the company), because the debt owed to the company of necessity arises only after it had gone into liquidation.[1] On the other hand, the right of a debtor of the company in liquidation to set off a claim he has against it which arose before the company went into liquidation is not destroyed by the liquidator assigning the debt which the debtor owes to the company, and the debtor can exercise the same right of set-off against the assignee from the liquidator as he could exercise in the winding up of the company itself.[2]

Inability to set off secured debts

Set-off of mutual claims in the liquidation of a company is effected only where the claimant against the company proves for the debt which is to be set off against the company's claim against him.

---

18 *Ascherson v Tredegar Dry Dock and Wharf Co Ltd* [1909] 2 Ch 401; *Thomas v Nottingham Incorporated Football Club Ltd* [1972] Ch 596, [1972] 1 All ER 1176.
19 *Re a Debtor (No 66 of 1955)* [1956] 3 All ER 225, [1956] 1 WLR 1226.
20 *Re Milan Tramways Co, ex p Theys* (1884) 25 Ch D 587.
 1 *Sankey Brook Coal Co v Marsh* (1871) LR 6 Exch 185; *Ince Hall Rolling Mills Co v Douglas Forge Co* (1882) 8 QBD 179.
 2 *Farley v Housing and Commercial Developments Ltd* [1984] BCLC 442, 1 BCC 99, 150; *Stein v Blake* [1995] 2 BCLC 94, [1995] BCC 543.

Consequently, if a creditor of the company is owed two debts by it, one of which is secured, and the creditor proves in the company's liquidation only for the unsecured debt, the liquidator cannot recover the amount by which a debt which the creditor owes the company exceeds the creditor's unsecured claim by setting the excess off against the amount of the creditor's secured claim for which he has not proved, but relied instead on his security.[3]

The inapplicability of the insolvency set-off rule where the company or the claimant has a security for the claim sought to be set off, but there is no personal liability in respect of it, is clearly illustrated by two cases where shareholders of a company had secured a loan made to it by its bank, which later went into liquidation, by making deposits with the bank equal to the amount of the loan and charging the deposits to the bank.[4] It was held that, because the shareholders incurred no personal liability for the loan to the company (ie they did not guarantee its repayment to the bank), they could not set off the company's indebtedness to the bank against the amount of the deposits which they had made with the bank and so treat the company's indebtedness to the bank as discharged.[4] If the shareholders had given guarantees to the bank in respect of the loan made to the company, however, the amount for which they were liable to the bank under the guarantees would be set off against the amount of the deposits made by them with the bank in the liquidation of the bank.[5] These decisions produce the peculiar result that the company and its shareholders who make deposits with the bank to secure loans by it to the company are in a better position in the liquidation of the bank if the shareholders guarantee the company's indebtedness than if they do not.

Notice of winding up petition or meeting

The legislation governing set-off in the winding up of an insolvent company provides that 'sums due from the company to [the other party] shall not be included in the account [to be taken in respect of mutual liabilities] if that other party had notice at the time they became due that a meeting of creditors had been summoned ... or (as the case may be) a petition for the winding up of the company was pending.'[6] This provision is derived from the former bankruptcy

---

3 *Re Norman Holding Co Ltd* [1990] 3 All ER 757, [1991] 1 WLR 10.
4 *Re Bank of Credit and Commerce International SA (No 8)* [1994] 1 BCLC 758; affd [1996] 2 All ER 121, [1991] 2 BCLC 254; sub nom *Morris v Agrichemicals Ltd* [1996] BCC 204.
5 *M S Fashions Ltd v Bank of Credit and Commerce International SA* [1993] BCLC 280, [1992] BCC 571; *(No 2)* [1993] BCLC 1200, [1993] BCC 360.
6 Insolvency Rules 1986, r 4.90(3).

set-off rule, which precluded a creditor of the bankrupt from setting off the liability of the bankrupt to himself against a liability which he had incurred to the bankrupt if he had notice of an available act of bankruptcy committed by the bankrupt when the creditor gave credit to him,[7] and under the former law governing liquidations this rule was applied by analogy so as to preclude a creditor of a company from setting off his own liability to the company against a liability of the company to him if he had notice of a winding up petition having been presented against it or a meeting having been called to pass a winding up resolution when the company incurred the liability to him.[8]

In the present insolvency set-off rule, the word 'due' is not used in the sense of 'immediately due and payable', and in the present context it can only refer to the time when the obligation to the creditor was entered into by the company or the time when the company's liability to the claimant was incurred, that is, when the contract creating an obligation of the company to make a payment to the creditor was entered into (whether the payment was to be made immediately or at a future date, and whether the obligation was absolute or was conditional or contingent), or when the obligation of the company arose otherwise than under a contract (eg a statutory obligation), or when the tort or other wrong by the company was committed.[9] If the word 'due' were given a different meaning in the present context, namely, when the time performance of the company's obligation under a contract has arrived, a creditor who extended credit to the company at a time when no winding up petition had been presented against it and no meeting had been called to pass a winding up resolution, would be unable to set off the amount of the company's indebtedness or liability to him against the amount of his own liability to the company if before the time the credit given by the creditor to the company expired a winding up petition had been presented against the company, or a meeting had been called to pass a winding up resolution, and the creditor had become aware of it. This would produce an impractical result, and would deprive creditors of their normal rights as a result of something over which they had no control.

It is, of course, immaterial that at the time when the creditor or claimant incurred a liability to the company he was aware that a

---

7 Bankruptcy Act 1914, s 31.

8 *Re Eros Films Ltd* [1963] Ch 565, [1963] 1 All ER 383.

9 Insolvency Rules 1986, r 13.12(1) to (3). A liability of the company in tort is for the purposes of the liquidation deemed to be an unconditional obligation incurred by the company when the cause of action arose (Insolvency Rules 1986, r 13.12(2)).

winding up petition had been presented against it or that a meeting had been called to pass a winding up resolution. Consequently, if a creditor gives credit to a company before winding up proceedings are initiated and later purchases assets from it on deferred payment terms at a time when he is aware of a pending winding up petition, the creditor's right of set-off is not impaired if a winding up order is subsequently made, and the purchase by the creditor can then be attacked only as a voidable preference if the necessary features are present.[10]

The mutual claims must be pecuniary and held beneficially

Set-off is possible in the liquidation of a company only if the obligations or liabilities of the company and the creditor or claimant are both to pay a sum of money to the other party, whether the sum is liquidated or not. If the obligation on either side is to transfer, deliver or restore property in specie, no set-off is possible.[11] But if the claimant's obligation under his contract with the company can be construed as an obligation to return or deliver assets of the company in his possession or to account for their value at his option, he is free to satisfy his obligation by paying money, and is therefore entitled to set off a monetary liability of the company to himself.[12]

Nevertheless, whatever the claimant's obligation to the company may be, he cannot set off a monetary claim which he has against it if he holds money or property in trust for it or in a fiduciary capacity on its behalf (eg as an agent for the company), because the money or property then belongs to the company beneficially, and the claimant is under an obligation to restore or to account for it in specie or to pay its value to the company as money held in trust. This is the situation when money is paid or assets are transferred by the company to the claimant for a particular purpose which is not, or cannot be, fulfilled, such as the claimant, as an agent, paying debts which the company owes to third persons, or the claimant paying dividends to the company's shareholders but the dividends cease to be payable when the company goes into liquidation.[13] The claimant must then restore the money or assets intact to the company, and cannot retain any part of them to satisfy a claim of his own against the company. Similarly, a director of a company who without

---

10 See p 225, ante.
11 *Eberle's Hotels and Restaurant Co Ltd v Jonas* (1887) 18 QBD 459.
12 *Rolls Razor Ltd v Cox* [1967] 1 QB 552, [1967] 1 All ER 397.
13 *Re Mid-Kent Fruit Factory* [1896] 1 Ch 567; *Re City Equitable Insurance Co Ltd (No 2)* [1930] 2 Ch 293; *Barclays Bank Ltd v Quistclose Investments Ltd* [1970] AC 567, [1968] 3 All ER 651; *Carreras Rothmans Ltd v Freeman Mathews Treasure Ltd* [1985] Ch 207, [1985] 1 All ER 155.

authorisation appropriates money of the company to satisfy a claim by him for severance pay which he anticipates the company will contest, must repay the amount appropriated without setting off the justified amount of his claim (for which he must prove in the company's liquidation); the director holds the amount which he appropriated as a fiduciary for the company because the appropriation was not authorised by its board of directors or by the director's service contract.[14] In contrast to these situations where the person liable to the company acted as a fiduciary for it, if a mortgagee of property of a company sells it for a price which more than suffices to discharge the mortgage debt and the mortgagee's costs and expenses, the mortgagee is simply under a personal liability to account for the surplus proceeds of sale to the company, and he does not hold them in trust for it; consequently, he may in the company's liquidation set off another unsecured debt which the company owes to him against the surplus in his hands.[15]

Contractual arrangements for set-off

While it is a going concern, a company may agree to whatever arrangements it wishes either extending or limiting or negativing its own or the other contracting parties' rights of set-off under the general law in respect of transactions between them, and such arrangements are effective and cannot be set aside in the company's subsequent liquidation in so far as they have already been carried out.[16] This applies equally to multipartite settlement arrangements between the company and several other parties by which they each periodically calculate their net indebtedness or net credit position as regards all the other participants taken together, and pay or receive net sums in settlement.[17]

All such arrangements terminate, as far as the company is concerned, when it goes into liquidation, and the contractual arrangements are mandatorily replaced by the insolvency set-off rule described above, which operates bilaterally between the company and each of its creditors individually, and precludes the set-off under contractual arrangements made before the liquidation of the amounts of obligations or liabilities which become due for payment

14 *Zemco Ltd v Jerrom-Pugh* [1993] BCC 275.
15 *Re H E Thorne & Son Ltd* [1914] 2 Ch 438.
16 *National Westminster Bank Ltd v Halesowen Presswork and Assemblies Ltd* [1972] AC 785, [1972] 1 All ER 641.
17 *British Eagle International Air Lines Ltd v Cie Nationale Air France* [1975] 2 All ER 390, [1975] 1 WLR 758.

or fulfilment only after the company goes into liquidation.[18] Furthermore, the mandatory insolvency set-off rule also supersedes the contractual arrangements between the parties as regards their current liabilities to each other when the company goes into liquidation, in so far as the amount of those liabilities has not already been settled between them.[19]

SECURED DEBTS

Nature of a secured debt

A creditor of a company in liquidation is treated as having security for his debt or claim if he holds any of the forms of security recognised by law (other than a guarantee of the company's indebtedness by a third person),[20] and it is immaterial whether the security was created by agreement or arose by operation of law. Securities, therefore, comprise mortgages and charges over any kind of property (including agreements to create mortgages or charges, which take effect in equity as securities and are immediately effective on the assets intended to be subject to the security being acquired by the company); floating charges over the company's whole undertaking or any class or classes of its assets; pledges of goods or negotiable instruments and certain transportation documents in respect of goods (eg bills of lading, rail consignment notes and air waybills); common law possessory liens over goods on which the creditor has bestowed labour, or which the creditor has sold to the company for a price which remains unpaid; maritime liens for supplies of goods or services to a ship and for unpaid seamen's wages; equitable liens in favour of a seller of land for the unpaid purchase price and other equitable liens securing the rights of trustees, agents and other fiduciaries; and finally, the charge which a judgment creditor obtains over assets of the company which are taken in execution. It must be remembered, however, that certain securities may be invalidated if the company goes into liquidation in an insolvent condition, in particular, those created by way of preference of a creditor,[1] and charges arising by law on the levying of execution on the company's assets if the

---

18 See p 317, ante.
19 *Midland Banking Co v Chambers* (1869) 4 Ch App 398; *Re Rees, ex p National Provincial Bank of England* (1881) 17 Ch D 98.
20 *Re Printing and Numerical Registering Co* (1878) 8 Ch D 535, 538 per Jessel MR; *Re National United Investment Corpn* [1901] 1 Ch 950.
 1 See p 225, ante.

execution has not been completed before the commencement of the winding up.[2]

Options for secured creditors

Surrender of the security

A secured creditor may pursue any one of four courses of action in a company's liquidation. He may in the first place surrender his security to the liquidator, and prove in the liquidation as an unsecured creditor for the whole amount owed to him.[3] By doing this the creditor renounces his right to be paid out of the proceeds of sale of the assets of the company comprised in his security in priority to the company's unsecured creditors, and he ranks for payment of a dividend in the liquidation for the whole amount owed to him in the same way as other unsecured creditors, but preserves his right to claim his debt as a preferential one if he is entitled to do so by the Insolvency Act 1986.[4]

A secured creditor is unlikely to surrender his security in practice, unless it is valueless or impossible or difficult to realise, or unless it is difficult to put a value on it and its value in any case is bound to be small. A secured creditor is taken to have surrendered his security if he proves in the liquidation for the whole amount for which the security was given and does not include mention of his security in his proof; he may then later revise his proof so as to include his valuation of the security and adjust the amount of the proof to the excess of the amount owing to him by the company over his valuation of his security, but he may do this only if the court gives him permission to do so on the ground that the omission of mention of his security in his original proof was inadvertent or the result of honest mistake, and the court may impose terms on the secured creditor in giving its permission.[5]

Valuation of the security

A secured creditor may, as an alternative to surrendering his security, include particulars of it and his valuation of it in a proof which he submits to the liquidator, and may then prove in the winding up for the excess of the amount owing to him over his

2 See p 249, ante.
3 Insolvency Rules 1986, r 4.88(2).
4 See p 303, ante.
5 Insolvency Rules 1986, r 4.96(1) and (2).

valuation of the security.[6] If the liquidator considers that the creditor has undervalued his security and has consequently lodged a proof for too large an unsecured excess, the liquidator may give the creditor 28 days' notice of his intention to redeem the security at the creditor's valuation for the benefit of the company's unsecured creditors, and unless the creditor within 21 days after receiving the notice revalues his security at a higher amount than his original valuation, the liquidator may redeem the security by paying the creditor the amount of his original valuation; if the creditor revalues the security within 21 days, the liquidator may redeem the security by paying the amount of the higher revaluation, and no further opportunity is given to the creditor to revise his valuation again.[7] Conversely, a creditor who has valued his security in his original proof may at any time call on the liquidator to elect whether he will or will not redeem the security at the creditor's valuation, and if the liquidator does not notify the creditor within six months that he intends to redeem the security at that figure, he loses his right to do so, and may redeem the security only by paying the amount owed to the creditor for which the security was given.[8]

Under the former law, the liquidator's failure to redeem the security at the creditor's valuation within six months after the creditor called on him to elect whether to do so prevented the liquidator from redeeming the security at all thereafter, and so operated as an automatic foreclosure of the company's right of redemption and vested an absolute title to the property comprised in the security in the secured creditor.[9] This is no longer so, and the effect of the failure of the liquidator to redeem within the six-month period is merely that the liquidator must pay the secured creditor the full amount of the secured debt owed to him if the liquidator redeems the security later.[9] The exercise or non-exercise by the liquidator of his right to redeem the security at the creditor's valuation does not affect the validity of the creditor's proof for his estimate of the unsecured surplus; if the liquidator considers that the creditor's estimate is too low, he must reject the proof within six months after it is determined.

If in a winding up by the court a secured creditor has lodged with the liquidator a proof containing a valuation of his security, he may amend the valuation upwards or downwards and so decrease or increase his proof for the unsecured excess of the secured debt over his valuation; however, he may do this only if the liquidator or the

6 Ibid, r 4.75(1).
7 Ibid, r 4.97(1) and (2).
8 Ibid, r 4.97(4).
9 Companies Act 1985, s 612(1); Bankruptcy Act 1914, Sch 2, para 13.

court permits; if the creditor was the petitioner who obtained the order under which the company is being wound up and valued his security in his petition, or if the creditor[10] has voted at a creditors' meeting in respect of the unsecured surplus of the amount owed to him by the company, he may amend his valuation only if the court permits.[11] Moreover, in any case where the liquidator is dissatisfied with the creditor's valuation or re-valuation of the assets of the company comprised in his security, the liquidator may require the property comprised in the security to be sold in such manner as the parties agree or the court directs,[12] and the proceeds of sale (less the expenses of the sale) are then applied in paying the secured debt to the creditor and any surplus is paid to the liquidator, or if the proceeds of sale are insufficient to discharge the secured debt, the secured creditor may amend his proof so as to prove as an unsecured creditor for the deficiency.[13]

Realisation of the security or reliance on it

A secured creditor's third alternative course of action is to realise his security and discharge the secured debt and the costs of realisation (except costs unreasonably incurred or of an unreasonable amount)[14] out of the proceeds of sale (so far as possible) and then to prove as an unsecured creditor in the winding up for any deficiency.[15] This is so whether the secured creditor has previously valued his security in a proof lodged with the liquidator or not.[13] If the company is wound up by the court, the secured creditor will need to obtain leave of the court in order to bring proceedings to obtain possession of the property comprised in his security from the company or in order to obtain a court order for the sale of that property,[16] but leave will normally be given as a matter of course.[17]

The final alternative open to a secured creditor is to rely on his security as sufficient to cover the amount owing to him, and to defer

10 The winding up petition may contain a valuation of the creditor's security in order to indicate the amount by which the secured debt owed to the petitioner exceeds the value of the security, and so enable the petitioner to vote in respect of that excess at meetings of creditors. There is no obligation on the petitioner to value his security in the petition, however.
11 Insolvency Rules 1986, r 4.95(1) and (2).
12 Ibid, r 4.98(1) and (2).
13 Ibid, r 4.99.
14 *Gomba Holdings (UK) Ltd v Minories Finance Ltd (No 2)* [1993] BCLC 7, [1992] BCC 877.
15 Insolvency Rules 1986, r 4.88(1).
16 Insolvency Act 1986, s 130(2); (see p 78, ante).
17 *Re David Lloyd & Co* (1877) 6 Ch D 339; *Re Joshua Stubbs Ltd* [1891] 1 Ch 187; on appeal [1891] 1 Ch 475; *The Zafiro* [1960] P 1, [1959] 2 All ER 537.

realising his security until need arises or until he wishes to recover that amount plus accrued interest and costs. He will then not prove for any part of his debt in the liquidation, and if the liquidator wishes to recover the property free from the security, he must redeem it by paying the whole amount owing to the creditor which is secured on the property. The secured creditor will exercise this option in practice only if the value of his security is substantially more than the amount secured on it and is likely to continue to be more than that amount (including accruing interest) for the foreseeable future. The secured creditor does not commit himself to defer the realisation of his security by not exercising his power of realisation for a particular length of time, and so subject to the limitation provisions mentioned below,[18] he may exercise his powers of realisation whenever he wishes.

Secured interest

A secured creditor may recover interest at the agreed rate calculated up to the date when he receives the proceeds of realisation of his security by paying himself such interest as well as the principal of the secured debt out of the proceeds of realisation. Similarly, if the liquidator seeks to redeem the security at the secured creditor's valuation or on the liquidator's own initiative, the secured creditor is entitled to be paid interest at the agreed rate calculated up to the date of redemption. But if a secured creditor of an insolvent company proves in its liquidation for the whole amount owing to him, or for the excess of that amount over the value of the property comprised in his security, his proof may only include interest at the agreed rate calculated up to the date of the winding up order or resolution.[19]

Because of this limitation on the amount of interest for which a proof may be lodged, a secured creditor who realises his security is required to appropriate the proceeds of sale primarily in paying the principal of the secured debt and interest calculated up to the date of the winding up order or resolution, so that any deficiency of the proceeds of realisation to satisfy the total amount owing to him will consist primarily of interest for the period after the commencement of the liquidation, which cannot be proved in the liquidation as an unsecured debt.[20] This does not necessarily mean that the secured

---

18 See p 331, post.
19 Insolvency Rules 1986, r 4.93(1); (see p 289, ante).
20 *Re London, Windsor and Greenwich Hotels Co, Quartermaine's Case* [1892] 1 Ch 639.

creditor loses all the interest on the secured debt for the period following the commencement of the liquidation, however, because if the proceeds of realisation are sufficient to satisfy the whole or part of such interest after discharging the principal of the secured debt and interest calculated to the date of the winding up order or resolution, the proceeds may be applied for that purpose.

The limitation period

It has already been observed that the limitation period for recovering unsecured debts and liabilities of a company in liquidation does not continue to run after the commencement of the winding up, and that the debt and claims are extinguished, and so excluded from proof, only if the limitation period in respect of them has expired before that time.[1] This is not so, however, as regards the application of a period of limitation in respect of the enforcement and continuing validity of a security held by a creditor of the company or by a claimant against it, because in so far as the creditor or claimant relies on his security it is immaterial whether the company is in liquidation or not.[2] Consequently, if the limitation period of 12 years from the date when the secured debt became due and immediately payable expires before or after the commencement of the company's liquidation, and the company has not acknowledged its indebtedness to the secured creditor in writing or made a part payment to him on account of principal or interest since that time, the security is extinguished,[3] and the debt becomes wholly unsecured. As an unsecured creditor, the formerly secured creditor may, of course, prove in the liquidation, provided that his personal claim against the company was not extinguished by the expiration of the appropriate limitation period before the liquidation began.

DISTRIBUTIONS TO MEMBERS

In the comparatively rare event of a company being wound up in a solvent condition, or being made solvent by the injection or recovery of money or assets by the liquidator in the course of the liquidation, the assets of the company remaining after meeting the costs and

1 See p 294, ante.
2 *Cotterell v Price* [1960] 3 All ER 315, [1960] 1 WLR 1097.
3 Limitation Act 1980, s 20(1) and (2), s 22(2) and (3), s 29(5) and s 30(1) (25 *Halsbury's Statutes* (4th edn)(1989 Reissue) 669 and 680).

expenses of the liquidation and paying all its debts and liabilities in full (including interest for periods since the company went into liquidation)[4] must be distributed among the members or shareholders of the company.[5] If varying amounts have been paid up on different shares issued by the company, the inequality between the different amounts paid up must be eliminated by the liquidator repaying the difference to shareholders who have paid up more on their shares than other shareholders, or by the liquidator making calls equal to the difference on shareholders who have paid up less on their shares.[6] Subject to any such adjustment, the remaining assets of the company must be distributed among the company's members or shareholders in proportion to the nominal values of their shares, and this is so whether the assets are more or less than sufficient to repay the nominal value of all the shares issued by the company.[7] If premiums have been paid on the issue of shares, they are not repayable when the company is wound up, and consequently shareholders are entitled to receive the same distribution out of the company's assets in respect of their shares, whether premiums were paid on the issue of their shares or not.[8]

The memorandum or articles of association of the company may vary the normal rules for the distribution of the company's assets between members or shareholders, but this must be by express provision and cannot be inferred.[9] The commonest variation found in articles of association is one providing for the repayment of the capital paid up on preference shares issued by the company, together with the unpaid amount (if any) of the preferential dividends thereon calculated up to the commencement of the liquidation, in priority to any distribution to other classes of shareholders.[10] Participating preference shares and preferred ordinary shares rarely carry the right to the repayment of the capital paid up on them in priority to the repayment of ordinary share capital, and unless their holders are expressly entitled to prior repayment of capital, they usually share the remaining assets of the company with the ordinary shareholders on the basis of equality after preference capital carrying priority for repayment of capital in a winding up has been repaid.

---

4 See p 291, ante.
5 Insolvency Act 1986, s 107, s 143(1) and s 154.
6 *Re Anglesea Colliery Co* (1866) 1 Ch App 555; *Re Hodge's Distillery Co, ex p Maude* (1870) 6 Ch App 51.
7 *Birch v Cropper* (1889) 14 App Cas 525.
8 *Re Driffield Gas Light Co* [1898] 1 Ch 451.
9 *Re Duncan Gilmour & Co Ltd* [1952] 2 All ER 871.
10 See *Pennington's Company Law* (7th edn) 263 to 268.

CHAPTER 7

Administration orders

The administration order procedure was introduced by the Insolvency Act 1986, as an alternative to the winding up of insolvent companies where there is a reasonable possibility that a company's business undertaking, or at least parts of that company's undertaking, may be made to survive its present financial difficulties, or that arrangements may be made with its creditors under which the survival of the company's business undertaking or part of it may be achieved, or that a more beneficial (because more extended and selective) winding up of the company's affairs may be facilitated. Administration order proceedings are broadly envisaged as a means of ensuring the continuance of the whole or part of a company's business undertaking and the avoidance of the piecemeal disposal of its assets at depressed prices, so protecting the interests of the company's shareholders and employees, and also safeguarding those of its creditors by requiring their approval of the proposals for the company's future management and the application of its assets. However, administration order proceedings can be of the most varied character, ranging at one extreme from the temporary management of a company's affairs by one or more qualified insolvency practitioners with a view to restoring it to solvency, to at the other extreme, proceedings which closely resemble a liquidation but for the fact that the whole or parts of the company's undertaking is disposed of as a going concern, and the disposal is effected in a measured way without undue despatch so as to obtain a better result for creditors and shareholders.

JURISDICTION

The jurisdiction to make administration orders is vested in the same courts as the jurisdiction to make winding up orders in respect of companies. Consequently, an administration order may be made in respect of any company by the Companies Court, and in respect of a company whose paid up capital does not exceed £120,000, by a county court.[1]

1 Companies Act 1985, s 744; Insolvency Act 1986, s 117(1), (2) and (4) and s 251. For the jurisdiction of the Companies Court and county courts to order the winding up of companies, see pp 11 and 12, ante.

The kinds of companies in respect of which administration orders may be made are, however, more restricted than those against which winding up orders may be made. The definition of a company for the purpose of an administration order is incorporated in the Insolvency Act 1986, by reference to the definition of a company in the Companies Act 1985, namely, a company registered under that Act or any of the earlier Companies Acts enacted in or since 1856.[2] Consequently, administration orders cannot be made in respect of unregistered companies or overseas companies, which are for certain purposes governed by the Companies Act 1985,[3] but such an order may be made in respect of an overseas company in exercise of the courts' duty to assist the courts of a country designated by the Secretary of State for Trade and Industry which has insolvency jurisdiction in respect of the overseas company.[4] An administration order may be made in respect of a partnership as though it were a company despite the fact that it is not incorporated,[5] but partnership administration orders are not dealt with in this book.

An administration order cannot be made against a company after it has gone into liquidation, that is, after a general meeting of its members has passed a resolution to wind it up voluntarily, or an order has been made that the company shall be wound up by the court.[6] If an application has been made to the court to review or rescind a winding up order made against a company or to stay the winding up, the company remains in liquidation until the winding up is rescinded or stayed, and so a petition for an administration order in respect of the company cannot be presented until that has happened.[7] But the fact that a petition for a company to be wound up by the court has been presented does not prevent the presentation of a petition for an administration order if the company or (it would seem) a substantial number of its creditors oppose the winding up petition; unless the petition for an administration order has clearly been presented to delay the winding up proceedings and is wholly without merit, the court will normally order that the winding up petition shall not be advertised or proceeded with until the petition

---

2 Companies Act 1985, s 735(1) to (3); Insolvency Act 1986, s 251.
3 Companies Act 1985, ss 680 to 703R.
4 Insolvency Act 1986, s 426(4), (5) and (11); *Re Maxwell Communications Corpn plc* [1992] BCLC 465, [1992] BCC 372; *Re Dallhold Estates (UK) Pty Ltd* [1992] BCLC 621, [1992] BCC 394; *Re Bank of Credit and Commerce International SA* [1993] BCC 787.
5 Insolvent Partnerships Order 1994 (SI 1994/2421), art 6(1). The order was made under the Insolvency Act 1986, s 420(1).
6 Insolvency Act 1986, s 8(4) and s 247(2).
7 *Re S N Group plc* [1994] 1 BCLC 319, [1993] BCC 808.

for an administration order has been disposed of,[8] but it has a discretion to allow the winding up petition to proceed if the petition for an administration order is unlikely to succeed.[9] Moreover, the court may restrain the advertisement of a creditor's winding up petition if the company or its directors or the solicitors acting for it undertake to present a petition for an administration order within a period fixed by the court, but the restraint ceases to be effective if they do not do so within that time.[10]

A petition for an administration order may be presented only in respect of one company, and so it is not possible in a single petition to request that administration orders shall be made in respect of a parent or holding company and one or more or all of its subsidiaries,[11] but separate petitions must be presented in respect of those companies in the group which it is sought to put into administration.

An administration order cannot be made against an insurance company governed by the Insurance Companies Act 1982,[12] but such an order may be made against an institution which is or has been authorised to accept deposits by the Bank of England under the Banking Act 1987, or by the Chancellor of the Exchequer under the Banking Act 1979.[13]

PETITIONERS AND GROUNDS FOR ADMINISTRATION ORDERS

Persons entitled to petition

The persons who may petition the court to make an administration order in respect of a company are the company itself, its directors and any one or more of its creditors, and a joint petition may be presented by any two or more of those persons together.[14] A petition may be presented in the names of the directors of the company if a board resolution has been passed to that effect, even if not all the directors concur in presenting the petition; this is because it is the

---

8 *Re a Company (No 001992 of 1988)* [1989] BCLC 9, 4 BCC 451; *Re a Company (No 001448 of 1989)* [1989] BCLC 715, 5 BCC 706.

9 *Re Manlon Trading Ltd* (1988) 4 BCC 455.

10 *Re a Company (No 001448 of 1989)*, supra; *Re Shearing and Loader Ltd* [1991] BCLC 764, [1991] BCC 232.

11 *Re Land and Property Trust Co plc* [1991] BCLC 845, [1991] BCC 446.

12 Insolvency Act 1986, s 8(4).

13 Ibid, s 8(1) and (1A). Section 8(1A) was inserted by the Banks (Administration Proceedings) Order 1989 (SI 1989/1276)).

14 Insolvency Act 1986, s 9(1).

duty of all the directors to give effect to the board resolution, despite their individual opposition, the resolution being binding on all of them.[15] For this reason, it would appear that a petition should be presented in the name of the company only if a general meeting of members or shareholders has so resolved, or if the company's articles of association expressly delegate the power to petition in the company's name to its board of directors and the board resolves to do so.[16] Individual members or shareholders cannot petition for an administration order in that capacity, however, and it is immaterial that they hold individually or collectively any particular fraction of the company's issued share capital, or even a majority of its issued shares.

It would appear that a creditor or creditors may petition for an administration order only if he or they would be treated as creditors for the purpose of petitioning for a winding up order.[17] It is expressly provided, however, that a creditor may petition, even though the debt owing to him is only contingent or prospective,[18] and so a petition may be presented by a creditor whose debt is not payable until a future date, or is payable only on the fulfilment of a condition or contingency which has not yet happened or been fulfilled, such as the claim of a person to be reimbursed for a debt of the company which he has guaranteed if he discharges it himself. A person who is a potential creditor of a company is not treated as a creditor however, and so a successful litigant against the company who has obtained an order against it for payment of his costs of the litigation is not a creditor for those costs until they have been quantified by taxation.[19]

A petition for an administration order to be made in respect of a company which is an institution authorised or formerly authorised under the Banking Acts 1979 or 1987, to accept deposits as part of a deposit-taking business, may be presented by the Bank of England alone or jointly with any one or more of the institution's depositors, if it defaults on an obligation to pay an amount which is due and payable in respect of a deposit made with it.[20] This does not, of course, prevent one or more depositors presenting a petition for an administration order in their capacity as creditors of the company,

---

15 *Re Equiticorp International plc* [1989] BCLC 597, 5 BCC 599.
16 *Smith v Duke of Manchester* (1883) 24 Ch D 611; *Re Galway and Salthill Tramways Co* [1918] 1 IR 62; *Re Emmadart Ltd* [1979] Ch 540, [1979] 1 All ER 599. These cases concerned winding up petitions, but the same reasoning would appear to apply.
17 See p 17, ante.
18 Insolvency Act 1986, s 9(1).
19 *Re Wisepark Ltd* [1994] BCC 221.
20 Insolvency Act 1986, s 8(1A) and s 9(1).

whether their deposits are repayable immediately or only at a future date or on the giving of a certain length of notice. Similarly, a petition for an administration order may be presented in respect of a company which is authorised to carry on investment business under the Financial Services Act 1986, either by the recognised self-regulating organisation of which it is a member or subject to whose rules it carries on business,[1] or by the recognised professional body which certified the company as authorised to carry on investment business incidentally to practising the profession regulated by the body,[2] or in the case of any other company authorised to carry on investment business under the Act, by the Securities and Investments Board.[3] Again, this does not prevent a company which is authorised to carry on investment business or its directors or creditors from themselves petitioning for an administration order to be made in respect of it.

Matters to be proved

The court may make an administration order on a petition presented by one or more competent petitioners only if it is satisfied that the company is, or is likely to become, unable to pay its debts within the meaning of that expression for the purpose of the court making a winding up order,[4] and the court considers that the making of an administration order would be likely to achieve one or more of four statutory purposes.[5]

A company may therefore be proved unable to pay its debts for the purpose of obtaining an administration order by showing either that a statutory written demand for payment of a debt exceeding £750 owed by it has been served on it by one of its creditors, and that the company has neglected to pay or secure the debt to the creditor's reasonable satisfaction within three weeks thereafter; or that execution has been issued to enforce a judgment debt owing by the company

---

1 There are three recognised regulating organisations, namely, the Securities and Futures Association, the Personal Investment Authority (PIA) and the Investment Managers Regulatory Organisation (IMRO).
2 The recognised professional bodies are the Law Society, the Law Society of Scotland, the Law Society of Northern Ireland, the Institute of Chartered Accountants in England and Wales, the Institute of Chartered Accountants of Scotland, the Institute of Chartered Accountants in Ireland, the Institute of Actuaries and the Insurance Brokers' Registration Council.
3 Financial Services Act 1986, s 74; Financial Services Act 1986 (Delegation) Order 1987 (SI 1987/942), art 3.
4 See p 42, ante.
5 Insolvency Act 1986, s 8(1).

and has been returned unsatisfied in whole or part; or that the company is otherwise unable to pay its debts as they fall due; or that the value of the company's assets is less than the total of its liabilities, taking its prospective and contingent liabilities into account.[6] These methods of proving the company's insolvency are alternatives, and so an order may be made where the company has ceased to pay its debts as they fall due, and is therefore presumptively unable to pay any of its debts, even though the company tenders evidence that its assets would realise an amount in excess of the total of its liabilities.[7] It would seem that if the petitioner seeks to prove that the company is likely to become insolvent, he cannot rely on any of the four statutory ways of proving its inability to pay its debts, because proof of any of these matters leads to the conclusion that the company is already insolvent. It would appear, therefore, that the likelihood that the company will become unable to pay its debts may be proved by the petitioner showing that if the company's financial situation continues to deteriorate in the way it has recently done (and there is no reasonable prospect of it improving), the company will become insolvent in the fairly near future.

The purposes to be achieved by an administration order

The four alternative purposes for whose achievement the court may make an administration order are:[8]

(a) the survival of the company and the whole or part of its undertaking as a going concern;

(b) the approval of a voluntary arrangement with the company's creditors by meetings of those creditors and the company's members under the provisions of the Insolvency Act 1986;[9]

(c) the sanctioning by the court of a compromise or arrangement between the company and its creditors, or any class or classes of its creditors, together with or without its members or any class or classes of them, under the provisions of the Companies Act 1985;[10]

(d) a more advantageous realisation of the company's assets than would be effected in a winding up.

---

6 Ibid, s 123(1) and (2).
7 *Re St Ives Windings Ltd* (1987) 3 BCC 634; *Re Business Properties Ltd* (1988) 4 BCC 684; *Re Imperial Motors (UK) Ltd* [1990] BCLC 29, 5 BCC 214.
8 Insolvency Act 1986, s 8(3).
9 For such arrangements, see p 407 et seq, post.
10 For such arrangements approved by the court, see p 434, et seq, post.

The survival of the whole or part of the company's undertaking

The first of these purposes envisages either that the company and its business undertaking will survive intact if the undertaking is managed for a period by an insolvency practitioner on the assumption that the company is temporarily relieved from the pressure of its creditors suing it, levying execution against its assets or enforcing any securities which they hold for their claims,[11] or, alternatively, that a part or parts of the company's whole undertaking, or the whole or part of one or more of several different kinds of undertakings carried on by the company will survive if that pressure by its creditors is temporarily removed. The emphasis is on the whole or part of the company's undertaking or undertakings surviving if an administration order is made, and the survival of the company, if necessary in an altered form and with reduced assets or with the benefit of the injection of fresh share or loan capital, is of less importance, and will readily be assumed by the court if it is shown that the whole or part of the company's undertaking may be made to survive. In practice, particularly where only parts of the company's undertaking can be preserved as a going concern or concerns, the viable parts will usually be vested in a new company or companies, and the shares of that company or those companies will be issued to the shareholders of the original company or, additionally, to persons who subscribe for new share capital, or the shares of the new company or companies will be issued in part to those shareholders and in part to subscribers for cash, adequate provision, of course, being made for the immediate or deferred payments of the original company's debts.

Where such a hiving down of the sound parts of a company's undertaking or undertakings has been effected under an administration order, and all that remains to be done is to dispose of the company's residual assets belonging to those parts of its undertaking which cannot survive, the court's inclination will be to make an administration order to facilitate the hiving down of the viable parts of the company's undertaking or undertakings, and when this has been done, to terminate the administration order and to replace it by a winding up order, under which a liquidator will be appointed to realise the company's remaining assets for cash and to distribute the proceeds to its creditors.[12] This cannot be anticipated by the court inserting conditions in the administration order, however, because administration orders, like winding up orders,

11 Insolvency Act 1986, s 10(1) and s 11(3); (see pp 355 and 358, post).
12 *Re Charnley Davies Business Services Ltd* (1987) 3 BCC 408; *Re Brooke Marine Ltd* [1988] BCLC 546.

must be made unconditionally.[13] It is for the administrator to apply to the court on the completion of the hiving down for an order terminating the administration order, and for him then to petition for a winding up order under which the former administrator or another insolvency practitioner will be appointed to be the liquidator in order to complete the winding up of the company. However, if after the administrator has achieved the purpose of the company and its undertaking surviving, there are sufficient residual assets of the company for him to discharge its debts and liabilities in full, he may do this without the need for an order of the court and without the company being wound up.[14]

Compromises and arrangements with creditors

The second and third purposes for which an administration order may be made are self-explanatory. It is not necessary that the terms of a compromise or arrangement with the company's creditors or a class or classes of them should already have been approved by a meeting of creditors, or by separate meetings of the classes of creditors involved, before the petition for an administration order is presented, nor in the case of an arrangement which the company's creditors or a class or classes of creditors under the Companies Act 1985, that the terms of the arrangement should have already been approved by the court. However, there is nothing to prevent this being done so as to provide the basis for an application for the court to make an administration order. The more usual manner of proceeding, however, is for an application to be made for an administration order when only the outline or skeleton of a proposed compromise or arrangement has been prepared, and before the proposals have been considered by a meeting of creditors. The detailed proposals for the compromise or arrangement are then elaborated by the administrator acting under the administration order, and submitted as his proposals to a meeting or meetings of creditors at a later stage. The advantage in proceeding in this way is that after the petition for the administration order has been presented

---

13 An administration order may be discharged by the court if the administrator does not obtain the approval of the company's creditors to his detailed proposals for the realisation of the company's assets at the meeting of creditors which must be held within three months after the order is made (Insolvency Act 1986, s 18(2), s 23(1) and s 27(1) and (4)). This does not, of course, require the approved proposals to be carried out within a particular period. The administrator may, nevertheless, find it necessary to apply to the court for an extension of the period of the administration order if the staged disposals of the company's assets cannot be carried out within that period.
14 *Re John Slack Ltd* [1995] BCC 1116.

and while the order remains in force, creditors of the company will be unable to bring actions against it, or to levy execution on its assets or to enforce any securities which they have over its assets, unless permission is given by the court or the administrator.[11]

The more advantageous realisation of the company's assets

The fourth and final purpose for which an administration order may be made envisages that the company will be fully wound up eventually, but the interposition of an administration order will facilitate the orderly disposal of the whole or part of the company's undertaking or undertakings, so as to realise a higher total price than would be realised by a rapid and probably piecemeal sale of the company's assets by a liquidator. The more advantageous realisation of the company's assets may be the consequence of the administrator spreading the disposal of the assets over a longer period than in a winding up in the expectation that the market for their sale will improve, or may result from the grouping of the company's assets into appropriate units so that they may each be sold by the administrator as a viable business undertaking at a price which includes an amount for goodwill.[15] On the other hand, the court will not make an administration order on the ground that it will facilitate a more advantageous realisation of the company's assets if the realisation will inevitably be protracted over several years, and until the later part of that time the company's income will unavoidably be less than its outgoings and expenses, so that it will accumulate increasing losses.[16]

The fourth statutory purpose which justifies the court making an administration order is closely related to the first, and administration orders are often made to achieve the first purpose or, alternatively, to achieve the fourth purpose if achieving the first purpose proves impracticable. The detailed proposals for the conduct of the administration are not known when the administration order is made, and so an order in this alternative form enables the administrator to make proposals for the hiving down of the viable parts of the company's undertaking, or where the company has carried on several undertakings, to make proposals for the preservation and continuance of one or more of them, and in either case the proposals will provide either for the retention of the hived down or preserved undertakings by the company or a successor

15 A liquidator may dispose of viable parts of a company's undertaking in this way, but he does so on his own responsibility and without the protection of the approval of his disposal plan by the company's creditors.
16 *Re Arrows Ltd (No 3)* [1992] BCLC 555, [1992] BCC 131.

company for the benefit of company's shareholders (adequate provision being made for the payment or satisfaction of the company's debts) or, alternatively, for the hived down or preserved undertakings to be transferred to successor companies whose shares will be issued to cash subscribers in order to raise money with which the company's debts will be discharged. The order then adds the alternative purpose that the company shall be wound up if the proposals for the hiving down of the company are not approved by a meeting of the company's creditors, or if they are so approved but prove impossible or impracticable to achieve.

The standard of proof

A court to which a petition for an administration order is presented has to decide an objective question of fact in determining whether the company concerned is unable to pay its debts or is likely to become unable to do so, and the normal standard of proof in civil cases, namely, that it is more probable than not that the company is, or is likely to become, insolvent can be applied without difficulty. The second matter which has then to be proved to the court's satisfaction, namely, that the making of an administration order would be likely to achieve one or more of the four statutory purposes set out above, is not susceptible of proof as a matter of fact, however, because a decision on the likelihood or otherwise of a statutory purpose being achieved requires a forecast to be made of the company's prospective or achievable destiny in the light of what is already known.

In some of the early applications for administration orders the court applied the normal civil standard of proof to this second question as well as the first, with the result that the burden of proof on the petitioner to show that it was more likely than not that the designated statutory purpose or purposes would be achieved under an administration order, was a very heavy one.[17] In later cases the predominant judicial view has been that the petitioner need merely prove that the statutory purposes or one of the statutory purposes which the petition alleges to be capable of achievement is reasonably likely to be achieved,[18] or that there is a real prospect that it will be achieved.[19] If the petition for an administration order seeks the

17 *Re Consumer and Industrial Press Ltd* [1988] BCLC 177, 4 BCC 68.
18 *Re Primlaks (UK) Ltd* [1989] BCLC 734, 5 BCC 710.
19 *Re Harris Simons Construction Ltd* [1989] 1 WLR 368, [1989] BCLC 202; *Re Primlaks (UK) Ltd*, supra; *Re SCL Building Services Ltd* [1990] BCLC 98, 5 BCC 746; *Re Rowbotham Baxter Ltd* [1990] BCLC 397, [1990] BCC 133.

making of the order to give effect to a compromise or arrangement to be approved by the company's creditors, the petitioner must prove that there is a real prospect that the required majority of creditors will approve the compromise or arrangement, whose general character is indicated in the petition and the supporting affidavit. If there is no or little likelihood of this approval being obtained, the court will dismiss the petition, however meritorious or attractive the proposals for a compromise or arrangement may be.[20]

The supporting affidavit

To assist the court in deciding whether the two matters mentioned above are established, the Insolvency Rules 1986, governing the procedure on petitions for administration orders, require such a petition to be presented to the court together with a supporting affidavit by one of the directors or the secretary of the company, or if the petition is presented by a creditor or creditors, by the petitioning creditor, or by one of several petitioning creditors, or by a person acting with the authority of all the petitioning creditors.[1]

The supporting affidavit must state the deponent's belief that the company is, or is likely to become, unable to pay its debts, and must specify which of the four statutory purposes is expected to be achieved by the making of an administration order; also the affidavit must contain a statement of the company's financial position, specifying, to the best of the deponent's knowledge and belief, the company's assets and liabilities, including contingent and prospective liabilities, and details must be given of securities known or believed to be held by creditors of the company together with a statement whether any of those securities is a general floating charge over the company's assets under which the secured creditor is entitled to appoint an administrative receiver, and whether to the knowledge of the deponent any petition has been presented for the winding up of the company by the court.[2] Additionally, the supporting affidavit must state any other matters known to the deponent which, in the opinion of the intending petitioner, will assist the court in deciding whether to make an administration order, and the affidavit must further state whether there has been prepared a report by an independent person (who may be the proposed administrator, but must not be a director, secretary, manager or employee of the company) to the effect that the making of an administration order and the appointment of an administrator would be expedient in

---

20 *Re Land and Property Trust Co plc (No 2)* [1991] BCLC 849, [1991] BCC 446.
1 Insolvency Rules 1986, r 2.1(1) to (3).
2 Ibid, r 2.3(1) to (4).

order to achieve one or more of the purposes for which an administration order may be made, and if no such report has been prepared, the affidavit must explain why it has not.[3]

The independent report

The information and insight afforded to the court by the affidavit in support of the petition for an administration order is, of course, of limited value, especially when the petition is presented by creditors who have no access to the company's accounting and trading records. Consequently, a full report in support of the petition, preferably by a qualified insolvency practitioner who is willing to be appointed as administrator if the court makes an administration order, is highly desirable, and has been indicated by the court as essential to enable it to give an informed judgment supported by expert opinion as to whether one or more of the four statutory purposes to be achieved by making an administration order are reasonably likely to be achieved.[4] The independent report should contain not only a statement of the company's assets and liabilities and its financial and trading history over a recent period, but also a prognosis of its likely future trading results and financial situation if it continues to carry on business, and as detailed an indication as possible of the steps which should be taken to halt the company's losses and to achieve one or more of the purposes for which an administration order is sought.

Because it is usually difficult, if not impossible, for creditors of a company in financial difficulties to obtain sufficient detailed information about the company's financial condition to prepare a proper affidavit in support of a petition for an administration order, and because creditors have no right to insist that the company shall permit a qualified insolvency practitioner to have access to its accounting and trading records in order to produce an independent report, it is rare in practice for creditors to petition for administration orders. It is simpler for a creditor who seeks to obtain payment of the amount owed to him to petition the court to wind up the company in a situation where its directors have not already taken the initiative by petitioning in their own or the company's name for an administration order to be made; the directors may then respond by presenting a petition for an administration order, and support their petition by an independent report. The petition for an administration order will then be heard first by the court, and the winding up

3 Ibid, r 2.2 and r 2.3(5) and (6).
4 *Re Newport County Association Football Club Ltd* [1987] BCLC 582.

petition will be advertised and proceeded with only if an administration order is not made.[5]

PROCEDURE FOR OBTAINING AN ADMINISTRATION ORDER

Presentation, filing and service of the petition

Contents of the petition and supporting affidavit

A petition for an administration order commences with a statement of the name and address or the names and addresses of the petitioner or petitioners, and in successive paragraphs there must be set out a statement of the company's name and the date of its incorporation, the address of its registered office, the amount of its nominal and paid up share capital and its principal objects as set out in its memorandum of association; the petition then continues with a statement of the petitioner's belief that the company is, or is likely to become, unable to pay its debts, and that an administration order would be likely to achieve one or more of the statutory purposes for which an administration order may be made, specifying which of those purposes are likely to be achieved, and that this is so for the reasons set out in the supporting affidavit; there then follows the petitioner's proposal that while an administration order is in force, the affairs, business and property of the company shall be managed by the qualified insolvency practitioner or practitioners named in the petition, whose written consent to act and a statement of whose qualification to so act are filed in court with the petition; the petition concludes with the petitioner's prayer to the court to make an administration order in respect of the company, and to appoint the named insolvency practitioner or practitioners to be the administrator or joint administrators; there is thereafter set out the names of the persons (including the company, if a creditor or creditors are the petitioners) on whom it is proposed to serve the petition, the name of the solicitors who issue the petition on the petitioner's behalf and their address for service.[6]

The affidavit made in support of the petition must have exhibited to it a copy of the petition, the written consent to act and statement

---

5 *Re a Company (No 001992 of 1988)* [1989] BCLC 9, 4 BCC 451; *Re Manlon Trading Ltd* (1988) 4 BCC 455; *Re a Company (No 001448 of 1989)* [1989] BCLC 715, 5 BCC 706.
6 Insolvency Rules 1986, r 2.4(1) to (5) and Sch 4, Form 2.1.

of the qualification of the qualified insolvency practitioner or practitioners whom the petitioner proposes for appointment as administrator or administrators, and any independent report supporting the petition which is to be filed with it.[7]

Filing, notification and service of the petition

The petition and supporting affidavit with its exhibited statement of consent to act by the nominated insolvency practitioner or practitioners and the independent report must be filed at the court to which the petition is presented with a sufficient number of copies for service; the petition and copies for service are sealed by the court and endorsed with a note of the date and time of filing and the date, time and place at which the petition will be heard.[8] Notice of the presentation of the petition must forthwith be given to any person who has appointed, or is entitled to appoint, an administrative receiver of the company's assets,[9] to any sheriff or other responsible officer of the court who to the petitioner's knowledge has received any writ or other process of execution against the company's property, and to any person who to the petitioner's knowledge has distrained on any property of the company.[10]

Copies of the petition which have been sealed for service and copies of the supporting affidavit and exhibits must be served by the petitioner's solicitor on the company (unless the petition is presented by the company itself or by its directors) and on any person who has appointed, or who is entitled to appoint, an administrative receiver of the company's assets, on any administrative receiver who has

---

7 Ibid, r 2.4(6) and Sch 4, Form 2.2.
8 Ibid, r 2.5(1) to (3).
9 Insolvency Act 1986, s 9(2). An administrative receiver may be appointed only by a creditor who is secured by a charge which, as created, was a floating charge over the whole or substantially the whole of a company's property, or by such a charge and one or more other securities (eg fixed or specific charges over property or classes of property of the company, such as land, investments or book debts at present owned or in the future acquired by, or vested in, the company), but the expression, administrative receiver, also includes a person who would be such a receiver but for the appointment of some other person as the receiver of part of the company's property (s 29(2)). The definition leaves it uncertain whether, if the company has created two or more floating charges over the whole or substantially the whole of its property, the appointment of an administrative receiver by the holder of the first ranking of those floating charges precludes the holders of the later ranking floating charges from themselves appointing administrative receivers (subject, of course, to the rights of the first ranking holder and of the administrative receiver appointed by him), and whether therefore, it is necessary to serve copies of the petition for an administration order on the holders of the later ranking floating charges.
10 Insolvency Act 1986, s 9(2); Insolvency Rules 1986, r 2.6A.

already been appointed, on any person who has presented a pending winding up petition against the company together with any provisional liquidator who has been appointed under the petition, and on the insolvency practitioner or practitioners proposed for appointment as administrator or administrators of the company.[11] Service of copies of the petition and the accompanying affidavit and exhibits to it must be effected by the petitioner or his solicitors or by a person instructed by him or them on all the persons to be served at their notified or usual or last known addresses, or in the case of the company, at its registered office, at least five days before the date on which the petition is to be heard,[12] and proper service must be verified by affidavits filed in court at least one day before the hearing of the petition.[13] Service may be effected at the appropriate address either by personal service on the person concerned, or by leaving the documents for him at that address, or by sending the documents to him at that address by first class post.[14]

The reason why a copy of the petition for an administration order must be served on any person or persons who have appointed, or who are entitled to appoint, an administrative receiver is that if an administrative receiver appointed by him or them holds office when the petition is heard, the court cannot make an administration order unless that person, or (if more than one) all such persons so entitled to appoint an administrative receiver consent, or unless the floating charge in respect of which an administrative receiver has been or could be appointed would be void against the administrator because it has not been registered at the Companies Registry,[15] or unless the floating charge would be void against the administrator under the provisions of the Insolvency Act 1986, relating to transactions at an undervalue or voidable preferences of particular creditors of the company, or the invalidation of floating charges created by the company within a limited period before a winding up or an administration order is made in respect of it.[16] Service of a copy of the petition for an administration order on a person who has appointed, or who is entitled to appoint, an administrative receiver and on any person who has presented a pending winding up petition against the company is required so as to enable them to appear on

11 Insolvency Rules 1986, r 2.6(1) and (2).
12 Ibid, r 2.7(1) to (4).
13 Ibid, r 2.8(1) and (2).
14 Ibid, r 2.7(5).
15 Companies Act 1985, ss 395, 399, 400 and 404 (see *Pennington's Company Law* (7th edn) 648 to 653).
16 Insolvency Act 1986, s 9(3); (see pp 221, 225 and 237, ante).

the hearing of the petition for an administration order in opposition to or in order to consent to such an order being made.[17]

Although copies of the petition for an administration order must normally be served on the company and the other persons mentioned above at least five days before the date fixed for the hearing of the petition, in a case of urgency the court can on the application of the petitioner, or it would seem, the company or its directors if the petition is not presented by them, order that the petition shall be heard, even though less than five days' notice of the hearing is given to a person who has appointed, or who is entitled to appoint, an administrative receiver, and if no such receiver has already been appointed, the court may appoint a suitable person to take and retain possession of the company's assets pending the hearing of the petition.[18]

Expedition of administration order proceedings

Obtaining an administration order or the appointment of an administrator may be a matter of extreme urgency, for example, because creditors of the company have presented winding up petitions against the company or are threatening to do so, or because secured creditors of the company are taking steps to realise their securities over assets of the company which are vital for the continuance of its business undertaking, or because the other parties to important contracts with the company are threatening to terminate them. The court has shown itself willing in such circumstance to modify the normal procedure for obtaining an administration order so as to expedite the proceedings and support them by making ancillary orders under its general jurisdiction. The court has in this connection appointed a manager of a company's business or a receiver of its assets and enjoined its directors from disposing of its assets when the applicant creditor undertook to present a petition for an administration order in respect of the company on the ground that a more advantageous realisation of its assets would thereby be achieved than by a winding up.[19] Furthermore, the court has made an administration order on a petition presented by a deposit-taking institution on the day when the petition was presented to the court where the making of an administration order was urgently necessary to preserve the company's business and to prevent the concerted

17 Insolvency Rules 1986, r 2.9(1).
18 *Re a Company (No 00175 of 1987)* [1987] BCLC 467, 3 BCC 124.
19 *Re Gallidoro Trawlers Ltd* [1991] BCLC 411, [1991] BCC 691.

withdrawal of deposits made with it by most of its depositors.[20] Again on an application to the court to appoint an administrator where the company's directors had ceased to carry on its business and its undertaking would be saleable at a substantial price only if its current contracts were carried out, the court made the appointment on the applicant's undertaking to present a petition for an administration order forthwith and filing with it in court an affidavit verifying the facts showing that such an order was justified.[1] Finally, the court has made an administration order which was to take effect immediately on a petition being presented to the court; the application for the order was made by the company's directors on the ground that administration order proceedings would result in a more advantageous realisation of the company's assets than a winding up, and the application was supported by an independent report prepared by an insolvency practitioner.[2] However, the court will permit departures from the normal procedure for obtaining an administration order only when the circumstances make the speedy obtaining of the order of special importance in order to preserve the company's business undertaking or assets, and in the absence of such circumstances the normal procedure must be followed.

The hearing, the making of an administration order and consequential proceedings

The court's functions

On the date fixed for the hearing of a petition for an administration order (which is endorsed on the petition), the petitioner and the company are entitled to be heard, and also any person who has appointed, or who is entitled to appoint, an administrative receiver who has already been appointed, any person who has presented a winding up petition against the company and the person proposed by the petition for appointment as administrator.[3] The company's directors are not entitled, as such, to be heard, but they will always in fact be heard either because they are the petitioners or because they represent the company.[4] Creditors of the company, too, are

---

20 *Re Cavco Floors Ltd* [1990] BCLC 940, [1990] BCC 589.
1 *Re Chancery plc* [1991] BCLC 712, [1991] BCC 171.
2 *Re Shearing and Loader Ltd* [1991] BCLC 764, [1991] BCC 232.
3 Insolvency Rules 1986, r 2.9(1).
4 The Insolvency Rules 1986, r 2.4(3) provides that if a petition is presented by the company's directors, it shall from and after its presentation be treated for all purposes as though it had been presented by the company. This provision would appear to eliminate any possibility of individual directors having a right to be heard.

not, as such, entitled to be heard unless they are the petitioners,[5] but the court may give leave for any person to be heard if he appears to have an interest justifying his appearance. The court will normally not hear shareholders of the company, even if they oppose the making of an administration order, but the court may do so if the shareholders can prove that, even though the company is unable to pay its debts as they fall due, its assets exceed its liabilities, and they therefore have an interest in it.[6]

The petition is heard by a judge or by the registrar of the court in open court, and after hearing the persons who are entitled or permitted to appear, he may make an administration order, dismiss the petition, adjourn the hearing conditionally or unconditionally, or make such other order as he thinks fit, including an interim order restricting the exercise of any of the powers of the directors of the company (whether by requiring the consent of the court or of a qualified insolvency practitioner to the exercise of any of their powers or otherwise).[7] This latter power is useful if the court adjourns the hearing, but wishes to prevent the disposal of any of the company's assets or any dealings with them before the adjourned hearing takes place. As an alternative to such a restriction, the court may appoint a suitable person (eg a qualified insolvency practitioner) to take and retain possession of the company's assets until the court's further order.[8] If petitions for administration orders are presented in respect of several companies belonging to the same group, the court must consider the petitions separately, and may make administration orders only in respect of those companies which taken alone will seek to fulfil one of the four statutory purposes for which an administration order may be made, it being insufficient that the group taken as a whole may be able to do so.[9]

If the court makes an administration order at the hearing or an adjournment of it, it must also appoint one or more qualified insolvency practitioners to be the administrator or administrators of the company.[10] The administrator(s) will usually be the insolvency practitioner(s) nominated in the petition if there is no objection to him or them raised at the hearing (eg because a nominated insolvency

5 Contrast the right of creditors to be heard individually on the hearing of a winding up petition (see p 69, ante).
6 *Re Chelmsford City Football Club Ltd* [1991] BCC 133.
7 Insolvency Act 1986, s 9(4) and (5).
8 *Re a Company (No 00175 or 1987)*, supra.
9 *Re Land and Property Trust Co plc (No 2)* [1991] BCLC 849, [1991] BCC 446.
10 Insolvency Act 1986, s 13(1) and s 230(1); Insolvency Rules 1986, Sch 4, Form 2.4.

practitioner has an interest in or connection with the company), but the court is at liberty to appoint another person as administrator, provided that he is currently qualified as an insolvency practitioner.[11]

An administration order may be, and normally is, made for a specified period.[10] If the purpose or purposes for which the order was made are not likely to be achieved within that period, an application may be made to the court to extend it; such an application must be supported by evidence that the purpose or purposes of the order are achievable within the extended period proposed, and the application must normally be made by the administrator, and not by the company, acting by its directors.[12]

If the court makes an administration order, the costs of the petitioner and of any other person who appears on the hearing of the petition and whose costs are allowed by the court are payable out of the assets of the company as an expense of the administration.[13] If the company or (it would seem) any other petitioner for any administration order does not appear in support of the petition at the hearing, and the court dismisses the petition and makes a winding up order against the company, the court may nevertheless order that the costs of the petition for an administration order shall rank as expenses of the winding up if the petition was presented in good faith.[14] The court will make such an order if the petition for an administration order was presented by the directors of the company and was supported by prima facie evidence, but the petition was withdrawn by the directors as soon as they realised that an overwhelming majority of the company's creditors were opposed to an administration order being made.[14] On the other hand, if directors in their own or the company's name present a petition for an administration order which has no prospect of success and their purpose is merely to obstruct or delay a creditor's winding up petition, the court on dismissing the directors' petition may order them to pay the costs of the proceedings personally after giving them an opportunity to argue against such an order being made.[15]

---

11 Ibid, s 388(1) and s 390.
12 *Re Newport County Association Football Club Ltd* [1987] BCLC 582, 3 BCC 635.
13 Insolvency Rules r 2.9(2).
14 *Re Gosscott (Groundworks) Ltd* [1988] BCLC 363, 4 BCC 372; *Re Land and Property Trust Co plc (No 2)* [1991] BCLC 849, [1991] BCC 446, on appeal [1994] 1 BCLC 232, [1993] BCC 462.
15 *Re Land and Property Trust Co plc (No 2)*, supra. The court's jurisdiction to order the directors to pay the costs of the abortive proceedings is conferred by the Supreme Court Act 1981, s 51(1) (as substituted by the Courts and Legal Services Act 1990, s 4(1) (11 *Halsbury's Statutes* (4th edn)(1991 Reissue) 1217).

Unavailability of administration order if an administrative receiver is appointed or the company is in liquidation

An administration order cannot be made by the court if the company has created a floating charge over the whole, or substantially the whole, of its assets which remains undischarged at the date of the hearing of the petition, and an administrative receiver has been appointed under the floating charge before that time, unless the holder of the charge consents to the making of the administration order or the court decides that the floating charge would be void against an administrator under various provisions of the Companies Act 1985 or the Insolvency Act 1986.[16] In order to give the holder of such a general floating charge an opportunity to appoint an administrative receiver if he has not already done so, the petitioner for an administration order must serve a copy of the petition on him at least five days (or such shorter period as the court directs) before the date for the hearing of the petition.[17] A general floating charge is effective to enable the person entitled to it to prevent an administration order being made by appointing an administrative receiver, even though the floating charge was created concurrently with fixed charges over the company's assets to secure the same debt, and the only assets which the company owned at the date when the floating charge was created or when an administrative receiver was appointed were assets which were subject to the fixed charges;[18] this is because the floating charge will nevertheless extend to assets which the company acquires later or during the existence of an administration order made by the court. The effect of an administration order being made with the consent of the holder of a general floating charge or because of its invalidity is that any administrative receiver appointed by him of the company's property automatically vacates office and the receivership terminates.[19] Moreover, any other receiver of any part of the company's property may be required to vacate office by the administrator,[20] and it would appear that the receivership terminates when the administrator's requirement is notified to the receiver.

An administration order cannot be made by the court if the company is already being wound up by the court or voluntarily when

16 Companies Act 1985, s 395(1); Insolvency Act 1986, s 9(3) (see pp 221, 225 and 237, ante).
17 Insolvency Rules 1986, r 2.6(1) and (2); *Re a Company (No 00175 of 1987)* [1987] BCLC 467, 3 BCC 124.
18 *Re Croftbell Ltd* [1990] BCLC 844, [1990] BCC 781.
19 Insolvency Act 1986, s 11(1).
20 Ibid, s 11(2).

the petition for the administration order is heard,[1] but the presentation of the petition for an administration order does not prevent the subsequent presentation of a winding up petition,[2] although the court will normally enjoin its advertisement and further proceedings on it until the petition for the administration order had been disposed of.[3] If a company is already being wound up by the court or voluntarily, a petition for an administration order in respect of it can only be heard if the court first orders that the proceedings on the winding up order or resolution shall be stayed.[4]

Publication of the administration order

When an administration order is made, the court gives notice of it to the person appointed as administrator, and he must advertise the order in the London Gazette and in a newspaper which he thinks most appropriate to bring the order to the attention of the company's creditors.[5] The administrator must then immediately give notice of the order in the prescribed form to any person who has appointed, or who would but for the making of the order be entitled to appoint, an administrative receiver of the company's assets, to any administrative receiver who has already been appointed, to any petitioner for a winding up order against the company which was pending when the administration order was made, to the provisional liquidator appointed in such proceedings (if any) and to the Registrar of Companies.[6]

Additionally, the administrator must on the making of an administration order forthwith give notice of it to the company in the prescribed form, and within 28 days after the administration order is made he must send a notice of it in the prescribed form to all creditors of the company of whose addresses he is aware, unless the court otherwise orders;[7] within 14 days after the order is made the administrator must send a sealed copy of the order to the Registrar of Companies.[8]

---

1 Ibid, s 8(4).
2 Ibid, s 10(2).
3 *Re a Company (No 001992 of 1988)* [1989] BCLC 9, 4 BCC 451; *Re a Company (No 001448 of 1989)* [1989] BCLC 715, 5 BCC 706.
4 Insolvency Act 1986, s 112(1) and s 147(1); (see p 76, ante).
5 Insolvency Rules 1986, r 2.10(1) and (2).
6 Ibid, r 2.10(3) and Sch 4, Form 2.6.
7 Insolvency Act 1986, s 21(1); Insolvency Rules 1986, Sch 4, Form 2.7.
8 Insolvency Act 1986, s 21(2).

THE EFFECT OF ADMINISTRATION ORDER PROCEEDINGS ON CREDITORS AND OTHERS

The effect of a petition for an administration order

After a petition for an administration order has been presented to the court and until the making of such an order or the dismissal of the petition, certain restrictions are imposed on the taking of proceedings against the company and on the enforcement of certain rights and securities against it. The purpose of these restrictions is to preserve the assets of the company which will be comprised in the administration if an administration order is made, and to prevent those assets being diminished by creditors of the company exercising remedies. During the period between the presentation and hearing of the petition the following restrictions are imposed, namely:[9]

(a) no resolution may be passed to wind the company up voluntarily and no order may be made that the company shall be wound up by the court, but a petition for a winding up order may nevertheless be presented and may be proceeded with if the petition for the administration order is dismissed;

(b) no steps may be taken to enforce any security[10] over the company's property or property in which the company has an interest (eg by selling it, appointing a receiver or taking possession of it), or to repossess goods in the company's possession under a hire-purchase agreement,[11] conditional sale agreement,[11] chattel leasing agreement[12] or retention of

9 Ibid, s 10(1).
10 A security is defined for this purpose as any mortgage, charge, lien or other security (Insolvency Act 1986, s 248(*b*)).
11 Hire purchase and conditional sale agreements have the same respective meanings as in the Consumer Credit Act 1974 (Insolvency Act 1986, s 436). Consequently, for the purpose of administration order proceedings, hire-purchase agreements are agreements under which goods are bailed or hired in return for periodical payments by the bailee or hirer, and the property in the goods will pass to that person if the terms of the agreement are complied with by him and he exercises an option to purchase them, or if he does any other specified act or any specified event occurs; and conditional sale agreements are agreements for the sale of goods or land under which the purchase price or part of it is payable by instalments, and the property in the goods or land is to remain vested in the seller (notwithstanding the purchaser being in possession) until the conditions as to payment of instalments or otherwise as specified in the agreement are fulfilled (Consumer Credit Act 1974, s 189(1)).
12 A chattel leasing agreement is defined as an agreement for the bailment of goods which is capable of subsisting for more than three months (Insolvency Act 1986, s 251).

title agreement,[13] or to repossess any land in the company's possession under a conditional sale agreement,[11] unless the court gives leave and subject to such conditions as the court imposes; and

(c) no other proceedings and no execution or other legal process may be commenced or continued against the company, and no distress may be levied against the company or its property, unless the court gives leave and subject to such conditions as the court imposes; the prevailing judicial opinion is that 'proceedings' mean litigation inter partes before a court, or similar contentious proceedings before a tribunal, and that proceedings do not include unilateral action taken by a person to assert or enforce a legal right (eg forfeiture of a lease by a lessor or landlord for non-payment of rent or breach of covenant);[14] the same view is taken of 'other legal process', namely, that its meaning is confined to action taken in the course of litigation or contentious proceedings, or for the purpose of enforcing or implementing a judgment or decision given in such proceedings, but in one case 'other legal process' was held to include unilateral action taken otherwise than in connection with litigation or contentious proceedings;[15] 'proceedings' have been held to include applications to a tribunal which acts judicially (eg an industrial tribunal to which an application for reinstatement is made by a dismissed employee of the company)[16] and proceedings before a foreign court or tribunal.[17]

These restrictions do not prevent a creditor secured by a charge created as a floating charge over the whole or substantially the whole of the company's property from appointing an administrative receiver, nor do they prevent such a receiver, whether appointed before or after the presentation of the petition, from carrying out his functions

---

13 A retention of title agreement is defined as an agreement for the sale of goods to a company, being an agreement which does not constitute a charge on the goods, but under which if the seller is not paid and the company is wound up, the seller will have priority over all other creditors of the company as respects the goods or any property representing them (Insolvency Act 1986, s 251).

14 *Air Ecosse Ltd v Civil Aviation Authority* 1987 SLT 751, 3 BCC 492; *Carr v British International Helicopters Ltd* [1994] 2 BCLC 474, [1993] BCC 855; *Re Olympia and York Canary Wharf Ltd, American Express Europe Ltd v Adamson* [1993] BCLC 453, [1993] BCC 154; *Scottish Exhibition Centre Ltd v Mirestop Ltd* [1994] BCC 845; *Re a Debtor (No 13A109 of 1994)* [1996] BCC 57.

15 *Exchange Travel Agency Ltd v Triton Property Trust plc* [1991] BCLC 396, [1991] BCC 341.

16 *Carr v British International Helicopters Ltd*, supra.

17 *Re Exchange Travel (Holdings) Ltd* [1991] BCLC 728, [1991] BCC 341.

and exercising his powers.[18] If a petition for an administration order is presented after the appointment of an administrative receiver, the restrictions mentioned above on winding up and other proceedings do not apply, unless and until the person who appointed the receiver consents to the making of an administration order.[19] After the presentation of the petition for an administration order, and unless and until the person who appoints, or who has already appointed, an administrative receiver consents to the making of an administration order, the only restrictions on the taking of enforcement proceedings against the company are those imposed by the general law in respect of the effects of floating charges on creditors' rights.

The right under the provisions of a lease for a lessor to forfeit it if the rent reserved by the lease is not paid or if the covenants contained in it are not performed and observed by the lessee, is treated as a security for the fulfilment of those obligations, and so if the lessee is a company in respect of which a petition for an administration order is presented, the leave of the court is required if the lessor is to forfeit the lease against the wishes of the company,[20] but the lessor may re-enter the premises comprised in the lease without leave of the court if the company agrees to him doing so or does not oppose re-entry.[1] If the security is conferred by law and not by contract (eg the lien of a solicitor over documents or moneys held by him as security for his professional fees), the enforcement of the security against a company in respect of which a petition for an administration order is pending nevertheless requires leave of the court.[2]

Securities over a company's property are defined widely for the purpose of the restrictions on their enforcement after a petition for an administration order has been presented. A security includes any right for a creditor to seize, possess, detain, restrain the use of any property of the company, or to sell or otherwise dispose of such property or an interest in it, if the right was conferred as a means of enforcing the creditor's claim against the company[3] or, it would

18 Insolvency Act 1986, s 10(2).
19 Ibid, s 10(3).
20 *Exchange Travel Agency Ltd v Triton Property Trust plc* [1991] BCLC 396, [1991] BCC 341.
1 *Re a Debtor (No 13A10 of 1994)* [1996] BCC 57.
2 *Re Euro Commercial Leasing Ltd v Cartwright & Lewis* [1995] 2 BCLC 618, [1995] BCC 830.
3 *Bristol Airport plc v Powdrill* [1990] Ch 744, [1990] 2 All ER 493 (where a statutory power for an airport authority to detain aircraft belonging to a company which had failed to pay amounts for landing charges or fuel supplied in respect of any of its aircraft, was held to be a security over the detained aircraft); *Re Sabre International Products Ltd* [1991] BCLC 470, [1991] BCC 694 (where an administrator was held entitled to recover goods consigned for carriage from the carrier who detained them in exercise of his lien for unpaid charges, but did not claim the right to sell the goods in order to pay the charges).

seem, as a means of completing or extending his security.[4]

The restrictions on the taking of possession of goods comprised in hire purchase or conditional sale agreements, or in chattel leasing or retention of title agreements apply whether the goods are in the immediate possession of the company or a person acting on its behalf, or whether they are in the possession of a person to whom the company has leased or hired them, or are in the possession of a person to whom the company has agreed to sell them, either conditionally or not or on terms of the company retaining title, or whether the goods are in the possession of a person to whom the company has disposed of them on hire-purchase terms.[5] In these latter situations the person in immediate possession of the goods holds them as a bailee of the company, and it is treated as being in possession of them by its bailee.[5]

The restriction on actions or other proceedings against a company being commenced or continued while a petition for an administration order is pending, presumably prevents the relevant limitation period continuing to run against the creditor or claimant while the restriction is effective, and if this is so, the limitation period will also not run while an administration order is in force. The reason why the court will probably so decide is the same as the reason for the suspension of limitation periods during the winding up of a company, namely, that the creditor's or claimant's right to sue on his own initiative and without any legal impediment is itself suspended.[6]

The effect of an administration order

When an administration order has been made in respect of a company, restrictions are imposed by the Insolvency Act 1986 on certain proceedings being initiated or continued against or in respect of the company and on the enforcement of certain rights and securities against it. The purpose of these restrictions is to preserve the company's assets intact while the administrator prepares his proposals to achieve the purpose or purposes for which the administration order was made, and when those proposals have been approved by a meeting of the creditors of the company, to

---

4 For example, the right which a bank in possession of shipping documents as security for advancing the purchase price of the goods represented by them, has to take delivery of the goods at the destination port and to sell them in order to recover its advance.

5 *Re Atlantic Computer Systems plc* [1991] BCLC 606, [1990] BCC 859.

6 *Re General Rolling Stock Co, Joint Stock Discount Co's Claim* (1872) 7 Ch App 646.

enable the administrator to carry out those proposals without the company's assets being interfered with or disposed of by its creditors individually.

During the period while an administration order is in force, that is from the date when the order is made until it is discharged by a subsequent order of the court, or by the expiration of the period for which the order was made if it is not renewed:[7]

(a) no resolution may be passed and no order may be made for the winding up of the company;

(b) no administrative receiver of the company's assets may be appointed;

(c) no steps may be taken to enforce any security over the company's property,[8] over any property in which the company has a interest,[9] or to repossess goods in the company's possession under any hire-purchase agreement,[9] conditional sale agreement,[9] chattel leasing agreement,[9] or retention of title agreement,[9] or to repossess any goods or land in the company's possession under any conditional sale agreement,[9] unless the administrator consents or the court gives leave, and leave may be given on such conditions as the court thinks fit; and

(d) no other proceedings and no execution or other legal process may be commenced or continued against the company, and no distress may be levied against the company or its property, unless the administrator consents or the court gives leave, and leave may be given on such terms as the court thinks fit.

An administrative receiver, who vacates office on the making of the administration order,[10] and any other receiver of any property of the company vacates office on being required to do so by the administrator,[11] but such receivers are, notwithstanding the foregoing restrictions, entitled to be paid his remuneration and any expenses properly incurred by him out of any property of the company which was in his custody or under his control at the date when he vacated office, and he is also entitled to be indemnified out of that property against any liabilities properly incurred by him; these rights take priority over any security held by the creditor by or on behalf of whom he was appointed to act,[12] and that

7 Insolvency Act 1986, s 11(3) and s 18(3).
8 The company's interest may take any form (eg a lease or hire contract in respect of equipment) (*Bristol Airport plc v Powdrill* [1990] Ch 744, [1990] 2 All ER 493).
9 See text supra at pp 354 to 355, footnotes 11 to 13.
10 Insolvency Act 1986, s 11(1).
11 Ibid, s 11(2).
12 Ibid, s 11(4).

security itself remains effective after the administration order is made although restrictions are imposed on its enforcement.[7] The two readily apparent differences in the position of creditors of a company between the presentation of a petition for an administration order and the date when the order is made, and their position after the order is made, are that before the order is made an administrative receiver, but not any other receiver, of the company's property may be appointed by a secured creditor who is entitled to make such an appointment, but after an administration order is made such a creditor cannot appoint any kind of receiver; and before an administration order is made, only the court can give leave to a creditor to exercise his powers and remedies which are restricted by the Insolvency Act 1986, whereas after the order is made either the court or the administrator may give permission for this to be done.

The court is disinclined to give leave for a secured creditor of the company to realise his security after an administration order has been made, if the administrator proposes to sell the subject matter of the security at a price which will be adequate to discharge the secured debt and the secured creditor's costs which have been properly incurred.[13] The court will therefore not give leave for a secured creditor to realise his security unless he shows good reason for criticising the administrator's proposals, bearing in mind that those proposals would be made in the interest of the company's secured and unsecured creditors generally.[13] On the other hand, if the administrator makes no proposals for the realisation of the subject matter of the security or for its employment in the continued carrying on of the company's business undertaking, or if the administrator has been unable to carry out his proposals in that respect and does not put forward new proposals within a reasonable time allowed to him by the court, the court will give leave for the secured creditor to realise his security.[14] Nevertheless, if the secured creditor has benefited from the administrator carrying on the company's business undertaking by using the property comprised in the security or otherwise, the court will be unwilling to give leave for the secured creditor to realise his security, even though there is a likelihood that the administrator will cease to carry on the company's undertaking himself, but will either sell its assets and undertaking as a going concern or will sell its assets piecemeal.[15]

The rights and interests of a secured creditor or a creditor who is prevented by the Insolvency Act 1986 from repossessing or

---

13 *Royal Trust Bank v Buchler* [1989] BCLC 130.
14 *Re Meesan Investments Ltd* (1988) 4 BCC 788; *Re Atlantic Computer Systems plc* [1991] BCLC 606, [1990] BCC 859.
15 *Bristol Airport plc v Powdrill* [1990] Ch 744, [1990] 2 All ER 493.

realising property in the possession of the company while an administration order is in force, are not terminated or even suspended, but are merely made temporarily unenforceable unless the court or the administrator permits the creditor to act.[16] The administrator should therefore give effect to the creditor's rights, unless to do so would prevent or impede the administrator achieving the purpose or purposes for which the administration order was made.[16] Consequently, the administrator of a company which has taken a lease of items of equipment and has sub-leased them to other firms, should pay the rentals and other contractual payments due under the lease to the lessor out of the sub-rental payments received by the administrator from the sub-lessees, even though the lessor has no effective, immediate right to enforce his claims against the company.[16] The only way in which a secured creditor, the owner of property comprised in a hire purchase, credit sale, chattel leasing or retention of title agreement may enforce his rights directly against the property comprised in the security or agreement, or his rights to collect payments in respect of the security or agreement, is by applying to the court for an order giving him leave to do so or directing the administrator to take the necessary action for his benefit.[17] On such an application the court must balance the interests of the applicant in recovering the amount owed to him or enforcing his proprietary rights against the interest of the administrator in devising and giving effect to proposals designed by him which are to achieve the purpose or purposes for which the administration order was made.[18] For this purpose the advantages which the parties would respectively gain and the detriments which they would respectively suffer if the court were to accede to or refuse the application must be taken into account, as must the conduct of the parties and the preservation (so far as possible) of the applicant's contractual and proprietary rights.[18]

The effect of administration order proceedings generally

There is no provision in the Insolvency Act 1986 in respect of administration order proceedings comparable to the provision in a winding up of a company by the court, that all dispositions of the property of the company after the date when the successful winding

---

16 *Re Atlantic Computer Systems plc*, supra; *Barclays Mercantile Business Finance Ltd v Sibec Developments Ltd* [1993] BCLC 1077, [1993] BCC 148.
17 Insolvency Act 1986, s 11(3); *Re Mirror Group (Holdings) Ltd* [1993] BCLC 538, [1992] BCC 972.
18 *Re Atlantic Computer Systems plc* [1991] BCLC 606, [1990] BCC 859; *Re David Meek Plant Ltd* [1994] 1 BCLC 680, [1993] BCC 175.

up petition was presented shall be void unless approved by the court.[19] During the period between the presentation of a petition for an administration order and the making of the order, the directors of the company may continue to exercise their powers and may dispose of the company's property by selling, leasing, mortgaging or charging it or by dealing with it in any other way. It is only creditors of the company who are inhibited by the provisions dealt with above from suing the company, levying execution on its assets, realising any security for their debts or repossessing goods or land of the company.[20]

Because the presentation of a petition for an administration order does not prevent disposals of the company's property, even if such an order is subsequently made, the directors of the company may continue to draw on the company's bank account after the presentation of the petition, and its bank is entitled to collect payments for the credit of the company's account, and may debit the amount of cheques, bills of exchange etc drawn against it. Furthermore, although the company's lessor or landlord is inhibited from distraining on the company's goods for arrears of rent during the period between the presentation of a petition for an administration order and the making of the order, he is not prevented from forfeiting the company's lease and retaking possession of the property comprised in it if the company agrees or does not oppose this being done, but he does need leave of the court to forfeit the lease and to recover possession of the property if the company opposes or resists this being done.[1] However, if a lessor does forfeit a lease held by the company without obtaining the necessary leave or the company's acquiescence, and then grants a new lease to a third person, the lessor cannot treat the forfeiture as invalid and seek to recover rent for periods after the forfeiture from the company, or seek to enforce the lessee's covenants against it in respect of matters occurring since the forfeiture.[2]

Although the Insolvency Act 1986 makes no express provision for the conduct of the company's affairs between the presentation of a petition for an administration order and the making of the order, and the court has no power to appoint an interim administrator, the court can appoint a suitable person (such as the insolvency practitioner proposed for appointment as administrator) to take and retain possession and control of the assets of the company pending

---

19 Insolvency Act 1986, s 127.
20 Ibid, s 10(1).
  1 *Exchange Travel Agency Ltd v Triton Property Trust plc* [1991] BCLC 396, [1991] BCC 341; *Re a Debtor (No 13A10 of 1994)* [1996] BCC 57.
  2 *Re AGB Research plc, Redleaf Investments Ltd v Talbot* [1995] BCC 1091.

the hearing of the petition, so as to prevent their dissipation or improper disposal.[3] However, it would appear that the court has no power to issue injunctions preventing the directors from exercising their normal powers conferred by the Companies Act 1985, and the company's memorandum and articles of association, unless it is proved that the proposed exercise of their powers will involve a breach of their fiduciary or other duties to the company or a breach of the Companies Act 1985.

When an administration order has been made in respect of a company and an administrator has been appointed by the court, the power to manage the company's affairs and to deal with its assets vests in the administrator,[4] and any powers conferred by the Companies Act 1985, or by the company's memorandum or articles of association on any other person (including the company's directors, officers and agents) which could be exercised in such a way as to interfere with the administrator's powers are not exercisable unless the court or the administrator consents.[5] The company's directors do not cease to hold office, however, although the administrator may remove any director and may appoint new directors, whether to fill a vacancy or otherwise, and the administrator may call meetings of members of the company in order to appoint directors or for any other purpose.[6] Moreover, the directors can exercise powers vested in them which do not involve disposal of the company's assets or interference with the administrator's functions (eg powers to call and hold general meetings or to register transfers of shares) and must do so when required by the Companies Act 1985 (eg calling and holding annual general meetings).

THE ADMINISTRATOR

Appointment, vacation of office, remuneration and contractual responsibilities

The court appoints an administrator or two or more administrators by the terms of the administration order which it makes in respect of a company.[7] If the court appoints two or more persons to be the

---

3 *Re a Company (No 00175 or 1987)* [1987] BCLC 467, 3 BCC 124; *Re Gallidoro Trawlers Ltd* [1991] BCLC 411, [1991] BCC 691.
4 Insolvency Act 1986, s 14(1).
5 Ibid, s 14(4).
6 Ibid, s 14(2).
7 Ibid, s 13(1).

administrators, it must direct whether any act required or authorised to be done by an administrator is to be done by all or any one or more of them (ie whether they must act jointly or may act individually).[8]

If a vacancy occurs in the office of administrator by death, resignation or otherwise, the court may fill the vacancy on the application of any continuing administrator, or where there is no such administrator, on the application of the creditors' committee,[9] or where there is neither a continuing administrator nor a creditors' committee, on the application of the company or its directors or any creditor or creditors of the company.[10] When the court makes an order filling a vacancy in the office of administrator, the order must be advertised in the same way as the original administration order.[11]

An administrator may resign because of ill health, or because he intends to cease to practise as an insolvency practitioner, or because there is some conflict of interest or change in his personal circumstances which precludes or makes impracticable the further discharge by him of the duties of an administrator, and he may resign with leave of the court for any other reason.[12] An administrator must give at least seven days' notice of his intention to resign to the continuing administrator or administrators, or if there are none, to the creditors' committee,[9] or if there is no continuing administrator nor a creditor's committee, to the company and its creditors.[13] The administrator's resignation is then effected by him giving notice of it to the court.[14]

An administrator may be removed by the court, apparently on the application of any interested person (eg a creditor or member of the company or the directors of the company).[14] An administrator automatically vacates office if he ceases to be qualified to act as an insolvency practitioner, or if the administration order is discharged by order of the court.[15]

The remuneration of an administrator must either be fixed as a percentage of the value of the property with which he deals in the administration (ie the company's assets at the date of the administration order plus any assets which the administrator recovers under the provisions of the Insolvency Act 1986, relating to gifts and disposals of the company's assets at a significant undervalue,

---

8 Ibid, s 231(1) and (2).
9 See p 390, post.
10 Insolvency Act 1986, s 13(2) and (3).
11 Insolvency Rules 1986, r 2.55.
12 Insolvency Act 1986, r 19(1); Insolvency Rules 1986, r 2.53(1) and (2).
13 Insolvency Rules, r 2.53(3).
14 Insolvency Act 1986, s 19(1).
15 Ibid, s 18(3) and s 19(2).

voidable preferences and invalidated floating charges,[16] and assets acquired by the company while the administration order is in force), or the administrator's remuneration must be calculated by reference to the time spent by him and his staff in carrying out his functions.[17] The amount or rate of the administrator's remuneration is fixed by the creditors' committee[18] (if there is one), or if there is no such committee or the committee does not decide on the remuneration to be paid, the administrator's remuneration is fixed by resolution of a meeting of creditors, but if no such resolution is passed, the court may fix the remuneration on the administrator's application.[19] If there are joint administrators, their remuneration is a single amount which is divided between them as agreed upon by them, but in the absence of agreement, the division of the remuneration may be referred for decision by the creditors' committee, by a meeting of creditors or by the court.[20] If the administrator considers that the amount or rate of his remuneration is inadequate, he may request a meeting of creditors to increase it if the remuneration was fixed by the creditors' committee,[1] and if the administrator's remuneration was fixed either by the creditors' committee or by a meeting of creditors, the administrator may apply to the court to increase it.[2]

When an administrator ceases to hold office or dies, his remuneration and his right to an indemnity for expenses properly incurred by him are charged on, and will be paid out of, any property of the company in his custody or under his control which is not subject to any security vested in another person, or which is subject only to a security which, as created, was a floating charge, in which case payment to the administrator is made in priority to that charge.[3] There is also charged on and payable out the same property and with the same priority debts and liabilities incurred by the administrator under contracts entered into by him or any of his predecessors as administrators of the company, and under contracts of employment adopted by him or any of his predecessors as administrators.[4] A contract of employment entered into by the company before the administrator's appointment is adopted by him if he gives effect to it (eg by accepting the employee's services and paying his remuneration) without the administrator expressly taking over the

---

16 See p 376, post.
17 Insolvency Rules 1986, r 2.47(1) and (2).
18 See p 390, post.
19 Insolvency Rules 1986, r 2.47(3), (5) and (6).
20 Ibid, r 2.47(1).
 1 Ibid, r 2.48.
 2 Ibid, r 2.49(1).
 3 Ibid, s 19(3) and (4).
 4 Ibid, s 19(3) and (5) to (7), as amended by Insolvency Act 1994, s 1.

contract as one made or confirmed by him, and the contract is adopted by the administrator giving effect to it even though he expressly disclaims any responsibility for the company's obligations contained in it when adopting it.[5] However, the administrator is not deemed to have adopted a contract of employment by reason of anything done or omitted by him written 14 days after his appointment.[6] The amount payable to an employee which is secured by the statutory charge comprises remuneration, holiday pay and employer's contributions to an occupational pension scheme which relate to the period after the administrator or a predecessor of his adopted the contract of employment until the administrator ceased to hold office as such.[4]

The administrator's legal status

In exercising his powers, an administrator is deemed to act as the agent of the company in respect of which he was appointed.[7] In this he resembles an administrative receiver, who also is deemed to be the company's agent until it goes into liquidation, but unlike an administrative receiver,[8] an administrator is not personally liable on contracts entered into by him in carrying out his functions and in respect of contracts of employment entered into by the company before his appointment which he subsequently adopts.[9] An administrator will, therefore, be personally liable on a contract made for the purpose of the administration only if when the contract is made he fails to make it clear that he is contracting in his capacity as administrator; if he does not do this, he will be personally liable on the contract in the same way as a director who enters into a contract without making it clear that he makes the contract on behalf of the company, and not himself.[10]

It is therefore surprising to find that when an administrator vacates office, the company's property in his custody or control is charged, not only with his remuneration and expenses properly incurred, but also with sums payable in respect of debts and liabilities incurred by him under contracts entered into by him or contracts of employment entered into by the company and adopted

5 *Powdrill v Watson* [1995] 1 BCLC 386, [1995] BCC 319.
6 Insolvency Act 1986, s 19(6).
7 Ibid, s 14(5).
8 Ibid, s 44(1).
9 *Re Olympia and York Canary Wharf Ltd (No 2)*, *Bear Stearns International Ltd v Adamson* [1993] BCC 159.
10 *Bridges and Salmon Ltd v The Swan (Owner)* [1968] 1 Lloyd's Rep 5.

by him.[6] The first part of this provision is intelligible in view of the fact that an administrator would be entitled to pay himself the remuneration earned by him and to indemnify himself in respect of expenses properly incurred by him by applying the company's assets accordingly while he remains in office, but in the absence of a statutory charge, he would not be able to realise the company's assets for that purpose after ceasing to hold office. The second part of the provision is unnecessary, however, because an administrator, unlike an administrative receiver does not incur personal liability by entering into contracts on behalf of the company for the purpose of carrying out his functions, or by adopting contracts of employment entered into by the company, and the effect of the statutory charge in respect of these matters is simply to turn the other parties to such contracts and the company's employees under employment contracts which the administrator has adopted into secured creditors, with a charge for their claims over the whole of the company's assets which are not subject to fixed or specific mortgages or charges created by it in favour of other persons.

Despite their similarity in certain respects, an administrator does not have the same legal status as an administrative receiver; unlike a receiver, an administrator is not free to disregard the contractual obligations of the company, unless it is necessary to do so in order to achieve the purposes for which the administration order was made.[11] It is therefore possible for the other party to an agreement entered into with the company before the administration order was made to obtain an injunction against both the company and the administrator to restrain the breach of restrictive promises by the company contained in the contract, unless the injunction would prevent the administrator from fulfilling the purposes for which the administration order was made.[11] Also in his capacity as an agent of the company, an administrator must conform to all statutory requirements which are imposed on the company, such as requirements to consult with representatives of the company's employees before making its employees redundant, but the court may nevertheless on the administrator's application direct him to sell the company's undertaking or assets with the result that contracts with its employees will terminate, and the administrator is then absolved from his duty of consultation.[12]

An administrator, like a director, must conform to the provisions of the company's memorandum and articles of association, and so cannot use the company's resources to carry on a business which

11 *Astor Chemicals Ltd v Synthetic Technology Ltd* [1990] BCLC 1, [1990] BCC 97.
12 *Re Hartlebury Printers Ltd* [1993] BCLC 902, [1992] BCC 428.

would be ultra vires the company.[13] On the other hand, an administrator is not affected by those provisions of the company's memorandum and articles which govern the exercise of its directors' powers to manage the company's undertaking and to dispose of its assets, nor is he affected by such provisions which require the consent of certain persons for the exercise of such powers; the administrator's own statutory powers, including his power to carry out his proposals approved by the company's creditors for the purpose of achieving the object or objects for which the administration order was made, override conflicting provisions of the company's memorandum and articles in this respect.[14]

The administrator's functions and powers

On his appointment it is the administrator's duty to take into his custody or under his control all the property to which the company is, or appears to be, entitled.[15] To enable him to do so and to conduct the administration, an administrator has the same statutory powers as a liquidator to obtain summary orders of the court for the delivery of property or the payment of money to him, to require information about the company's property and affairs and to apply to the court for the private examination of persons in possession of such information.[16]

If in exercising his powers, an administrator seizes or takes possession of property which does not belong to the company, or if he disposes of any such property, and at the time of seizure or taking possession of the property or disposing of it he believes on reasonable grounds that he is entitled to do so (ie he believes it to be property to which the company is entitled), the administrator is not liable to any person for any loss or damage resulting from the seizure, taking possession or disposal unless the loss or damage is caused by the administrator's negligence, and the administrator has a lien or first charge on the property or the proceeds of selling it for his expenses incurred in connection with the seizure or disposal.[17]

Subject to the statutory provisions dealt with below by which an administrator may seek the invalidation of certain transactions entered into by the company in administration,[18] an administrator

---

13 *Re Home Treat Ltd* [1991] BCLC 705, [1991] BCC 165.
14 *Re P & C and R & T (Stockport) Ltd* [1991] BCLC 366, [1991] BCC 98.
15 Insolvency Act 1986, s 17(1).
16 Ibid, s 234(1) and (2), s 235(1) to (3) and s 236(1) to (3); (see pp 115, 177, 179 and 210, ante.
17 Ibid, s 234(1), (3) and (4).
18 See p 376 et seq, post.

has no better right to recover or retain assets or to enforce rights against third persons than the company has itself. Consequently claims by the administrator to recover property of the company or alleged to belong to it may be met by defences based on contractual or other rights for the defendant to retain possession which he could rely on against the company.[19] Moreover, the administrator is bound by express, implied and constructive trusts on which the company holds property or assets (eg the earnings of franchisees of the company which are collected by the company and are payable by it to them subject to certain agreed declarations).[20]

The administrator's functions before and after approval of his proposals

The administrator's primary functions are to manage the affairs, business and property of the company and to prepare proposals for achieving the purpose or purposes for which the administration order was made.[1] Before the proposals prepared by him are approved by a meeting of creditors of the company, the administrator must manage the company's affairs, business and property in accordance with any directions given by the court.[2] This does not mean that at this stage of the administration the administrator requires the court's approval for each transaction which he enters into; on the contrary, he is given a general power to do all such things as are necessary for the management of the company's affairs, business and property,[3] and he must manage its affairs on his own initiative. The only materials which the administrator has to guide him in deciding whether to enter into particular transactions before he has completed the preparation of his proposals for approval by a meeting of the company's creditors, are the purposes specified in the administration order as those which the administration is intended to achieve, when read with the independent report on the company's financial position which was filed with the petition for the administration order and was accepted by the court in making it. These materials will provide only a general and somewhat vague framework within which the administrator can decide on making disposals of the company's assets and entering into new contracts, or terminating, continuing or renewing existing ones. The administrator should not, however, make disposals of assets or enter

---

19 *Re Atlantic Computer Systems plc* [1991] BCLC 606, [1990] BCC 859; *Barclays Mercantile Business Finance Ltd v Sibec Developments Ltd* [1993] BCLC 1077, [1993] BCC 148.
20 *Re Lewis's of Leicester Ltd* [1995] 1 BCLC 428 [1995] BCC 514.
1 Insolvency Act 1986, s 17(2) and s 23(1).
2 Ibid, s 17(2)(*a*).
3 Ibid, s 14(1)(*a*).

into or break contracts, if to do so would seriously and adversely affect the fulfilment of the proposals which he intends to submit to the company's creditors, or which will prevent any such proposals being prepared.[4]

When the administrator has prepared his proposals for achieving the purpose or purposes for which the administration order was made and those proposals have been approved by a meeting of creditors of the company, the administrator must manage the affairs, business and property of the company in accordance with those proposals, as revised from time to time by the administrator with the approval of meetings of creditors.[5] An administrator is required to submit revisions of the proposals which were originally approved by the company's creditors to a further meeting of creditors only if the revisions appear to him to be substantial.[6] Consequently, minor departures by him from the originally approved proposals in managing the company's affairs are permissible if they do not endanger the achievement of the purposes for which the administration order was made, or involve substantial changes in the results sought to be achieved by the original proposals or in the manner of achieving them. In cases of doubt the administrator can, of course, apply to the court for directions.[7]

The administrator's specific powers

An administrator is given a number of specific powers to enable him to fulfil his functions both before and after the approval of his proposals by a meeting of the company's creditors. The specific powers conferred on an administrator should enable him to do almost all the things and to enter into almost all the transactions which he is likely to need to do in the context of any administration, whatever the nature or contents of his proposals to the company's creditors may be. The statutory list of the administrator's powers is not intended to be exhaustive, however, and if any act were necessary or appropriate in order to achieve the purposes for which the administration order was made, the administrator would be authorised to do it under his general statutory power to do all such things as may be necessary for the management of the affairs, business and property of the company.[8] A person dealing with an administrator is, in any case, protected if that person acts in good

4 *Re Charnley Davies Business Services Ltd* (1987) 3 BCC 408.
5 Insolvency Act 1986, s 17(2)(*b*).
6 Ibid, s 25(1) and (2); (see p 388, post).
7 Ibid, s 14(3).
8 Ibid, s 14(1).

faith and for value, and any transaction with him is valid whether it is within the administrator's powers or not.[9]

The specific powers of an administrator are listed in the Insolvency Act 1986,[10] and are similar to those of a liquidator,[11] but in some respects are more extensive. Like a liquidator, an administrator has power to take possession of, collect and get in the property of the company, and to sell or otherwise dispose of such property by public auction or by private contract, and to do all such things (including the carrying out of works) as are necessary for the realisation of the property of the company.[12] An administrator also has power to grant or take a lease of property, and to make or accept a surrender of a lease.[13] To enable him to manage the company's affairs, business and property, an administrator has power to raise or borrow money and to create securities for borrowed money over the property of the company; to appoint an agent to do any business which he is unable to do himself or which may more conveniently be done by an agent; to appoint a solicitor, accountant or other professionally qualified person to assist him; to appoint and dismiss employees; to effect and maintain insurance of the property and business of the company; to make payments which are necessary or incidental to the performance of his functions; to use the company's common seal; to do acts and to execute instruments and documents in the company's name and on its behalf; and to draw, make, accept and indorse bills of exchange, cheques and promissory notes in the company's name and on its behalf.[14]

An administrator has power to carry on the company's business in order to achieve the purpose or purposes for which the administration order was made,[15] and not merely for the purpose of selling or disposing of it, like a liquidator; unlike a liquidator, he also has power to form subsidiaries of the company and to transfer to such subsidiaries or existing subsidiaries of the company the whole or any part of its business and property.[16] If an administrator sells or disposes of the whole or any part of the company's business undertaking as a going concern, the rights, powers, obligations and liabilities of the company as regards its employees in its undertaking, or in the part of its undertaking which is disposed of, are transferred

---

9 Ibid, s 14(6).
10 Ibid, s 14(1)(*b*) and Sch 1.
11 See p 145 et seq, ante.
12 Insolvency Act 1986, Sch 1, paras 1, 2 and 12.
13 Ibid, Sch 1, para 17.
14 Ibid, Sch 1, paras 3, 4, 7 to 11 and 13.
15 Ibid, Sch 1, para 14.
16 Ibid, Sch 1, paras 15 and 16.

by operation of law to the purchaser or disponee.[17] Like a liquidator, an administrator may bring or defend any action or other legal proceedings in the company's name and on its behalf; may make arrangements and compromises on the company's behalf; may prove in the bankruptcy or winding up of any person or company which is indebted to the company of which he is the administrator; and unlike a liquidator, an administrator may submit any question concerning the company to arbitration, and may present or defend a petition for the winding up of the company by the court.[18] Finally, an administrator may call up and recover uncalled capital of the company, and may change the address of its registered office.[19]

All the powers of an administrator are exercisable on his initiative and at his discretion. Unlike a liquidator, he does not require the consent of any other person or the court before exercising any of his powers.

The administrator's report on directors' conduct and the removal or continuance in office of directors

An administrator must submit to the Secretary of State for Trade and Industry a report on persons who are or have been directors or shadow directors of the company at the date of the administration order or within three years beforehand in the same circumstances and for the same purposes as the liquidator of a company in voluntary liquidation must do.[20]

An administrator may remove any director of the company from office, and may appoint any person to be a director of the company, whether to fill a vacancy or otherwise.[1] Directors do not automatically cease to hold office on the making of an administration order, as they do on the making of a winding up order. Instead, directors continue in office notwithstanding the administration order, and they retire and may be re-elected or become disqualified to hold office in the same way as before. As indicated above,[2] the directors may continue to exercise their functions in the same way as before the administration order provided that they do not obstruct or interfere with the

---

17 Transfer of Undertakings (Protection of Employment) Regulations 1981 (SI 1981/1794), reg 3(1) and (2) and reg 5(1) and (2), as amended by Trade Union Reform and Employment Rights Act 1993, s 33.
18 Insolvency Act 1986, Sch 1, paras 5, 6, 18, 20 and 21.
19 Ibid, Sch 1, paras 19 and 22.
20 Company Directors' Disqualification Act 1986, s 7(3); Insolvent Companies (Reports on Conduct of Directors) Rules 1996 (SI 1996/1909), r 3(1) and (2) and r 4(1) and (2) and Schedule, Forms D7, 2 and 3 (see p 186, ante).
1 Insolvency Act 1986, s 14(2)(a).
2 See p 362, ante,

exercise of the administrator's functions,[3] and except so far as the Insolvency Act 1986 provides otherwise, directors continue to be subject to the same duties and restrictions under the Companies Acts 1985 and 1989, as though no administration order were in force.

A director who is removed by an administrator presumably has no claim against the company for damages or compensation for loss of office, unless he has a service contract with the company which so provides, or which entitles him to compensation or damages if he ceases to be a director for any reason.[4] In any other situation, it would seem that a director who has served the company on the terms of the company's articles of association without having a separate service contract would have no claim for damages against the company because the administrator removes him from office in exercise of his statutory power to do so, or without removing him, excludes him from exercising his former functions.[5]

Because the continued exercise by the directors of their management functions is entirely at the discretion of the administrator, he may authorise them or any of their number to do such acts, or to manage or supervise such parts of the company's business activities, as the administrator thinks fit. If the administrator does so, it would seem that no new contract of employment is made between the company and the director whose services are retained, unless the parties expressly agree to that effect, but it may be that the whole or part of the director's remuneration during the period for which he continues to act with the administrator's authority or consent will be an expense of the administration payable with the same priority as other such expenses.

The disposal of the company's assets free from charges

Fixed and specific mortgages and charges; goods subject to hire purchase agreements etc

An administrator may apply to the court for leave to dispose of any property of the company which is subject to a mortgage, charge, lien or other security (other than a floating charge), or for leave to dispose of goods in the possession of the company which are comprised in a hire-purchase agreement, conditional sale agreement, chattel leasing agreement or retention of title agreement,[6] as if the

3 Insolvency Act 1986, s 14(4).
4 *Southern Foundries (1926) Ltd v Shirlaw* [1940] AC 701; [1940] 2 All ER 445;
   Taupo Totara Timber Co Ltd v Rowe [1978] AC 537, [1977] 3 All ER 123.
5 *Newtherapeutics Ltd v Katz* [1991] Ch 226, [1991] 2 All ER 151.
6 For the definition of these terms, see pp 354 and 355, ante, footnotes 11 to 13.

property were not subject to the security, or as if ownership of the goods were vested in the company.[7] If the court is satisfied that the disposal in that way of the property or goods (with or without other assets) would be likely to promote one or more of the purposes for which the administration order was made, the court may authorise the administrator to dispose of the property or goods accordingly.[7]

The court must make it a condition of the authorisation given by it that the net proceeds of the disposal (after meeting the expenses of carrying it out) and, if those proceeds are less than the net amount which the court considers would be realised on a sale of the property or goods in the open market by a willing seller, an addition to the net proceeds of disposal made out of the company's general assets to make the net proceeds equal to that amount, shall be applied toward discharging the sum secured by the security, or the sum payable under the hire purchase or other agreement; if the property disposed of is subject to two or more securities, the net proceeds must be applied toward discharging those securities in the order of priority in which they rank between themselves.[8]

The effect of those provisions is that with leave of the court an administrator can sell or dispose of any property of the company which is subject to a mortgage, charge or lien, as though it were in the company's unencumbered ownership; and with such leave, the administrator may likewise sell or dispose of any goods in the company's possession of which it has not yet acquired ownership under the hire-purchase or other agreement with the owner by which it obtained possession, and the administrator may make such dispositions as though the company already owned the goods. In both situations the rights of the secured creditor or creditors or the rights of the owner of the goods are transferred to the proceeds of sale or disposal in the administrator's hands, augmented by any addition ordered by the court if the net amount realised on the disposal by the administrator is less than the open market realisable value of the property or goods. Presumably, the administrator holds the net proceeds of the disposal in trust for the secured creditor or creditors or for the former owner of the goods, and any addition ordered by the court to equate with the open market value will be an expense of the administration for which the secured creditor or former owner will be subrogated to the administrator's right to an indemnity.

The value of the facility available to the administrator to dispose of property or goods which are subject to a secured creditor's or owner's rights is that the administrator may be able to obtain a better

7 Insolvency Act 1986, s 15(2), (3) and (9), s 248(*b*) and s 251.
8 Ibid, s 15(5) and (6).

price for them by selling them together with other assets of the company which are not subject to such rights (eg the sale of a mortgaged factory together with the plant and equipment used in it; the sale of stock in trade, some of which is owned by the company, and the remainder of which is subject to the retention of title by the unpaid supplier). The authorisation for the administrator to dispose of property or goods in an unencumbered condition will be given by the court, however, only if the disposal will clearly assist the achievement of the purpose or purposes for which the administration order was made. If the administrator has not yet prepared or submitted his proposals for the achievement of those purposes to a meeting of the company's creditors for their approval, the court has shown itself disinclined to authorise the administrator to sell the various classes of the company's assets free from specific or fixed charges on them merely because the administrator wishes to sell the goodwill attached to part of the company's business[9] together with those assets.[10] On the other hand, the fact that there is a dispute between the administrator and the holder of a fixed charge over property of the company as to the market value of the property, will not induce the court to refuse leave for the administrator to dispose of the property, and to permit the secured creditor to sell it instead, provided that the court is satisfied that the administrator will realise a sufficient amount from the disposal to discharge the whole of the secured indebtedness, or at least, if there is any deficiency, that the company's general assets in the administrator's hands will be sufficient to make it good.[11] Moreover, where the administrator of a construction company sought unsuccessfully to raise finance needed to complete an uncompleted construction project with a view to selling it, the court refused to permit a mortgagee of the uncompleted structures to exercise his power to sell them without first giving a reasonable opportunity to the administrator to find a purchaser to whom the court would authorise him to dispose of the structures free from the mortgage.[12]

The court's function on hearing an administrator's application to the court for authorisation to dispose of property free from a fixed mortgage or charge which incumbers it, whether there is a counter-application by the secured creditor for leave to realise his security or not, is to balance the conflicting interests of the secured creditor and the company's creditors generally, taking account of any detriment

9 The goodwill in the case in question was the publicity value attached to magazine titles published by the company.
10 *Re Consumer and Industrial Press Ltd (No 2)* (1987) 4 BCC 72.
11 *Re ARV Aviation Ltd* [1989] BCLC 664, 4 BCC 708; *Royal Trust Bank v Buchler* [1989] BCLC 130.
12 *Re Meesan Investments Ltd* (1988) 4 BCC 788.

which the secured creditor may suffer by the administrator being given leave to realise the property; unless the administrator's proposals are open to serious criticism, however, the court will incline toward authorising him, and not the secured creditor, to dispose of the property if there is some benefit to be obtained as a result by the company's creditors generally.[13]

Floating charges

In addition to his power with the court's approval to dispose of assets of a company in administration free from any specific mortgages or charges, an administrator may dispose of or otherwise exercise his powers (eg to make a transfer to a newly created subsidiary of the company) in respect of property of the company which is subject to a charge which, as created, was a floating charge, as though the charge did not extend to that property, and the administrator does not require the approval of the court or anyone else to do this.[14] The effect of such a disposition or exercise of the administrator's powers is that the person to whom the disposition is made or in whose favour the powers are exercised takes the ownership of the property or rights over it free from the floating charge, even if it has already crystallised or has become a fixed charge, and free also from any restrictions imposed on the company's power to dispose of or to deal with the property which were imposed by the charge. This provision applies to all floating charges, and not only to those which comprise the whole or substantially the whole of the property of the company, so that, for example, the administrator of a company which had created a floating charge over its existing and future book debts is able to sell and transfer them free from the charge to a factoring concern which purchases book debts at a discount.

The exercise of the administrator's power of disposal does not destroy the floating charge, however, nor if the charge has crystallised or become a fixed charge at the date of the disposition by the administrator, does that disposition prevent the charge from extending to later acquisitions of assets of the class or classes charged.[15] Moreover, the holder of a charge created as a floating charge has the same security over property of the company directly or indirectly representing the property disposed of as he would have

---

13 *Re ARV Aviation Ltd,* supra; see also for the principles on which the court grants or withholds authorisation, *Re Atlantic Computer Systems plc* [1991] BCLC 606, [1990] BCC 859.

14 Insolvency Act 1986, s 15(1) and (3).

15 *N W Robbie & Co Ltd v Witney Warehouse Co Ltd* [1963] 3 All ER 613, [1963] 1 WLR 1324; *Business Computers Ltd v Anglo-African Leasing Ltd* [1977] 2 All ER 741, [1977] 1 WLR 578.

had in respect of the property originally subject to the security.[16] In other words, whether or not the floating charge has crystallised or become a fixed charge before the disposal by the administrator, the proceeds of the disposal and any property acquired by the administrator with those proceeds will be subject to the floating charge, or as the case may be, the floating charge which has become a fixed charge by crystallisation or otherwise, in the same way as the property disposed of was subject to the charge before the disposal, and the charge will have the same priority as regards those proceeds and property acquired with them as it formerly had as regards the property disposed of. This will be so, whatever the character of the derivative property may be. Consequently, if an administrator sells book debts of the company which are subject to a floating charge and uses the proceeds of sale to purchase further stock in trade, the floating charge which has been overreached will continue as a floating charge with the same priority over the acquired stock in trade. This could give rise to problems in identifying the derivative property, because in the example given the holder of the floating charge would have such an extended charge only over the stock in trade acquired with the proceeds of the book debts which have been sold, and not over the company's stock in trade generally. In practice, administrators are likely to use their power to overreach floating charges only if they extend to the company's whole assets and undertaking (with or without the exclusion of assets subject to fixed or specific charges vested in the holder of the floating charge), and in that situation tracing and identifying derivative property should not present difficulties.

Invalidation of transactions by the company

When an administration order has been made in respect of a company, the administrator may apply to the court in the same circumstances as a liquidator in a winding up for orders invalidating gifts and transactions entered into by the company at a significant undervalue,[17] or invalidating voidable preferences given by the company to its creditors or guarantors of its obligations,[18] setting

---

16 Insolvency Act 1986, s 15(4).
17 Ibid, s 238(1) to (4), s 423(1) to (3) and s 424(1); (see pp 221 and 233, ante).
   Applications to invalidate transactions at an undervalue entered into by the
   company for the purpose of putting its assets beyond the reach of its creditors or
   otherwise prejudicing its creditors may also be made by victims of the transactions
   (s 424(1)).
18 Insolvency Act 1986, s 239(1) to (5); (see p 225, ante).

aside extortionate credit transactions with the company,[19] or declaring the invalidity of floating charges created by the company for no new consideration within certain periods before the administration order proceedings.[20] The periods preceding the administration order proceedings within which the gifts, transactions at a significant undervalue or voidable preferences must have been effected, or the floating charges created, if they are to be invalidated and appropriate restoration, repayment or compensation orders made by the court, are the same as in a winding up, and the same differential periods are prescribed depending on whether the beneficiary of a voidable preference or grantee of a floating charge was or was not connected with the company at the time of the transaction.[1] The relevant periods are calculated from the date on which the petition was presented on which the administration order was made,[2] but if an administrator seeks to have an extortionate credit transaction with the company set aside, he must show that the company entered into it within three years preceding the date of the administration order.[3]

The effect of the invalidation in administration proceedings of gifts, transactions at a significant undervalue, voidable preferences, extortionate credit transactions or floating charges created for no new consideration, is to augment the assets of the company in the administrator's hands which he may use or dispose of in order to achieve the purpose or purposes for which the administration order was made, or at least, to diminish the company's liabilities or the amount of its assets encumbered by charges or other securities. Although an administration order may be made in order to achieve short-term purposes and to avoid the company going into liquidation (eg an order made to enable the company and its business undertaking to survive a period of insufficient cash flow to meet its obligations), the invalidation pronounced by the court and the automatic invalidation on the making of an administration order of certain floating charges for which the company has received no new consideration, are permanent in effect, and the orders made by the court for the restoration of assets to the company, the repayment of money received from it or the payment of compensation to it are not terminated or cancelled by the discharge of the administration order by the court, except so far as the court expressly orders.[4]

19 Ibid, s 244(1) to (3); (see p 235, ante).
20 Ibid, s 245(1), (2) and (4); (see p 237, ante).
 1 Ibid, s 240(1) and s 245(3); (see pp 229 and 240, ante).
 2 Ibid, s 240(3) and s 245(5).
 3 Ibid, s 244(2).
 4 Ibid, s 18(3).

THE ADMINISTRATOR'S PROPOSALS

The preparation of proposals

The administrator's duty to prepare proposals

Within three months after an administration order is made or such longer period as the court allows, the administrator must send to the Registrar of Companies and (so far as he is aware of their addresses) to all creditors of the company a statement of the administrator's proposals for achieving the purpose or purposes specified in the administration order, and the administrator must within the same period lay a copy of his proposal before a meeting of the company's creditors for their approval.[5] An application to the court to extend the period of three months should be made by the administrator, and not in the name of the company, or by a creditor or other interested person.[6] The administrator must also within the same three month period or an extension thereof allowed by the court either send a copy of the statement of his proposals to all members of the company (so far as he is aware of their addresses), or he must publish in the London Gazette and the newspaper in which the administration order was advertised a notice giving an address at which members of the company may apply for copies of the administrator's statement of his proposals to be sent to them free of charge.[7]

The statements of the company's affairs

To assist him in preparing the statement of his proposals, the administrator may require any persons who are or have been directors or officers of the company, or who have taken part in the company's formation within one year before the administration order was made, or who are or have been within that year employees of the company, or officers or employees of another company which is, or was within that year, an officer of the company, to make out and submit to him a statement of the company's affairs in the prescribed form.[8] The Insolvency Act 1986 is expressed to impose an obligation on the administrator to require some or all of the persons indicated above to submit a statement of affairs, but the

---

5 Ibid, s 23(1) and s 24(1).
6 *Re Newport County Association Football Club Ltd* [1987] BCLC 582, 3 BCC 635.
7 Insolvency Act 1986, s 23(2); Insolvency Rules 1986, r 2.17.
8 Insolvency Act 1986, s 22(1) and (3); Insolvency Rules 1986, r 2.11(1).

administrator is also empowered to release any person who may be called on to make or join in making such a statement from his duty to do so,[9] and so it would appear that the administrator may dispense with a statement of affairs altogether, if he considers that he already has sufficient information about the company's affairs, for example, from his inquiries made to enable him to prepare his report in support of the petition for the administration order.

The statement of affairs must be in the prescribed form,[10] and must be verified by the affidavit of the person or persons making it, and supported by concurring affidavits made by any of the persons indicated above whom the administrator requires to verify the whole or part of the statement; such concurring affidavits may be qualified in respect of any of the matters included in the statement if the deponent does not agree with the principal deponent(s).[10] The statement of affairs must set out particulars of the company's assets, debts and liabilities, the names and addresses of its creditors, the securities held by them respectively (if any) with the dates on which such securities were created, the amount of the company's debts and liabilities which would be preferential payments in a liquidation, and the estimated amount of the deficiency of the company's assets to satisfy its preferential debts and liabilities, and to satisfy both its preferential and ordinary debts and liabilities combined, or as the case may be, the estimated surplus of the company's assets after satisfying all those liabilities.[11]

The administrator must file the statement of the company's affairs and the verifying and concurring affidavits in court,[12] where they are open to inspection by any member of the public, whether a creditor or member or shareholder of the company or not.[13] If the administrator considers that it would prejudice the conduct of the administration if the whole or any part of the statement of affairs were open to public inspection, he may apply to the court for an order, either that the statement of affairs shall not be filed in court, or that the relevant parts of it shall be filed separately and shall not be open to inspection unless the court gives leave.[14]

---

9 Insolvency Act 1986, s 22(5). If the administrator refuses to give a release, the person required to make or verify the statement may apply to the court for a release from his obligation.

10 Insolvency Act 1986, s 22(2); Insolvency Rules 1986, r 2.12(1) to (3) and Sch 4, Form 2.9.

11 Insolvency Act 1986, s 22(2); Insolvency Rules 1986, r 2.12(1) and Sch 4, Form 2.9.

12 Insolvency Rules 1986, r 2.12(6).

13 Ibid, r 7.28(1).

14 Ibid, r 2.13(1) and (2).

Power of the administrator to obtain information, records and property of the company

In addition to the requirement that directors and other persons connected with the company shall submit a statement of the company's affairs in a standardised form in order to assist the administrator in fulfilling his functions, the administrator has the same powers as a liquidator in a winding up to require any person who has in his possession or control any property, books, papers or records of the company to deliver them to the administrator, and he may apply to the court summarily for an order to that effect if the requirement is not complied with.[15] The administrator may also require any person who could be called on to make and verify, or to join in verifying a statement of the company's affairs, to give to the administrator such information about the company's promotion, formation, business, dealings, affairs or property as he reasonably required.[16]

Furthermore, the court may on the application of the administrator order the examination by it in the same way as in a winding up of any officer of the company, or any person known or suspected to have in his possession any property of the company or supposed to be indebted to the company, or any person whom the court thinks capable of giving information about the promotion, formation, business, dealings, affairs or property of the company; the court may on such an examination summarily order the delivery to the administrator of any property of the company in the possession of the person examined, or the payment by him to the administrator of any debt which he owes to the company.[17] The court may exercise its power of examination either by requiring the person in question to attend the court and to answer questions put to him orally, or it may require him to submit an affidavit dealing with the matters in question or to answer interrogatories on affidavit.[18] The procedure in respect of these matters is the same as on an examination in a winding up.[19]

The purpose of conferring power on the court to conduct examinations is to assist the administrator to ascertain the company's assets and liabilities, the nature and effect of transactions entered into by the company and the availability of steps to invalidate them, and to enable the administrator to decide whether to litigate in the company's name or by making applications to the court in the

15 Insolvency Act 1986, s 234(1) and (2); (see p 177, ante).
16 Ibid, s 235(1) to (3); (see p 115, ante).
17 Ibid, s 236(1) to (3) and s 237(1) and (2); (see p 178, ante).
18 Ibid, s 236(2) and (3).
19 Insolvency Rules 1986, rr 9.1 to 9.5; (see p 179, ante).

administration proceedings. The power to interrogate persons from whom the administrator seeks information is a wide one, but will not be ordered by the court where it would be oppressive to do so; consequently, if the administrator already has sufficient information to enable him to decide whether to take proceedings in his own or the company's name against the person whom he seeks to have examined, the court will not order the examination of that person merely in order to provide the administrator with evidence by way of admissions or otherwise with which he may prove his case in litigation.[20]

The contents of the administrator's proposals

The proposals prepared by the administrator for the achievement of the purpose or purposes for which the administration order was made must set out in detail the way in which the administrator proposes to conduct the administration. The proposals must therefore set out which of the company's assets he intends to dispose of or to retain, which parts of the company's business undertaking (if any) he intends to carry on, the way in which the continuation of the company's business or parts of it will be financed (eg by using the proceeds of disposal of assets which are to be sold, by raising loans, or by the company issuing further shares[1]) and the manner in which the company's indebtedness is to be dealt with, either by deferring the dates when debts or some of them will become due and payable, by the company's creditors releasing certain debts or a certain percentage of the company's indebtedness, or by creditors releasing securities for some or all of the company's indebtedness.

The nature of the administrator's proposals will, of course, depend on the company's financial situation and prospects, but the varieties of proposals which may be made by the administrator are almost infinite, ranging from the temporary deferment of payment of the company's debts in the expectation that the administrator will be able to carry on its business profitably and restore it to a sound financial condition, to proposals for the winding up of the company's affairs over an extended period, or the hiving down of the company's undertaking and the vesting of the viable parts of it in a newly formed company or companies with or without the company raising new finance by the issue of share or loan capital. Where the administrator's

---

20 *Re Cloverbay Ltd* [1991] BCLC 135.
1 The issue of further shares of the company would require the concurrence of its directors or its existing shareholders.

proposals involve the cancellation or modification of the rights of shareholders or debt security holders, the administrator will prepare a scheme of arrangement or, in a straightforward case involving only creditors' rights, a voluntary arrangement to which special rules apply. This subject is dealt with separately in the following chapter.

The prescribed form for the administrator's proposals unavoidably sets out only its formal contents, leaving the expression of the substance of the proposals to his discretion.[2] However, there must be annexed to the copies of the proposals delivered to the Registrar of Companies and laid before the meeting of the company's creditors called to approve the proposals, a statement by the administrator containing:[3]

(a) details of the administrator's appointment, the purpose or purposes for which the administration order was applied for and made, and any subsequent variation of those purposes which have been made;[4]

(b) the names of the directors and secretary of the company;

(c) an account of the circumstances giving rise to the application for an administration order (ie a brief history of the company's trading activities and financial condition during the period preceding the administration proceedings);

(d) if a statement of affairs has been submitted, a copy or summary of it with the administrator's comments, if any;

(e) if no statement of affairs has been submitted, details of the company's financial position at the latest practicable date, not being earlier than the date of the administration order, unless the court otherwise orders;

(f) a statement of the manner in which the affairs and business of the company have been managed and financed since the administrator's appointment, and the manner in which they will continue to be managed and financed if the administrator's proposals are approved by the meeting of the company's creditors; and

(g) such other information as the administrator considers necessary to enable the company's creditors to decide whether or not to vote for the adoption of the administrator's proposals.

---

2 Insolvency Rules 1986, Sch 4, Form 2.21.
3 Insolvency Act 1986, s 23(1); Insolvency Rules 1986, r 2.16(1).
4 See p 387, post.

Approval of the administrator's proposals by the creditors

Convening the meeting of creditors

When he has prepared his proposals, the administrator must call a meeting of the company's creditors to approve them by giving at least 14 days' notice to each of the creditors who is identified in the statement of the company's affairs, or who is known to the administrator to have claims against the company at the date of the administration order.[5] Notice of the meeting must at the same time be sent to directors and officers of the company whose attendance at the meeting the administrator requires.[6] The meeting must be advertised in the newspaper in which the administration order was advertised.[7]

The meeting of creditors is presided over by the administrator, or by a person nominated by him who is either a qualified insolvency practitioner, or an employee of the administrator who is experienced in insolvency matters.[8] If within 30 minutes after the time fixed for the commencement of the meeting no person entitled to act as chairman is present, the meeting is adjourned to the same time and place in the following week.[9] The chairman additionally has power to adjourn the meeting for not more than 14 days after the date on which it was to have commenced.[10]

Creditors' entitlement to attend and vote at the creditors' meeting

A creditor is entitled to attend and vote at the creditors' meeting only if he has given to the administrator, not later than 12 noon on the business day preceding the day fixed for the meeting, details in writing of the debt claimed by him from the company, and the claim must have been admitted in whole or part by the chairman of the meeting.[11] The chairman's rejection of a claim in whole or part is subject to an appeal to the court by the creditor concerned, and any other creditor may appeal against the admission of a claim, but the appeal must be made within 28 days after the administrator reports the result of the meeting to the court.[12] If the chairman is in doubt whether to admit or reject a claim, he must mark it as objected to and

---

5 Insolvency Act 1986, s 23(1) and s 24(1); Insolvency Rules 1986, r 2.18(1).
6 Insolvency Rules 1986, r 2.18(3).
7 Ibid, r 2.18(2).
8 Ibid, r 2.20(1) and (2).
9 Ibid, r 2.19(6).
10 Ibid, r 2.19(7).
11 Ibid, r 2.22(1) and r 2.23(1).
12 Ibid, r 2.23(2) and (5).

allow the claimant to vote, subject to the subsequent disallowance of his vote if the objection to it is sustained.[13] If on an appeal to the court the decision of the chairman as to the right of a claimant to vote, or as to the amount of indebtedness in respect of which he may vote, is reversed or varied, the court may order another meeting of creditors to be held in place of the original meeting, or may make such other order as it thinks just (eg a declaration that a resolution has or has not been validly passed at the meeting).[14]

A creditor may appoint a proxy to attend the meeting of creditors and to vote on his behalf, and the notice of the meeting sent to each creditor must be accompanied by a proxy appointment form which a creditor who wishes to appoint a proxy must complete and deliver to the administrator, together with the notification of details of the debt which he claims from the company.[15] Company and other corporate creditors may appoint proxies, or may appoint representatives authorised by their boards of directors or similar bodies by a resolution authenticated under the company's common seal, or by a director or secretary of the company in writing, and each representative may attend the meeting of creditors and vote on his company's behalf.[16]

Approval of the administrator's proposals

A resolution of the creditors' meeting approving the administrator's proposals is effective only if a majority in value of the creditors present and voting at the meeting in person or by proxy or (in the case of corporate creditors) by representative vote in favour of it, but the resolution will not be valid if those voting against it include more than one half in value of the creditors to whom notice of the meeting was sent and who are not persons connected with the company, that is, directors or shadow directors of the company and persons associated with them or the company.[17] This means that if the majority in value of the company's creditors who vote for the approval of the administrator's proposals includes the votes of creditors connected with the company, the value of their debts must be deducted from the total amount of the debts owed to creditors voting to approve the proposals, and the resolution of approval is then ineffective if the net amount of debts owed to creditors voting to approve the proposals, is less than the total debts owed to

13 Ibid, r 2.23(3).
14 Ibid, r 2.23(4).
15 Ibid, r.19(5) and r 2.22(1) and Sch 4, Form 8.2.
16 Ibid, r 8.7(1) and (2).
17 Insolvency Rules 1986, r 2.28(1) and (1A). For the definition of persons connected with the company, see Insolvency Act 1986, s 249 and p 150, ante.

creditors who vote against approval being given and are not themselves connected with the company. The purpose of this rule is to prevent proposals becoming binding on creditors of the company who are not connected with it as the result of connected creditors (ie directors and persons associated with them) providing the votes which are essential to procure a majority for approval. In effect the rule requires a double majority vote by the company's creditors for the administrator's proposals to be validly approved, namely, an initial majority vote of all creditors of the company, whether connected with it or not, who vote at the creditors' meeting, and secondly a majority vote of creditors of the company who are not connected with it; this does not mean that two separate votes must be taken, however, but that the chairman must ascertain whether the result of the votes taken on a single resolution is that both majorities have been attained.

Valuation of debts and claims

The value of debts owed by the company is taken for voting purposes to be their nominal amount or face value, and no deduction is made from that amount because debts are payable at a future date or are subject to conditions or contingencies. The value of a debt is taken as at the date of the administration order, including interest calculated up to that date, but amounts paid in respect of a debt after that date must be deducted.[18] Votes may not be cast in respect of claims for unliquidated amounts or debts whose amounts are uncertain, but the chairman of the creditors' meeting may agree to put an estimated minimum value upon such a debt or claim, and may admit it for voting at that value.[19] There has been a conflict of authority as to whether this provision means that the chairman may admit the creditor's claim for an estimated amount only if the chairman and the creditor agree on that amount (as was held in one case),[20] or whether the only agreement required is the unilateral consent of the chairman to admit the claim for voting purposes at his estimate of its value, and the acceptance of this by the creditor is not required (as was held in another case);[1] the latter view, which has been upheld by the Court of Appeal, would appear to be the correct one.[2]

18 Insolvency Rules 1986, r 2.22(4).
19 Ibid, r 2.22(5).
20 *Re Cranley Mansions Ltd, Saigol v Goldstein* [1995] 1 BCLC 290, [1994] BCC 576.
 1 *Doorbar v Alltime Securities Ltd* [1995] 1 BCLC 316, [1994] BCC 994, *(No 2)* [1995] BCC 728.
 2 [1996] 1 BCLC 487, [1995] BCC 1149.

Certain creditors are required to make deductions from their claims for voting purposes. Secured creditors may vote only in respect of the excess of their debts over their estimate of the value of the property comprised in their security;[3] the chairman may reject the claim of a secured creditor for that excess if he considers that the security is undervalued, but the secured creditor may appeal to the court against the rejection.[4] Creditors holding bills of exchange or promissory notes to which the company is a party must likewise treat the liability of every person whose liability on the instrument is antecedent to that of the company as a security, and deduct the value of that security from their claims.[5] Likewise, sellers of goods to the company who have by agreement retained the ownership of the goods until the price or any other indebtedness of the company is paid, must deduct from their claims their estimate of the value of their rights to recover the goods or to claim the proceeds of reselling them.[6] On the other hand, owners of goods under hire-purchase or chattel leasing agreements entered into with the company and sellers of goods to the company under conditional sale agreements are entitled to vote only in respect of the amounts due and payable to them at the date of the administration order (ie unpaid instalments or rental already accrued due), but leaving out of account amounts becoming payable under the agreement only by reason of the presentation of the petition for an administration order or the making of the order (ie amounts payable under acceleration provisions by which the outstanding balance of future rental or instalments of the price of the goods become immediately payable).[7]

A creditor may divide the total amount of indebtedness in respect of which he is entitled to vote on a resolution, and may cast an affirmative vote in respect of part of it and a negative vote in respect of the balance.[8] This is a useful facility when the creditor is a trustee of the indebtedness for two or more persons who are beneficially entitled to separate parts of it, and they give him conflicting instructions as to the manner in which he shall vote.

After the conclusion of the creditors' meeting, the administrator must report the results to the court, and must notify those results to the Registrar of Companies and each creditor of the company to whom notice of the meeting was sent and to each other creditor of whom the administrator has since become aware.[9] The report or

3 Insolvency Rules 1986, r 2.24.
4 Ibid, r 2.23(1) and (2).
5 Ibid, r 2.25.
6 Ibid, r .2.26.
7 Ibid, r 2.27(1) and (2).
8 *Re Polly Peck International plc* [1991] BCC 503.
9 Insolvency Act 1986, s 24(4); Insolvency Rules 1986, r 2.30(1).

notification must have annexed to it details of the proposals and of any revisions or modifications of them which were considered by the meeting.[10]

Modifications and revisions of the administrator's proposals

The creditors' meeting convened to approve the administrator's proposals may approve them with modifications, but unless such modifications are consented to by the administrator, they are treated as ineffective and the administrator's proposals are then treated as not approved by the creditors' meeting.[11] If the creditors' meeting is willing to accept the proposals only if modifications called for by the creditors are made to them, the administrator must decide whether to accept the modifications so that the administration may proceed, or whether to reject them, in which case the court will either discharge the administration order or make an interim order enabling the administrator to submit revised proposals to another meeting of creditors for their approval.[12] The court has no power itself to make modifications to the administrator's proposals, or to consent to proposals called for by the creditors if the administrator refuses to consent to them. If the administrator consents to suggested modifications to his proposals, a resolution accepting each modification must be put to the vote of the creditors, and when all the suggested modifications have been so disposed of, a final vote of the creditors must be taken to approve the administrator's proposals incorporating the modifications which the creditors' meeting has adopted.

When an administrator's proposals have been approved by the meeting of creditors with or without modifications consented to by the administrator and approved by the meeting, it is the administrator's duty to conduct the administration in accordance with the approved proposals with the approved modifications (if any).[13] As the administration proceeds, the administrator may find that the approved proposals require revision, either because measures envisaged by the original proposals turn out to be impracticable or inappropriate for achieving the purposes for which the administration order was made (eg it proves impossible to effect the originally intended sale of some part of the company's assets, or to raise new share or loan capital), or because the economic conditions whose continuance formed the basis of the original proposals undergo an

10 Insolvency Rules 1986, r 2.29.
11 Insolvency Act 1986, s 24(2).
12 Ibid, s 24(5).
13 Ibid, s 17(2).

important change (eg a major improvement or deterioration occurs in the market for the products or services which the company supplies, or in the availability of the goods or materials which the company requires for carrying on its business). The administrator may revise his originally approved proposals in order to deal with such developments, and if the revisions are substantial, he must send to all the creditors of the company a statement in the prescribed form of the revisions which he proposes should be made in his original proposals as approved by the creditors, and must submit the revisions for approval by a further meeting of creditors convened by giving them not less than 14 days' notice.[14] The administrator must also either send copies of the statement to all members of the company of whose addresses he is aware, or must publish in the London Gazette and the newspaper in which the administration order was advertised a notice giving an address at which members of the company may apply for copies of the statement of the administrator's revised proposals.[15]

It may be difficult to draw a distinction between situations where substantial revisions of the administrator's proposals should be made, and situations where changes in carrying out his original proposals are not sufficiently important to require the approval of a creditors' meeting. This is because the question whether a revision is substantial is essentially one of degree. If the purpose for which the administration order was made is still capable of achievement, but the administrator is in doubt whether the original proposals are adequate to accommodate the changes in the measures which he wishes to take, he may, if the matter is urgent, apply to the court for directions that he shall effect those changes, and it will not then be necessary for him to submit revised proposals to a creditors' meeting.[16] However, if the administrator has disposed of the major part of the company's assets, he should not protract the administration by preparing and submitting revised proposals, but should apply to the court to discharge the administration order.[17]

An administrator should not submit revisions of his proposals to the creditors if they involve an alteration of the purpose or purposes for which the administration order was made; in that situation the administrator should apply to the court to vary the terms of the administration order so as to add or substitute the purpose which is appropriate in the circumstances,[18] and if the court

14 Ibid, s 25(1) and (2); Insolvency Rules 1986, Sch 4, Form 2.22.
15 Insolvency Act 1986, s 25(3); Insolvency Rules 1986, r 2.17.
16 Insolvency Act 1986, s 14(3); *Re Smallman Construction Ltd* [1989] BCLC 420, 4 BCC 784.
17 *Re Charnley Davies Ltd* [1988] BCLC 243.
18 Insolvency Act 1986, s 18(1).

accedes to his application, the administrator must submit new proposals to a creditors' meeting for approval in order to achieve the new or substituted purpose,[19] and the original proposals approved by the creditors will cease to have effect.

Meetings of creditors convened to approve revisions in the administrator's proposals are governed by the same rules as creditors' meetings called to approve the original proposals, and the creditors' voting rights and the calculation of the majority required to approve the revisions are also the same, as is the power of the creditors' meeting to approve the revised proposals with modifications to which the administrator consents.[20] After the conclusion of the creditors' meeting called to approve revised proposals, the administrator must notify the result to the Registrar of Companies and to each creditor of the company in the same way as he was obliged to notify the results of the creditors' meeting which approved his original proposals.[1] Revised proposals can themselves be revised by the administrator adopting the same procedure.

CONDUCT OF THE ADMINISTRATION

The administrator's duties; meetings of creditors and members

The administrator is responsible for conducting the administration in order to achieve the purpose or purposes for which the administration order was made, and he must do so in accordance with the proposals and revised proposals (if any) which have been approved by the creditors' meeting and are currently in force.[2] If the administrator is in doubt as to the propriety of any act which he proposes to do or as to any transaction which he proposes to enter into, he may apply to the court for directions.[3] The court will not substitute its opinion for that of the administrator in exercising his discretionary powers, however.

There is no provision in respect of administration order proceedings that the court or the administrator may or shall have regard to the wishes of the creditors or members of the company in carrying out his functions, as there is in a winding up as regards the

---

19 *Re St Ives Windings Ltd* (1987) 3 BCC 634.
20 Insolvency Act 1986, s 25(1) to (5); Insolvency Rules 1986, rr 2.19 and 2.20 and rr 2.22 to 2.28.
 1 Insolvency Act 1986, s 25(6); Insolvency Rules 1986, rr 2.29 and 2.30(1).
 2 Insolvency Act 1986, s 17(2).
 3 Ibid, s 14(3).

court and the liquidator,[4] nor is there, as in a winding up by the court, a statutory power for any creditor or member of the company to apply summarily to the court to give directions to the administrator as regards the exercise or proposed exercise of any of his powers.[5] Nevertheless, an administrator may at his discretion call meetings of creditors or members of the company in order to ascertain their wishes,[6] and he must call a meeting of creditors if directed by the court, or if requested in writing to do so by creditors to whom is owed at least one-tenth of the company's total indebtedness and they specify the purpose of the proposed meeting.[7] The rules governing the convening and holding of meetings of creditors and their voting rights at such meetings are the same as for creditors' meetings called to approve the administrator's proposals,[8] except that at least 21 days' notice of the meeting must be given to each creditor.[9] If an administrator is requested to call a meeting of creditors by the requisite fraction of their number, he must call the meeting to be held not later than 35 days after he received the request and must give at least 21 days' notice of the meeting to each creditor.[10] The administrator may require the requisitionists to deposit with him an amount equal to his estimate of the expenses which he will incur in calling and holding the creditors' meeting, but the meeting may resolve that the expenses so incurred shall be paid out of the company's assets as an expense of the administration, and the deposit is then refunded.[11]

Meetings of members of a company subject to an administration order are called by the administrator and held in accordance with the rules governing general meetings of members; they are presided over by the administrator by or a person nominated by him who is either a qualified insolvency practitioner, or an employee of the administrator or his firm who is experienced in insolvency matters.[12]

The creditors' committee

The meeting of creditors which approves the administrator's proposals for the conduct of the administration may resolve to

---

4 Ibid, s 195(1).
5 Ibid, s 167(3).
6 Ibid, s 14(2)(*b*).
7 Ibid, s 17(3); Insolvency Rules 1986, r 2.21(1).
8 Insolvency Rules 1986, r 2.19, r 2.20 and rr 2.22 to 2.28.
9 Ibid, r 2.19(4A) and r 2.21(2).
10 Ibid, r 2.21(2).
11 Ibid, r 2.21(3) to (6).
12 Ibid, r 2.31(2), (3) and (5).

establish a creditors' committee to exercise the functions conferred on it by the Insolvency Act 1986, and the rules made under the Act.[13] The committee consists of at least three and not more than five creditors elected by the creditors' meeting by the votes of a simple majority in value of creditors voting in person or by proxy or by the representative of a corporate creditor.[14] The chairman of the creditors' meeting may put a single resolution to the meeting naming all the candidates for election to the creditors' committee, and may declare those of them who obtain the greatest number of votes to be elected; the chairman may alternatively put separate resolutions for the election of each of the candidates individually and declare those of them in whose favour the greatest number of net votes are cast(ie votes cast for minus votes cast against) to be elected.[15] If an elected creditor is a company or corporation, a representative appointed by its board of directors attends meetings of the creditors' committee on its behalf.[16] Individual members of the creditors' committee may also appoint other individuals by a written authority to act as their representatives and to vote on their behalf at meetings of the committee.[17]

A member of the creditors' committee may resign or may be removed by resolution of a meeting of creditors, and a vacancy in the membership of the committee from any cause may be filled by the administrator appointing another creditor to be a member of the committee with the agreement of a majority of its members, but such an appointment is essential only if the membership of the committee would otherwise fall to less than three.[18]

The creditors' committee must assist the administrator in carrying out his functions, and the scope of its activities is determined by agreement between the committee and the administrator.[19] Meetings of the creditors' committee are called by the administrator at his discretion, but a meeting must be called by him if requested by a member of the committee or his representative, and the meeting must then be held within 21 days after the request is made.[20] The first meeting of the creditors' committee must be held within three months after it is established, and every meeting must be called by the administrator giving at least seven days' notice of it to each member of the committee or his representative.[1] Meetings of the

13 Insolvency Act 1986, s 26(1).
14 Insolvency Rules 1986, r 2.32(1).
15 *Re Polly Peck International plc* [1991] BCC 503.
16 Insolvency Rules 1986, r 2.32(4).
17 Ibid, r 2.37(1), (2) and (4).
18 Ibid, r 2.38, r 2.40 and r 2.41(2) and (3).
19 Ibid, r 2.34(1).
20 Ibid, r 2.34(2) and (3) and r 2.37(1) and (2).
 1 Ibid, r 2.34(3) and (4).

committee are presided over by the administrator or by a person nominated by him who could be appointed to preside over a meeting of creditors.[2] The quorum at a meeting of the creditors' committee is two members of the committee present personally or by their representatives.[3] The committee may require the administrator to attend any of its meetings and to provide the committee with such information about the carrying out of his functions as it reasonably requires.[4]

Resolutions of the creditors' committee are passed by the affirmative votes of a majority of its members or their representatives present at a meeting, each member or his representative having one vote.[5] However, the administrator may obtain the approval of the members of the creditors' committee which is treated as the equivalent of a resolution by soliciting the consent of the members of the committee in writing, and the majority of them giving their written consent, but any member may require the administrator to call a meeting of the committee to consider the proposed resolution.[6] A resolution by the written consents of members of the committee is deemed to be passed when the administrator receives the written approval of the resolution from a majority of the members.[7]

Abstract of receipts and payments

An administrator must send to the court, the Registrar of Companies and each member of the creditors' committee within two months after the end of six months from his appointment, and thereafter within two months after the end of each succeeding period of six months and after he ceases to act as administrator, an abstract of his receipts and payments during the relevant six-month period or, on the administrator ceasing to act, from the end of the period for which he last submitted such an abstract.[8] The abstract must contain details of the amounts received and paid by the administrator during the relevant period, together with the totals of amounts received and paid by him since his appointment up to the beginning of the period to which the abstract relates, and the receipts and payments during the relevant period must be added to those totals at the conclusion

2 Ibid, r 2.35(1) and (2); (see p 383, ante).
3 Ibid, r 2.36.
4 Insolvency Act 1986, s 26(2); Insolvency Rules 1986, r 2.44(1).
5 Insolvency Rules 1986, r 2.42(1).
6 Ibid, r 2.43(1) to (3).
7 Ibid, r 2.43(4).
8 Ibid, r 2.52(1) and (3) and Sch 4, Form 2.15.

of the abstract.[8] The court may extend the time within which the administrator must submit his abstracts of receipts and payments.[9] The administrator's abstracts are not audited, and he is not required to keep the detailed accounting records which a liquidator must keep, or to pay amounts received by him into the Insolvency Services Account at the Bank of England.[10] Nevertheless, in order to maintain his authorisation to act as an insolvency practitioner granted to him by the Secretary of State for Trade and Industry, an administrator will keep detailed accounting records showing individual items of receipts and expenditure and the acquisition and disposal by him of individual items of property.[11]

Liability of the administrator

An administrator is undoubtedly under a duty to the company whose affairs, business and property he administers to fulfil the functions of his office properly, and to do so in accordance with his proposals which have been approved by the company's creditors in order to achieve the purposes for which the administration order was made.[12] In fulfilling these functions and carrying out his duties, an administrator is subject to the same equitable fiduciary obligation to the company to act in its interests, and not in the interests of any particular section of its creditors or members, as the obligation imposed on a liquidator in the winding up of a company.[13] An administrator is also under a duty to exercise proper professional skill and care in fulfilling his functions.[13]

It appears that it is a breach of duty for an administrator to cause the company to break a contract which it has entered into and which has not been terminated by or in consequence of the administration order being made; this duty is similar to the duty of a receiver not to cause such a breach of contract.[14] The administrator will not be liable to the other contracting party for such a breach of contract, of course, because there is no contractual relationship between them,[15] but, unless the administrator has good reason to disregard the contract in order to achieve the purpose for which the administration

9 Ibid, r 2.52(2).
10 See pp 188 and 191, ante.
11 Insolvency Practitioners Regulations 1990, reg 17(1).
12 Insolvency Act 1986, s 17(1) and (2), s 23(1) and (2) and s 25(1) to (3).
13 *Re Sheridan Securities Ltd* (1988) 4 BCC 200; *Re Charnley Davies Ltd (No 2)* [1990] BCC 605.
14 *Re Newdigate Colliery Ltd* [1912] 1 Ch 468; *Astor Chemicals Ltd v Synthetic Technology Ltd* [1990] BCLC 1, [1990] BCC 97.
15 *Said v Butt* [1920] 3 KB 497.

order was made, it would appear that by causing the contract to be broken, he is guilty of a breach of his duty to the company to protect and promote its interests and not to cause it a loss of goodwill.

The enforcement of the administrator's duties to the company while the administration order remains in force at first sight presents some difficulty. Apart from the statutory remedy of a creditor or member of a company to petition the court for relief from the unfairly prejudicial conduct of the administration, which is dealt with below,[16] the Insolvency Act 1986 makes no provision for applications to the court for redress against an administrator while an administration order is in force. Nevertheless, it would appear that actions for breaches of fiduciary duty may be brought against the administrator in the company's name or in the names of minority shareholders of the company suing on behalf of themselves and all the other shareholders of the company in a derivative action.[17] On the other hand, it would not be possible for creditors to sue the administrator in the company's name or in a derivative action, because the cause of action would be vested in the company and its creditors have no legal power to represent it. It is uncertain whether directors of a company in administration are inhibited from exercising their power to initiate litigation in its name which is conferred by the company's articles of association or by the general law[18] while the administration order remains in force; this doubt arises because of the statutory prohibition on them exercising their powers in a way which interferes with the exercise by the administrator of his powers.[19] However, it would seem unlikely that the court would interpret the inhibition as preventing the company's directors from seeking redress for the administrator's breaches of duty to the company, even if the relief sought is an injunction against the administrator.

The summary procedure for obtaining injunctive, compensatory or restitutive remedies against liquidators in the winding up of a company[20] is not available against an administrator while an administration order is in force, but if the administration order is discharged by the court and the company is subsequently wound up by the court or voluntarily, such summary proceedings may be taken in the winding up against the former administrator on the initiative of the liquidator or a creditor or contributory.[1] An administrator

16 See p 396, post.
17 *Re Charnley Davies Ltd (No 2)*, supra.
18 *Gray v Lewis* (1873) 8 Ch App 1035; *Russell v Wakefield Waterworks Co* (1875) LR 20 Eq 474, 479; *Burland v Earle* [1902] AC 83, 93.
19 Insolvency Act 1986, s 14(4).
20 Ibid, s 212(1) to (3); (see p 173, ante).
 1 Ibid, s 212(2).

obtains his release from liability in respect of his acts and omissions in the administration and his conduct as administrator when the court so orders on his application,[2] which is usually made at the same time as his application to the court to discharge the administration order.[3] The release of the administrator granted by the court prevents any action or other proceedings subsequently being brought against him for breaches of his duties, whether such proceedings are initiated by the company or by any of its creditors or members, but the release does not prevent summary proceedings for breaches of duty to the company being taken against the administrator in the subsequent liquidation of the company if the court gives leave for such proceedings to be brought.[4] Because a release will make the administrator immune from other proceedings, the court will defer granting the administrator's release if such proceedings against him are pending or intended.[5]

Despite the limitations on the remedies mentioned above, the court has indicated that while an administration order is in force, it will avoid any impasse which would otherwise arise from creditors or members of the company not being able to seek relief against the administrator for breaches of his obligations to conduct the administration proceedings properly and competently, and not to exceed or abuse his powers.[6] The court will do this by exercising its inherent jurisdiction to direct the administrator, as an officer of the court, to do or abstain from doing any act, and an application for such an order may be made to the court by an interested creditor or member of the company.[6] In practice, dissatisfied members or creditors will avail themselves of this procedure, which is speedy and direct, instead of relying on the remedy of an action commenced by writ, and in most situations an application to the court, resulting in a corrective direction to the administrator, will be more appropriate and expeditious than the statutory remedy of a petition for relief from the unfairly prejudicial conduct of the administration, which is dealt with below. On hearing an application to exercise its inherent jurisdiction, the court can give directions to the administrator in respect of his future conduct, including the remedying of wrongful acts or defaults already committed; the court may also direct the administrator to pay compensation to persons who have suffered loss as a result of his breach of duty or other wrongful conduct, and

2 Ibid, s 20(1) and (2).
3 Ibid, s 18(1).
4 Ibid, s 212(4).
5 *Re Sheridan Securities Ltd* (1988) 4 BCC 200.
6 *Re Atlantic Computer Systems plc (Nos 1 and 2)* [1990] BCLC 729, [1990] BCC 439; revsd on another ground [1991] BCLC 606, [1990] BCC 859; *Re Mirror Group (Holdings) Ltd* [1993] BCLC 538, [1992] BCC 972.

may order, or decline to order, that the company shall indemnify him in respect of the payment of such compensation.[7]

Relief against the unfairly prejudicial conduct of an administration

At any time while an administration order is in force, a creditor or member of the company may apply to the court for relief on the ground:

    (a) that the company's affairs, business and property are being or have been managed by the administrator in a manner which is unfairly prejudicial to the interests of the company's creditors or members generally, or to the interests of some part of the company's creditors or members (including at least himself); or

    (b) that any actual or proposed act or omission of the administrator is or would be so prejudicial.[8]

If the court finds that the complaint against the administrator is proved, it may make such order as it thinks fit to give relief in respect of the matters complained of, or the court may adjourn the hearing conditionally or unconditionally (eg on the administrator giving undertakings as to the future conduct of the administration), or the court may make any other order which it thinks fit.[9] The court may, in particular, by its order regulate the future management by the administrator of the company's affairs, business and property; or require the administrator to abstain from doing or continuing to do any act complained of by the petitioner, or require him to do any act which the petitioner complains he has omitted to do; or require the convening and holding of a meeting of members or creditors of the company to consider such matters as the court directs; or discharge the administration order and make such consequential provisions as the court thinks fit.[10]

    However, the court cannot make an order which prejudices or prevents the implementation of a voluntary arrangement with the

---

7 *Barclays Mercantile Business Financial Ltd v Sibec Developments Ltd* [1993] BCLC 1077, [1993] BCC 148.

8 Insolvency Act 1986, s 27(1). The application to the court is made by way of an originating application (Insolvency Rules 1986, r 7.2(1)).

9 Ibid, s 27(2).

10 Ibid, s 27(4). If the court discharges the administration order the administration must within 14 days send a copy of the court's order to the Registrar of Companies (s 27(6)).

company's creditors which has been approved by them under the Insolvency Act 1986,[11] or a compromise or arrangement with the company's creditors or members which the court has sanctioned under the Companies Act 1985;[12] and the court may not make an order which affects proposals or revised proposals for the achievement of the purpose or purposes for which the administration order was made, if the petition is presented more than 28 days after those proposals were approved by a meeting of creditors called by the administrator.[13]

This provision for the relief of unfairly prejudiced creditors or members of a company in administration is obviously modelled on the provision in the Companies Act 1985, which enables a member of a company to petition the court for relief from the unfairly prejudicial conduct of a company's affairs by its directors or majority shareholders, and the court has the same wide power under the present provision to give whatever form of relief it considers appropriate and to make such order as it thinks fit.[14] Presumably, decisions of the court on petitions for relief presented by minority shareholders under the Companies Act 1985, will be relevant in determining the circumstances in which relief should be given on petitions by creditors or members of companies in administration, particularly where under the administrator's proposals approved by the creditors he is to carry on the company's business for an extended period or is to dispose of all or some of its assets over such a period. If decisions of the court as to the interpretation and application of the provisions of the Companies Act 1985, are treated as relevant in the application of the present provision of the Insolvency Act 1986, it will suffice for the petitioner to prove that he and other creditors or members have been treated unfairly in consequence of the acts or omissions to act of the administrator, whether he acted deliberately, intending to bring about unfair results, or not.[15] However, it will not seem possible for a petitioner to seek relief if his complaint is merely that the administrator did not exercise the highest measure of skill and care in carrying out his functions,[16] nor it would seem, that he is not sufficiently skilled or

---

11 Insolvency Act 1986, s 4(1) and s 5(1) and (2). An application may be made to the court to revoke the approvals of the voluntary arrangement given by meetings of the company's creditors and of its members within 28 days after the reports of those meetings are delivered by the administrator to the court (Insolvency Act 1986, s 6(1) to (3)); (see p 429, post).
12 Companies Act 1985, s 425(1) and (2); (see p 434, post).
13 Insolvency Act 1986, s 27(3).
14 Companies Act 1985, s 459(1) and s 461(1).
15 *Re H R Harmer Ltd* [1958] 3 All ER 689, [1959] 1 WLR 62.
16 *Re Five Minute Car Wash Service Ltd* [1966] 1 All ER 242, [1966] 1 WLR 745.

experienced to manage the company's business and affairs so as to achieve the purposes for which the administration order was made, but the court may give relief if the administrator failed to make decisions or to take steps which were obviously necessary for the proper conduct of the company's affairs, or if he took decisions which would foreseeably result in loss to the company.[17] It may be that the court will be more critical of the conduct of administrators than of directors and controlling shareholders in proceedings for the relief of minority shareholders under the Companies Act 1985, on the ground that administrators, as insolvency practitioners, must be qualified professionally, whereas directors are not required to be. If the court adopts this position it could well decide that conduct by an administrator which has caused, or threatens to cause, loss to the company or its creditors or members should entitle creditors to relief under the present provision in the Insolvency Act 1986.

It will not be possible in proceedings brought for the relief of creditors or members of a company from the unfairly prejudicial conduct of its affairs under an administration order for the petitioner to challenge the exercise of the administrator's discretion in deciding on the measures to be taken to carry out his proposals which have been approved by the company's creditors, at least if the administrator's decisions are not proved to be actuated by bad faith, or shown to be decisions which no reasonable person would make. This corresponds to the conclusion of the court that it is not possible to challenge the wisdom of business decisions made by directors or majority shareholders in a minority shareholder's petition for relief[18] unless the decisions were made in bad faith or are wholly unreasonable. The more effective remedy of a creditor or member who complains that the administrator has exercised, or proposes to exercise, his discretion in a defective or harmful way would be to apply to the court to remove him and appoint another insolvency practitioner in his place.[19]

A creditor's or member's petition for relief in administration proceedings is not an appropriate remedy if the petitioner complains merely of an act or omission by the administrator which is in breach of his fiduciary duties to the company,[20] or a failure by the administrator to apply the company's assets in satisfying the petitioner's claim in accordance with a direction by the court,[1] and

---

17 *Re Macro (Ipswich) Ltd* [1994] 2 BCLC 354, [1994] BCC 781.
18 *Re Blue Arrow plc* [1987] BCLC 585, 3 BCC 618; *Re a Company (No 003096 of 1987)* (1987) 4 BCC 80; *Re Sam Weller & Sons Ltd* [1990] Ch 682, [1990] BCLC 80.
19 Insolvency Act 1986, s 13(2) and s 19(1).
20 *Re Charnley Davies Ltd (No 2)* [1990] BCC 605.

in either case there is no evidence of discrimination by the administrator between creditors or a realisation by him that his acts would bring about results which are unjust or unfair to creditors or any of them. The proper remedy in that situation is for the creditors or members who are affected to apply to the court to give directions to the administrator in respect of the matter of which they complain in exercise of its inherent jurisdiction to ensure that affairs appointed by it fulfil their functions correctly.

THE CONCLUSION OF AN ADMINISTRATION

The discharge of an administration order

An administrator may at any time apply to the court to discharge the administration order in respect of the company,[2] and he must make such an application if it appears to him that the purpose or each of the purposes for which the order was made has been achieved or is incapable of achievement, or if the administrator is required to make the application by a resolution passed by a meeting of the company's creditors.[3] On hearing the administrator's application, the court may by order discharge the administration order and make such consequential orders as it thinks fit, or it may adjourn the hearing or make an interim order or such other order as it thinks fit.[4] If the administration order is discharged, the administrator must within 14 days send an office copy of the order of discharge to the Registrar of Companies.[5]

The usual reason for an application being made to the court to order the discharge of an administration order is that the purposes for which the administration order was made cannot be achieved, or that the administrator's proposals for achieving them have not been approved by the creditors' meeting called for the purpose, or that the company has been made solvent by the administrator's exercise of his powers and its management should be returned to its board of directors (in practice, a rare reason).[6] The court has also discharged an administration order on the ground that it was made in consequence of misrepresentations of the relevant facts or failure to

1 *Re Atlantic Computer Systems plc (Nos 1 and 2)* [1990] BCLC 729, [1990] BCC 439.
2 Insolvency Act 1986, s 18(1).
3 Ibid, s 18(2).
4 Ibid, s 18(3).
5 Ibid, s 18(4).
6 Ibid, s 24(5).

disclose relevant facts to the court,[7] or because the administrator has prepared no proposals during the three months following the making of the administration order or such longer period as the court has allowed and has disposed of most of the company's assets,[8] or because the administration order was made with a view either to preserving the company's business undertaking or selling it as a going concern, if that proved impracticable, and the one likely purchaser of the business has withdrawn.[9] If an administration order has been procured by misrepresentation or the non-disclosure of material facts, the court may, as an alternative to discharging the administration order, make an order rescinding it, and it is then treated as not having been made.[10]

If the purpose for which an administration order was made cannot be achieved, but an alternative purpose for which such an order could be made is practicable, the administrator may apply to the court to vary the original order by adding the alternative purpose to the original one,[11] and it would also appear to be possible for the court to substitute the alternative purpose for the original one. The procedure on such an application is the same as on an application to discharge an administration order.

An administrator obtains his release from such time as the court orders,[12] and the application for his release may be made at the same time as an application for the discharge of the administration order. The effect of the release is to discharge the administrator from liability in respect of his acts or omissions in the administration and in relation to his conduct as administrator, but if the company subsequently goes into liquidation, summary proceedings in the liquidation may still be taken against the administrator in respect of such acts, omission or conduct while the administration order was in force.[13]

Consequences of the discharge of an administration order; winding up

The discharge of an administration order restores the company to its condition immediately before the order was made, and so the

---

7 *Re Sharps of Truro Ltd* [1990] BCC 94.
8 *Re Charnley Davies Business Services Ltd* (1987) 3 BCC 408.
9 *Re Synthetic Technology Ltd* [1990] BCLC 378.
10 *Cornhill Insurance plc v Cornhill Financial Services Ltd* [1993] BCLC 914, [1992] BCC 818. The court's power to rescind an administration order is conferred by Insolvency Rules 1986, r 7.47(1).
11 Insolvency Act 1986, s 18(1); *Re St Ives Windings Ltd* (1987) 3 BCC 634.
12 Ibid, s 20(1).
13 Ibid, s 20(2) and (3).

restrictions on its creditors pursuing their normal legal remedies against the company and on realising and enforcing securities for their debts come to an end. Disposals of the company's assets during the administration by or with the authorisation of the administrator or the court are effective against the company after the discharge of the administration order, as are acquisitions of assets by him in the company's name or on its behalf during the administration, and contracts entered into by the administrator in the conduct of the administration continue to be binding on and enforceable by the company. Dispositions and transactions by the company which have been invalidated by the court in the administration proceedings as gifts or transactions at a significant undervalue, or as voidable preferences, or as extortionate credit transactions,[14] remain invalid after the discharge of the administration order; but because the discharge of the administration order causes the administrator to vacate office,[15] neither he nor any other person may apply to the court to invalidate such dispositions or transactions thereafter, even though there were grounds for making such an application while the administration order was in force. A floating charge over the company's undertaking or property which was invalidated on the making of the administration order[16] remains invalid, despite the subsequent discharge of the order, and so the charge does not affect property of the company at the date of the discharge of the administration order or property subsequently acquired by the company. On the other hand, applications to the court to invalidate transactions entered into by the company before an administration order was made in respect of it where the transactions were entered into for the purpose of putting assets of the company beyond the reach of its creditors or otherwise prejudicing their interests[17] may be made by victims of those transactions at any time, notwithstanding the discharge of the administration order.

Administration orders are most frequently discharged because the company ought to be wound up in the absence or impracticability of proposals by the administrator to achieve the purpose for which the order was made, or because the company's creditors have not approved his proposals. The court cannot make an order for the winding up of the company on the administrator's application for the discharge of the administration order, but a winding up petition must be presented in separate proceedings.[18] Nevertheless, the

14 Insolvency Act 1986, s 238(2) and (3), s 239(2) and (3) and s 244(2) and (4); (see p 221 et seq, ante).
15 Ibid, s 19(2).
16 Ibid, s 245(1) and (2); (see p 237, ante).
17 Ibid, s 423(1) to (3); (see p 233, ante).
18 Insolvency Act 1986, s 14(1) and Sch 1, para 21.

court may direct the administrator to exercise his statutory power[18] to present a petition for a winding up order upon the administration order being discharged by the court.[19] However, the court will not give such a direction if the discharge of the administration order is made subject to a condition (eg if the administrator does not find a purchaser of the company's business undertaking within a limited period), because on the condition being satisfied the discharge of the administration order takes effect, and then any creditor of the company may petition for it to be wound up.[20] If the court directs the administrator to petition for a winding up order, it may also direct that he shall be the provisional liquidator as from the presentation of the petition[1] so that he will be able to retain possession and control of the company's assets, and the court may then appoint him to be the liquidator of the company when it makes a winding up order,[2] so avoiding the official receiver becoming the liquidator and calling meetings of creditors and contributories to appoint a liquidator.[3] If the court makes a winding up order following the discharge of an administration order, the court will not appoint an additional liquidator who is directed to inquire into possible breaches of the administrator's duties while the administration order was in force, but will leave the question of the administrator's defaults to be explored and appropriate remedies to be pursued (eg summary proceedings for the administrator's wrongdoing) in the normal way in the winding up.[4]

When an order is made by the court discharging an administration order and the company then immediately goes into liquidation under an order of the court or voluntarily, the court may in the winding up proceedings invalidate gifts and transactions entered into by the company at a significant undervalue,[5] or set aside voidable preferences given by the company for the benefit of any of its creditors or of guarantors of any of its debts or liabilities,[6] within certain prescribed periods before the onset of the company's insolvency.[7] If no administration order had been made in respect of

19 *Re Charnley Davies Business Services Ltd* (1987) 3 BCC 408; *Re Brooke Marine Ltd* [1988] BCLC 546.
20 *Re Synthetic Technology Ltd* [1990] BCLC 378.
1 The appointment of a provisional liquidator by the court can take effect only after a petition for a winding up order has been presented (Insolvency Act 1986, s 135(1)).
2 Insolvency Act 1986, s 140(1); *Re Charnley Davies Business Services Ltd*, supra.
3 See p 115, ante.
4 *Re Exchange Travel (Holdings) Ltd* [1993] BCLC 887, [1992] BCC 954.
5 Insolvency Act 1986, s 238(1) to (3); (see p 221, ante).
6 Ibid, s 239(1) to (3); (see p 225, ante).
7 Ibid, s 240(1) and (2).

the company, or if an interval had occurred between the discharge of the administration order and the company subsequently going into liquidation by a winding up order being made or a winding up resolution being passed, the onset of the company's insolvency would be taken to be the date of the commencement of its winding up.[8] But where a winding up order is made or a winding up resolution is passed immediately after the discharge of an administration order, the onset of the company's insolvency is taken to be the date when the petition for the administration order was presented, and the relevant prescribed periods are extended retrospectively by the duration of the administration order proceedings.[9]

8 Ibid, s 240(3)(*b*); (see pp 228 and 229, ante).
9 Ibid, s 240(3)(*a*).

CHAPTER 8

Compromises and arrangements

Companies may need to enter into agreements compromising claims or modifying rights which other persons have against them, or which they have against other persons, either because the company or other party cannot perform its obligations as originally agreed upon, or because a change of circumstances has made it appropriate for the rights or liabilities of the parties to be altered. Such compromises or arrangements may be called for when a company is insolvent, when they will usually, but not necessarily, be made with the company's creditors or one or more classes of them, but compromises and arrangements may also be made when a company is fully able to satisfy its debts but is in dispute with its creditors as to the amounts payable to them or lacks the liquid resources to pay them immediately. A company has an implied power to compromise disputes in which it is involved with outsiders or with its own members,[1] and it probably also has implied power to enter into arrangements with such persons modifying the undisputed rights which they or the company have. In any case, an express power to do these things is usually inserted in the objects clause of the company's memorandum of association. Furthermore, in the winding up of a company by the court or voluntarily, the liquidator may enter into compromises or arrangements with any of its creditors and may enter into compromises with any of its present or past members.[2] Such compromises or arrangements must be entered into by agreement between the liquidator and each creditor or member concerned, however, the liquidator has no power to coerce a creditor or member into accepting a compromise or arrangement merely because it has been accepted or agreed to by a majority of his fellow creditors or members.[3]

The reason why the subject of compromises and arrangements is deserving of separate treatment is that rights enforceable against companies are often vested in numerous persons with whom it would be practically impossible to negotiate individually, and in such cases machinery is required by which the claims of the

---

1 *Re Norwich Provident Insurance Society, Bath's Case* (1878) 8 Ch D 334.
2 Insolvency Act 1986, s 165(2) and s 167(1) Sch 4, paras 2 and 3 (see p 149, ante). The power can be exercised by the liquidator only if he obtains the appropriate consent.
3 *Re Trix Ltd* [1970] 3 All ER 397, [1970] 1 WLR 1421.

interested persons collectively may be compromised or their rights modified with the assent of a majority of their number given at meetings called for the purpose. This machinery may be provided by the original agreements between the company and the classes of persons entitled to the rights concerned, but whether such machinery is provided by agreement or not, it is also provided by the Companies Act 1985 and the Insolvency Act 1986.

A compromise has been described[4] as an agreement terminating a dispute between parties as to the rights of one or more of them, or modifying the undoubted rights of a party which he has difficulty in enforcing. An arrangement, as the expression is used in the Companies Act 1985 and the Insolvency Act 1986, embraces a far wider class of agreements, and it need be in no way analogous to a compromise. Arrangements include agreements which modify rights about which there is no dispute and which can be enforced without difficulty, where the purpose of the agreement is simply to alter the rights originally conferred.[5] Arrangements also include compositions with a company's creditors, that is to say, arrangements by several creditors or all the creditors of a company, or all its creditors of a particular class, under which they are to be paid a percentage of their debts in full discharge of the company's liability to them; or under which such creditors are to be paid the whole or part of their debts at dates later than those on which the debts fell due for payment, or are to be paid by instalments, some or all of which will be paid after those dates; or agreements by which the rights of the company's creditors are otherwise abrogated or modified, but they nevertheless remain creditors of the company.[6]

Where compromises or arrangements are initiated or effected under provisions of the Companies Act 1985 or the Insolvency Act 1986 dealt with in this chapter, the debts of the company include debts which are immediately due and payable, debts which will become payable only at a future time and debts which are contingent or conditional. Where compromises or arrangements are purely contractual, however, the debts which are caught by them are ascertained by reference to the express or implied terms of the contract concerned defining the debts, rights or claims to which it applies.

4 *Sneath v Valley Gold Ltd* [1893] 1 Ch 477 at 494; *Mercantile Investment and General Trust Co v International Co of Mexico* [1893] 1 Ch 484n at 489, 491.
5 *Re Guardian Assurance Co* [1917] 1 Ch 431, not following Buckley LJ in *Re General Motor Cab Co Ltd* [1913] 1 Ch 377.
6 *Re Hatton* (1872) 7 Ch App 723, 726; *Slater v Jones* (1873) LR 8 Exch 186, 193; *Re Cancol Ltd* [1996] 1 BCLC 100, [1995] BCC 1133; *R v Smith* [1996] 2 BCLC 109.

COMPROMISES AND ARRANGEMENTS
BINDING CONTRACTUALLY

When a company issues shares or debt securities (ie debentures, debenture stock, unsecured loan stock or unsecured loan notes) to numerous subscribers, it is usual for a provision to be inserted in the company's articles of association or, in the case of debt securities, in the securities themselves or in the trust deed which is executed contemporaneously by the company and a trustee or trustees for the security holders, that the rights of the holders of the shares or debt securities may be varied with the assent of a certain majority of their number. Such provisions for the variation of rights attached to classes of shares and their regulation by the Companies Act 1985, are dealt with in the standard textbooks on company law.[7] The usual provision in the case of debt securities is that the holders of the securities may by an extraordinary resolution passed at a meeting of their number[8] agree as regards all of them: (a) to any variation or modification of their rights; (b) to the release of the company from liability for the whole or part of the debt secured by the debt securities or the covering trust deed; (c) to any scheme for the reconstruction, merger or division of the company; and (d) to the conversion of the debt securities into shares or other classes of debt securities of the company carrying such rights as are specified in the resolution, or into shares or debt securities of any other company formed under, or participating in, a reconstruction, merger or division of the company.[9]

Under a provision by which the rights of debt security holders may be 'modified', the meeting of security holders may resolve to release part[10] but not the whole,[11] of the debt to which the securities relate; to allow the company to create mortgages or debt securities ranking before their own securities;[12] to accept the conversion of debt securities with a fixed redemption date into perpetual or

---

7 See *Pennington's Company Law* (7th edn) p 273, et seq.

8 That is, a resolution passed by a majority of three-quarters in value of the debt security holders present in person or by proxy and voting at a meeting called for the purpose.

9 See the precedent of a debenture trust deed in 6 *Encyclopaedia of Forms and Precedents* (4th edn), 1267, 3rd Sch, para 12; and *Palmer's Company Precedents* (16th edn) Vol 3, p 273, 3rd Sch, para 16.

10 *Re Madras Irrigation Co* (1882) unreported, but cited in *Re Alabama, New Orleans, Texas and Pacific Junction Rly Co* [1891] 1 Ch 213 at 228.

11 *Mercantile Investment and General Trust Co v International Co of Mexico* [1893] 1 Ch 484n at 489 per Lindley LJ.

12 *Follit v Eddystone Granite Quarries* [1892] 3 Ch 75.

irredeemable debentures;[13] to accept shares in place of their debt securities;[14] and to release a guarantor of the amount payable to the debt security holders.[15] If the debt securities also empower the meeting to assent to the reconstruction, merger or division of the company, the meeting may resolve that the debt security holders shall take shares or debt securities of the new company or companies to be formed under the reconstruction, merger or division, in place of their original debt securities,[16] and probably this may be done even if the securities merely empower the meeting to assent to a 'modification' of the debt security holders' rights.[17]

It is, of course, obvious that a company does not require the approval of debt security holders to a transaction or measure which does not affect their rights, even if the relevant clause in their securities or the covering trust deed is ambiguous and appears literally to extend to matters which would not affect their rights as well as matters which would. Consequently, it was held that where debentures secured only by a floating charge contained a condition empowering the company to issue further debentures ranking in priority to the original ones if the original debenture holders consented by an extraordinary resolution, the consent of the original debenture holders was unnecessary for the issue of further debentures secured by a fixed charge on certain of the company's assets, because under the general law such a charge would have priority over the floating charge held by the original debenture holders, even if created without their consent.[18]

VOLUNTARY ARRANGEMENTS WITH CREDITORS

Scope

Under the Insolvency Act 1986 it is possible for a proposal to be made on behalf of a company for approval by meetings of its creditors and of its members under which a composition in satisfaction

13 *Northern Assurance Co Ltd v Farnham United Breweries Ltd* [1912] 2 Ch 125.
14 *Mercantile Investment and General Trust Co v International Co of Mexico*, supra, per Fry LJ, at 491.
15 *Goodfellow v Nelson Line (Liverpool) Ltd* [1912] 2 Ch 324.
16 *Re W H Hutchinson & Son Ltd* (1915) 31 TLR 324.
17 *Sneath v Valley Gold Ltd* [1893] 1 Ch 477, where such a scheme was held validly approved under a power to sanction 'any modification or compromise of the rights of debenture holders', the court holding, on the facts, that the scheme was a compromise.
18 *Cox Moore v Peruvian Corpn Ltd* [1908] 1 Ch 604.

of the company's debts or a scheme of arrangement of its affairs (ie a voluntary arrangement) will become binding on all its creditors and on the company.[19] If the approved proposal is expressed to be for a composition and is accepted by the company's creditors and its members in the manner described below, the company's original indebtedness ceases to exist and is replaced by the substituted obligations under the terms of the proposal, with the result that third persons who were liable in respect of the company's original indebtedness (eg guarantors) cease to be so liable.[20] On the other hand, if an approved proposal is for a scheme of arrangement of a company's affairs, its original indebtedness will not cease to exist, and third persons liable for that indebtedness as guarantors or otherwise will not be released, unless the scheme expressly provides for the company's release and so, consequentially, for the release of those third persons[20] whether the proposal is for a composition or an arrangement with the company's creditors, there is no need for the company's memorandum or articles of association to empower the company to make and give effect to the proposal; the power to do so is conferred by law on all companies registered under the Companies Acts.

If a company is not in liquidation or subject to an administration order, a proposal for a composition of its indebtedness or a scheme of arrangement of its affairs must be made by its directors (presumably pursuant to a resolution of a board of directors);[1] if the company is in liquidation, the proposal must be made by the liquidator, or if it is subject to an administration order, the proposal must be made by the administrator.[2]

A proposal for a voluntary arrangement made by directors of the company must provide that one or more persons qualified to act as insolvency practitioners (the nominee or nominees) shall report to the court on the proposal, and in the report shall express an opinion whether meetings of creditors and members of the company should be convened to consider the proposal.[3] No such report is prepared if the proposal is made by the liquidator or administrator of the company and no other insolvency practitioner is nominated by the proposal to report to the court on it; the submission to the court will then consist only of the arrangements with the company's creditors

19 Insolvency Act 1986, s 1(1).
20 *R A Securities Ltd v Mercantile Credit Co Ltd* [1994] 2 BCLC 721, [1994] BCC 598; *March Estates plc v Gunmark Ltd* [1996] 2 BCLC 1.
1 *D'Arcy v Tamar, Kit Hill and Callington Rly Co* (1867) LR 2 Exch 158; *Re Haycraft Gold Reduction and Mining Co* [1900] 2 Ch 230; *Re Equiticorp International plc* [1989] 1 WLR 1010, [1989] BCLC 597.
2 Insolvency Act 1986, s 1(1) and (3).
3 Ibid, s 1(2) and s 2(1) and (2).

which the liquidator or administrator proposes. If a proposal by the liquidator or administrator does not nominate another insolvency practitioner to report on it, the liquidator or administrator himself is deemed to be the nominee, even though he prepares no report on his own proposal, and if the proposal is then approved by the meetings of creditors and of members, the liquidator or administrator becomes the supervisor of the arrangement with responsibility for carrying it out.[4]

It is not essential that the company should be insolvent or likely to become insolvent for a proposal of a voluntary arrangement to be made in respect of it, but if the proposal is made by the liquidator in a creditors' voluntary winding up or in a winding up by order of the court on a creditor's petition, the company will in all probability be insolvent. If the proposal is made by an administrator, the company must have been proved to be, or to be likely to become, unable to pay its debts[5] for an administration order to have been made in respect of it.

The Insolvency Act 1986, does not define the debts of a company for the purpose of voluntary arrangements with its creditors, but such debts will include not only liabilities of the company to pay liquidated amounts of money which are immediately due and payable, but also such liabilities which will or may accrue in the future, whether subject to conditions or contingencies or not. Debts of the company will also include liabilities for unliquidated damages or other amounts, whether for breach of contract, tort or under statutory liability, but not obligations of the company under executory contracts for the performance of acts other than the payment of money unless the obligations of the company have been broken.[6] Nor will debts include a claim for costs by a creditor of the company who has petitioned for it to be wound up by the court, but whose petition will be dismissed if the proposed voluntary arrangement is approved by meetings of the company's creditors and members.[7] It is clear from the provisions of the Insolvency Act 1986 that such a wide meaning of debts is intended in respect of winding up and administration order proceedings,[8] but there are no such indications in the part of the Act which deals with voluntary arrangements, apart from the availability of voluntary arrangements in winding-up and

---

4 Ibid, s 2(1).
5 Ibid, s 8(1). The test of the company's liability to pay its debts is the same as in the proceedings for a winding up order (Insolvency Act 1986, s 123(1) and (2); (see p 42, ante).
6 *Burford Midland Properties Ltd v Marley Extrusions Ltd* [1995] 1 BCLC 102, [1994] BCC 604; *Re Cancol Ltd* [1996] 1 BCLC 100, [1995] BCC 1133.
7 *Re Wisepark Ltd* [1994] BCC 221.
8 See Insolvency Act 1986, s 8(1)(*a*), s 22(2) (*a*), s 123(2) and s 131(2)(*a*).

administration order proceedings, where the purposes of the Act in respect of which will obviously be best achieved by treating the debts of a company as comprising all monetary liabilities of the company.

Voluntary arrangements with creditors of companies under the Insolvency Act 1986 may be proposed only in respect of companies registered under the Companies Act 1985, or the earlier Companies Acts, and not in respect of unregistered companies or overseas companies which may be wound up under the Insolvency Act 1986.[9] However, voluntary arrangements under the Insolvency Act 1986 may be entered into by the members, liquidators or administrators of insolvent partnerships with the same effect as voluntary arrangements in respect of companies.[10]

Voluntary arrangements may be proposed in respect of companies registered under the Companies Act 1985, or any of the earlier Companies Acts without any other concurrent insolvency proceedings being taken against it (ie winding up, administration or administrative receivership), but the company is then unprotected against actions brought by claimants against it, or against the realisation of mortgages, charges or other securities held by its creditors, or the levying of execution on its assets by its judgment creditors. In this respect corporate voluntary arrangements differ from voluntary arrangements by individual creditors under the Insolvency Act 1986, where temporary protection of the debtor and his property from realisation by his creditors is given by the Act.[11]

In practice, voluntary arrangements with a company's creditors are often proposed by an administrator, and the proposal for the arrangement is then an extension of the proposals made by the administrator for the conduct of the administration. The proposal for a voluntary arrangement is necessary, because it is intended that the rights of some or all of the company's creditors shall be altered, curtailed, deferred or cancelled, or that securities to which they are entitled shall be reduced, postponed, modified or cancelled by the arrangement. An administrator may not propose a voluntary arrangement with the company's creditors for approval by them and the company's members unless this is the purpose, or one of the purposes, for which the administration order was expressed to be made,[12] or if it was not, unless the administrator has first applied

---

9 This is because of the restricted definition of the term 'company' for the purposes of the Insolvency Act 1986, s 251, incorporating Companies Act 1985, s 735(1).
10 Insolvent Partnerships Order 1994 (SI 1994/2421) art 4(1) and art 5(1).
11 Insolvency Act 1986, ss 252 to 254.

successfully to the court for the administration order to be varied so as to make the approval of such a proposal a purpose of the order.[13]

A voluntary arrangement proposed under the Insolvency Act 1986 may provide for a composition to be entered into between the company and its creditors, or for a scheme of arrangement of the company's affairs affecting its creditors to be carried out; nevertheless its terms may not cancel, alter or affect the right of a secured creditor to enforce his security,[14] or cancel, alter or postpone the right of a creditor whose debt or claim would be preferential in a winding up[15] to be paid in priority to other creditors and rateably with other preferential creditors, unless the secured or preferential creditor concerned agrees.[16] Moreover, rights of the company's members may not be modified or cancelled by a voluntary arrangement under the Insolvency Act 1986. A meeting of the company's creditors and a separate meeting of its members must be held to consider the proposal for every voluntary arrangement, and the approval of both those meetings is required to make the arrangement effective. The arrangement then takes effect as if it had been made by the company at the creditors' meeting and had been assented to by every creditor who was entitled to vote thereat,[17] but the arrangement is not deemed to have been assented to by the members or shareholders of the company individually. It follows that the subject matter of the voluntary arrangement must relate exclusively to the rights of the company's creditors, and must not extend to the rights of its members or shareholders.

Initial procedure

Proposal by the company's directors

If the proposal for a voluntary arrangement is made by the directors of the company, or if the proposal is made by the liquidator or administrator of the company and he nominates a qualified insolvency practitioner (other than himself) to report on it, the nominee mentioned in the proposal must within 28 days after he is notified

12 Ibid, s 8(3)(*b*).
13 Ibid, s 18(1).
14 A lessor or landlord is deemed to be a secured creditor in respect of a right conferred on him by the lease to forfeit it if the rent reserved is unpaid or if the lessee's covenants are not performed or observed (*March Estates plc v Gunmark Ltd* [1996] 2 BCLC 1).
15 See p 303, ante.
16 Insolvency Act 1986, s 1(1) and s 4(3) and (4).
17 Ibid, s 5(1) and (2).

of it (or such longer period as the court allows) submit a report on the proposal to the court, stating whether, in his opinion, meetings of the creditors and of members of the company should be summoned to consider the report, and if so, the date on which and the time and place at which he proposes the meetings should be held.[18] The court to which the nominee's report should be submitted is any court which has jurisdiction to order that the company shall be wound up, and it may therefore be the Companies Court, or if the company's paid up share capital does not exceed £120,000, a county court.[19]

To assist the nominee to prepare his report on a proposal made by the directors of the company, the directors must provide the nominee with a document setting out the terms of the proposal and, within seven days after doing so or within such longer period as the nominee allows, they must provide him with a statement of the company's affairs, setting out: the company's assets divided into appropriate categories showing the estimated value of each category; particulars of securities for claims against the company and the persons entitled to them, with a statement of the amounts secured and the reason for, and dates of, the creation of the securities; particulars of the preferential creditors of the company and the amounts of their respective claims, and similar particulars of the company's unsecured creditors; particulars of any debts owed to the company by its directors or shadow directors or by persons associated with them and particulars of debts owed by the company to such persons;[20] a list of the company's members and of their respective shareholdings; and any other information which the nominee may require for the purpose of preparing his report.[1]

The statement of affairs must be made up to a date not earlier than two weeks before the date on which the proposal is notified to the nominee, or up to such earlier date not more than two months before the notification as the nominee permits, but in that case the nominee must in his report on the proposals give his reasons for permitting the statement of affairs to be made up to the earlier date.[2] The preferential debts of the company which must be specified in the statement of affairs are those debts and liabilities which would be payable by a liquidator of the company in priority to other debts and claims against it.[3] According to the Insolvency Act 1986, the

18 Ibid, s 1(2) and s 2(1) and (2).
19 Companies Act 1985, s 744; Insolvency Act 1986, s 117(1), (2) and (4) and s 251 (see p 11, ante).
20 For persons associated with directors or shadow directors, see p 150, ante.
 1 Insolvency Act 1986, s 2(3); Insolvency Rules 1986, r 1.5(1) and (2).
 2 Insolvency Rules 1986, r 1.5(3).

date up to which such debts and claims should be calculated is the date on which the proposal is approved by meetings of the company's creditors and members,[4] but as this date will not have been reached when the statement of affairs is made out, it would seem that the company's preferential debts, like its other debts and liabilities, should be set out as at a date not more than two weeks before the date of the statement of affairs, or such earlier date as the nominee permits, not being more than two months before the notification of the proposal to him.[1] If the voluntary arrangement is proposed under an administration order made in respect of the company, the statement of affairs must set out the preferential debts of the company calculated as at the date of the administration order.[4] The statement of affairs must be certified as correct to the best of their knowledge and belief by two directors of the company, or by one director and the company's secretary, not being a director.[5]

Proposal by a liquidator or administrator

If the proposal is made by a liquidator or administrator and the proposal nominates a qualified insolvency practitioner other than himself who is to report on it, the liquidator or administrator must provide the nominee with a document setting out the terms of the proposal and a copy of the statement of affairs prepared in respect of the company when it went into liquidation or when an administration order was made in respect of it.[6] The nominee must then deliver a report on the proposal to the court within 28 days after he is notified of it, or within such longer period as the court allows.[7] If a proposal made by a liquidator or administrator does not name another qualified insolvency practitioner who is to report on it, no report is prepared before the proposal is submitted to the meetings of creditors and of members of the company, and no copy of the proposal is delivered to the court.[8] If the company is being wound up by the court, however, whether a nominee reports on the proposal or not, a copy of the proposal must be sent to the official receiver.[9]

Nominee's requirement of further information

3 Insolvency Act 1986, s 4(7) and s 386(1) and Sch 6; Insolvency Rules 1986, r 1.5(2)(c).
4 Insolvency Act 1986, s 387(1) and (2).
5 Insolvency Rules 1986, r 1.5(4).
6 Insolvency Act 1986, s 2(3); Insolvency Rules 1986, r 1.12(1), (2) and (5).
7 Insolvency Act 1986, s 2(2).
8 Ibid, s 2(1).
9 Insolvency Rules 1986, r 1.10(2) and r 1.12(6).

If a proposal is submitted to a nominee so that he may report on it, and the nominee considers that he does not have adequate information to prepare his report on the basis of the contents of the proposal and the statement of the company's affairs supplied to him, he may require the directors, liquidator or administrator who prepared the proposal to provide him with further information as to the circumstances in which, and the reasons why, the company is insolvent or threatened with insolvency, particulars of any previous proposals in respect of the company which have been made under the Insolvency Act 1986, and any further information about the company's affairs which the nominee considers necessary for him to prepare his report.[10] Furthermore, the nominee may require the directors of the company or the liquidator or administrator who prepared the proposal to inform him whether any person who is, or within two years before the notification of the proposal to the nominee, has been a director or officer of the company, has been concerned in the affairs of any other company which has become insolvent, or has himself been adjudged bankrupt or made a composition with his creditors.[11] Finally, and probably of even greater importance, the nominee is entitled to have access to the company's accounts and records for the purpose of preparing his report.[12]

Delivery of the nominee's report to the court

With his report to the court on a proposal submitted to him by a company's directors or by its liquidator or administrator, the nominee must deliver a copy of the proposal, including any amendments made to it by its initiators with the nominee's consent, and he must also deliver to the court a copy or summary of the statement of the company's affairs which the nominee received from the initiators of the proposal.[13] If the nominee in his report expresses the opinion that meetings of creditors and of members of the company should be convened to consider the proposal, the report must have the nominee's comments on the proposal annexed to it.[14]

When the nominee's report is delivered to the court the date of delivery must be endorsed on it, and the proposal and report are then open to inspection by any director, creditor or member of the company.[15] The nominee must also send a copy of his report and his

10 Ibid, r 1.6(1) and r 1.12(4).
11 Ibid, r 1.6(2) and r 1.12(4).
12 Ibid, r 1.6(3) and r 1.12(4).
13 Ibid, r 1.7(1) and r 1.12(7).
14 Ibid, r 1.7(2) and r 1.12(7).

comments on the proposal to the company.[16]

Replacement of the nominee

Because the nominee's functions as such are completed when he has both delivered his report on a proposal made by the company's directors, liquidator or administrator and called and held meetings recommended by him of the company's creditors and members to consider the proposal, it is rarely necessary to have a succession of nominees appointed. However, to cover the situation where a nominee dies, or ceases to be qualified to act as an insolvency practitioner, or fails to submit his report on a proposal within the proper time, the court is empowered on an application by the person or persons who initiated the proposal to direct that the nominee shall be replaced by another person qualified to act as an insolvency practitioner.[17] The applicant or applicants for the replacement of a nominee must give him at least seven days' notice of the application.[18]

Contents of the proposal

Proposal by the company's directors

A proposal for a voluntary arrangement made by a company's directors must contain a short explanation of why in their opinion the arrangement is desirable, and must state why the company's creditors may be expected to concur in it.[19] The proposal must also give the following information:[20]

(a) particulars of the company's assets and estimates of their respective values, a statement of the extent to which they are charged in favour of creditors and a statement of the extent to which any of the company's assets are to be excluded from the voluntary arrangement;

(b) particulars of any property other than the company's which it is proposed to include in the arrangement, the source of such property and the terms on which it is available for inclusion;

(c) the nature of the company's liabilities, the manner in which

15 Ibid, r 1.7(3) and r 1.12(7).
16 Ibid, r 1.7(4) and r 1.12(7).
17 Insolvency Act 1986, s 2(4).
18 Insolvency Rules 1986, r 1.8 and r 1.12(7).
19 Ibid, r 1.3(1).
20 Ibid, r 1.3(2).

they are proposed to be met, modified, postponed or otherwise dealt with (eg by partial payment in full discharge, or by deferred payment, or by the company issuing notes or other securities), and in particular there must be stated:

  (i)   how it is proposed to deal with preferential creditors[1] and creditors who are, or claim to be, secured;

  (ii) how creditors who are directors or shadow directors of the company or persons associated with them (connected persons)[2] are to be treated under the arrangement;

  (iii) whether there are circumstances which make it possible that if the company were wound up, transactions entered into by it and acts done by it might be invalidated as gifts or transactions at a significant undervalue,[3] or as voidable preferences,[4] or as extortionate credit transactions,[5] or as floating charges created without new consideration being received by the company,[6] and whether and how it is proposed that the company shall be indemnified in respect of such transactions under the voluntary arrangement;[7]

(d) whether any, and if so what, guarantees have been given of the company's debts and liabilities by other persons, specifying which of the guarantors (if any) are persons connected with the company;[2]

(e) the proposed duration of the voluntary arrangement;

(f) the proposed dates of distributions to creditors and the estimated amounts of such distributions;

(g) the amount to be paid to the nominee as remuneration and to meet his expenses;

(h) the manner in which it is proposed to remunerate the supervisor, who will carry out the voluntary arrangement, and to defray his expenses;

(i) whether guarantees for the carrying out of the arrangement

---

1 This means creditors whose claims would be preferential in a winding up if the claims were calculated as at the date on which the proposal is approved by the meetings of creditors and of members (Insolvency Act 1986, s 4(7), s 386(1) and s 387(1) and (2)).

2 See p 150, ante.

3 See pp 221 and 223, ante.

4 See p 225, ante.

5 See p 235, ante.

6 See p 237, ante.

7 Such transactions will not be invalidated by or in consequence of the voluntary arrangement unless the company is already in liquidation or subject to an administration order or subsequently goes into liquidation or has an administration order made against it.

are to be given or offered by directors of the company or by other persons, and whether any security for such guarantees is to be given or sought;

(j) the manner in which funds held for the purposes of the voluntary arrangement are to be banked, invested or otherwise dealt with pending distribution to creditors of the company;

(k) the manner in which funds held for payment to creditors and not so paid are to be dealt with on the termination of the voluntary arrangement;

(l) the manner in which the company's business is to be conducted while the voluntary arrangement is being carried out (eg by the directors or subject to the supervision of a committee of creditors);

(m) particulars of any further credit facilities which it is intended to arrange for the company in connection with the voluntary arrangement, and how debts incurred under such facilities are to be paid (eg bank loan or overdraft facilities to finance the continued carrying on of the company's business);

(n) the functions which will be undertaken by the supervisor of the voluntary arrangement (eg managing the company's business or realising all or some of its assets); and

(o) particulars of the person proposed for appointment as supervisor of the voluntary arrangement and confirmation that (so far as the directors or the liquidator or administrator who make the proposal is or are aware) he is qualified to act as an insolvency practitioner, as the Insolvency Act 1986 requires.[8]

The information listed above is the minimum which any proposal made by directors of a company must contain. Obviously, in order to provide a workable arrangement which will be acceptable to the company's creditors, a proposal for a voluntary arrangement must contain a great deal more detail, and in particular, must set out a programme for the carrying out and completion of the arrangement, and it will probably require the supervisor to obtain the consent of a creditors' meeting or of a committee representing creditors if the supervisor is to enter into or carry out major commitments or disposals of the company's assets which are not dealt with in detail by the proposal. Usually the proposal is prepared by or with the collaboration of the insolvency practitioner who reports on it as nominee, and who will, if the proposal is approved by meetings of the company's creditors and of its members, carry out the arrangement proposed as the supervisor. This ensures an economy

8 Insolvency Act 1986, s 388(1) and s 390.

of effort and expense, and the nominee's professional status and experience should ensure that the arrangement proposed is a proper one and stands a reasonable chance of proving successful.

Proposal by a liquidator or administrator

The contents of a proposal made by the liquidator or administrator of a company are the same as those of a proposal made by directors, but there must be included additionally in a proposal by an administrator particulars of the creditors of the company who would be preferential creditors in a winding up if their claims were calculated up to the date on which the administration order was made.[9]

Whether the proposal is made by a liquidator or an administrator, if no other insolvency practitioner is nominated by him to report on it to the court, the proposal must include such other information and material as the liquidator or administrator considers appropriate to ensure that creditors and members of the company are enabled to reach an informed decision on the proposal.[10] The reason for requiring this latter material and explanation is to provide creditors and members of the company with the same supplemental information and comment as they would expect to find in a nominee's report.

The meetings of creditors and of members

Convening the meetings

When a nominee named in a proposal for a voluntary arrangement has reported to the court that meetings of creditors and of members should be convened to consider the proposal, he must call those meetings to be held at the times and places mentioned in his report, unless the court otherwise directs.[11] If the proposal is made by the liquidator or administrator of a company and he does not nominate another insolvency practitioner to report on it, the meetings of creditors and of members must be convened by the liquidator or administrator to be held on such date and at such time and place as he thinks fit.[12]

The two meetings of creditors and of members must be held on

---

9 Ibid, s 4(7), s 386(1) and s 387(2); Insolvency Rules 1986, r 1.10(1) and r 1.12(3).
   If the proposal is made by the liquidator, it need merely show how it is proposed to deal with the claims of preferential creditors in the liquidation (Insolvency Rules 1986, r 1.3(2) and r 1.12(3)).
10 Insolvency Rules 1986, r 1.10(1) and s 1.12(3).
11 Insolvency Act 1986, s 3(1).
12 Ibid, s 3(2).

the same day and at the same place, but the meeting of creditors must be called for a time before the commencement of the meeting of members.[13] If the meetings are convened by the nominee who has reported on the proposal, they must be held not less than 14 days and not more than 28 days after his report is delivered to the court.[14] At least 14 days' notice of the meeting of creditors must be sent by the nominee to each of the creditors of the company mentioned in the statement of affairs delivered to the nominee by the directors, liquidator or administrator of the company (as the case may be) and to any other creditors of whom the nominee is otherwise aware, and at least 14 days' notice of the meeting of members must be sent by the nominee to all persons who are, to the best of his belief, members of the company.[15] If the meetings are convened by the liquidator or administrator of the company because no nominee was named to report on a proposal made by him, at least 14 days' notice of the creditors' meeting must be given to each of the creditors mentioned in the statement of the company's affairs prepared at the commencement of the winding up or administration and to any other creditors of whom the liquidator or administrator is aware; correspondingly, at least 14 days' notice of the members' meeting must be given to all persons who are, to the best of the liquidator's or administrator's belief, members of the company.[16]

Each notice of a creditors' or members' meeting must be accompanied by a copy of the proposal for a voluntary arrangement to be considered by the meeting and the comments of the nominee on the proposal and a copy or summary of the statement of the company's affairs delivered to the nominee, or if no nominee was named to report on the proposal, a copy or summary of the statement of the company's affairs prepared at the commencement of its winding up or on an administration order being made.[17] The notices of creditors' and members' meetings must also specify the court to which the nominee's report on the proposal (if any) has been delivered and the requisite majority of creditors who must vote to approve the proposal at their meeting if it is to be effective.[17]

Meetings of creditors and of members are presided over by the nominee, liquidator or administrator who convened the meeting, but if he cannot attend the meeting, he may nominate another person who is a qualified insolvency practitioner, or who is an employee of the convener of the meeting and is experienced in

13 Insolvency Rules 1986, r 1.13(3).
14 Ibid, r 1.9(1).
15 Insolvency Act 1986, s 2(3); Insolvency Rules 1986, r 1.9(2) and r 1.12(7).
16 Insolvency Act 1986, s 2(3); Insolvency Rules 1986, r 1.11(1).
17 Ibid, rr 1.9(3), 1.11(2) and 1.12(7).

insolvency matters, to act as chairman in his place.[18] The convener of the meetings of creditors and members of the company must give at least 14 days' notice of both meetings to each director of the company, and may give such notice to any other person whose attendance at the meetings the convener requires because they are officers of the company or have been directors or officers of it within the preceding two years.[19] On the other hand, the chairman of a meeting may exclude from the whole or any part of the proceedings any present or former director or officer of the company if he thinks fit.[20]

Voting rights

At the creditors' meeting or any adjournment of it, every creditor who was given notice of the meeting is entitled to vote in person or by proxy,[1] and to ensure that creditors are aware of their right to vote by proxy, the notices convening the meeting must be accompanied by proxy appointment forms which enable a creditor to authorise his proxy to vote for or against each resolution proposed at the meeting.[2]

Votes at a creditors' meeting are cast according to the amount of the creditor's debt or claim at the date of the meeting, or if the company is in liquidation or subject to an administration order, at the date of the winding up order or resolution, or (as the case may be) the date of the administration order.[4] A creditor may vote at a creditors' meeting only if his claim and its amount are admitted by the chairman of the meeting;[5] the chairman must make his own decision as to the validity of the creditor's claim and as to its proper amount, and the chairman cannot without inquiry admit claims and their amounts as they are shown in the company's statement of affairs.[6] A creditor may not vote in respect of an unliquidated claim or a debt whose amount is unascertained, unless the chairman agrees to put an estimated minimum value on it for the purpose of voting.[7] There has been a conflict of authority as to whether this provision means that the chairman may admit the creditor's claim for an estimated amount only if the chairman and the creditor agree

18 Ibid, r 1.14(1) and (2).
19 Ibid, r 1.16(1).
20 Ibid, r 1.16(2).
 1 Ibid, r 1.17(1).
 2 Ibid, r 1.13(4) and r 8.1(6) and Form 8.1.
 3 *IRC v Conbeer* [1996] BCC 189.
 4 Insolvency Rules 1986, r 1.17(2).
 5 Ibid, r 1.17(4).
 6 *Beverley Group plc v McClue* [1995] 2 BCLC 407, [1995] BCC 751.
 7 Ibid, r 1.17(3).

on that amount (as was held in one case),[8] or whether the only agreement required is the unilateral assent of the chairman to admit the claim for voting purposes at his estimate of its value and the acceptance of this by the creditor is not required (as was held in another case);[9] the latter view, which has been upheld by the Court of Appeal,[10] would appear to be the correct one.

The chairman may admit or reject a creditor's claim to vote, or may admit the claim in respect of part of the debt claimed by the creditor, but the chairman's decision is subject to appeal to the court within 28 days after he reports the result of the meeting to the court.[11] Such an appeal dies if the chairman puts a minimum estimated value on an unliquidated claim or on a claim of uncertain amount, and the creditor does not accept the chairman's decision.[12] If the court reverses or varies the chairman's decision on the right of a creditor to vote, or the amount for which a claim must be admitted, or declares a vote invalid, it may order another meeting to be held or make such other order as it thinks just (eg an order declaring a resolution to have been passed or defeated), but the court may exercise its power to make any such order only if it considers the matter complained of gave rise to unfair prejudice or involved a material irregularity.[13] If the chairman is in doubt whether to admit or reject a creditor's claim to vote, he must mark the claim as objected to and allow the creditor to vote, subject to his vote subsequently being declared invalid if the objection is sustained.[14] Only one meeting of creditors is held, at which they may all attend and vote, irrespective of the nature or categories of their debts or claims against the company. The procedure set out above for the admission and quantification of the debts and claims of creditors of the company relates only to the right of creditors to vote at the meeting of their number called to approve or reject the proposed voluntary arrangement and to the proportion of votes which they may cast at that meeting. It does not relate to the quantification of creditors' claims for the purpose of implementing the voluntary arrangement once it has been approved by the creditors' and members' meetings; for that purpose creditors' claims are valued at

---

8 *Re Cranley Mansions Ltd, Saigol v Goldstein* [1995] 1 BCLC 290, [1994] BCC 576.

9 *Doorbar v Alltime Securities Ltd* [1995] 1 BCLC 316, [1994] BCC 994, *(No 2)* [1995] BCC 728.

10 [1996] 1 BCLC 487, [1995] BCC 1149.

11 Insolvency Rules 1986, r 1.17(4), (5) and (8).

12 *Doorbar v Alltime Securities Ltd* [1995] 1 BCLC 316, [1994] BCC 972; affd [1996] 1 BCLC 487, [1995] BCC 1149.

13 Insolvency Rules 1986, r 1.17(7).

14 Ibid, r 1.17(6).

their actual worth, subject to any provisions in respect of valuation contained in the approved voluntary arrangement itself.

The right to vote at the members' meeting called to approve a voluntary arrangement is governed by the provisions of the company's memorandum or articles of association, but if a member's shares carry no voting rights under those instruments, he is nevertheless entitled to vote as though the memorandum or articles imposed no restriction on his right to vote.[15] This does not appear to confer full or proportionate voting rights on all members, but merely to confer normal voting rights on members who by the company's memorandum or articles have no voting rights at all. If the company's articles confer differential voting rights on different classes of shareholders, the voting rights exercisable at the members' meeting will be those differential rights. Only one meeting of members is held, at which they may all attend and vote in person or by proxy without any distinction being drawn between the holders of different classes of shares. A member may vote at a members' meeting in person or by proxy, and proxy appointment forms enabling a member to authorise his proxy to vote for or against each resolution proposed at the meeting must be sent out with notices of the meeting.[16]

The meetings of creditors and of members must decide whether to approve the proposed voluntary arrangement with or without modification.[17] In particular, a modification may be resolved upon to confer the functions of the supervisor, who is responsible for carrying out the approved arrangement, on another qualified insolvency practitioner instead of the nominee who reported on the proposal.[18] The substitution of another insolvency practitioner to be the supervisor is possible, whether the proposal for the voluntary arrangement is prepared by the directors or the liquidator or administrator of the company, and in the latter case, whether the liquidator or administrator or another insolvency practitioner is the nominee. However, no modification may be resolved upon which would cancel, alter or affect the right of a secured creditor of the company to enforce his security, or which would cancel, alter or postpone the right of a creditor whose debt or claim would be a preferential claim in a winding up to be paid rateably with other preferential creditors in priority to unsecured creditors of the company, unless the secured or preferential creditor concerned

15 Ibid, r 1.18(1) and (2).
16 Ibid, r 1.13(4) and r 8.1(6) and Form 8.1.
17 Insolvency Act 1986, s 4(1).
18 Ibid, s 4(2).

agrees.[19]

The majority required for the approval at a creditors' meeting of a proposed voluntary arrangement or of a modification to it is the affirmative votes of creditors holding more than three-quarters in value of the company's total indebtedness in respect of which votes are cast in person or by proxy on the resolution.[20] There must be left out of account when determining whether the required majority has been attained, however, the vote of a creditor:

(a) who has not given written notice of his debt or claim to the chairman or convener of the meeting before or at the time when it is held; or

(b) whose debt or claim is wholly or partly secured; or

(c) whose debt or claim is under a bill of exchange or promissory note, unless the creditor is willing to treat the liability of every party to it prior to the company (unless he has been adjudged bankrupt or is a company or corporation which has gone into liquidation) as a security for his claim and to deduct the estimated value of that security from the amount in respect of which he votes.[1]

If the whole of a claim is secured on assets of less value than the amount of the claim, the creditor may vote in respect of the amount of his claim in excess of the value of those assets.[2]

A resolution approving a proposed voluntary arrangement or a modification to it is invalid if the creditors who voted against it comprise more than half in value of the creditors to whom notice of the meeting was given, whose votes are not required to be left out of account under the preceding provision, and who are not to the best of the chairman's belief directors or shadow directors of the company or persons associated with them or with the company (connected person.[3] In other words, if the requisite majority for the approval or modification of the proposed voluntary arrangement is procured by the votes of creditors who are directors, shadow directors or persons associated with them or with the company, or by their votes plus the votes of other creditors who are entitled to vote and the total value of whose debts or claims is less than the total value of the debts and claims of other creditors who are entitled to vote and who vote to

19 Ibid, s 4(3) and (4). A judgment creditor of the company who has issued a writ of execution under which the sheriff has seized goods of the company is a secured creditor for this purpose (*Peck v Craighead* [1995] 1 BCLC 337, [1995] BCC 525).

20 Insolvency Rules 1986, r 1.19(1).

1 Ibid, r 1.19(3).

2 *Calor Gas Ltd v Piercy* [1994] 2 BCLC 321, [1994] BCC 69.

3 Insolvency Rules 1986, r 1.19(4). For connected persons, see p 150, ante.

reject the arrangement, the approval of the arrangement by the creditors' meeting is not given. The situation is therefore similar to that of a resolution passed at a meeting of creditors called to approve the proposals of an administrator under an administration order, namely, that the proposed voluntary arrangement must be approved by the requisite majority in value of all the creditors entitled to vote and voting in person or by proxy, and also by the requisite majority in value of creditors so entitled to vote and voting who are not persons connected with the company. The requisite majority for the approval of a voluntary arrangement is of course higher than that needed for the approval by creditors of an administrator's proposals under an administration order (ie more than three-quarters in value of the creditors' admitted claims, as against a simple majority in value of those claims) and, moreover, a proposed voluntary arrangement must be approved by both the meeting of creditors and the meeting of members, whereas an administrator's proposals under an administration order do not require the approval of the company's members.

A voluntary arrangement proposed by an administrator authorised to do so by the administration order under which he acts may be submitted to a meeting of the company's creditors for approval as the proposal of the administrator under the administration order itself.[4] A single resolution passed by the creditors' meeting approving the proposed voluntary arrangement will suffice also as the creditors' approval of the administrator's proposals under the administration order, but the resolution should make it clear by its terms that it is passed for both those purposes.

Other resolutions passed at a meeting of creditors in connection with a proposed or actual voluntary arrangement (whether at the meeting which approves the arrangement or a separate meeting) are passed by the affirmative votes of more than half in value of the creditors voting on the resolution in person or by proxy (eg a resolution to adjourn the meeting), but the resolution is not treated as passed if it is procured only by the votes of creditors who are directors or shadow directors of the company or persons associated with them, and the same rule applies in this respect as that relating to resolutions approving a proposed voluntary arrangement which are so procured.[5]

Resolutions are passed at the meeting of members called to approve the proposed voluntary arrangement if they are supported by more than half of the votes cast by members attending the

4 Insolvency Act 1986, s 23(1) and (2) and s 24(1); (see p 340, ante).
5 Insolvency Rules 1986, r 1.19(2) and (4).

meeting in person or by proxy.[6] This applies to resolutions to approve or modify the arrangement as well as to other resolutions (such as a resolution to adjourn the meeting).

The meetings of creditors and of members called to approve a voluntary arrangement may be adjourned; also the chairman may if he thinks fit hold both meetings or adjournments of them at the same time so that the approval of the creditors and members for the arrangement is obtained simultaneously.[7] If approval of a voluntary arrangement is not given at the first meeting of creditors or of members, the chairman may, and if the meeting so resolves, must adjourn it for not more than 14 days, but neither meeting may be adjourned to a day later than 14 days after it was first held.[8] If neither meeting approves the arrangement at its first meeting, adjournments of both meetings must be to the same day.[9]

Report and notice of the result of the meetings

Within four days after the meetings of creditors and of members are held, the chairman must file a report in court stating whether each meeting resolved to approve the voluntary arrangement with or without modification, setting out the resolutions passed at each meeting and listing the creditors and members who attended the meetings in person or by proxy and the value of the debts or the amount of shares in respect of which they respectively voted.[10] Immediately after filing his report in court, the chairman must give notice of the result of each meeting to the persons to whom were sent notices convening it.[11] The supervisor appointed to carry out the approved voluntary arrangement must send a copy of the chairman's report to the Registrar of Companies when the report has been filed in court.[12]

The possibility of further meetings to consider a proposed voluntary arrangement

If either of the meetings of creditors and members of a company called to approve a proposed voluntary arrangement disapproves it or fails to approve it, the arrangement obviously does not take effect,

---

6 Ibid, r 1.20(1).
7 Ibid, r 1.21(1).
8 Ibid, r 1.21(2) and (3).
9 Ibid, r 1.21(4).
10 Insolvency Act 1986, s 4(6); Insolvency Rules 1986, r 1.24(1) to (3).
11 Insolvency Act 1986, s 4(6); Insolvency Rules 1986, r 1.24(4).
12 Insolvency Rules 1986, r 1.24(5).

but the question then arises whether further meetings of creditors and members (as distinct from adjournments of the original meetings) may be called to approve the proposed arrangement so that it will then become effective. In a bankruptcy case[13] it has been held that a second meeting of the debtor's creditors may not be called to approve a proposed voluntary arrangement which was rejected by the original meeting, and if such a meeting is held and resolves to approve the proposed arrangement, its approval is ineffective. It is true that where an individual debtor proposes a voluntary arrangement, the court, on approving the nominee's report that a meeting of creditors should be called to consider the proposal, makes an interim order which temporarily prevents creditors of the debtor from taking proceedings against him or levying execution or pursuing any legal process against him or his assets, whereas there are no such restrictions imposed when a company's directors propose a voluntary arrangement.[14] However, this would not appear to be a relevant distinction where a voluntary arrangement is proposed in respect of a company, because whether the debtor is a company or an individual, the relevant meetings are called by the nominee, the purpose of the meetings is the same and the nominee reports to the court on the result of the meeting in both cases. It therefore appears that if the original meetings of creditors and members of a company called to approve a proposed voluntary arrangement do not both approve it, the whole procedure must be re-commenced, and even though the new proposed arrangement is identical in terms with the original one, a new report by a nominee must be prepared and submitted to the court before meetings of creditors and members of the company are called to approve the new proposal.

Effect and implementation of the arrangement

The effect of both the meetings of creditors and of members of a company approving a proposed voluntary arrangement is that the arrangement (with any modifications agreed upon by both meetings) takes effect as though it had been made by the company at the creditors' meeting, and is binding on every creditor who had notice of that meeting and was entitled to vote at it as if he were a party to the arrangement, whether or not he attended the meeting in person or by proxy.[15] The voluntary arrangement is therefore binding on

---

13 *Re Symes, Kent Carpets Ltd v Symes* [1995] 2 BCLC 651, [1996] BCC 137.
14 Insolvency Act 1986, s 252(2) and s 255(1) and (2).

the company and its creditors who had notice of the creditors' meeting either by it being delivered to them, or by them being informed of it in some other way (eg by a creditor being notified of a meeting of members from which he must have concluded that a meeting of creditors had been called for the same day).[16] But this is so only if the creditor was entitled to vote at the meeting of creditors, whether he did so or not, being immaterial; the voluntary arrangement is equally binding on an assignee of the debt owed to a creditor who would be bound by the arrangement.[17] However, the approved voluntary agreement is not binding on a creditor who did not have notice of the creditors' meeting,[18] or whose claim to vote at it was rejected by the chairman;[19] if a creditor claims in respect of a debt for an amount less than he should have claimed, he is bound by the approved voluntary arrangement in respect of the whole of that debt,[20] and if the chairman puts a value on a claim of uncertain amount or on an unliquidated claim, the claimant is similarly bound in respect of the whole of the claim at that valuation, unless he successfully appeals to the court, in which case he is bound at the court's valuation.[1]

Although the approval of the members' meeting is essential for a voluntary arrangement to be effective as between the company and its creditors, the rights of members are not, and cannot be, affected by the arrangement (eg by requiring them to subscribe share or loan capital which the arrangement provides shall be raised to finance it, or by binding them to guarantee that the arrangement will be carried out). If an arrangement is to affect the interests of members of the company, in particular by modifying or extinguishing the rights attached to their shares or by imposing new obligations on them, the arrangement must be effected, so far as the members are concerned, under the provisions of the company's memorandum and articles or of a scheme of arrangement approved by the court under the Companies Act 1985.[2]

If the company is in liquidation when the voluntary arrangement becomes effective, the court may stay the winding up proceedings and terminate the liquidation; the liquidator is then discharged and

---

15 Insolvency Act 1986, s 5(1) and (2).
16 *Beverley Group plc v McClue* [1995] 2 BCLC 407, [1995] BCC 751.
17 *Burford Midland Properties Ltd v Marley Extrusions Ltd* [1995] 1 BCLC 102, [1994] BCC 604.
18 *Re a Debtor (No 64 of 1992)* [1994] 1 WLR 264, [1994] BCC 55.
19 *Re Cranley Mansions Ltd, Saigol v Goldstein* [1995] 1 BCLC 290, [1994] BCC 516.
20 *Re Cancol Ltd* [1996] 1 BCLC 100, [1995] BCC 1133.
1 *Doorbar v Alltime Securities Ltd* [1996] 1 BCLC 487, [1995] BCC 1149.
2 See p 434, post.

the supervisor under the arrangement is entitled to administer the company's assets.[3] If the company is subject to an administration order when the voluntary arrangement becomes effective, the court may discharge the order, and the administration thereupon terminates.[3] As an alternative if the company is in liquidation or subject to an administration order, the court may give such directions as it thinks appropriate in respect of the conduct of the winding up or administration in order to facilitate the implementation of the voluntary arrangement.[3]

Upon a voluntary arrangement being approved by the meetings of creditors and of members of a company, the nominee who reported on the proposal, or the insolvency practitioner appointed to replace him by the court or by an approved modification of the arrangement, becomes the supervisor, whose task is to carry out the arrangement by exercising the functions conferred on him by it.[4] Whether the supervisor is the same person as the nominee or not, he must be a qualified insolvency practitioner; curiously, the Insolvency Act 1986, does not so provide expressly (as it does in respect of a liquidator, an administrator, or an administrative receiver),[5] but it is a criminal offence for a person to act as the supervisor of a voluntary arrangement by a company unless he is a qualified insolvency practitioner.[6]

The directors of the company or its liquidator or administrator (if not himself the supervisor) must do everything necessary to put the supervisor in possession of the assets of the company comprised in the arrangement.[7] The supervisor may apply to the court for directions in carrying out his functions, and a creditor of the company or any other person who is dissatisfied with an act, omission or decision of the supervisor may apply to the court, which may confirm, reverse or modify the act etc, or give the supervisor directions, or make such other order as the court thinks fit.[8] The court may replace or fill a vacancy in the office of supervisor by appointing another qualified insolvency practitioner to be the supervisor where it is inexpedient, difficult or impracticable to effect the replacement or fill the vacancy in any other way.[9]

A voluntary arrangement which has been approved by the requisite majorities at meetings of the company's creditors and members takes effect as a contract between the company and the

3 Insolvency Act 1986, s 5(3).
4 Ibid, s 7(1) and (2).
5 Ibid, s 230(1) to (4).
6 Ibid, s 388(1) and s 389(1).
7 Insolvency Rules 1986, r 1.23(1).
8 Insolvency Act 1986, s 7(3) and (4).
9 Ibid, s 7(5).

creditors who are bound by it and between the creditors themselves, as well as having a statutory effect.[10] It has also been held that the supervisor of the arrangement holds the assets of the company vested in him, or available to him, under a voluntary arrangement as a trustee for the creditors who are to benefit under it, and they presumably acquire equitable interests in those assets.[11] It would appear that the beneficiaries of the trust are the creditors of the company as defined by the terms of the voluntary arrangement, and their interests in the property and assets of the company comprised in the arrangement (which may be the whole or only part of the assets of the company) are likewise defined by the terms of the voluntary arrangement. Creditors of the company who are not bound by the voluntary arrangement are, of course, free to pursue their claims against assets of the company which are not included in the arrangement, but where the arrangement extends to the whole of the company's assets, they are more likely to petition for the company to be wound up than to resort to particular assets of the company on the ground that they are not caught by it.

If a voluntary arrangement becomes effective in respect of a company which is in liquidation or subject to an administration order, the supervisor must out of the assets of the company of which he takes possession discharge any amount due to the liquidator or administrator in respect of his proper remuneration and any fees, costs, charges or expenses payable in connection with the liquidation or administration and any advances made by him for carrying it out, and the liquidator or administrator has a statutory charge on the assets of which the supervisor takes possession for the payment of those amounts.[12]

Revocation and suspension of a voluntary arrangement

Within 28 days after the filing of his report by the chairman who presided at the meetings of creditors and members which approved a voluntary arrangement with the creditors of a company, or such longer period as the court permits, an application may be made to the court to revoke or suspend the approval of the voluntary arrangement by the meetings of creditors and of members; such an application may be made to the court by any person entitled to vote at the meetings of creditors or members which approved the

10 Insolvency Act 1986, s 5(1) and (2).
11 *Re Leisure Study Group Ltd* [1994] 2 BCLC 65.
12 Insolvency Rules 1986, r 1.23(2) and (4).

arrangement, or by the nominee specified in the proposal for the arrangement, or by any person appointed to replace him by the court or substituted as nominee by a modification of the arrangement made by the meetings which approved it; if the company is in liquidation or is the subject of an administration order, the application may also be made by the liquidator or administrator.[13] The application to the court is made by way of an originating application setting out the names of the parties, the grounds on which the application is made and particulars of the persons on whom it is intended to serve copies of the application.[14]

The grounds on which the application to the court may be made are either: (a) that the approved voluntary arrangement unfairly prejudices the interests of a creditor, member or contributory of the company; or (b) that there has been some material irregularity at, or in relation to, either of the meetings of creditors or of members of the company which approved the arrangement.[15] The first of these grounds is obviously modelled on the provision of the Companies Act 1985, which empowers the court to give minority shareholders relief from the conduct of a company's affairs in a way which is unfairly prejudicial to the whole or some part of the company's members, or against any actual or proposed act which is or would be so prejudicial.[16] It nevertheless differs from that provision in that the complaint of unfair prejudice is directed against the terms or effect of the voluntary arrangement, and not the conduct of the supervisor in carrying it out, or the inadequacy of the resources available to the supervisor in order to carry it out, or the financial unreliability of a person who has guaranteed the carrying out of the voluntary arrangement.[17] The situations in which the court can give relief are therefore the same as, or similar to, those where the court would refuse to sanction a scheme of arrangement made under the Companies Act 1985,[18] or to enforce an arrangement made under a contractual provision contained in debt securities or the trust deed covering their issue, namely, that the arrangement is unreasonable or unfair, or was not proposed in good faith.[19]

The second ground for an application to the court to revoke or

---

13 Insolvency Act 1986, s 6(1) to (3).
14 Insolvency Rules 1986, r 7.2(1) and r 7.3(1) and (2).
15 Insolvency Act 1986, s 6(1).
16 Companies Act 1985, s 459(1); (see p 396, ante).
17 *Re a Debtor (No 259 of 1990)* [1992] 1 All ER 641, [1992] 1 WLR 226 (decided under the identical provisions of the Insolvency Act 1986 as to voluntary arrangements by individual debtors).
18 Insolvency Act 1986, s 425(1) and (2); (see p 449, post).
19 See p 451, post.

suspend a voluntary arrangement would apply in situations where the court would invalidate a resolution passed by a general meeting of a company because of procedural irregularities, including material misstatements or omissions in the statement of the company's affairs or in copies of the proposed voluntary arrangement sent out by the nominee,[20] or the miscalculation of votes at the meeting of creditors or members, or an incorrect declaration of the result of the votes cast, or because the approval of the arrangement by a meeting of creditors or members has been procured by improper means.[1] The refusal of the chairman of a creditors' meeting to allow a creditor to vote in respect of the admitted amount of his debt is a material irregularity, but the court will not revoke the approval of the voluntary arrangement if it would have been approved by the requisite majority even if the applicant for revocation had been able to vote against it.[17] A claimant whose claim to vote at the creditors' meeting has been rejected by the chairman should in any case not apply to the court to revoke the approval of the voluntary arrangement; his proper remedy is to appeal against the chairman's decision excluding his claim to vote.[17] Similarly, a creditor who contends that persons were permitted to vote at the creditors' meeting who were not entitled to do so and that this resulted in a spurious majority vote to approve the proposed arrangement, should not apply to the court to revoke the approval of the arrangement by the creditors' meeting; his proper remedy is to appeal to the court against the admission by the chairman of the right of those persons to vote and his consequential declaration that the resolution of approval was not passed.[17]

If on the hearing of an application to revoke or suspend the approval of a voluntary arrangement, the court is satisfied that either or both of the grounds for the application have been proved, the court may revoke or suspend the approval of the arrangement by the meetings of creditors and members, and/or direct the convening of further meetings to consider any revised proposal to be made by the person or persons who made the original one, or if the consent of the meetings is revoked because of a material irregularity, to direct the convening of further meetings to consider the original proposal.[2] If the court directs that meetings shall be convened to consider a revised proposal, it must revoke the direction and revoke or suspend the approval of the arrangement given at previous meetings if the court is later satisfied that the person who made the original proposal does not intend to make a revised proposal.[3] The person

---

20 *Re a Debtor (No 87 of 1993) (No 2)* [1996] 1 BCLC 63, [1996] BCC 74.
1 See *Pennington's Company Law* (7th edn) p 857.
2 Insolvency Act 1986, s 6(4).

who obtains an order of the court revoking or suspending the approval of a voluntary arrangement must serve sealed copies of it on the supervisor of the arrangement and on the directors or the liquidator or administrator who made the proposal for the arrangement, and if the court's order directs the convening of further meetings, notice of the order must be served on the person who is to convene them.[4] On receiving a copy of the court's order, the directors or the liquidator or administrator must give notice of it to all persons who were sent notice of the original meetings of creditors and members and to all other persons who are affected by the order, and if the court's order calls for a revised proposal, within seven days of receiving a copy of the court's order, the directors or the liquidator or administrator must give notice to the court whether it is intended to prepare a revised proposal.[5]

If no application is made to the court to revoke or suspend the approval of a voluntary arrangement within the 28-day period, the approval of the arrangement by a meeting of creditors or members cannot be invalidated because of any irregularity at or in relation to either meeting of creditors or members.[6] This would still appear to leave it open to any creditor or member of the company to seek the invalidation of the arrangement itself after the 28-day period has expired by bringing an action by writ for a declaration of the invalidity or ineffectiveness of the arrangement and an injunction to restrain its implementation, on the equitable grounds that it is unfair, or was not proposed in good faith, or because no sensible creditor acting reasonably would have approved it.[7]

The supervisor's accounts and reports

If a voluntary arrangement authorises or requires the supervisor to carry on the business of the company or to trade in its name or on its behalf, or to realise assets of the company, or otherwise to administer or dispose of any of its funds, the supervisor must keep accounts and records of his acts and dealings, including in particular, accounts of his receipts and payments of money.[8] Not less often than every 12 months following his appointment, such a supervisor must, unless the court otherwise directs, send an abstract of his receipts and payments with his comments on the progress and efficacy of the

3 Ibid, s 6(5).
4 Insolvency Rules, r 1.25(1) to (3).
5 Ibid, r 1.25(4).
6 Insolvency Act 1986, s 6(7).
7 See p 449, post.
8 Insolvency Rules 1986, r 1.26(1).

voluntary arrangement to the court, the Registrar of Companies, the company and each of the members and creditors of the company who is bound by the arrangement[9] and, if the company is not in liquidation, to its auditors.[10] If a supervisor is not authorised to carry on the company's business etc, he must not less often than every 12 months following his appointment send to the court and the persons mentioned above a report on the progress and efficacy of the voluntary arrangement.[11]

The Secretary of State for Trade and Industry may at any time while the voluntary arrangement is being carried out or after its completion, require the supervisor to produce for inspection his records and accounts and copies of the annual abstracts and reports sent out by him, and may cause his records and accounts to be audited.[12]

Within 28 days after the completion of a voluntary arrangement, the supervisor must send to the court, the Registrar of Companies and to each of the creditors and members of the company who is bound by the arrangement, a notice that the voluntary arrangement has been fully implemented and a report by the supervisor summarising his receipts and payments in connection with carrying out the arrangement, and explaining any difference between its actual implementation and the proposal for the arrangement which was approved by the meetings of creditors and of members.[13]

The effect of a subsequent liquidation or administration order

A voluntary arrangement by a company with its creditors would appear not to be terminated or rescinded automatically if the company is subsequently wound up by order of the court or voluntarily, or if an administration order is subsequently made in respect of the company.[14] The supervisor of the company's voluntary arrangement may petition the court to wind up the company or to make an administration order in respect of it.[15] The grounds on

9 This would appear to require copies of the abstract to be sent to all the current members of the company, but not necessarily to persons who were members when the arrangement was approved.
10 Insolvency Rules 1986, r 1.26(2) and (5).
11 Ibid, r 1.26(4).
12 Ibid, r 1.27(1) and (3).
13 Ibid, r 1.29(1) to (3).
14 There is no judicial decision to this effect, but it has been held that a voluntary arrangement by an individual debtor with his creditors under the Insolvency Act 1986 is not terminated by him subsequently being adjudged bankrupt (*Re Bradley-Hole* [1995] 2 BCLC 163, [1995] BCC 418; *Davis v Martin-Sklan* [1995] 2 BCLC 483, [1995] BCC 1122).

which he may petition for a winding up order are the same as those on which a creditor or contributory may petition, (principally the company's inability to pay its debts, or that it would be just and equitable to wind the company up); the reasons why a supervisor would be likely to petition for a winding up order are the impossibility or impracticability of carrying out the voluntary arrangement or serious breaches by the company of the obligations imposed on it by the arrangement.

There is no provision in the Insolvency Act 1986, comparable to that in respect of voluntary arrangements by individual debtors, under which the court may make a bankruptcy order against the debtor if he fails to comply with his obligations under the voluntary arrangement, or to do all things reasonably required of him by the supervisor for the purpose of carrying it out, or if he has supplied materially false or misleading information to his creditors in connection with a proposed arrangement.[16] It has been held that if a bankruptcy order is made for any of those reasons, the voluntary arrangement terminates,[17] but if a winding up order were made in similar circumstances against a company which has entered into a voluntary arrangement on the ground that it was just and equitable to wind it up,[18] it is questionable whether the voluntary arrangement would terminate. The question nevertheless remains whether in the liquidation or administration of a company the court could treat the voluntary arrangement approved by its creditors and members as invalid or ineffective on the equitable grounds that it is unreasonable or unfair or was not proposed in good faith.[19] There would appear to be no reason why the court should not have jurisdiction to do this in the same way as if the company were not in liquidation or administration.

COMPROMISES AND ARRANGEMENTS APPROVED BY THE COURT

The Insolvency Act 1986 provides a procedure by which comparatively straightforward compositions and arrangements between a company and its creditors may be made binding and effective without the need to obtain the approval of the court. For

15 Insolvency Act 1986, s 7(4).
16 Ibid, s 264(1)(*c*) and s 276(1).
17 *Davis v Martin-Sklan*, supra.
18 Insolvency Act 1986, s 122(1)(*g*); (see p 47, ante).
19 See p 449, post.

more complex compromises and arrangements by a company with its creditors and for arrangements between a company and any class or classes of its members which cannot be effected under the provisions of its memorandum or articles of association,[20] the Companies Act 1985 provides an alternative and more complicated procedure under which the court's approval of the scheme is essential.

If a scheme for a compromise or arrangement is proposed between a company and its creditors, or any class of them, or between the company and its members, or any class of them, the court may on the application of the company, or any of its members or creditors, or if the company is in liquidation or administration, on the application of its liquidator or administrator, direct meetings to be held of the creditors or members or class of creditors or members concerned; if each of the meetings so directed approves the compromise or arrangement by a resolution passed by a majority in number representing three-quarters in value of the persons present and voting in person or by proxy, the court may sanction the scheme, and when a copy of the court's order has been delivered to the Registrar of Companies, the compromise or arrangement becomes binding on all the creditors or members of the class or classes concerned.[1] For the purpose of this provision the value of shares is taken to be their nominal value and the value of creditors' claims is taken as their nominal or face value, or in the case of claims for unliquidated or uncertain amounts and claims which are contingent or conditional, at a fair estimate of their value. Compromises and arrangements may be approved by the court under this provision, whether the company in question is registered under the Companies Act 1985, or any of the earlier Companies Acts or is an unregistered or overseas company which may be wound up by order of the court, but compromises and arrangements may not be effected under the present provisions in respect of insolvent partnerships.[2] Moreover, the court's approval may be given whether the company is in liquidation or administration or not, and an administration order may be made in respect of a company registered under the Companies Acts in order to give effect to a compromise or arrangement with its creditors or any class of them which is to be submitted to the court for its sanction.[3]

---

20 See *Pennington's Company Law* (7th edn) p 273 et seq.
  1 Companies Act 1985, s 425(1) to (3).
  2 Ibid, s 425(6).
  3 Insolvency Act 1986, s 8(3)(*c*); (see p 340, ante).

Limitations on the court's powers

Wide as the court's powers are to sanction a scheme for a compromise or arrangement under the Companies Act 1985, there are, nevertheless four limitations upon them.

In the first place, the court can sanction a scheme only if it would be valid without the court's sanction if every creditor or member of the company concerned agreed to it. In other words, the only power which the court has is to make the scheme binding on non-assenting creditors or members; it has no power to sanction something which the parties could not do by unanimous agreement.[4] Consequently, the court cannot sanction an arrangement which requires the company to do an act or to engage in a transaction which is outside the objects of the company,[5] nor can it sanction the transfer of a contract which is not assignable, such as a contract of employment,[6] unless the transfer is under a scheme by which the whole or part of the company's undertaking is transferred to another company which is to become the employer of the original company's employees in that undertaking.[7]

Secondly, the court cannot sanction an act being done if the law permits it only if certain conditions are fulfilled and the arrangement seeks to dispense with those conditions. Thus, the court has refused to sanction a scheme for converting preference shares into redeemable preference shares, because the Companies Act 1985,[8] by permitting the issue of redeemable shares, impliedly prohibits shares being made redeemable after they have been issued as non-redeemable shares.[9]

Thirdly, the court cannot sanction a scheme which can be effected under some other provision of the Companies Act 1985. Thus, the court refused to approve a scheme which merely provided for the reduction of the company's capital,[10] and in the case cited above[9] where the court refused to approve a scheme for the conversion of preference shares into redeemable preference shares, a second reason given for its decision was that the company could carry out

4 *Re Guardian Assurance Co* [1917] 1 Ch 431 at 441, per Younger J.
5 *Re Oceanic Steam Navigation Co* [1939] Ch 41, [1939] 3 All ER 740.
6 *Nokes v Doncaster Amalgamated Collieries Ltd* [1940] AC 1014, [1940] 3 All ER 549.
7 Transfer of Undertakings (Protection of Employment) Regulations 1981 (SI 1981/1794), paras 3(1) and 5(1) and (2). The transfer of the contracts of employment will take effect by operation of law on the transfer of the company's undertaking or part of it.
8 Companies Act 1985, s 159(1).
9 *Re St James' Court Estate Ltd* [1944] Ch 6.
10 *Re Cooper, Cooper and Johnson Ltd* [1902] WN 199.

the scheme by issuing new redeemable preference shares for cash and using the proceeds to pay off the existing preference shares on a duly authorised reduction of capital. But there seems to be no reason why a company should not seek the court's sanction to a modification of the rights of its shareholders or the rights of its debt security holders merely because there are provisions in the company's memorandum or articles of association, or in the debt securities or the trust deed executed to cover them, under which the modification could be effected without the need for the sanction of the court.[11] Moreover, it has been held that when a scheme of arrangement was submitted for the transfer of control of a company's undertaking by the acquisition of all its shares, the fact that the transfer of control could be effected by an offer by the intending acquirer to acquire the shares coupled with the power to compel non-assenting shareholders to transfer their shares under the Companies Act 1985,[12] did not prevent the court from approving the scheme.[13]

Fourthly and finally, the court cannot approve a scheme unless it is either proposed by the company or its liquidator or administrator, or if it is proposed by someone else, unless the company has consented to the submission of the scheme for the approval of the class or classes of the members or creditors concerned by a resolution passed by its board of directors or a general meeting.[14] In practice schemes for compromises or arrangements are always proposed by the board of directors or liquidator of the company concerned, or if an administration order has been made in respect of the company in order that a scheme of arrangement shall be effected, by the company's administrator.

Examples of schemes approved by the court

Within the limits set out above, the court allows companies the greatest freedom in devising schemes to meet the exigencies of their financial situations or their plans for the future conduct of their undertakings, and the court approves such schemes if they are fair to the company's members and creditors whose interests are affected.

11 The reorganisation of share capital in *Carruth v ICI Ltd* [1937] AC 707, [1937] 2 All ER 422, by converting the company's issued deferred shares into ordinary shares with a lower total nominal and paid up value, was effected by a normal reduction of capital combined with a variation of class rights under a provision in the company's articles of association, but the House of Lords did not say that it was obligatory to carry out the reorganisation in this way.
12 Companies Act 1985, s 428(1) to (4).
13 *Re National Bank Ltd* [1966] 1 All ER 1006, [1966] 1 WLR 819.
14 *Re Savoy Hotel Ltd* [1981] Ch 351, [1981] 3 All ER 646.

The court has deliberately laid down no rules to which schemes must conform in order to obtain the court's approval, and has thus left companies free to initiate schemes of the widest variety. Nevertheless, the kinds of schemes which are proposed in practice do fall into three broad categories.

Insolvent and capitally insufficient companies

The first category comprises schemes of arrangement which modify the rights of a company's members or creditors when the company becomes insolvent, or when the value of its assets shown in its accounts less the total of its debts and liabilities is not matched by the company's total paid up share capital, so that the company carries a deficit of assets in its balance sheet. Such schemes may provide for the payment of the company's unsecured trading debts in whole or part, even though its long-term loan capital is to be partly cancelled or converted into share capital,[15] or the scheme may provide for the payment of part of the company's unsecured trading debts and the conversion of the remainder into secured indebtedness, which may be made to rank before the company's existing debt securities.[16] Although this involves a reversal of the normal order of priority between creditors in the insolvency of a company, it is acceptable to the court, because the purpose of the scheme is to enable the company to continue carrying on its business and avoid being wound up, and if the company were to continue carrying on business and avoid going into liquidation without there being any scheme at all, its unsecured trade creditors would probably be paid in point of time before the company's medium or long-term indebtedness became due for payment, or before the holders of securities for such indebtedness became entitled to enforce their securities.

As between the company's unsecured creditors themselves, it has been suggested that the same priority should be given as in a winding up to creditors whose debts would then rank as preferential payments,[17] but the court has never laid this down as a binding rule. Other ways in which the rights of debt security holders may be modified is by converting accrued interest on the company's

15 *Re Empire Mining Co* (1890) 44 Ch D 402.
16 *Re Dorman, Long & Co* [1934] Ch 635.
17 *Re Richards & Co* (1879) 11 Ch D 676 at 679, per Fry J. For preferential payments in a winding up, see p 303, ante. Voluntary arrangements under the Insolvency Act 1986 cannot displace the priority rights of creditors for preferential payments without their individual consent (Insolvency Act 1986, s 4(3) and (4); (see p 422, ante)).

indebtedness into an addition to the principal bearing the same rate of interest; or by accumulating accrued and future interest (often at a higher rate) during a certain period; or by making accrued or future interest payable only out of profits;[18] or by converting part of each debt security into a deferred income bond on which interest is payable only out of the company's future profits;[19] or where the company needs to raise additional loan capital, by empowering the company to issue a new series of debt securities ranking before the existing ones.[20] Even though a company is insolvent, the scheme of arrangement need not throw the whole of the loss on the shareholders. Thus, schemes have been approved by which the rights of holders of a company's debt securities have been seriously reduced in order to allow the company's paid up share capital to be only partly reduced,[1] or not reduced at all.[19]

Reorganisations

The second category of schemes of arrangement comprises those where the company's assets are worth more than the total of its paid up share capital and its unsecured debts and liabilities, and the scheme is designed to modify shareholders' or debt security holders' rights in order to meet an eventuality which has occurred (such as a default under the terms of issue of the company's debt securities which could accelerate the date for repayment of the amount secured), or to enable the company to raise new capital, or to reorganise its existing capital structure. Thus, the court has approved schemes which released the guarantor of a company's debt securities because of his insolvency;[2] which empowered the company to issue debt securities ranking in priority to those which it had already issued;[3] which consolidated the company's issued ordinary and deferred shares into one class of ordinary shares;[4] and which divided the company's partly paid ordinary shares into a class of fully paid preference shares and a class of ordinary shares with a correspondingly smaller amount paid up.[5]

18 *Re White Star Line Ltd* [1938] Ch 458, [1938] 1 All ER 607.
19 *Re Alabama, New Orleans, Texas and Pacific Junction Rly Co* [1891] 1 Ch 213.
20 *Re Dorman, Long & Co Ltd* [1934] Ch 635.
 1 *Re Tea Corpn Ltd, Sorsbie v Tea Corpn Ltd* [1904] 1 Ch 12.
 2 *Shaw v Royce Ltd* [1911] 1 Ch 138.
 3 *Re Dominion of Canada Freehold Estate and Timber Co Ltd* (1886) 55 LT 347.
 4 *Carruth v Imperial Chemical Industries Ltd* [1937] AC 707, [1937] 2 All ER 422.
   The court went into the merits of the scheme, even though, technically, the only petition before it was for its sanction to a reduction of capital.

Reconstructions, mergers and divisions

The third and final category of schemes of arrangement comprises reconstructions, mergers and divisions of a company's undertaking and the acquisitions of controlling shareholdings in a company by the cancellation of all its issued shares, or all its shares carrying voting rights, except those held by the acquiring concern. These are complex arrangements and are partly governed by special statutory provisions, which are outside the scope of this book.[6]

Creditors and members

In all the varieties of schemes of arrangement mentioned above, the term 'creditor' has been given the widest possible meaning by the court, and has been held to include all persons who have, or who will or may have, any pecuniary claim against the company, whether the claim is liquidated or not, and whether it is subject to a condition or contingency or not.[7] Thus, the holders of life insurance policies which have not yet matured have been held to be creditors of the insurance company which issued them,[8] and a lessee who assigned a lease to a company and who therefore had a right to be indemnified by its against his continuing liability to the lessor for future rent and future performance of the lessee's covenants, was held to be a creditor of the company in respect of his right to an indemnity.[9] The interpretation given by the court is also wide enough to include persons who have claims for unliquidated damages against the company for breaches of contract or for torts committed by it, or claims for compensation or an indemnity under statutory provisions.[10]

The term 'member' has also been given a wide meaning in connection with schemes of arrangement, and has not been confined to persons who are registered as holders of shares in the company in its register of members. Consequently, schemes have been approved which affected the rights of the holders of share warrants or share certificates to bearer,[11] or the rights of the holders of letters of allotment

5 *Re Guardian Assurance Co* [1917] 1 Ch 431.

6 Companies Act 1985, s 427A and Sch 15A (inserted by Companies (Mergers and Divisions) Regulations 1987 (SI 1987/1991), reg 2 and Schedule, Part I); Companies Act 1985, s 428 to s 430F (inserted and substituted by Financial Services Act 1986, s 172(1) and Sch 12).

7 *Re Midland Coal Coke and Iron Co, Craig's Claim* [1895] 1 Ch 267 at 271, per Wright J and Lindley LJ at 277.

8 *Sovereign Life Assurance Co v Dodd* [1892] 2 QB 573.

9 *Re Midland Coal Coke and Iron Co,* supra.

10 *Soden v British and Commonwealth Holdings plc* [1995] 1 BCLC 686, [1995] BCC 531; affd [1997] BCC 249.

11 *Re Wedgwood Coal and Iron Co* (1877) 6 Ch D 627.

of shares when no entry yet appeared in respect of their holdings in the company's register of members relating to the shares or their holders.[12] Whether a person who has a right to acquire shares in a company is to be treated as a member (eg a person who has contracted to purchase a specified number of shares) has not yet been decided, but it has been held that a person who has an option to purchase shares has no interest in them until he has exercised the option.[13]

Procedure

Summons for directions to call meetings

The meetings of creditors and members held to approve a scheme of arrangement proposed in respect of a company, must be called under the directions of the court.[14] The first step, therefore is for the company pursuant to a resolution of its board of directors or general meeting, or if the company is in liquidation or is subject to an administration order, its liquidator or administrator, to apply to the Companies Court by originating summons returnable before the registrar of the court in chambers for an order giving such directions.[15] If the application is made otherwise than by the company or its liquidator or administrator, the applicant must show that the company consents to the scheme.[16]

The applicant must ensure that the meetings requested are separate meetings of the creditors and members who belong to different classes; if at the applicant's request the registrar directs the holding of meetings which are not separate, and those meetings resolve to approve the scheme of arrangement, the court will either refuse its approval of the scheme, or will defer consideration of it until proper separate meetings have been held.[17] It is often extremely difficult to decide whether creditors, and to a lesser extent, shareholders form one class or several separate classes. The only very general guidance which the court has given in this respect is contained in the following words of Bowen LJ:[18]

'It seems plain that we must give such a meaning to the term "class" as will prevent the section being so worked as to result in confiscation and

---

12 *Dey v Rubber and Mercantile Corpn Ltd* [1923] 2 Ch 528.
13 *Sainsbury plc v Connor* [1991] 1 WLR 963.
14 Companies Act 1985, s 425(1).
15 RSC Ord 102, r 2(1); Practice Note dated 27 November 1996, para 3.
16 *Re Savoy Hotel Ltd* [1981] Ch 351, [1981] 3 All ER 646.
17 *Practice Note* [1934] WN 142.
18 *Sovereign Life Assurance Co v Dodd* [1892] 2 QB 573 at 583.

injustice, and that it must be confined to those persons whose rights are not so dissimilar as to make it impossible for them to consult together with a view to their common interest.'

Consequently, it has been held that the holders of life insurance policies issued by a company which have matured form a distinct class from the holders of such policies which have not yet matured;[18] that where a company had issued shares, some of which were fully paid, others partly paid, and others partly paid but the unpaid balance of capital on them had been paid up in advance of calls, the shareholders formed three distinct classes, and a single meeting could, therefore, not be held for the holders of fully paid shares and the holders of partly paid shares who had paid up the balance of capital on their shares in advance of calls;[19] and that under a scheme for the acquisition of the whole of a company's shares by another company, the ordinary shares already held by the acquiring company and its subsidiaries in the first company formed a distinct class from ordinary shares held in that company by other shareholders, because the acquiring company and its subsidiaries (which for this purpose must be identified with it) were in effect purchasers of the shares of the other shareholders, whose interest in the scheme was that of sellers.[20]

It is uncertain whether unsecured creditors may be treated collectively as one class under a scheme of arrangement; probably unsecured creditors whose claims would be preferential payments in a winding up should be treated as a distinct class from other unsecured creditors, at least if the company is insolvent. Secured creditors should probably be treated as belonging to different classes if their debts are secured on different properties or assets of the company, or if they are secured on the same property or assets but rank in some order of priority as between themselves. Debt security holders whose loans are secured on the same property and assets of a company and whose respective debt securities rank pari passu or equally, however, form one class, and it makes no difference that some of the debt security holders have been issued with debentures or debenture stock certificates under seal, whilst others still hold letters of allotment which they have not yet exchanged for debentures or debenture stock certificates.[1]

Surprisingly, it has been held that where a scheme of arrangement provided for the issue of new senior and junior unsecured bonds by a company in place of an existing series of unsecured bonds with a

19 *Re United Provident Assurance Co Ltd* [1910] 2 Ch 477.
20 *Re Hellenic and General Trust Ltd* [1975] 3 All ER 382, [1976] 1 WLR 123.
 1 *Dey v Rubber and Mercantile Corpn Ltd* [1923] 2 Ch 528.

nominal value some six times greater than the bonds to be substituted for them, the fact that banks which sponsored the issue of the original bonds would under the scheme receive guarantees from the company's solvent parent company and its subsidiaries of the banks' rights under the substituted bonds taken by them, whereas other holders of substituted bonds would not be given any guarantees, did not result in the banks and those other bondholders forming separate classes of creditors.[2] The reason given for treating all the original bondholders as a single class was that the profits earned by the borrowing company's subsidiaries would be available to pay dividends to the company and so enable it to meet its obligations under the substituted bonds, so that the banks, as holders of guarantees by the parent company and its subsidiaries would be in no preferred position. This reasoning holds goods only if the borrowing company's subsidiaries made sufficient profits and remained solvent, and it ignores the fact that the banks became creditors of the parent company and its subsidiaries under the guarantees whereas the other bondholders did not.

The only meetings which the registrar need direct to consider the proposed scheme of arrangement are meetings of creditors or members whose rights are affected by the scheme. Consequently, if the company is insolvent and the scheme provides that its business undertaking and assets shall be transferred to another company, it is not necessary for the scheme to be approved by a meeting of the first company's shareholders, because they would receive nothing if the company were wound up, and so they have no rights which are affected by the scheme.[3] Similarly if the terms of issue of subordinated loan stock provide that claims under it shall be paid only after the claims of all unsecured creditors of the company, which is insolvent, a scheme of arrangement affecting the rights of secured creditors, unsecured creditors and the holders of non-subordinated loan stock does not require the approval of the holders of subordinated loan stock, because they would receive nothing in the company's liquidation.[4] The rights of creditors or members will be treated as affected by a scheme of arrangement only if they are cancelled or substantially modified, or if new rights of a different kind are substituted for them (eg if debt security holders are to be issued shares in place of their existing securities). Consequently, where the company's articles of association were silent as to the dividends to

2 *Re Heron International NV* [1994] 1 BCLC 667.
3 *Re Brownfields Guild Pottery Society* [1898] WN 80.
4 *Re British and Commonwealth Holdings plc (No 3)* [1992] BCLC 322, [1992] BCC 58; *Re Maxwell Communications Corpn plc (No 2)* [1994] 1 BCLC 1, *(No 3)* [1993] BCC 369.

be paid to its ordinary shareholders, it was held that a scheme to increase the preferential dividend payable to its preference shareholders did not require the assent of a meeting of ordinary shareholders, because their right was to be paid dividends only out of the company's residual profits after satisfying its other obligations, and that right was not affected by the scheme.[5] It is doubtful whether this case was correctly decided on the facts, however; the ordinary shareholders' dividend rights were not varied literally, it is true, but they were varied in substance, because ordinary share dividends would after the increase in the preference dividend be payable only out of a smaller residue of profits unless the company's profits increased sufficiently to cover the higher preference dividend.

On hearing the summons for directions for the holding of meetings of creditors and members of the company, the registrar settles the form of notice of the meetings to be sent to them, and also directs one or more newspaper advertisements of the scheme to be published if individual notices may not reach all the persons concerned, for example, when the scheme affects the holders of debt securities in bearer form, or shares represented by share warrants or bearer share certificates or renounceable letters of allotment. With the notice of the meetings sent to each creditor and member there must be sent a statement explaining the effect of the scheme of arrangement, and stating what interests the directors of the company (and if the scheme affects debt security holders) the trustees under any trust deed covering the debt securities, have in the scheme, and how their interests are affected differently by it from the interests of other persons, if that is so.[6] If such interests are accurately stated in the statement, but are changed in nature or extent before the scheme comes before the court for its approval, the court will not give its approval of the scheme unless an appropriately revised statement is first circulated.[7] If the registrar directs newspaper advertisements of the scheme to be published, each advertisement must state where interested persons may obtain copies of the statement, and copies must be furnished to them on request free of charge.[8] Notices sent to registered share and debt security holders who have, and have notified the company of, their addresses overseas must be sent to those addresses, even if the company's articles of association or the terms of issue of the debt securities require notices of meetings to be sent to them only if they have notified the company of an address in the United Kingdom for that purpose.[9]

5 *Re Stewart Precision Carburettor Co* (1912) 28 TLR 335.
6 Companies Act 1985, s 426(1), (2) and (4).
7 *Re Jessel Trust Ltd* [1985] BCLC 119; *Re Minster Assets plc* [1985] BCLC 200.
8 Companies Act 1985, s 426(3) and (5).
9 *Re English, Scottish and Australian Chartered Bank* [1893] 3 Ch 385.

Holding of the directed meetings

Persons entitled to vote at a meeting of creditors or members may attend either in person or may be represented by proxy.[10] The forms appointing proxies are settled by the registrar, and are always 'two way' proxy forms, that is, the form may be filled in by a creditor or member so as to show on its face whether the proxy is to vote for or against the scheme. Proxy appointments in a form different from that approved by the registrar are valid, however, and there is no need for the document appointing a proxy to be delivered to the company before the meeting, it being sufficient that the proxy produces it at the meeting.[11] Members or creditors of the company which are themselves companies or corporations may be represented at meetings of members or creditors by representatives appointed by their respective boards of directors, and they may exercise the company or corporation's rights to speak and vote,[12] but this does not prevent a company or corporation from being represented by a proxy if it so wishes. The holders of debt securities in bearer form, or of share warrants, bearer share certificates or renounceable letters of allotment or their proxies must produce the document evidencing their title to the securities or the title of the person whom they represent at the meeting in order to prove their right to vote.[13] It appears that proxies may both speak and vote at meetings of creditors or members, and that the inability of proxies for members to speak at general meetings of a public company[14] does not apply to meetings called to approve schemes of arrangement.

The vote on the scheme of arrangement at each meeting of members or creditors is taken by a poll,[15] and for a resolution approving the scheme to be passed, the persons who are present in person or by proxy or corporate representative at the meeting and who vote on the resolution must comprise a majority in number of all those persons who hold between them three-quarters in value of the interests[16] of all such persons.[17] The number and the value of the

10 Companies Act 1985, s 425(2).
11 *Re Dorman, Long & Co Ltd* [1934] Ch 635 at 662.
12 Companies Act 1985, s 375(1) and (2).
13 *Re Wedgwood Coal and Iron Co* (1877) 6 Ch D 627.
14 Companies Act 1985, s 372(1).
15 That is, by the voters filling in ballot forms on which they state the amount or value of their interest and whether they vote for or against a resolution.
16 Value means the nominal value of shares, the nominal value or any greater amount payable on the redemption of redeemable shares or debt securities the redemption date for which has passed, the amount owed in the case of debts, and the estimated value in the case of other debts and claims, including contingent and conditional claims and claims for unliquidated damages.
17 *Re Bessemer Steel and Ordnance Co* (1875) 1 Ch D 251.

interests of persons who do not attend and are not represented at the meeting, or who do attend but abstain from voting, are irrelevant, and do not enter into the calculation at all. Likewise, the interests of persons who appoint proxies or corporate members or creditors who appoint representatives are disregarded if the proxies or representatives do not attend the meeting, or do attend but do not vote. Since votes are computed according to the value of the interests of the persons who cast them, multiple or weighted voting rights conferred on certain shareholders by the memorandum or articles of association of the company cannot be exercised at a meeting of a class of members; also provisions in a company's memorandum or articles of association which disentitle certain shareholders to vote do not apply, and they can vote proportionately to the nominal value of their shares. If the scheme affects the rights of shareholders with multiple or weighted voting rights or non-voting shareholders differently from other shareholders, however, they would appear to form different classes, and separate meetings must then be held for them.

Petition for the court's sanction

When the requisite resolutions approving the scheme of arrangement have been carried by meetings of each class of creditors and members affected by its provisions, the company or, it would seem any interested creditor or member of the company, may present a petition[18] to the Companies Court or (in an appropriate case) the county court to sanction the scheme. The petition must set out the name and date of incorporation of the company, its objects and the fact that the company has carried on business since its incorporation or a more recent date, the company's issued and paid up share capital; the facts and events leading up to the preparation of the scheme and the effects which the scheme will have if the court sanctions it (the terms of the scheme being set out in a schedule to the petition); the registrar's order directing the meetings of creditors and members; and the numbers of persons attending each of the meetings in person and by proxy and the result of the voting at each meeting. The petition should conclude with a prayer that the court will sanction the scheme under s 425 of the Companies Act 1985, and should be supported by an affidavit or affidavits verifying the facts set out in the petition, which should be filed in court at the same time as the petition.

The petition for the court's sanction of a scheme of arrangement is heard by a judge of the court to which the petition is presented.[19]

---

18 RSC Ord 102, r 4(1)(*f*).
19 Practice Note dated 27 November 1996, para 2.

On the hearing of the petition the court will, before giving its sanction to the scheme, need to satisfy itself that proper meetings of the different classes of creditors and members have been held, and that the requisite resolutions approving the scheme have been passed, but if an unnecessary meeting has been held of a class of persons who have no interest in the scheme, the court will disregard the proceedings at that meeting, and may approve the scheme despite the rejection of the scheme by it.[20] If the scheme involves a reduction of the company's share capital by the reduction of shareholders' liability for unpaid capital or by the return of capital to shareholders, the additional steps required by the Companies Act 1985, for the protection of creditors must be taken before the court's sanction may be given to the scheme.[1]

The court's powers on the hearing of the petition are limited to giving or refusing its sanction to the scheme of arrangement,[2] and so the court may not give its approval subject to conditions, or subject to amendments being made to the scheme. If the court finds the scheme unacceptable, however, it may indicate that it would be prepared to sanction the scheme if certain changes were made in it, and on the application of the proponents of the scheme the court will then direct that further meetings of the classes of creditors and members affected shall be held to ascertain whether they will approve the changes by the same majorities as were required for the original scheme. Moreover, without directing further meetings to be held, the court may sanction a scheme on the company giving an undertaking not to implement it until certain steps have been taken, for example, that the company will discharge its unsecured debts before its business and assets are transferred to another company under the scheme.[3]

When an office copy of the court's order sanctioning a scheme of arrangement has been delivered to the Registrar of Companies, the scheme takes effect,[4] and it becomes binding on all interested persons, even though it provides for something to be done which is ultra vires the company and the court has overlooked this.[5] But the scheme is not binding on creditors or members for whom a separate meeting should have been held, but was not, and they retain their original rights unaffected by the scheme.[6] However, if a proper

20 *Re Tea Corpn Ltd, Sorsbie v Tea Corpn Ltd* [1904] 1 Ch 12.
 1 Companies Act 1985, s 136(2) to (4); *Re White Pass and Yukon Rly Co Ltd* [1918] WN 323 (see *Pennington's Company Law* (7th edn), 226 et seq).
 2 Companies Act 1985, s 425(2).
 3 *Re Needhams Ltd* (1923) 130 LT 256.
 4 Companies Act 1985, s 425(3).
 5 *Nicholl v Eberhardt Co* (1889) 59 LJ Ch 103.
 6 *Sovereign Life Assurance Co v Dodd* [1892] 2 QB 573.

meeting of the class in question was called, but a quorum was not present or there was some other irregularity of procedure, the scheme is nevertheless binding on all persons who could have attended the meeting, whether they attended or were represented at it or not.[7] A scheme does not bind anyone until the court has approved it and an office copy of the court's order has been delivered to the Registrar of Companies,[4] and so, unless the company is being wound up or is subject to an administration order, the court has no jurisdiction to restrain a creditor from suing the company or from levying execution on its property merely because a scheme is pending which will prevent him from doing those things if the scheme is approved by the court.[8] When a scheme has become effective, it cannot be modified, extended or cancelled by agreement between the company and the interested parties; a variation can then be made only by a supplemental scheme which is approved by meetings of creditors and members of the company and sanctioned by the court by the same procedure as an original scheme of arrangement.[9] Moreover, a scheme approved by the court can be cancelled or invalidated because it contravenes a rule of law (eg the unlawful acquisition of a company's shares by itself) only by the court which approved the scheme giving a judgment to that effect in proceedings brought for the purpose, and not merely by the court ruling that the scheme is defective in that way incidentally in litigation principally concerned with another matter.[10]

If the court's order approving a scheme of arrangement provides for the transfer of property for a consideration, it is a conveyance on sale for the purpose of stamp duty, and the office copy delivered to the Registrar of Companies must accordingly be stamped ad valorem.[11]

The protection of dissenters from a scheme of arrangement

In describing the function of the court when petitioned to sanction a scheme of arrangement under the predecessor of the Companies Act 1985, s 425, Lindley LJ said:[12]

---

7 *Re Plymouth Breweries Ltd, Plymouth Breweries Ltd v Penwill* (1967) 111 Sol Jo 715.
8 *Booth v Walkden Spinning and Manufacturing Co Ltd* [1909] 2 KB 368.
9 *Srimati Premila Devi v Peoples Bank of Northern India Ltd* [1938] 4 All ER 337.
10 *Barclays Bank plc v British and Commonwealth Holdings plc* [1996] 1 BCLC 1, [1995] BCC 19; affd [1995] BCC 1059.
11 *Sun Alliance Insurance Ltd v IRC* [1972] Ch 133, [1971] 1 All ER 135.
12 *Re Alabama, New Orleans, Texas and Pacific Junction Rly Co* [1891] 1 Ch 213 at 238.

'... What the court has to do is to see, first of all, that the provisions of that statute have been complied with; and secondly, that the majority has been acting bona fide. The court also has to see that the minority is not being overridden by a majority having interests of its own clashing with those of the minority whom they seek to coerce. Further than that, the court has to look at the scheme and see whether it is one which persons acting honestly, and viewing the scheme laid before them in the interests of those they represent, take a view which can be reasonably taken by business men.'

The court therefore protects creditors or members who have voted against the scheme or have not voted for it and do not assent to it, by refusing to make it binding on them (a) if it is so unreasonable that no sensible creditor or member of the company acting reasonably would have approved it; or (b) if the majority who voted for the scheme did not vote to promote the interests of their own class, but to foster some extraneous interest; or (c) if the scheme is unfair on the face of it.

Unreasonableness

It is rare that a scheme of arrangement is held to be unreasonable. The court is strongly influenced by the size of the majority vote, and often discounts an objection that the scheme is unreasonable by referring to the small number of dissenters who opposed it. Lindley LJ once went so far as to say that the court should only overrule the decision of the majority if there had been 'some material oversight or miscarriage' on their part.[13] Lord Maugham expressed a reservation on this willingness to bow to the majority, however, when he said:[14]

'Both Eve J, and the Court of Appeal seem to have laid considerable stress on the well known proposition ... that shareholders acting honestly are usually much better judges of what is to their commercial advantage than the court can be. I do not intend to throw the smallest doubt on this general proposition, which I have had occasion more than once to repeat, but I doubt very much whether it is of great value as a guide when it is proved that the majority of the class voted in the way they did because of their interests as shareholders of another class.'

But whatever view it takes of its functions, the court is in any case ill-equipped to examine the detailed implications of a scheme submitted for its approval,[15] and it can rarely do more than exercise the judgment of a reasonable man possessed of the limited information which an investor usually has.

13 *Re English, Scottish and Australian Chartered Bank* [1893] 3 Ch 385 at 409.
14 *Carruth v ICI Ltd* [1937] AC 707 at 769, [1937] 2 All ER 422 at 461.
15 In the United States schemes which affected creditors (whether or not the company was insolvent) had formerly to be submitted to the Securities and

The court's judgment is therefore invariably a broad commonsense one, paying particular regard to suspect motives and substantial disproportions between the proposed treatment of different classes of interests, and is not based on a minute analysis of the details of the scheme or a comparison of alternative ways of dealing with the problems which the scheme seeks to solve. If a scheme provides for the cancellation of rights without compensation in the form of a cash payment or the conferment of substituted rights, the court will always condemn it as unreasonable.[16] Indeed, it is doubtful whether such a scheme is an arrangement at all for the purposes of the Companies Act 1985, or the memorandum or articles of a company, or within the terms of debt securities or a covering trust deed.[16] On the other hand, if a scheme provides for the payment or provision of compensation on the cancellation of rights, the court will not refuse to approve it merely because the compensation is not equivalent in value to the rights which are cancelled.[16]

In the few cases where schemes of arrangement have been held unreasonable, there has usually been evidence to show that the votes in favour of it were cast to promote a sectional interest or were improperly procured, and this has induced the court to examine the scheme with a more critical eye than usual. For example, in one case[17] the court refused to sanction a scheme by which a vendor company was to sell a mine which it had bought for £425,000 and on which it had expended £17,000, and was also to transfer its liquid assets, worth £85,000, to a purchasing company for 130,000 of the latter's 10s shares, whose market value was about 13s 9d each. The scheme also involved the sale of two other companies' undertakings to the purchasing company for shares in it, and no evidence was tendered of the value of those undertakings. One of these other companies held a majority of the shares in the vendor company, and had procured the resolution for the sale of the vendor company's assets by using its majority vote. The court weighed together the

Exchange Commission (a government authority with wide supervisory and regulatory powers over the issue of securities and transactions in them), and the court considered the report of the Commission before sanctioning the scheme; (Federal Bankruptcy Act, ss 572 to 574 (now repealed)). The Commission could also and still can, appear as amicus curiae on the hearing of the petition for the court's sanction (Federal Bankruptcy Act, s 608). The value of the Commission's power to intervene is that it will probably possess or have access to detailed information about the company and its history, and is therefore able to detect latent defects in the scheme more readily than the court can do from the information put before it by the company and members and creditors who oppose its confirmation by the court.

16 *Re NFU Development Trust Ltd* [1973] 1 All ER 135, [1972] 1 WLR 1548.
17 *Re Consolidated South Rand Mines Deep Ltd* [1909] 1 Ch 491.

disparity between the probable value of the vendor company's assets and the market value of the shares which it was to receive, and the likelihood that the company which held a majority of the vendor company's shares devised the scheme in order to profit at the expense of the minority shareholders of the vendor company, and the court therefore concluded that the scheme was unreasonable, because no reasonable business man, apprised of those facts, would accept it. It is possible that the scheme in this case was in fact a perfectly fair one; it would have been fair if the real value of the vendor company's assets was less than a fifth of the value attributed to them by the company's balance sheet, or if the other two companies were also to transfer their undertakings to the purchasing company in exchange for a fifth of their value in terms of the current market value of the purchasing company's shares. But there was no evidence presented to the court of either of these possibilities, and the court could therefore only conclude that there was a serious risk of the vendor company disposing of its undertaking at a substantial undervalue.

Absence of good faith

The second ground for the court's refusal to sanction a scheme of arrangement under the Companies Act 1985, is also a ground on which it will annul any compromise or arrangement made without the approval of the court under a power in the company's articles of association or under the provisions of debt securities or a covering trust deed (or possibly) under a voluntary arrangement entered into under the Insolvency Act 1986. It is that the resolution approving the scheme was not passed in good faith. Viscount Haldane particularised the duty of the majority who vote for the scheme in the following words:[18]

'There is, however, a restriction of such powers, when conferred on a majority of a special class in order to enable that majority to bind a minority. They must be exercised subject to a general principle, which is applicable to all authorities conferred on majorities of classes enabling them to bind minorities; namely, that the power given must be exercised for the purpose of benefiting the class as a whole, and not merely individual members only.'

But this does not mean that every person who votes for the scheme as a member or creditor of the company must do so altruistically. The court applies an objective test, and interferes only when the majority have so far disregarded the interests of their class that there

---

18 *British America Nickel Corpn v O'Brien* [1927] AC 369 at 371.

is a substantial risk that the minority will be treated oppressively or unfairly.[19] Thus, Parker J said in one case:[20]

> 'The powers conferred by the trust deed on the majority of the debenture holders, must, of course, be exercised bona fide, and the Court can no doubt interfere to prevent unfairness or oppression, but, subject to this, each debenture holder may vote with regard to his individual interests, though these interests may be peculiar to himself and not shared by other debenture holders.'

In most of the cases where the court has interfered because of an absence of good faith, the evidence has shown that the majority shareholders or debt security holders have either sought to obtain an improper advantage for themselves, or have been induced to vote as they did by other persons who sought an improper advantage. Thus, a resolution passed at a meeting of debenture holders by which they agreed to surrender their debentures secured on the company's property in exchange for new debentures charged only on the company's profits, was held void because the holder of a majority of the debentures had agreed with the directors to vote for the resolution in consideration of receiving a gratuitous allotment of fully paid shares.[1] Again, where the holders of debentures of a company which were charged on its undertaking resolved that its undertaking should be sold to another company in exercise of their powers of realisation, and that they would accept debentures in the other company in exchange for their existing debentures, the court refused to sanction the sale, because it thought it probable that certain shareholders who owed large sums to the company for unpaid share capital had induced the holders of the majority of the debentures to vote as they did; those shareholders hoped by the scheme to avoid having to pay the capital unpaid on their shares, which would be needed for the company to pay the amount secured by the debentures if the scheme were not carried out.[2] But the mere fact that a majority share or debt security holder obtains an advantage under the scheme which the other share or debt security holders will not enjoy, will not induce the court to annul the scheme if the advantage is disclosed and is not an improper one. Thus, the court upheld a resolution passed by a meeting of debenture holders by which the majority debenture holder was released from a guarantee of the debt secured by the debentures which he had given, and in consideration of the release the rate of debenture interest was to be

---

19 *Goodfellow v Nelson Line (Liverpool) Ltd* [1912] 2 Ch 324.
20 Ibid, at 333.
 1 *British America Nickel Corpn v O'Brien* [1927] AC 369.
 2 *Re Wedgwood Coal and Iron Co* (1877) 6 Ch D 627.

increased by reducing the guarantor's remuneration as trustee under the debenture trust deed.[3] Parker J said:[4]

'... where, as in this case, there is, as between different holders, a diversity of interest, it may be necessary or advisable, as a matter of business fairness, to make special provision for special interests, and I do not think there is any equity precluding a debenture holder voting for or against a scheme containing such special provision merely because he is interested thereunder.'

Unfairness

It is very rare that the court annuls a scheme because it is unfair on the face of it. The court did this, however, in one case[5] where a meeting of debenture holders resolved to accept a scheme by which part of the company's assets would be used to pay off those debenture holders who were willing to surrender their debentures at the lowest price. Swinfen Eady J said:[6]

'Though full effect is given to majority clauses in debenture trust deeds, it would be going beyond any previous authority to hold that a majority of debenture holders can in effect determine to divide the property amongst some only of their number. Such a proceeding is not authorised by the terms of the trust deed, and is not allowed by law.'

If this scheme had required the sanction of the court instead of being effected out of court under a provision in the debentures, the court would undoubtedly have rejected it as unreasonable. In the absence of judicial decision, the fact that a scheme is unreasonable may or may not be a ground on which the court can interfere when the court's positive approval of the scheme is not required; but having regard to the reluctance of the court to hold that a scheme submitted for its sanction is unreasonable when the scheme is well supported by the persons affected by it, there is good reason for concluding that unreasonableness and unfairness are merely facets of the same ground for judicial intervention, and that any scheme which is likely to be held invalid because unreasonable is also likely to be held unfair on the face of it, and vice versa. This conclusion is supported by another decision[7] where the court refused to sanction a reduction of capital by cancelling redeemable preference shares and substituting for them unsecured loan stock whose redemption dates were between 15 and 20 years later than that of the preference shares, and whose

---

3 *Goodfellow v Nelson Line (Liverpool) Ltd* [1912] 2 Ch 324.
4 Ibid, at 333.
5 *Re New York Taxicab Co* [1913] 1 Ch 1.
6 Ibid, at 9.
7 *Re Holders Investment Trust Ltd* [1971] 2 All ER 289, [1971] 1 WLR 583.

holders would be entitled to a rate of interest one per cent higher than the preference dividend, but several percentage points below current long-term borrowing rates. The court held that the scheme was patently unfair, because it was not shown that the dissenting preference shareholders would be adequately compensated for being prevented from re-investing their capital at the market interest rates prevailing at the time when their preference shares would otherwise have been redeemed.

CHAPTER 9

Remedies of a company's secured creditors

Secured creditors of an insolvent company may rely on the rights to realise the securities vested in them by agreement or by law (eg legal and equitable liens for the value of work done or services rendered, or for unpaid purchase money) and to apply the proceeds of realisation in satisfying their secured claims. To the extent that they are able to satisfy the amounts which the company owes them by doing so, they are preferred (subject to statutory exceptions) to the unsecured creditors of the company who, if it is wound up, will be paid only out of the proceeds of the liquidator realising the other assets of the company and the surplus (if any) of the proceeds of realising the securities held by the secured creditors after the amounts owed to them and their costs have been discharged.

This chapter is concerned only with the remedies of creditors whose securities are created by agreement with the company, and not with the law governing the remedies of the holders of securities arising by operation of law (ie the holders of legal and equitable liens, landlords and others who exercise rights to distrain on goods and execution creditors). Creditors whose securities are created by agreement comprise the holders of legal or equitable mortgages over the property of a company, the holders of equitable charges over such property and the holders of floating charges over the whole or substantially the whole of the assets of a company, or over a class or classes of its assets.[1] The remedies of the holders of such mortgages and charges created by a company to enable them to recover amounts owed to them may for convenience be divided into three heads, namely: (a) remedies apart from enforcing any security held by them; (b) remedies for enforcing their securities without the assistance of the court; and (c) remedies for enforcing their securities with the assistance of the court.

---

1 For such mortgages and charges, see *Pennington's Company Law* (7th edn), Chapter 12.

REMEDIES APART FROM ENFORCING THE CREDITOR'S SECURITY

Action of debt

Availability and restrictions on the action

A mortgage, charge or debt security created by a company (other than debenture stock or loan stock issued under a contemporaneous trust deed and expressed to be subject to, and with the benefit of that deed) always contains a promise by the company to pay the principal and interest of the loan or other debt to which it relates on the due dates to the mortgagee, chargee or other security holder, who is thereby made a creditor of the company. Consequently he may recover the principal or interest in respect of his secured debt when it is in arrear by bringing an action of debt or for breach of contract against the company.

When a series of debentures issued by a company is secured by a trust deed under which the trustees are not bound to enforce the company's covenants (including its covenant to pay principal and interest) unless requested to do so by a certain fraction of the debenture holders, and the trust deed provides that no debenture holder may bring an action 'for the execution of the trusts' of the trust deed unless the trustees have been requested to sue by that fraction, any debenture holder may sue for the principal or interest which the company has promised to pay him by the terms of his debentures, even though the requisite fraction of debenture holders has not requested the trustees to sue.[2] This is because the plaintiff sues to enforce the promise made to him by the company, and not for the execution by the trustees of the trusts of the trust deed. If in such a case the securities issued were debenture stock or loan stock, however, by the terms of which the entire debt owed in respect of stock of the same series is owed to the trustees for the stockholders, who are entitled simply to proportionate equitable interests in the global stock, an individual stockholder would not be able to sue the company without the support of the trustees or the requisite fraction of his fellow stockholders specified in the covering trust deed, because the company's promise in the covering trust deed to pay principal and interest would then have been made not to the individual stockholder, but to the trustees exclusively, and so the enforcement of the promise would involve the execution of the trusts of the trust deed.[2]

Furthermore, if in debentures containing a promise by the company to pay principal and interest to the individual debenture

---

2 *Mortgage Insurance Corpn Ltd v Canadian Agricultural, Coal and Colonization Co Ltd* [1901] 2 Ch 377; *Cleary v Brazil Rly Co* [1915] WN 178.

holders, there is a provision by which none of them may bring an action under his debentures without the consent of a certain fraction of the other debenture holders, no individual holder may sue without obtaining that consent, because his action to enforce the company's promise to pay principal and interest to him is brought under his debentures, whether it is framed as an action for breach of contract or an action of debt.[3] In practice trust deeds covering an issue of debentures or of debenture or loan stock usually preserve the right of each debenture holder or debenture stockholder to sue for the principal or interest payable to him, even though the trustees are not obliged to sue themselves until requested by a certain fraction of holders of the class concerned.[4]

Effect of a pari passu clause

When debentures are issued in a series and by the terms of issue or by the covering trust deed they are to rank pari passu or equally, any debenture holder may bring a representative action on behalf of himself and all other holders of debentures of the same series[5] for a judgment that all the holders shall be entered as judgment creditors of the company for the respective fractions of the whole debenture debt payable to them, including all interest which is in arrear on those fractions.[6] Consequently, one debenture holder may in effect sue for the benefit of them all collectively. It has been held that after proceedings have been taken for the enforcement of the debenture holders' security and an interim receiver of the assets comprised in the security has been appointed by the court pending a hearing on the merits, an individual debenture holder may only sue for such a collectively beneficial judgment, and may not steal a march over his fellow debenture holders by suing for the principal or interest payable to him alone and by levying execution for his individual judgment debt on property of the company which is subject to the security created for the benefit of all the debenture holders.[7] But where proceedings for the enforcement of the debenture holders' security were merely pending and no judgment had been given or receiver appointed, and no steps had been taken to enforce the

---

3 *Pethybridge v Unibifocal Co* [1918] WN 278.

4 See, for example, the precedent of a debenture trust deed in 10 *Encyclopaedia of Forms and Precedents* (5th edn) 700, cl 43; and *Palmer's Company Precedents* (16th edn), Vol 3, 273, cl 50.

5 For a detailed account of representative actions, see *Pennington's Company law* (7th edn), 867 et seq.

6 *Hope v Croydon and Norwood Tramways Co* (1887) 34 Ch D 730.

7 *Bowen v Brecom Rly Co, ex p Howell* (1867) LR 3 Eq 541.

8 *Cleary v Brazil Rly Co* [1915] WN 178.

security out of court, it was held that there was nothing to prevent an individual debenture holder from suing in debt for a judgment in his own favour alone.[8]

The prohibition of individual actions only after judgment has been given in an action for the enforcement of the debenture holders' security or, at least, only after a receiver or an interim receiver has been appointed by the court, is in accord with another decision in which it was held that where the company has made unequal payments to different debenture holders in respect of principal or interest, the debenture holders who have received the larger payments are not compelled to bring them into account when the assets subject to the security are realised, unless the unequal payments were made after the court had given judgment in the debenture holders' action or had appointed a receiver of the assets subject to the security.[9] On the other hand, it has been held that if one of the debenture holders has been given a collateral security for the debenture debt owing to him, and he realises that security after proceedings have been initiated to enforce the principal security for the whole debenture debt, he must bring the proceeds of sale of the collateral security into account,[10] but, presumably, he need not account if he sells the collateral security before such proceedings are taken.

In the present state of the decided cases it is impossible to say definitely what restrictions are imposed on an individual debenture holder's right to pursue remedies exclusively for his own benefit by a pari passu clause in the debenture or trust deed. If restrictions are thereby imposed on suing and levying execution, realising a collateral security or accepting payment from the company, and the debentures are secured by a floating charge over the company's undertaking, it appears that the restrictions do not apply before the floating charge crystallises or becomes a fixed charge over the company's assets, and probably the restrictions do not apply until the court has appointed a receiver in a debenture holders' action or given judgment for the payment of the total amount payable to all the debenture holders in a representative action brought on their behalf by one or more of their number or by the trustees of the covering trust deed.

Debenture stockholders and loan stockholders

When a company issues debenture stock or loan stock it promises the trustees in the covering trust deed to repay to each stockholder when the stock becomes due for repayment the nominal amount of

---

9 *Re Midland Express Ltd, Pearson v Midland Express Ltd* [1914] 1 Ch 41.
10 *Landowners West of England and South Wales Land Drainage and Inclosure Co v Ashford* (1880) 16 Ch D 411 at 439 per Fry J.

his stock, which represents the amount of his contribution toward the total amount of the loan or indebtedness secured by the trust deed; the company also promises the trustees to pay each stockholder interest periodically on the nominal value of his stock until that nominal value is actually repaid.[11] Such a promise may be enforced by the trustees, and they may recover the whole nominal value of the loan or indebtedness and interest on it themselves, even though the company has promised the trustees that it will make payment directly to the stockholders.[12] The promise does not make each stockholder a creditor of the company, however, because the company's promise is made to the trustees, and not to the stockholders, who are not parties to the contract between the company and the trustees.[13] Consequently, a stockholder can sue the company for the principal or interest payable to him personally only if he joins the trustees as co-plaintiffs or co-defendants in his action, so that the court may order that the trusts of the trust deed shall be carried out by ordering that judgment for the whole of the amount owing in respect of the debenture stock or loan stock shall be entered in the names of the trustees against the company, and the court may declare that the trustees will hold the amount recovered from the company in trust for the debenture stockholders or loan stockholders according to their respective interests.[14]

Petition for winding up

By relying on the company's promise to pay the debt secured by a mortgage or charge over its property or by an issue of debentures, the holders of such debt securities may, as creditors, petition for an order that the company shall be wound up, if it fails to pay either the principal or interest of their debts.[15] Debenture stockholders and loan stockholders, however, cannot petition for a winding up order, because they are not creditors of the company,[16] but a petition may

11 If the stock is repayable at a premium in addition to its nominal value, the observations in this paragraph apply to both the nominal amount of the stock and the premium.
12 *Lamb v Vice* (1840) 6 M & W 467; *Stansfeld v Hellawell* (1852) 7 Exch 373; *Lloyd's v Harper* (1880) 16 Ch D 290; *Beswick v Beswick* [1968] AC 58, [1967] 2 All ER 1197.
13 *Re Uruguay Central and Hygueritas Rly Co of Monte Video* (1879) 11 Ch D 372 *Re Dunderland Iron Co Ltd* [1909] 1 Ch 446.
14 *Tomlinson v Gill* (1756) Amb 330; *Gregory and Parker v Williams* (1817) 3 Mer 582; *Affréteurs Réunis SA v Leopold Walford (London) Ltd* [1919] AC 801.
15 Insolvency Act 1986, s 124(1).
16 *Re Dunderland Iron Ore Co,* supra.

be presented by the trustees of the covering trust deed as creditors, because the legal title to the total indebtedness of the company under the issue of debenture stock or loan stock is vested in them, and it is immaterial that it is held by them in trust for the debenture stockholders or loan stockholders. If the trustees refuse to petition, any stockholder can sue them to compel them to carry out the trusts of the covering trust deed, and may request the court to direct them to present a winding up petition. A stockholder is only likely to pursue this course if the debenture stock is unsecured (that is, if it is loan stock), however, because if the trust deed creates a security over the company's property, stockholders would do better to apply to the court to order that the security shall be realised in order to pay off the whole amount of the stock, rather than seek to have this done indirectly by means of a winding up. In any event, it is not possible for a stockholder to avoid a preliminary action against the trustees by presenting a winding up petition himself and joining the trustees as parties to it. Winding up petitions are a statutory creation, and the proceedings on them are governed by rules which make no provision for the joinder of parties other than the company against which the petitioner seeks a remedy.[17]

REMEDIES FOR ENFORCING THE SECURITY WITHOUT THE ASSISTANCE OF THE COURT

It is outside the scope of this book to deal in general with the remedies available to the holders of legal and equitable mortgages and charges in reliance on their securities, as distinct from the peculiarities of those remedies and the extension of them by statute or otherwise where the owner of the property comprised in the security is a company. The following account therefore presupposes a knowledge of the general law relating to the enforcement and realisation of mortgages and charges.[18]

Statutory remedies

The holders of mortgages, charges and debentures may exercise the statutory remedies given by the Law of Property Act 1925, if their

---

17 Insolvency Act 1986, s 117(1); Insolvency Rules 1986, r 4.7(1) and r 4.10 and Form 4.2.
18 For this, see Fisher and Lightwood, *The Law of Mortgages* (9th edn), Part V; 32 *Halsbury's Laws of England* (4th edn), para 785 et seq.

mortgages, charges or debentures are executed under the company's seal or are signed by two of the company's directors or by a director and the company's secretary and expressed to take effect as a deed.[19] If the mortgage or charge on the company's property is vested in the trustees of a trust deed securing an issue of debentures or debenture stock, it is the trustees, and not the holders of the debentures or debenture stock, who can exercise the statutory remedies. These remedies are to sell the company's property which is subject to the mortgage or charge, and to appoint a receiver of the income of such property,[20] but the remedies can only be exercised if the principal of the debt secured by the mortgage or charge is due and payable and has remained unpaid for three months after a written demand for its payment has been made on the company, or if interest on that debt is in arrear and unpaid for two months, or if the company has broken some other obligation imposed on it by the mortgage, debentures or debenture trust deed (as the case may be).[20] Additionally, the person in whom the mortgage or charge is vested may grant leases of the company's land if he takes possession of it personally or by a receiver.[1]

If the statutory remedies are exercisable by a person in whom a floating charge over property of the class in question or over a company's whole assets and undertaking is vested, it would not be possible for him to exercise the remedies in the event of the company's default until after the floating charge had crystallised by the company going into liquidation or otherwise, because until then the floating charge does not attach specifically to any property of the company.[2] It has been held, however, that a floating charge on a company's undertaking was not a mortgage within the definition in the Conveyancing Act 1881,[3] which is substantially repeated in the Law of Property Act 1925.[4] Consequently, it has been held that the proprietor of a floating charge cannot exercise the statutory powers of sale and realisation conferred on a mortgagee.[5] It is, nevertheless, doubtful whether this is correct. The Law of Property Act 1925 provides that a 'mortgage' includes any charge or lien on any property for securing money or money's worth',[3] and this certainly seems to be wide enough to include a floating charge. Moreover, if

---

19 Law of Property Act 1925, s 101(1) (37 *Halsbury's Statutes* (4th edn) 222); Companies Act 1985, s 36A(4) and (5), inserted by Companies Act 1989, s 130(2).
20 Law of Property Act 1925, s 103 and 109(1).
 1 Ibid, s 99(2) and (19).
 2 See *Pennington's Company Law* (7th edn) 562.
 3 Conveyancing Act 1881, s 2(vi).
 4 Law of Property Act 1925, s 205(1)(xvi).
 5 *Blaker v Herts and Essex Waterworks Co* (1889) 41 Ch D 399.

a floating charge were not a mortgage for the purposes of the Law of Property Act 1925, it would also not be a general equitable charge over unregistered land for the purpose of the Land Charges Act 1972, and would therefore not be registrable as such under that Act, which would make purposeless the express exemption of floating charges from registration contained in the Act.[6]

The probable explanation of the judicial decision which excluded floating charges from the statutory definition of mortgages is that the court was impressed by the obvious conflict between the inability of the holder of a floating charge to realise his security before the floating charge crystallised and the immediate availability of the mortgagee's statutory powers if the debt secured by his mortgage was not paid after three months' notice calling for payment had been given to the mortgagor. The conflict is best resolved, however, not by treating floating charges as excluded altogether from the statutory definition, but by implying in the instrument creating a floating charge a term that the statutory powers may not be exercised until the floating charge has crystallised. In practice debt security agreements and trust deeds securing issues of debenture stock avoid uncertainty by expressly incorporating the statutory remedies of mortgagees under the Law of Property Act 1925, and by providing that as regards property comprised in a floating charge, those powers shall be exercisable only after the occurrence of an event which causes the floating charge to crystallise or to become or be converted into a fixed or specific charge.

Remedies conferred by debt security agreements, debentures or covering trust deeds

When a series of debentures or debenture stock is issued to a large number of subscribers, it is obviously impracticable for them to rely on the statutory powers given by the Law of Property Act 1925 for the realisation of their security. In the first place, the debenture holders or debenture stockholders will be too numerous to exercise the statutory powers effectively. This difficulty has been largely overcome by the use of a trust deed securing the debentures, under which trustees are appointed in whom fixed and floating charges over the company's assets are vested, and who are therefore able to exercise the statutory powers on the debenture holders' or debenture stockholders' behalf. In the second place, whether the secured loan is made by one lender or by a small group of lenders (eg a syndicate

6 Land Charges Act 1972, s 3(7) and (8) (37 *Halsbury's Statutes* (4th edn) 411).

of banks) or by many contributory lenders, the statutory powers of sale and appointing a receiver have been found inadequate to enable debt security holders to realise their security in all situations where there is a risk of the security deteriorating or being dissipated. Because of this, debt security agreements and trust deeds securing issues of debentures or debenture stock always contain their own special provisions for the realisation of the security they confer, and these provisions are much more extensive than the statutory powers.

Events of default

The standard provision in debentures, debt security agreements and trust deeds covering issues of debenture stock is that on the occurrence of any one or more of certain events, the security created by the security agreements or trust deed shall become enforceable, and the loan security holder or trustees shall have power to appoint a receiver of the company's assets comprised in the security. The events which make the security enforceable are usually: (*a*) the principal of the secured loan or other secured indebtedness or any part of it not being repaid on the date when it falls due, or interest being in arrear for a specified period, usually not more than one month; (*b*) the company being wound up by order of the court or voluntarily otherwise than for the purpose of an amalgamation or reconstruction approved by the lender or by the debenture holders or the trustees for debenture stockholders; (*c*) an application being made to the court that an administration order shall be made in respect of the company;[7] (*d*) a receiver being appointed of any of the company's assets by the court or otherwise, or execution being levied on any of the company's property or assets by a judgment creditor; (*e*) the company failing to prepare proper annual accounts in conformity with the requirements of the Companies Act 1985 (as amended), or preparing annual accounts which in the opinion of the lender or debt security holders or of the trustees of the covering trust deed show that the continued carrying on of the company's business would endanger the security for the loan or other indebtedness; (*f*) the company's assets, liquid assets or earnings falling below stipulated minima, or its secured or unsecured liabilities rising above stipulated maxima or exceeding a stipulated proportion of its assets; (*g*) the company altering its memorandum of association in a way which the

---

7 This ground for enforcing a floating charge over the whole or substantially the whole of the company's property by appointing an administrative receiver (see p 489, post) is implied in debt security agreements and in debentures where the floating charge was created before the Insolvency Act 1986 came into operation on 29 December 1986 (Insolvency Act 1986, s 437 and Sch 11, para 1(1)).

debt security holder or trustees consider detrimental without first obtaining their consent; (*h*) the company breaking any condition or obligation imposed on it by the debt security agreement or the covering trust deed; and (*i*) the company ceasing to pay its debts or, without the consent of the lender, debt security holders or the trustees for debenture stockholders, ceasing to carry on its business.[8]

Often the loan documentation designates the events listed above as events of default, whether they involve a breach of a contractual or other obligation on the part of the company or not; the lender, debt security holders or trustees for debenture stockholders are then empowered to require immediate payment of the total amount owed by the company, and to enforce the security vested in them or trustees for them if such payment is not made on demand. If the debt security agreement is entered into to secure any amount overdrawn on the company's bank account, or all moneys which the company for the time being owes to the bank, it is usual to provide that the bank may call for payment of the whole amount owing to it either immediately or within a short period, such as seven days, and that the bank's security shall become enforceable if payment is not duly made. Whether the debt security agreement empowers its holder to call for immediate payment of the amount secured by it on the occurrence of an event of default, or whether the debt security agreement secures an amount which its holder may require to be paid immediately on demand, the debt security holder need give only such length of notice demanding payment as is necessary to enable the company to make payment on the assumption that it has sufficient funds readily available to do so (half an hour's notice having been held sufficient for this purpose); if the debt security holder proceeds to exercise his remedies (eg the appointment of a receiver) immediately on the expiration of that time, the exercise is valid and effective, as it is also if exercised before the expiration of that time if the company admits that it is unable to make payment immediately.[9]

On the security created by debt security agreement or a trust deed covering an issue of debenture stock becoming enforceable, the agreement or trust deed invariably empowers the holder of the security or the trustees to appoint a receiver, who may take possession of the company's business and property, carry on its business, sell

---

8 See, for example, the precedents of a debenture trust deed in 10 *Encyclopaedia of Forms and Precedents* (5th edn) 687, cl 19, and *Palmer's Company Precedents* (16th edn) Vol 3, 273, cl 11.

9 *Cripps (Pharmaceuticals) Ltd v Wickenden* [1973] 2 All ER 606, [1973] 1 WLR 944; *Bank of Baroda v Panessar* [1987] Ch 335, [1986] 3 All ER 751; *Sheppard and Cooper Ltd v TSB Bank plc* [1996] 2 All ER 654.

any of its assets comprised in the security and exercise other ancillary powers.[10] Sometimes a trust deed provides that the trustees can appoint a receiver only with the consent of a certain fraction of the debenture holders or debenture stockholders, or that such a fraction of debenture holders or of debenture stockholders may appoint a receiver on their own initiative, or may require the trustees to appoint a receiver. In deciding whether to appoint a receiver, a lender, debt security holder or debenture holders or debenture stockholders may have regard exclusively to their interests as creditors of the company or as beneficiaries of the global debenture debt held by the trustees, and they need not take into account the adverse consequences which the appointment will inevitably have for the company and its members.[11] An appointment of a receiver purporting to be made on a ground specified in the debt security agreement, or the debentures, or the debenture trust deed is void if that ground does not exist, unless the appointment could have been made on another ground which is so specified and does exist although not mentioned in the instrument of appointment,[12] but an appointment made on a ground so specified which does not exist is not validated by the fact that an application could have been made to the court to appoint a receiver in the actual circumstances.[13]

An appointment of a receiver must be made by a written instrument,[14] and if it is made pursuant to a resolution passed by a meeting of debenture holders or debenture stockholders, or to a requisition made to the trustees of the covering trust deed by a certain fraction of their number in exercise of a power conferred on them by the trust deed, the appointment must be made in writing by the persons designated to make the appointment by the covering trust deed, usually the trustees of that deed. The appointment takes effect only when it is communicated to the receiver and is accepted by him, but if it is not accepted by the end of the business day following its notification to the receiver, the appointment is ineffective.[14] Unless the receiver's acceptance of his appointment is communicated in writing to the person who appointed him, it must be confirmed in writing to that person within seven days after the acceptance is given, and the confirmation must state the times and dates when the instrument of appointment was received by the

---

10 See 10 *Encyclopaedia of Forms and Precedents* (5th edn), 690, cll 22 and 23, and *Palmer's Company Precedents* (16th edn) Vol 3, 282, cl 25.

11 *Re Potters Oil Ltd (No 2)* [1986] 1 All ER 890, [1986] 1 WLR 201; *Shamji v Johnson Matthey Bankers Ltd* [1986] BCLC 278; affd [1991] BCLC 36.

12 *Byblos Bank SAL v Al-Khudhairy* [1987] BCLC 232.

13 *Cryne v Barclays Bank plc* [1987] BCLC 548.

14 Insolvency Act 1986, s 33(1).

receiver and when the appointment was accepted by him.[15] It is not necessary for the appointment of a receiver to be communicated to the company to make it effective.[16] Often a trust deed covering an issue of debentures or debenture stock provides that when the security created by it becomes enforceable, the trustees may exercise the same powers to take possession of and to realise the company's assets comprised in the security and to carry on its business as may be exercised by a receiver appointed by them. Debt security agreements may similarly empower the security holder or holders to take possession of the company's property comprised in the security and to manage or realise it. However, it is rare for trustees to act personally, because by appointing a receiver instead they can avoid the possibility of incurring personal liability for mismanagement of the company's affairs or for failure to realise a sufficient price for its assets; if a receiver is appointed, trustees will be liable only if they participate actively in the receiver's wrongdoing.

If a debt security holder or trustees for debenture holders or debenture stockholders appoint a receiver because the company has gone into liquidation, or if such a security holder or trustees, or a receiver appointed by them or by the debenture holders or debenture stockholders, sells the company's property under a power of sale conferred by the debt security agreement, or debentures or the covering trust deed because the company has gone into liquidation, it does not appear to be necessary to obtain the approval of the court to the appointment of the receiver or the sale under the statutory provision to that effect in respect of mortgages.[17] This is because the statutory provision would seem to apply to the appointment of a receiver only when his powers are confined to those conferred by the same statute, namely, collecting and applying the income of the mortgaged property, which the powers of a receiver appointed under a debt security agreement or debentures or a trust deed covering debentures or debenture stock are not, and also because

---

15 Insolvency Rules 1986, r 3.1(2), (3) and (5).
16 *Windsor Refrigerator Co Ltd v Branch Nominees Ltd* [1961] Ch 375, [1961] 1 All ER 277; *Cripps (Pharmaceuticals) Ltd v Wickenden* [1973] 2 All ER 606, [1973] 1 WLR 944.
17 Law of Property Act 1925, s 110(1) and s 205(1)(i) (37 *Halsbury's Statutes* (4th edn) 237 and 331). It is questionable whether s 110(1) applies when the mortgagor is a company, since it is expressed to apply only when a power to sell or appoint a receiver is exercised by the mortgagee in consequence of the mortgagor 'committing an act of bankruptcy or being adjudged bankrupt', and s 205(1)(i) merely equates the term 'bankruptcy' with the winding up of a corporation without equating 'being adjudged bankrupt' with the making of a winding up order or the passing of a winding up resolution. Moreover, even while the Bankruptcy Act 1914 was in force, a company or corporation could not commit an act of bankruptcy.

the power of sale is exercisable by the receiver or by the trustees for the benefit, not of themselves, but of the debt security holder or the debenture holders or debenture stockholders whose interests they are appointed to protect. The position of the trustees as disinterested intermediaries is often reinforced by the debentures or the trust deed containing an irrevocable appointment of them by the company as its attorneys to realise its assets and to satisfy its obligations in respect of the secured loan out of the proceeds of realisation.[18]

If the security created by a debt security agreement or by a trust deed covering debentures or debenture stock is a floating charge, it does not automatically crystallise when one of the events occurs which makes the security enforceable under the terms of the agreement or trust deed,[19] but the floating charge does crystallise when the debt security holder or the trustees for debenture holders or debenture stockholders appoint a receiver because of the occurrence of that event.[20] If the debt security agreement or the trust deed provides that the floating charge shall crystallise immediately when any of the stipulated events happen, or when notice effecting crystallisation is given to the company following the occurrence of any such event, however, the floating charge crystallises on the event happening, or on such notice being given to the company after it has happened (as the case may be), and not on the later date when a receiver is appointed.[1]

Status of a receiver

A receiver appointed by a debt security holder or by debenture holders or by trustees for debenture holders or for debenture stockholders (other than an administrative receiver)[2] is presumed to be his or their agent. Consequently, he or they are liable as his principals upon contracts which the receiver enters into during the receivership,[3] and he or they are accountable similarly for the receiver's defaults, so that if through the receiver's deliberate or negligent act he fails to realise as high a price on the sale of the company's assets as he could have done, the debt security holder or

---

18 Powers of Attorneys Act 1971, s 4(1) (1 *Halsbury's Statutes* (4th edn) 57).
19 *Governments Stock and Other Securities Investment Co Ltd v Manila Rly Co* [1897] AC 81.
20 *Re Panama, New Zealand and Australian Royal Mail Co* (1870) 5 Ch App 318; *Re Florence Land and Public Works Co, ex p Moor* (1878) 10 Ch D 530.
1 *Re Woodroffes (Musical Instruments) Ltd* [1986] Ch 366, [1985] 2 All ER 908; *Re Brightlife Ltd* [1987] Ch 200, [1986] 3 All ER 673; *Re Permanent Houses (Holdings) Ltd* [1988] BCLC 563, 5 BCC 151.
2 Insolvency Act 1986, s 44(1)(*a*).
3 *Deyes v Wood* [1911] 1 KB 806. For the receiver's personal liability in respect of contracts made by him, see p 520, post.

the debenture holders or the debenture stockholders or their trustees who made the appointment will be treated as having received the highest price which could have been obtained.[4] The provision in the Law of Property Act 1925,[5] that a receiver appointed by a mortgagee shall be deemed to be the agent of the mortgagor, applies only when the receiver is appointed to receive the income of the mortgaged property under the power conferred by the Act,[6] and does not extend to a receiver invested with the far wider powers of realisation conferred by a debt security agreement or by a trust deed covering debentures or debenture stock.[7]

The debt security agreement, the debentures or the covering trust deed may expressly provide that the receiver shall be deemed to be the company's agent, however, and in practice will always do so; in that case the company is liable as the receiver's principal in respect of the contracts which he makes during the receivership, and the debt security holder or the debenture holders or debenture stockholders and their trustees are not so liable;[8] furthermore, losses suffered by the company as a result of the receiver's acts or defaults are borne by the company and not by the debt security holder or by the debenture holders or debenture stockholders or their trustees,[9] unless they are personally guilty of wrongdoing. But a receiver who is deemed by the terms of the loan documentation to be an agent of the company does not owe the duties of a real agent to the company,[9] other than a duty to act honestly and with reasonable skill and care,[10] and the company cannot give him instructions as to the way in which he shall exercise his powers.

The one exception to the rule that the loan documentation must expressly provide that a receiver appointed under its terms shall be the agent of the company, and not that of the persons who appoint him, in order to achieve that result is the administrative receiver, that is, a receiver or manager of the whole, or substantially the whole, of a company's property appointed by or on behalf of the holders of any debentures of a company secured by a charge which, as created was a floating charge, or by such a charge and one or more

4 *White v City of London Brewery Co* (1889) 42 Ch D 237.
5 Law of Property Act 1925, s 109(2).
6 Ibid, s 101(1).
7 *Re Vimbos Ltd* [1900] 1 Ch 470; *Robinson Printing Co Ltd v Chic Ltd* [1905] 2 Ch 123, as explained by *Deyes v Wood*, supra.
8 *Central London Electricity Ltd v Berners* [1945] 1 All ER 160.
9 *Re B Johnson and Co (Buildings) Ltd* [1955] Ch 634, [1955] 2 All ER 775.
10 *Standard Chartered Bank Ltd v Walker* [1982] 3 All ER 938, [1982] 1 WLR 1410; *American Express International Banking Corpn v Hurley* [1985] 3 All ER 564, [1986] BCLC 52.

other securities.[11] An administrative receiver is by the Insolvency Act 1986 deemed to be the company's agent until it goes into liquidation or until he vacates office.[12] Most receivers appointed under powers conferred by security agreements, debentures and trust deeds covering debentures and debenture stock are administrative receivers.

If the company is wound up by order of the court[13] or voluntarily,[14] a receiver ceases to be the company's agent, whether he is an administrative receiver or any other kind of receiver appointed under the terms of loan documentation; nevertheless, the receiver can still exercise the same powers as before for the realisation of the security held by the debt security holder or by the trustees for the debenture holders or for debenture stockholders,[15] and he does not become their agent so as to make them liable for his acts,[16] unless they expressly appoint him to be their agent, or do so impliedly by giving him instructions which he accepts.[17] In fact, the only consequence of the receiver ceasing to be the company's agent on its going into liquidation appears to be that he can no longer make contracts on its behalf.[18] The appointment of a receiver after the commencement of the company's liquidation is valid, and does not require leave of the court, even if the debt security agreement or debentures or the covering trust deed provides that the receiver shall be deemed to be an agent of the company.[13] Moreover, if a receiver is appointed after the company goes into liquidation, the provision that the receiver shall be the company's agent is effective to the extent that the company, and not the debt security holder or the debenture holders or debenture stockholders or the trustees for them, bear the consequences of his acts and defaults, and the receiver may dispose of the company's assets without the concurrence of the liquidator if he is given a general power of realisation by the debt security agreement or a covering trust deed or, in the case of an administrative receiver, by law.[19]

If a receiver or a debt security holder, or debenture holders or

---

11 Insolvency Act 1986, s 29(2). For the full definition of an administrative receiver, see p 489, post.

12 Insolvency Act 1986, s 44(1).

13 *Gosling v Gaskell* [1897] AC 575.

14 *Thomas v Todd* [1926] 2 KB 511.

15 *Sowman v David Samuel Trust Ltd* [1978] 1 All ER 616, [1978] 1 WLR 22.

16 *Gosling v Gaskell* [1897] AC 575.

17 *American Express International Banking Corpn v Hurley* [1985] 3 All ER 564, [1986] BCLC 52.

18 *Re Northern Garage Ltd* [1946] Ch 188, [1946] 1 All ER 566.

19 *Re Northern Garage Ltd*, supra; *Sowman v David Samuel Trust Ltd*, supra; Insolvency Act 1986, s 42(1) and Sch 7, paras 1 and 2.

debenture stockholders or trustees for them are by the terms of the loan documentation given a power of attorney by the company to enable them to realise its assets, the power of attorney, being given for value, is not revoked by the company going into liquidation.[20] Likewise, if the loan documentation provides that the debt security holder and any receiver appointed by him shall be authorised to act as attorneys of the company, the appointment of a receiver by the debt security holder vests in the receiver the powers of an attorney, and he may execute deeds and conveyances of land on the company's behalf.[1] However, if a receiver who is expressed to be the company's agent or attorney initiates or continues an action brought in the company's name as plaintiff after it goes into liquidation, the court may order him personally to pay the defendant's costs if the action is dismissed, but if the receiver has acted properly, the court will also direct that he may indemnify himself for such costs out of the company's assets subject to the receivership.[2] The Court of Appeal in Northern Ireland has similarly held that if a receiver continues to defend an action brought against the company before his appointment and judgment is given for the plaintiff, the court may order the receiver to pay the plaintiff's costs personally with a right to an indemnity out of the assets of the company to which the receivership extends.[3]

Remuneration of a receiver

When a receiver is appointed by a debt security holder, or by debenture holders or by debenture stockholders or by trustees acting on their behalf, loan documentation usually provides that the receiver's remuneration shall be fixed by the person or persons who appoint him, and shall be paid out of the company's assets. The debt security holder or the debenture holders or debenture stockholders have no incentive to limit the remuneration to a reasonable amount when the company's assets are more than sufficient to pay the secured debt and the costs incidental to realising the company's assets, but the company and its unsecured creditors suffer in those circumstances if excessive remuneration is paid to the receiver. Consequently, statute provides that if the company is wound up, the liquidator may apply to the court to fix the amount of remuneration to be paid to a person appointed to be a receiver or manager of a company's property; the court may then reduce the remuneration to be paid to the receiver or manager in the future, even for work which he has already done, and if there

20 *Sowman v David Samuel Trust Ltd*, supra.
1 *Phoenix Properties Ltd v Wimpole Street Nominees Ltd* [1992] BCLC 737.
2 *Bacal Contracting Ltd v Modern Engineering (Bristol) Ltd* [1980] 2 All ER 655.
3 *Andersons Hyde* [1996] 2 BCLC 144.

are special circumstances, the court may make the order retrospective and require the receiver to account for any remuneration which he has already received for a past period in excess of that allowed by the court.[4] The court may on the application of the liquidator or the receiver or manager vary any order which it has made fixing his remuneration.[5] In practice the court is reluctant to exercise its power to reduce a receiver's remuneration, unless it is obviously excessive by any standard, and the court will not order a reduction where it is at a rate no greater than that to which a liquidator would be entitled in a winding up.[6] If the loan documentation expressly incorporates the provisions of the Law of Property Act 1925 relating to receivers, a receiver appointed by the debt security holder, or by debenture holders or debenture stockholders or by trustees acting on their behalf, is entitled to the remuneration specified by that Act in the absence of any different stipulation in the loan documentation, and this is so even if the receiver's functions are more extensive than merely collecting income;[7] consequently, such a receiver is entitled to commission on the gross amount of assets which he recovers at the rate fixed by the document appointing him, or if no such rate is fixed, at the rate of five per cent or such other rate as the court decides on an application made by him.[8]

Position of the directors

If a receiver is appointed otherwise than by the court, the directors of the company which created the security which he is to enforce do not cease to hold office automatically, even if the security extends the company's whole assets and undertaking;[9] the directors may continue to exercise their powers to the extent that the receiver does not decide to exercise equivalent powers himself, so excluding the directors from doing so, but in exercising their retained powers, the directors must not impede the proper conduct of the receivership.[10]

4 Insolvency Act 1986, s 36(1) and (2).
5 Ibid, s 39(3).
6 *Re Potters Oil Ltd (No 2)* [1986] 1 All ER 890, [1986] 1 WLR 201.
7 *Marshall v Cottingham* [1982] Ch 82, [1981] 3 All ER 8.
8 Law of Property Act 1925, s 109(6) (37 *Halsbury's Statutes* (4th edn) 234). The receiver must bear the costs, charges and expenses incurred by him as receiver out of this commission, unless the loan security agreement or trust deed otherwise provides.
9 *Re Foster Clark Ltd's Indenture Trusts* [1966] 1 All ER 43 [1966] 1 WLR 125; *Griffiths v Secretary of State for Social Services* [1974] QB 468, [1973] 3 All ER 1184; *Newhart Developments Ltd v Co-operative Commercial Bank Ltd* [1978] QB 814, [1978] 2 All ER 896.
10 *Newhart Developments Ltd v Co-operative Commercial Bank Ltd*, supra. It has been held that directors may not initiate or defend litigation to which the company is a party after the appointment of a receiver (*Tudor Grange Holdings Ltd v Citibank NA* [1992] Ch 53, [1991] BCLC 1009).

REMEDIES FOR ENFORCING THE SECURITY
WITH THE ASSISTANCE OF THE COURT

The elaboration of the documentation for the creation of debt securities and for the issue of debentures or debenture stock and the inclusion in that documentation of provisions by which the holders of such securities are empowered to realise the mortgages or charges to which they are entitled (usually by means of appointing a receiver) has made it rarely necessary for them to apply to the court to make orders and direct steps to be taken for that purpose. Nevertheless, occasions do occur when resort to the court is unavoidable, and a consideration of the relevant procedure, of the circumstances in which the court can act and the remedies which the court can give is therefore necessary.

Form and initiation of a mortgagee's, chargee's or debenture holder's action

The holder of a security, whether a legal or equitable mortgage or a charge or a floating charge, may apply to the court for any of five remedies available in respect of his security, namely, an order for the payment to him of the amount secured, an order for the sale of the property or assets comprised in the mortgage or charge, an order of foreclosure, an order for the delivery to him of possession of the property mortgaged or charged, or an order appointing a receiver to take possession or control of that property or of those assets and to deal with them as directed by the court. The application may be made in an action or summarily by originating summons in the Chancery Division.[11] The summons may be taken out by a mortgagee or chargee, or by a debenture holder or debenture stockholder suing on his own behalf,[12] or by a debenture holder or debenture stockholder making a representative application on behalf of himself and all other debenture holders or debenture stockholders of the same class or series as himself.[13] If the security which a debenture holder or debenture stockholder wishes to realise is vested in the trustees of a debenture trust deed, the applicant must join the trustees as co-plaintiffs in his originating summons, or if they refuse to be co-plaintiffs, he must join them as co-defendants together with the company.[14]

11 RSC Ord 30, r 1(1) and Ord 88, r 1(1).
12 *Sadler v Worley* [1894] 2 Ch 170.
13 *Oldrey v Union Works Ltd* [1895] WN 77.
14 *Franklin v Franklin* [1915] WN 342; *Mortgage Insurance Corpn v Canadian Agricultural, Coal and Colonization Ltd* [1901] 2 Ch 377.

When there a numerous debenture holders or debenture stockholders, there are usually complex accounts to be taken and enquiries to be made, particularly with regard to the title of the persons who claim to be debenture holders or debenture stockholders and the amount payable to each of them, and the court is unwilling to deal with such complexities on an originating summons, which it regards as a summary procedure to be used only in fairly straightforward cases. For this reason, when a large number of persons hold debentures or debenture stock of the same class or series, it is usual for a debenture holder's action to be commenced by writ.[15] The plaintiff then brings a representative action on behalf of himself and all the other debenture holders or debenture stockholders of the same class or series. The trustees of the covering trust deed (if there is one) may be joined as plaintiffs if they consent; if not, they must be joined as defendants so that the court may order that the trusts of the trust deed shall be executed, and that the security vested in the trustees shall be realised.[14] The indorsement on the writ usually claims: (a) the execution of the trusts of the trust deed; (b) a declaration that the property charged by the debentures or by the trust deed stands charged with payment of the loan or the debt to which the plaintiffs and the persons they represent are entitled; (c) an order that all necessary accounts shall be taken and enquiries made; (d) an order that the amount to which the debenture holders or debenture stockholders are entitled shall be paid to them; (e) the appointment of a receiver and manager; and (f) an order that the property comprised in the charge shall be sold.

It is not necessary for prior or subsequent mortgagees, chargees or other encumbrancers of the property or assets charged with payment of the secured debt to be made co-defendants with the company in a debenture holder's action. If their interests are affected by proceedings taken subsequently to judgment, they should be added as co-defendants then, either on their own application or on the application of the plaintiff debenture holder.[16] To this general rule there is one exception. If the plaintiff debenture holder or debenture stockholder seeks a foreclosure order by his writ, all subsequent encumbrancers, including debenture holders or debenture stockholders of a later class or series who have as their security merely a floating charge which has not yet crystallised,[17] must be made defendants. Moreover, although a plaintiff debenture holder or debenture stockholder may seek a foreclosure order in a

---

15 8 RSC Ord 88, r 1(1).
16 Direction of the Chancery Judges dated 12 May 1909.
17 *Oldrey v Union Works Ltd* [1895] WN 77. Applications for foreclosure orders by mortgagees or in debenture holders' actions are extremely rare.

representative action brought on behalf of himself and his fellow debenture holders or debenture stockholders,[18] debenture holders or debenture stockholders of another class who rank for payment after the class represented by the plaintiff cannot be made defendants in a foreclosure action by the plaintiff suing one or a few of their number on behalf of himself or themselves and all the other debenture holders or debenture stockholders of the later ranking class, nor can the court make a representation order to that effect.[19] Instead, all the debenture holders or debenture stockholders of the later ranking class must be made individual defendants, however numerous they may be.[19] If the security which the debenture holders of the later ranking class have over the property in respect of which the first class seek a foreclosure order is a mortgage or charge which is vested in trustees, however, or if the later ranking class consists of debenture stockholders whose security is necessarily vested in trustees, those trustees may be made defendants, and it is then unnecessary to join the debenture holders or debenture stockholders of the later ranking class themselves.[20]

Subsequent procedure

After the close of pleadings in an action brought by a debenture holder or debenture stockholder, the case is set down for trial. If the company does not dispute the plaintiff's claim, pleadings may be dispensed with by the plaintiff making an interlocutory application for the appointment of a receiver immediately after serving the writ, and by the parties agreeing to treat the hearing of this application as the trial of the action. If no such agreement is reached, the plaintiff may wish to have a receiver or manager appointed or the company's property sold before the case comes on for trial. Interlocutory applications can be made for these purposes on notice of motion or summons,[1] but an interlocutory order for sale can be made only if the plaintiff sues in a representative action on behalf of himself and his fellow debenture holders or debenture stockholders, and not merely on his own behalf.[2]

On the trial of the action, or with the consent of the parties, on the hearing of the application for the appointment of a receiver, the

---

18 *Wallace v Evershed* [1899] 1 Ch 891.
19 *Westminster Bank v Residential Properties Improvement Co Ltd* [1938] Ch 639, [1938] All ER 374.
20 RSC Ord 15, r 14(1).
 1 Supreme Court Act 1981, s 37(1) (11 *Halsbury's Statutes* (4th edn) 792); RSC Ord 30, r 1(1) (receiver); *Re Crigglestone Coal Co* [1906] 1 Ch 523 (sale).
 2 *Parkinson v Wainwright & Co* [1895] WN 63.

court may make the orders sought by the plaintiff if he proves his case, or if the company consents to judgment being given against it. But the court will not declare that the property charged by the debentures or by the trust deed covering the debentures or debenture stock stands charged with payment of the debenture debt, even though the company consents, unless the plaintiff proves that the charge is valid and subsisting,[3] or unless the company is being wound up and the liquidator admits the validity of the charge.[4] This is because such a declaration would estop the company and its liquidator (if the company subsequently went into liquidation) from disputing the validity of the charge in later proceedings, and a declaration made by consent would obviously unfairly prejudice the company's shareholders and unsecured creditors if the security created by the debentures or by the covering trust deed were for some reason invalid or not binding on them.

By its judgment, the court usually orders the following accounts to be taken and enquiries made:[5] (*a*) an account of the amount payable to the debenture holders or debenture stockholders; (*b*) an enquiry as to the property which is specifically charged, and as to the property and assets which are subject to a floating charge created by the debentures or by the covering trust deed; (*c*) an enquiry whether there are any encumbrances ranking in priority to the debentures or debenture stock in respect of which the action is brought, and if so, an account of the amount payable to the persons entitled to such encumbrances; and (*d*) an enquiry whether there are any unsecured debts of the company which are preferential payments in a receivership, and which will consequently rank for payment out of property subject to the floating charge before the debt secured by it.[6] These accounts and enquiries are taken and made by a master in chambers, and his certificate is filed in court by the plaintiff in the debenture holder's action.

When judgment has been given in a debenture holder's action, the plaintiff should serve an informal notice of the substance of the judgment[7] on all the debenture holders or debenture stockholders on whose behalf he sues, so that they may claim payment of the amounts to which they are respectively entitled out of the company's

3 *Re Gregory Love & Co* [1916] 1 Ch 203 at 209.
4 *Marwick v Lord Thurlow* [1895] 1 Ch 776.
5 *Re Wolverhampton District Brewery Ltd* [1899] WB 229; *Re Addressograph Ltd* [1909] WN 260; *Re Burradon and Coxlodge Coal Co Ltd* [1929] WN 15.
6 See p 532, post.
7 Direction of the Chancery Judges dated May 1896; *Re Commonwealth Oil Corpn Ltd, Re Pearson v Commonwealth Oil Corpn Ltd* [1917] 1 Ch 404. If debentures in bearer form have been issued, the court orders the publication of its judgment in the London Gazette and such other newspapers as it thinks fit.

assets. The other debenture holders or debenture stockholders may appear before the master in the proceedings subsequent to judgment, however, only if they apply to him to be added as defendants and he permits this to be done.[8]

The court may order a receiver appointed by it to keep a register of transfers and transmissions of debentures or debenture stock of the class or series for the benefit of whose holders he is appointed, and debenture holders or debenture stockholders at the date of judgment in the debenture holder's action and persons claiming under them may on proving their titles require the receiver to enter appropriate particulars of their holdings in the register.[9] The function of the register is merely to assist the receiver and the master in making distributions to the persons entitled to the debentures or debenture stock when the distribution is made however,[10] and entries in it have no effect on the proprietary rights of persons interested or claiming to be interested in the debentures or debenture stock. These rights continue to be regulated by the same rules as before the receiver's appointment,[11] and the register of debenture holders or debenture stockholders kept by the company or the trustees of the covering trust deed must therefore be maintained and entries made in it accordingly when there is a transfer or transmission of the title to any of the debentures.

Jurisdiction of the court to enforce the security

The court may order the sale of property comprised in the security held by a secured creditor or by or on behalf of debenture holders or debenture stockholders, or the court may appoint a receiver or manager of that property with a view to its sale, if any of the following events has occurred.

1. Principal or interest in arrear

If payment of the principal or an instalment of principal of the secured debt, or if payment of interest on that debt for an interest period which has expired, is not made on the date when payment falls due, the court may intervene. If interest is in arrear, it is not necessary that the principal should also be immediately payable

---

8 *Re W Mate & Sons Ltd* [1920] 1 Ch 551.
9 RSC Ord 87, rr 1, 2, 4 and 5. There is provision for the rectification of the register in similar terms to the Companies Act 1985, s 359(1) (ibid, r 3).
10 RSC Ord 87, r 6.
11 See *Pennington's Company Law* (7th edn) 609 et seq.

under the terms of an acceleration provision. Consequently, where debentures provided that if interest was in arrear and unpaid for a certain length of time, the principal should also become immediately due and payable, it was held that the court could appoint a receiver even though that period had not expired.[12] If a secured lender or a debenture holder or a debenture stockholder applies to the court for the appointment of a receiver because the principal or an instalment of principal of the debt is due and unpaid, it is not necessary that the principal or instalment should have become due before the application to the court is made, provided that it is due and unpaid when the action is tried.[13]

2. Commencement of winding up

The court will always intervene at the request of a secured creditor, or of a debenture holder or debenture stockholder, if the company has gone into liquidation, whether voluntarily or by order of the court. This is so even though the secured debt is not immediately payable, and the debt security agreement or the debentures or the trust deed covering debenturers or debenture stock do not provide expressly that the principal of the debt and unpaid interest shall become payable in the event of the company being wound up.[14] It has, moreover, been held that the court may appoint a receiver even though the company is wound up merely for the purpose of a reconstruction of the company by the formation of a new company with a different capital structure to take over its undertaking, or for the purpose of a merger or amalgamation of the company with another company or companies; this is so even though the security agreement or the debentures or the trust deed covering the debentures or debenture stock provide that the security shall not become enforceable in that event. The correctness of this decision is doubtful in cases where the secured lender, or the debenture holders or debenture stockholders, have contracted out of their right to treat a floating charge over the company's assets and undertaking, to which they are entitled, as having crystallised in consequence of the reconstruction, merger or amalgamation of the company. Loan agreements, debentures and deeds covering debentures or debenture stock frequently provide that if a reconstruction, merger or amalgamation is proposed, the persons entitled to a specified fraction of the principal of the loan or a specified fraction of the outstanding debentures or debenture stock may on behalf of them

---

12 *Bissill v Bradford Tramways Co Ltd* [1891] WN 51.
13 *Re Carshalton Park Estate Ltd* [1908] 2 Ch 62.
14 *Wallace v Universal Automatic Machines Co* [1894] 2 Ch 547.

all accept a charge on the property or assets of the reconstructed, merged or amalgamated company in substitution for the original security,[16] and if the requisite fraction of those persons accepts the substituted security, the court will not intervene and appoint a receiver at the instance of a dissenting lender or debenture holder or debenture stockholder and so impede the reconstruction, merger or amalgamation.[17]

If a company which has borrowed on security or has issued debentures or debenture stock is ordered to be wound up by the court, a debenture holder or debenture stockholder cannot commence an action for the enforcement of his security, nor continue a pending action for that purpose, unless he first obtains leave of the Companies Court or the court which made the winding up order,[18] which is always given as a matter of course.[19] The action by the debenture holder or debenture stockholder will have to be a representative one brought on behalf of himself and all other debenture or debenture stockholders of the same series, because the purpose of the action is the realisation of the security to which they are all entitled.[20]

3. Jeopardy

The court has always had power to protect any mortgagee or secured creditor from losing his security by exercising its discretionary power to allow him to take possession of the property charged with payment of his loan or the debt owed to him if there is a risk of the security being lost.[1] The court can allow a mortgagee to take possession, even though the principal and interest of the secured loan or debt are not overdue and the debtor has broken none of his obligations. But the court will exercise its discretion in the secured creditor's favour only if there is an immediate and substantial risk of his security disappearing, or being dissipated, or falling substantially in value. The risk is clearly greatest if the security is a floating charge created over a company's assets and undertaking, or over some class of its assets, but there may also be such a risk if the security is a specific or fixed charge over property which can fluctuate in value,

---

15 *Re Crompton & Co Ltd, Player v Crompton & Co Ltd* [1914] 1 Ch 954.
16 The security for the loan or debenture debt should be improved on a merger or amalgamation, because the substituted security will comprise the assets of both or all of the participating companies. Whether this in fact happens depends on the level of secured indebtedness of the acquiring company.
17 *Re Crompton & Co Ltd, Player v Crompton & Co Ltd,* supra.
18 Insolvency Act 1986, s 130(2); (see p 77, ante).
19 *Re David Lloyd & Co* (1877) 6 Ch D 339.
20 *Bowen v Brecon Rly Co., ex p Howell* (1867) LR 3 Eq 541.
 1 *Barclays Bank Ltd v Bird* [1954] Ch 274, [1954] 1 All ER 449.

such as investments in other companies (particularly if not listed on a stock exchange) or the goodwill of a business, or if the security is a fixed charge over property which is likely to be seized and sold by judgment creditors of the mortgagor, such as plant and machinery.[2] When debentures or debenture stock have been issued by a company to numerous persons in a series, it is obviously impossible for the court to allow them all to take possession of the company's property comprised in their charge, and so the court will instead appoint a receiver and order that the property shall be sold.[3] In fact, these remedies have been found so effective that it is usual for them to be sought when recourse to the court is necessary, even though the debt security agreement has been entered into by the company with only one or a few persons, or where there has been an issue of debentures or debenture stock to one or a small number of persons who could quite easily take possession themselves.

The circumstances in which the court will hold the security for a loan or debt to be in such jeopardy as to warrant the appointment of a receiver cannot be catalogued exhaustively, because the court's jurisdiction is a discretionary one, and new situations may justify an extended exercise of the discretion. The cases so far decided, however, fall into three classes.

Where the company is being seriously pressed by its creditors, who are likely to seize or sell the property subject to the security, the secured lender's or debenture holders' or debenture stockholders' security will be in jeopardy. Consequently, the security is in jeopardy if a judgment creditor has levied execution on the property comprised in it,[4] or has threatened to do so,[5] or is in a position to do so although he has as yet taken no action.[6] The security is also in jeopardy if the company is insolvent and its creditors are threatening to sue it or to petition for it to be wound up,[7] or if the company is insolvent and its creditors are abstaining from suing it only because its directors have undertaken to be personally responsible for payment of its debts.[8] If creditors of the company have actually presented a winding up petition, the security is deemed to be in jeopardy, even though the secured lender or the debenture holders or debenture stockholders cannot prove that the company is insolvent.[9] On the other hand, if

2 *Grigson (or Gregson) v Taplin & Co* (1915) 85 LJ Ch 75.
3 *Re London Pressed Hinge Co, Campbell v London Pressed Hinge Co* [1905] 1 Ch 576 at 683 per Buckley J.
4 *Edwards v Standard Rolling Stock Syndicate* [1893] 1 Ch 574.
5 *Grigson v Taplin & Co*, supra.
6 *Re London Pressed Hinge Co*, supra.
7 *McMahon v North Kent Ironworks Co* [1891] 2 Ch 148.
8 *Re Braunstein and Marjorlaine Ltd* (1914) 112 LT 25.
9 *Re Victoria Steamboats Ltd* [1897] 1 Ch 158.

there are no pending or threatened proceedings against the company, the security is not in jeopardy merely because the company's assets are worth less than the total amount of the secured debt, but this is so only so long as the company continues to carry on its business and there is some prospect of its assets eventually proving sufficient to discharge the secured debt.[10]

The second category of cases where the court has held that the security held by a secured lender, or by debenture holders or debenture stockholders, is in jeopardy is where the company has ceased to carry on its business,[11] or intends to do so shortly,[12] or has ceased to carry on any of the principal business activities authorised by its memorandum of association.[13] In most of these cases the company was also insolvent, but this is not a vital part of the secured creditor's case. Consequently, when a company which was not shown to be insolvent, although it probably was, had ceased to carry on its business because all its directors were dead, it was held that jeopardy was established.[14] Similarly, a receiver was appointed when a solvent company had ceased to carry on any of its activities because of the outbreak of war.[13] The fact that a company has ceased to carry on business has been held to cause a floating charge created by it to crystallise and to become a fixed charge over its assets at the moment when the company's business ceased,[15] and for that reason alone the court will intervene and appoint a receiver without the need for the applicant to prove that his security is otherwise in jeopardy.

The final category of cases is really an extension of the second. If a company proposes to distribute its assets among its shareholders,[16] or to transfer them to another person,[17] and after the distribution or transfer the company will be unable to continue carrying on its business, a security over its assets and undertaking will be put in jeopardy, and the court will forestall the disposal of the company's assets by appointing a receiver. But if the company sells all its assets

10 *Re New York Taxicab Co Ltd* [1913] 1 Ch 1, where the deficiency was caused by the failure of the insurers of some of the company's assets to satisfy the company's claims for their value when the assets were destroyed.
11 *McMahon v North Kent Ironworks Co* [1891] 2 Ch 148; *Re Levison & Steiner Ltd, Wissner v Levison and Steiner* [1900] WN 152.
12 *Re Braunstein and Marjorlaine Ltd* (1914) 112 LT 25.
13 *Higginson v German Athenaeum Ltd* (1916) 32 TLR 277.
14 *Re Newport Construction Co Ltd* [1948] Ch 217, [1948] 1 All ER 365.
15 *Re Woodroffes (Musical Instruments) Ltd* [1986] Ch 366, [1985] 2 All ER 908; *Re Brightlife Ltd* [1987] Ch 200, [1986] BCLC 418; *Re Real Meat Co Ltd* [1996] BCC 254.
16 *Re Tilt Cove Copper Co Ltd* [1913] 2 Ch 588. The proposed distribution was otherwise lawful, as the law then stood, because the assets represented undistributed profits.
17 *Hubbuck v Helms* (1887) 56 LJ Ch 536.

to another company in return for shares in the purchasing concern, and the selling company intends to continue in existence as a holding company, there is no jeopardy, at least if the selling company's memorandum of association empowers it to effect such a sale, and the shares in the purchasing company have a substantial value.[18] There is even less cause for creditors secured by a charge over a company's whole assets and undertaking to seek the appointment of a receiver if the company was formed to carry on two or more businesses, and it disposes of one of them for an adequate consideration in cash or shares, but will continue to carry on the other business as before.[19] It is uncertain whether a distribution of the company's assets to its shareholders causes jeopardy if it does not prevent the company from carrying on its business, but does make the company's remaining assets worth less than the total amount of the secured debt. An insufficiency of assets caused by a trading loss does not of itself bring about jeopardy,[20] but probably such an insufficiency resulting from a deliberate distribution of assets to the company's shareholders would be held to do so. Such a distribution by a public company would, in any case, be illegal under the present statutory rules governing distributions,[1] and this would almost inevitably be so in the case of a private company as well.[2] The illegality of the distribution would not of itself entitle secured creditors or debenture holders or debenture stockholders to the appointment of a receiver by the court, but it is a factor which the court could take into consideration in assessing the risk of their security being lost.

Appointment of a receiver and manager

Selection and powers of a receiver or a manager

The court may appoint any person whom it considers competent and suitable to be a receiver of a company's assets, and in the

---

18 *Re Borax Co, Foster v Borax Co* [1901] 1 Ch 326. The adequacy of the consideration given for the company's assets was not considered in this case, but the deliberate acceptance by the company of a consideration worth less than its assets, and also worth less than the secured debt, would jeopardise the secured creditors.

19 *Re H H Vivian & Co Ltd* [1900] 2 Ch 654.

20 *Re New York Taxicab Co Ltd* [1913] 1 Ch 1. The debt security agreement, debentures or trust deed covering debentures or debenture stock usually guard against this by making the security enforceable if the company's assets become inadequate in the opinion of the secured lenders or the debenture holders or debenture stockholders or their trustees (see p 463, ante).

1 Companies Act 1985, s 264(1) and (2) (see *Pennington's Company Law* (7th edn) 533).

2 Companies Act 1985, s 263(1) and (3). See *Pennington's Company Law* (7th edn) 531.

absence of substantiated objections, it will usually appoint the person nominated by the plaintiff mortgagee or chargee, or by the plaintiff debenture holder or debenture stockholder, or by the trustees of the trust deed covering debentures or debenture stock. A receiver appointed by the court, unlike an administrative receiver appointed out of court under the provisions of a debt security agreement or of debentures or a trust deed covering debentures or debenture stock,[3] need not be a qualified insolvency practitioner, but the court is unlikely, save in exceptional cases, to appoint a receiver who is not so qualified. If the company is already being wound up under an order of the court when the application to the court is made for the appointment of a receiver, the court is inclined to appoint the liquidator in the winding up to be the receiver in order to save expense in administering the company's assets,[4] and this was also done when the winding up was a voluntary one continued under the supervision of the court.[5] However, it is unlikely that the court would appoint the liquidator in a voluntary winding up of the company to be the receiver if this was contrary to the wishes of a secured lender or the debenture holders or debenture stockholders of the company. In a winding up by the court the official receiver[6] may be appointed to be the receiver,[7] apparently whether he is acting as the liquidator in the winding up or not. When a receiver has been appointed on the application of a secured creditor, or in a debenture holder's or debenture stockholder's action, before the court has made a winding up order, the court may remove him and appoint the liquidator to be the receiver in his place,[8] but if this would be of no advantage to the secured creditors or the debenture holders or debenture stockholders in the realisation of their security, because, for example, the receiver is in possession of all the assets of the company and does not need the wider powers of realisation which a liquidator possesses,[9] the court will not remove and replace the original receiver.[10] The fact that a receiver has been appointed by a

---

3 Insolvency Act 1986, s 230(1) and (2).
4 *Re Joshua Stubbs Ltd* [1891] 1 Ch 475.
5 *Perry v Oriental Hotels Co* (1870) 5 Ch App 420. Voluntary winding up subject to supervision was abolished by the Insolvency Act 1986, s 438 and Sch 12.
6 The official receiver is appointed by the Secretary of State for Trade and Industry, and is attached to the court for the purposes of bankruptcy and winding up (Insolvency Act 1986, s 399(1) and (2)).
7 Insolvency Act 1986, s 32.
8 *Campbell v Compagnie Générale de Bellegarde* (1876) 2 Ch D 181; *Tottenham v Swansea Zinc Ore Co Ltd* (1884) 53 LJ Ch 776; *British Linen Co v South American and Mexican Co* [1894] 1 Ch 108.
9 See p 145, ante.
10 *Re Joshua Stubbs Ltd* [1891] 1 Ch 475.

secured creditor or by debenture holders or debenture stockholders or by trustees for them does not prevent the court from appointing another person to be a receiver in his place,[11] but if the court does not replace the receiver appointed out of court, it will assist him in collecting the company's assets, and will order the liquidator in the company's winding up to deliver assets in his possession to the receiver if they are comprised in the security.[12] The court may appoint a receiver of a company's assets and undertaking who has been appointed out of court also to be the receiver of the assets of a 'phoenix' or successor company which has been formed by the controlling shareholders of the original company to take a transfer of its assets and undertaking with a view to avoiding the company's obligations.[13]

In addition to appointing a receiver, the court may appoint a manager to carry on the company's business for a limited time with a view to it being sold.[14] The manager so appointed may be the same person as the receiver, or another person may be appointed, but when the court appoints the official receiver to be the receiver of the company's assets and undertaking, it always appoints someone else to be the manager, preferably a person with business experience, which the official receiver, as an official of the Department of Trade and Industry, usually lacks. A manager can be appointed only if the secured creditor or the debenture holders or debenture stockholders who seek his appointment, or trustees for them, have a charge on the company's business undertaking as distinct from the premises where, or the assets with which, it is carried on;[15] but a charge on 'the undertaking and property'[15] or on 'the property,[16] of a company includes a charge on its business undertaking, and so a manager may always be appointed to assist in the realisation of a floating charge over the whole or substantially the whole of the company's assets, which must of necessity include its business undertaking.

The powers of a receiver appointed by the court are fixed by the court in the order for his appointment, and can be as general or restricted as the court thinks fit. If the company's business undertaking is to be carried on with a view to sale, the receiver and manager (if any) are given the necessary powers for the purpose, but the court

11 *Re Slogger Automatic Feeder Co Ltd* [1915] 1 Ch 478.
12 *Re Henry Pound, Son and Hutchins Ltd* (1889) 42 Ch D 402.
13 *Bank of Credit and Commerce International SA v Kumar Bros Ltd* [1994] 1 BCLC 211.
14 *Re Victoria Steamboats Ltd* [1897] 1 Ch 158.
15 *Whitley v Challis* [1892] 1 Ch 64; *Gloucester County Bank v Rudry Merthyr Steam and House Coal Colliery Co* [1895] 1 Ch 629.
16 *Re Leas Hotel Co* [1902] 1 Ch 332.

may require certain transactions to be approved by it before they are entered into, either because of their size or character, or because of their significance in achieving an orderly realisation of the company's assets.

Security by a receiver for the performance of his duties

The court normally requires a receiver appointed by it to give security for the proper performance of his duties.[17] If the receiver is appointed subject to giving security, his appointment is not effective, and he may not act, until he has done so;[18] but if the applicant for his appointment undertakes to be responsible for the receiver's acts and defaults until he does give security, the court may give the receiver liberty to act immediately, and the appointment is then effective as from the date it is made.[19] The order appointing the receiver always fixes a date by which he must give security, and if he fails to do so by that date, his appointment is automatically cancelled, or if the court has permitted him to act meanwhile, his appointment is terminated.[19] If the receiver provides the security required by the court after the time permitted by it has expired, the court may re-appoint the receiver and may confirm and retrospectively validate acts done by him after his original appointment terminated; but the effective date of the receiver's appointment (eg in order to cause the crystallisation of a floating charge) will be that of his re-appointment.[20] The security given by a receiver appointed by the court takes the form of a guarantee entered into by the receiver and an insurance company for an amount fixed by the master in chambers after considering an affidavit by the receiver showing the probable value of the company's assets of which he is to take possession.[1]

A receiver is an officer of the court and not an agent

A receiver or manager is an officer of the court which appointed him, and is not the agent of either the company or of the secured creditor who procured his appointment, or of the debenture holders or debenture stockholders for whose benefit the appointment was made, or of the trustees of the trust deed covering such debentures or debenture stock.[2] Consequently, if the receiver enters into

---

17 RSC Ord 30, r 2(1).
18 *Re Roundwood Colliery Co* [1897] 1 Ch 373.
19 *Re Sims and Woods Ltd* [1916] WN 223.
20 *Smith v Keely* (14 June 1996, unreported).
　1 RSC Ord 30, r 2(2) and (3).
　2 *Moss SS Co Ltd v Whinney* [1912] AC 254; *Parsons v Sovereign Bank of Canada* [1913] AC 160 at 167.

contracts during the receivership, neither the company[3] nor the secured creditor, nor the debenture holders or debenture stockholders[4] are liable to the other contracting parties. The receiver or manager alone is personally liable on such contracts,[5] but if the contract is a proper one for carrying out his functions, he has a right to be indemnified against the cost of carrying it out from the assets of the company of which the court appointed him to be the receiver or manager;[6] but his right to be indemnified cannot prejudice the rights of holders of securities over the property comprised in the receivership which rank in priority to the security in respect of which the receiver was appointed.[7] Because the receiver is not the agent of the secured creditor or of the debenture holders or debenture stockholders, they are not accountable for his defaults, and so will not be treated as having received any sum which the receiver could have realised out of the company's assets, but which he failed to realise because of his negligence.

A receiver's remuneration

The remuneration of a receiver or manager is fixed by the court which appoints him.[8] The receiver's remuneration is usually fixed at a percentage of the amount which he realises by selling and getting in the company's assets to which his appointment relates, but there is no standard scale. A manager's remuneration always takes the form of a salary, but when the same person is appointed to be both a receiver and manager, the court often allows him simply a percentage of the amount of assets realised as the remuneration of both offices. The secured creditors who obtain the appointment of a receiver by the court, or the debenture holders or debenture stockholders for whose benefit the receiver is appointed, are not responsible for payment of the receiver's remuneration or for indemnifying him against expenses and liabilities incurred by him if the company's assets prove to be insufficient,[9] but in appropriate circumstances the court may order that they shall be so liable to the receiver as a condition of ordering his appointment.[10]

3 *Burt, Boulton and Hayward v Bull* [1895] 1 QB 276.
4 *Boehm v Goodall* [1911] 1 Ch 155.
5 *Moss SS Co v Whinney*, supra.
6 See p 531, post.
7 *Choudhri v Palta* [1994] 1 BCLC 184, [1992] BCC 787.
8 RSC Ord 30, r 3.
9 *Boehm v Goodall* [1911] 1 Ch 155; *Evans v Clayhope Properties Ltd* [1988] 1 All ER 444 [1988] 1 WLR 358.
10 *Evans v Clayhope Properties Ltd*, supra.

The geographical extent of a receiver's functions

The powers of a receiver appointed by the court to realise a floating charge over a company's assets are effective throughout the United Kingdom, and he may recover such assets and realise them without being appointed afresh by the courts of the part of the United Kingdom where the assets are situate.[11] Consequently, if a receiver is appointed by the High Court to take possession of and to realise the assets and undertaking of a company which has property in Scotland or Northern Ireland, he may realise that property without his appointment being confirmed by the Scottish or Northern Irish courts, and conversely, a receiver appointed by a court in either of those countries may freely realise assets of the company in England or Wales. It is not necessary for this purpose that the company should be registered in the part of the United Kingdom by whose courts the receiver is appointed, and so an appointment by the High Court of a receiver of a company registered in Scotland or Northern Ireland which has assets in England or Wales, is effective to empower him to realise other assets of the company in Scotland or Northern Ireland. The appointment of a manager of a company's business in addition to the appointment of a receiver has the like territorial effect.[12] However, there is no provision in the international agreements for the enforcement of judgments entered into by the United Kingdom by which the appointment of receivers by a court in the United Kingdom takes effect in Commonwealth or foreign countries, or vice versa.

Order for the sale of the property comprised in the security

If the court orders the sale of any land comprised in a security held by or on behalf of the secured creditor or debenture holders or debenture stockholders for whose benefit the court has appointed a receiver, the receiver may be directed to arrange for the sale subject to the control and approval of the court at each stage of the negotiations and transfer.[13] Alternatively, the court may empower the receiver to sell the property in such manner as he thinks fit,[13] in which case he conducts the negotiations and carries out the transfer without further approval by the court. But the court will permit the receiver to effect the sale of the company's land as he thinks fit only if all mortgagees, debenture holders and other secured creditors

11 Administration of Justice Act 1977, s 7(1) (8 *Halsbury's Statutes* (4th edn) 103).
12 Ibid, s 7(2).
13 RSC Ord 31, r 2(1).

who rank after the holders of the securities for whose benefit the receiver was appointed, are parties to the action in which the sale is directed,[14] and if they were not parties originally, they may be added as defendants for the purpose.

In a debenture holder's or debenture stockholder's action the court usually orders the sale of the company's property comprised in the debenture holders' or debenture stockholders' security as part of its judgment, unless there is evidence that the company's liquid resources (ie cash and readily saleable investments) will suffice to satisfy the total amount payable to the debenture holders or debenture stockholders and the costs of the action. Initially the order for sale is made in general terms, and the receiver then negotiates piecemeal sales of the company's assets comprised in the security. If the security extends to the whole or substantially the whole of the company's assets and undertaking, the court may direct that the company's business undertaking and assets shall be sold as a going concern (if that is possible); the receiver must then apply to the court by summons for its approval of the terms of a sale which he is able to negotiate before entering into a contract with the purchaser. If the court initially orders that the receiver may sell the assets comprised in the security as he thinks fit, there is, of course, no need for the receiver to seek the court's approval for the terms which he negotiates for the sale of the company's business undertaking as a going concern, but he may nevertheless do so out of caution.

RECEIVERSHIPS

The purpose of a receivership

The primary functions of receivers are to take possession and control of, and to realise, the property and assets comprised in the security created for a loan to, or indebtedness of, the company which is entitled to those assets, or for the indebtedness of other companies in the same group, or of other companies or individuals, for whose benefit the company has created the security; to apply the net proceeds of realisation after meeting the incidental expenses in discharging the secured loan or indebtedness; and to return any surplus proceeds or unrealised assets to the company, which may then continue carrying on its undertaking, or go into liquidation if it is insolvent or has insufficient assets left to continue as a going concern.

14 *Re Crigglestone Coal Co* [1906] 1 Ch 523.

A receivership does not necessarily bring about the termination of the company's activities or its liquidation, although this will be the inevitable result if its assets realise insufficient to pay what is due to the secured creditors or holders of debentures or debenture stock, and they are unwilling to enter into an arrangement cancelling at least part of the amount owing to them, or deferring the date or dates on which the company's indebtedness to them becomes due for payment, or providing further funds to enable the company to continue in business. Even if the company's activities cease, however, it does not inevitably follow that its undertaking will be broken up and its assets sold piecemeal, for the receiver may be able to sell the company's undertaking or part of it as a going concern, and for this purpose he may be appointed manager of the company's undertaking to carry it on pending the negotiation of a contract for its sale, or so as to improve the company's financial position and effect a more beneficial sale.

In exceptional circumstances receivers have been able to discharge the company's indebtedness which they were appointed to recover by carrying on the company's business successfully and discharging that indebtedness out of the profits so realised or the income of the company's property or investments, or by doing this in combination with selling some of the company's assets. This is not the normal method of recovery, although if successful, it does produce the benefit that the company's business undertaking or a major part of it remains intact and will be returned to the management of its directors on the conclusion of the receivership.

The outcome of receiverships may therefore be very varied, ranging from the realisation of all the company's saleable assets as in a liquidation, to the preservation of the company's business undertaking as a going concern. The interest of the secured creditors for whose benefit the receiver is appointed is to be paid what is owed to them as quickly as possible, and the receiver and the trustees of any covering trust deed are usually under considerable pressure to see that this is done. Because of that, most receiverships result in the piecemeal sale of the company's assets fairly rapidly after the receiver is appointed, or occasionally, the sale of the whole or part of the company's business undertaking for cash.

Administrative and other receivers

The Insolvency Act 1986 makes a clear distinction between administrative receivers and other receivers (including those appointed by the court), and the Act confers statutory powers and imposes requirements on administrative receivers which do not apply to other receivers.

Definition

An administrative receiver is defined as a receiver or manager of the whole, or substantially the whole, of the property of a company who is appointed by or on behalf of the holders of any debentures or debenture stock of the company secured by a charge, which as created, was a floating charge, or by such a charge and one or more other securities.[15] Such a receiver may be appointed by the holder of a floating charge created by a debt security agreement entered into with a single lender or a few lenders (eg a loan agreement with a bank or a syndicate loan agreement with several banks) as well as by or on behalf of holders of debentures or debenture stock issued as a series; this is because the definition of a debenture is wide enough to include such debt security agreements.[16] A receiver appointed by the court is not an administrative receiver, even though he is appointed to realise a floating charge over the whole or substantially the whole of a company's property; this is because such a receiver is not appointed by or on behalf of the holders of the floating charge.[15] On the other hand, an administrative receiver may be appointed in respect of an unregistered company which the court may order to be wound up under the Insolvency Act 1986, or in respect of an overseas company,[17] provided that the receiver is appointed by or on behalf of the holders of the securities and they take the form of a floating charge over the whole, or substantially the whole, of the company's property, either with or without additional fixed charges.[15]

The floating charge created by a debt security agreement, or by debentures or by a trust deed executed to secure debenture stock, under which an administrative receiver is appointed, must be a general charge over the whole or substantially the whole of the company's assets and undertaking, if a receiver appointed under it or them is to be an administrative receiver; this is because a receiver can be appointed only in respect of the assets or classes of assets comprised in the security which he is appointed to enforce. However, under the definition of an administrative receiver, it is the range of assets which he is appointed to administer that determines his status, and so if under a floating charge over the whole or substantially the whole of a company's property and assets, a receiver is appointed to realise only a class or certain classes of the company's assets (eg

---

15 Insolvency Act 1986, s 29(2)(a).
16 Companies Act 1985, s 744; Insolvency Act 1986, s 251; *Levy v Abercorris Slate and Slab Co* (1887) 37 Ch D 260, 264 per Chitty J; *Knightsbridge Estates Trust Ltd v Byrne* [1940] AC 613, [1940] 2 All ER 401 (see *Pennington's Company Law* (7th edn) 560).
17 *Re International Bulk Commodities Ltd* [1992] BCLC 1074, [1992] BCC 463.

the company's book debts and other debts owing to it), he will not be an administrative receiver. On the other hand, if the instrument creating a floating charge also creates fixed or specific charges over certain assets or classes of assets of the company, and the floating charge is expressed to extend only to those of its other assets which are not subject to the fixed charges, a receiver appointed under both the fixed and the floating charges will be an administrative receiver, provided that the assets of which he is appointed receiver comprise in total the whole or substantially the whole of the company's property at that time.[18]

A receiver will also be an administrative receiver if he is prevented from qualifying as such under the above definition only by the fact that another person has been appointed to be a receiver of part of the company's property.[19] Consequently, the fact that a receiver has already been appointed of particular properties of a company, or of all its assets of a particular class (eg book debts), by another creditor who has a fixed or floating charge over that property or those assets, or who has been appointed by the court on his application, will not prevent the holder of a floating charge over the whole or substantially the whole of the company's assets (other than assets comprised in fixed charges vested in the same person) from appointing an administrative receiver of all the company's assets charged to him. This extension of the statutory definition of an administrative receiver does not apply, however, if a receiver has already been appointed by another creditor in respect of the whole or substantially the whole of the company's property, namely, an administrative receiver appointed by another creditor who is secured by a general floating charge over the whole or substantially the whole of the company's property, whether that other creditor's security ranks in priority or not. Consequently, there cannot be two or more concurrent appointments of administrative receivers by creditors secured by different general floating charges over the whole or substantially the whole of the same company's property; the first such receiver to be appointed will be the only administrative receiver, and an administrative receiver can be appointed by the holder of another floating charge only if the appointment of the administrative receiver currently holding office is terminated. If the person entitled to the other general floating charge ranks in priority for his charge over the floating charge under which the administrative receiver has been appointed,[20] he may apply to the court to remove

---

18 *Re Croftbell Ltd* [1990] BCLC 844, [1990] BCC 781.
19 Insolvency Act 1986, s 29(2)(*b*).
20 For the order of priority between two or more floating charges, see *Pennington's Company Law* (7th edn) 576, 654 to 659 and 691 to 695.

the administrative receiver,[1] and if the court so orders, he may then appoint his own nominee to be the administrative receiver. The mere appointment of his own nominee without the previous removal of the original administrative receiver by the court will not displace that receiver, however, because an administrative receiver can be removed only by the court, and the attempted appointment of the second administrative receiver would be invalid.[1]

Power to appoint an administrative receiver

The Insolvency Act 1986 does not confer power on the holder of a floating charge over the whole or substantially the whole of a company's property to appoint an administrative receiver if the company defaults on its obligations in the debt security agreement, debentures or trust deed in respect of debentures or debenture stock, or if any of the conditions or contingencies have occurred which make the floating charge enforceable by the terms of the instrument which created it. Consequently, the power to appoint an administrative receiver in those circumstances must be conferred expressly by the instrument creating the floating charge, or by an instrument which is supplemental to it, but it is not necessary for the power to be expressed to be one to appoint 'an administrative receiver' in those identical words, provided that it is a power to appoint a receiver of the whole or substantially the whole of the company's property under a floating charge, with or without other securities. This is a matter of importance as regards the appointment of administrative receivers under powers to appoint a receiver of a company's whole assets and undertaking conferred by an instrument executed before the Insolvency Act 1986 came into force on 29 December 1986, because the term 'administrative receiver' had no technical meaning before that date. Conversely, the fact that an instrument confers a power to appoint an administrative receiver, or that an appointment purports to be the appointment of an administrative receiver, will not give an appointee the status of an administrative receiver, unless he is effectively appointed to be a receiver of the whole or substantially the whole of the company's property under a floating charge, or under such a charge together with one of more other securities.[2]

If two or more persons are appointed by the same holder or holders of securities to be administrative receivers of the property of a company, the instrument of appointment must state whether any act required or authorised by any enactment to be done by an

1 Insolvency Act 1986, s 45(1).
2 Ibid, s 29(2)(*a*).

administrative receiver is to be done by all, or by any one or more, of the persons who for the time being are administrative receivers of the company.[3] Administrative receivers may therefore be appointed to act jointly or individually, or certain of their powers may be made exercisable only jointly with the concurrence of them all, whilst other powers may be made exercisable by them individually. It is not essential than the instrument appointing administrative receivers should state whether powers conferred on them by an instrument (eg an extension of an administrative receiver's statutory powers conferred by a debt security agreement, or by debentures, or by a trust deed covering debentures or debenture stock) shall be exercisable individually or jointly by the receivers, but for clarity it is desirable that the instrument of appointment or the debt security agreement should do so.

The acts of an administrative receiver are valid notwithstanding any defect in his appointment or qualifications,[4] and so a person who deals with him in good faith, even though aware of such a defect, is fully protected. It would seem by analogy with the similar statutory provision in respect of the acts of directors who are defectively appointed,[5] that even directors or officers of a company who deal with its administrative receiver may rely on the statutory validation of his acts, despite any defect in his appointment or qualifications.[6]

Qualification and status as an agent of the company

An administrative receiver, like a liquidator or administrator must be qualified to act as an insolvency practitioner, and a person (other than the official receiver) who acts as an administrative receiver without being so qualified commits a criminal offence.[7] The appointment of a person who is not a qualified insolvency practitioner is void,[7] and so is ineffective to cause the floating charge in respect of which he is appointed to crystallise or to become a fixed or specific charge under a provision to that effect in the debt security agreement, debenture or covering trust deed. A receiver or manager other than an administrative receiver, whether appointed by the court or out of court under the terms of a debt security agreement, debentures or a trust deed covering an issue of debentures debenture stock, is not required by law to be qualified to act as an insolvency practitioner.

---

3 Ibid, s 231(1) and (2).
4 Ibid, s 232.
5 Companies Act 1985, s 285.
6 *Dawson v African Consolidated Land Trading Co* [1898] 1 Ch 6.
7 Insolvency Act 1986, s 230(2), s 388(1) and s 389(1) and (2).

An administrative receiver is deemed to be the agent of the company, unless and until it goes into liquidation,[8] and so the debt security holder, or debenture holders or debenture stockholders or trustees for them who appoint an administrative receiver are not responsible for his acts or defaults unless they participate in them actively.[9] Because an administrative receiver is treated by law as being an agent of the company until a winding up order is made in respect of it or a winding up resolution is passed by a general meeting of its members, it is unnecessary for the instrument creating the floating charge under which he is appointed to provide expressly that he shall be deemed to be the company's agent. Consequently, contracts made by an administrative receiver and acts done by him in the course of his receivership are automatically binding on the company as his principal,[10] and losses caused by his acts or defaults are attributed to the company, but without prejudice to its right to recover damages from him if he acts dishonestly or without proper skill and care.[11] The fact that an administrative receiver ceases to be an agent of the company when it goes into liquidation does not prevent him from continuing to exercise his powers in order to carry out his receivership,[12] and he does not become the agent of the persons who appointed him so as to make them responsible for his acts or defaults in doing so.[13] In these respects the rules relating to administrative receivers are the same as those relating to receivers of assets of a company who are not administrative receivers.

Powers and functions

The Insolvency Act 1986 confers the same powers on an administrative receiver for the fulfilment of his functions as the Act confers on an administrator appointed by the court when an administration order is made by the court in respect of a company.[14] These powers may be diminished or supplemented by the terms of the security agreement, or by the terms of the debentures or the trust deed in respect of debentures or debenture stock, under which the receiver is appointed,[14] but a person who deals with an administrative

---

8 Ibid, s 44(1)(*a*).
9 *Re B Johnson and Co (Builders) Ltd* [1955] Ch 634, [1955] 2 All ER 775.
10 *Central London Electricity Ltd v Berners* [1945] 1 All ER 160.
11 *Standard Chartered Bank Ltd v Walker* [1982] 3 All ER 938, [1982] 1 WLR 1410; *American Express International Banking Corpn v Hurley* [1985] 3 All ER 564, [1986] BCLC 52.
12 *Sowman v David Samuel Trust Ltd* [1978] 1 All ER 616, [1978] 1 WLR 22.
13 *Gosling v Gaskell* [1897] AC 575.
14 Insolvency Act 1986, s 42(1) and (2) and Sch 1. For an administrator's powers, see p 369, ante.

receiver in good faith is not concerned to inquire whether he is acting within his powers.[15] It is, of course, no longer necessary to confer these powers expressly on an administrative receiver, because they are now vested in him by law in the absence of a contrary provision.[14]

Although the powers of an administrative receiver are the same as those of an administrator, subject to any variation made by the instrument under which the administrative receiver is appointed, their functions are entirely different. An administrative receiver is appointed to recover the secured debt by realising the company's assets, and he may carry on the company's business or part of it temporarily for the purpose of recovering (with the proceeds of sale of the company's business undertaking, if it is sold) sufficient to pay the amount owed to the secured creditors for whose benefit he was appointed; he would act improperly and would incur liability to those secured creditors if he exercised his powers, as an administrator might exercise them, with a view to ensuring the survival of the company's business undertaking, even at the expense of the secured creditors going wholly or partly unpaid. Such an attempt should be made by an administrative receiver only with the consent of the secured creditors by or for whose benefit he was appointed, or if there are numerous secured creditors, such as debenture holders or debenture stockholders of the same class, with the approval of a meeting of those creditors held under the provisions of the instrument by which the security was created and which facilitate such departures from the receiver's normal duties.[16]

The powers conferred on administrative receivers by the Insolvency Act 1986 consist mostly of the powers which traditionally were expressly conferred on receivers appointed under instruments creating floating charges over a company's whole undertaking and assets before the Insolvency Act 1986 came into force. The statutory powers of an administrative receiver which call for special mention are the following, namely: power to use the company's seal to execute deeds and other sealed documents in its name and on its behalf;[17] (so dispensing with the need for the instrument creating the floating charge under which the receiver is appointed to contain an irrevocable power of attorney in favour of such a receiver); power to do all such things (including the carrying out of construction works) as may be necessary for the realisation of the assets of the company;[18] power to carry on the business of the company (presumably, only for the purpose of realising it by selling it as a going concern, or

15 Ibid, s 42(3).
16 See p 466, ante.
17 Insolvency Act 1986, Sch 1, para 8.
18 Ibid, Sch 1, para 12.

discharging the secured debt out of the profits generated by the business);[19] power to establish subsidiaries of the company, and to transfer the whole or parts of the company's undertaking or the whole or parts of its property to any of its subsidiaries, whether formed by the receiver or not, and to sell or otherwise dispose of shares in its subsidiaries held by the company;[20] power to call up any share capital of the company which has not previously been called up;[1] and power to petition the court to order the winding up of the company.[2] The statutory powers of an administrative receiver are similar to those of a liquidator,[3] but are more extensive in that an administrative receiver (unlike a liquidator) has a statutory power to carry on the company's business generally (and not only for the purpose of winding up the company), and power to form subsidiaries of the company or to transfer the whole or part of the company's business or property to any one or more of its subsidiaries.

Application of the rules relating to receivers

Administrative receivers are a particular species of receiver, and not a distinct category of corporate officers or functionaries, despite the fact that special and distinctive rules in the Insolvency Act 1986 govern them. Because administrative receivers are members of the same category as receivers of other kinds, the general rules of law which apply to receivers appointed out of court under powers conferred by an instrument apply to administrative receivers, except so far as those rules are inconsistent with the special statutory rules governing them. In the following account of receiverships, therefore, administrative receivers and other receivers will be dealt with together, and exceptions from the general rules as they apply to administrative receivers will be pointed out in the context of those rules, and the special rules which apply only to administrative receivers will be presented within the framework of the general law.

Disqualifications for appointment as receiver or manager

A corporation cannot be appointed to be the receiver of property of a company either by the court, or by secured creditors or by debenture holders or debenture stockholders or by trustees for them

19 Ibid, Sch 1, para 14.
20 Ibid, Sch 1, paras 2, 15 and 16.
 1 Ibid, Sch 1, para 19.
 2 Ibid, Sch 1, para 21.
 3 Ibid, s 165(1) to (3) and s 167(1) and Sch 4 (see p 145 to 149, ante).

acting under powers conferred by an instrument.[4] A company cannot be the receiver of another company's property, but there seems to be nothing to prevent it from being appointed the manager of another company's business, provided that a receiver who is an individual is also appointed.[5] The prohibition on corporate receivers also extends to the appointment of a corporation to be the receiver of the income of property mortgaged by a company where the mortgagee makes the appointment under the power conferred by the Law of Property Act 1925.[6] The appointment of a corporation to be a receiver is absolutely void, so that not only will the appointee be unable to act,[7] but the appointment will also be ineffective to cause a floating charge to crystallise or to bring into operation any of the statutory rules which apply when a company goes into receivership. The prohibition on corporate receivers applies to administrative receivers, although the prohibition is superfluous so far as they are concerned, because administrative receivers must be qualified insolvency practitioners,[8] and such practitioners must be individuals.[9]

An undischarged bankrupt commits an offence if he acts as receiver or manager of the property of a company, unless he is appointed by the court.[10] The appointment of an undischarged bankrupt as a receiver or manager under powers conferred by a debt security agreement, or by debentures or a trust deed covering debenture stock, is not void, however, and so it would be effective to cause a floating charge to crystallise. The same applies to the appointment of a bankrupt as a receiver of the income of property mortgaged by a company.[11] Furthermore, the fact that a receiver or manager becomes bankrupt after he is appointed does not terminate his appointment or bring the receivership to an end. But if a receiver were bankrupt when appointed, or subsequently became bankrupt, the court would undoubtedly restrain him from acting at the request of any interested person, and would remove him from office. The appointment of a bankrupt to be an administrative receiver of a

---

4 Insolvency Act 1986, s 30.
5 In practice the court always appoints individuals to be managers.
6 Law of Property Act 1925, s 109(1); *Portman Building Society v Gallwey* [1955] 1 All ER 227, [1955] 1 WLR 96.
7 A company is liable to a fine if it does act as a receiver of another company's property (Insolvency Act 1986, s 30).
8 Insolvency Act 1986, s 230(2).
9 Ibid, s 390(1).
10 Ibid, s 31. In practice the court would not appoint a bankrupt to be a receiver or manager.
11 Law of Property Act 1925, s 109(1).

company's property is void, and such a receiver who becomes bankrupt automatically ceases to hold office. This is because an administrative receiver must be a qualified insolvency practitioner,[8] and a person who is in other respects qualified to act as an insolvency practitioner ceases to be qualified if he is adjudged bankrupt.[12]

If the court makes a disqualification order against a person under the Company Directors' Disqualification Act 1986,[13] the appointment of that person to be a receiver or manager of any property of a company is void if made during the period of disqualification, unless the appointment is made with leave of the court, and if a disqualification order is made against a receiver or manager who has already been appointed, it operates to terminate his appointment.[14] This provision applies to administrative receivers in the same way as to other receivers, and in respect of the former is reinforced by a provision in the Insolvency Act 1986, which disqualifies a person from acting as an insolvency practitioner if a disqualification order is made against him under the Company Directors' Disqualification Act 1986.[15]

Notification and publicity in respect of a receivership

A person who obtains an order of the court appointing a receiver or manager of any property of a company, or who appoints a receiver out of court under powers conferred by debt security agreement, debentures, or a trust deed covering an issue of debentures or debenture stock, or under powers conferred by the Law of Property Act 1925,[16] must notify the Registrar of Companies within seven days from the date of the court's order or the appointment out of court, and the Registrar must file the notification of the appointment in the register of charges over the property and assets of companies which he keeps.[17]

When a receiver or manager of the property of a company has been appointed, every invoice, order for goods or business letter issued or sent out by or on behalf of the company, or by the receiver or manager, or by the liquidator of the company, must, if the

---

12 Insolvency Act 1986, s 390(4)(*a*).
13 Company Directors' Disqualification Act 1986, ss 2 to 6 and s 8 (see *Pennington's Company Law* (7th edn) 717 to 723.
14 Company Directors' Disqualification Act 1986, s 1(1).
15 Insolvency Act 1986, s 390(4)(*b*).
16 Law of Property Act 1925, s 109(1).
17 Companies Act 1985, s 405(1). For the register of charges created by a company, see *Pennington's Company law* (7th edn) pp 635 to 662.

company's name appears in it, contain a statement that a receiver or manager has been appointed.[18]

When an administrative receiver is appointed, he must forthwith notify the company of his appointment, and must advertise it in the London Gazette and a newspaper which he thinks appropriate to ensure that it comes to the notice of the company's creditors.[19] Within 28 days after his appointment, an administrative receiver must send a notice of it to all the creditors of the company of whose addresses he is aware, unless the court otherwise orders.[20] The notices of his appointment sent by an administrative receiver to the company and to its creditors and the advertisements of his appointment must state the registered name of the company and any other name with which it has been registered within the preceding 12 months, any name other than its currently registered name in which the company has traded during that 12 months, the name, address and date of appointment of the administrative receiver and the name of the person who appointed him, and the date of the debt security agreement, debentures or trust deed securing debenture stock which conferred power to appoint the receiver and a brief description of that instrument and of the assets of the company (if any) to which the receiver's appointment does not extend.[1]

Statement of affairs in an administrative receivership; report on directors' conduct

An administrative receiver must on his appointment require the present and former directors and officers of the company, persons who have taken part in the company's formation within one year before his appointment, and persons who are or have within that year been employees of the company, or directors or officers of another company which is or has within that time been a director or officer of the company, or some of such persons who can provide the necessary information, to make out and submit to the administrative receiver a statement of the company's affairs in the prescribed form, setting out particulars of the company's assets, debts and liabilities, the names and addresses of its creditors and any securities held by them respectively with the dates of such securities, particulars of the preferential creditors of the company[2] and debts of the company

18 Insolvency Act 1986, s 39(1).
19 Ibid, s 46(1); Insolvency Rules 1986, r 3.2(1) and (3).
20 Insolvency Act 1986, s 46(1).
 1 Insolvency Rules 1986, r 3.2(2) and (4).
 2 For preferential claims on the crystallisation of a floating charge, see p 303 et seq, ante.

secured by floating charges, a statement of the company's issued and called up share capital and an estimate of the excess or deficiency of the company's assets to satisfy its preferential debts, its debts secured by floating charges and its creditors generally.[3] The persons whom the administrative receiver requires to submit a statement of the company's affairs must submit such a statement to him verified by affidavit within 21 days or within such longer period as he permits.[4] The administrative receiver may require any of the persons whom he could require to submit a statement of affairs to submit instead affidavits concurring in the statement of affairs by other persons, and such affidavits may be qualified if the deponent does not concur in all the statements contained in the statement of affairs.[5] The administrative receiver must pay out of the assets of the company in his hands any reasonable expenses incurred by the deponents in making the statement of affairs.[6]

The administrative receiver must within three months after his appointment or such longer period as the court allows, send to the Registrar of Companies, to persons who are trustees for secured creditors of the company (including the trustees of trust deeds other than the one under which the administrative receiver was appointed) and to all secured creditors of the company of whose addresses he is aware, copies of a report by the administrative receiver which summarises the statement of affairs submitted to him and his comments on it, and which sets out the events leading to the appointment of the administrative receiver, particulars of disposals or intended disposals by him of property of the company and of the carrying on or intended carrying on by him of the company's business, a statement of the principal and interest payable to the secured lenders or to the debenture holders or debenture stockholders by or on behalf of whom the receiver was appointed, a statement of the amounts payable to the company's preferential creditors and the amount (if any) which is likely to be available to pay its other creditors.[7] The administrative receiver must additionally within three months after his appointment send copies of his report (including a summary of the statement of affairs submitted to him and his comments on it) to all unsecured creditors of the company of whose addresses he is aware, or alternatively, he must publish in the newspaper in which his appointment was advertised a notice of

---

3 Insolvency Act 1986, s 47(1) to (3); Insolvency Rules 1986, r 3.4(1) and Form 3.2.
4 Insolvency Act 1986, s 47(4) and (5); Insolvency Rules 1986, r 3.4(1) and (4).
5 Insolvency Rules 1986, r 3.4(2) and (3).
6 Ibid, r 3.7(1).
7 Insolvency Act 1986, s 48(1) and (5).

an address to which unsecured creditors may apply for a copy of his report to be sent to them free of charge.[8]

The administrative receiver must, unless the court otherwise orders, call a meeting of the company's unsecured creditors to be held within three months after his appointment, and he must lay before the meeting a copy of his report (including a summary of the statement of affairs and his comments on it).[9] The copy of the administrative receiver's report which he sends to the Registrar of Companies is open to inspection by any member of the public,[10] but if the administrative receiver considers that disclosure of the whole or any part of the statement of affairs or of his report would prejudice the conduct of the receivership, he may apply to the court for an order that the copy of the statement of affairs or the receiver's report filed at the Companies Registry, or part of it, shall not be available for public inspection.[11]

An administrative receiver must furthermore submit to the Secretary of State for Trade and Industry a report on persons who are or have been directors or shadow directors of the company at the date of the receiver's appointment or within three years beforehand in the same circumstances and for the same purposes as the liquidator of a company in voluntary liquidation must do so.[12]

Removal and resignation of a receiver or manager and new appointments

The court may remove a receiver appointed by it, or a receiver appointed under the provisions of a security agreement or of debentures or a trust deed covering debentures or debenture stock, and may appoint another person to be the receiver in his stead.[13] The court will be particularly ready to do this if the original receiver has not diligently sought to protect and enforce the rights of the secured creditors on whose behalf he was appointed.[14] A receiver or manager appointed out of court under the terms of an instrument (other than an administrative

---

8 Ibid, s 48(2); Insolvency Rules 1986, r 3.8(1).

9 Insolvency Act 1986, s 48(2).

10 Companies Act 1985, s 709(1) (substituted by Companies Act 1989, s 126(2)).

11 Insolvency Rules 1986, r 3.5(1) to (3) and r 3.8(3).

12 Company Directors' Disqualification Act 1986, s 7(3); Insolvent Companies (Reports on Conduct of Directors) Rules 1996 (SI 1996/1909), r 3(1) and (2) and r 4(1) and (2) and Schedule Forms D7, 2 and 3 (see p 186, ante).

13 *Mitchell v Condy* [1873] WN 232; *Re Slogger Automatic Feeder Co Ltd* [1915] 1 Ch 478.

14 *Re Maskelyne British Typewriter Ltd* [1898] 1 Ch 133.

receiver) may also be removed and replaced in accordance with that instrument by the persons empowered by it to do so (eg the secured lender who appointed the receiver, or the trustees of a trust deed covering debentures or debenture stock), but an administrative receiver may be removed only by an order of the court.[15]

A receiver or manager appointed out of court may resign his appointment and the receivership therefore terminates. However, a receiver or manager appointed by the court may resign only with leave of the court.[16] An administrative receiver may resign by giving seven days' notice of resignation to the person or persons who appointed him, to the company and its liquidator (if any) and to the members of the creditors' committee (if any).[17] An administrative receiver who completes the administration of the company's assets comprised in the receivership is (it appears) taken to resign automatically, and he must give notice of his implied resignation accordingly, but not necessarily to the person or persons who appointed him.[18] It would be more practical in these circumstances if the administrative receiver were required to give notice of the conclusion of the receivership, and if the termination of his receivership were to take effect from the notice being given. A receiver or manager ceases to hold office if a disqualification order is made against him by the court, unless the court gives leave for him to continue to act.[19] Additionally, an administrative receiver vacates office if he ceases to be qualified to act as an insolvency practitioner.[20] The appointment of a successor to a receiver, manager or administrative receiver who has ceased to hold office is made in the same way as the original appointment.

A receiver or manager appointed under powers conferred by an instrument must notify the Registrar of Companies when he ceases to act,[1] and if a new receiver or manager is appointed in his place, whether by the court or otherwise, the person who appoints him, or who obtains an order of the court appointing him, must also notify the Registrar of the appointment.[2] An administrative receiver who vacates office must notify that fact to the Registrar of Companies within 14 days.[3] When his successor is appointed it is not necessary

15 Insolvency Act 1986, s 45(1).
16 An application is made to the court by the receiver by summons in the action in which the receiver was appointed.
17 Insolvency Rules 1986, r 3.33(1). For the creditors' committee, see p 525, post.
18 Ibid, r 3.35(1).
19 Company Directors' Disqualification Act 1986, s 1(1).
20 Insolvency Act 1986, s 45(2).
 1 Companies Act 1985, s 405(2).
 2 Ibid, s 405(1).
 3 Insolvency Act 1986, s 45(4).

for a further statement of affairs to be submitted to the new receiver if a statement has already been submitted to his predecessor.[4]

There are no statutory provisions, corresponding to those in a liquidation,[5] by which an administrative or other receiver appointed otherwise than by the court may obtain his release from liability for breaches of duty by him during his receivership. In the absence of provisions for that purpose in the debt security agreement or in the debentures or the covering trust deed under which he was appointed, he will remain liable for such breaches of duty until the expiration of the applicable limitation period. A receiver or manager appointed by the court may be discharged from acting as such by order of the court (eg on completion of the receivership), and the court may order that he shall be released from liability to the persons for whose benefit he was appointed.[16]

Duties of receivers and managers to the company

A receiver, whether appointed by the court or under a power contained in a debt security agreement, debentures or a trust deed covering an issue of debenture or debenture stock, owes a duty to the company and to holders of later ranking charges and securities to exercise his powers honestly and with reasonable skill and care.[6] Consequently, he is liable in damages to the company and to the holders of such securities if he causes the company or such security holders loss by deliberate wrongdoing or by his negligence, for example, by realising its assets too rapidly without seeking alternative offers, or by realising them in temporarily adverse circumstances, so that a substantially reduced amount is obtained for the company's assets than would have been obtained on an arms' length sale in the market for the assets in question.[6] The loss suffered by the company which it can recover from the receiver is the difference between the full saleable value of the assets sold by the receiver and the lower amount which he actually realised, a proper allowance being made for the costs of realisation. If a claim against the receiver is made by a secured creditor whose security ranks after that in respect of which the receiver was appointed, the recoverable loss will be at most the

---

4 Ibid, s 46(2).
5 See pp 197 and 201, ante.
6 *Standard Chartered Bank Ltd v Walker* [1982] 3 All ER 938, [1982] 1 WLR 1410; *American Express International Banking Corpn v Hurley* [1985] 3 All ER 564, [1986] BCLC 52; *Downsview Nominees Ltd v First City Corpn Ltd* [1994] 1 BCLC 49, [1993] BCC 46.

same as for the company's claim but will be restricted to the part of that amount which would have been available to pay the later ranking secured creditor's debt if the receiver had sold the assets for their full value, bearing in mind that that amount owed to the secured creditor for whose benefit the receiver was appointed would have to be paid first. The receiver's duty to act honestly and with care is also owed to guarantors of the secured debt which he was appointed to recover, and if the duty is not fulfilled, they may recover from him as damages the loss which they suffer as a result of their personal liability to the secured creditors being increased by the shortfall in the proceeds of sale of the company's assets.[7] Presumably a manager is under a similar duty to act honestly and with reasonable skill and care in managing the company's business.

In only two cases has it been held that a receiver's duty to the company and the holders of later ranking securities is limited to acting in good faith for the purpose of realising the company's assets comprised in the receivership as beneficially as possible for the benefit of the secured creditor for whose benefit the receiver was appointed.[8] In one of these cases, however, the liability of a receiver to pay damages or compensation was not in question,[9] and in the other case the conduct for which the receiver was held liable was not designed to achieve the proper realisation of the company's assets, but to carry on the business activities of the company after it had ceased to be a viable concern, so that the receiver would inevitably have been found guilty of negligence if the court had ruled it to be ground of liability.[10]

Although a receiver owes a duty to the company to realise its assets at the best price reasonably obtainable, the company and its directors are not entitled to impede him from fulfilling his functions by arranging for the disposal of the company's assets in a way which they allege will realise a higher price than the receiver is likely to obtain.[11] The court will restrain a receiver from proceeding with a sale or disposal which he has negotiated only if the company or its directors tender the amount required to discharge the security under which the receiver was appointed, or if the proceeds of realisation of the company's assets already in the receiver's hands are sufficient for that purpose, and in either case the amount

---

7 *Standard Chartered Bank Ltd v Walker*, supra (overruling *Latchford v Beirne* [1981] 3 All ER 705).
8 *Rottenberg v Monjack* [1993] BCLC 374, [1992] BCC 688; *Downsview Nominees Ltd v First City Corpn Ltd*, supra.
9 *Rottenberg v Monjack*, supra.
10 *Downsview Nominees Ltd v First City Corpn Ltd*, supra.
11 *Gomba Holdings UK Ltd v Homan* [1986] 3 All ER 94, [1986] 1 WLR 1301; *Downsview Nominees Ltd v First City Corpn Ltd*, supra.

available will also be sufficient to indemnify the receiver and the trustees for the security holders for costs and expenses properly incurred by them.[11]

If a secured lender, debenture holder or trustees for debenture holders or debenture stockholders instruct the receiver or manager to act in a way which involves a breach of his duties to the company and he does so, they too are vicariously liable for the loss which he causes to the company and to its other security holders; if the instructions were given by the persons beneficially entitled to the secured debt or the debentures or debenture stock, the company may recover the loss by setting its amount off against the secured debt to which they are entitled, and guarantors of that debt are correspondingly relieved from personal liability.[6] If a receiver or manager incurs personal liability to the company by causing it loss deliberately or negligently, it would appear that by analogy with the position of agents[12] and trustees,[13] he cannot claim an indemnity out of the company's assets subject to the charge created by the debt security agreement, or by the debentures or covering trust deed, or from the debenture holders or debenture stockholders or their trustees.

ASSETS AND LIABILITIES IN A RECEIVERSHIP

Assets

The extent of the assets

The assets and property of a company which a receiver may realise are the assets comprised in the fixed mortgage or charge or the floating charge in respect of which he is appointed at the time of his appointment. Additionally, if the charge is a floating charge, the charge extends by implication to assets acquired by the company after the receiver's appointment which are within the class or classes of assets comprised in the floating charge.[14] This includes the company's assets caught by a floating charge over the whole of its assets and undertaking, but not, it would seem, assets acquired by the company after the commencement of its liquidation; on that

---

12 *Lewis v Samuel* (1846) 8 QB 685; *Duncan v Hill* (1873) LR 8 Exch 242; *Lage v Siemens Bros & Co Ltd* (1932) 42 Ll L Rep 252.

13 *Benett v Wyndham* (1862) 4 De GF & J 259; *Re Raybould, Raybould v Turner* [1900] 1 Ch 199; *Ecclesiastical Comrs v Pinney* [1900] 2 Ch 736.

14 *N W Robbie & Co Ltd v Witney Warehouse Co Ltd* [1963] 3 All ER 613, [1963] 1 WLR 1324; *Business Computers Ltd v Anglo-African Leasing Ltd* [1977] 2 All ER 741, [1977] 1 WLR 578.

happening, the company's assets are held in trust to discharge the amounts which it owes to its unsecured creditors, subject only to mortgages and charges which have already attached specifically to its assets.[15] Moreover, if the company is already in liquidation or is wound up after the receiver's appointment, the floating charge under which he was appointed will not extend to assets recovered by the liquidator under statutory provisions intended to protect or benefit unsecured creditors of the company,[16] such as the provisions by which the liquidator may recover assets which the company has disposed of at a significant undervalue, or assets which the company has paid, transferred or charged by a voidable preference,[17] or compensation recovered by the liquidator from directors or others who have carried on the company's business by way of fraudulent or wrongful trading.[18] It would seem that if a company creates a fixed or specific charge over a class of its assets, including assets of that class which the company acquires in the future (eg present and future book debts), the charge will extend to assets of that class which the company acquires after the receiver is appointed, but not to assets acquired after the company goes into liquidation.[15]

Recovery of assets by the receiver

Debt security agreements, debentures and trust deeds covering issues of debentures or debenture stock which confer power to appoint a receiver, always empower the receiver to take possession and to dispose of all assets of the company which are comprised in the security,[19] and for that purpose and also for the purpose of enforcing rights of action which the company has against other persons, the receiver is empowered to bring actions in the company's name. This power is undoubtedly valid,[20] and may be used by the

---

15 *IRC v Olive Mill Spinners Ltd* [1963] 2 All ER 130, [1963] 1 WLR 712; *Pritchard v M H Builders (Wilmslow) Ltd* [1969] 2 All ER 670, [1969] 1 WLR 409; *Ayerst v C & K (Construction) Ltd* [1976] AC 167, [1975] 2 All ER 537.

16 *Willmott v London Celluloid Co* (1886) 31 Ch D 425; *Re Yagerphone Ltd* [1935] Ch 392; *Re Oasis Merchandising Services Ltd* [1995] 2 BCLC 493, [1995] BCC 911; *Re Ayala Holdings Ltd (No 2)* [1996] 1 BCLC 467.

17 Insolvency Act 1986, ss 238, 239 and 423 (see p 221, et seq, ante).

18 Ibid, s 213(1) and (2) and s 214(1) and (2)(see p 253, ante).

19 A receiver is not entitled to possession of the books and records which the company is required to keep under the Companies Act 1985, nor to other books and records which relate exclusively to the management of the company's affairs and not to the company's title to assets comprised in the debenture holders' security (*Engel v South Metropolitan Brewing and Bottling Co* [1892] 1 Ch 442; *Gomba Holdings UK Ltd v Minories Finance Ltd* [1989] 1 All ER 261, [1989] BCLC 115).

20 *M Wheeler & Co Ltd v Warren* [1928] Ch 840.

receiver to obtain possession of the company's tangible assets which are under the control of its officers or other persons, and also to obtain payment of debts owed to the company. It has been held that in exercise of such a power a receiver may continue an action brought in the company's name after it commences to be wound up,[1] but it has been doubted whether he may institute new actions after the commencement of the winding up.[2] An administrative receiver has full powers to obtain possession of the assets of the company to which he is appointed and to bring or defend actions in the company's name, subject to any restrictions imposed by the instrument under which he was appointed,[3] and these powers are exercisable whether the company is in liquidation or not.

A receiver or manager appointed by the court may be empowered by it to bring an action in the company's name in order to enforce or realise the security in respect of which he was appointed.[4] Any interested person may apply to the court for an order directing the receiver to bring such an action, even against the person who obtained his appointment.[4] If the assets which the receiver wishes to recover are under the control of the company's officers or agents, however, it is not necessary for him to bring an action against them. The judgment in the action in which the receiver was appointed will require the company to deliver its assets to the receiver, and so all that is necessary for the receiver to recover such assets is for the plaintiff in the action to initiate the appropriate process to enforce the court's order against the company,[5] or to apply for the committal of the company's officers for contempt of court in failing to make delivery.[6]

An administrative receiver has the same power as a liquidator to apply to the court summarily for an order directing any person who has in his possession or control any property, books, papers or records to which the company appears to be entitled, to pay, deliver, transfer or surrender that property etc to the receiver.[7] Additionally, present and former directors, officers and employees of the company, or of any other company which has been a director or officer of the

---

1 *Gough's Garages Ltd v Pugsley* [1930] 1 KB 615.
2 *Re Henry Pound, Son and Hutchins Ltd* (1889) 42 Ch D 402 at 421 per Cotton LJ. If this were correct, the receiver could apply to the court for a direction that the liquidator should sue in the company's name for the benefit of the secured creditors on whose behalf the receiver was appointed (Insolvency Act 1986, s 112(1) and (2), s 167(3) and s 168(5)).
3 Insolvency Act 1986, s 42(1) and (2) and Sch 1, paras 1 and 5.
4 *Viola v Anglo-American Cold Storage Co* [1912] 2 Ch 305.
5 *Hawkes v Holland* [1881] WN 128.
6 RSC Ord 45, r 5(1).
7 Insolvency Act 1986, s 234(1) and (2); (see p 210, ante).

company, are under an obligation to give to an administrative receiver such information about the company and its business, dealings, affairs or property as the receiver reasonably requires.[8] Furthermore, if an administrative receiver finds it necessary for the purposes of his receivership, he may apply summarily to the court for an order that any director or officer of the company, or any person known or suspected to have any property of the company in his possession or to be indebted to it, or any person who is able to give information about the promotion, formation, business, dealings, affairs or property of the company, to attend the court for examination, or to submit to the court an affidavit setting out relevant information which he has.[9] This provision is the same as that which enables a liquidator to apply to the court to examine any such person, and is subject to the same rules and limitations.[10]

Uncalled and unpaid share capital

If the secured debt, debentures or debenture stock in respect of which a receiver is appointed is or are secured on the uncalled share capital of the company, a receiver cannot make calls on the shareholders on his own initiative,[11] unless he is an administrative receiver,[12] nor despite an obiter dictum to the contrary,[13] does it appear that the court may authorise a receiver who is not an administrative receiver to do so. The practice where the receiver has been appointed by the court is for the court to order the directors, or if the company is being wound up, the liquidator,[14] to make the appropriate call and to deliver the proceeds of it to the receiver,[15] and if any shareholders do not pay the call, the court may authorise the receiver to sue them in the company's name.[16]

If a call has been made by the directors or liquidator before the receiver is appointed by the court, it may authorise him to sue for it in the company's name in the same way as it may authorise him to

---

8 Ibid, s 235(1) to (3).
9 Ibid, s 236(1) to (3).
10 See p 178, ante.
11 Unless the articles of association authorise the directors to delegate their power to make calls and they have conferred the power on the receiver by the terms of the security (see Table A, art. 71 of the Companies (Tables A to F) Regulations 1985 (SI 1985/805)).
12 Insolvency Act 1986, s 42(1) and (2) and Sch 1, para 19.
13 *Re Phoenix Bessemer Steel Co* (1875) 44 LJ Ch 683 at 695 per Jessel MR.
14 An application for an order against the liquidator must be made in the winding up proceedings, and not in the action in which the receiver was appointed (*Fowler v Broad's Patent Night Light Co* [1893] 1 Ch 724).
15 *Fowler v Broad's Patent Night Light Co*, supra; *Sadler v Worley* [1894] 2 Ch 170.
16 *Re Westminster Syndicate Ltd* (1908) 99 LT 924.

sue for any other debt owed to the company. Likewise, the debt security agreement, debentures or trust deed covering debentures or debenture stock may empower a receiver to sue shareholders for unpaid capital which has fallen due for payment in the same way as those instruments may authorise a receiver to sue for debts owed to the company.[17] An administrative receiver can, of course, exercise his power to sue in the company's name[18] in order to recover unpaid amounts of share capital, whether comprised in calls made by the company's directors or liquidator or falling due for payment by the terms of issue of the shares.

The rights and interests of third persons

A receiver appointed by the court or out of court under a floating or a fixed or specific charge created by a debt security agreement, debentures or a trust deed covering an issue of debentures or debenture stock, takes the assets of the company in the same condition and subject to the same encumbrances and obligations in favour of third persons and the same rights of such persons as the company holds those assets itself, except so far as the secured creditor or debenture holders or debenture stockholders have rights which rank in priority to those matters under the general law.[19]

Retention of title agreements

If a company has purchased goods on terms that ownership shall remain vested in the seller until they are paid for, and the company is not authorised by the seller to re-sell or dispose of the goods, until that happens, the receiver and the security holders on whose behalf he was appointed cannot resist a claim by the seller for the return of goods which the company has neither paid for nor sold, nor a claim by the seller to the proceeds of sale of goods which the company has sold without the seller's authorisation, and therefore wrongfully.[20] If the terms of sale reserve the ownership of the goods to the unpaid seller, he may recover them in specie from the company or the

---

17 *M Wheeler & Co Ltd v Warren* [1928] Ch 840.
18 Insolvency Act 1986, s 42(1) and (2) and Sch 1, para 5.
19 See *Pennington's Company Law* (7th edn) 569 to 584, 648 and 649 and 653 to 659.
20 *Aluminium Industrie Vaassen BV v Romalpa Aluminium Ltd* [1976] 2 All ER 552, [1976] 1 WLR 676; *Clough Mill Ltd v Martin* [1984] 3 All ER 982, [1985] 1 WLR 111; *Armour v Thyssen Edelstahlwerke AG* [1991] 2 AC 339, [1990] 3 All ER 481.

receiver, even though they have been attached to or made a component of other products, provided they can be identified and physically separated from those other products (eg diesel engines bolted to the other components of electricity generating machinery).[1] But the unpaid seller can claim the return of goods supplied by him only if they are still identifiable and are substantially unchanged, and he cannot claim to be the owner of products which the company has manufactured by combining the goods in question with other goods, or by subjecting the goods in question to processing; this is so whether or not the seller's retained ownership of the original goods is expressed to extend to the resulting products as well.[2] Although an unpaid seller who has retained the ownership of goods until they are paid for has an absolute right to them at common law, the court may exercise a discretion in equity not to issue an injunction requiring the receiver to return the goods to the seller if they are required for the continued carrying on of the company's business and its disposal as a going concern, provided that the receiver is willing to give a personal undertaking to apply the proceeds of disposing of the goods or any products in which they are embodied in paying the amount owing to the unpaid seller.[3]

Where a contract for the sale of goods to a company reserves the ownership of them to the seller until the price is paid, but permits the company to re-sell the goods or products manufactured with them on condition that the proceeds of sale shall belong to the unpaid seller, or shall be charged in his favour with the amount owing to him, the unpaid seller's rights in respect of the proceeds of resale, however expressed, are deemed to be an equitable charge on them.[4] Consequently, unless the seller registers the charge at the Companies Registry under the Companies Act 1985,[5] it will be invalid against a liquidator or administrator of the company and against any other creditor of the company who has a security over the

---

1 *Hendy Lennox (Industrial Engines) Ltd v Grahame Puttick Ltd* [1984] 2 All ER 152, [1984] 1 WLR 485.
2 *Borden (UK) Ltd v Scottish Timber Products Ltd* [1981] Ch 25, [1979] 3 All ER 961; *Re Peachdart Ltd* [1984] Ch 131, [1983] 3 All ER 204; *Clough Mill Ltd v Martin*, supra; *Specialist Plant Services Ltd v Braithwaite Ltd* [1987] BCLC 1, 3 BCC 119; *Modelboard Ltd v Outer Box Ltd* [1993] BCLC 623, [1992] BCC 945.
3 *Lipe Ltd v Leyland DAF Ltd* [1994] 1 BCLC 84, [1993] BCC 385.
4 *Hendy Lennox (Industrial Engines) Ltd v Grahame Puttick Ltd*, supra; *Re Andrabell Ltd (in liquidation), Airborne Accessories Ltd v Goodman* [1984] 3 All ER 407; *E Pfeiffer Weinkellerie-Weineinkauf GmbH & Co v Arbuthnot Factors Ltd* [1988] 1 WLR 150, [1987] BCLC 522; *Tatung (UK) Ltd v Galex Telesure Ltd* (1988) 5 BCC 325.
5 Companies Act 1985, s 395(1) and s 396(1)(e).

same proceeds of sale.[6] Similarly, if an unpaid seller of goods to a company has reserved the ownership of them, but ownership has passed to the company because the goods have lost their original identity by being processed or manufactured (with or without other goods) into a product, the seller's interest in the resulting goods and the proceeds of their resale by the company is treated as an equitable charge on them. Like a charge on the proceeds of sale of unaltered goods, such a charge will, if not registered under the Companies Act 1985, be invalid against the liquidator or administrator of the company and against a creditor of the company who has a security over the altered goods, or the proceeds of the company reselling them.[7] It follows that because a receiver is appointed to enforce the rights and realise the assets comprised in the debenture holders' security, he can disregard the unpaid seller's claim to the proceeds of sale of goods supplied to the company, and the unpaid claim to derivative products made by the company with such goods and the proceeds of sale of such products, unless in their case the seller's claims have been duly registered.

Rights of set-off

A receiver appointed to realise a floating charge over assets of a company can enforce the rights of the company against third persons only to the same extent as the company itself could do at the time when the floating charge crystallised.[8] The receiver can therefore recover debts owed to the company which are comprised in the floating charge and are due for payment either before or after the floating charge crystallises, only subject to the debtors' rights to set off claims which they have against the company.[8] Such claims must either be for specific sums which were due and immediately payable by the company before the floating charge crystallised,[9] or they must be for amounts which became unconditionally owing before the floating charge crystallised, even though they were not due for payment until afterwards.[10] If the debtor's claim arises under the same transaction of a transaction closely related to the one under

---

6 Ibid, s 395(1), as amended by Insolvency Act 1985, s 109 and Sch 6, para 10.
7 Ibid, s 395(1) and s 396(1)(c) and (e).
8 *Parsons v Sovereign Bank of Canada* [1913] AC 160; *Rother Iron Works Ltd v Canterbury Precision Engineers Ltd* [1974] QB 1, [1973] 1 All ER 394. References in this paragraph to a floating charge crystallising include the floating charge being converted into a specific charge by its terms, by agreement or by the occurrence of any stipulated event.
9 *Biggerstaff v Rowatt's Wharf Ltd* [1896] 2 Ch 93.
10 *Business Computers Ltd v Anglo-African Leasing Ltd* [1977] 2 All ER 741, [1977] 1 WLR 578.

which the company's claim against the debtor arises, however, the debtor may exercise his right of set-off, even though his own claim arises or becomes unconditional only after the appointment of a receiver or the crystallisation of the floating charge.[11]

A right of set-off by a debtor of the company exists even when the debtor's claim against the company is for an amount which is payable under a security which ranks after the floating charge under which the receiver was appointed, so that by setting off his secured debt against the debt which he owes the company, the holder of the later ranking security obtains payment of his debt in full, although the debt secured by the prior ranking security goes wholly or partly unpaid.[12] Similarly, if a shareholder who is indebted to the company for an unpaid call or instalment of the issue price of shares also has a claim against the company for an unpaid debt, the receiver can recover the call only subject to the shareholder's right to set off the amount of his claim.[13] On the other hand, if the right of set-off arises or becomes unconditional only after a floating charge over a debt owed to the company crystallises, and the debtor's claim against the company arises under a separate transaction from its claim against him, the debtor's right of set-off is not available against the debenture holders or other secured creditors for whose benefit the receiver was appointed, because they cannot be deprived of their right to enforce claims belonging to the company by subsequent events.[14]

Where debts owing to a company are mortgaged, assigned or charged by it as security and the charge is a fixed or specific (eg a fixed charge over a company's present and future book or trading debts owed or becoming due to it from its customers), the set off rules set out above apply to the set-off of claims by the company's

---

11 *Handley Page Ltd v Customs and Excise Comrs and Rockwell Machine Tool Co Ltd* [1970] 2 Lloyd's Rep 459; *British Anzani (Felixstowe) Ltd v Marine International Marine Management (UK) Ltd* [1980] QB 137, [1979] 2 All ER 1063.

12 *Edward Nelson & Co v Faber & Co* [1903] 2 KB 367.

13 This is in contrast to the position in a winding up, where a set-off against calls is not permitted (*Re Overend, Gurney & Co, Grissell's Case* (1866) 1 Ch App 528; *Re General Works & Co, Gill's Case* (1879) 12 Ch D 755).

14 *H Wilkins and Elkington Ltd v Milton* (1916) 32 TLR 618 (the company's debtor held a debenture of a later series which became immediately repayable upon the appointment of a receiver under the debentures of the first series); *N W Robbie & Co Ltd v Witney Warehouse Co Ltd* [1963] 3 All ER 613, [1963] 1 WLR 1324 (assignment of a debt owed by the company to the company's debtor after crystallisation); *Business Computers Ltd v Anglo-African Leasing Ltd*, supra (the company's debtor had leased equipment to it under a separate contract, which was terminable before the appointment of the receiver, but which was only terminated afterwards, whereupon the debtor acquired a claim for liquidated damages against the company).

debtors against the company when the chargees of the debts which they owe to the company, or a receiver for those chargees, seeks to recover those debts. The only difference when the security over debts owed to the company is a fixed charge (and not a floating charge) is that set-off is not possible if the company's debtor has a claim against it which has not become one for a debt or liquidated sum before he is notified of the fixed or specific security over the debt which he owes the company.[15] If the debtor's claim against the company is for such a debt or liquidated sum, it may be set off even if the debtor is notified of the fixed charge over the debt which he owes the company between the time when it becomes owing and the later date when it becomes due for payment.[15]

Third person's rights under insurance

If a company has insured against a liability which it has incurred to a third party, whether in contract, tort or otherwise, the third party can compel the insurance company to pay him the insurance money directly when the company has gone into liquidation or a receiver has been appointed under a floating charge over the company's business undertaking or property, and the receiver and the persons on whose behalf he was appointed have no prior claim to the insurance money.[16] This is the case also if the persons entitled to the benefit of the floating charge take possession of the company's business undertaking or property without a receiver being appointed.[16]

Disposal of third persons' property by a receiver

A receiver or administrative receiver is, of course, not entitled to take and dispose of the property of persons other than the company without their consent for the purpose of the receivership, and if he does so he cannot confer a good title on the person to whom he makes the disposal. Furthermore, a receiver who disposed of tangible movables (goods) which belonged to a person other than the company at common law committed the wrong of conversion, and was liable to the true owner in damages equal to the value of the goods; it was no defence that the receiver had acted honestly and carefully. Now, however, an administrative receiver (but not any

---

15 *Watson v Mid Wales Rly Co* (1867) LR 2 CP 593; *Christie v Taunton, Delmard, Lane & Co* [1893] 2 Ch 175; *Re Pinto Leite and Nephews, ex p Visconde des Olivaes* [1929] 1 Ch 221.
16 Third Parties (Rights Against Insurers) Act 1930, s 1(1), (4) and (5) (4 *Halsbury's Statutes* (4th edn) 688); (see also p 219, ante).

other receiver) is protected by statute,[17] which provides that if he takes possession or disposes of any property or assets which do not belong to the company and the receiver has reasonable grounds for believing that he is entitled to do so, he is not liable to any person for loss or damage suffered by them in consequence, except so far as it is caused by the receiver's own negligence. This provision does not, however, confer any title to the property disposed of by the receiver on the person to whom the disposal is made, even if that person acts honestly, and such a person cannot pass title to anyone else.

The company's existing contracts

Enforcement against the company's assets

The appointment of a receiver to enforce a specific or a floating charge which extends to contracts which the company enters into in carrying on its business (as would a floating charge over a company's whole assets and undertaking), does not affect the validity of such contracts which the company has already entered into, whether the appointment is made under the terms of a debt instrument or by the court.[18] The other contracting parties can enforce the company's obligations under such contracts subject, of course, to the secured interests of the holders of debt securities or the debenture holders or debenture stockholders in the assets of the company which the receiver has been appointed to realise. Consequently, if a person has contracted to purchase particular assets of a company before a receiver is appointed under a floating charge over the company's undertaking and assets, and has acquired an equitable interest in the assets by virtue of his contract, he may obtain an order for specific performance of the contract against the company, despite the receivership.[19] Likewise, the receiver appointed to enforce a floating charge over the assets of a company which manufactured plastic moulding equipment and which had contracted to sell it to a user of such equipment at a price equal to the highest price offered by any other person, was required by the court's order to notify the other contracting party of the prices offered by other persons and not to sell the equipment to any of them if the other party to the contract partly matched their highest offer.[20]

---

17 Insolvency Act 1986, s 234(1), (3) and (4).
18 *Parsons v Sovereign Bank of Canada* [1913] AC 160; *Forster v Nixon's Navigation Co Ltd* (1906) 23 TLR 138; *Re Leyland DAF Ltd* [1994] 2 BCLC 106, [1994] BCC 166.
19 *Freevale Ltd v Metrostore (Holdings) Ltd* [1984] Ch 199, [1984] 1 All ER 495.
20 *Ash and Newman Ltd v Creative Devices Research Ltd* [1991] BCLC 403.

Also it has been held that the other contracting party may enforce rights given to him by a contract entered into with the company before the appointment of a receiver to realise a floating charge over the company's undertaking and assets, even though those rights entitle the other contracting party to take possession of assets of the company, and he may sell such assets and apply the proceeds of sale in discharging a debt of the company which was owing before the receiver's appointment.[1]

In situations like those in the last two cases mentioned in the preceding paragraph, the other contracting party relies on a purely contractual right to possess or acquire the assets in question and not on a mortgage, charge or proprietary interest in those assets, but the effect of the enforcement of those contractual rights is to destroy the security over the assets of the persons for whose benefit the receiver was appointed; it is therefore doubtful whether the other contracting party should be able to gain priority over the interests of those persons in such circumstances when a mortgagee or chargee of the assets would not be able to do so. In two similar cases where a party to a contract entered into with the company before the receiver was appointed, sought an order of specific performance of a promise to transfer or charge assets of the company to him, it was held that specific performance could be ordered against the company and the receiver, even though the effect of the order would be to take assets out of the receiver's hands which he would otherwise be entitled to realise,[2] but such an order is effective against the persons for whose benefit the receiver was appointed only if the contract created an interest in the company's assets which is binding on them under the general rules governing the priority of securities over the same assets of a company.[3] It follows from this, of course, that a party to a contract with the company cannot enforce it by an unsecured claim in debt or for damages against the assets of the company comprised in the security which the receiver is appointed to enforce, except where the claim is for a preferential debt and the receiver was appointed under a charge which, as created, was a floating charge.[4]

Although the court has no power to modify contracts which a company has entered into when it goes into receivership, it can in equity grant relief to the receiver and the secured creditors for whose benefit he is appointed against the enforcement of contracts entered

---

1 *George Barker (Transport) Ltd v Eynon* [1974] 1 All ER 900, [1974] 1 WLR 462.
2 *Swiss Bank Corpn v Lloyds Bank Ltd* [1979] Ch 548, [1979] 2 All ER 853; affd [1982] AC 584, [1981] 2 All ER 449; *Freevale Ltd v Metrostore (Holdings) Ltd*, supra.
3 See *Pennington's Company Law* (7th edn) 575 to 584.
4 Insolvency Act 1986, s 40(1) and (2); (see p 303, ante).

into by the company, where the company's assets would thereby be substantially diminished (eg the termination by the owner of hire purchase agreements of trucks and vans let to the company when the outstanding balance of the hire purchase price is small, the receiver is able and willing to pay that balance within a fairly short period and the vehicles are essential for the continuance of the company's business).[5]

Contracts of employment

If a receiver is appointed by the court, all contracts of employment between the company and its employees are automatically terminated.[6] It is immaterial that the receiver continues to carry on the company's business, for he does not do so as an agent for the company, and employees who continue to work for him do so under new contracts of employment entered into with him.[6] The appointment of a receiver under the provisions of a debt security agreement, or of debentures or a trust deed covering debentures or debenture stock, apparently does not terminate existing contracts of employment. If the debt security agreement, debentures or covering trust deed provide that the receiver shall be deemed to be the agent of the company in exercising his powers, or if he is an administrative receiver, and so is deemed by law to be the company's agent,[7] existing contracts of employment with the company are definitely not terminated,[8] unless the employees are directors or managers and the continued exercise of their functions would conflict with the exercise of the receiver's powers, which is not inevitable even in the case of a managing director.[9] Employees of the company are not dismissed automatically when the receiver's status as the company's agent is terminated by the company subsequently going into voluntary liquidation,[10] but it would appear that employees are automatically dismissed if a winding up order is made against the company.[11] If a

---

5 *Transag Haulage Ltd v Leyland DAF Finance plc* [1994] 2 BCLC 88, [1994] BCC 356.
6 *Reid v Explosives Co Ltd* (1887) 19 QBD 264. This exception to the general rule that the company's contracts are unaffected by the appointment of a receiver has been attributed to the personal nature of contracts of employment (*Midland Counties District Bank Ltd v Attwood* [1905] 1 Ch 357 at 362, per Warrington J).
7 Insolvency Act 1986, s 44(1)(a).
8 *Re Foster Clark Ltd's Indenture Trusts* [1966] 1 All ER 43, [1966] 1 WLR 125; *Re Mack Trucks (Britain) Ltd* [1967] 1 All ER 977, [1967] 1 WLR 780.
9 *Griffiths v Secretary of State for Social Services* [1974] QB 468, [1973] 3 All ER 1184; *Newhart Developments Ltd v Co-operative Commercial Bank Ltd* [1978] QB 814, [1978] 2 All ER 896.
10 *Deaway Trading Ltd v Calverley* [1973] 3 All ER 776.
11 *Re General Rolling Stock Co, Chapman's Case* (1866) LR 1 Eq 346; *Measures Bros Ltd v Measures* [1910] 2 Ch 248.

receiver appointed out of court sells the assets comprised in the company's business or closes it down, however, all contracts of employment which have not already been terminated are thereby brought to an end.[12] Nevertheless, this does not happen if the receiver sells or transfers the whole or part of the company's business undertaking carried on by the receiver in the United Kingdom as a going concern.[13] In that case the rights, powers, obligations and liabilities of the company toward persons employed in the undertaking or the part of an undertaking which is sold or transferred are transferred by law to the purchaser or transferee,[14] and the employee's rights against the purchaser or transferee are the same as though the company and the purchaser were the same legal person. However, this does not prevent any employee terminating his employment without notice if a substantial change is made in his working conditions, or if the change in the identity of his employer is of significance and, in the circumstances, is detrimental to him, or if he informs the receiver or the purchaser or transferee of the whole or part of the company's business that he objects to becoming employed by the purchaser or transferee.[15]

Novation

A receiver or manager is not personally responsible for the performance of the company's contracts which were concluded before his appointment and were executory at that time, and no novation will be inferred from the fact that he carries out any part of those contracts.[16] If the company has entered into a contract of a continuing character, and the receiver accepts the benefit of the contract, for example, by using or occupying property or availing himself of services provided by the other party,[17] or by accepting the delivery of goods under a standing supply contract,[18] the receiver is not taken thereby to have entered into a new contract himself.

---

12 *Re Foster Clark Ltd's Indenture Trusts* [1966] 1 All ER 43, [1966] 1 WLR 125; *Re Mack Trucks (Britain) Ltd* [1967] 1 All ER 977, [1967] 1 WLR 780.

13 Transfer of Undertakings (Protection of Employment) Regulations 1981 (SI 1981/1794), regs 3(1) and (2) and 5(1) and (2), as amended by the Trade Union Reform and Employment Rights Act 1993, s 33.

14 Ibid, reg 5(2).

15 Ibid, reg 5, as amended by the Trade Union Reform and Employment Rights Act 1993, s 33.

16 *Parsons v Sovereign Bank of Canada* [1913] AC 160; *Forster v Nixon's Navigation Co Ltd* (1906) 23 TLR 138; *Nicoll v Cutts* [1985] BCLC 322, 1 BCC 99, 427.

17 *Hay v Swedish and Norwegian Rly Co* (1892) 8 TLR 775; *Re J W Abbott & Co Ltd, Abbot v J W Abbot & Co Ltd* (1913) 30 TLR 13.

18 *Re Ryland's Glass Co York etc, Bank v Ryland's Glass Co* (1904) 49 Sol Jo 67.

Nevertheless, the appropriate part of the consideration to be given by the company under the contract for the benefits accepted by the receiver will be treated as an expense of the receivership, and will be recoverable by the other contracting party in priority to the claims of the secured creditors for whose benefit the receiver was appointed.[19]

There is one statutory exception to the rule that a receiver is not personally liable in respect of contracts entered into by the company before his appointment. Whether he is an administrative receiver or not, a receiver or manager appointed under the provisions of a debt security agreement, or debentures or of a trust deed covering debentures or debenture stock, is personally liable on contracts of employment entered into by the company which he adopts, but nothing done or omitted by him within 14 days after his appointment is to be regarded as an adoption of such a contract.[20] A receiver adopts a contract of employment if he informs the employee to that effect, even if he disclaims any personal responsibility for the company's obligations; he also adopts a contract of employment if he merely allows the employee to perform his obligations under the contract,[1] but anything less than an express adoption will not be binding on the receiver if it is done during the 14 days immediately following his appointment. The extent of the receiver's personal liability to employees of the company was held by the House of Lords to extend to the payment of remuneration, holiday pay and employers' contributions to occupational pension funds accruing on or after the receiver's appointment and during the continuance of his receivership.[1] However, statute has now confined the personal liability of an administrative receiver to such payments which relate to services rendered by the employee during the period from when the receiver adopts the contract of employment until he ceases to hold office, either by the receivership being concluded or by the receiver being removed or superseded by another appointee.[2] A receiver who makes payments required to satisfy his personal liability to employees under these provisions is entitled to an indemnity out of the company's assets comprised in the receivership in the same way as in respect of other payments properly made by him.[3]

---

19 See p 531, post.
20 Insolvency Act 1986, s 37(1) and (2) and s 44(1) and (2), as amended by Insolvency Act 1994, s 2(1) and (2).
1 *Powdrill v Watson* [1995] 1 BCLC 386, [1995] BCC 319, HL.
2 Insolvency Act 1986, s 44(2) to (20), as amended by Insolvency Act 1994, s 2.
3 Insolvency Act 1986, s 37(3) and s 44(3).

Breach of company's contracts

Although a receiver or manager is not personally bound by contracts entered into by the company before his appointment, he should not break such contracts without the leave of the court if the breach is likely to injure the company's goodwill. The court will not give leave for this purpose if the receiver merely shows that it will be of immediate advantage to the secured creditors for whose benefit he was appointed to break the contract in question, for the receiver or manager owes a duty to the company, as the owner of the property subject to the security, as well as to the secured creditors themselves, not to diminish the value of the company's assets, which include its goodwill.[4] But if breach of the contract will not injure the company's goodwill, or if the company's goodwill is valueless, the court will not require the receiver or manager to carry out the contract,[5] and in any case, if he cannot perform the contract without borrowing, the court will not compel him to do so.[6]

It has been suggested that a receiver appointed by the court who breaks a contract made by the company might be liable to the other contracting party for the tort of procuring the company to commit a breach of the contract, unless he acts with the permission of the court.[7] Whether this is so or not, it is certain that a receiver appointed out of court under the terms of an instrument who is declared by a debt security agreement, or debentures or by the trust deed covering an issue of debentures or debenture stock, to be an agent of the company, or who is an administrative receiver and is therefore deemed by law to be the company's agent,[8] is not liable in tort for causing breaches of contracts which the company has entered into, because agents who in the course of exercising their authority effect, advise or procure the breach of contracts made by their principals are not responsible for the loss thereby caused to the other contracting parties or to other persons.[9] Moreover, a person who is owed a debt, or who will have a claim for damages against the company if his contract with it is broken, cannot obtain an injunction to restrain a receiver of the company's assets or undertaking from

---

4 *Re Newdigate Colliery Co Ltd* [1912] 1 Ch 468, where the receiver unsuccessfully sought leave to break a contract by the company for the sale of coal on the ground that the market price obtainable for the coal on the delivery date was higher than the contract price.

5 *Re Great Cobar Ltd* [1915] 1 Ch 682.

6 *Re Thames Ironworks, Shipbuilding and Engineering Co Ltd* [1912] WN 66.

7 *Re Botibol, Botibol v Botibol* [1947] 1 All ER 26.

8 Insolvency Act 1986, s 44(1)(*a*).

9 *Said v Butt* [1920] 3 KB 497; *Lathia v Dronsfield Bros Ltd* [1987] BCLC 321; *Welsh Development Agency v Export Finance Co Ltd* [1992] BCLC 148, [1992] BCC 270.

applying its assets so that the debt is not paid, or so that the contract is broken, and this is so whether the receiver is the company's agent or not.[10] On the other hand, if a contract made by the company before the receiver's appointment vests a proprietary interest in any of its property in the other contracting party (eg a contract conferring an option to purchase any of the company's assets), the receiver will be liable in tort to the other party if he knowingly causes the company to breach the contract, thereby infringing the other party's proprietary interest.[11]

Contracts made by the receiver or manager

If a receiver or manager appointed by the court makes a contract in the course of the receivership, he is personally liable to the other party for its performance, and the company is not so liable, because the receiver or manager is not its agent.[12] But if the receiver or manager is in control of the company's business and the other contracting party believes him to be a duly appointed director of the company or a manager appointed by its board of directors, it may be that the other party can treat the company as bound by the contract under the rule in *Royal British Bank v Turquand*.[13] In any event, the receiver or manager is entitled to be indemnified against his personal liability out of the property comprised in the security in respect of which he was appointed; if he becomes insolvent, the persons with whom he contracts are subrogated to his right to an indemnity, and their claims must be satisfied before payment of the debt for which the security was given.[14] The other parties to contracts made by a receiver or manager have no greater rights to an indemnity than the receiver or manager himself, however, and so if he fails to recover or account for some assets comprised in the security in breach of his duty to act honestly and with reasonable skill and care, his right to an indemnity is correspondingly reduced, and so is the amount available to satisfy the other parties with whom he contracted.[15] Furthermore, the principle of subrogation does not enable persons who have promised to make payments to the company or to the receiver in contracts which they have entered into with him, to set off claims against the company which they have acquired during the

10 *Airlines Airspares Ltd v Handley Page Ltd* [1970] Ch 193, [1970] 1 All ER 29n.
11 *Telemetrix plc v Modern Engineers of Bristol (Holdings) plc* [1985] BCLC 213.
12 *Moss SS Co Ltd v Whinney* [1912] AC 254.
13 Ibid, at 266, per Lord Atkinson (see *Pennington's Company Law* (7th edn), 136.
14 *Re Ryland's Glass Co, York etc, Bank v Ryland's Glass Co* (1904) 49 Sol Jo 67.
15 *Re British Power Traction and Lighting Co Ltd* [1910] 2 Ch 470.

receivership but which did not arise out of contracts made with the receiver.[16] The reason for this is that the claims sought to be set off are merely claims against the company, and are not fresh liabilities for which the receiver is himself entitled to be indemnified out of the security in respect of which he was appointed.

If a receiver appointed out of court under the provisions of a debt security agreement or debentures, or under a trust deed covering an issue of debentures or debenture stock, enters into contracts during his receivership and before the company is wound up, he does so either as an agent for the secured creditors or the debenture holders or debenture stockholders for whose benefit he was appointed, or as an agent for the company, depending on the terms of the instrument under which he was appointed.[17] If he is an administrative receiver, he will be deemed by law to be an agent of the company until it goes in liquidation, unless the debt security agreement, debentures or covering trust deed otherwise provide.[18] At common law the receiver was not personally liable in respect of such contracts, but whether he is an administrative receiver or not, he is now personally liable by statute on all contracts made by him in carrying out his functions, in the same way as a receiver appointed by the court, and he has the same right to an indemnity.[19] This is so even if the debt security agreement, debentures or the trust deed covering an issue of debentures or debenture stock provides that the receiver shall be deemed to act as the company's agent in respect of all transactions entered into by him, and shall not be personally liable to the other parties to them.[20] Because of the personal liability of a receiver, only he can ratify transactions entered into by persons wrongly pretending to have authority to act on his behalf; a subsequently appointed receiver or the company itself cannot ratify such transactions, for if the ratification were effective, it would retrospectively cast liability on the first receiver without his consent.[1]

---

16 *N W Robbie & Co Ltd v Witney Warehouse Co Ltd* [1963] 3 All ER 613, [1963] 1 WLR 1324 (a buyer of goods of the company sold by a receiver appointed to realise a floating charge sought unsuccessfully to set off against the price a debt owed by the company to a third party before crystallisation of the floating charge, when the third party had assigned the debt to the buyer after the receiver was appointed).

17 See p 467, ante. A receiver appointed out of court is, and has always been, personally liable on contracts made by him after the company goes into liquidation because, even if he was initially an agent of the company, his agency terminated on the company going into liquidation.

18 Insolvency Act 1986, s 44(1)(*a*); (see p 468, ante).

19 Insolvency Act 1986, s 37(1) and (3) and s 44(1)(*b*) and (3).

20 *Hill Samuel and Co Ltd v Laing* [1991] BCC 665.

1 *Lawson v Hosemaster Machine Co Ltd* [1965] 3 All ER 401, [1965] 1 WLR 1399.

For this reason, the same rule should apply to a receiver appointed by the court.

There is nothing to prevent a receiver contracting on terms that he shall not be personally liable to the other party to the contract, or that he shall be liable only so far as the company's assets are sufficient for the fulfilment of the contract.[2] A contract which completely excludes the receiver's personal liability is most inadvisable for the other contracting party, however. Because the receiver has no personal liability under such a contract, he has no right to an indemnity out of the company's assets, and the other contracting party will therefore not even have a claim against the company's assets by subrogation if the receiver breaks the contract.[3]

Borrowing by receiver or manager

A receiver or manager may borrow in order to carry on the company's business undertaking comprised in the security in respect of which he is appointed, or to enable him to carry out his other duties, and an administrative receiver has a general power to borrow and to create mortgages, charges and other securities over the property of the company.[4] For the reasons already given, the receiver or manager will be personally liable to repay any loan which he contracts, but he will have a right to an indemnity out of the property comprised in the security in respect of which he was appointed. However, a receiver or manager cannot create a mortgage or charge ranking in priority to the security in respect of which he was appointed in order to secure a loan raised by him;[5] he may do this only if the instrument under which he was appointed expressly empowers him to do so, or if the receiver was appointed by the court in a representative action brought on behalf of all the debenture holders or debenture stockholders of the series concerned, in which case the court may make an order binding on those debenture holders or debenture stockholders giving the receiver authority leave to create such a charge.[6]

If with the authority of the court a receiver appointed by the court creates a charge in favour of a lender which is expressed to be a 'first charge' on property comprised in the security in respect of which he was appointed, the charge has priority over that security,

2 *Re Ernest Hawkins & Co Ltd* (1915) 31 TLR 247.
3 *Re A Boynton Ltd* [1910] 1 Ch 519.
4 Insolvency Act 1986, s 42(1) and (2) and Sch 1, para 3.
5 *Moss SS Co Ltd v Whinney* [1912] AC 254.
6 *Greenwood v Algesiras (Gibraltar) Rly Co* [1894] 2 Ch 205.

but not over the receiver's right to an indemnity for the expenses which he has incurred in carrying out his duties. In the earlier cases in which this was decided,[7] the loan raised by the receiver was made by one of the original debenture holders, and the court treated it as being made for the benefit of the debenture holders generally, so that there was no reason why the receiver, acting for the benefit of them all, should not have his normal indemnity. But in a later case it was held that it is immaterial whether the loan is made by one of the original security holders or one of the original debenture holders or debenture stockholders or by a stranger.[8] If the lender is to have priority over the receiver's right to an indemnity, therefore, his charge must expressly so provide. The point is of practical importance, because receivers often do not undertake personal liability for the advances which they raise, but merely charge the company's assets with the amount of the advance and interest; in that situation, if the lender's charge is postponed to the receiver's right to an indemnity for the expenses of the receivership, the lender will not even be able to share in the company's assets by subrogation rateably with creditors whose claims arise under other contracts made by the receiver, but the lender will be repaid his loan only after all such other creditors have been paid.[8]

If the court authorises a receiver or manager to borrow a certain amount, whether on the security of a charge having priority over the security in respect of which he was appointed or not, he should not borrow more than that amount, unless the excess is urgently required and he cannot reasonably be expected to defer borrowing it until authorisation by the court has been obtained.[9] If the receiver or manager unjustifiably borrows more than the court has authorised, his right to an indemnity is limited to the maximum amount which the court did authorise him to borrow,[9] and this of course, limits the lender's right to recover his loan by subrogation or by relying on the charge over the company's assets which the receiver has created in his favour.

An administrative receiver may exercise his statutory power to borrow and to create mortgages or charges over the company's property only to enable him to fulfil his functions properly, but a person who makes a secured loan to him in good faith is not concerned to enquire whether the loan is required for that purpose,[10]

---

7 *Strapp v Bull Sons & Co* [1895] 2 Ch 1; *Re Glasdir Copper Mines Ltd* [1906] 1 Ch 365.
8 *Re A Boynton Ltd*, supra.
9 *Re British Power Traction and Lighting Co Ltd* [1906] 1 Ch 497. For a practical example of the application of the principle laid down in this case, see the subsequent proceedings reported [1907] 1 Ch 528.
10 Insolvency Act 1986, s 42(3).

and can recover the loan made by him and enforce any security taken by him for the loan, even if the receiver raises it for an improper purpose. An administrative receiver had no statutory power to create charges ranking in priority to the charge in respect of which he was appointed. His position in this respect and his right to an indemnity for borrowing and other liabilities which he has properly incurred are therefore the same as those of any other receiver appointed otherwise than by the court.

THE CONDUCT OF A RECEIVERSHIP

The receiver's autonomy

A receiver carries out on his own initiative the functions of realising the company's assets subject to the security in respect of which he was appointed and, if he chooses to do so, carrying on the company's business under a power vested in him. Unless the debt security agreement, debentures or trust deed under which he was appointed otherwise provide, a receiver is not required to obtain the approval of the secured lenders or debenture holders or debenture stockholders for whose benefit he was appointed before exercising any of his powers. Correspondingly, a receiver appointed by the court is not required to obtain its approval before exercising the powers conferred on him by the terms of his appointment. Nevertheless, if a receiver is appointed under the terms of an instrument, his powers may be restricted by it or by the conditions of his appointment, and in particular, the consent of the persons for whose benefit he is appointed may be required for certain acts or transactions or the exercise of his powers in certain circumstances. This is so in respect of administrative receivers as well as other receivers and managers appointed out of court, but a person who deals with an administrative receiver in good faith and for value is not concerned to inquire whether he is acting within his powers, and is protected if he is not (eg if he disregards restrictions imposed on his powers, or conditions for their exercise imposed by the instrument by which he was appointed).[11]

A receiver or manager appointed out of court, whether an administrative receiver or not, may apply summarily to the court for directions in respect of any particular matter arising in connection with the performance of his functions, and on hearing the application the court may give the receiver or manager such directions and may

---

make such order declaring the rights of interested persons as it thinks just.[12] An application to the court under this provision may also be made by any person by or on whose behalf a receiver or manager was appointed out of court, such as a secured lender or a debenture holder or a debenture stockholder.[12] It has been held that on an application under this provision the court may not only resolve doubts which a receiver has as to the extent of his powers in a particular instance, or where he is in disagreement with the secured creditor or debenture holders or their trustees who appointed him, but the court may also direct that the receiver shall be entitled to an indemnity for expenses which he has incurred or intends to incur in doing acts or entering into transactions approved by the court, and that the persons by or on whose behalf he was appointed shall put him in funds to meet those expenses.[13] On the other hand, it appears that the court will not on such an application exercise a discretion which the receiver is empowered by law to exercise (eg as the price at which, or the terms on which, he will dispose of the company's assets) in the same way as the court will not interfere with the exercise of a liquidator's powers,[14] in the absence of evidence of bad faith on his part, the use of the power for an improper purpose, or the receiver's decision being one which no reasonable person could reach. The costs of an application for directions by the court made by a receiver or other person are usually awarded against the unsuccessful party, but if the company's creditors generally have an interest in the outcome of the application, the court may in its discretion order the costs to be paid out of the company's assets comprised in the receivership.[15]

A receiver appointed by the court may apply to it for directions on a summons issued in the debenture holders' action in which he was appointed, but the court has indicated that the receiver should make the application only if the plaintiff in that action declines to do so, and no other debenture holder or debenture stockholder of the class in question is willing to request the court to make him a party to that action so that he may apply for directions to be given to the receiver.[16]

12 Ibid, s 35(1) and (2).
13 *Re Therm-a-Stor Ltd, Morris v Lewis* [1996] 2 BCLC 400, [1997] BCC 301. See also *Anderson v Hyde* [1996] 2 BCLC 144, a decision of the Court of Appeal of Northern Ireland.
14 See p 169, ante.
15 *Re Westdock Realisations Ltd* [1988] BCLC 354, 4 BCC 192.
16 *Parker v Dunn* (1845) 8 Beav 497; *Debenture Corpn v De Murrieta & Co Ltd* (1892) 8 TLR 496.

The creditors' committee

In a receivership other than an administrative receivership, there is no provision for the holding of meetings of creditors of the company, or for the appointment of a committee to represent them, comparable to the meetings of creditors and the appointment of persons to represent them on the liquidation committee in the winding up of a company by the court or in a creditors' voluntary winding up.[17] In an administrative receivership, however, the meeting of the company's unsecured creditors which the administrative receiver is required to call within three months after his appointment, unless the court dispenses with the need to call it,[18] may resolve to establish a creditors' committee; on giving the administrative receiver seven days' notice at any time during the receivership, such a committee may require him to attend before it at a reasonable time in order to provide it with such information about the carrying out of the administrative receiver's functions as the committee reasonably requires.[19]

The creditors' committee in an administrative receivership is constituted in the same way as the component of a liquidation committee which represents creditors in a winding up. The committee comprises between three and five creditors whose claims to vote at creditors' meetings have not been rejected, and who are elected by their number at the meeting of creditors which establishes the committee; a corporate creditor elected to be a member may be represented at meetings of the committee by a representative appointed by its board of directors.[20] The creditors' committee comes into being and can act only when the administrative receiver certifies to that effect; its members must each agree to act, and the receiver cannot certify the constitution of the committee until at least three of its members have agreed to do so.[1] The creditors' committee must assist the administrative receiver in exercising his functions, and must do so in such manner as is from time to time agreed between them.[2]

Meetings of the creditors' committee are called by the administrative receiver as and when he thinks fit, but the first

17 See p 127 and 141, ante.
18 See p 500, ante.
19 Insolvency Act 1986, s 49(1) and (2). A notice requiring the administrative receiver to attend a meeting of the committee in order to provide it with information about the receivership must be signed by a majority of the members of the committee (Insolvency Rules 1986, r 3.28(1) and (2)).
20 Insolvency Rules 1986, r 3.16(1) to (3).
1 Ibid, r 3.17(1), (2) and (2A), as amended by SI 1987/1919.
2 Ibid, r 3.18(1).

meeting of the committee must be held not later than three months after it is established; also meetings of the committee must be called by the receiver if and when the committee so resolves, or if any member of the committee so requests, and in this latter case the meeting must be held not more than 21 days after the request is made.[3] The quorum at a meeting of the creditors' committee is two members of it present in person or by representatives appointed by them in writing;[4] the chairman is the administrative receiver or a person nominated by him who is a qualified insolvency practitioner, or an employee of the receiver or his firm who is experienced in insolvency matters.[5] Each member of the creditors' committee has one vote, and resolutions are passed by a simple majority vote.[6] It is possible for resolutions to be passed by a postal vote if the administrative receiver circulates a resolution which he proposes shall be passed in this way to all members of the committee, but any member of the committee may within seven days after the receiver sends out the proposal require a meeting of the committee to be called so that the resolution may be considered and voted on in the normal way.[7] In the absence of such a requirement, a resolution is deemed to be passed by a postal vote when a simple majority of the members of the committee or their representatives notify the receiver in writing that they concur with it.[7]

The creditors' committee is not in a strong position to influence the conduct of an administrative receivership. The committee is representative only of unsecured creditors of the company and of secured creditors in respect of the company's indebtedness to them in excess of their valuation of their respective securities. Apart from preferential creditors, who are entitled to be paid their claims out of the proceeds of realising assets of the company subject to a charge which was created as a floating charge in priority to the debt secured by the charge,[8] unsecured creditors are entitled to be paid out of the company's assets only when its indebtedness secured on those assets has been discharged in full, and their interests as creditors are therefore entitled to the least consideration by the receiver. The creditors' committee may, therefore, acts as a channel of communication between an administrative receiver and the unsecured creditors of the company, and may seek to persuade the receiver to act in a way which will preserve the interests of those

3 Ibid, r 3.18(2) and (3).
4 Ibid, r 3.20 and r 3.21(1) and (2).
5 Ibid, r 3.19(1) and (2).
6 Ibid, r 3.26(1).
7 Ibid, r 27(1), (3) and (4).
8 See p 303, post.

creditors where possible, but the committee cannot control or even supervise the receiver's conduct of the receivership, or prevent him from doing acts or entering into transactions of which it disapproves.

Power to dispose of property free from securities

An administrative receiver (but no other kind of receiver) may apply to the court for authority to dispose of any property of the company which is comprised in the floating charge or any other mortgages or charges created by the same transaction in respect of which he was also appointed, free from any mortgages, charges or other securities (including securities arising by operation of law) which are vested in persons other than those entitled to the floating charge and which rank in priority to that floating charge or any other mortgage or charge to which the receiver's appointment relates.[9] If it considers that the disposal of any such property (whether alone or with other property of the company) free from the prior ranking securities would be likely to promote a more advantageous realisation of the company's assets than would otherwise occur, the court may authorise the disposal of the property by the administrative receiver free from the prior ranking securities, and when the disposal is made by him, it will take effect accordingly.[9] An example of a situation where this provision would be useful is where an administrative receiver wishes to sell the whole assets and undertaking of the company, but the floating charge over them in respect of which he was appointed is subject to a mortgage to a third person of the premises where the company's business is carried on to secure part of the cost of its acquisition by the company, and is also subject to a floating charge in favour of another third person over the machinery and equipment from time to time in or at those premises which ranks in priority to the floating charge under which the receiver was appointed. The administrative receiver would probably obtain a better price on selling the company's business if he were able to sell the whole of its assets free from the mortgage of the company's business premises and the floating charge over the machinery and equipment, and were to discharge the mortgage and charge out of the proceeds of sale, instead of selling the company's business subject to those encumbrances.

If the court authorises an administrative receiver to dispose of property of a company free from securities which rank in priority to the floating charge under which he was appointed, the receiver must apply the net proceeds of the disposal primarily in discharging those

9 Insolvency Act 1986, s 29(2), s 43(1), (2) and (7) and s 248(*b*).

prior ranking securities, and if those net proceeds are less than the amount determined by the court as the net amount which would be realised on the sale of the property on the open market by a willing seller, it must be a condition of the court's authorisation that the receiver shall make good the deficiency so far as is necessary to discharge those prior ranking securities.[10] This condition would not appear to impose a personal obligation on the receiver to pay the deficiency himself, but it does seem to make it his duty to ensure that he has sufficient available assets of the company comprised in his receivership to make good the deficiency before he disposes of the property in question, and if he fails to do this, he will apparently be liable to the holders of those securities in damages for his negligence.

In applying the net proceeds of realisation of property disposed of with the authorisation of the court and any amount required to make good any deficiency of the proceeds to meet the open market value of the property, the administrative receiver must give effect to the rights of priority of two or more holders of securities charged on the same property as between themselves.[11] It would also seem that where two or more properties are disposed of by the administrative receiver with the authority of the court, and more of those properties are subject to one of the prior ranking securities than are subject to another such security, the principle of marshalling must be applied to the proceeds of the disposal and the amount of any deficiency which the receiver is required to make good, so that the secured creditor whose security extends to fewer properties receives the maximum payment possible out of the proceeds and the amount of any such deficiency made good by the receiver in respect of those properties, and so that the other secured creditor or creditors are required to resort first to the proceeds and any deficiency contribution in respect of the other properties which are not comprised in the first security but are subject to their security or securities.

The statutory provision which enables an administrative receiver with the authority of the court to dispose of property of a company free from prior ranking securities is similar to, but not identical with, that which enables an administrator to dispose free from encumbrances of property of a company which is subject to fixed or specific charges.[12] The administrative receiver's power of disposal with the court's authorisation extends to property of the company which is subject to any kind of security (including a floating charge), which ranks in priority to the floating charge or additional charge under which the receiver was appointed; in this respect his power is

10 Ibid, s 43(3).
11 Ibid, s 43(4).
12 Ibid, s 15(2), (3) and (5); (see p 372, ante).

narrower than that of an administrator, who may dispose of property subject to a floating charge and so liberate it from that charge without the need to obtain the authority of the court, which is required only when an administrator seeks to dispose of property of the company which is subject to a fixed or specific charge or charges.[13] Furthermore, the power of an administrative receiver to dispose of property of the company free from securities ranking in priority to the security in respect of which he was appointed applies only when all the securities involved are mortgages, charges, liens or other similar securities over land or movables,[14] whereas an administrator may also exercise his similar statutory power where the interests involved are those of the owner of goods in course of acquisition by the company under hire purchase, chattel leasing, conditional sale or retention of title agreements.[15] Moreover, when an administrator disposes of property of a company in administration which is subject to a floating charge, the charge is transferred to the proceeds of the disposal,[16] but the administrator is not required to discharge the debt secured by it immediately; if an administrative receiver realises assets which are subject to a prior ranking floating charge with the court's authorisation, however, the proceeds must be applied immediately in paying the debt formerly secured by that charge.[17]

Taxation

If a company's business is carried on by a receiver or manager, the profits or capital gains realised by him are subject to corporation tax as though the receiver had not been appointed and the company were carrying on the business itself.[18] The tax payable is an expense of the receivership for which the receiver is entitled to be indemnified out of the company's assets, and although an assessment to tax may be made on him personally, whether he is appointed out of court under the provisions of a debt security agreement or of debentures or a covering trust deed[19] or by the court in a debenture holder's action,[20] the receiver is liable to the Inland Revenue for tax only to

13 Ibid, s 15(1) to (3).
14 Ibid, s 43(1) and s 248(b).
15 Ibid, s 15(1), (2) and (9).
16 Ibid, s 15(4).
17 Ibid, s 43(4).
18 Income and Corporation Taxes Act 1988, s 6(1) and s 12(1) to (3) (44 *Halsbury's Statutes* (4th edn) 32 and 39).
19 *IRC v Thompson* [1937] 1 KB 290, [1936] 2 All ER 651.
20 Taxes Management Act 1970, s 75(1) (42 *Halsbury's Statutes* (4th edn) (1993 Reissue) 227.

the extent of the assets of the company comprised in the receivership. Similarly if a receiver or manager carries on the company's business and in the course of doing so receives from the company's customers amounts in respect of value added tax on goods or services supplied by him, he must account to the Commissioners of Customs and Excise for the payments so received, even though he is not personally liable for the tax.[1] Presumably the same rule applies if the receiver charges the company's customers prices which include value added tax without specifying its amount.

Distribution of the company's assets

At the end of a receivership when the company's assets comprised in the receivership have been realised, there will be a sum of money in the receiver's hands or (if the receiver was appointed by the court) in court representing the proceeds of sale or disposal of the company's property, together with the amount of debts owed to the company which the receiver has collected and any unpaid capital on shares issued by the company which has been collected by the receiver. If the receiver was appointed by the court, he must apply to the master on summons for an order setting out the way in which the money in his hands or in court is to be distributed among the various claimants to it.[2] This will protect the receiver against personal liability to claimants if the order of application directed by the master is incorrect. The remedy of a claimant who considers that the master's directions as to distribution are wrong is to appeal against the master's order. If the receiver was appointed out of court under the terms of an instrument, he distributes the money in his hands without an order of the court, but he must observe the same order of application as a master would order in a debenture holder's action, so far as relevant.

A receiver is personally liable to make payments in the proper order only to the extent of the assets in his hands. However, if he has assets in his hands which result from the realisation of a charge which was created as a floating charge over the whole of the company's assets and undertaking, or over any class or classes of its assets, he must apply those assets in discharging preferential debts and claims against the company which accrued by the date when the receivership commenced before paying the amount secured by the floating charge to the persons entitled to it.[3] The receiver is personally

---

1 *Re John Willment (Ashford) Ltd* [1979] 2 All ER 615, [1980] 1 WLR 73.
2 RSC Ord 44, r 11.
3 Companies Act 1985, s 196(1) to (3) (substituted by Insolvency Act 1986, s 439(1) and Sch 13, Part I; Insolvency Act 1986, s 40(1) and (2); (see p 303, ante).

liable to the preferential creditors of the company to an amount equal to the value of those assets if he distributes them to the persons entitled to the floating charge without first discharging the company's preferential debts and other preferential claims,[4] and the receiver's duty and liability to preferential creditors does not terminate because he has already realised sufficient to discharge the amount secured by the floating charge.[5] This does not, of course, apply to the proceeds of realising assets of the company which were comprised in fixed or specific charges.

Order of application

The proceeds of realisation and other money in the receiver's hands or in court must be applied in making the following payments in the order in which they are set out, omitting those items which cannot apply to a particular receivership because of its nature (ie where the receiver is appointed out of court):[6]

1. The cost of selling the property and assets, collecting the debts and enforcing the claims of the company against third persons in order to realise the security created by the debt security agreement, by the debentures or by the trust deed, covering an issue of debentures or debenture stock, but not the cost of preserving such assets with a view to realisation.[7]

2. All other proper expenses of the receiver and manager and their remuneration. It is to this right of indemnity that persons who enter into contracts with the receiver or manager are subrogated if he becomes insolvent.

3. The costs and expenses of the trustees of the trust deed covering an issue of debentures or debenture stock[8] and also their remuneration if the trust deed directs that it shall be paid before the loan or other debt secured by the debentures or the trust deed,[9] but not if the company has merely undertaken to pay that remuneration, when it will rank for payment after the loan or other secured debt.[10]

4 *Westminster City Council v Treby* [1936] 2 All ER 21; *Westminster Corpn v Haste* [1950] Ch 442, [1950] 2 All ER 65; *IRC v Goldblatt* [1972] Ch 498, [1972] 2 All ER 202.
5 *Re Pearl Maintenance Services Ltd* [1995] 1 BCLC 449, [1995] BCC 657.
6 *Batten v Wedgwood Coal and Iron Co* (1884) 28 Ch D 317; *Re Glyncorrwg Colliery Co* [1926] Ch 951.
7 *Lathom v Greenwich Ferry Co* (1895) 72 LT 790.
8 *Mortgage Insurance Corpn v Canadian Agricultural Coal and Colonization Co Ltd* [1901] 2 Ch 377.
9 *Re Piccadilly Hotel Ltd, Paul v Piccadilly Hotel Ltd* [1911] 2 Ch 534.
10 *Re Accles Ltd, Hodgson v Accles* (1902) 18 TLR 786.

4.   The costs of the debenture holder's action (if any). The plaintiff debenture holder is entitled to costs on a full indemnity basis if there will be no surplus left after paying the loan or debt secured by the debentures or covering trust deed, because in that case no other person is prejudiced by the payment of a larger amount of costs than costs on a standard basis, and the debenture holders or debenture stockholders themselves cannot complain, because they have benefited from the bringing of the action.[11] But if there will be a surplus returnable to the company, or available to pay later ranking secured creditors or debenture holders or debenture stockholders of a later ranking series, the plaintiff is entitled to be paid only standard costs (formerly party and party costs) out of the proceeds of realisation.[12] The solicitor acting for the plaintiff in the successful debenture holder's action is entitled to recover his solicitor and client costs as against the debenture holders or debenture stockholders of the series concerned, however, and he may obtain a charging order for those costs on the total amount payable to the debenture holders or debenture stockholders of that series.[13]

5.   If the loan or other debt which the receiver was appointed to recover is secured by a charge which, as created, was a floating charge, the debts and liabilities of the company which are preferential payments must next be discharged out of the proceeds of the company's assets comprised in the floating charge which have not been applied under the preceding heads 1 to 4.[14] The relevant preferential payments are those which would rank as such in a liquidation of the company under a winding up order made or a winding up resolution passed on the date when the appointment of the receiver by the court or out of court became effective.[14] If the company had already gone into liquidation before that date, the relevant date will be the earlier date on which a winding up order was made or a winding up resolution was passed in respect of the company, or the earlier of those dates if the company has been wound up by the court after going into voluntary liquidation.[14] If the receiver was appointed by the court, these debts will be certified by the master at the

---

11   *Re New Zealand Midland Rly Co* [1901] 2 Ch 357; *Re A Boynton Ltd* [1910] 1 Ch 519.
12   *Re Queen's Hotel Co, Cardiff Ltd* [1900] 1 Ch 792.
13   *Re W C Horne & Sons Ltd, Horne v W C Horne & Sons Ltd* [1906] 1 Ch 271.
14   Companies Act 1985, s 196(1) to (3) (substituted by Insolvency Act 1986, s 439 and Sch 13, Part I); Insolvency Act 1986, s 40(1) and (2), s 175(2), s 386(1) and (2), s 387(3) and (4) and Sch 6.

conclusion of the enquiries which he is directed to make by the judgment in the debenture holder's action. If the proceeds of assets of the company comprised in the floating charge have been applied in discharging the expenses listed under headings 1 to 4 above, but there are other assets of the company or the proceeds of realising them which are subject to fixed or specific charges to secure the same debt or liability, it would appear that those assets or proceeds must be marshalled so as to throw the expenses so listed as far as possible on them and so as to leave as large a fund as possible (not exceeding the value of the assets comprised in the floating charge) available to satisfy the company's preferential debts and liabilities.

6. The loan or other indebtedness of the company which is secured by the debt security agreement, or by the debentures or the trust deed securing debentures or debenture stock, together with interest thereon calculated up to the date of payment. If those documents provide that the principal of the secured loan or debt shall be repaid on a certain date, and do not enable the secured creditors or the debenture holders or debenture stockholders or their trustees to call for payment or to realise their security before then, the loan or debt nevertheless becomes immediately payable or repayable when judgment is given in an action for the appointment of a receiver or for a sale, and the amount of the loan or debt must be paid in full out of the money in the receiver's hands without allowing any discount for the fact that it is being paid before the stipulated date.[15] The same applies if an acceleration provision in a debt security agreement or in debentures or a covering trust deed provides that the secured debt shall become immediately payable on the company committing any breach of its obligations, or on the occurrence of any event of default, or on the person entitled to the security giving notice to the company demanding immediate payment on the occurrence of any specified events (one at least of which has happened), and such a demand has been made.

Indebtedness of debenture holders to the company

If a debenture holder or debenture stockholder is indebted to the company and the debt forms part of the security to which all the debenture holders or debenture stockholders of the same series are entitled, he must pay the debt to the receiver before he can share in the

15 *Wallace v Universal Automatic Machines Co* [1894] 2 Ch 547.

proceeds of the company's assets or other funds (eg the proceeds of enforcing guarantees) which are available for redeeming the debentures or debenture stock.[16] This rule is confined to debts owed to the company by a debenture holder or debenture stockholder, and does not apply where the company has a claim against him for unliquidated damages for breach of contract or tort.[17] In practice, the debenture holder or debenture stockholder discharges the debt which he owes by having it set off against his share of the total fund, including the debt, which is available for distribution,[18] but this does not mean that the rule is merely an application of the company's own right of set-off.[19] The company's right of set-off is confined to debts owed to it by the original holder of the debentures or debenture stock, whereas the present rule applies to debts owed by the holder of the debentures or debenture stock when the proceeds of sale of the debenture holder's security fall to be distributed. Furthermore, the company's right of set-off is exercised by treating the amount payable to the debenture holder or debenture stockholder as reduced by the amount owed by him to the company,[20] whereas the present rule requires the debenture holder or debenture stockholder to contribute the amount which he owes the company into the fund available for all the debenture holders or stockholders of the same series before he shares in it at all.

It is uncertain whether the present rule applies when some debenture holders or debenture stockholders have paid the issue price of their debentures or debenture stock in full and others have paid it only in part. At common law a company had merely a right to sue for unliquidated damages if a debenture holder failed to pay the issue price of the debentures for which he had subscribed, and so he was not required to contribute specifically the unpaid amount in order to ensure equality between himself and his fellow debenture holders.[1] But now that a company may specifically enforce a

---

16 *Re Rhodesia Goldfields Ltd* [1910] 1 Ch 239.

17 *Re Smelting Corpn* [1915] 1 Ch 472.

18 Thus if A and B are each holders of £50,000 of debentures of the same series ranking pari passu, and A owes the company £20,000, and its other assets are worth £40,000, on the assumption that A and B are the only debenture holders, A will pay the £20,000 into the common fund, and the whole £60,000 will be divided between A and B equally. The same result is achieved if the £40,000 is applied in paying A £10,000 (viz his share in the total fund, £30,000, less the debt which he owes, £20,000), and in paying B £30,000.

19 *Re Rhodesia Goldfields Ltd*, supra, at 246 to 247.

20 In the example given in footnote 18, if A and B were proving as unsecured creditors in the winding up of the company, A's claim would be for £30,000 (ie £50,000 debenture debt less £20,000 which he owes the company) and B's claim would be for £50,000, and the assets of £40,000 would be divided rateably, so that A would receive £15,000 and B £25,000.

1 *Re Smelting Corpn* [1915] 1 Ch 472.

contract to subscribe for debentures or debenture stock,[2] it may be that the court will put the debenture holder or debenture stockholder in the same position as if an order of specific performance had already been made, in which case the issue price would be payable by him as a debt owed to the company, and he would have to pay it before sharing in the total fund available for distribution among all the debenture holders or debenture stockholders.[3]

Prior encumbrances

If the secured lenders or debenture holders or debenture stockholders whose security has been realised rank for payment after prior encumbrancers, such as the holders of a prior ranking series of debentures or debenture stock, the prior encumbrances must be discharged out of the proceeds of realisation of the company's assets in the receiver's hands before payment of the amount due to the debenture holders or debenture stockholders for whose benefit the receiver was appointed. But the receiver and the plaintiff in the debenture holder's action (if any) are entitled to have their costs and expenses reimbursed before the prior encumbrances are discharged,[4] because the prior encumbrancers have benefited from their efforts.[4] However, the remuneration and expenses of the trustees of a trust deed securing the debentures or debenture stock will have priority over the amount payable to prior encumbrancers only so far as they relate to work done and expenses incurred in connection with the debenture holders' action (if any) and the realisation of the debenture holders' security.[4] If the receiver was appointed by the court, the prior encumbrances which he must discharge will be certified by the master at the conclusion of the enquiries which he is directed to make by the judgment in the debenture holders' action.

Receivers' and managers' accounts and records

A receiver appointed by the court must submit accounts of his receivership periodically to such persons (normally the debenture holders or debenture stockholders and their trustees) as the court

---

2 Companies Act 1985, s 195.
3 This may be inferred from the remarks of Horridge J, in *Kuala Pahi Rubber Estates Ltd v Mowbray* (1914) 111 LT 1072 at 1073.
4 *Batten, Proffitt and Scott v Dartmouth Harbour Comrs* (1890) 45 Ch D 612; *Carrick v Wigan Tramways Co* [1893] WN 98. The costs allowed would presumably always be standard (formerly party and party) costs.

directs,[5] but he is not required to submit accounts to the court itself as was formerly the practice. Any person to whom the receiver is required to submit accounts may, either personally or by an agent, inspect the books and papers in the receiver's possession relating to the accounts,[6] and if any such person is dissatisfied with the receiver's accounts, whether because of the omission or the inclusion of matters in them, he may object to particular items and require the receiver to lodge the accounts in court.[7] The receiver must then lodge his accounts and take an appointment before a master so that the objections may be dealt with; notice of the appointment must be given by the receiver to all the persons to whom he is required to submit his accounts, and any of them may be heard on the objections raised. The court may order the receiver to pay moneys in his hands into court periodically or otherwise, or may permit him to maintain a bank account himself or jointly in the names of himself and other persons.[8] If a receiver fails to submit his accounts as directed by the court, or to attend before a master for the examination of his accounts, or to pay money into court as directed by it, the court may disallow the whole or part of his remuneration and charge him with interest at the rate currently payable on judgment debts on the amount of money which he has wrongfully retained.[9]

An administrative receiver is required to keep the same records of the progress of the receivership as an insolvency practitioner is required to keep in respect of any insolvent estate which he administers,[10] but an administrative receiver is not required by law to keep the detailed financial records and accounts which a liquidator must keep in the winding up of a company by the court or in a creditors' voluntary liquidation.[11] Nevertheless, an administrative receiver will in practice keep accounting records showing his receipts and payments with details of the proceeds of realisation of the company's assets, of the expenses which he incurs in connection with the receivership and of the payments which he makes to the secured creditors or debenture holders or debenture stockholders by or on whose behalf he was appointed and to other creditors of the company. The keeping of such accounting records will be relevant when the Secretary of State considers whether the administrative receiver is a fit and proper person to continue to act as an insolvency

---

5 RSC Ord 30, r 5(1).
6 Ibid, r 5(2).
7 Ibid, r 5(3).
8 Ibid, r 6.
9 Ibid, r 7(2).
10 Insolvency Practitioners Regulations 1990 (SI 1990/439), reg 17(1) and Sch 3.
11 See p 191, ante.

practitioner, and whether his authorisation to act as an insolvency practitioner should be renewed.[12]

An administrative receiver must within two months after each successive anniversary of his appointment and within two months after he ceases to act, or within such longer period than two months as the court permits, send to the Registrar of Companies, to the company, to the company's liquidator (if any), to the person or persons by whom he was appointed and to each member of the creditors' committee(if any) an account in the form of an abstract of his receipts and payments during the twelve month period to which the account relates, or in the case of the account delivered upon the administrative receiver ceasing to act, during the period from the end of the most recently completed twelve months' accounting period until the receiver ceased to act.[13] Each such abstract must also show the total amounts of the administrative receiver's receipts and payments since his appointment which are brought forward from the immediately preceding twelve month period.[13]

Any receiver or manager of a company's property (other than an administrative receiver) who was appointed under powers conferred by an instrument (for example, a receiver of the income of property appointed by a mortgagee under the Law of Property Act 1925) must within one month after the anniversary of his appointment, and thereafter within one month after the end of each successive six-month period of the receivership and after ceasing to act, deliver to the Registrar of Companies an abstract of his receipts and payments during the period to which the abstract relates.[14] The abstract must also show the total amount of the receiver's receipts and payments brought forward from earlier periods.

If a receiver or manager fails to deliver any abstract of his receipts and payments to the Registrar of Companies or to any other person entitled to a copy of it within 14 days after receiving a notice requiring him to do so, or if he fails to render proper accounts of his receipts and payments to the liquidator of the company at his request at any time and to pay to the liquidator any cash balance properly payable to him, the Registrar of Companies, or in an appropriate case, the liquidator or any member or creditor of the company may apply to the Companies Court for an order directing the receiver to make good his default.[15] There is, however, no provision for an audit of a receiver's accounts or of abstracts of his receipts and payments.

12 Insolvency Act 1986, s 393(2) and (3).
13 Insolvency Rules 1986, r 3.32(1) to (3) and Sch 4, Form 3.6.
14 Insolvency Act 1986, s 38(1) and (2); Insolvency Rules 1986, Sch 4, Form 3.6.
15 Insolvency Act 1986, s 41(1) and (2).

The statutory accounting obligations of a receiver appointed under the provisions of a debt security agreement, or under debentures or a trust deed covering an issue of debentures or debenture stock, or under the statutory powers conferred by the Law of Property Act 1925, do not exclude his obligation in equity to account in detail to the company or its liquidator on the conclusion of the receivership;[16] presumably the company may challenge the accuracy of the items and details of the accounts submitted and require reasonable amplifications and explanations as though the accounts were those of an agent.[17] The equitable obligation of a receiver to account to the company and its liquidator applies to a receiver or manager, whether or not the instrument or enactment under which he was appointed provides that he shall be deemed to be an agent of the company,[17] but it does not apply to a receiver or manager appointed by the court, who as an officer of the court is accountable only to it or as it directs.

During any receivership the directors of the company may request the receiver to supply them with a statement of the amount required to discharge the secured debt in respect of which the receiver was appointed together with the receiver's costs and expenses, or to supply them with particulars of the company's assets which the receiver has not so far disposed of and of contracts which he has entered into for disposing of such assets; however, the receiver is under an obligation to supply this information only if the directors can satisfy the court that the company has available sufficient funds to discharge the secured debt and the receiver's costs and expenses.[18] The reason for this limitation on the receiver's obligation is to avoid him being compelled to incur purposeless expense in obtaining information and preparing accounts when the company either cannot, or does not intend to, discharge the secured debt in the near future.[18]

On the conclusion of a receivership the books, papers, records, correspondence and memoranda kept by the receiver appointed under powers conferred by an instrument belong to the company insofar as they relate to the management of its business and the disposal of its assets; on the other hand, such documents belong to the secured creditor, or to the debenture holders or debenture stockholders for whose benefit the receiver was appointed, insofar as the documents etc were brought into existence to keep them informed about the progress of the receivership; and finally, such

16 *Smiths Ltd v Middleton* [1979] 3 All ER 842.
17 *Gray v Haig* (1854) 20 Beav 219; *Cheese v Keen* [1908] 1 Ch 245.
18 *Gomba Holdings UK Ltd v Homan* [1986] 3 All ER 94, [1986] 1 WLR 1301.

documents belong to the receiver himself insofar as they were prepared to enable him to fulfil his functions properly or to obtain information or advice for that purpose.[19]

19 *Gomba Holdings UK Ltd v Minories Finance Ltd* [1989] 1 All ER 261, [1989] BCLC 115.

Index